Competition and Regulation in the Postal and Delivery Sector

ADVANCES IN REGULATORY ECONOMICS

Series Editors: Michael A. Crew, *Professor of Economics, Director, Center for Research in Regulated Industries (CRRI) and the CRRI Scholar, Rutgers, The State University of New Jersey, Newark, USA and* Paul R. Kleindorfer, *Anheuser-Busch Professor Emeritus, The Wharton School, University of Pennsylvania, Philadelphia, USA and INSEAD, Fontainebleau, France*

Edited by Michael A. Crew and Paul R. Kleindorfer, this series aims to advance research in theory, practice and policy in the area of regulatory economics. While regulation is all-pervasive in the modern economy and touches almost every aspect of economic life, this series focuses on micro-economic issues in regulation rather than macro policies. Topics of interest include contributions in the following areas: network industries, environmental, health and safety, risk and insurance, and financial services. Regulatory economics deals with both direct instruments affecting profits and prices in these industries and governance structures in regulated industries, including self-regulation. Contributions may address specific instruments across industries as well as in-depth sector-specific studies.

Titles in the series include:

Liberalization of the Postal and Delivery Sector
Michael A. Crew and Paul R. Kleindorfer

Competition and Regulation in the Postal and Delivery Sector
Michael A. Crew and Paul R. Kleindorfer

Competition and Regulation in the Postal and Delivery Sector

Edited by

Michael A. Crew

Center for Research in Regulated Industries (CRRI), Rutgers, The State University of New Jersey, Newark, USA

Paul R. Kleindorfer

The Wharton School, University of Pennsylvania, USA and INSEAD, France

ADVANCES IN REGULATORY ECONOMICS

Edward Elgar
Cheltenham, UK • Northampton, MA, USA

Published by
Edward Elgar Publishing Limited
Glensanda House
Montpellier Parade
Cheltenham
Glos GL50 1UA
UK

Edward Elgar Publishing, Inc.
William Pratt House
9 Dewey Court
Northampton
Massachusetts 01060
USA

A catalogue record for this book
is available from the British Library

ISBN 978 1 84720 507 0

Printed and bound in Great Britain by MPG Books Ltd, Bodmin, Cornwall

Contents

List of contributors

José Ansón, Economist, Universal Postal Union

Francis Bloch, GREQAM, Université de la Méditerranée and Warwick University

François Boldron, La Poste

Lawrence G. Buc, President, SLS Consulting, Inc.

Catherine Cazals, Researcher, University of Toulouse (IDEI–GREMAQ)

Margaret M. Cigno, Postal Rate and Classification Specialist, US Postal Regulatory Commission

Robert Cohen, Independent Consultant

Luis Correia da Silva, Managing Director, Oxera

Helmuth Cremer, Professor, Toulouse School of Economics (IDEI and Institut universitaire de France)

Michael A. Crew, CRRI Scholar and Director – CRRI, Rutgers Business School, Rutgers University

Gonzales d'Alcantara, Senior Lecturer, University of Antwerpen and Economic Expert, d'Alcantara Economic Consulting

Patrick de Bas, Consultant Competition & Regulation, ECORYS

Philippe De Donder, Professor, Toulouse School of Economics (GREMAQ–CNRS and IDEI)

Karen Dewulf, La Poste

Luigi Di Paola, Poste Italiane

Alex Dieke, Head of Department – Postal Services and Logistics, WIK Wissenschaftliches Institut für Infrastruktur und Kommunikationsdienste

Paul Dudley, Head of Regulatory Economic Analysis, Royal Mail Group

Richard Eccles, Partner, Bird & Bird

Lawrence Fenster, Economist, US Postal Regulatory Commission

Jean-Pierre Florens, Professor, University of Toulouse (IDEI–GREMAQ)

Alessandra Fratini, Partner, Fratini Vergano, European Lawyers

Axel Gautier, Associate Professor, HEC, Univeristé of Liège and CORE, Université Catholique de Louvain

Matthew C. Harding, Assistant Professor of Economics, Stanford University

John Hearn, Project Manager – Postal Regulation, Commission for Communications Regulation (ComReg) and Vice-Chair CERP (European Committee for Postal Regulation)

Christian Jaag, Economist, Swiss Post and University of St. Gallen

Luis Jimenez, Senior Vice President and Chief Industry Policy Officer, Pitney Bowes, Inc.

Denis Joram, Chief Economist, European and National Regulation Division, La Poste

Paul R. Kleindorfer, Professor Emeritus, The Wharton School, University of Pennsylvania; and Research Professor, INSEAD

J.P. Klingenberg, Consultant

Pauline Kuipers, Partner, Bird & Bird

Michael Lintell, Director, Future of the Mailstream, Pitney Bowes, Inc.

Shoji Maruyama, Senior Manager, Japan Post Service Co., Ltd

Leonardo Mautino, Senior Consultant, Oxera

Diane Monaco, Economist, US Postal Regulatory Commission

James Pierce Myers, Executive Vice President and Counsel, Parcel Shippers Association

Heikki Nikali, Research Director, Business Intelligence, Itella Corporation

Andrei Obrea, Senior Fellow, Pitney Bowes, Inc.

Clémence Panet, La Poste

Elizabeth Payling, Service Performance Measurement Manager, Royal Mail Group

Edward S. Pearsall, Economist, US Postal Regulatory Commission

Leon A. Pintsov, Pitney Bowes Fellow and Vice President, Pitney Bowes, Inc.

David Rawnsley, President, Postal Services International Ltd

Robert A.F. Reisner, President, Transformation Strategy Inc.

Alan Robinson, Analytic Business Services

Matthew H. Robinson, Postal Rate and Classification Specialist, US Postal Regulatory Commission

Frank Rodriguez, Head of Economics, Royal Mail Group

Bernard Roy, Director, European and National Regulation, La Poste

Sonja Schölermann, Economist, WIK Wissenschaftliches Institut für Infrastruktur und Kommunikationsdienste

Renée Sheehy, Evaluator, United States Postal Service Office of the Inspector General

Soterios Soteri, Senior Economist, Royal Mail Group

Joëlle Toledano, Commissioner, Autorité de Régulation des Communications Electroniques et des Postes

Urs Trinkner, Economist, Swiss Post and University of Zurich

Nick van der Lijn, Director Macro and Sector Policies, ECORYS

Joost Vantomme, Director Regulatory Affairs, La Poste / De Post Belgium

Olivier Vialaneix, La Poste

Vincenzo Visco Comandini, Chief Economist, ISIMM, and University of Rome 'Tor Vergata'

Richard Waterman, Analytic Business Services and the Wharton School, University of Pennsylvania

Spyros Xenakis, Economist, US Postal Regulatory Commission

List of sponsors

Royal Mail
Deutsche Post World Net
United States Postal Service
Bank of America
Canada Post Corporation
FedEx
La Poste
La Poste / De Post
Österreichische Post AG
R.R. Donnelley & Sons Company
UPS
Swiss Post
CTT Correios de Portugal S.A.
Pitney Bowes
Postcomm – Postal Services Commission
Siemens AG
United States Postal Regulatory Commission
Posten AB
Itella Corporation
Canadian Union of Postal Workers
International Post Corporation
Anacom
An Post
ARCEP
A.T. Kearney GmbH
Communication Workers Union
LECG
NERA Economic Consulting
Poste Italiane
Posten Norge AS
Postwatch
Sidley Austin LLP
TNT Post
IBM Global Business Services
Haldi Associates
Bird & Bird
Commission for Communications Regulation (ComReg)
Frontier Economics
O'Connor and Company
Oxera
Association for Postal Commerce
d'Alcantara Economic Consulting
Kirkpatrick & Lockhart Preston Gates Ellis LLP
London Economics
National Association of Letter Carriers
New Zealand Post
Parcel Shippers Association
SLS Consulting, Inc.
Venable LLP

Preface and acknowledgments

This book is a result of the Center for Research in Regulated Industries' (CRRI) 15th Conference on Postal and Delivery Economics, which was held on May 30 to June 2, 2007 in Semmering, Austria. The conference and the book follow our earlier conferences and workshops. In 1990, the first Conference on Postal and Delivery Economics was held at Coton House, Rugby, England, July 22–25, 1990, in honor of the 150th anniversary of the Penny Post and the contributions of Sir Rowland Hill. To date, there have been 15 conferences, three workshops and now 14 edited volumes as part of CRRI's program on Postal and Delivery Economics. The conference has grown significantly from 65 participants in 1990 to 216 in 2007.

The 2007 conference was made possible by the support of the following organizations: CRRI, Rutgers Business School, Rutgers University; Royal Mail; Deutsche Post World Net; United States Postal Service; Bank of America; Canada Post Corporation; FedEx; La Poste; La Poste / De Post; Österreichische Post AG; R.R. Donnelley & Sons Company; UPS; Swiss Post; CTT Correios de Portugal S.A.; Pitney Bowes; Postcomm – Postal Services Commission; Siemens AG; United States Postal Regulatory Commission; Posten AB; Itella Corporation; Canadian Union of Postal Workers; International Post Corporation; Anacom; An Post; ARCEP; A.T. Kearney GmbH; Communication Workers Union; LECG; NERA Economic Consulting; Poste Italiane; Posten Norge AS; Postwatch; Sidley Austin LLP; TNT Post; IBM Global Business Services; Haldi Associates; Bird & Bird; ComReg; Frontier Economics; O'Connor and Company; Oxera; Association for Postal Commerce; d'Alcantara Economic Consulting; Kirkpatrick & Lockhart Preston Gates Ellis LLP; London Economics; National Association of Letter Carriers; New Zealand Post; Parcel Shippers Association; SLS Consulting, Inc.; and Venable LLP.

We would like to thank sponsors not only for financial support, but also for their advice and encouragement, and for serving on the organizing committee. In particular, we would like to thank Nabil Allaf, José Amado da Silva, John Baldwin, Kristin Bergum, Jody Berenblatt, Robert Bernau, Geoff Bickerton, Lawrence Buc, Bernhard Bukovc, Philip Burns, João Castro, Sophie Colman, Jeff Colvin, Julien Coulier, Robert Curry, Gonzales d'Alcantara, Bernard Damiens, Gene Del Polito, John Dodgson, Jane Dyer, Richard Eccles, Jutta Fabjan, Charles Fattore, Stephen Ferguson, Alessandra Fratini, Beat Friedli, Stefano Gori, John Haldi, Catherine Harper, John Hearn, Jan Bart Henry, George Houpis, Helen Jenkins, Luis Jimenez, Robert L. Kee, Daniel Krähenbühl, Ian Leigh, David M. Levy, Walter Maschke, Leonardo Mautino, Richard Moriarty, Heikki Nikali, Louis O'Brien, Chris Osborne, Wolfgang Pickave, James Pierce Myers, Alberto Pimenta, Leon Pintsov, Frank Rodriguez, Bernard Roy, Jim Sauber, Michael Scanlon, Gennaro Scarfiglieri, Michael Shinay, Nancy Sparks, Gregory Swinand, Joëlle Toledano, Marie Turrell, David Treworgy, Urs Trinkner, Mark van der Horst, Anton van der Lande, Ian Volner, Sture Wallander, John Waller, Ingo Willems, and David Williams.

The host country plays an important role in these conferences. This year's conference, the 15th Conference on Postal and Delivery Economics, benefited greatly from the efforts of our host PO, Österreichische Post. Their representative Jutta Fabjan, and her colleagues Peter Koppe, Alexandra Nagle, Dietlinde Wagner, and Sophie Weiner, were gracious hosts. As well as arranging two wonderful excursions for the conference participants, they provided both advice and assistance on numerous occasions and contributed greatly to the success of the event.

We would like to thank our distinguished dinner speakers, Louis F. O'Brien, Stefan Keh, and Anton Wais. In the tradition of these conferences, we very much enjoyed the speech by Anton Wais, Chief Executive Officer of Österreichische Post AG. His keynote speech provided an outlook on the future of postal and delivery networks from the unique perspective of Österreichische Post. Louis F. O'Brien, Senior Vice President of Parcels, Canada Post, gave an interesting discussion of postal reform and challenges facing Canada Post. Stefan Keh discussed the role of technology in the future direction of postal and delivery services.

Finally, we would like to thank Jeremy Guenter, Assistant Director of CRRI, for his assistance and efforts on behalf of the conference and this book. We would like to thank him not only as editors but also on behalf of the authors, speakers, discussants, chairs, and participants to whom he provided considerable assistance.

The usual disclaimers are applicable. In particular, the views expressed reflect the views of the authors and are not necessarily those of the sponsors.

Michael A. Crew and Paul R. Kleindorfer

PART I

Universal Service Obligation

1. Regulation and the USO under entry*

Michael A. Crew and Paul R. Kleindorfer

The postal sector is now in the midst of major change, especially in Europe as the EU moves to open up postal markets to competition. Some countries, notably the United Kingdom in 2006 and Sweden in 1993, have already opened their markets to competition. According to the proposal for a Third Postal Directive, approved by the European Parliament on July 11, 2007, markets in most of the EU-15 member states will be open for competition in 2011, with all EU states open to competition by 2013.[1] Given the market dominant position of incumbent postal operators at the beginning of full market opening (FMO), and the requirement for continuing funding of the universal service obligation (USO), FMO will not mean the end of regulation, which will remain an essential element of governance for postal markets for the foreseeable future. Notwithstanding the importance of regulation under FMO, appropriate models for postal regulation have been slow to emerge, and there still remains considerable variety across countries in this respect (e.g., WIK-Consult, 2006). We will argue that insufficient consideration has been given to how regulation will function and its impact on funding the USO in the absence of a reserved area. The chapter will examine how the USO might be funded under FMO without explicit subsidies, focusing on the role of regulation.

Attitudes about competition in the postal sector also vary widely across countries. Certainly, one of the major concerns is that the USO could not be readily funded without the traditional reserved area (PwC, 2006). Indeed, with the abolition of the reserved area the competition faced by POs might be greater than that faced by traditional network industries, in part because there are fewer sunk costs and hence lower entry barriers. So if the proposal by the EU to abolish the reserved area in Europe in 2011 is approved, postal markets may arguably be subject to more competition than other network industries and may lack the wherewithal to fund the USO. This already is giving rise to an increasing role for regulation in the postal sector. This increased regulation arises for a number of reasons: concern over preserving the USO after FMO, and increased commercialization and privatization leading to demands by competitors for a level playing field under FMO.

Both a concern for maintaining the USO and a concern for creating competitive markets are serious issues for regulators under FMO. Failure to address these issues adequately could cause major problems in the postal and delivery sector. For example, a regulator might impose a USO that is not adapted to the changes in market structure under FMO, or the regulator might *de facto* subsidize entrants by policies aimed at a level playing field. The problem has not apparently received much attention from policy makers. There seems to be a tendency on the part of policy makers and regulators to allow the process to work itself out as it goes along rather than having a reasonably clear objective and approach in mind. Similarly, despite the critical importance of the role of regulation under FMO, relatively little scholarly effort has been devoted to analyzing how the regulator should act under FMO. As a result, a wide spectrum of regulatory policies and models from micromanagement to *laissez-faire* has emerged. This chapter takes a first step in providing a framework for analyzing and resolving the role of regulation under FMO. We will restrict our attention to regulation at the national level, though some of the issues we address will have implications for restrictions and policies set at the regional level (e.g., the EC).

Section 1 of the chapter will examine how the USO might be funded under FMO. For purposes of this chapter we will assume that a USO can be funded without explicit subsidies from the government. Section 2 will examine the role of regulation consistent with funding the USO, focusing on Price Cap Regulation (PCR), which is essentially ubiquitous in the postal sector. Given that most postal operators (POs) are public enterprises, this *prima facie* raises questions concerning the impact of PCR on efficiency since the efficiency properties of PCR rely on the assumption of residual claimants driving profit-seeking behavior, and residual claimants are absent under public enterprise. We note how preferences of stakeholders such as postal management, labor, and large customers might conflict with profits, undermining the basic presupposition of PCR of a profit-seeking residual claimant. Various proposals for realigning these preferences are suggested. Section 3 examines the further the integration of PCR with competition, including the treatment of access prices under PCR. Section 4 is by way of conclusions and implications. Although the problem of residual claimants raised in Section 2 remains unresolved, we conclude that PCR should remain the dominant regulatory form in the postal sector, but subject to a number of caveats and prescriptions that are intended to align better the interests of management and labor with efficiency, making these stakeholders what we might call 'pseudo residual claimants'.

1. FUNDING THE USO UNDER FMO

The traditional USO implies ubiquitous delivery at a uniform stamp price at least for letter mail. In addition, it implies ubiquitous counter service. The nature of the USO has been the subject of an extensive literature, which we will not review here.[2] It was traditionally funded primarily by the reserved area. Typically, this was determined by a weight limit below which POs had a legal monopoly. Absent this it was argued that the cross-subsidy going from low-cost to high-cost areas would result in cream-skimming entry, making the situation unsustainable absent a reserved area. So, what is different about 2011? What reasons are there to believe that a USO would be sustainable without a reserved area in 2011? Have some miraculous new funding opportunities emerged? They have not. They have potentially always been there. FMO in 2011 is intended to unlock and leverage other areas than the reserved area as the means of supporting the USO.

Under FMO the reserved area would disappear. The alternatives to funding the USO include the following:

1. Scale economies: POs derive scale economies from local delivery that may provide some cost advantages and some protection against entry.
2. Scope economies: POs expect to have scope economies between say letters and other products, particularly, parcels and financial services.

3. Market dominance: POs may derive market power from a number of sources including ubiquitous coverage and name recognition.
4. Increase in the uniform price of single-piece mail.
5. Reducing the scope and therefore the obligation of the USO.
6. Increased X-efficiency.
7. The extent of pricing flexibility allowed by regulators.

Currently, the first two items on the list apply. Indeed, scale economies have traditionally provided the principal rationale for the existence of natural monopoly and its regulation. So there is nothing new about the first item. Similarly, scope economies have for a long time been a major feature of POs. Some have been more successful than others in exploiting them. Notably, USPS has lost the majority of the B2B and B2C parcel business to UPS and FEDEX. On the other hand some European POs, notably TNT and Deutsche Post, have sought ways to make their offerings more attractive to business customers. Success in the parcel area will depend not only on scope economies but also on the introduction of tighter business practices, investment in more automated handling, better logistics, and information technology.

The third item, market dominance, has again always existed for POs. Because of their status as public enterprises and the absence of a profit motive and residual claimants, it has not received much attention until recently. The cap on prices provided by the single-piece uniform price had, at least for many years, been thought of as a rough and ready control on monopoly exploitation. Under FMO market dominance would no longer be latent, especially in case of privatized POs, where it will be not only a means of funding the USO but also a source of profits. Even in the case of public enterprise POs, market dominance will require careful monitoring by governments and regulators, as it will not only be a source of funding for the USO but has the potential, by its very nature, to damage competition. Thus, balancing the benefits of funding the USO and potential harm to competition is likely to be a major issue for regulators and antitrust authorities whether or not the PO is privately or publicly owned.

The fourth and fifth items, raising the uniform stamp price and reducing the burden of the USO, are at the core of the problems raised by FMO. In effect, they imply that 'you can't have guns and butter'. Changes are very likely to be required in these two fundamental aspects of the USO. The tradeoffs required may in some cases be painful. The concept of a 'reasonable' uniform single-piece price is a tradition in the postal service going back to Roland Hill. It is a rough and ready form of consumer protection and safeguard against monopoly exploitation. Raising it in real terms may be inevitable based on past experience. For example, the successful case of FMO in Sweden involved a significant real price increase in single-piece rates. The rationale for increasing the single-piece price under FMO derives from the interactions between this single-piece price and business products for outlying areas. Prior to FMO, this price has tended to be set without much attention paid to the interaction of single-piece and bulk rates, with the result that the single-piece rate often embodied significant cross-subsidies from low-cost urban areas to high-cost rural areas. Aligning prices and costs, a requirement under FMO, will require that these cross-subsidies be reduced or even eliminated. Otherwise, the single-piece price will be the *de facto* price by the incumbent PO for service to high-cost areas for business customers, including entrants. Under FMO, this could lead to inefficiencies and financial difficulties for the incumbent PO, some of which can be addressed only by raising the single-piece rate.[3]

An alternative to increasing rates would be to reduce USO costs, especially in rural areas. However, reducing the USO is likely to meet resistance. Measures that result in significant cost savings, for example, post office closures and reduction in delivery frequency in outlying areas, are going to face vigorous opposition. Governments, particularly their regulators, are going to have to assess the tradeoffs in order to achieve a balance between financial viability for the PO and the loss of benefits from a reduced USO.

Item six provides probably the primary *raison d'être* for FMO. The intent of FMO is to introduce entry and therefore competition into a market that was previously a monopoly guaranteed by government policy. Competition has the benefit in economic theory of bringing about allocative efficiency. In the neoclassical model of perfect competition, price is driven to marginal cost and a Pareto optimum is achieved where net benefits are maximized, making it impossible to make one individual better off without making others worse off. In real-world markets like the postal sector, perfect competition will not be attained. However, the basis of the argument for FMO relies on increased efficiency as a result of entry. Competition has the property of driving prices closer to cost. This is one of the fundamental tenets underlying FMO – that POs, as a result of competition, will improve internal or X-efficiency. A second tenet underlying FMO is that POs will have stronger incentives to introduce new products that achieve greater value for customers. The argument is along the lines that a monopoly, especially if it is in the form of a public enterprise, will lack incentives for efficient operations, including internal restructuring and redesign of its product portfolio to meet market needs. Inefficiencies might include a bloated labor force and under-development and adoption of labor-saving technologies. They might also include product design features, including service quality and reliability that are not aligned with the willingness-to-pay of specific customer segments. The pressures of FMO might then be expected to result in improvements in both product portfolios and X-efficiency, with impacts on labor in the form of reduced wages and force reductions. The latter might be mitigated by growing demand, which may be the result of lower prices and product innovations.

The final element to funding the USO under FMO is the extent to which regulators will allow pricing flexibility. It seems almost inevitable for most POs that they will not have the complete pricing flexibility allowed in a fully deregulated market. Indeed, given the market dominant position of incumbent POs, if regulators allowed complete pricing flexibility, it is possible that POs would run afoul of the antitrust authorities. Controls placed on pricing flexibility by a regulator have two effects. The first is to immunize, at least partially, the PO from intervention from the antitrust authorities.[4] The second is to reduce the PO's ability to compete and reduce its profit/USO-funding potential. Typically, the constraints brought about by the latter are likely to exceed the benefits from the former. Most POs would take the risk of antitrust action for the benefits of increased pricing flexibility.

2. THE ROLE OF REGULATION UNDER FMO

The role of regulation is going to be a critical element in the mix of instruments that determine whether FMO will live up to its promises or have seriously negative consequences.

European postal regulation has a significant reach, with primary areas including: USO regulations scope, accessibility conditions and quality standards, competitive and level playing field issues (such as customs clearance and value-added tax uniformity), accounting separation and structure, and authorization/licensing of operators (WIK-Consult, 2006). Our focus here will be on two interrelated issues at the center of postal regulation, namely (a) funding of the USO and (b) tariff/price regulation. For purposes of clarity of discussion of these issues, we are taking the definition of the scope and conditions associated with the USO as given.

Wrong regulatory decisions can result in serious problems. One regulatory decision that has been made concerns the form of regulation. PCR has been widely adopted. *Prima facie* this is a positive sign. In his report to the Department of Trade and Industry proposing the system of regulation for British Telecom, Littlechild (1983) argued that PCR has a number of beneficial efficiency properties relative to other forms of existing regulation, including cost-of-service regulation, also known as rate-of-return regulation (ROR), which was prevalent in the US at the time. His arguments have been explored more formally in many subsequent papers (e.g., Braeutigam and Panzar, 1989, 1993; Crew and Kleindorfer, 1996, 2001). PCR would provide high-powered incentives for cost economy or X-efficiency that were absent under ROR. These efficiency arguments for PCR were driven by a presumption that profit-oriented residual claimants would attempt to reap the benefits of PCR through the additional flexibility in pricing and in the ability to appropriate the benefits of increased cost efficiency in the short run. These arguments considered, often only implicitly, the privately owned firm as the model by which PCR would operate. The owners of a privately owned firm are the residual claimants, and profit maximization and therefore cost minimization are natural corollaries of private ownership. However, in the postal sector, most POs are public enterprises. Public enterprises do not have residual claimants, or at least not of the usual profit-oriented character.

Because of the absence of residual claimants in the public enterprise structure typical of most incumbent operators in the postal sector, it is important to reexamine the foundations of PCR as these might apply to this sector. One benefit that PCR does provide is potential for lower transactions costs and price flexibility, which are likely to be required for FMO to succeed. Maintaining these benefits of PCR in a public enterprise structure, while continuing to meet a USO, will certainly require some rethinking of the design and operation of PCR. Our approach to this will be to first review PCR under private ownership and then examine the implications for PCR for public enterprise, finally addressing further challenges associated with the USO under PCR.

Braeutigam and Panzar (1989), hereafter B-P, provide a discussion of the efficiency properties of PCR for the profit-maximizing firm. Their approach is particularly apt to the postal sector in that they address an issue of considerable importance in the postal sector under FMO, namely, whether PCR provides incentives for fair competition. They show that PCR provides not only incentives for internal or X-efficiency but also incentives not to cross-subsidize, thereby eliminating one major source of unfair competition. In some respects their analysis might be viewed as presenting PCR in its best possible light, even though they are clear in noting its qualifications. Applying their analysis to public enterprise *prima facie* presents a problem because of the absence of residual claimants.

Nonetheless, we will first state their results briefly as a benchmark before presenting our analysis of PCR as applied to public enterprise.

B-P examine a case of a single product PCR profit-maximizing firm that makes a decision to enter into a competitive market, where it is a price taker. The move is assumed to be profitable because of the existence of economies of scope, which is reflected in the cost function they employ, namely, $TC = F + c_1 f_1(x_1) + c_2 f_2(x_2)$. This simplified cost function *prima facie* reflects the existence of scale and scope economies in the postal sector. Product 1 is the regulated monopoly product and product 2 is a product supplied by a competitive industry. Because of scope economies the regulated firm can compete profitably with the competitive fringe. They show that under PCR the profit-maximizing regulated firm has no incentive to cross-subsidize the competitive product. Their result is driven by the existence of residual claimants. This result is important in the postal sector but raises a number of regulatory problems. One implication is that, for a profit-maximizing firm, claims by competitors of unfair competition and cross-subsidization may be unfounded. Squeals of protest by competitors about low prices may not be because POs cross-subsidize competitive products but because of the scope economies inherent in the PO's network operations. One problem with too rapid an adoption of this argument is that most POs are public enterprises and may, indeed, not be profit maximizers. Indeed, this notion that public enterprises are not profit maximizers clearly underlies the critique of Sappington and Sidak (2003), henceforth S-S.

The origins of S-S go back half a century. Notably, Baumol (1967)[5] developed a theory of the firm based upon sales revenue maximization. Williamson (1963)'s theory of expense preference was based upon the notion that management maximized a preference function that included its own emoluments and its preference for some expense categories over others. For example, he argued that expenditures on additional staff might be preferred to expenditures on shopfloor labor. Baumol argued that in his experience of management in private corporations, which was considerable, managers did not maximize profit but sales revenue. Both employed basic optimization models. S-S draw from both approaches. They argue that a public enterprise is likely to be a sales revenue maximizer. They view sales revenue maximizing as a proxy variable reflecting management's desire for a 'quiet life'.[6] Because managers in public enterprises are not allowed to receive a level of compensation as high as those in private enterprise, the desire for labor peace and other aspects of the quiet life may be a significant part of their preferences. S-S argue that these kinds of preferences will be translated into the desire to increase the size of the enterprise, and particularly the level of employment, of the enterprise. Niskanen's (1971) economic theory of bureaucracy provides another foundation to their approach in that he argues that the bureaucrat's objective is to expand the size of his department. Public enterprises, in many respects, have many of the same features as government agencies. The S-S model incorporates these types of notions by having the public enterprise maximize sales revenue. Unlike Williamson, who has separate variables for expense preference, S-S use sales revenue to capture such effects. Arguably, this simple one-variable approach is a reasonable abstraction for the case S-S have in mind. Given that public enterprise management is normally not going to be able to attain the level of compensation of private managements, it is at least arguable that it will want to reduce conflict and obtain the benefits of reduced managerial effort implied by this.

Adoption of an S-S type of sales revenue maximization would throw a monkey wrench into the attainment of PCR's properties of X-efficiency and prevention of cross-subsidization. In the Technical Appendix we develop a general model of the firm subject to PCR. This model allows the behavior of the firm to be compared under different single objectives and under a mixture of different objectives including the S-S sales revenue maximizing approach, maximizing the average wage, profit maximization, and welfare maximization. Under the S-S approach the efficiency properties of PCR would be significantly attenuated. Especially noteworthy is that, in contrast to B-P, cross-subsidy would not be avoided under PCR. This occurs because under sales maximization there would be an underweighting of cost relative to the Ramsey Rule, which could even lead to charging less than marginal cost for some products (those with relatively high elasticity).

While S-S's approach is a simple characterization of the behavior of a public enterprise, the objectives of public enterprise may be too diverse to be captured by a one-variable model. So we develop in the Technical Appendix a more general model, which addresses objectives beyond simple sales revenue maximization.[7] Our model takes a multi-product enterprise, regulated by PCR, but with diverse objectives that are represented as a weighted sum of (a) sales, (b) average payments to labor, and (c) welfare, and are further subject to a break-even constraint on profits. Different weights on the different objectives (or required profit level) represent situations in which different factions or stakeholders in the enterprise have greater bargaining power. The sales revenue maximizing case is addressed in our model by giving this variable a unit weight and giving the other variables zero weights. In addition, by manipulating the required level of profits, we can also mimic the profit-maximizing enterprise. The results for the labor-managed firm imply that less than the optimal amount of labor will be employed as labor maximizes the wages of those employed (Ward, 1958). In reality, other objectives of labor may be present, including 'solidarity', which may work in the opposite direction. In either case the amount of labor employed will be inefficient but such effects can be attenuated as the profit constraint is tightened, driving the labor-managed firm to behave more like a profit-maximizing firm.

The results of the analysis show that if, indeed, objectives other than profit maximization, which is driven by residual claimants, are pursued, then the efficiency properties of price caps are lost. However, the model does imply that as profit maximization is given greater weight that more of the efficiency benefits of PCR are attained. An implication is that the more they are required to behave like profit maximizers, thereby constraining expense preference behavior, the greater are the efficiency benefits that will arise from PCR. The results of the model raise a number of questions. What are the types of policies and reforms that might bring about achieving this? How do FMO and commercialization relate to the attainment of this goal?

To the extent that FMO puts POs under greater pressure from competition in the product market, they may be less free to pursue objectives other than profitability. Indeed, objectives other than profit maximization are feasible only under conditions of market power. In the limiting case of perfect competition, profit maximization is the only feasible objective for firm survival. However, under FMO POs will still have residual market power. So the discipline of the product market will be in the right direction but would not be complete. In addition, as a public enterprise it will not face the discipline of the capital market, nor does it face the threat of bankruptcy. So FMO, by itself, is not going to be enough to secure the efficiency gains expected from FMO and PCR. Indeed, to attain the full benefits of PCR requires residual claimants. Under public ownership these cannot be fully attained. However, where for political or policy reasons a country is not prepared to privatize its PO, what alternatives are available to it? One alternative would be to subsidize the PO that is unable to compete under FMO, which we exclude from consideration here.[8] The more likely approach is for regulators to attempt to implement more detailed regulations to 'fix' the problems that the absence of a residual claimant causes. This approach typically leads to a spiral of ever increasing regulatory complexity, and it too should therefore be ruled out.

A more promising approach begins with the proposition that efficiency gains from PCR can be achieved to the extent that commercialization drives the PO toward profit-maximizing behavior. Thus, promoting commercialization of the PO itself should be the primary objective of regulation under FMO. Commercialization would then drive a better alignment of the PO's profits with the incentives faced by various stakeholders, and with an improved market and customer orientation that accompanies commercial operations. This approach may be thought of as attempting to make stakeholders in the PO into 'pseudo residual claimants'. For management, this means greater reliance on the profit-alignment of executive compensation. For labor, this means profit sharing and employment contracts and work rules that are more in tune with market realities and profitability of the enterprise. For regulators, this means providing the flexibility to the enterprise to behave like a commercial enterprise, and not just a regulated entity saddled with many public missions and no commercial mission. For the current provider of capital, the government, this means setting up a corporate structure for the PO. Initially, this would naturally give rise to profit targets on the PO, including reasonable returns on invested capital. Subsequently, it may allow the enterprise to move toward competitive sourcing of capital.

The creation of a corporate structure with an enterprise charged to make profits, either for itself or for the government, will imply changes in incentives for management and labor. Executive compensation will have to be modified along the lines employed in private companies. However, absent private ownership these will be limited by the inability to motivate management through stock ownership, options, and the like. Some form of profit sharing may move in the direction of aligning incentives even under public ownership. For example, management could be compensated based on a simple linear incentive scheme, along the lines of Compensation $= A + b(\Pi - \Pi^0)^+$, where A is a constant salary component, b is management's share of profits Π in excess of some minimal level, Π^0 (where for any number x, $x^+ = \max(x, 0)$, so that the '+' in this expression implies that compensation is guaranteed to be at least equal to A). Setting parameters, A, b, and Π^0 will be a non-trivial problem requiring judgment, and some of the flexibility to apply judgment to executive compensation must be left to the PO itself. Along with incentive compensation, there must be a clear accountability for enterprise outcomes. As part of this, subsidies must be ruled out and the commercial aspects of the undertaking must dominate. Similarly, attempts at micromanagement by regulators, dictating to the enterprise what it should do at every step of the way, should be avoided as misguided and detracting from both efficiency and the establishment of a commercial culture.[9]

Commercialization can enable POs to move in the direction of attaining the benefits of PCR, but it cannot attain all the benefits under public ownership because the best that can be achieved is a form of pseudo residual claimants. At best, only the carrot of residual claimants, namely profits, is present, and this in attenuated form. The stick of bankruptcy and takeover are completely absent. We recognize this as placing serious limits on the benefits that can be attained from pseudo residual claimants. Despite all the qualifications, we conclude that the adoption of PCR is appropriate when it is accompanied by commercialization and FMO.[10] PCR is superior to the alternatives and has the benefit of flexibility, low transactions costs, and the ability to accommodate competition. For these reasons PCR has been widely adopted in the postal sector and some POs, the Netherlands, Germany, and Austria, have adopted varying degrees of private ownership. FMO can be expected to promote further moves in this direction, and in the direction of creating pseudo residual claimants of current stakeholders whose interests are not aligned with profits and the innovation potential required to prosper under competition.

3. IMPLEMENTING PCR UNDER FMO IN THE POSTAL SECTOR

PCR enjoys considerable advantages over other approaches to price regulation when markets are open to competition. In the early stages of liberalization, where the incumbent PO continues to have significant market power, the regulator can require *ex ante* review of rates, and can impose additional restrictions on access pricing and on new product development. As the sector becomes more competitive, PCR can move to an *ex post* light-handed regime that concentrates on single-piece rates and protection for the small customer, leaving competition to assure quality, pricing, and product innovation for large customers. As noted in the B-P analysis reviewed in the previous section, the decoupling of cost and price under PCR also assures that incentives for cross-subsidy in the profit-oriented firm are minimized.

Notwithstanding these potential benefits of PCR, there are several major issues associated with its implementation. These include setting initial values for the price cap, determining the review period for PCR, regulatory commitment (treatment of excess profits and losses), setting the 'X factor', and basket design. These have been noted already in previous research and a sizeable literature on both theory and practice exists on these issues, so we will not take them up again here. Perhaps the central issue in implementing PCR in the postal sector is the degree of flexibility in pricing that is allowed the PO under price caps. We illustrate this issue by discussing one aspect of PCR, the inclusion of access prices under price caps in what has come to be known as 'global price caps'.

3.1 The Structure of PCR

The well-known structure of PCR (Crew and Kleindorfer, 1996) involves separating major products and services offered by the regulated company into a set of 'baskets' and capping price increases for each basket according to some index of prices. The most common index employed is the Laspeyres Index, which we use here to illustrate the operation of PCR. For a particular basket with n products, $i = 1, 2, \ldots, n$, PCR constrains the vector of prices P_{it+1}, $i = 1, \ldots, n$, for year $t+1$ of the regulated company (possibly subject to further constraints on the structure of these prices, some of which are noted below in the context of access pricing) according to the following rule:

$$\frac{\sum_{i=1}^{n} P_{it+1} Q_{it}}{\sum_{i=1}^{n} P_{it} Q_{it}} \leq (1 + \Delta CPI_t - X) + Y.$$

In the above, ΔCPI is the change in the consumer price index (or similar index), and the X factor indicates how much consumers can expect to gain in real terms from PCR.[11] The Y factor represents additional adjustments that the regulator may allow based on changes in exogenous factors; for example, tax law or other effects outside the control of the company.[12]

PCR can give considerable pricing flexibility to the PO. For example, one form giving close to maximum flexibility could take the form of a regulated basket for letters, primarily the single-piece USO prices for a number of weight steps. This basket might also include services like registered mail and COD. There could also be a single-piece parcels basket. All other products would then be in the competitive basket and not subject to any regulatory requirements. However, given the market dominant position of an incumbent PO, this level of flexibility may not be acceptable, as there would be a concern that prices and conditions of access be offered on a non-discriminatory basis to both the PO's customers of the USP as well as to third-party competitors seeking access to the PO's network. Just what level of pricing flexibility should be left to the PO while its market dominant is a key issue in implementing PCR. We illustrate this for what will certainly be a center-piece of this issue, the treatment of worksharing and access regulation.

3.2 PCR and Access Regulation

Access is a critical element of FMO, as it enables entrants to utilize the incumbent's network to provide national coverage for their customers without duplicating network elements in high-cost areas. Access pricing is the method by which potential entrants (be they customers of the PO, consolidators, or transportation organizations) are provided incentives to undertake activities in the postal value chain. Access can occur at various points in the (USP) network, corresponding to different levels of upstream activities provided by entrants and customers, ranging from collection and consolidation activities, various steps in mail processing, and possibly also transportation to the USP's delivery areas. For some products, entrants will bypass the USP's network altogether, where it is profitable. The more work that is done upstream, the greater the worksharing content of the mail and the less work for the PO to accomplish final delivery.

Several approaches have been proposed for setting access prices (and their associated worksharing discounts). It is not our purpose to review the theory and practice of postal access pricing here, as this has been done in several recent studies.[13] We use the terminology WSP = Worksharing Provider to designate an entrant or a customer of the PO that is a potential user of the PO's network and access products. Our concern here is focused only on incorporating worksharing and access prices into the PCR structure.

Including access prices in the price cap index under PCR has come to be called 'global price caps'. The approach was first developed by Crew and Kleindorfer (1994) and was subsequently termed 'global price caps' by Laffont and Tirole (1996). It attempts to strike a balance between imposing price limitations while retaining meaningful price flexibility for the PO. This can be done by including a weighted average of all access products in the regulated basket along with all other regulated products to which the traditional price-cap formula applies. In addition, there would be a competitive basket to which the price cap would not apply and for which the PO could change its prices without regulatory approval, as in the case of private carriers.[14]

Irrespective of the form of access pricing, if every conceivable form of worksharing discount is subject to regulatory review, the regulatory process will become extremely complicated. So our basic conclusion is that under FMO PCR should be restricted to a few generic products, allowing flexibility to the PO to adjust their prices for other access products subject only to floors and ceilings implied by respective generic products that embody less worksharing content and E2E products. It is important that sufficient flexibility be granted the PO/USP under FMO so that customization of products to individual customer segments can be achieved without excessive intervention by the regulator.

To clarify alternative approaches to access pricing and global price caps under PCR, let us first note the arboreal structure for access products (see Figure 1.1). This figure shows two typical E2E products, which we label First-Class and Second-Class mail. Each of these products goes through a number of stages prior to final delivery, where the amount of work to be done by the PO depends on the quality and extent of worksharing undertaken by the WSP prior to tendering the mail to the PO. The remaining work to be accomplished by the PO also may depend, at each node in Figure 1.1, on the volumes tendered, the times at which these are received by the PO, and other characteristics of the operational and accounting processes linking the WSP and the PO. For concreteness, let us refer to these additional features of incoming mail streams as WSP attributes.

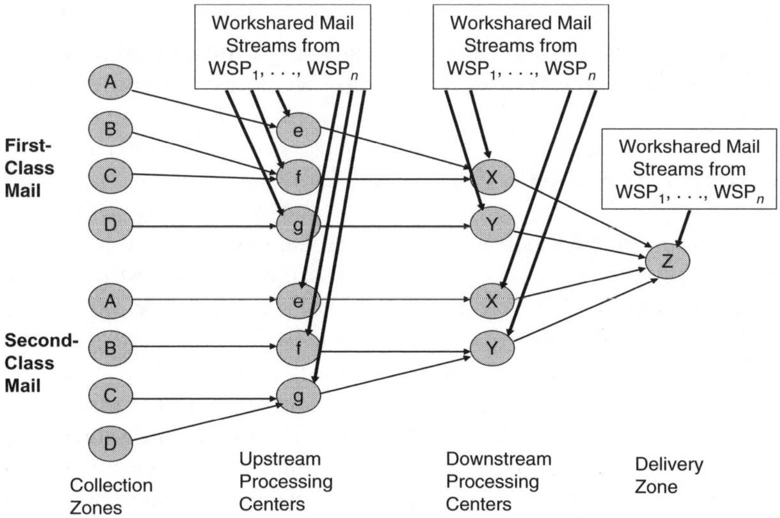

Figure 1.1 Illustrating the structure of access services

Under global price caps, access services could be defined, and their prices regulated through the logic of PCR, for every one of the nodes and WSP attributes evident in Figure 1.1, which could allow for different prices for every delivery zone. However, there is a tradeoff not evident in this approach. Given the structure in Figure 1.1, the key tradeoff we wish to highlight is in the detail or granularity of the design of the PCR regulated basket containing access products and associated regulatory oversight. Two basic approaches suggest themselves:

1. A very detailed accounting for every access product, and separately for various WSP attributes (e.g., various volume categories) could be employed. This would give rise to a weighted average of access products with a very large number of product and WSP attribute distinctions.
2. An alternative is that only a few products such as basic downstream access and the E2E rate for the underlying non-workshared product (e.g., $D+1$, $D+3/4$, $D+6/7$) could be included in the price-cap formula. Then there would be the requirement that the prices for all other access products be subject to the floor and ceiling prices of the single-piece rate and the (possibly zone-specific) applicable delivery zone rate, leaving otherwise the determination of pricing for all intermediate forms of access and WSP attributes entirely to the discretion of the incumbent.[15]

A variation on the second case would leave discretion entirely in the hands of the incumbent, but would require non-discriminatory treatment across all WSPs (i.e., including both the PO's customers and entrants), possibly enforced by *ex post* posting (and availability) of any particular agreements reached with individual customers or WSPs.

The point here is that the more inclusive the regulation of the details of access prices in the price-cap formula, the greater is the control that the regulator will have over access prices, but also the greater is the rigidity of the resulting access regimes in responding to market conditions. When the PO has significant market power, arguably more detailed regulatory control over access prices might be warranted. However, as FMO develops, it will be important to increase the flexibility allowed to the PO. A center-piece of this flexibility will certainly be the approach to which such access prices are reflected in PCR.

4. SUMMARY AND CONCLUSIONS

FMO in 2011 has serious implications for funding the USO and the future of postal and delivery services within the EU. We have examined some of the adjustments that POs, governments, and regulators will be required to make to achieve viability under the major shock of FMO. We reviewed how the USO might be funded. We argued that until the market itself provides adequate coverage for universal services that these be financed by adjusting the flexibility of PCR, including its coverage of access services. This would allow POs sufficient commercial freedom to finance their operations, including the USO. In terms of pricing flexibility, our general recommendations are based on the strong conviction that external subsidies will lead to considerable inefficiencies and loss of customer orientation by the PO. We discussed regulation of access prices, which would be included in the price-cap (business products basket) in the form of a global price cap, with the granularity of the access services included determined with due regard for the tradeoff between the transactions cost of regulation and its benefits in restraining market power of the PO. Ways of assessing the tradeoff between regulatory control of access and pricing flexibility will become of increasing interest, particularly in Europe, as more countries open their markets to competition.

We reviewed PCR at a basic level. PCR had been widely adopted by POs, which are public enterprises, without concern that PCR's efficiency properties are driven by the profit objective of the residual claimants. We concluded that the more competitive the market and the more commercialized the public enterprise POs, the more they will mimic a profit-maximizing firm. So the increased commercialization that we have been observing clearly is in line with the adoption of PCR. For a USO to be funded under FMO not only must POs become more commercially oriented but also governments and regulators have to recognize that the USO cannot be funded without some accommodation. If subsidies are to be avoided, this implies that POs have to take advantage of scale and scope economies and be allowed pricing flexibility. This can be achieved by a form of PCR that balances considerations of market dominance with the financial viability of the PO.

NOTES

* The authors gratefully acknowledge the support of Royal Mail Group in the preparation of this chapter. The views expressed are solely those of the authors and do not necessarily reflect those of Royal Mail Group. We thank Paul Dudley and Frank Rodriguez for valuable comments.

1. For details on the EU Parliament proposal, which still must be approved by the Council of Ministers to take effect, see http://www.europarl.europa.eu/news/expert/infopress_page/056-8955-190-07-28-909-20070706IPR08902-09-07-2007-2007-true/default_en.htm
2. See Crew and Kleindorfer (2007) for the most recent of our own contributions to this literature.
3. The interactions between single-piece tariffs and business product pricing are explored in Crew and Kleindorfer (2007). In addition, higher single-piece prices can lead to increased consolidation and e-substitution, and the increased price elasticity implied also limits the degree to which single-piece prices can be used to raise revenue.
4. Sector regulators may choose to deregulate to share or transfer the burden of profit or price regulation to antitrust authorities or to the competition regulator, but more often than not sector regulators are reluctant to relinquish control. It is therefore usually only by legislative decision that sector regulation is fundamentally shifted from one agency to another.
5. Baumol first published this book in 1959 and revised in 1967.
6. This notion goes back to an even earlier literature, namely, Hicks (1935), whose notion was that the greatest of all monopoly profits was the quiet life.
7. Vickers and Yarrow (1988) examine objectives of public enterprises.
8. Various public missions and responsibilities may still be imposed on the PO as part of the USO, and some of these could be explicitly funded by the government; for example, as a result of public tenders or a transparent identification of the mission and its cost. See Crew and Kleindorfer (2007) for a discussion. Our point here is that subsidies beyond very well identified public missions will undermine both efficiency and the commercial culture of the PO, which must be considered the main objectives of FMO.
9. The Postal Accountability and Enhancement Act of 2006 adopted PCR but failed to take any meaningful steps toward commercialization and FMO along the lines argued here. It is an exercise in micromanagement that fails to address the underlying problems.
10. Littlechild (1983) and Crew and Kleindorfer (2001) also discuss issues of regulatory commitment under PCR. Where PCR is successful in improving efficiency with resultant high profits, the regulator may 'renege' and lower the price cap. This has a potentially serious impact on the ability of PCR to attain efficiency. This is compounded with the fact that, with a public enterprise, government ownership of the enterprise will clearly affect regulator behavior and the likelihood of reneging. We do not explore the impact of commitment here, but it is clearly important under PCR.

11. There is a continuing confusion about the nature of the *X* factor among many regulators. Instead of being considered nothing more than the real reduction in prices to be provided to customers, the *X* factor has often been coupled directly with predicted productivity growth of the company or the economy at large. Prices would then be allowed to rise not by the CPI minus the *X* factor but by the CPI minus the estimated 'productivity offset', where the productivity offset was intended to reflect the productivity of the firm. Although the practice of setting the *X* factor based upon the productivity offset is rather widespread, it is inappropriate. Setting the *X* factor involves several factors other than the productivity offset, including expected growth in the market, estimates of internal inefficiency in the firm that PCR is intended to remedy, required returns on capital, and other factors. See Crew and Kleindorfer (1996).
12. Estimating *X* and determining the scope of *Y* require considerable judgment, especially in the initialization phase. In addition to these complexities, setting the level of initial prices in a manner that will give customers and the PO a fair chance of profiting from PCR is a further matter requiring judgment. Given that initially at least single-piece prices may be lower than required, it is important to allow for the possibility for a gradual upward adjustment of these rates in the initial (e.g., five-year) price-cap regime. Recent history in the US and the UK indicates that this initialization process may involve reviewing enormous amounts of data. Such detailed examination is misplaced under PCR; the key element is to assure that small customers are protected by a reasonable setting of the *X* factor, while larger customers are served through increased pricing flexibility and the pressures of competition.
13. See Billette de Villemeur et al. (2002, 2003, 2007), Calzada (2006), Crew and Kleindorfer (2004, 2007), De Donder (2006), and Panzar (2002).
14. It would, however, not be exempt from antitrust law.
15. Both of these forms of access price regulation have been discussed in the literature, and the inclusion of access prices in the price-cap formula has come to be known as 'global price-cap regulation'. For details, see Crew and Kleindorfer (1994), Laffont and Tirole (1996) and Billette de Villemeur et al. (2003).

REFERENCES

Aoki, Masahiko (1980), 'A model of the firm as a stockholder–employee cooperative game', *The American Economic Review*, **70** (4), 600–10.

Baumol, William J. (1967), *Business Behavior Value and Growth*, revised edition, New York, NY: Harcourt, Brace and World.

Billette de Villemeur, Etienne, Helmuth Crémer, Bernard Roy and Joëlle Toledano (2002), 'Pricing and worksharing discounts in the postal sector', in M.A. Crew and P.R. Kleindorfer (eds), *Postal and Delivery Services: Delivering on Competition*, Boston, MA: Kluwer Academic Publishers, pp. 33–48.

Billette de Villemeur, Etienne, Helmuth Crémer, Bernard Roy and Joëlle Toledano (2003), 'Optimal pricing and price-cap regulation in the postal sector', *Journal of Regulatory Economics*, **24** (1), 49–62.

Billette de Villemeur, Etienne, Helmuth Crémer, Bernard Roy and Joëlle Toledano (2007), 'Worksharing, access and bypass: the structure of prices in the postal sector', *Journal of Regulatory Economics*, **32** (1), 67–85.

Braeutigam, Ronald R. and John C. Panzar (1989), 'Diversification incentives under "price-based" and "cost-based" regulation', *RAND Journal of Economics*, **20**, 373–91.

Braeutigam, Ronald R. and John C. Panzar (1993), 'Effects of the change from rate-of-return to price-cap regulation', *American Economic Review*, **83**, 191–8.

Calzada, Joan (2006), 'Worksharing and access discounts in the postal sector with asymmetric information', *Journal of Regulatory Economics*, **29** (1), 69–102.

Crew, Michael A. and Paul R. Kleindorfer (1979), 'Managerial discretion and public utility regulation', *Southern Economic Journal*, **45** (3), January: 696–709.

Crew, Michael A. and Paul R. Kleindorfer (1994), 'Pricing, entry, service quality, and innovation under a commercialized postal service', in J. Gregory Sidak (ed.), *Governing the Postal Service*, Washington, DC: AEI Press, pp. 150–77.

Crew, Michael A. and Paul R. Kleindorfer (1996), 'Incentive regulation in the United Kingdom and the United States: some lessons', *Journal of Regulatory Economics*, **9** (3), 211–25.

Crew, Michael A. and Paul R. Kleindorfer (2001), 'A critique of the theory of incentive regulation:

implications for the design of Performance Based Regulation (PBR) for postal service', in M.A. Crew and P.R. Kleindorfer (eds), *Future Directions in Postal Reform*, Boston, MA: Kluwer Academic Publishers, 37–66.
Crew, Michael A. and Paul R. Kleindorfer (2004), 'Access and the USO for letters and parcels', in M.A. Crew and Paul R. Kleindorfer (eds), *Competitive Transformation of the Postal and Delivery Sector,* Boston, MA: Kluwer Academic Publishers, pp. 3–42.
Crew, Michael A. and Paul R. Kleindorfer (2007), 'Approaches to the USO under entry', in M.A. Crew and P.R. Kleindorfer (eds), *Liberalization of the Postal and Delivery Sector*, Cheltenham, UK and Northampton, MA, USA: Edward Elgar, pp. 1–18.
De Donder, Philippe (2006), 'Access pricing in the postal sector: theory and simulations', *Review of Industrial Organization*, **28**, 207–326.
Hicks, J.R. (1935), 'Annual survey of economic theory: the theory of monopoly', *Econometrica*, **3** (1), 1–20.
Kleindorfer, Paul R. and Murat R. Sertel (1980), 'Labor-management and codetermination in regulated monopolies', in Bridger Mitchell and Paul R. Kleindorfer (eds), *Regulated Industries and Public Enterprise: European and United States Perspectives*, Lexington, MA: Lexington Books, pp. 139–68.
Laffont, Jean-Jacques and Jean Tirole (1996), 'Creating competition through interconnection: theory and practice', *Journal of Regulatory Economics*, **10** (3), 227–56.
Littlechild, Stephen C. (1983), *Regulation of British Telecommunications' Profitability*, London: Department of Trade and Industry.
Niskanen, William A. Jr. (1971), *Bureaucracy and Representative Government*, Chicago: Aldine Atherton.
Panzar, John C. (2002), 'Reconciling competition, downstream access, universal service in postal markets', in M.A. Crew and P.R. Kleindorfer (eds), *Postal and Delivery Services: Delivering on the Competition*, Boston, MA: Kluwer Academic Publishers, pp. 93–118.
PricewaterhouseCoopers (PwC) (2006), 'The impact on Universal service of the full market accomplishment of the postal internal market in 2009', Brussels.
Sappington, David E.M. and J. Gregory Sidak (2003), 'Incentives for anticompetitive behavior by public enterprises', *Review of Industrial Organization*, **22** (3), 183–206.
Vickers, John and George Yarrow (1988), *Privatization: An Economic Analysis*, Cambridge, MA: The MIT Press.
Ward, Benjamin (1958), 'The firm in Illyria: market syndicalism', *The American Economic Review*, **48** (4), 566–89.
WIK-Consult GmbH (2006), 'Main developments in the postal sector (2004–2006)', Bad-Honnef.
Williamson, Oliver E. (1963), 'Managerial discretion and business behavior', *The American Economic Review*, **53** (5), 1032–57.

TECHNICAL APPENDIX

Alternative Objectives for the Regulated Enterprise

We consider a multi-product enterprise, regulated by price caps, but with diverse objectives that are represented as a weighted sum of (a) sales, (b) average payments to labor and (c) welfare, and are further subject to a break-even constraint on profits. (By manipulating the required level of profits, we can also mimic the profit-maximizing enterprise.) Different weights on the different objectives (or profit level) represent situations in which different factions or stakeholders in the enterprise have greater bargaining power.[1]

Except for excess labor, we do not consider further objectives reflecting expense preferences including purely wasteful activities (Williamson, 1963; Crew and Kleindorfer, 1979). Including these would not change the basic message below, which is that if different stakeholders have the power to set prices and other operating decisions of the enterprise, then the outcomes for the regulated enterprise will reflect the objectives of these stakeholders. The fact that this is so from a mathematical point of view is the result of the usual deductive tautology that arises in formal modeling from tracing through the consequences of assumptions to their logical conclusions. The point we wish to underline is, however, not tautological. Our deeper point, as noted in the text, is that the incentives of various stakeholders in regulated enterprises need to be aligned with efficient outcomes. Under regulated monopoly, failure to align these incentives results in inefficiency that is paid for by the consumer through higher prices and lower quality. However, under competition, the result could be even worse, with the collapse of the entire enterprise, and ensuing pleas for rescue and subsidy that could have long-term effects on the efficiency of both the enterprise and its competitors. Our basic message is that merely imposing price caps or some other regulatory regime on an enterprise is considerably more complicated, and may not suffice to ensure efficient outcomes when a stakeholder with bargaining power or key decision rights derives utility from something other than efficient outcomes.

We employ the following notation:

$i \in N = \{1, \ldots, n\}$ = product index

$P_i(Q_i)$ = inverse demand curve for product i; P_i also represents price of product i; we assume that the demands for the N products are independent

Q_i = demand for product i = enterprise output

H_i = units (say hours) of labor input required to produce product i

w_C = competitive wage rate

$C_{iL} = H_i w_C$ = labor cost/unit to produce product i, evaluated at the competitive wage rate w_C

$L = \sum_{i \in N} H_i Q_i$ = total labor required by the enterprise

C_{iO} = unit costs of (other) non-labor inputs required to produce product i

$\sum_{i \in N} C_{iO} Q_i$ = total cost of other (non-labor) inputs required by the enterprise

$w(Q)$ = wage rate for enterprise employees, where $w(Q) \geq w_C$ is required

F = fixed costs per period, including any required profit payments to shareholders in the enterprise

The model of the price-cap regulated enterprise with general objectives can be stated as follows.

Price-cap regulated, multiple-stakeholder enterprise model

$$\text{Max } \alpha_1 R(Q) + \alpha_2 w(Q) + \alpha_3 W(Q) \tag{1.A1}$$

Subject to: $Q = (Q_1, \ldots, Q_n) \geq 0$ and

$$\Pi(Q) = \sum_{i \in N} P_i(Q_i)Q_i - \sum_{i \in N} C_{iO}Q_i - w_C L - F \geq 0 \tag{1.A2}$$

$$R(Q) = \sum_{i \in N} P_i(Q_i)Q_i \tag{1.A3}$$

$$L \geq \sum_{i \in N} H_i Q_i \tag{1.A4}$$

$$w(Q) = \frac{\Pi(Q)}{L} + w_C \tag{1.A5}$$

$$W(Q) = \Pi(Q) + \sum_{i \in N} \int_0^{Q_i} [P_i(q) - P_i(Q_i)]\,\mathrm{d}q \tag{1.A6}$$

$$\sum_{i \in N} A_i P_i(Q_i) \leq B \tag{1.A7}$$

where the parameters A_i and B in the price-cap equation (1.A7) are positive, and where the weights $\alpha_1, \alpha_2, \alpha_3 \geq 0$ reflect the relative bargaining power, respectively, of management (with revenue being a proxy for the size of the enterprise), labor (interested in maximizing their wage level), and the efficiency-oriented regulator (interested in maximizing the traditional welfare generated by the enterprise). Without loss of generality, we can assume that the weights $\alpha_1, \alpha_2, \alpha_3 \geq 0$ are normalized so that they sum to one.

We note the following concerning (1.A1)–(1.A7). First, (1.A2) and (1.A5) assure that the actual wages paid $w(Q)$ will exceed the competitive wage level, which is required in order to attract and retain employees in the enterprise. Second, the definition (1.A5) means that whatever surplus remains after paying the fixed costs F (which could include a profit component to shareholders of the enterprise) go to labor.

Substituting for $R(Q)$, $w(Q)$, and $W(Q)$ into (1.A1), we obtain the following equivalent problem:

$$\text{Max } \alpha_1\left(\sum_{i \in N} P_i(Q_i)\,Q_i\right) + \alpha_2\left(\frac{\Sigma_{i \in N}(P_i(Q_i) - C_{iO})Q_i - F}{L}\right) + \alpha_3\left(\Pi(Q) + \sum_{i \in N} \int_0^{Q_i} [P_i(q) - P_i(Q_i)]\,\mathrm{d}q\right) \tag{1.A8}$$

Subject to: (1.A2), (1.A4), and (1.A7).

Associate Lagrange multipliers λ, μ, and ν, respectively, to the constraints (1.A2), (1.A4) and (1.A7). Forming the Lagrangian $G(Q, \lambda, \mu, \nu)$ and proceeding in the usual fashion, we obtain the following derivatives:

$$\frac{\partial G}{\partial Q_i} = \alpha_1[P_i'Q_i + P_i] + \frac{\alpha_2}{L}[(P_i - C_{iO}) + P_i'Q_i] + \alpha_3[P_i - C_{iO}] + \lambda[P_i'Q_i + P_i - C_{iO}] - \mu H_i - \nu A_i P_i', \quad (1.A9)$$

$$\frac{\partial G}{\partial L} = \mu - \frac{\alpha_2}{L}\left[\frac{\sum_{i \in N}(P_i(Q_i) - C_{iO})Q_i - F}{L}\right] - (\alpha_3 + \lambda)w_C. \quad (1.A10)$$

Simplifying and regrouping terms in (1.A9) and setting the result to zero, we obtain the following FOCs:

$$\left(\alpha_1 + \frac{\alpha_2}{L} + \lambda - \nu A_i\right)P_i'Q_i + \left(\alpha_1 + \frac{\alpha_2}{L} + \alpha_3 + \lambda\right)(P_i - C_{iO}) + \alpha_1 C_{iO} - \mu H_i = 0, \quad i \in N. \quad (1.A11)$$

We can rewrite (1.A11) in the following form:

$$\frac{P_i - \xi C_{iO} - \zeta C_{iL}}{P_i} = \frac{\delta_i}{\eta_i}, \quad i \in N, \quad (1.A12)$$

where elasticity $\eta_i = -P_i/P_i'Q_i$, and where (using the identity $C_{iL} = H_i w_C$),

$$\xi = \frac{\frac{\alpha_2}{L} + \alpha_3 + \lambda}{\alpha_1 + \frac{\alpha_2}{L} + \alpha_3 + \lambda} \leq 1, \quad (1.A13)$$

$$\zeta = \frac{\mu}{\alpha_1 + \frac{\alpha_2}{L} + \alpha_3 + \lambda} = \frac{\frac{\alpha_2}{L}w(Q) + (\alpha_3 + \lambda)w_C}{\left(\alpha_1 + \frac{\alpha_2}{L} + \alpha_3 + \lambda\right)w_C} \geq \frac{\frac{\alpha_2}{L} + \alpha_3 + \lambda}{\alpha_1 + \frac{\alpha_2}{L} + \alpha_3 + \lambda}, \quad (1.A14)$$

$$\delta_i = \frac{\alpha_1 + \frac{\alpha_2}{L} + \lambda - \nu A_i}{\alpha_1 + \frac{\alpha_2}{L} + \alpha_3 + \lambda}, \quad i \in N, \quad (1.A15)$$

where in (1.A13) we have used (1.A2) to infer that $w(Q) = (\Pi(Q) + w_C L)/L \geq w_C$.

Various cases can be analyzed from the above results, depending on the values of the weights α_i. We note a few of the interesting ones here.

Welfare-maximizing/Ramsey solution: $\alpha_1 = \alpha_2 = 0$, $\alpha_3 = 1$, $B = \infty$
The familiar inverse elasticity Ramsey rule obtains from (1.A12) when welfare is maximized and the price-cap constraint (1.A7) is non-binding (implying $\nu = 0$).

Profit-maximizing price-cap regulated firm: $\lambda \to \infty$
If λ is large relative to all the weights α_i, then (1.A12) reduces to the following:

$$\frac{P_i - (C_{iO} + C_{iL})}{P_i} = \left(\frac{\lambda - \nu A_i}{\lambda}\right)\frac{1}{\eta_i}. \tag{1.A16}$$

We see that price caps have the expected effect of mitigating prices relative to the pure profit-maximizing solution (the solution corresponding to $\nu = 0$). Their relative impact would be proportional to the parameters A_i.

Revenue-maximizing solution: $\alpha_1 = 1$, $\alpha_2 = 0$, $\alpha_3 = 0$
In this case, the optimal pricing rule (1.A12) reduces to the following:

$$\frac{P_i - \frac{\lambda}{1+\lambda}(C_{iO} + C_{iL})}{P_i} = \left(\frac{1 + \lambda - \nu A_i}{1 + \lambda}\right)\frac{1}{\eta_i}. \tag{1.A17}$$

From this, three basic properties of the 'revenue-maximizing' rule are evident:

1. As noted by Sappington and Sidak (2003), there is an underweighting of cost relative to the Ramsey Rule, which could even lead to charging less than marginal cost for some products (those with relatively high elasticity).
2. Price caps can counterbalance departures from Ramsey pricing in that setting the parameters A_i appropriately could counteract the relative underweighting associated with the revenue-maximizing objective.[2] As expected from the logic of price-cap regulation, the larger the weight A_i in the price-cap formula, the larger the relative adjustment to the price of product *i*.
3. As the profit constraint becomes more binding (so that λ increases), the revenue-maximizing firm sets its prices more and more like a profit-maximizing firm.

Wage-maximizing solution: $\alpha_1 = 0$, $\alpha_2 = 1$, $\alpha_3 = 0$
In this case, the optimal pricing rule (1.A12) results in:

$$\frac{P_i - C_{iO} - \frac{w(Q) + \lambda L w_C}{w_C + \lambda L w_C} C_{iL}}{P_i} = \left(\frac{1 + \lambda L - \nu A_i L}{1 + \lambda L}\right)\frac{1}{\eta_i}. \tag{1.A18}$$

From this, three basic properties of this 'wage-maximizing' rule are evident:

1. Kleindorfer and Sertel (1980) built upon Ward (1958) to show that in regulated labor-managed firms, the average wage objective leads to a rule that over-weights the cost of labor relative to the Ramsey Rule, which would naturally lead to hiring less labor than efficient, thus increasing the average wage of those in the enterprise. This assumes that labor is freely adjustable downward. However, for solidarity or other reasons, if the

work force in the enterprise has the bargaining power and the desire to impose a constraint that $L \geq L_0$, where L_0 is the initial labor force, then, if L_0 is larger than the wage-maximizing solution, this implies that constraint (1.A4) will be non-binding in the optimal solution ($\nu = 0$ in (1.A18)). The consequence would be that the firm would behave like a price-cap regulated profit-maximizing firm, but with an inefficiently sized labor force, and with prices and outputs that reflected both of these effects.

2. Price caps can counterbalance departures from Ramsey pricing for the wage-maximizing firm, in that a proper choice of the parameters A_i could restore the relative underweighting associated with the wage-maximizing objective. As expected from the logic of price-cap regulation, the larger the weight A_i in the price-cap formula, the larger the relative adjustment to the price of product *i*.
3. As the profit constraint becomes more binding (so that λ increases), the wage-maximizing firm sets its prices more and more like a profit-maximizing firm.

Other cases could be analyzed, including extending the analysis to the same multi-stakeholder regulated enterprise facing competition of one sort or another. However, the basic points we wish to emphasize are already clear from the above. First, the price-cap regulated enterprise will behave very differently depending on the objectives of the stakeholder group that, for one reason or another, controls the decisions of the enterprise. Second, these differences arise even in the case where the stakeholder group with major bargaining power is the residual claimant to all profits generated by the enterprise. For example, in the wage-maximizing case examined, labor is effectively the residual claimant. However, if incentives are not aligned with enterprise profit, well-known distortions can arise in enterprise behavior. Finally, price caps can have some counterbalancing effect to the various forms of inefficiency examined, but applying them effectively is obviously more complicated when the regulator must counteract not only cost inefficiencies arising from monopoly, but also inefficiencies that arise from objectives not aligned with profit. All of this leads to our basic conclusion that regulation must start with aligning the incentives of the enterprise with value creation as measured by profit.

NOTES

1. Similar models have been analyzed in the context of labor-managed firms by Kleindorfer and Sertel (1980). See Aoki (1980) for a general formulation of this multi-stakeholder argument in the context of labor and investors as stakeholders, with labor providing firm-specific capital that provides some benefits to the firm while also yielding additional bargaining leverage to labor.
2. In practice, this result may not be of great significance that the A_i are themselves not set by the regulator, but rather are determined via a price index and previous prices and quantities determine the A_i. We are merely noting the algebraic fact that, in principle, some counterbalancing of the inefficiencies caused by revenue maximization could occur through price-cap regulation. As far as we know, it is an open research question whether one or another pricing index would be more efficient in the price-cap structure when regulating a revenue-maximizing firm. We do not analyze this here, as our basic message is that incentives (e.g., executive compensation and profit sharing) should be adopted to align the incentives of the regulated firm with profits, rather than accepting its initial governance and objectives (be they revenue maximizing or some other) as given.

2. Social costs and benefits of the universal service obligation in the postal market*

Helmuth Cremer, Philippe De Donder, François Boldron, Denis Joram and Bernard Roy

1. INTRODUCTION

The universal service obligation (USO) is a cornerstone of regulatory policy in the postal sector. In the EU, where the sector is headed towards full liberalization, the USO is the major argument used to advocate some residual regulation. In the postal sector, like in many other network industries, universal service was historically provided by a monopolistic public or regulated operator. While the need for monopoly protection has been increasingly disputed, the very idea of universal service has remained relatively uncontested during the early stages of the liberalization process. The debate was not that much about the appropriate extent of the USO but about the most efficient (or least costly) way to make it competitively neutral, or at least as compatible as possible with competition. This in itself is a challenging question.

More recently, however, the USO in itself has increasingly been questioned. The question is whether the social benefits associated with the USO are significant enough to justify its cost, and in particular the impediment to competition it often implies. The spectacular development of electronic communications is likely to further fuel this debate, because email and telephone tend to supplant the postal sector as provider of universal access to communications.

To ensure a sound design of the future regulatory context in the postal sector, it is important not to restrict this debate to political or ideological considerations. The underlying economic aspects are of crucial importance and have to be given thorough consideration. While there are some papers in the literature that deal with this issue, it appears fair to say that most of the contributions on USO have concentrated on the 'how' (to implement) rather than on the 'why' (to impose it and to what extent). This is true to some extent for all network industries but even more so for the postal sector.[1]

This chapter provides a detailed analysis of the benefits and costs of the USO in the postal sector. We present and assess alternative economic justifications of the USO. These include the idea that a USO may be used as a remedy for network externalities, that a USO is a form of redistributive pricing policy, and that it can be a channel to supply a public good or an instrument of regional policy.

Among these, the redistributive pricing argument is probably the most unexpected one and needs some further elaboration. Prices are referred to as 'redistributive' when they are not solely set according to (private or social) efficiency considerations. We argue that USO is first and foremost a constraint on pricing; the obligation to provide service without an affordable pricing requirement would be an empty constraint. We show that USO may be an optimal second best policy, and that this is true even within the sender pays context of the postal sector. We also identify the (social) costs of USO and suggest some avenues along which a formal cost–benefit analysis of USO can be carried out.

Another aspect that will be explored is the role of the postal network as 'intermediary' between firms and consumers (who interact through the 'platform' provided by the postal network). This is related to the notion of network externality that has traditionally been used to justify the USO in telecommunications. However, the recent literature on two-sided markets has taken a fresh look at these forms of interactions. Specifically, it has brought together the notions of usage and membership externalities and studied their implications on the pricing rules. One of the messages that has emerged from this literature is that 'membership fees' on one side of the market may be below cost (or even negative). We shall examine if and to what extent the view of the postal network as a two-sided market can provide a rationale for a USO.

Before proceeding, it is useful to briefly review the definition of a USO. It involves the obligation of an operator to supply a specific package of goods and services, of a determined quality, to all users at 'affordable' rates. In the European Union, a minimum definition is contained in the EU directives. It can be reinforced by individual member countries according to the principle of subsidiarity. In Germany or in France, for instance, the requirement concerning the delivery frequency goes beyond the minimal EU requirements of five days a week. In addition, many EU countries have specific 'accessibility' conditions as part of their USO, not required by EU directives, which impose density and distance restrictions on collection boxes and counter services. Similarly, uniformity of prices is not an obligation but just a possible option. Nevertheless, many Member States (including the UK, Denmark, and France) have transposed in their law a uniformity obligation (for products within the scope of USO) rather than just an 'affordability' requirement.[2]

Studying the rationale of USO involves two different questions. First, we can look for a justification of the USO on welfare grounds, taking into account the various constraints that the policy makers may face. Alternatively, one can adopt a positive approach and explain why the USO is effectively imposed in most network industries. In this chapter, we focus on the first aspect while keeping the issue of political constraint in mind. We present a critical review of the major arguments that can justify a USO in the postal sector.

2. REDISTRIBUTION

2.1. The Basic Idea

The USO can be seen as a special case of *redistributive pricing*; that is, a policy meant to achieve redistribution through prices instead of (or in addition to) income taxation and/or 'direct' transfers. This statement may come as a surprise, and the reader may wonder why we refer to USO as a *pricing* policy and why we qualify it as *redistributive*. Consequently, two clarifying remarks are in order. First, one has to keep in mind that the USO is primarily a constraint on pricing. The restrictions on pricing are a crucial ingredient in its definition. Without such a restriction, the obligation to provide service would be an empty constraint. An operator who can charge a price that is sufficiently large to cover cost has no reason to refuse the provision of service. Second, the term 'redistributive' is used here to designate considerations that are not covered by efficiency. In other words, redistributive prices are prices that differ from those set on pure efficiency grounds (e.g., marginal cost driven).

Observe that a USO may imply two types of redistribution. First, there is redistribution towards high-cost customers (e.g., single-piece mail users) or addressees (e.g., mail sent to rural households). This is achieved through uniform pricing or whenever price differentials (between consumer groups) fall short of cost differentials. Second, there may be redistribution towards low-income (or otherwise needy) individuals. Illustrations are social tariffs (in telecommunications or electricity). In the postal sector, the first aspect appears to be the most relevant.[3] However, in reality, cost and income may be correlated: in France, low-income people are more likely to live in rural areas.[4] They benefit from universal service in two ways: first, as individual senders, they benefit from the 'affordable' redistributive price of the single-piece stamp; and second, as addressees, they benefit from uniform pricing (see Section 3).

When viewed as redistributive pricing, a USO bears some similarities with policies involving 'public provision of private goods' or in-kind transfers. The basic feature of these policies is that some essentially private goods like education, child care, or health care are provided either free of charge or at (sometimes highly) subsidized prices.

2.2. The Economic Background

These policies can be justified in two ways. The first justification relies on the notion of *specific egalitarism* introduced by Tobin (1970). According to this view, some goods are considered as essential in that they satisfy basic needs. Consequently, they ought to be made available to everyone irrespective of income, location, or other considerations. This argument is often used to justify universal provision of health care or education, but it can also apply to basic postal services. It is considered as debatable by many authors because it relies on the notion of paternalistic, non-Paretian preferences. Nevertheless, it is a very popular view that typically draws a good deal of political support.

A more subtle (and less *ad hoc*) justification can be found in the public economics literature, where it has been shown that such policies can be optimal in a second-best setting; that is, when policy makers do not have the necessary information to implement (potentially) more efficient policies like direct transfers. A detailed survey of this literature would go beyond the scope of this chapter and we shall restrict ourselves to reviewing the arguments that are most relevant for the problem under investigation.

The gist of the argument is that the use of price subsidies makes it easier to target redistribution. Consider the case of health care. Provision at subsidized prices may create overconsumption and thus imply an inefficient outcome. Consequently, if the objective of the public authorities is to help the less-healthy individuals, it would appear more efficient to do so directly, through a personalized transfer. Now, this is certainly true in a (hypothetical) world where public authorities can perfectly observe individual characteristics and can distinguish the needy from the well-off individuals. In reality, this is hardly the case and direct transfers to less-healthy individuals may be difficult to implement. Specifically, if sick individuals are entitled to some transfer, everyone has an incentive to pretend that he is needy and the verification of these claims would be impossible or very costly. However, if instead healthcare expenses are subsidized, the redistribution appears to be better targeted, even though it may come at the expense of some inefficiency (over-consumption).

To sum up, though potential generators of inefficiencies, price subsidies (or public provision at free or highly subsidized rates) may be an effective instrument of redistributive policies if alternative instruments (like personalized transfers) are not feasible for informational (or other) reasons. Observe also that political considerations may prevent direct transfers. This is most striking in the context of agricultural policy, but in the postal sector the replacement of USO by direct aid to rural residents may not be politically feasible either.

2.3. Redistributing through USO in a Sender-pays Sector

The view of the USO in the postal sector as a redistributive policy may give rise to two objections. First, in this sector, cost differentials arise mainly because of the locations (and types) of the addressees; the paying customers, on the other hand, are the senders. Second, the postal budget of a typical household is small and one can thus argue that the redistribution achieved is rather insignificant.

To establish that a USO can effect significant redistribution between, say, urban and rural individuals, it thus has to be shown that the eventual beneficiaries of the USO are not so much the senders, but rather the addressees, and specifically the high-cost households. This claim is supported by at least three arguments.

First, the existence of cost differentials according to the location of the addressee is, to a certain extent, due to the USO. It is because operators face the obligation of delivering to the addressees' mailbox at a given frequency that rural delivery is more expensive. In the absence of a USO, reduced frequency, post office box delivery, or similar measures could be implemented by the operator in order to eliminate the excess costs in rural delivery.[5] Such an adjustment would certainly have a much more significant impact on rural households than on the senders of the various mail items.

Second, in the absence of a USO, the postal operators could charge rural households for the delivery cost differentials by imposing a (periodic) fixed fee on those who opt for home delivery (rather than at some collective delivery point). In reality, such 'connecting charges' do, of course, not exist in the postal sector (at least not in Europe), but this does not mean that the operators might not find such a pricing scheme optimal if the USO were removed. Now, the arguments, which oppose such differential fees (and which may make them hard to accept on political grounds), are essentially of redistributive nature. From that perspective, the redistributive role of the USO is that it precludes certain (non-linear) pricing schemes that would impose a heavier burden on high-cost customers.

Third, most mail products are *inputs rather than final goods*. A large proportion of letters (and mail items in general) are sent by businesses, and economic analysis shows that firms generally manage to shift (at least part of) their costs to customers. Put differently, cost increases in postal items will, in general, lead to price increases for final goods or services, using mail as an input. Under uniform pricing in the postal sector, banks, for instance, have no reason to charge rural customers more for the mailing of their bank statements than they charge their urban customers. However, if mailing costs were different, banks might find it profitable to differentiate fees according to the location of a customer. A similar argument goes through for many other types of businesses and, in particular, for mail-order corporations. It is very likely that the burden of a removal of the uniform pricing requirement would eventually fall on the high-cost customers.

Consequently, the USO does effectively redistribute between high- and low-cost customers, and the significance of this redistribution goes beyond the budget that rural customers *directly* spend on mail. The crucial point is that this redistribution is achieved indirectly, because it concerns an input the cost of which will be reflected in the price of final goods. For example, the budget spent by each household (including small businesses) as a sender is about €68 per annum in France. As an addressee, the average household receives a 'mail budget' of €425; that is, more than six times the direct postal expenditures. A formal model that illustrates and substantiates this argument is presented in Appendix A.

So far, we have focused on equity issues. We now examine if and how a USO can be justified on efficiency grounds.

3. NETWORK EXTERNALITIES AND ECONOMIC INTERMEDIATION

3.1. The Traditional View

Network externalities are a classical justification of USO in telecommunications (see, e.g., Riordan, 2001). They arise when the benefits from using a network depend on the number of individuals who are connected to the network. Telecommunications provide a prominent example: the number of subscribers determines the number of individuals any particular user can communicate with. Consequently, any individual's decision to subscribe or not directly affects the utility of other individuals. However, when deciding upon participation, any particular consumer will only take his own (private) benefits into account. These externalities may lead to an inefficient outcome in an unregulated market and have an adverse effect on the development of the network. Specifically, one can expect participation rates to be too low. These inefficiencies may be reduced through regulatory measures promoting the affordability of access to the network, such as USO. From that perspective, USO can be seen as a device to correct market inefficiencies in the presence of network externalities.

This traditional view relies on a symmetric view of externalities where all subscribers are potential callers and receivers. This view is probably of limited relevance for the postal sector.

3.2. Externalities, Intermediation and the Two-sided Market Approach

A more modern approach to network externalities is provided by the 'two-sided markets' framework. In this setting, a market is viewed as a platform (intermediary) for exchanges between agents on its two sides. The membership and/or usage on one side of the market affect the utility or profit opportunities on the other side. This gives rise to membership and/or usage externalities that are no longer symmetric. Take the prominent example of credit/debit cards. The utility of a cardholder depends on the number of outlets that accept the card. Conversely, the benefits to, say, a restaurant from accepting the card depend on the number of cardholders. These externalities affect pricing policies and in many circumstances it is desirable to 'subsidize' membership or usage on one side of the market.

While the postal sector differs in several respects from the sectors that have been studied in the two-sided market literature, this view of externalities has interesting implications for the interpretation of a USO.[6] The postal sector acts as an intermediary between firms and households. Firms' benefits from relying on postal products (as opposed to alternative media) depend on the number of households that can be reached (with a given quality of service). Conversely, households may benefit from the presence of a large number of firms. A USO can then be seen as a device to internalize these externalities. For instance, a direct application of two-sided market models to the case of pricing of usage and 'membership' would show that making addressees pay for home delivery is not likely to be optimal. The free home delivery mentioned above for its redistributive merits could thus also be justified on efficiency grounds. We do not further pursue the issue of addressee's payments here, since a fully fledged study of postal sector pricing from a two-sided market perspective would go beyond the scope of this chapter and is left for future research.[7]

Instead, we use some ingredients of the two-sided market approach, but focus on quality rather than pricing. In Appendix B, we consider a simple model where the benefits of senders depend on coverage of the delivery network at a certain level of service (defined, for instance, by the number of deliveries per week). More precisely, the senders' surplus (and thus their demand) depends on the number of addressees that can be reached via, say, six deliveries per week. In other words, when some addressees cannot be reached at all – or more realistically, when they can only be reached with a lower quality of service – demand decreases. We show that a profit-maximizing (monopoly) operator can be expected to choose a degree of coverage that is too small. This means, for instance, that the part of the territory subject to six days a week delivery tends to be too small under profit-maximizing behavior. We also show that this argument is reinforced when there is a 'call externality' according to which an addressee's utility depends on the number of mail items he receives.[8]

This problem can be solved, or at least mitigated, through a USO. Under these circumstances, USO thus appears to be justified on efficiency grounds. Specifically, it is efficiency enhancing when the profit-maximizing operator spontaneously sets a degree of coverage (a level of quality) that is too low.

This argument is likely to be reinforced if there is competition. In that case, the coverage of the incumbent may spill over to entrants' demands, which in turn increases surplus in that segment.[9] A profit-maximizing operator has no reason to take this effect into account and an under-provision of quality is even more likely.

4. OTHER ARGUMENTS

4.1. Public/Merit Good

It can be argued that a uniform and universal postal network presents the character of a 'public good' because it 'binds the nation together' or it is essential for the functioning of a democracy or because, for ethical reasons, society finds it unacceptable that anyone be excluded from communications services. The argument relies on the idea that the existence of the network is valuable in itself, *independently of the specific services it provides* to the consumers. In other words, a universal postal network produces externalities that are non-rival in nature. Consequently, this argument may apply even when the provided service is essentially a private good. From that perspective, a USO can be seen as a mechanism for the provision of this public good. Observe that this argument can be combined with the one given in Section 2. It can then explain why redistributive pricing ought to be used in network industries rather than in other sectors where the public good aspect may not be present.

The importance of this aspect has been re-enforced in the recent Directive project launched by the Commission on October 2006. In this project, the accessibility of the postal network (which is a component of universal service) is meant to promote social and territorial cohesion.[10]

4.2. Regional Policy

The USO can also be an instrument of regional policies. For instance, uniform pricing can be a way to subsidize rural customers, in order to encourage households and firms to locate in rural areas (or to prevent them from moving away). Similarly, maintaining basic public services (like post offices) in small villages may contribute toward preventing the decline of rural areas. Many initiatives at the European level, such as the *European Regional Development Fund* or the *European Spatial Development Perspective*, pursue the objective of a balanced and sustainable spatial development. They are intended to achieve economic and social cohesion, to preserve cultural heritage, to manage natural resources and to obtain a more balanced competitiveness of the European territory.[11] Universal service obligations in the postal sector can be seen as instruments to pursue these objectives.

5. CONCLUSION

We have presented two complementary perspectives on the benefits of USO. First, we have argued that a USO is a form of redistributive pricing that achieves redistribution between low-cost and high-cost consumers. We have shown that within the sender-pays framework adopted in the postal sector this redistribution is operated *indirectly*, through the firms that use postal products as inputs (and sell their final goods to households). Second, we have presented an argument that relies on externalities and intermediation to show that USO can also be justified on efficiency grounds. A delivery network, with a widespread coverage and a high level of quality, increases demand for postal products (specifically, for commercial mail products). A profit-maximizing operator does not appropriately account for this effect and sets a suboptimal level of coverage/quality. This effect is reinforced when there is a 'call externality' (addressees obtain utility from receiving mail) and/or when there is competition.

What are the lessons we can learn from this analysis regarding the future role of the USO in a postal world of enhanced electronic communications? First of all, it appears that abolishing a USO and replacing it by (say) the provision of subsidized stamps to households is *not* a solution. This is because the relevant benefits of a USO are all related to the role of postal products as inputs and thus to the industrial mail segment. Furthermore, one can notice that the redistributive role of a USO is not *directly* related to the availability of the Internet. These two points suggest that a USO does have a role to play in the future. However, we also have to keep in mind that all benefits considered depend on the demand for postal products and the role that the sector plays in the economy. The central question that has to be asked is whether this channel of communication will remain a crucial input for firms.

As for now, the recent debate in Europe and elsewhere reveals the continued importance of USO, at least for the foreseeable future. It is thus important to provide some guidelines on how to assess the proper scope and financing of USO, since the benefits associated with USO come at a certain cost. First, there are the distortions to prices and competition. These costs depend on the design of the USO and related pricing policies and, in particular, on the financing mechanism that is used. Second, there is the danger that quality is overprovided. For instance, it may not effectively be socially optimal to deliver six times per week on the entire territory. To avoid or mitigate this second type of costs, proper studies are necessary to ensure that appropriate standards are set, in terms of reliability and accessibility, or of delivery frequency. Our chapter has not addressed these questions, but rather has underscored the importance of providing adequate answers to them in view of the continuing importance of USO.

NOTES

* We thank Michael Crew, Ruth Goldway, Paul Kleindorfer, Alberto Rovero, and Vincenzo Visco-Comandini for their comments. The opinions expressed in this chapter are those of the authors and do not necessarily reflect the positions of the Groupe La Poste.

1. Exceptions are Cremer et al. (1997) and Cremer et al. (2001). Crew and Kleindorfer (1998) study the relationship between USO and reserved area under entry. Doing this they also discuss the nature of and justification for the USO. In particular, they stress the issue of transaction costs which are avoided by uniform pricing. Some further discussion is also provided by Crew and Kleindorfer (2007). While transaction costs associated with non-uniform pricing may be a relevant problem for single-piece mail, they do not appear to be a significant issue for commercial mail. In any event, where they are relevant, the operator may spontaneously adopt uniform pricing even if this is not required by a USO. This argument is most obvious when the transaction falls directly on the operator. However, even when the transaction cost is on the demand side, it may be borne in part by the operator (through a 'tax incidence' effect).
2. See Ambrosini et al. (2006) for a description of the obligations in the different countries according to three dimensions: scope of products, quality requirements and price regulation.
3. This is true at least for mail services. Some financial services provided by post banks fall into the second category.
4. See Roy (1999) for an analysis of cost drivers in postal delivery and Bernard et al. (2002), for a comparison between France and the USA, studying the costs of delivery rural areas and/or to low-income households.
5. See Boldron et al. (2006) for a study of the cost savings associated with a decrease in the number of routes in rural areas.
6. Panzar (2006) applies the two-sided market approach to the postal sector but concentrates on PO boxes.
7. In any event, addressees' payments for delivery do not appear to be a significant issue for the time being, at least not in Europe. Note, however, that some types of delivery, such as to a PO box, are not free and represent an interesting example of a receiver payment (albeit on a membership rather than on a usage basis).
8. Riordan (2001) considers such an externality for the telecommunications sector.
9. In the monopoly case, the problem arises because (under linear pricing) the operator cannot capture the entire surplus created by an increase of the degree of coverage; part of the extra surplus is absorbed by the

customer. When there is competition, the competitors also profit from the extra demand and the argument is reinforced.

10. It is the induced social cohesion and not the network in itself that represents the public good for the sake of this argument. In particular, it is a nonrival good that is jointly 'consumed' by all residents of a given country.
11. See, Boldron et al. (2007) for more details on those policies.

REFERENCES

Ambrosini, X., F. Boldron and B. Roy (2006), 'Universal service obligations in the postal sector: economic learnings from cross-country comparisons', in M.A. Crew and P.R Kleindorfer (eds), *Progress towards Liberalization of the Postal and Delivery Sector*, New York: Springer.

Bernard, S., R.H. Cohen, M.H. Robinson, B. Roy, J. Toledano, J.D. Waller and S.S. Xenakis (2002), 'Delivery cost heterogeneity and vulnerability to entry', in M.A. Crew and P.R. Kleindorfer (eds), *Postal and Delivery Services: Delivering on Competition*, Boston, MA: Kluwer Academic Publishers Publishers.

Boldron, F., D. Joram, L. Martin, B. Roy (2006), 'From the size of the box to the costs of universal service obligations: a cross-country comparison', in M.A. Crew and P.R. Kleindorfer (eds), *Liberalization of the Postal and Delivery Sector*, Cheltenham, UK and Northampton, MA: Edward Elgar.

Boldron, F., K. Dewulf, D. Joram, C. Panet, B. Roy and O. Vialaneix (2007), 'The accessibility of the postal retail network and the objectives of social cohesion and economic development', to be presented at the 15th Conference on Postal and Delivery Economics, Semmering, Austria.

Cremer, H., M. De Rycke and A. Grimaud (1997), 'Cost and benefits of universal service in the postal sector', in M.A. Crew and P.R. Kleindorfer (eds), *Managing Change in the Postal and Delivery Industries*, Boston: Kluwer Academic Publishers.

Cremer, H., F. Gasmi, A. Grimaud and J.J. Laffont (2001), 'Universal service: an economics perspective', *Annals of Public and Cooperative Economics*, **72**, 5–43.

Crew, M. and P. Kleindorfer (1998), 'Efficient entry, monopoly and the universal service obligation in Postal Service', *Journal of Regulatory Economics*, **14**, 103–25.

Crew, M. and P. Kleindorfer (2007), 'Multi-national policies for the universal service obligation in the postal sector under entry', *Review of Network Economics*, **2**(2), 1–19.

Panzar, J. (2006), 'PO box access: competition issues in a two-sided postal market', presented at the fourth conference on Regulation, Competition and Universal Service in the Postal Sector, Toulouse, France.

Riordan, M. (2001), 'Universal residential telephone service', in M. Cave, S. Majumdar and I. Vogelsang (eds), *Handbook of Telecommunications Economics*, Amsterdam: Elsevier Science.

Roy, B. (1999), 'Technico-economic analysis of the costs of outside work in postal delivery', in M.A. Crew and P.R. Kleindorfer (eds), *Emerging Competition in Postal and Delivery Services*, Boston, MA: Kluwer Academic Publishers.

Tobin, J. (1970), 'On limiting the domain of inequality', *Journal of Law and Economics*, **13**(2), 263–77.

Varian, H. (1987), *Intermediate Microeconomics: a Modern Approach*, New York: W.W. Norton.

APPENDIX A

Redistributive Pricing under the Sender Pays Principle

There are N individuals and two areas indexed u (urban) and r (rural). The proportion of individuals living in the urban area is denoted by α. The (constant) marginal delivery costs of one item of mail differ according to the location of the addressee and are given by $c^u < c^r$. All individuals consume some good y (e.g., banking services) that use mail services as input. The production of one unit of y requires one unit of mail. The cost of all other inputs required for producing a unit of y is constant (and independent of location) and given by k. Let p^i denote the prices paid by the producers of y for mail sent to area $i = u,r$. The price of y in area $i = u,r$ is denoted q^i. Assuming that y is produced by a competitive industry, we have $q^i = p^i + k$. With this linear technology, the cost of the input is entirely shifted to the consumer.[1] The indirect utility of a consumer located in area i is given by $v(q^i)$, while demand for y is denoted by $y(q^i)$; in other words, all other prices and incomes are considered as given (and mail is only used as input).[2]

The pricing problem of a (postal) regulator who cares for efficiency and redistribution can then be expressed as the maximization of a social welfare function subject to a break-even constraint:

$$\begin{aligned} &\max_{p^u,p^r} \alpha N\Psi[v(p^u+k)] + (1-\alpha)N\Psi[v(p^r+k)] \\ &\text{s.t. } \alpha N(p^u - c^u)y^u + (1-\alpha)N(p^r - c^r)y^r - F = 0, \end{aligned} \tag{2.A1}$$

where F is the postal operator's fixed cost, $y^i = y(q^i)$, $i = u,r$, and where Ψ is an increasing and concave function. The degree of concavity reflects the importance of redistribution in the regulator's objective. For instance, we can set

$$\Psi = \frac{v^{1-\rho}}{1-\rho},$$

with $\rho \geq 0$. For this specification, $\rho = 0$ yields a utilitarian welfare function, which with quasi-linear preferences implies that there are no benefits associated with redistribution (social welfare is measured by total surplus). At the other extreme, $\rho \to \infty$ yields the Rawlsian welfare function: social welfare is measured by the utility of the worst-off individual. Observe that this problem illustrates the *indirect* redistribution argument presented in Section 2 above. The price of the input (mail products) affects the price of the final good bought by rural and urban consumers.

Differentiating the Lagrangian expression associated with this problem yields the following pricing rules:

$$\frac{p^u - c^u}{p^u} = \frac{\lambda - \Psi'_u}{\varepsilon^u}, \tag{2.A2}$$

$$\frac{p^r - c^r}{p^r} = \frac{\lambda - \Psi'_r}{\varepsilon^r}, \tag{2.A3}$$

where ε^i, $i = u,r$ is the absolute value of demand elasticity while λ is the multiplier of the break-even constraint. To interpret these expressions, consider first the case where $F = 0$. When Ψ is linear ($\Psi' = 1$; $\rho = 0$) the solution implies marginal cost pricing with $c^r > p^r \geq p^u > c^u$. When Ψ is strictly concave, $\Psi'_u < \Psi'_r$ yielding $p^r = c^r > p^u = c^u$. In other words, the price differential is smaller than the cost differential. In the Rawlsian case prices will be equal. Finally, when $F > 0$, we have simple Ramsey pricing when $\Psi' = 1$ and this implies $p^r > p^u$ (unless ε^r is much smaller than ε^u).[3] Strict concavity of Ψ continues to imply $\Psi'_u < \Psi'_r$ and the price differential will decrease with the degree of concavity. In the Rawlsian case prices will again be equal.

APPENDIX B

Optimal versus Profit-maximizing Coverage

Let μ denote the proportion of the N addressees (ranked in order of total costs of service) that can be reached through the postal network with some specified quality of service – like, for instance, home delivery on a $D + 1$ basis. The utility of the representative customer sending x units of mail at price p to each addressee is given by[4]

$$US = N\mu v(x,\mu) - N\mu px.$$

Observe that μ plays two roles in this expression. It multiplies v and x, which are defined on a per-addressee basis, to yield total utility and output. Furthermore, it is an argument of v to capture the idea that the degree of coverage of the network is perceived by the sender as a quality attribute of mail.

We also introduce the possibility that receiving mail generates a 'call externality'.[5] Each addressee's utility from receiving mail is given by $h(x)$, so that the sum of addressees' utilities is given by

$$UA = N\mu h(x). \tag{2.A4}$$

The cost of the postal operator is specified by

$$C = F(\mu) + N\mu cx,$$

with $F' > 0$ and $F'' > 0$ so that profit is

$$\pi = N\mu px - F(\mu) - N\mu cx.$$

For simplicity, we assume here that the *marginal* delivery cost does not depend on the addressee's location. However, the fixed cost of maintaining the network depends on location; this supports our assumption that F is a strictly convex function of μ.

B.1 Socially optimal solution

To determine the optimal solution (x^*,μ^*), we maximize a utilitarian welfare W (equivalent here to total surplus).[6] We have

$$W = US + UA + \pi \tag{2.A5}$$
$$= N\mu v(x,\mu) + N\mu h(x) - F(\mu) - N\mu cx. \tag{2.A6}$$

Differentiating with respect to x and μ yields:

$$\frac{\partial W}{\partial x} = \left[\frac{\partial v}{\partial x} + h'(x) - c\right]\mu = 0, \tag{2.A7}$$

$$\frac{\partial W}{\partial \mu} = N[v(x,\mu) + h(x) - cx] + N\mu\frac{\partial v}{\partial \mu} - F'(\mu) = 0. \tag{2.A8}$$

The two conditions have straightforward interpretations. Equation (2.A7) states that the marginal benefit of x (accounting for the call externality $h'(x)$) equals its marginal cost. Similarly, in (2.A8) the first two terms measure the marginal benefit of an increase in μ while the last term represents the marginal cost.

B.2 Profit-maximizing solution

Writing profits as a function of μ and x yields

$$\pi = N\mu p(x,\mu)x - F(\mu) - N\mu cx,$$

where $p(x,\mu)$ is the inverse demand function. Differentiating yields the following FOCs:

$$\frac{\partial \pi}{\partial x} = N\mu\left[x + \frac{\partial p}{\partial x} - c\right] = 0 \tag{2.A9}$$

$$\frac{\partial \pi}{\partial \mu} = N\mu\frac{\partial p}{\partial \mu}x + N[p(x,\mu)x - cx] - F'(\mu) = 0 \tag{2.A10}$$

Based on (2.A7)–(2.A8) and (2.A9)–(2.A10), the comparison between the social optimum (x^*,μ^*) and the profit-maximizing solution (x^π,μ^π) is not entirely obvious. One easily shows that $x^\pi < x^*$, but the comparison between μ^π and μ^* is ambiguous.[7]

We can gain some further insight by noting that for any level of x, the derivative of W with respect to μ, at the profit-maximizing level of μ is simply

$$\frac{\partial W}{\partial \mu} = \frac{\partial US}{\partial \mu} + \frac{\partial UA}{\partial \mu} + \frac{\partial \pi}{\partial \mu} = \frac{\partial US}{\partial \mu} + \frac{\partial UA}{\partial \mu},$$

because $\partial\pi/\partial\mu$ vanishes by definition when profit is maximized. Thus, profit maximization yields a level of coverage that is too low (given x) when consumer surplus (counting both the senders and the addressees) increases in μ. It is clear from (2.A4) that $\partial UA/\partial\mu > 0$. Furthermore, we have

$$\frac{\partial US}{\partial \mu} = N[v(x,\mu) - px] + N\mu\left[\frac{\partial v}{\partial \mu} - \frac{\partial p}{\partial \mu}x\right] \tag{2.A11}$$

This first term in this expression is positive. Intuitively, the quantity sold by a profit-maximizing monopolist is too small at both the intensive and the extensive margin and this term captures the extensive margin. The second term is the quality term whose sign depends on the sign of $\partial p^2(x,\mu)/\partial x \partial \mu$ (see Varian, 1987).

NOTES

1. With more general technologies we would get partial shifting: an increase in p of Δ would lead to an increase of q of $\gamma\Delta$, with $0 \leq \gamma \leq 1$. This would complicate the analysis, but our argument would remain valid.
2. For simplicity, we assume that preferences are quasi-linear so that utility and surplus are equivalent.
3. The equation of the demand elasticity in both areas is the same, because utility functions are identical, but the values taken at equilibrium will in general differ.
4. This is a simplified version of the utility function used by Cremer et al. (2001).
5. On this terminology, see Riordan (2001).
6. For simplicity, we concentrate on the first-best solution and do not impose a break-even constraint on the operator. This does not affect the results pertaining to the determination of μ.
7. This is similar to the problem of quality choice by a profit-maximizing monopoly (see Varian, 1992, pp. 239–41).

3. The distribution of post offices in Italy and the United States*

Robert Cohen, Luigi Di Paola, Renée Sheehy and Vincenzo Visco Comandini

1. INTRODUCTION

The post is considered a basic and fundamental service throughout the industrialized world. The universal service obligation (USO) for postal services always includes a mandate to render effective and regular service to all areas (including rural ones). This in turn influences the distribution of post offices. This chapter presents the distribution of post offices in the US and Italy. It then compares these distributions with the distribution of pharmacies in the US and banks in Italy. The distribution of the latter two is the result of the operation of economic forces, while the distribution of post offices reflects historical factors that may or may not be relevant today, political forces, and social needs. The distribution of post offices would, therefore, be expected to be different from those of banks and pharmacies.

The chapter finds that service outlets for pharmacies and banks in the United States and Italy appear to be driven by population density, as expected for market-determined services. However, the distribution of post offices in these countries exhibits a rather different pattern. The data show for both countries that rural areas receive a higher quality of retail service than do urban areas, because of the disproportionate number of post offices relative to population. This in turn makes the provision of counter service to rural populations much more expensive than to urban populations. These results are probably true for most if not all industrialized economies and they point to the key policy implication of this study: namely, post offices in rural areas will become an increasing burden and are likely to be a more visible political issue than in the past as a result of increasing direct and indirect competition for universal service providers to keep costs down and to align their costs with the value of services produced.

The pressure to align cost and profitability of postal service outlets is already visible in many postal administrations. Thus, Table 3.1 shows that almost all postal administrations are reducing the number of post offices. Most of the offices closed are in rural areas. The table suggests that there is no fixed level of retail counter service required to fulfill the USO and that postal administrations in most countries have latitude in how they fulfill the USO with respect to counters. Table 3.1 also shows that the United States has relatively few offices, as it ranks third in terms of the average number of persons served. The United States has over 700 pieces of mail per capita, and so it spreads the cost of counters over more pieces than any other postal administration. Counter services comprised five percent (or $3.5 billion) of total USPS cost in 2004. On the other hand, the burden

Table 3.1 Comparison of selected countries

Country	People per post office (rank)				Number of post offices		
	1988		2003		1988	2003	% Change
Australia	3650	(9)	5120	(8)	4489	3853	−14%
Austria	2856	(13)	4043	(12)	2676	2007	−25%
Belgium	5392	(5)	7931	(2)	1838	1301	−29%
Denmark	4032	(7)	5264	(6)	1270	1019	−20%
Finland	1690	(16)	3868	(13)	2926	1346	−54%
France	3313	(12)	3560	(15)	16949	16992	0%
Germany	3527	(10)	6102	(5)	17410	13514	−22%
Greece	7768	(1)	4949	(9)	1296	2218	71%
Ireland	1676	(17)	2386	(19)	2103	1658	−21%
Italy	3939	(8)	4183	(11)	14373	13728	−4%
Japan	5135	(6)	5165	(7)	23871	24715	4%
Luxembourg	3504	(11)	4196	(10)	106	108	2%
Netherlands	5625	(4)	6267	(4)	2624	2577	−2%
Norway	1540	(18)	3067	(16)	2728	1478	−46%
Portugal	1371	(19)	2844	(17)	7259	3537	−51%
Spain	6122	(3)	12283	(1)	6368	3343	−48%
Switzerland	1783	(15)	2634	(18)	3763	2722	−28%
United Kingdom	2683	(14)	3733	(14)	21030	15868	−25%
United States	6258	(2)	7825	(3)	40117	37579	−6%

Source: UPU.

of counter services in Italy and in many other countries is shared with financial services (and/or governmental services) or has been extensively outsourced, thus reducing the burden on mail. The cost of post offices, other than in the United States, exceeds 5 percent of total cost – at least, for postal administrations that do not share the cost of counters or have not franchised extensively.

While several postal administrations have converted many post offices (especially in rural areas) to franchises, using franchises is politically very difficult or even impossible in many countries. This is certainly the case in Italy and the United States. Franchising can produce substantial savings, especially for postal administrations that do not provide financial services. For example, in 2004 a small rural office in the United States cost about $63 000 to operate (including salaries, rent and utilities). The average revenue for such an office was about $31 000. A contract or franchise office cost about $17 000 annually, for a saving over half. Frequently, there are strong objections from the community when an office is converted to a contract office. In the United States, these conversions are opposed almost as much as an outright closing.

It is generally conceded that many small rural offices cannot be justified on economic grounds, because they have relatively few transactions and they have considerable fixed cost.[1] Postal administrations and commercial mailers who provide most postal revenue argue that these offices are not necessary to provide adequate postal services to the rural communities they serve. However, defenders of these offices argue that they are vital to the well-being of the communities and that they are included in the USO of the post.[2] It is interesting to note that the authors have found no quantitative studies in either the United States or Italy that analyze the value of these offices to the communities that they serve.[3] Nevertheless, the large-scale closing of small rural offices is a political 'nonstarter' in both the United States and Italy.

2. RETAIL SERVICES PROVIDED BY RURAL CARRIERS USING A ROADSIDE MAIL BOX

In the United States and in other countries, rural carriers provide retail services to recipients along their routes. USPS patrons can meet the carrier or, more commonly, leave money or a check in their rural roadside mail box with a note of instructions. In this way, they can obtain virtually every service offered to consumers and small businesses. In communities where post offices have been closed, there are few if any businesses catering to the residents. When it is inconvenient to use a rural carrier, a customer can visit a post office in a nearby community while shopping. Whenever the USPS closes a post office, it claims that rural carriers can provide whatever service is supplied by the closed facility. In most cases, however, customers of closed offices feel that rural carrier service is an inadequate substitute. Currently, Poste Italiane carriers do not offer retail services.

3. GROWTH AND DECLINE OF RURAL POST OFFICES IN THE UNITED STATES

In 1890, only a quarter of the US population received free mail delivery, which was only available in cities. Most people lived on farms or in small farming towns and had to travel, often miles, to a post office to pick up mail. Figure 3.1 shows the increase in the US population and the increase and then decline of the number of post offices in the United States from 1790 through 2001.[4] There is a very high correlation between population and post offices until 1901, when the number of post offices peaked. The advent of Rural Free Delivery (RFD) caused a sudden reversal. RFD, as it was called, began as an experiment in 1896 and continued to cover more and more of the country. By 1915, virtually the entire nation was served, eliminating the need for many rural offices.[5] The Post Office Department announced a policy to abolish all small rural offices that duplicated the new delivery service (Fuller, 1964, p. 85). Only those offices from which the newly established routes originated would remain open.[6] With the advent of RFD, there was no need for farmers and other rural residents to travel to a post office in town to pick up mail or to post letters.[7]

The legacy of a largely rural population means that there remain a disproportionate number of rural communities relative to the number of urban communities. Generally, each community has a post office (as in Italy), which results in a disproportionate number of post offices in rural areas.

The USPS has continued to close post offices at a slowing rate to the present day (see Table 3.2).

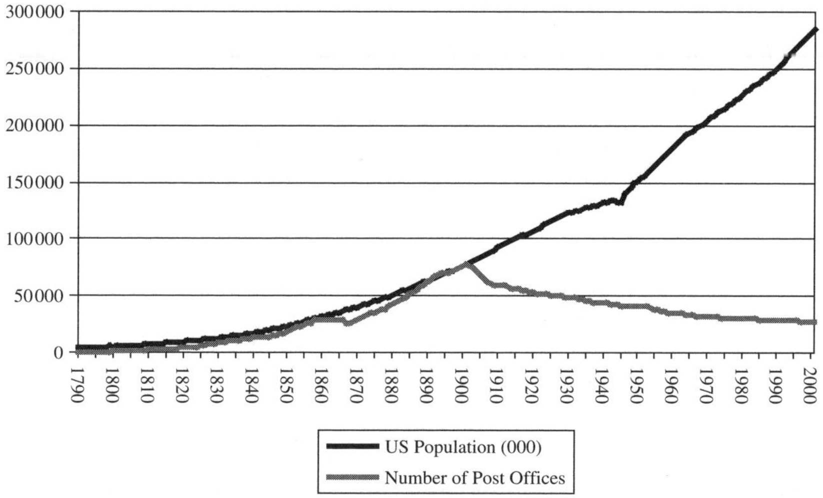

Figure 3.1 Comparison of US population with total number of post offices

Table 3.2 Average annual post office closures by decade

Decade	Closures
1901–10	1737
1911–20	659
1921–30	309
1931–40	470
1941–50	227
1951–60	595
1961–70	295
1971–80	162
1981–90	128
1991–2000	103
2001–6	55

From 2001 to 2005, USPS has closed only 558 post offices (2 percent) on a net basis. The slowing of the rate of closings can be largely attributed to Congressional pressure, which led to a temporary four-year moratorium on closings in 1998.[8] The long-standing policy of USPS is only to close an office when the postmaster leaves, retires, or dies.[9]

4. THE DEVELOPMENT OF POST OFFICES IN ITALY

In Italy, regular delivery service was furnished by horse riders (*cavallari*) during the Middle Ages and the Renaissance. In 1859, two years before national unification, there were 1632 post offices in north and central Italy, excluding Venice and Rome. When Italy was first unified in 1861, Rowland Hill's reforms (a uniform tariff and payment by the

Table 3.3 The development of the Italian postal network

Year	Population (thousands)	Post offices	People per post office
1895	31948	5965	5356
1915	37067	10442	3550
1920	36431	10812	3369
1925	39941	10676	3741
1926	40268	10992	3663
1932	42192	11278	3741
1935	43194	11352	3805
1942	45752	11735	3899
1957	49311	11735	4202
1989	56694	14400	3937
2000	57844	13950	4147
2002	57321	13787	4158

sender) were quickly adopted (Castronovo, 2003). Delivery was furnished by postmen in urban areas and usually contracted out in rural areas to individuals (*procaccia*). Table 3.3 presents the data from 1895 to 2002.

There are two main reasons for the gradual increase in the number of post offices in Italy despite the existence of regular delivery service in both rural and urban areas. In the first years after unification, Italy was an aggregation of provinces with huge differences in education, culture, economic development, language, customs, politics, and infrastructure. A national postal network providing ubiquitous service was seen as an effective way to pull the nation together.[10] In addition, the newly established postal network enjoyed significant economies of scope between communication (telegraph and telephone) and financial (savings and money transfer) services. Postal savings was a particularly important way to develop trust in the post. The post in Italy adopted the French institutional model of creating a bank entirely devoted to financing public infrastructure investments (*Cassa Depositi e Prestiti*). Historically, the post has been the most important provider of financial services in poor areas of the country, because they are underserved by banks.[11]

The number of inhabitants per post office gradually increased until the early 1960s.[12] In the 1950s, Poste Italiane was profitable and it financed the cost of the retail network. Financial services only broke even at this time.[13] However, in the 1960s, politicians began to use postal service for patronage. They engaged in corrupt contracting practices, and established new post office branches and hired labor for political reasons.

In the 1980s inefficiencies were spread over the whole postal network, with inefficient rural post offices and inefficient urban offices. Today, the problem lies primarily in rural areas. Nearly 20 percent of post offices in Italy have revenue less than the cost of operating, but the cumulative difference in 2004 was less than €143 million.[14] The real issue is their cost of sales relative to the countrywide average. As in most countries, local politicians in Italy traditionally oppose the closure of unprofitable rural post offices (most of which conduct fewer than three daily transactions). In the last few years a new strategy has emerged because of the corporatization and commercialization of Poste Italiane. Its aim is to create incentives for a Coasian bargain[15] between the postal administration and local authorities. The closure of post offices is avoided in exchange for local governments contracting out some clerical activities to them. The aim of this strategy is to utilize spare capacity caused by clerk waiting times at rural post offices for window service. This reduces the net burden, and avoids the political cost of closing facilities.

Another strategy to reduce operating losses from rural post offices is Poste Italiane's recent application for a Virtual Mobile Operator (VMO) license. The Italian Postal Administration is planning to become a VMO (i.e., a telecommunication mobile operator with its own brand, but using a third-party (Vodafone) network). Subscriptions to Poste Italiane's mobile service will be sold in all POs. VMO service revenues come from both the spread between wholesale and retail prices and termination charges, and are expected to contribute to net income. Poste Italiane will set lower rates for mobile services to attract marginal customers, most of who live in rural areas. Recently, there has been a small reduction in the number of post offices, and there have been efforts to reduce the number of days a week facilities with high cost of sales are open.[16]

In Italy, and perhaps in other OECD countries, contracting out counter services (letter and parcel clearance, money collection) may not be practical. There may be no savings if the potential franchisees (e.g., tobacconists or newspaper kiosk owners) have a politically strong association and demand compensation that equals postal cost. In most industrial countries, the distribution of post offices appears to be largely a political rather than a technical matter. Italy has adopted a unique approach (where politicians actively push towards reducing the burden of what might be called the political rent of maintaining small rural offices) by increasing income from rural offices and reducing their costs.

The actual average value of 4.2 post offices per thousand inhabitants in Italy cannot be considered either as low (with respect to the United States) or high (with respect to France), because this figure is the result of the distribution of population and efficiency in allocating post offices given the bundle of services provided and geographic factors.[17] There are 8100 communes in Italy. Three thousand have less than 2000 inhabitants and one thousand have fewer than 1000 inhabitants. Communes without a post office are in rural areas or in urban areas near larger cities. Thus, as in the United States, it would be expected that there are a disproportionate number of rural post offices in Italy.

5. A COMPARISON OF THE DISTRIBUTION OF POSTAL RETAIL FACILITIES AND PHARMACIES IN THE UNITED STATES

Arguably, pharmacies are at least as important to the average citizen as post offices. Comparing the geographic distribution of a commercial service, like pharmacies, with the distribution of post offices illustrates what the distribution of post offices might look like if it were driven by market forces. The rows in Table 3.4 present statistics on five-digit postal code ('ZIP code') tabulation areas grouped into semi-deciles based on population densities.[18] Group Number 1 contains the least densely populated five-digit ZIP code areas in the country; Group Number 20 contains the most densely populated.

There are 1579 five-digit ZIP code areas in each semi-decile.[19] The average number of people per postal retail facility appears in column 2.[20] It can be seen that this ranges from a low of 454 per retail facility in the least densely populated areas to a high of 24 030 in

Table 3.4 The numbers of persons served by USPS retail facilities and pharmacies in Census ZIP Code Tabulation Areas (ZCTAs) ranked by population density[a]

Semi-decile	Average no. of people per USPS retail facility	Average no. of people per pharmacy	Average land area per ZCTA (sq. miles)
1	454	6738	369
2	976	4825	218
3	1215	5647	139
4	1404	5760	107
5	1697	5801	96
6	2143	5250	94
7	2391	5049	82
8	3049	4751	86
9	3510	5105	81
10	4007	4598	73
11	5119	4702	72
12	6143	4657	66
13	7615	4916	56
14	9321	5090	47
15	10128	4944	32
16	11921	4900	21
17	14501	4778	13
18	16100	4705	9
19	18842	5138	6
20	24030	5347	3

Note: [a] Only ZCTAs in the continental United States are included.

Source: US Census Bureau 2000 ZCTA data, National Council for Prescription Drug Programs, Inc. (NCPDP) Pharmacy Database (2002), and USPS facilities data (2002).

the most densely populated areas, a remarkably wide span. The average number of people per pharmacy is shown in column three and ranges from a low of 4702 to a high of 6738; a much tighter span.[21] The average land area for each five-digit ZIP code area is shown in column four. The average land area decreases consistently as the population density of the five-digit ZIP code areas increase.

The discrepancy in the number of people per postal facility versus the number per pharmacy in the first nine semi-deciles is a legacy of the period before RFD, when farmers needed to travel to the post office to get mail and there were very few pharmacies. The number of people per post office does not exceed the number of people per pharmacy until semi-decile 11. This is the same semi-decile where the number of people per post office exceeds the number of people per bank branch in Italy. The comparative uniformity of the number of people per pharmacy results from the fact that it takes a certain number of people to support a pharmacy. Competition seems to keep the number relatively constant. The fact that many postal facilities serve far more people than pharmacies in the semi-deciles with greater population densities reflects the fact that most people visit post offices much less frequently than they visit pharmacies.

6. THE DISTRIBUTION OF BANKS AND POST OFFICES IN ITALY

Unlike the US comparison of post offices with pharmacies, the Italian comparison is post offices with bank outlets (BO) because the number and the location of pharmacies are strictly regulated in Italy, whereas the distribution of bank outlets is not. Services offered by bank branches are arguably more important to most people in Italy than mail-related services provided by post offices. In recent years, however, post offices have become more useful to many Italians as a result of significant changes in Poste Italiane's financial services.[22]

The Post Office (PO) network was originally set up on a political rather than business basis, with each commune (the first level of local government in Italy) having its own local retail post office. Often small remote villages belonging to a commune were also granted an office.

Table 3.5 shows that the number of bank outlets is more highly correlated than post offices with respect to population, income, and number of local firms. Square kilometers show a lower correlation with banks than with POs. Not surprisingly, bank outlets, much more than post offices, go where there are people, money, and businesses.[23]

In Table 3.6, communes are split into three groups: (1) communes with at least two post offices and two bank outlets, (2) communes with one post office and one bank outlet, and (3) communes not served by a bank or a post office. The distribution of post offices in the three groups differs from that of bank outlets. While almost half of banks are located in communes with several postal and bank facilities, less than a third of post offices belong to Group 1. The vast majority of post offices (67 percent) are located in small communes served by only one PO and BO. The most striking difference between PO and BO distribution is in Group 3. Only 4.5 percent of communes are without PO, while 26.8 percent are not served by a BO. Sorting the same data further (communes with at least one PO but without a BO) allows for a rough estimate of the uneconomic allocation of PO. Twenty-one percent of communes fall into this group.

Another source of information comes from the Poste Italiane's post office data set for 2002.[24] Table 3.7 shows that the number of households per postal facility is consistently

Table 3.5 Correlation coefficients of post offices and bank outlets with population, family disposable income, local firm branches and square kilometers in Italy

	Population	Family disposable income	Local firm branches	Square km
Post offices (PO)	0.711	0.719	0.747	0.476
Bank outlets (BO)	0.901	0.97	0.969	0.22

Table 3.6 The banking and post office network in Italian communes

	Banking network (%)	Postal network (%)
Communes with more than one outlet	43.7	28.8
Communes with only one outlet	29.5	66.8
Communes not served	26.8	4.4

Table 3.7 The average numbers of households in 2002 served by Poste Italiane retail facilities and bank branches, ranked by population density

Semi-decile	Households per post office	Households per bank branch
1	103	1 291
2	176	819
3	235	849
4	286	742
5	335	728
6	389	655
7	449	604
8	515	643
9	589	648
10	680	903
11	795	586
12	938	580
13	1 103	573
14	1 314	597
15	1 596	574
16	1 938	612
17	2 406	591
18	3 098	606
19	4 371	642
20	10 453	1 057

lower than the number of people per bank outlet through semi-decile 11. Moreover, the average number of households is monotonically increasing in each semi-decile, while the number of bank outlets is nearly constant in all but the first and last semi-deciles (5-percent groupings).[25] This is remarkably similar to the US data on post offices and pharmacies. The fact that many postal facilities serve far more people than bank outlets in the semi-deciles with greater population densities reflects the fact that people visit post offices much less frequently than they visit banks. The highest post office density in Italy is in the mountain areas of the north and south. Bank branches, on the other hand, are disproportionately located in the north, because it is significantly richer and more densely populated.

7. CONCLUDING REMARKS

Both Italy and the United States have a disproportionate percentage of their post offices located in rural areas (see Table 3.8). It is likely that the distribution of post offices in most postal administrations is disproportionately rural. Bank branches in Italy and pharmacies in the United States have a market distribution that is very different, as their location is driven by economic forces.

When postal administrations enjoyed strong monopolies, this kind of non-economic distribution was quite acceptable. The monopoly forced everyone to pay for various types of non-economic behavior. However, postal administrations face increasing indirect com-

Table 3.8 A comparison of the distribution of population, post offices and pharmacies/bank branches in the US and Italy, in percent

Country	Population		Post offices		Pharmacies/bank branches	
	Urban	Rural	Urban	Rural	Urban	Rural
US	79	21	49	51	88	12
Italy	92	8	67	33	90	10

petition from the Internet and (the prospect of) direct competition from liberalization. It is likely that bulk mail and not single-piece mail will be subject to direct competition as in Sweden. If so, it will be difficult to charge the cost of the retail network to competitive bulk mail, since most mail-related retail activities are for single-piece mail. New entrants will not be saddled with a network of post offices. In order to have competitive prices, incumbents will have to allocate costs based on causation, and bulk mail will pay only for the small portion of the retail network cost that it imposes.

Thus, under a competitive scenario, the network of post offices would largely be paid for by single-piece revenue,[26] or by some external funding mechanism such as a government subsidy in Italy. This would be a heavy burden to place on single-piece mailers or taxpayers. Of course, the burden may be ameliorated if counters are shared with financial services, are heavily outsourced or are redistributed on a market basis. Notwithstanding, there will be considerable pressure to move toward a more commercial distribution of retail services, outsourcing or both under a liberalized scenario.

NOTES

* This chapter does not necessarily reflect the opinion of Poste Italiane or of the Office of the Inspector General, US Postal Service.

1. Records of post office closings that have come before the US Postal Rate Commission indicate that many small rural offices have fewer than 20 counter transactions daily. Poste Italiane defines 'marginal POs' as those having fewer than 30 transactions daily.
2. For a good description of the perceived benefits to small rural communities from their post office, see Margolis (1980).
3. A recent paper by Cremer et al. (2007) opens a promising research stream on the economic impact of post offices in rural communities.
4. Figure 3.1 includes only classified post offices. It excludes other retail facilities such as stations, branches, and contract facilities.
5. There were 43 718 rural routes by 1915.
6. The Post Office Department was only partly successful in carrying out this policy.
7. Until 1952, the Post Office Department provided what was known as Postal Savings accounts that paid a nominal rate of interest. These accounts were never important enough to justify maintaining a post office.
8. The moratorium extended from March 16, 1998 to April 5, 2002.
9. It is not known how long this policy has been in effect, but it is mentioned in an annex to the Kappel Commission report (see Arthur D. Little, Inc., 1968).
10. In the early years of independence of the United States, the post was also seen as an effective means of unification (John, 1995).
11. In areas that lack bank branches, the per capita sale of postal bonds is still nearly three times the average for the country.
12. Note the decrease in population between 1915 and 1920 due to deaths in World War I.
13. Traditionally, the main device for steering financial results of postal financial services to a desired target

has been the implicit interest rate paid by the State to the Post Office on postal savings. Today, this is still important but not decisive. However, the Italian bank association, ABI, in a recent antitrust case, claimed that the monopoly granted to Poste Italiane provides improper financing and therefore distorts competition. The implicit interest rate should be evaluated using an opportunity cost approach: Would the banking system charge less for a task that is likely to affect its own deposits?

14. This total is based on an estimate from the NERA study (1998).
15. See the classic article of Ronald Coase (1960).
16. Poste Italiane's employees generally work six days a week, including Saturday morning openings, which is considered an advantage in competing with banks.
17. Let's suppose two communes, a and b, with the identical population and territory. In a, the inhabitants are located in two villages far away from one another, while in b there is only one urban center. Fulfilling the demand for postal services requires two post offices in a, but only one in b.
18. ZIP code tabulation areas correspond quite closely with five-digit ZIP code areas.
19. Semi-deciles 1, 7, and 14 contain 1580.
20. A retail facility can be a post office or a branch or station of a large post office.
21. These are pharmacies that serve the general public.
22. Italy is an example of an established network of post offices with excess capacity that was revitalized to compete for commodity financial services (e.g., checks, savings, bond sales, etc.). The Post's financial services revitalization program included improving service and employee training while offering lower prices and Saturday hours. The number of customers increased from 600 000 in 1998 to 4.5 million in 2006. Poste Italiane does not explicitly compete with banks in loans, because legislation forbids non-bank organizations (such as POs) from lending money. However, loan services of other banks are supplied in some large retail postal outlets with the PO acting as the agent of bank firms.
23. Post office data is from the 1999 Poste Italiane Post Office database. The population data source is ISTAT (Italian Bureau of Census), and bank outlets are from the 2001 Bank of Italy database. The number of observations is 8012. There are 14 084 post offices and 27 117 bank outlets.
24. The available data set for Italy is organized by commune. In Italy, communes exhibit very large differences (purely due to local history) in both territory extension and population (from less than 500 people in some villages in the north up to Rome, with a population of more than 3.1 million people). This is why Table 3.6 does not show, as Table 3.3, the landmass of each semi-decile.
25. There is a disproportionate number of households per BO in the first semi-decile because of the absence of bank branches (the average is weighted) and in the last semi-decile is because in large city facilities, economies of scale allow an increase in the size of the area served.
26. The cost of counter services in the United States in 2004 was over 12 percent of total single-piece revenue and the cost of small rural offices in the United States was 3 percent of single-piece revenue. Single-piece First-Class Mail® volume was 45 billion pieces in 2004 (out of a total of 205 billion) and its revenue was $20.5 billion (out of a total of $69 billion).

REFERENCES

Arthur D. Little, Inc. (1968), 'Postal Problems and their Causes', contractor's report in *Towards Postal Excellence* by the President's Commission on Postal Organization, Washington, DC: Government Printing Office, Annex 3, 2–32.

Castronovo, V. (2003), *Le Poste in Italia da amministrazione pubblica a sistema d'impresa*, Laterza & Figli: Roma, Bari.

Coase, R. (1960), 'The problem of social cost *Journal of Law and Economics*, **3**, 1–44.

Cremer H., P. De Donder, F. Boldron, D. Joram, and B. Roy (2007), 'Social costs and benefits of universal service obligations in the postal market', paper presented at the 15th Conference on Postal and Delivery Economics, Semmering Austria, 30 May–3 June 2007.

Fuller, W. (1964), *RFD: The Changing Face of Rural America*, Bloomington: Indiana University Press.

John, R. (1995), *Spreading the News: The American Postal System from Franklin to Morse*, Cambridge and London: Harvard University Press.

Margolis, R. (1980), *At the Crossroads: an Inquiry into Rural Post Offices and the Communities They Serve*, US Postal Rate Commission.

NERA (1998), 'Costing and financing of universal service in the postal sector in the European Union', in *Costing & Financing of Universal Services in the Postal Sector in the European Union*, Report to European Commission, DGXIII, London, October.

4. Accessibility of the postal retail network, social cohesion and economic development*

François Boldron, Karen Dewulf, Denis Joram, Clémence Panet, Bernard Roy and Olivier Vialaneix

En tout lieu, ce qui est proche a plus d'influence que ce qui est éloigné.
P.P. Combes, T. Mayer and J.F. Thisse (2006)

1. INTRODUCTION

Social and territorial cohesion are strategic goals of the European Union (EU). Indeed, those objectives have been inscribed in the original Treaty of Rome of 1957 (in Articles 130 and 131 in particular). Following the treaty, the European Regional Development Fund was created in 1975. The main objective of this fund is to give financial aid to less-developed regions of Europe or to revitalise regions affected by serious industrial decline. More recently, in the Lisbon Strategy, the EU has promoted an ambitious objective: 'to become the most competitive and dynamic knowledge-based economy in the world capable of sustainable economic growth with more and better jobs and greater social cohesion'. Social and territorial cohesion is a pillar of the European Union policies.

The accessibility of the postal retail network is a component of universal service provision. This provision takes the shape of a general guideline: '. . . Member States shall take steps to insure that the density of the points of contact (. . .) takes account of the needs of users'. The contribution of universal service to social and economic cohesion has always been present in the Postal Directives, and has been recalled in the Directive project launched by the Commission in October 2006. However, quite surprisingly, the influence of postal presence on social welfare has never been studied, such that the concept remains rather vague.

Most European countries have incorporated the accessibility component of the Universal Service Obligation (USO) through the establishment of different accessibility criteria along the Member States (see Ambrosini et al., 2006). The application of these criteria leads to 'oversized' retail networks, as compared to the ones that would have been sustained in a purely commercial objective. For instance, in Great Britain, Royal Mail is required to maintain about 8000 rural post offices, even though its commercial rural network would be composed of 1300 offices, as is clearly set out in the decisions of the European Commission (see European Commission, 2003; 2006). In France, the postal network is constituted of about 17 000 post offices' whereas a profit-maximizing behavior would lead to only around 3000 retail outlets. This oversized retail network means net USO costs that are borne[1] by the universal service providers (USP) through their reserved area (when it exists). With full market opening of the sector comes the question of the financing of this net cost, which is quite complex to set in the postal sector from a theoretical point of view as well as from a practical one (see Crew and Kleindorfer, 2006; Oxera, 2007).

Another approach could be to reduce the net cost through a proper understanding of local economic development and coordination between public intervention and commercial environment. State intervention can be expected, through a combined policy of different services (e.g., public services, services of general economic interest, etc.), to launch positive spillovers in the local economy. If more public services in rural areas attract more commercial services, additional demand for public services could be generated. Applied to postal counters this means that the presence of commercial services combined with public services creates demand for postal services, and increases the takings for retail outlets, thereby reducing the net cost of the accessibility constraint.

The principal objective of this chapter is to show that there exists a link between the number of public services, in particular postal services, and the commercial activity. This chapter is the first attempt at addressing the role of postal counters in rural economic development. To highlight this link we have collected data on different types of outlets in France. In Section 2, we will present a broad picture of these outlets, having either strictly commercial purposes (bakeries, bars) or responding to more basic needs that we associate with a public objective (pharmacies, hospitals, schools, postal outlets, etc.). These descriptions and the associated comparison of accessibility show that retail outlet networks are spread throughout the territory in various ways, leading to great variations of presence, particularly in rural areas. In Section 3, we attempt to establish a link between the provision of public services and the intensity of commercial activity estimated by the number of commercial stores. We focus our analysis on rural towns, because of the obvious prevalence of population, to explain commercial activity in big cities. We build a 'public service indicator' that measures the concentration of public services in similar areas in terms of population, and that should be compared to an activity or commercial indicator such as the PIB in future studies. We show that there is a direct link between 'public' services and commercial behavior. We then attempt to identify a specific combination of public services that leads to more commercial activity. Finally, we draw some avenues for future studies to better isolate the influence of the public service presence on the local development. In Section 4 we summarize the main findings and present some concluding remarks and our future research agenda.

2. HETEROGENEITY OF NETWORKS: THE FRENCH CASE

In order to highlight an empirical link between public service and commercial outlets, we have collected French data for 19 different kinds of services. These data concern services used by people in their daily lives, like administrative services, consumption goods, or service of general economic interest.[2] These data have been collected and encoded at a very thin level. Indeed, the French territory has been divided into 275 925 areas (named *Ilots*).

In order to drive an urban/rural analysis, we have used the French statistics office (INSEE) definition of an urban area. An urban area is a city or an aggregation of cities in which we find a residential zone of at least 2000 inhabitants and where no dwelling is at more than 200 meters from the next one. Moreover, each city concerned must have more than a half of its population living in this residential area.

The next section presents a broad picture of those networks and analyzes their differences by comparing their accessibility levels, as Cohen et al. (2006; Chapter 3, this volume) have done for Italy and the United States.

2.1 General Description

In our description, we would like to stress the differences between 'public services' and 'commercial goods'. So, in Table 4.1 the first four families of services are the ones that will be called public services, because they meet basic needs such as health or education, or because their presence is decided by the public authority. The last family of goods is commercial services. Table 4.1 also presents the total number of locations and the average distance[3] from a consumer to the closest point of the network.

Those types of networks are of very different sizes – between 963 and 56 234 points – and their accessibility across the territory is heterogeneous. Indeed, the average distance to the nearest point varies from 509 meters (for a primary school) to 6178 meters (courthouse).

Table 4.1 A comparison of networks

	Network	Number of location	Average distance* (m)
Health	General practitioner	37 428	1 037
	Dentist	36 244	1 507
	Pharmacy	22 450	1 151
	Hospitals	8 580	3 576
	Medical laboratory	4 492	3 956
Education	Primary school	56 234	509
	Secondary education	9 212	2 251
	Nursery	8 351	3 056
Other public services	Library	2 907	4 268
	Museum	1 936	5 221
	Courthouse	1 854	6 178
	Emergency services, fire department	963	5 750
Postal services	Post office counters	16 609	934
Commercial services	Bakeries	39 511	821
	Bar/tobacco dealer	41 350	1 077
	Bank branch (except *Banque Postale*)	22 696	1 813
	Groceries	25 249	1 340
	Newspaper stall	18 296	1 979
	Gas station	6 453	3 224

Note: * Between a random inhabitant and the closest outlet.

Some of these services face constraints that differ from each other. It is required to have a licence to open a bar, the number of pharmacies is determined by a 'per inhabitant rule', there exist accessibility constraints for postal counters, and the location choice of public hospitals depends on the health ministry, while for many goods/services commercial freedom is the rule (as for bakeries or groceries). These constraints, when they exist, are mainly imposed by national planning and regional policies. Their objectives are mainly to safeguard the accessibility of some public services in remote areas.

Figure 4.1 illustrates that the accessibility issue in term of distance[4] is essentially relevant in rural areas. Indeed, these areas are the ones within the sample with the highest dispersion of average distance between inhabitants and the nearest service.

Two effects appear clearly from this graph. The first one is the 'size effect': the more numerous the points, the more accessible is the network. Indeed, if the primary schools constitute the most accessible network in France with only 500 meters on average to cover, it is also the largest (more than 56 000 points). On the contrary, the emergency services and fire departments have the lowest numbers of points (less than 1000) and are the least accessible (5700 meters on average).

The second effect is the heterogeneity in accessibility between the rural and urban areas. Indeed, in the urban areas the average distance varies from 400 meters to 4420 meters, and 15 out of 19 services are at less than 2000 meters from the inhabitants. In the rural areas, for each service, only 3 out of 19 services (primary schools, bakeries, and post office counters) are at less than 2000 meters. The issue of accessibility is critical in rural areas, because the critical mass of consumers, which makes a commercial service profitable, is more difficult to gather.

One last striking feature of Figure 4.1 is the specificity of the postal network, which performs better in terms of accessibility in rural areas than the bakeries network, which has more points (39 511 points, compared to 16 609 points[5] for the post offices network). This is the result of the constraints imposed on the French postal network, linked to its

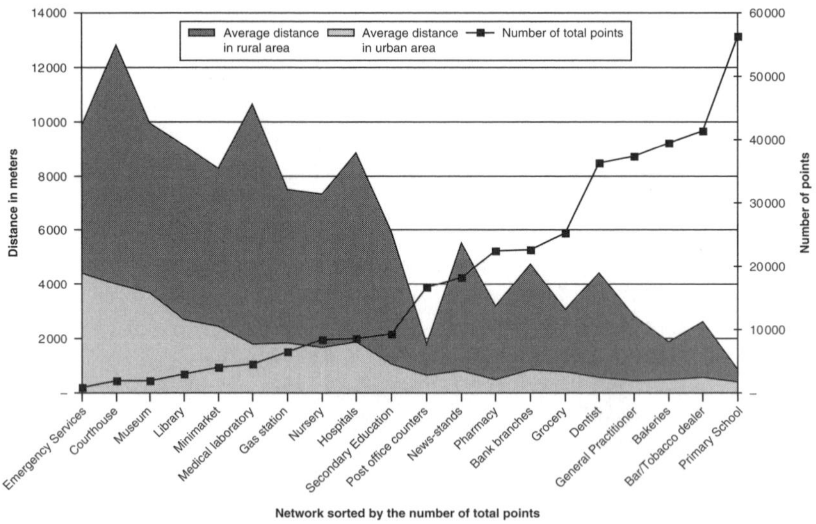

Figure 4.1 Average distances in urban and rural areas

universal service and regional policy objectives, constraints that are binding mainly in rural areas. Indeed, the postal service has the particularity that its urban service locations are commercially determined[6] while the location and density of service centers in rural areas are more aligned with a public service purpose.

In order to analyze the accessibility between services independently of the size effect, we compare, in Section 3.2, the accessibility of different networks that have the same number of total points. Next, we will focus on the accessibility levels in rural areas.

2.2 A Comparison of Accessibility Independent of the Size Effect

In this section we compare services with comparable numbers of points in order to isolate the size effect. We first compare the postal network, which is subject to constraints, with the news-stands network, which has no legal obligation concerning the location of points.

Figure 4.2 shows that the network density in urban and rural areas is very different from one network to another. Indeed, La Poste's retail network has almost 60 percent of its points in rural areas, whereas the news-stands network, which only operates with profit-maximizing behavior, has only 11 percent of its points in rural areas.

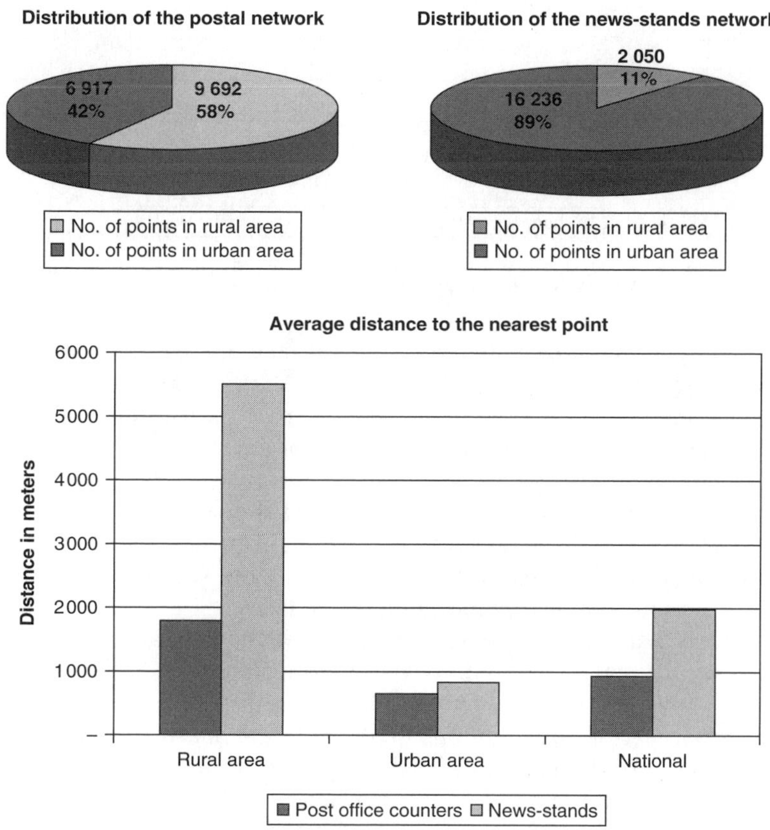

Figure 4.2 A comparison between the post offices network and the news-stands network

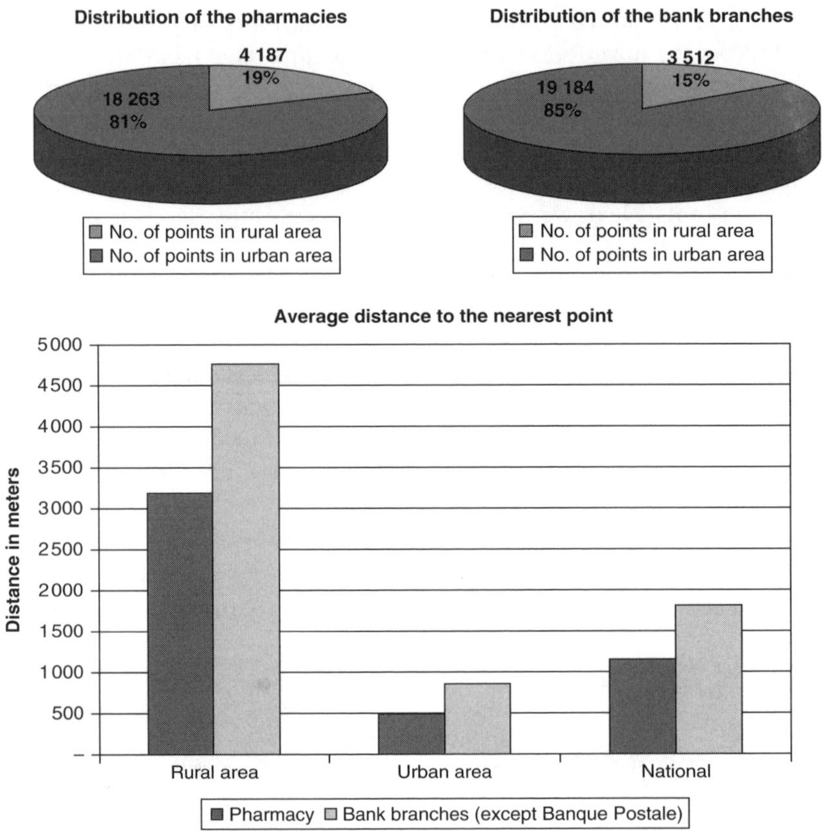

Figure 4.3 A comparison between the pharmacy network and the bank branches network

In terms of networking, those differences are reflected in the accessibility: the average distance of the population from a postal counter is less than 1800 meters, whereas the distance from a newspaper stall is more than 5500 meters. This accessibility gap is less pronounced at the national level, and the concentration of news-stands in urban areas makes it almost nil.

We now turn to the comparison of two networks of the same size and with almost the same split between points in rural areas and points in urban ones – the pharmacies network, which faces constraints, and the bank branches (except *La Banque Postale*) network, which is grounded on a purely commercial basis.

Figure 4.3 shows that these two networks do not have the same accessibility even if they have the same number of points. Indeed, the pharmacies are more accessible despite a lower number of points (200 points fewer). This better distribution all over the territory is explained by the rules of implantation laid down to the pharmacies. Indeed, a bill[7] set a per inhabitant rule for pharmacies, which limits a concentration effect in urban area and allows them to offer a better distribution everywhere.

The bank branches network includes several branded banks that all have commercial aims. The concentration illustrates an interesting behavior: banks choose to be closer to each other than a Hotelling approach would suggest. One could argue that banks should try to spread out better and get far away from each other, to benefit from a more captive local customer base due to transportation costs. But it seems that, on the contrary, there are 'bank areas', where the co-location of competitors can create an interesting form of externality, which offers mutual benefits.

In this chapter, we will not study in more depth the question of co-location strategies of competing services, although this phenomenon is very well known, especially in many industries.[8] This explains why the difference in accessibility between these two networks is less marked in urban areas than in rural areas. To access to a bank branch, a consumer has to cover 260 meters more than to access to a pharmacy in urban areas (but he or she will have more choice once the distance has been covered). This difference in distance becomes 1500 meters in rural areas.

To conclude, we can say that different constraints put on network locations obviously lead to a different topography of networks. The number of points is then not the main criterion for the measurement of accessibility. Indeed in the rural areas we can see that with almost the same number of points in rural areas, accessibility levels of two kinds of services might be quite different.

2.3 Networks in Rural Areas: a Closer Look

As we have seen previously, the accessibility of different services is very sensitive to the geographical area. The transition from an urban area to a rural area is always accompanied by an increase of the average distance of the population from the nearest point. However, this increase is not uniform across the services examined. Indeed, for each service, we have derived the ratio between the average distance in rural areas and the average distance in urban areas. Being in a rural area is 'most costly' in terms of access to services provided by unconstrained networks than in terms of services provided by constrained networks (see Figure 4.4).

A rural citizen has to cover a distance that is twice as big in a rural area than in an urban area to encounter a school, whereas he or she has to cover a distance that is seven times as big to encounter a newspaper stall. There is a clear dichotomy between the constrained public services networks (such as primary schools, post office counters, courthouses and so on) and the networks that fulfill a public utility role but that network on a purely commercial basis. For instance, in rural areas the distance to a dentist is eight times that in urban areas.

This comparison does not reflect a relatively low accessibility level in rural areas. For instance, even if general practitioners and pharmacies networks have a high ratio of their average distance between urban and rural areas (roughly a factor of six), they offer good accessibility in rural areas, with 48 percent of the population at less than 200 meters from a general practitioner and 40 percent from a pharmacy.

3. THE INFLUENCE OF PUBLIC SERVICES ON COMMERCIAL ACTIVITY

We have seen that there are differences between the accessibility of public services and the accessibility of commercial services between constrained and unconstrained networks.

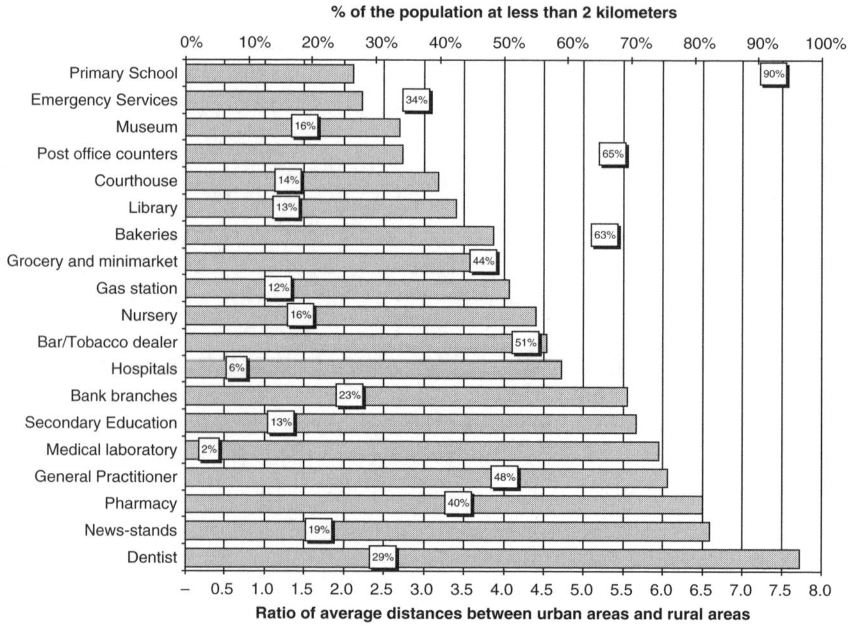

Figure 4.4 A comparison of the average distance between urban and rural areas and accessibility at 2 kilometers in rural areas

Broadly speaking, commercial services networks tend to be concentrated in urban areas and tend to offer much better accessibility in urban areas than in rural areas. This is in line with economic geography theory, which assesses that there exists an economical movement of concentration. The objective of this section is to try to empirically verify or illustrate that more public services in a given area could lead to more commercial services, even in rural areas.

A first look at the data, aggregated by cities (see Table 4.2), shows that first of all, the population has a direct impact on the density of commercial and public services.

The larger cities in terms of inhabitants have the highest number of commercial and public services. We have then to isolate the population effect[9] in order to establish the link between the number of public services and the number of stores. We can then drive our analysis on rural cities with comparable populations. We have split the 30 611 rural villages in five categories.

In each of those five categories (see Table 4.3), we have ranked the rural villages by the number of public services provided ('portfolio'). This means that if there are two schools in the village and no other public services, the village appears here with one type of public service.[10] Within those cities with the same public services 'portfolio', we have derived the average number of commercial services.

Figure 4.5 can be read as follows: in the villages with, for instance, four types of public service and with a population of between 250 and 500 inhabitants, the average number of commercial services is 3. Firstly, we can learn from this figure that for cities of comparable size, greater provision of public services implies more commercial service points

Table 4.2 The number of public and commercial services by semi-deciles of city

Population	Number of cities	Population		Number of public services outlets		Number of commercial outlets	
		Average	Total	Average	Total	Average	Total
< 64	1 830	44	79 913	0.0	47	0.0	84
64 to 93	1 830	79	143 924	0.1	175	0.1	151
94 to 119	1 831	107	195 214	0.2	317	0.1	211
120 to 146	1 830	132	242 300	0.3	498	0.1	257
147 to 175	1 830	161	293 968	0.4	822	0.2	387
176 to 206	1 831	191	349 188	0.6	1 104	0.3	465
207 to 241	1 830	223	408 272	0.7	1 346	0.4	674
242 to 280	1 830	260	475 733	0.9	1 688	0.4	776
281 to 327	1 831	302	553 753	1.1	1 995	0.5	1 006
328 to 381	1 830	353	645 198	1.3	2 326	0.7	1 216
381 to 446	1 830	412	753 133	1.5	2 722	0.9	1 584
447 to 526	1 831	486	890 402	1.7	3 172	1.1	1 990
527 to 624	1 830	573	1 049 215	2.0	3 745	1.4	2 601
625 to 751	1 830	684	1 252 119	2.5	4 565	1.7	3 130
752 to 930	1 831	834	1 527 560	3.2	5 781	2.3	4 149
931 to 1 190	1 830	1 051	1 923 661	4.2	7 619	3.0	5 548
1 190 to 1 639	1 830	1 392	2 546 563	5.8	10 696	4.3	7 789
1 640 to 2 506	1 831	2 016	3 690 921	8.3	15 209	6.0	10 923
2 507 to 5 007	1 830	3 485	6 377 245	13.6	24 890	10.3	18 896
> 5 009	1 831	19 181	35 120 230	64.8	118 586	52.4	95 956
Total	36 607	1 599	58 518 512	5.7	207 303	4.3	157 793

Table 4.3 Categories of rural cities

	Number of villages	Population		Surface (km²)		Average density (inhabitants per km²)
		Average	Total	Average	Total	
< 250	13 230	137	1 818 624	10.4	136 994	20
251–500	7 798	356	2 779 639	14.3	111 761	39
501–750	3 929	610	2 395 858	17.2	67 619	58
751–1 000	2 044	861	1 760 352	19.3	39 617	73
> 1 000	3 610	1 543	5 570 490	25.6	92 482	96
Total	30 611	468	14 324 963	14.6	448 472	42

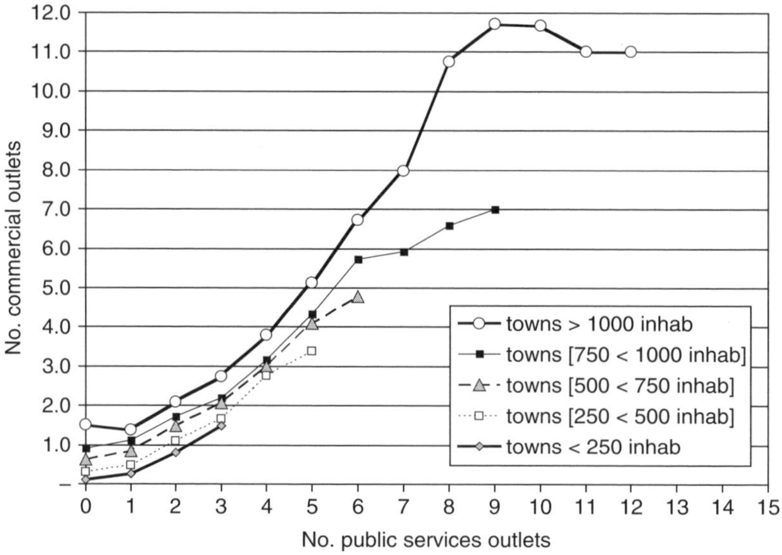

Figure 4.5 The link between the number of commercial outlets and the diversity of public services, for rural towns

(indeed, all the curves are 'increasing'). Secondly, less populated cities may have more commercial service points than bigger cities if they provide more public services. For instance, villages with 500–750 inhabitants with six types of public services have, on average, more commercial services than cities with more than 1000 inhabitants but between one and five types of public services. Thirdly, a saturation effect of the impact of the number of public services provided exists. For instance, in cities of more than 1000 inhabitants one can show that the number of commercial outlets ceases to increase when more than ten public services are provided.

It is not clear whether all these public services have the same influence, or if some combinations of those services perform better than others. It seems that all these public

Table 4.4 The performance of combinations of public services

		Average number of commercial outlets		Average number of commercial outlets
Two public services	Post office + primary school	1.43	All other combination of two public services	0.97
Three public services	Post office + primary school + pharmacy	3.26	All other combination of three public services	2.09

services do not have the same impact on commercial activity. We have not compared all the possible combinations of public services that could be provided – mainly because of data issues,[11] but this phenomenon might be illustrated if we focus on pharmacies, post offices and primary schools.

Table 4.4 shows that on average there are more commercial services in rural cities where two public services, post offices and primary schools, exist than in cities with any other combination of two public services. We obtain the same kind of results with towns with three public services. On average, the combination of post office, primary school and pharmacy attracts more commercial outlets than any other combination of three public services.

Post office counters appear to provide a potentially efficient tool for local economic development, but it also appears that a post office counter must be combined with appropriate public services to have a significant impact. A regional policy could not be based solely on a constraint upon postal retail offices. However, further research is needed to determine whether the link between public services provided – in particular, postal counters – and the number of commercial locations is strong. Moreover, it might be very interesting to compare the number of public services provided with other location macroeconomic data, such as the local GDP, for instance.

4. CONCLUDING REMARKS

In French rural areas, postal counters are more accessible than any other services (except primary schools); in particular, pharmacies or bank branches. This finding is in line with the results of Cohen et al. (2008). At first sight, this accessibility might be judged too high for postal services. However, such a conclusion would ignore and deny the role that postal services play in local economic development by generating spillovers and positive demand externalities for commercial services.

Postal counters have the characteristic that they can be considered both as commercial services and as public services. More precisely, they are located in urban areas for commercial purposes, and in rural areas for public service purposes. The accessibility of postal counters is a tool for social cohesion and economic development in rural areas, and fulfills its purpose within the universal service objectives.

Postal counters create an externality over their immediate environment that serves commercial services, and therefore contributes to economic development. A policy of constraining the retail postal network is nevertheless costly. The net cost of presence in the territory is borne by the USO provider, as the reserved area pays for it. However, the introduction of competition leads to external financing problems that can be quite complex to solve.

The demand created by proximity and co-location is undoubtedly an efficient way to reduce the net cost. By coordinating public services – by co-locating public services, for instance – public decision makers can create a critical mass by giving the market the opportunity to make commercial services profitable. By coordinating public services, public authorities not only act more efficiently on economic development, but they also reduce the net cost of the postal presence. Indeed, in return, the presence of commercial services combined with public services creates demand for postal services, and increases the takings for retail outlets – and therefore reduces the net cost of the constraint. This need for coordination pleads in favor of a 'location choice' policy for public services.

Another way of increasing efficiency through demand externality is to co-locate public services and commercial services at the same point. Like many operators before them, La Poste develops partnerships with commercial storekeepers. The efficiency also comes from the spreading of costs between commercial and public services.

NOTES

* The views expressed in this chapter are those of the authors and do not necessarily reflect the views of La Poste.

1. Note that it is partly financed through public subsidies in Great Britain.
2. The services we study are much closer to those studied by the Swiss *Office Fédéral de la Statistique* in its 2006 reports on accessibility.
3. The average distance has been derived by considering that inhabitants are located at the center of the *Ilot*.
4. Note, however, that the question of accessibility could be set in other ways. For instance, one can focus on accessibility in deprived urban areas or accessibility of buildings for disabled people.
5. The total number of post offices in 2005.
6. It is actually a little more complicated than this. La Poste's counters are also present in 'sensitive urban areas' by law, where profit-maximizing behavior would lead to the closure of these offices. We do not deal with this aspect in this chapter.
7. The bill stipulated that these cannot be more than one pharmacy per 3000 inhabitants in a city of more than 30 000 inhabitants, more than one per 2500 inhabitants in a city of more than 5000 inhabitants and less than 30 000 inhabitants, and more than one per 2000 inhabitants in a city of less than 5000 inhabitants.
8. Jewelers, clothes shops, restaurants, cinemas, and so on are categories of services that tend to co-locate, to create a center of attraction. They are competitors, but by co-locating they attract a higher mass of clientele (that they share) than when surrounded with other types of non-competing services.
9. Within a city, the correlation coefficient between the number of inhabitants and the number of public services is equal to 0.97. The correlation coefficient between the number of inhabitants and the number of commercial services is equal to 0.94.
10. We have driven an analysis with the total number of public services locations, but the results seem to be less clear.
11. The statistical problem that we face lies in the fact that for some combinations we have only few observations (one or two cities). As a consequence, we cannot find out what the best and statistically significant combination is.

REFERENCES

Ambrosini, Xavier, François Boldron and Bernard Roy (2006), 'Universal service obligations in the postal sector: economic learnings from cross-country comparisons', in M.A. Crew and

P.R. Kleindorfer (eds), *Progress toward Liberalization of the Postal and Delivery Sector*, New York: Springer, pp. 23 37.

Cohen, Robert H., Matthew Robinson, Renee Sheehy, Tom Sharkey, John Waller and Spyros Xenakis (2006), 'The conflict about preserving small rural post offices: difference in the distribution and post offices', paper presented at the Winton M. Blount Symposium on Postal History, Washington, DC.

Combes, Pierre-Philippe, Thierry Mayer and Jean-Francois Thisse (2006), Economie geographique: I' integration des regions et des nations, Economica.

Crew, Michael A. and Paul R. Kleindorfer (2006), 'The welfare effects of entry and strategies for maintaining the USO in the postal sector', in M.A. Crew and P.R. Kleindorfer (eds), *Progress toward Liberalization of the Postal and Delivery Sector*, New York: Springer, pp. 3–22.

European Commission (2003), *Government Rural Network Support Funding, Debt Payment Funding and Rolling Working Capital Loan to Post Office Limited*, State Aid N 784/2002, Brussels.

European Commission (2006), *Government Rural Network Support Funding to Post Office Limited*, State Aid N 166/2005, Brussels.

Office Fédérale de la Statistique (2006), *Services à la population: accessibilité entre 1998 et 2001*, Neuchâtel, Switzerland.

Oxera (2007), *Funding Universal Service Obligations in the Postal Sector*, Oxford.

PART II

Demand

5. Forecast uncertainty in dynamic models: an application to the demand for mail*

Catherine Cazals, Jean-Pierre Florens, Frank Rodriguez and Soterios Soteri

1. INTRODUCTION

National postal operators use a variety of techniques to generate projections of the mail market to inform financial and strategic planning decisions. In the UK, for example, Royal Mail uses econometric time series models to produce business projections and to provide a framework to analyse and understand the evolving nature of the demand for mail in the UK (Nankervis et al., 2002). Other national postal operators, such as Finland Post and the United States Postal Service, also possess detailed econometric models which they use extensively for projection and scenario analysis purposes. However, while the reporting and use of such models has tended to be reasonably well documented within the postal economics literature,[1] relatively little quantitative analysis has been undertaken on the uncertainty surrounding volume projections.

Understanding the nature and extent of mail volume uncertainty is necessary to assess appropriately business and policy-related risks. This chapter attempts to bridge this information gap. In particular, we use an econometric time series model of the demand for mail to identify potential sources of model-based projection errors and via the use of Monte Carlo simulation techniques obtain quantitative estimates of the uncertainty surrounding such projections. The results provide a number of insights into the level of uncertainty surrounding projections of mail volumes using time series econometric models.

We proceed as follows. Section 2 provides an overview of the nature of forecasting errors that could arise from time series econometric models. Section 3 briefly describes the econometric model and Monte Carlo simulation methodology used to derive quantitative estimates of forecast uncertainty. Section 4 highlights a number of practical issues that postal operators and policy makers face in using mail market projections that are subject to such levels of uncertainty.

2. FORECAST ERRORS USING TIME SERIES ECONOMETRIC MODELS

The traffic model used in this chapter is estimated by applying time series econometric techniques and a standard error correction model specification such that

$$dq_{it} = \theta_i[q_{it-1} - \xi_i' x_{it-1}] + \Sigma\xi_{ik}\, dx_{it-k} + \Sigma\theta_{ik}\, dq_{it-k} + \varepsilon_{it}, \qquad (5.1)$$

where t denotes time in annual quarters, i refers to a specific stream of mail traffic, q_i denotes the logarithm of type i traffic volume (v_i) per household (h), $dq_{it} = q_{it} - q_{it-1}$, x is a vector of explanatory variables, and ξ and θ are vectors of estimated coefficients.

In order to abstract from issues related to whether the functional form and the explanatory variables included in the model are a good representation of the underlying data generating process over the period that the model was estimated, we analyse the uncertainty associated with model-based volume projections using Monte Carlo simulation techniques. In particular, we use our model and the data used to estimate it to differentiate between, first, forecast errors that are due to random error (that is, associated with the residual term ε_t in expression (5.1)) and, secondly, those related to estimated parameters (i.e. θ and ξ) and the future evolution of the explanatory variables (x_t). The distribution of volume projection forecast errors of this type are then used in this chapter to quantify *within-model* risk. However, in addition, there is also a second type of risk related to structural changes in the demand for mail that occur outside the model estimation period. Such risk, referred to as *off-model* risk, can lead to considerable systematic forecast errors.[2] Within this framework, therefore, the commonly held belief of most national postal operators that changes in technology are creating structural changes in the demand for mail can be interpreted as raising the likelihood that out-of-sample model projections may suffer systematic forecast failure if such off-model risks are ignored.

Projections using dynamic time series models are usually constructed by econometricians conditionally on a forecast of the explanatory variables. These forecasts are in general constructed as the conditional means of these variables given the conditioning set of available information. The range of uncertainty surrounding these projections, estimated in the form of confidence intervals, tends to be constructed using the residual term (ε_t) only. However, as noted above, at least two other sources of within-model uncertainty exist. The errors associated with estimated parameters (that is, θ and ξ) are well known (given the values of the explanatory variables) and are very often assumed to be negligible in comparison to the residual term. But this is not necessarily the case and this point needs to be analysed more carefully. For example, small variations to the parameter values of the macro-economy or time trend variables in dynamic models of the demand for mail are likely to affect mail volume forecasts in an important way, given that forecast errors cumulate in dynamic models as the forecast period increases. Similarly, forecast errors associated with specific scenarios of the explanatory variables could lead to cumulative projection errors over time. It is necessary to consider the distribution of the explanatory variables, which may be asymmetric around the mode (see Wallis, 1999), to assess more appropriately the extent to which explanatory variable uncertainty affects mail volume projection uncertainty (see Hendry and Ericsson, 2001; Hendry and Clements, 2003).

In order to emphasise the importance of taking parameter and explanatory variable uncertainty into account when assessing model-based projection uncertainty (i.e. within-model risks), we undertake an exercise using Monte Carlo simulations. This framework is then used to demonstrate the importance of off-model risk and to highlight the types of issues that national postal operators confront when using models to project the demand for mail.

3. ASSESSING FORECAST UNCERTAINTY FOR TIME SERIES MODELS USING MONTE CARLO SIMULATIONS

3.1 The Econometric Model

The econometric model used is estimated using quarterly data over the period 1976q1 to 2003q2 and, as noted in Section 2, uses a standard error correction model specification. The variables and the estimated coefficients are reported in Table 5.1. The model itself comprises three individual equations, one for each of the following streams of traffic: public tariff next-day service (First Class); public tariff two or three day service (Second Class); and all other mail (mainly presorted traffic). The key drivers of the model for delivered mail are similar to the model reported in Nankervis et al. (2002), namely economic growth, demographic factors and price variables.

3.2 The Monte Carlo Simulation

The Monte Carlo simulation constructed to analyse forecast uncertainty follows a four-step procedure. Step 1 estimates models for all the explanatory variables contained in the econometric model of demand for mail reported in Table 5.1. This exercise uses data observed at the time the model was estimated (that is, 1976q1 to 2003q2). In particular, the following model specifications were used: a VAR(4) for *y* and *p*; AR(4) for *h*; AR(2) for *qos*; AR(1) for *pa*.[3]

Step 2 generates 200 samples of 130 quarterly observations, covering the period 1976q1 to 2008q2, for all the explanatory variables and three streams of traffic. This is 20 observations more than the number used to estimate the econometric models. The observations for the explanatory variables were generated using the models estimated in step 1 as follows:

$$x_t^s = \hat{x}_t + u_t^s, \tag{5.2}$$

where $\hat{x}_t$ is the predicted value of the explanatory variable predicted by the models estimated in step 1[4] and u_t^s are randomly drawn values from a Normal distribution $N(0,\hat{\sigma})$, where $\hat{\sigma}$ is the estimated standard error of the residual of the model, for each sample $s = 1, \ldots, 200$. A similar methodology was adopted to generate volume data for the three streams of traffic data using the equations reported in Table 5.1.

Step 3 assumes that an econometrician observes only the first 110 observations (representing the period from 1976q1 to 2003q2, corresponding to the period used to estimate the econometric model) for each of the 200 simulated samples. The data are then used to estimate the models specified for the explanatory variables in step 1 and the econometric model reported in Table 5.1.[5]

Finally, step 4 uses the models estimated in step 3 to obtain forecasts for the explanatory variables. These are in turn entered into the mail traffic models to predict mail volumes for First Class, Second Class and other inland letter traffic for each of the 200 simulated samples, for up to 20 quarters ahead (that is, corresponding to the period from 2003q3 to 2008q2).

Table 5.1 Econometric demand for mail model

First Class			Second Class			Other (mainly presort)		
Dependent variable dq1			Dependent variable dq2			Dependent variable dq3		
Estimation method least squares			Estimation method least squares			Estimation method least squares		
	Estimated coefficient	*t*-value		Estimated coefficient	*t*-value		Estimated coefficient	*t*-value
ECT1(−1)*	−0.46	−5.0	ECT2(−1)*	−0.52	−7.6	ECT3(−1)*	−1.01	−9.3
p1(−1)	−0.34	−2.8	p1(−1)	0.29	2.2	T	0.0125	9.2
p2(−1)	0.25	2.9	p2(−1)	−0.24	−2.2	T97	−0.0093	−7.8
T87	−0.0035	−4.2	qos(−1)	0.25	3.0			
			T	−0.0068	−6.6			
			T87	0.0042	4.7			
In addition, each equation includes a set of deterministic variables (i.e. a constant and seasonal plus other dummy variables)								
$\hat{\sigma}_1$	0.0261		$\hat{\sigma}_2$	0.0358		$\hat{\sigma}_3$	0.0314	
Estimation period	1976Q3 2003Q2		Estimation period	1976Q1 2003Q2		Estimation period	1983Q2 2003Q2	
ECT1 = q1 − 1.37*y			ECT2 = q2 − 0.44*y			ECT3 = q3 − 1.15*y + 0.32(p3 − pa)		
Constructed using DOLS estimation. See appendix for further details.								
Long-run coefficients			Long-run coefficients			Long-run coefficients		
y	1.37		y	0.44		y	1.15	
p1	−0.72		p1	0.55		p3	−0.32	
p2	0.53		p2	−0.47		pa	0.32	
T87	−0.0076		qos	0.49		T	0.0124	
			T	−0.0130		T97	−0.0092	
			T87	0.0080				

Variable definitions:
q1 = log of 1C traffic per household (v1/h)
q2 = log of 2C traffic per household (v2/h)
q3 = log of other inland traffic (mainly presort) per household (v3/h)
y = log of GVA weighted by each sector's contribution to letter demand
p1 = log of 1C tariff index deflated by all items RPI
p2 = log of 2C tariff index deflated by all items RPI
p3 = log of 3C tariff index deflated by all items RPI
pa = log of price of non-mail advertising
qos = log of quality of service for 1C
T = time trend
T87 = time trend starting in 1987
T97 = time trend starting in 1997
T02 = time trend starting in 2002

3.3 Confidence Intervals of Within-model Forecast Errors

If the behaviours driving mail traffic growth in the future are similar to those in the past (that is, the underlying data generating process is stable), the uncertainty associated with the within-model forecast projections is adequate for assessing true forecast risk. In this case, the Monte Carlo simulation results generated in steps 1–4 of Section 3.2 can be used to compute confidence intervals of forecast error. In particular, the differences between the traffic volume forecasts in step 4 and the traffic volumes generated in step 2 are used to construct true within-model confidence intervals of forecast errors for the five-year forecast period from 2003q3 to 2008q2. The confidence intervals computed take into account uncertainties associated with parameter uncertainty and the future evolution of explanatory variables, as well as the standard element of random error.

Figure 5.1 reports Monte Carlo simulation results for the sum of the three streams of traffic, which is broadly equivalent to the total addressed inland mail market in the UK. In particular, it contains estimates for the mean forecast error (predicted value minus observed value), confidence intervals of forecast errors, computed in the standard way by econometricians (that is, those computed by taking into account only the uncertainty from residual terms in the models) and the true confidence intervals of within-model forecast errors as outlined in Section 3.2.[6] Within the 'fan chart', it can be seen that the mean value of the true forecast error is close to zero and tends to drift slightly downwards, suggesting there is a small negative forecast bias over time (that is, predicted traffic tends to be slightly less than actual traffic).

However, there are two other results contained in Figure 5.1 that are more significant. First, the level of forecast uncertainty increases substantially over the forecast time horizon. This is due to the cumulation of errors in the dynamic modelling as discussed in Section 2. These arise from errors in the estimated parameters and also in the forecasts for explanatory variables in the model, such as economic growth.

Secondly, there is the considerable extent to which the uncertainty of forecasts, and hence of volume risk, is underestimated over the medium and long term if reliance is placed on standard econometric estimates of confidence intervals. For example, in the econometric model for mail demand analysed in this chapter, and as shown in Figure 5.1, the true risks measured through 95 per cent confidence intervals associated with total traffic projections are approximately double those estimated by standard econometric techniques two years into the forecast horizon. They are over three times greater five years into the forecast horizon.

3.4 Assessing Risks Associated with Off-model Forecast Errors

It is not possible to conduct statistical tests within the estimation period of the model to quantify *ex ante* the risk that the behaviour of mail senders will change in the future if the factors driving this change in behaviour, say new technology, are qualitatively different to those in the past. However, an econometric model's forecasting properties can be used *ex post* to provide valuable information as to whether events of this kind have taken place and the extent to which they may have and are generating off-model forecast errors. In order to examine this difficult forecasting issue further, we develop an illustrative example and analyse it using the Monte Carlo simulation methodology outlined in Section 3.2. In particular, it is assumed that the model reported in Table 5.1 is used in 2003q3 to project

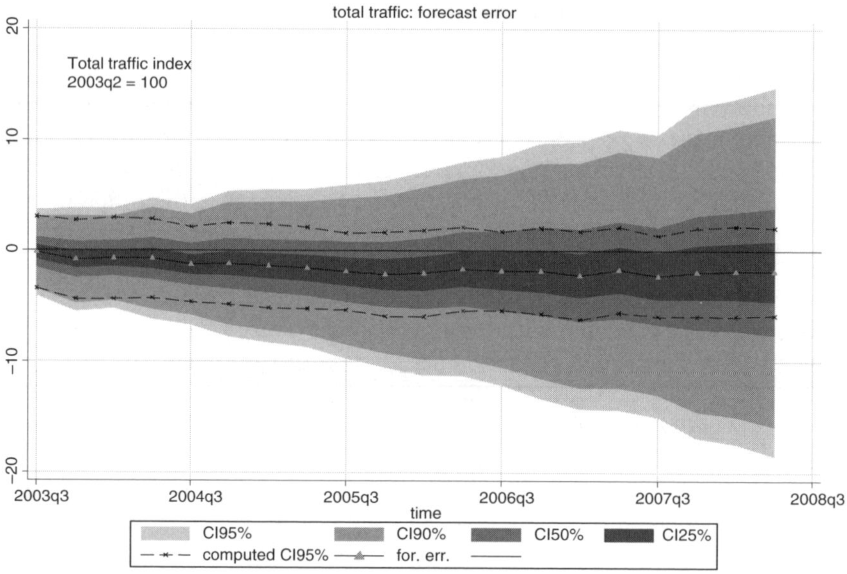

Figure 5.1 Confidence intervals of forecast errors for total traffic

mail volumes but that, unknown at the time of the forecast, structural factors relating to changes in technology are reducing the demand for mail relative to what it would otherwise have been by 6 per cent a year for First Class, 3 per cent for Second Class and 3 per cent for other mail (equal to a reduction of around 3.5 per cent a year for total traffic).[7] It should be stressed that these values are hypothetical and are used here to illustrate the application of our methodology to the examination of the potential impact on forecast errors of off-model developments.

In order to estimate the impact of using the econometric model to project forwards, each of the three equations in Table 5.1 has been augmented with an additional trend variable that reduces traffic by the amount required in the example from 2003q3 onwards. The Monte Carlo simulation exercise reported in Section 3.2 has then been repeated to generate a new set of actual values. The traffic projections using the original model specification (that is, not including the new trend terms) are then compared to the simulated actual values, including the new trend terms. The results are reported for total traffic in Figure 5.2, which shows that, in general, the characteristics highlighted in the previous section still hold, but the mean forecast error suffers from systematic and increasing upward bias. Indeed, in this example the model tends to overestimate mail traffic and the gap between predicted and real values increases considerably over time.

A further point to note is that the mean forecast error reported in Figure 5.2 would not lie outside the standard but narrow 95 per cent confidence interval reported in Figure 5.1 until at least a year after the post-estimation period. Indeed, the mean forecast error would not lie outside the true 95 per cent confidence interval over the full five-year simulation period. However, we would observe continuous and increasing forecast error, signalling clearly the risk that the model suffers from systematic forecast failure unless projections are modified in an appropriate way.

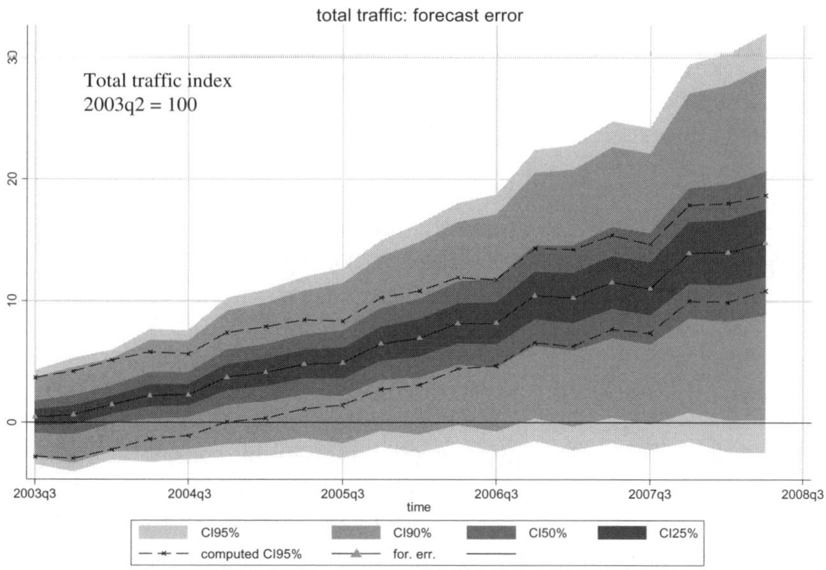

Figure 5.2 Forecast errors and associated confidence intervals when model contains unknown break in trend

4. MAIL MARKET PROJECTION UNCERTAINTY AND IMPLICATIONS FOR POSTAL OPERATORS AND POLICY MAKERS

This chapter has applied Monte Carlo simulation analysis to a model of the demand for mail to identify and quantify risk surrounding volume projections. The analysis yields a number of key conclusions. First, the true risks associated with model-based-volume projections, measured through confidence intervals that reflect fully the various sources of error in econometric estimation and projection, are large and tend to increase over time. Secondly, this risk is considerably greater than suggested by confidence intervals as normally presented in econometric reporting, which tend to focus only on a subset of these sources of error. Thirdly, while models can be used to assess within-model risk, changes in the external environment can lead to substantial changes in demand and hence forecast errors. It is important to try to take such developments into account, albeit outside the econometric model, when assessing forecasting risk. Fourthly, the forecast properties of econometric models should be regularly reviewed to inform assessments of the likely presence, and potential extent of, off-model forecast risk as well as the underlying robustness of the existing model. Fifthly, the knowledge gained from points three and four should provide valuable information, such that future re-estimation of the volume models can incorporate measures to account for previous events, and are hence more robust (Hendry and Clements, 2001, p. 63).

A number of implications for policy flow from our conclusions. First, postal operators and policy makers will underestimate substantially the potential risks associated with model-based volume projections if they rely on confidence intervals produced by standard econometric reporting. In particular, sensitivity ranges for volume projections used to appraise investment projects, stress test business strategies, evaluate break-even rates of return and inform regulatory targets and incentives are likely to be too narrow if they are informed by confidence intervals computed on this basis, which focus only on risks associated with random error. Within a stable structural environment, confidence intervals that take into account risks associated with future values of explanatory variables and errors in parameter estimates as well as in random error will inform postal operators and policy makers more appropriately of risk related to volume projections.

Secondly, risks associated with events that are not covered by the models themselves (that is, off-model risk) should not be ignored. Risks of this type are related to events and changes in behaviour that take place after the model has been estimated and hence by definition they are not, and cannot be, included in the model itself. When off-model risks of this type occur, they could lead to systematic and increasing forecast errors over time. However, in the early stages of the post-estimation time horizon, observed forecast errors that are in fact due to factors external to the model may be difficult to detect, especially if such forecast errors lie within a relatively small and tolerable forecast range.

Thirdly, it may be necessary to modify model based projections using additional information in order to try to reduce the risk of systematic forecast error in the future. In practice, it is recommended that such modifications should adopt a blend of within-model adjustments, using 'intercept shift' adjustments once a sequence of forecast errors is observed,[8] and forward looking adjustments based, for example, on business expert knowledge of the industry and other information that may help improve a forecast.

NOTES

* The analysis contained in this chapter reflects the views of the authors and may not necessarily be those of Royal Mail Group.
1. See Nikali (2001, 2007), Thress (2006) and Tolley (2001).
2. See Kay (2006) for a discussion of within-model and off-model risks.
3. These are reported in the Appendix.
4. For mail tariffs, a slightly different procedure was adopted for the 20 observations beyond the econometric model estimation period that more appropriately reflects the terms of the price control that Royal Mail currently operates within. In particular, mail tariffs were predicted to change in the second quarter of the calendar year and the change was set equal to the average percentage change in the all items retail prices index in the second and third quarters of the previous year plus: 0 per cent in the case of q_1 and q_2; and minus 2 per cent in the case of q_3.
5. Note also that the long-term relationships (that is, the error correction terms) are also estimated with the same specification as that generated by the econometric model (see the Appendix).
6. The values on this graph have been rescaled such that the mean (over the simulated samples) total traffic index in 2003q2 is equal to 100.
7. This illustrative example reduces the long-term projection for total volume growth in the model reported in Table 5.1 from around 3 per cent a year to around −0.5 per cent a year.
8. For example, Hendry and Ericsson (2001, p. 40) state: 'when the first of a sequence of forecasts is in error, the remaining forecasts often suffer similarly. Consequently, an "intercept shift", equal to the last observed error, can considerably improve forecast performance.'

REFERENCES

Hendry, D.F. and M.P. Clements (2001), *Forecasting Non-stationary Economic Time Series*, Cambridge, MA: The MIT Press.

Hendry, D.F. and M.P. Clements (2003), 'Economic forecasting: some lessons from recent research', *Economic Modelling*, **20**, 301–29.
Hendry, D.F. and N.R. Ericsson (eds) (2001), *Understanding Economic Forecasts*, Cambridge, MA: The MIT Press.
Kay, J. (2006), 'Amaranth and the limits of mathematical modelling', *Financial Times*, 10 October.
Nankervis, J., S. Richard, S. Soteri and F. Rodriguez (2002), 'Disaggregated letter traffic demand in the UK', in M.A. Crew and P.R. Kleindorfer (eds), *Postal and Delivery Services*, Boston, MA: Kluwer Academic Publishers, pp. 203–18.
Nikali, H. (2001), 'Demand models for letter mail in the competitive targeted communication market', draft paper presented at Institut D'Economie Industrielle Second Conference on Competition and Universal Service in the Postal Sector.
Nikali, H. (2007), 'Substitution of letter mail in different sender–receiver segments', paper presented at 15th Conference on Postal and Delivery Economics.
Thress, T.E. (2006), 'Direct testimony of Thomas E. Thress on behalf of the United States Postal Service', Postal Rate Commission, Docket No. R2006-1.
Tolley, G.S. (2001), 'Direct testimony of George S. Tolley on behalf of the United States Postal Service', Postal Rate Commission, Docket No. R2001-1.
Wallis, K. (1999), 'Asymmetric density forecasts of inflation and the Bank of England's Fan Chart', *National Institute Economic Review*, **167**, 106–12.

APPENDIX

In the following tables, dx_t is the first difference of x (that is, $x_t - x_{t-1}$), S*i* are quarterly dummies, T*i* are trends, and $\hat{\sigma}$ is the standard error of regression.

A.1 Long-term Relations: Estimated Coefficients

First class (dependent variable: $q1_t$)		Second class (dependent variable: $q2_t$)		Other (dependent variable: $q3_t$)	
c	−4.39	c	−2.65	c	−5.06
y_t	1.369	y_t	0.44	y_t	1.15
$p1_t$	−0.89	$p1_t$	0.36	$p3_t - pa_t$	−0.32
$p2_t$	0.53	$p2_t$	−0.44	T83	0.01
T87	−0.008	qos_t	0.69	T97	−0.008
S1	0.03	T75	−0.01	S1	0.04
S2	0.01	T87	0.007	S2	−0.02
S3	−0.03	S1	−0.01	S3	−0.08
dy_t	−0.27	S2	−0.03	dy_t	0.59
dy_{t+1}	1.08	S3	−0.09	dy_{t+1}	1.08
$dp1_t$	0.95	dy_t	−0.67	$dp3_t$	0.21
$dp1_{t+1}$	0.49	dy_{t+1}	1.26	$dp3_{t+1}$	0.08
$dp2_t$	−0.53	$dp1_t$	−0.19		
$dp2_{t+1}$	−0.42	$dp1_{t+1}$	−0.2		
		$dp2_t$	0.36		
		$dp2_{t+1}$	−0.18		
		$dqos_t$	−0.38		
		$dqos_{t+1}$	−0.17		

A.2 Models for Exogenous Variables

VAR(4) model for (y, p)

	Equation for dy_t		Equation for dp_t	
	Coefficient	*Std error*	Coefficient	*Std error*
c	0.02	*(0.004)*	0.004	*(0.004)*
dy_{t-1}	0.05	*(0.103)*	0.21	*(0.09)*
dy_{t-2}	−0.004	*(0.098)*	−0.19	*(0.089)*
dy_{t-3}	0.28	*(0.095)*	−0.01	*(0.086)*
dy_{t-4}	−0.07	*(0.096)*	0.09	*(0.087)*
dp_{t-1}	0.03	*(0.093)*	0.53	*(0.084)*
dp_{t-2}	−0.34	*(0.107)*	0.07	*(0.97)*
dp_{t-3}	0.05	*(0.110)*	−0.01	*(0.099)*
dp_{t-4}	−0.19	*(0.093)*	0.09	*(0.084)*
S1	−0.009	*(0.003)*	−0.0008	*(0.003)*
S2	−0.004	*(0.002)*	0.01	*(0.002)*
S3	−0.007	*(0.003)*	−0.009	*(0.003)*
T75	−0.0001	*(3.5E-05)*	−0.00003	*(3.2E-05)*
$\hat{\sigma}$	*0.0061*		*0.0055*	

AR(2) model for dqos

	Coefficient		*Std error*
c	0.01		*(0.002)*
$dqos_{t-1}$	−0.36		*(0.051)*
$dqos_{t-2}$	−0.09		*(0.038)*
S1	−0.01		*(0.004)*
$\hat{\sigma}$		*0.02*	

AR(1) model for dpa

	Coefficient		*Std error*
c	0.001		*(0.0005)*
dpa_{t-1}	0.8		*(0.048)*
T87	−0.00002		*(1.6E-05)*
$\hat{\sigma}$		*0.0029*	

AR(4) model for dh

	Coefficient		*Std error*
c	0.00004		*(3.5E-06)*
dh_{t-1}	0.93		*(0.083)*
dh_{t-2}	0.58		*(0.123)*
dh_{t-3}	−0.03		*(0.123)*
dh_{t-4}	−0.5		*(0.082)*
T76	−9E-08		*(1.5E-08)*
$\hat{\sigma}$		*3.8E-06*	

6. The impact of economic and demographic dispersion on aggregate mail volumes*

Luis Jimenez, Matthew C. Harding and Michael Lintell

1. INTRODUCTION

Mail demand is an important object of study in the economics of regulated industries. While some of the main drivers of aggregate mail demand (e.g., GDP) are well understood, the relationship between the mail drivers of demand across mail streams disaggregated by sender–receiver pair is often poorly predicted by macroeconomic aggregates. The aim of this chapter is to analyze the extent to which the dispersion in some of the drivers of mail demand can be used to explain variation in mail demand across time and across countries. This research is the third contribution to the series on aggregate mail demand across countries.

Harding (2005) provides a comprehensive review of the econometric and qualitative models developed over the past 30 years and notes that so far no econometric model of mail demand has been constructed that takes advantage of combining multiple time series of mail volumes across countries. Although many useful and interesting time series models exist in the literature (e.g., Trinkner and Grossmann, 2006), they focus on explaining mail volumes in one country only. Given the limitations on the availability of past data and the risk of structural breaks occurring if we investigate events that happened too many years into the past, time series based models find it difficult to investigate a large number of potential drivers.

Harding (2006) tries to overcome this limitation by investigating the demand jointly across several developed economies. It constructs a unique dataset consisting of an extensive number of drivers and employs two related multivariate techniques, a detailed clustering analysis and a panel regression analysis. Although a panel model of mail demand based on a number of macroeconomic and demographic controls appears to describe the evolution of mail demand during the sampling period, it nevertheless finds that a substantial amount of unobserved heterogeneity remains unexplained and is required to reconcile the observed volumes with those predicted by the employed mail drivers. This is particularly important for understanding the cross-country variation in mail volumes.

This study attempts to explain the unobserved heterogeneity in the data by examining the role the dispersion of some of the main drivers has on the overall mail volumes. The focus of this chapter is on Business-to-Household (B2H) and Business-to-Business (B2B) mail flows and does not consider mail originating from households.

Business originating mail accounts for close to 85 percent of the world's mail. Business-originating mail refers to, in this instance, addressed letter mail from businesses, as either correspondence and transaction (C&T), or Direct Marketing (DM) destined for households or for other businesses. B2H letter mail accounts for approximately 50–65 percent of a country's total mail volume, while B2B mail is about 15–20 percent. Business-to-Household mail continues to grow in volume in most countries due in part to the growth in the number of financial accounts held by households (OECD, 2006) and the continued growth in the mail channel as an effective advertising and direct marketing medium. B2B mail volumes are in decline for a variety of plausible reasons. B2H mail is more visible and measured due to the nature of the content and its volume. B2B mail is not as commonly visible or measured. In addition to the large percentage of the total mail volume that business-originating mail represents, data is more widely available on household statistics in most countries over time and thus can be more effectively evaluated statistically when combined into the mail demand models.

1.1 Theoretical and Empirical Reasons for the Dispersion Hypothesis

Recent work in macroeconomics and political economy has started to emphasize the role that income inequality plays in a variety of economic policies and outcomes. The question has become especially salient given wide differences across developed economies in their levels of income inequality. Evidence over the past 60 years indicate persistent and large differences in levels of inequality between the US and European countries, as well as within Europe. Over the last decade, income inequality has also rapidly increased in the US, while household surveys from Europe show that in most countries their inequality has either not changed much or declined over the same period. Inequality is a function both of levels of poverty and levels of income dispersion in the highest-earning segment of the labor market. Additionally, in large part, these differences in income inequality across the OECD countries relate to large differences in the size of the welfare states – for example, the US government's general expenditure accounts for 30 percent of its GDP, while in France it is 49 percent and in Sweden it reaches 52 percent.[1] Beyond the size of public spending, inequality is also associated to many microeconomic factors (wage inequality, consumption behavior, and educational disparities) and macroeconomic institutions and policies (structure of labor markets, growth and investment policies).

There are two channels through which income inequality would be particularly important for mail demand. The first relationship is on the demand side. As the distribution of income among consumers widens, we observe a 'hollowing out' of the middle class, with a potentially large number of consumers who ordinarily receive mail becoming either increasingly rich or more likely poor. Because mail received is likely to follow general consumption patterns, and inequality of income translates into inequality of consumption, we can expect that increasing inequality will have a direct effect on consumer use for mail. This effect of inequality on consumer use for mail will be low if the marginal increase in demand for mail is high as consumers move from low income to middle income bracket, and marginal increase in demand for mail lower when more individuals move from middle-income to higher-income bracket.[2] As consumer use of mail changes over time, this may also affect B2B mail demand patterns as businesses aim to change their models in order to adapt to the new market structure.

The second channel through which income inequality could be affected by inequality is macroeconomic performance. Here, on the output side, inequality affects the supply of labor. In a standard Meltzer–Richard (1981) model, income inequality arises from heterogeneity of skills and productivity levels. In democracies such as the United States, the voters then set taxes and the size of government spending, which in turn redistributes income to compensate those with lower productivity. However, due to loss of efficiency that comes with raising taxes and government spending, there is maximum optimum tax, past which even those with lower productivity have no incentive to demand more taxation and redistribution. In addition to redistribution, inequality can also create different demands for social insurance provided by the government, to protect workers against the risk of unemployment and income shocks (Moene and Wallerstein, 2001). Together, the demand for redistribution and social insurance has combined with the shift to a service economy and economic openness to shape the dramatic growth of the welfare state in Europe following the Second World War (Iversen and Cusack, 2000).

To understand the effects of these macroeconomic consequences of inequality on mail demand, it is also necessary to understand how the size of the welfare state shapes business practices and economic performance across OECD countries. The size of the welfare state directly relates to a broader host of institutions that regulate how businesses relations are coordinated. Large welfare states, redistributing resources and decreasing post-tax inequality, correlate with more hierarchical and long-term investment relationships and horizontal coordination of firms across industry sectors (Hall and Soskice, 2001). A large welfare state also translates into various government-provided social insurance institutions, including those that structure education and training and more tightly regulate labor markets (Saint-Paul, 1996; Estavez-Abe et al., 2001). Hence these differences affect how businesses operate, and how they use mail to communicate with other businesses and their consumers. Mail demand therefore reflects the patterns and practices of B2B and B2H communication.

In addition, inequality can influence economic performance, which in turn affects mail demand. The original work on the role of inequality in economic performance dates back to Kuznets (1955), in which he put forward a theory that inequality has an inverse U-shaped relationship to economic output. According to the theory, both complete leveling-down of income and very high rates of inequality would hurt performance. More recently, economic theory and evidence is divided over under what conditions inequality can be harmful or helpful for growth (Alesina and Rodrik, 1994; Persson and Tabellini, 1994; Bénabou, 1996; Perotti, 1996; Aghion and Bolton, 1997; Aghion et al., 1999; Barro, 2000). The major channels through which inequality can potentially affect performance include loss of efficiency that arises with high rates of income taxation, social instability that can result from very high inequality, and various effects on human capital and investment that high levels of inequality may have. Together, through all of these channels inequality may affect demand for mail in as much as mail demand follows general long-term patterns of economic performance.

Effects of social and economic inequality on health of a society are substantial. In countries with public healthcare systems, individuals are entitled to receive the same quantity of healthcare, however there are large geographic differences in the healthcare provided based on societal variances including population density, multicultural characteristics, and unequal economic growth. Various international studies have documented a strong association between income inequality and high mortality. In a study by Kennedy et al., income inequality was shown to directly affect the total mortality in a given population [$p < 0.05$] (Kennedy et al., 1996). Additionally, the growth of private healthcare sector is seen as a boon; however, it adds to ever-increasing social dichotomy. The dominance of the private sector not only denies access to poorer sections of society, but also skews the balance towards urban-biased, tertiary-level health services with profitability overriding equality, and rationality of care often taking a back seat. The services offered at a very high price are excellent but are unaffordable for the common man. This re-emphasizes the role socio-economic inequality plays in healthcare delivery.

2. DISPERSION MEASURES

Measures of dispersion describe the spread in the data from a central value. Two distinct values may have the same mean or median but completely different levels of variability. Based on the model developed by Harding, primary drivers of mail volume demand across countries consisted of aggregate economic and socio-economic measures; for example, GDP, bankable households and so on. Expanding on the Harding model, we test the hypothesis that measures of inequality and dispersion of the primary driving variables would further explain the unobserved heterogeneity of mail demand between countries. The primary drivers from the Harding model with large standard deviations were examined. Economic inequality (GINI index), income distribution, age distribution, and measures of social cultural dispersion were given consideration for inclusion on the expanded demand model. Each of these measures alone describes differences between the countries and shows that there are substantial differences between these countries in their economic and social structures.

2.1 Income Distribution Inequality

In many studies, Household Income and Personal Income aggregates are noted as principal factors contributing to aggregate mail demand. As economic activity increases, mail demand increases due to the volume of financial transactions, number of financial accounts, the increase in the number of business relationships, and so on. In many empirical studies, it is shown that as a nation becomes fully industrialized, the distribution of wealth within that country begins to concentrate in the upper and lower quartiles. There are a variety of measures of the distribution of income equality, absolute income (e.g., the Poverty Line – the absolute measure of income to subsist in a society), and relative measures (e.g., percentile distributions and indicies). This distribution of income is most notably measured by the GINI coefficient – the summary statistic used to quantify the extent of income inequality depicted in a particular Lorenz curve (the locus of points used to display the relative inequality in a distribution of income values – a society's total income is ordered according to income level and the cumulative total is then graphed). The GINI coefficient can vary over time and does vary from country to country. Overall, North America, Northwest Europe, (as well as Japan, and Australia) have a stable income ratio between 1980 and 2005 at more than three times mean world income, with slower growing incomes and growing inequality in Asia, Latin America, Eastern Europe, and Africa.

2.2 Demographics

2.2.1 Age variables

Income inequality metrics and other measures of economic dispersion often ignore life cycle effects. In most industrialized societies, an individual starts life with little or no income, gradually increases income until about age 50, after which incomes will decline, eventually becoming negative. This will have the effect of significantly overstating inequality. It has been estimated (Blinder, 1973) that 30 percent of measured income inequality is due to the inequality individuals experience as they go through the various stages of life. As previously studied, economic patterns and mail demand are correlated to life stage and income (Jimenez et al., 2006). As an individual becomes economically active, the volume of mail demand for this individual increases following the similar patterns of the economic life stages. There are a number of measures of age distributions of populations from population pyramids that graphically depict the age/gender distribution. These are normally used to find the number of economic dependents being supported in a particular population. By evaluating the age range distributions of each country in the model, it can be determined to what extent the age range and distribution of the population may contribute to the mail demand.

There are a number of ways in which countries differ from both social and economic perspectives. Many of these are not easily captured statistically. Given that social and economic measures of households are shown to be principal components of mail demand, the need to identify the variability between countries over time of the different social and economic variables is a pertinent issue to more accurately understand the demand for mail. A perfectly homogeneous population would allow for clearer understanding of the drivers of mail demand. In effect, all countries have some degree of demographic heterogeneity among their populations (e.g., age distribution, household income, urbanization, education, language spoken, ethnic background, etc). This study utilized the standard economic and demographic variables and additionally utilized linguistic and ethnolinguistic fractionalization (ELF). Ethnolinguistic fractionalization is the ethnic diversity of a country, in terms of number of different ethnic groups. According to Roeder, it is the likelihood that two individuals, chosen at random, will be from different ethnic groups. Thus, the higher the ELF, the more ethnically diverse a country, and the more ethnic groups in the population. The US and Switzerland are highly fractionalized (higher diversity), while Denmark, Italy, Norway, and Sweden are least fractionalized (lower diversity). The ELF index was chosen as it provides a stable measurement for levels of language and ethnic diversity. Since we could not isolate and test for all sources of social and economic heterogeneity, it is important to include these (ELF) demographic measures, as they contribute to the homo- or heterogeneity of a country's population and would in turn contribute to mail volume demand.

3. ECONOMETRIC MODELS OF DISPERSION

3.1 The Baseline Panel Data Model

We model the evolution of mail demand for each country over time as a function of observed drivers, country-specific unobserved effects, and stochastic shocks. This approach treats the marginal effects of the drivers of mail demand as constant, but at the same time allows the elasticities to vary with the volumes. The approach explains changes in demand across time for different periods and allows us to focus on explaining these trends as a function of clearly interpretable drivers.

The estimation of mail demand is performed using panel data econometric methods. Our approach takes into account both variation over time and across countries, models unobserved heterogeneity as country-specific fixed-effects, and allows us to estimate within-country determinants of mail demand as our main quantity of interest. In particular, we employ a mixed specification:

$$\text{Demand}_{it} = \beta_1 \log x_{it}^1 + \beta_2 \log x_{it}^2 + \ldots + \beta_K x_{it}^K + a_i + u_{it},$$

where Demand_{it} is the time series of mail demand for country i in year t of a particular mail stream under consideration: B2B or B2H. Different drivers of mail demand are included in the analysis as either $\log x_{it}^j$ or x_{it}^K, and they are the observed economic, social, and demographic characteristics of a country i at time t. The remaining terms estimated include the country-specific fixed effect a_i and the error term u_{it}. The advantage of the fixed effects set-up is that it models statistically unobserved mail drivers, which cannot be included in the model due to data limitations. The country-specific fixed effect is constant over time but differs across countries, capturing the effect of various country characteristics that include institutions, culture, history, and business practices. The error terms are corrected for autocorrelation and heteroskedasticity by estimating robust covariance matrices. Finally, the set of unknown coefficients β_K corresponds to estimated quantitative relationship between different mail drivers and demand.

We employ a unique dataset of mail demand volumes and associated drivers, developed through in-depth consideration of plausible demand channels and extensive interviews of industry practitioners. The variables included in the model are summarized in Table 6.1. Here, we focus our attention on two particular mail streams, defined by sender–receiver pair: Business-to-Consumer (B2H) and Business-to-Business (B2B). Various data sources used include the World Bank, EU databases, and postal data provided by postal operators in Austria, Denmark, France, Germany, Finland, Italy, Switzerland, the United Kingdom, and the United States. The time series for each country in the period between 1995 and 2004 are included in the panel. Special attention was taken to minimize missing variables in the data, both by in-depth research to code any missing data and by the use of a range of statistical imputation techniques to extrapolate the most likely values in the few cases where no data was available.

Finally, we perform all our estimation on two samples: one including the US and one without the US. The advantage of this approach is that the US is often an outlier in terms of both mail volumes and economic and demographic dispersion, and therefore estimating different models allows us to assess both the general effect of drivers in the whole sample, and the more specific effect when the US is excluded.

In the baseline model of mail demand, important drivers of mail demand include population size and income. In addition, B2H mail demand is also driven by the number of households, and of Internet and cellphone users. The substitution effect of new technologies is somewhat stronger in the case of B2H than in the case of B2B. As expected in the B2H case, it is both the size of the population and the number of households that plays a role in driving mail demand.

B2B mail demand is in addition negatively affected by high levels of unemployment, indicating the importance of economic performance as a determinant of B2B mail demand. We observe no statistically significant effect of Internet and cellphone users on B2B mail demand, and only the number of telephone lines seems to affect demand, but this effect vanishes when the US is excluded from the sample.

Furthermore, the main difference between the samples that include and exclude the US is that in the US sample mail demand also depends on C&T mail price, while in the sample without US there is no statistically significant relationship between C&T mail price and demand.

3.2 GINI and Income Inequality

To measure the effect of economic dispersion we use the GINI coefficient. The GINI coefficient ranges from 0 (perfect income equality) to 1 (highest level of inequality) and is constructed as a function of the area under the Lorenz curve. Precisely, the Lorenz curve is a derived relationship between the cumulative distribution of population in different income brackets and the cumulative share of income earned by the portion of a population in a given income bracket. The GINI coefficient quantifies the deviation of the Lorenz curve from a perfect 45-degree uniform distribution line (representing complete equality of incomes); the GINI coefficient is calculated as the ratio, with a numerator being the area between the Lorenz curve and 45-degree line, and the denominator being the area under the 45-degree.

We include the GINI coefficient as its own driver, as well as the interactions between the GINI coefficient with GDP and growth, separately. These two interactions are important because they allow us to test whether economic performance and the level of income in a given country condition the effect of inequality on mail demand. By this empirical strategy, we are able to explore in part not only whether income dispersion has an effect on mail demand but also whether the channel by which it affects demand corresponds to the above-discussed theories about inequality and economic performance.

Considering B2H mail demand first, the results indicate that the effects of the GINI coefficient alone are not always statistically significant, but rather that it is important to look both at the GINI coefficient and its interaction with economic performance variables. Once the entire demand model is estimated, the results show that income inequality on its own is positively correlated with B2H mail demand. However, this direct effect is mediated by an opposite effect of the two interactions. At times of good economic performance (measured by increased income and economic growth), the positive effect of inequality on mail demand is more limited.

These results show strong support for above-discussed theories that one main channel through which income inequality affects demand is through economic performance. In other words, economic performance conditions the effects of inequality. When the economy is doing well, with high growth and higher living standards, these effects can potentially limit the positive correlation between inequality and mail demand. However, the results also indicate that when the economy is doing poorly, increasing inequality of incomes may still increase B2H mail demand in some parts of the market.

Our regression analysis also indicates that this mechanism is not sensitive to the inclusion of the US, since the relationship estimated is largely identical to that with the US excluded from the sample.

Second, considering B2B demand, the GINI coefficient is overall a statistically significant predictor of demand. Both with and without the US included, we observe that when countries have higher levels of inequality, their B2B main demand goes down. The relationship between B2B mail demand and inequality suggests a pattern where higher income and higher growth offset the negative effects of inequality and drive B2B mail demand up, even in the presence of high income inequality. However, once the US is included in the sample, the relationship becomes less robust. On its own, higher inequality is still associated with lower B2B mail demand, but the interaction effects cannot be estimated precisely enough to draw reliable inference. This result can be explained by the fact that the United States is an outlier both when it comes to the levels of income inequality and to income. Together, these two factors conspire to increase the variance of our estimates, decreasing the predictive power of the model.

3.3 Quartiles of Income Distribution

Going beyond the GINI coefficient, our next task was to examine what causes the effect of income inequality on aggregate mail volumes. Given that the relationship between income inequality and B2H mail demand was very robust, we examined how the ratio of low- to high-income households is related to B2H mail demand. The estimated relationship generally supports the findings above, although statistical precision of the estimates is not high enough to make very reliable predictions. Overall, having more high-income households tends to drive up B2H mail demand on the national level. This relationship is more important at times of poorer economic performance, indicated by the opposite effect that the number of high-income households has on B2H mail demand when interacted with growth and income.

In the entire sample, including the US, we found some evidence that the number of high-income households is a statistically significant driver of B2H mail demand and that the interaction of high-income households and income has the opposite effect. Excluding the US, we found that the interaction of the number of low-income households with income has a positive effect on B2H mail demand. This finding is consistent with the theory that economic performance and income are important channels through which income inequality works, and that good economic performance may function to offset the direct effect that income inequality has on B2H mail demand.

Our estimation of B2B mail demand also found that the number of high-income households might serve to drive up demand. In the sample with the US included, we also find relatively robust results that the number of low-income households drives down B2B mail demand. The interaction with economic conditions in this case did not add much explanatory power. When the US is excluded from the sample, we find that the relationship becomes more uncertain and more difficult to discern whether it is the relative number of high- and low-income households, or the interaction of this variable with economic performance variables that drives B2B mail demand.

Hence, our conclusion from these analyses is that the data on high- and low-income households provides further evidence that income dispersion is an important driver of aggregate mail demand, but that significant differences may exist in how this driver operates when we consider the US or when we exclude it from the analysis, as well as when we compare B2H and B2B mail demand.

3.4 The Inequality Mechanism: the Effect of Government Transfers

Given that our results above supported the economic theory intuition that income inequality functions in interaction with macroeconomic performance, we proceeded to directly test the role that different welfare states, identified through government transfers, have on mail demand. This presents the test of the efficiency hypothesis, which argues that increased government transfers may inhibit economic performance, as well as being accompanied by the creation of rigid labor markets and less competitive business relations. If this is the case, large government transfers should eventually decrease mail volumes as market competition is replaced by elements of market coordination.

The results of our regression analysis indicate that across most specifications government transfers have a negative effect on both B2H and B2B mail demand. Lower government transfers are also a statistically significant driver of B2H mail demand in our entire sample. When the US is excluded from the sample, the relationship is no longer statistically significant. In the case of B2B mail demand we found that government transfers have a statistically significant negative effect on demand, but only when the United States is excluded from the sample. This relationship is relatively robust even when we control for inequality by including the GINI coefficient in the analysis.

While the analysis indicates a negative relationship between government transfers and mail demand, there is relatively little variance in the size of the government transfers, especially if the US is excluded, over the period from 1990 to 2004. For these reasons, there are limitations to using government transfers to provide very precise estimates of demand.

These results, however, show that dispersion in the main drivers of mail demand may have both first and second order effects. Thus, income inequality affects consumer purchasing power and the extent to which customers can benefit from direct mail. But income dispersion also affects overall government policy, which in turn affects the business climate. Government transfers affect the business climate and influence firms incentives in interacting with their customers.

3.5 Age Demographics

The mail volume received by households will differ across countries depending on the age (life stage) and income of the primary household occupant. As noted by Jimenez et al. (2006):

> Life stage and economic activity, not generational affiliation, are largely responsible for changes in mail use. This research indicated there is no pattern of increases or decreases in the mail volume received by different age groups that can be attributed to the members' birth years and, consequently, their generation. In short, the study concluded that business senders do not take into account the 'technology adroitness' or the generational affiliation of the recipient in making decisions to mail to them, but chiefly consider the recipient's age and income.

Building on the generational model introduced by Jimenez, this chapter considers the level of dispersion in the ages of the country's population and its effect on mail demand. The age distributions in four primary age groupings of the economically active population were compiled for each country examined. The age groupings were 20–29, 30–39, 40–49, and 50–59.

As seen in Jimenez et al. (2006) and in other studies analyzing age and mail usage, the younger population group aged 20–29 were a lower level driver of business-to-household mail than that of the older age groups, meaning that the younger age groups are still emerging economically and businesses have fewer reasons to mail to these individuals. Additionally, the higher share of the population in the 30–39 age groups lowers demand for B2H mail volume. Lastly, consistent with findings from Jimenez, the 50–59 age group attracts more mail and is a significant driver of B2H mail demand (for the model inclusive of the US). This supports findings that at the peak income earning capacity of households, mail demand also reaches the peak as businesses use the mail channel to communicate, transact, and solicit business for those households earning more income.

In the business-to-business mail flow segments, the same age group data were used. Most significantly, the higher distribution percentage of the 40–49 and 50–59 age groups were found to be significant drivers of B2B mail demand. This finding supports the hypothesis that the decision making management of companies would fall within these age groups. In being consistent with the B2H pattern of mail demand, businesses' decision makers would both choose to send and also receive mail as a communication channel for transacting and soliciting business with other businesses.

4. GOODNESS OF FIT

While in general there is no perfect measure of the goodness of fit of a specific econometric model, it is common to consider measures such as the R^2 of a regression fit or the value of the maximized likelihood. The R^2 measures the proportion of the variance in dependent variable, which can be predicted from the independent variables. In the case of panel data, however, we can decompose this variance further and look at the ability of the model to predict *within* and *between* variation separately. The within variation corresponds to the variation of the model variables after each of them was de-meaned. Thus, it only looks as the correlation of the variables above or below their mean values. The between R^2, on the other hand, looks at the correlation between the mean levels of variables in our model. Thus, it tells us to what degree the mean levels of the explanatory variables can explain the mean levels of mail volumes over the time period under consideration for each of the countries in the sample. Table 6.2 presents a summary view of the R^2 statistics for the main models used in our analysis.

In the initial model discussed by Harding, the baseline model of business-to-household mail demand (without the US) saw a good fit ($R^2 = 0.9$). The effects of the unobserved heterogeneity contributed to the underperformance of the model and led to the hypothesis that the dispersion within the variables contributes to the levels of heterogeneity of mail demand across countries. Following the analysis, the addition of the dispersion variables improves the model in most cases. For models inclusive of the US mail demand, the dispersion variables improved the model performance and in some cases substantially.

In the baseline model of B2H overall (with US) R^2 equals 0.563: by adding GINI this improves to 0.587, by including the income distribution the R^2 improves to 0.666, and including the age distribution the R^2 improves to 0.763. Without the US, the baseline model R^2 (overall) equals 0.898. By including GINI, Income, and Age distributions, the R^2 improves to 0.899, 0.906, and 0.556, respectively.

In the baseline model of B2B within R^2 (with the US) equals 0.668: by adding GINI this improves to 0.725, by including the income distribution the RSQ improves to 0.736, and including the age distribution the R^2 improves to 0.772. Without the US, the baseline model R^2 (within) equals 0.678. By including GINI, Income, and Age distributions, the R^2 improves to 0.709, 0.714, and 0.753, respectively. Additional details are listed in Table 6.2.

The notable improvement of the performance of the model of B2B (with the US) clearly demonstrates that the dispersion in these variables dramatically affects the model performance. This allows the conclusion that the dispersion of the variables matters more for the US than the other countries included in the models.

5. CONCLUSION

Cross-country mail demand over the past decade can be modeled with reference to a small set of economic and demographic variables. The model fit, however, allows for substantial cross-country heterogeneity, which remains unobserved. Technically, this means that the demand for mail depends on a set of unobserved country specific fixed effects. These are driving forces distinct from those explicitly included in the model and which are not observed by the econometrician. They capture the difference in mean levels of demand from country to country that cannot be explained by the variables included in the model.

This chapter tests the hypothesis that dispersion in some of the aggregate variables within each country can be used to explain cross-country differences in demand. Thus, we explore the extent to which aggregation may hide relevant information in modeling demand. The aim is to improve on existing models of mail demand by reducing the role of the unobserved fixed effects and relating demand directly to some observable characteristic of the country.

The dispersion in the variables can be measured in several ways (Mean, Standard Deviation, Coefficient of Variation) as well as by index measures such as GINI. In an early attempt to show that that dispersion measures may provide increased precision of the mail demand model, in effect the dispersion of the variables proved a more accurate statistical measure in explaining the unobserved heterogeneity. Thus, we focused our investigation on dispersion in income, as measured by the GINI coefficient, and the age distribution for B2C and B2B C&T mail flows. These are key dispersion measures for the main economic and demographic factors influencing mail demand. By utilizing these measures in the model, the performance of the model increased, with a between 20 percent to over 100 percent improvement in the descriptive power of the model. It is therefore considered that a certain degree of heterogeneity will remain unexplained and that econometric analysis of aggregate demand may have reached the maxima of explanatory power in this industry.

The key implications that exist for a business or industry-level strategy are to understand the market and its underlying heterogeneity. In exploring the heterogeneity, demand models consistently focus on exogenous forces to mail demand (e.g., GDP) in which little can be done to affect change in the aggregate demand. By evaluating the distribution of the factors of demand (dispersion), regional or market segments may have substantially different compositions than that of aggregate demand. Therefore, a more detailed analysis of the dispersion of the demand factors may enable a more effective stimulus to aggregate demand.

While the exact causal mechanism through which dispersion affects mail demand appears to be fairly complex, involving several layers of interaction between consumers, businesses, and government, the performance of a market-level model of mail demand is nevertheless significantly improved after accounting for within-country heterogeneity.

Thus, it appears that although dispersion variables can reduce the impact of unobserved heterogeneity in models of mail demand, they nevertheless leave a substantial amount of variation in mean levels of demand unexplained. Further factors will need to be considered in order to improve the fit of mail demand models.

NOTES

* We are grateful for the excellent contributions of Wenbo Dang and Anna Owsiany to this research project. Additionally, the authors wish to thank Dr. Ingo Willems and Gene DelPolito for their discussion at the 15th Conference on Postal and Delivery Economics and Dr. Michael Crew for his constructive comments.

1. Figures from 2000. Source: OECD Economic Outlook Database (no. 71), quoted in Alesina and Glaeser (2004, p. 17).
2. Additionally, income inequality has been associated with lower social capital and deterioration of community networks in developed democracies, particularly the United States. As such, inequality may also have effects on H2H mail demand; but we do not address that topic directly here, since our focus is on B2B and B2H. See Putnam (2001) on how income inequality affects communities and social networks.

REFERENCES

Aghion, P., E. Caroli and C. García-Peñalosa (1999), 'Inequality and economic growth: the perspective of the new growth theories', *Journal of Economic Literature*, **37**, 1615–60.

Aghion, P. and P. Bolton (1997), 'A trickle-down theory of growth and development with debt overhang', *Review of Economic Studies*, **64**, 151–72.

Alesina, Alberto and Edward L. Glaeser (2004), *Fighting Poverty in the US and Europe*, Oxford: Oxford University Press.

Alesina, Alberto and D. Rodrik (1994), 'Distributive politics and economic growth', *Quarterly Journal of Economics*, **109**, 465–90.

Barro, R.J. (2000), 'Inequality and growth in a panel of countries', *Journal of Economic Growth*, **5**, 5–32.

Bénabou, R. (1996), 'Equity and efficiency in human capital investment: the local connection', *Review of Economic Studies*, **63**, 237–64.

Blinder, A.S. (1973), *The Decomposition of Inequality*, Cambridge, MA: The MIT Press.

Estevez-Abe, Margarita, Torben Iversen and David Soskice (2001), 'Social protection and the formation of skills: a reinterpretation of the welfare state', in Peter A. Hall and David Soskice (eds), *Varieties of Capitalism: the Institutional Foundations of Comparative Advantage*, Oxford: Oxford University Press.

Harding, Matthew C. (2005), 'Mail demand models', mimeo.

Harding, Matthew C. (2006), 'A panel data study of mail demand in advanced economies', mimeo.

Hall, Peter A. and David Soskice (2001), *Varieties of Capitalism; the Institutional Foundations of Comparative Advantage*, Oxford: Oxford University Press.

Iversen, Torben and Thomas Cusack (2000), 'The causes of welfare state expansion: deindustrialization or globalization?' *World Politics*, **52** (April), 313–49.

Jimenez, L., A. Owisiany and C. Szeto (2006), 'Scenarios of mail receipt patterns across generations', in Michael A. Crew and Paul R. Kleindorfer (eds), *Liberalization of the Postal and Delivery Sector*, Cheltenham, UK and Northampton, MA: Edward Elgar, pp. 293–306.

Kennedy, B.P., I. Kawachi and D. Prothrow-Stith (1996), 'Income distribution and mortality: cross sectional ecological study of Robin Hood Index in the United States', *BMJ*, **312**, 1004–7.

Kuznets, S. (1955), 'Economic growth and income inequality', *American Economic Review*, **45**, 1–28.

Meltzer, Allan H. and Scott. F. Richard (1981), 'A rational theory of the size of government', *Journal of Political Economy*, **89**, 914–27.
Milanovic, Branko (2006), 'Global income inequality, What it is and why it matters', World Bank Research.
Moene, Karl Ove and Michael Wallerstein (2001), 'Inequality, social insurance and redistribution', *American Political Science Review*, **95**(4), 859–74.
OECD (2006), 'OECD factbook', *Economic, Environmental and Social Statistics*, Paris: OECD, pp. 95–129.
Perotti, R. (1996), 'Growth, income distribution, and democracy: what the data say', *Journal of Economic Growth*, **1**, 149–87.
Persson, T. and G. Tabellini (1994), 'Is inequality harmful for growth?' *American Economic Review*, **84**, 600–21.
Putnam, Robert (2001), *Bowling Alone: The Collapse and Revival of American Community*, New York: Simon and Schuster.
Saint-Paul, Gilles (1996), 'Exploring the political economy of labour market institutions', *Economic Policy*, **23**, 265–300.
Trinkner, Urs and Martin Grossman (2006), 'Forecasting Swiss mail demand, in M.A. Crew and P.R. Kleindorfer (eds), *Progress Toward Liberalization of the Postal and Delivery Sector*, New York: Springer, pp. 267–80.

APPENDIX

Table A6.1 Summary statistics of variables used in the models

Variable description	Max.	Min.	Mean	Std	Median
Demographics and income					
Population (in millions)	296.5	5.11	62.84	82.89	57.59
Number of households (in millions)	111.22	2.29	24.98	30.95	22.23
Total population of age group 20–29 (in millions)	40.81	0.63	8.47	11.42	7.54
Total population of age group 30–39 (in millions)	44.89	0.66	9.76	12.71	8.58
Total population of age group 40–49 (in millions)	45.32	0.74	9.2	12.49	7.76
Total population of age group 50–59 (in millions)	37.44	0.57	7.32	9.26	6.42
Number of households earning < $25 000 per year (in millions)	28.89	0.17	6.76	7.84	4.4
Number of households earning > $50 000 per year (in millions)	64.86	0.05	9.27	15.99	3.93
Macroeconomic					
GDP per capita (US$)	37 574.10	17 084.95	25 489.99	5 338.74	23 814.08
GDP annual growth rate	6.25	−0.35	2.27	1.27	2.19
GINI index	46.4	22.2	32.13	7.01	30.9
Government transfer: social benefits	1 484 000	21 047	268 051.67	329 909.40	195 422
Financial services					
Unemployment (in millions)	8.79	0.06	2.13	2.31	1.56
Median household income (US$)	63 990.00	23 170.00	38 475.35	9 746.02	36 220.00
Number of bankable households (in millions)	104.6	2.11	23.81	28.61	21.9
Lending per bankable household (in millions)	0.33	0.03	0.11	0.06	0.09
Telecom and IT					
Internet users (per 1000 people)	886	5	306.73	211.98	307
Telephone mainlines (per 1000 people)	745	434	577.3	83.41	573
Mobile phone subscribers (per 1000 people)	1 277	23	548.29	336.42	586
Personal computers (per 1000 people)	891	84	393.67	179.35	360
Postal related					
Correspondence and transaction mail price (€ 1/100)	0.75	0.28	0.47	0.11	0.47
B2C correspondence and transaction mail volume (in billions)	52.2	0.19	7.87	14.46	2.27
B2B correspondence and transaction mail volume (in billions)	43.44	0.21	5.02	10.13	1.18

Source: World Bank, Economist Intelligence Unit, Universal Postal Union, OECD and WIDER.

Table A6.2 R^2 *comparison*

	CT B2C			CT B2B		
	Within	Between	Overall	Within	Between	Overall
Baseline model with US	0.629	0.573	0.563	0.668	0.241	0.229
Baseline model without US	0.702	0.901	0.898	0.678	0.688	0.684
Model adding GINI variable with US	0.631	0.597	0.587	0.725	0.710	0.666
Model adding GINI variable without US	0.708	0.902	0.899	0.709	0.691	0.689
Model adding income distribution variables with US	0.637	0.675	0.666	0.736	0.747	0.701
Model adding income distribution variables without US	0.724	0.908	0.906	0.714	0.695	0.693
Model adding age variables with US	0.704	0.767	0.763	0.772	0.804	0.797
Model adding age variables without US	0.767	0.557	0.556	0.753	0.666	0.665

Note: A more detailed set of appendices and full presentation are available online at www.postinsight.com

7. Substitution of letter mail for different sender–receiver segments

Heikki Nikali

1. INTRODUCTION

As far as the development of addressed mail is concerned, the following trends are to be observed in many countries: B2B volume is decreasing, B2C volume is growing or at least remaining stable, and the volume of C2C is falling (Critelli, 2005). These differences may be explained by differences in how the implementation of new technology succeeds in specific segments. It is not only a question of the economic opportunities afforded by new technology, but also of the desire and ability to use it. Further, the pricing of letters can be made to vary according to segment, which also affects letter services demand.

When the development of letter[1] volumes in Finland is analysed in different sender–receiver segments, considerable variation is to be observed. Volumes are shown in Figure 7.1. The total number of B2B letters has steadily decreased since 1991 for the whole period under review. Yet during the 2000s the decrease in volume in this sector has began to acquire new features: although the trend is downwards, the changes that occur vary considerably from year to year. In the B2C sector volume has grown, which has meant that total volume has remained fairly stable. The number of letters sent by consumers grew slightly during the whole of the 1990s, but since 2000 there has been continual decrease. It can therefore be stated that all sectors behave differently. Letter pricing cannot explain these differences, because from the point of view of the enterprise, the price will be the same regardless of whether the recipient is another enterprise or a domestic household. The causes behind the pattern of volume in the different sectors are to be found in the effect of changes that have taken place in the economic activities of households or in the influence of new technologies.

The reduction in letter mail traffic between organisations means that the volume of letter mail does not follow the general economic trend. This is not exclusively a Finnish phenomenon, since this has taken place in all of the developed European countries, in North America, and also when analysed globally (Nader, 2004). Until the 1990s the number of letters continued to grow rapidly and closely mirrored the growth in GDP. Finland suffered a major economic recession at the beginning of the 1990s. During the period 1990–3 GDP volume fell by 11 per cent, whereas for the same period letter volume only dropped by a little over 3 per cent. After the slump and since 1993, GDP has grown by 60 per cent, although letter volume has only risen by 5 per cent over the same period. At the beginning of the 1990s technological innovations meant for targeted communication were developed, which were quickly adopted during the period of intense economic activity that followed the recession. Innovations of this type were e-mail and

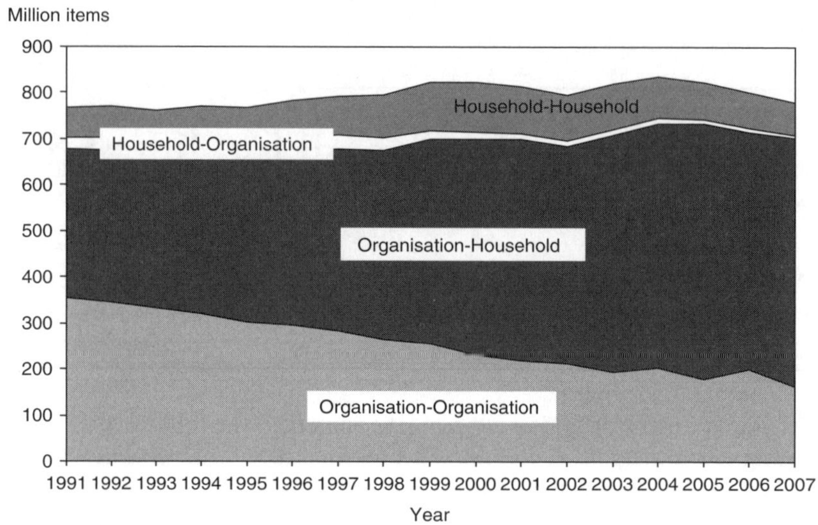

Figure 7.1 Domestic first and second class letter volumes in different sender and receiver segments in Finland

mobile phone text messages. At the same time, the prices of services connected to these fell swiftly. The possibilities for the substitution of letters with these channels took an entirely new direction.

The objective of this research is to analyse those factors that affect letter demand in different sender–receiver segments, with particular attention being paid to estimating the form of substitution function required for each sector. This research is based on time series analyses for the years 1991–2007.

The value of this research is that it not only clarifies the concept of substitution, but it also quantifies it. These results help us to understand the most critical factors concerning letter services demand, and in this way facilitate the making of real forecasts in the new competitive environment into which the traditional letter has been led by the development and resultant low cost of technology. Now, for the first time, results have been calculated for the letter services demand sectors, so that the effect of substitution can be more accurately measured than earlier. Further, new technologies are introduced in quite different stages in different segments. The abilities and preferences needed for different kinds of communication services vary when comparing large and small companies, as well as households. Of particular interest in this connection is to analyse substitution in the B2C sector, that is, how these two parties are able to encounter each other through the use of common electronic channels.

2. THE NATURE OF THE SUBSTITUTION EFFECT

Substitution of letters by electronic communication is not a uniform process. The common approach of a single *s*-curve, $f_t = f_t(y)$, where t is time and y is technology, is not

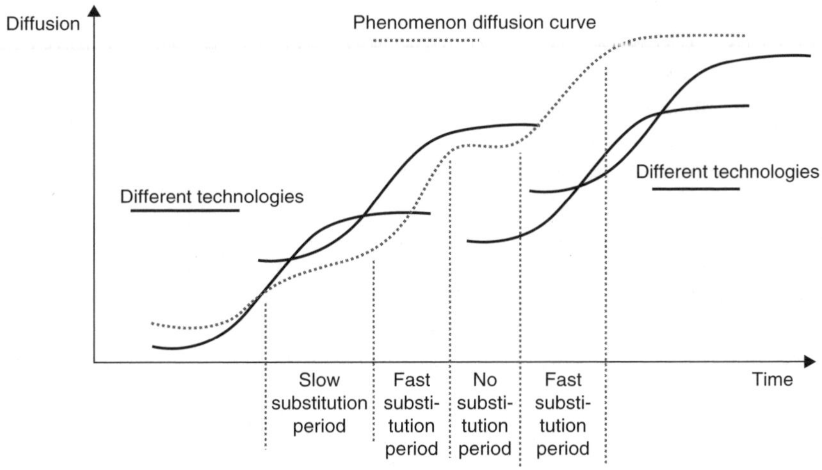

Figure 7.2 Substitution of letters by diffusion with different technologies

adequate, given the need to take into account the effects of multiple technologies. A better representation is a combination of different diffusion curves $g_{it} = g_t(f_t(y_i))$, for the respective technologies $i = 1, \ldots, n$, which means that the curve for substitution is reminiscent of a large corrugated *s*-curve. This is illustrated in Figure 7.2.

Depending on how new technologies are adopted, substitution can be fast or slow. If there are few technological advances or senders of letters do not make much use of these, substitution may come to a standstill. In Finland it has been observed that structural changes in letter volume depend on the speed of substitution: structural changes in the flow of letters are to be associated with a phase of rapid substitution, whereas during a period of slow substitution structures remain somewhat stable (Nikali and Heino, 2007). This implies that the speed of substitution not only depends on the senders' and receivers' ability to use new technology, but also on the strong effect of the purpose and content of the communication. For example, paper invoices can quickly be transferred to the Internet in communication between companies, regardless of the fact that substitution in the B2B sector as a whole or the substitution of paper invoices in the B2C sector is negligible.

The reasons for substitution can be crystallised as follows: companies seek economies in processes and consumers in ease of communication (Elkelä et al., 2001a, b). That is, no party argues for transference from paper to electronic channels on account of postal expenditure.

From the standpoint of substitution the most critical sector is B2C, because a communication common denominator in addition to the conventional letter is a challenge both to the sender and to the receiver. Even though over half of consumers in Finland already use e-mail as a personal communication channel, companies are unaware of their e-mail addresses and are therefore unable to communicate with them in this way. Nor do companies know consumers' messaging habits and so they do not take the chance of sending an invoice, for example, by e-mail. The risk for a company of not eventually receiving due payment is too great. It is easy and quick to send information by mobile concerning, for example, picking up a car from a service station, using a text message. Before the SMS age, this type of information was transmitted either by telephone or not at all. No letter was sent because this would have been too slow, so that in this instance it is not a question of a letter being substituted, but rather substituting a short message service (SMS) for a phone call. In several studies this complementariness of communication channels or increased communication generated by new forms of electronic means leads to the conclusion that there is no actual substitution for a paper letter, nor will there be one (Harding, 2005; Nader, 2005; Nader and Jimenez, 2005; Jimenez, 2006; Jimenez et al., 2006). Because of the difficulty in locating a common targeted channel of electronic communication used by both companies and consumers, the B2C sector will be the last area in which the paper letter will be substituted by an electronic channel. For companies and consumers to find each other in this sense, a third party must be available to act as a common information bank for the other two parties. This third link in the chain could be service operators specialised in this task or banks, in the case of invoices. The Internet would play an important part in this process, such as filling in and transmitting different kinds of forms.

Why are the conditions in Finland favourable for substitution to take place and for studying its effects? The prices of telecommunications in Finland were high at the end of the 1970s, but since then prices have really toppled. The present prices of telecommunication services have, in real terms, fallen to one-fifth of what they were at the beginning of the 1980s. The real prices of calls in Finland in 2007 are only 40 per cent of what they were in 1991 (Ministry of Transport and Communications Finland (MoTC), 2007). At the same time, the real prices of letters being sent by companies have fallen by a few per cent and the price of the consumer letter has risen by a half. It is clear that this change in the price ratio of letters and telecommunications must have an effect on competition between services and through this also on substitution.

This erosion of prices and the development of technology in Finland have made the Finnish communication culture fertile ground for substitution. Compared with elsewhere in Europe, prices of telecommunications in Finland are extremely low. Finland is the cheapest in a 15-country comparison survey (MoTC, 2006). Looking at the pricing basket, the price in Finland is only one-third that of the most expensive country, Germany, and as far as averages are concerned the Finland basket is 60 per cent cheaper than the average. From the point of view of the substitution phenomenon Finland is also in a favourable situation in that in Finland the structure of letter volume and volumes in different sender and receiver sectors have been monitored regularly over a period of 17 years now (Nikali and Heino, 2007). It is easy for substitution studies to remain simply descriptive, if a database for quantitative modelling of letter communication is not available. Pure substitution is more easily found in areas other than letter communication; for example, the recording industry (Nader and Jimenez, 2005; Jimenez, 2006). The total volume of letter mail could rise again, even though substitution is taking place continuously in certain sub-parts of the communication area under consideration. The periodic diffusion of substitution, shown in Figure 7.2, hampers the quantitative modelling of the phenomenon. When customers are asked about the future of letter communication, the question of substitution is always given preference, even though in modelling the demand for letters the significance of substitution is of less consequence (Koppe and Bosch, 2006).

3. SUBSTITUTION MODELS

The substitution effect in different sender–receiver segments is estimated as a totality by the demand model

$$Q_t = Q_t(g_t,P_t,K_t,T_t,S_t) = Q_t\{g_t(f_t(y_i)),P_t,K_t,T_t,S_t\}, \tag{7.1}$$

where Q is the volume of letters, g describes substitution, P is the price of letter mail, K is the price of competitive service, T is the trend and S is the business cycle variable.

Substitution is the total degree of substitution, not annual changes in the state of substitution. Substituting letters with electronic means of communication requires that the receiver also has the possibility of using the same electronic channel of communication. Decisions to convert to electronic operations are carried out patiently, because continually changing from paper to electronic and then back again would become too expensive. Another attribute of substitution is that a letter, once substituted, does not generally return to become paper, despite possible improvements in the paper relative to electronic forms of communication; that is, substitution is not a bidirectional phenomenon (Nikali, 1998). If the degree of penetration of an electronic channel is used as a descriptive variable for substitution, practice has shown that not even this penetration moves bidirectionally (Nikali and Heino, 2007). It is rare for penetration to diminish. If an electronic messaging device is abandoned, it will usually be compensated for with an even more technological innovation. In such event that the population grows, but the use of the electronic messaging form grows less than this, the degree of penetration could diminish. Nevertheless, the growth in the size of the population (companies, their manpower and normal consumers) takes place so slowly that the significance of such variation in penetration is negligible.

The electronic channels concerned in the research are e-mail, text message, phone call and telefax. The collective variable formed from these $g_t = g_t(f_t(y_i), i = 1, \ldots, n)$, where t is time and y is technology, did not, however, prove to be the best variable for describing the substitution variable. Its place was taken by the use of e-mail at work and at home. The telephone dropped out of the model, because its penetration during the period under study (1991–2007) has been, practically speaking, 100 per cent in Finland. However, during this time, as far as the telephone is concerned, a considerable change has taken place, from the fixed-line telephone to the mobile phone (Statistics Finland, 2007a). The substitution effect of telefax diminished as early as the beginning of the 1990s (Nikali, 1998). The text message, especially in communication between consumers, has had a clear substitution effect, but it has mostly affected postcards, which only account for 10 per cent of letter mail. Neither text messaging between companies nor from companies to consumers has acquired many of the characteristics of letter substitution. Mobile content services will alter the current situation considerably, but in the wider perspective this is for the future.

The e-mail indicator in this study describes the spread of the use of e-mail in Finland. The incidence of e-mail use in companies, p^c, does not measure how many companies have e-mail, but how many employees have personal access to e-mail at work. For households penetration, p^h, describes how large a proportion of people also use e-mail at home. E-mail use has grown from 17 per cent in organisations and close to zero in households in 1991 to 70 per cent and 53 per cent respectively, at the end of 2006 (Nikali and Heino, 2007).

If the possibility of using e-mail in different sender and receiver sectors is considered, it can be defined according to how great a proportion of both senders and receivers use it. The descriptive variable for substitution, g_t, in different sectors is obtained by the following functions:

$$\text{B2B sector} \quad g_t^{B2B} = p_t^c * p_t^c = (p_t^c)^2, \tag{7.2}$$

$$\text{B2C sector} \quad g_t^{B2C} = p_t^c * p_t^h, \tag{7.3}$$

$$\text{C sector} \quad g_t^C = p_t^h * p_t^h = (p_t^h)^2. \tag{7.4}$$

Because the size of the population affects the demand for communication, it must also be taken into consideration in the substitution factor. The size of the work force is represented by the variable w_t, and the population in Finland of 15 years and over by the variable h_t. The final substitution variables by sector are obtained:

$$\text{B2B sector} \quad G_t^{B2B} = \frac{w_t}{w_{1991}} * g_t^{B2B} = \frac{w_t}{w_{1991}} (p_t^c)^2, \tag{7.5}$$

namely, relative change in the work force and the possible use of e-mail in B2B communication;

$$\text{B2C sector} \quad G_t^{B2C} = \frac{w_t}{w_{1991}} * \frac{h_t}{h_{1991}} * g_t^{B2C} = \frac{w_t}{w_{1991}} * \frac{h_t}{h_{1991}} * p_t^c * p_t^h, \tag{7.6}$$

namely, relative changes in work force and population, and possible use of e-mail in B2C communication; and

$$\text{C sector} \quad G_t^C = \frac{h_t}{h_{1991}} * g_t^C = \frac{h_t}{h_{1991}} * (p_t^h)^2, \tag{7.7}$$

namely, relative change in population and possible use of e-mail in C2C communication.

The demand models for letters in different sender and receiver segments have the following form:

$$q_t^i = \alpha_i * T_t^{\beta_i} * S_t^{\phi_i} * P_t^{i\,\chi_i} * K_t^{\delta_i} * e^{\varphi_i * G_t^i} * \varepsilon_t^i. \tag{7.8}$$

where; i = segment (B2B, B2C or C) and t = time (the years 1991–2007)

q_t^i = domestic first and second class letter volumes in segment i

T_t = general economic activity variable

S_t = business cycle variable

P_t^i = real tariff index of letters in segment i

K_t = real tariff index of phone services

G_t^i = variable for describing the possibility of using replaceable electronic forms of communication in segment i

ε_t^i = residual error

The analysis is made on the basis of annual time series. The demand for letter services by sector has been measured since the beginning of 1991, whereby there are observations for 17 years, which is rather few for time series analyses. Nevertheless, by constructing a model some ideas can be gained as to whether the demand factors for letter services are different in different sectors. It is of particular interest to analyse the importance of substitution in different sectors, because the preconceived hypothesis is that substitution progresses in different ways in different sectors.

The pricing of letter services is different from the point of view of companies and consumers. In both the B2B and B2C sectors, there are no differences in pricing, because the price is not influenced by who the recipient of the letter is. In general, the real price of the company letter has been falling. The real price in 2007 is lower than it was in 1991. For the corresponding period the real consumer price for the letter has risen, on average, 2.8 per cent annually. There was a quite substantial rise in the price of the consumer letter in 1994, when it became subject to the value-added tax, at 22 per cent. Without that change, the real price of the consumer letter would have risen, on average, by 1.8 per cent annually. Companies send out 90 per cent of letters in Finland, and consumers 10 per cent (Nikali and Heino, 2007). The proportion of B2B letters of total volume in 2007 is 21 per cent and the proportion for B2C is 69 per cent. The corresponding figures for 1991 were B2B 46 per cent, B2C 42 per cent and C 12 per cent. The total letter volume for 2007 is 1.3 per cent greater than for the year 1991.

4. RESULTS

4.1 B2B Letters

The volume of B2B letters in Finland in 2007 is less than half that in 1991. The reduction in volume was quite steady during the years 1993–2003. Since then volume has risen and fallen from year to year. However, as a whole the trend is downwards. There have been three significant periods of economic development during this time: at the beginning of the 1990s there was a deep recession lasting three years, at the end of the 1990s the economy expanded exceptionally rapidly and the 2000s have been marked by considerable fluctuation.

The use of services that replace letters, particularly e-mail and text message, has grown phenomenally since 1991. At the beginning of the 1990s the use of these services in working life was limited, e-mail was rarely used and the text message not at all (Nikali and Heino, 2007; Statistics Finland, 2007a). Penetration of e-mail at work moved at a steady pace during the period 1991–2002 to become quite common. Penetration has not grown since then. For e-mail to continue to intensify, new processes in working life will need to found. Congruent with the increase in penetration, services have become more user-friendly and more diverse than before, but above all the price has become considerably lower. On average, for the period under review the prices of telecommunications have fallen by 5 per cent annually. The largest reduction, −22 per cent, occurred in 2005 (MoTC, 2007). Almost 90 per cent of e-mail traffic in Finland nowadays uses broadband (FiCom, 2007). The utilisation of broadband has multiplied tenfold during the last four years, and the price of broadband services halved in Finland from 2003 to 2006 (MoTC, 2007).

The B2B letter demand and substitution function is as follows:

$$q_t^{B2B} = 1331.68 * S_t^{0.11} * \left(\frac{P_t^{B2B}}{K_t}\right)^{-0.37} * e^{-0.0077 * G_t^{B2B}} * \varepsilon_t \tag{7.9}$$

Variable	Coefficient	t-value
Constant	1331.68	22.73
S_t	0.11	1.98
P_t^{B2B}	−0.37	−6.10
K_t	0.37	6.10
G_t^{B2B}	−0.0077	−8.80

Parameter	Value
t	1991–2007
R^2	0.98
s	0.041
Durbin-Watson statistic	2.37

This model is extremely reliable statistically. Surprisingly, GDP is not the trend variable in the model; rather, in the B2B sector the cornerstone of letter demand has in recent years been the rapidly fluctuating business cycles. This explains why the volume of letters in the B2B sector has no longer fallen steadily in the past few years. When the business cycle makes an abrupt upturn in Finland, it generates new business, which increases correspondence between companies, and between companies and government offices. When a business has gained a foothold, the number of paper messages targeted at the end-product users – that is, consumers – increases.

No corresponding B2B sector demand model has yet been made in Finland, but several models for first class and second class letters have been made. Even in the models made in the 1980s and before that time, the cross-elasticity in relation to telecommunications prices was an important factor in clarifying letter demand in Finland (Teräsvirta, 1966; Soininvaara, 1974; Mäkinen and Nikali, 1980). But as the prices of the telecommunications fell rapidly, the effect of cross-elasticity on letter services demand vanished (Nikali, 1986, 1992, 1997, 2002, 2004). At the same time, the price elasticity of the letter itself grew. Now, in the B2B sector letter demand model, cross-elasticity has come back into the picture. This is not in itself so remarkable, because in the B2B sector companies have the possibility of using electronic channels instead of letters, and electronic service charges have also continued to fall significantly in the 2000s.

The price elasticity that has now been attained in the B2B sector is, in respect of its own price, very much in harmony with other studies that have been carried out in Finland (Nikali, 2004). Its absolute value is slightly higher than the average of earlier estimated first and second class letter price elasticities, and companies are now sending approximately just as many first and second class letters (Nikali and Heino, 2007). It would appear that letter services demand continues on its course towards even greater price sen-

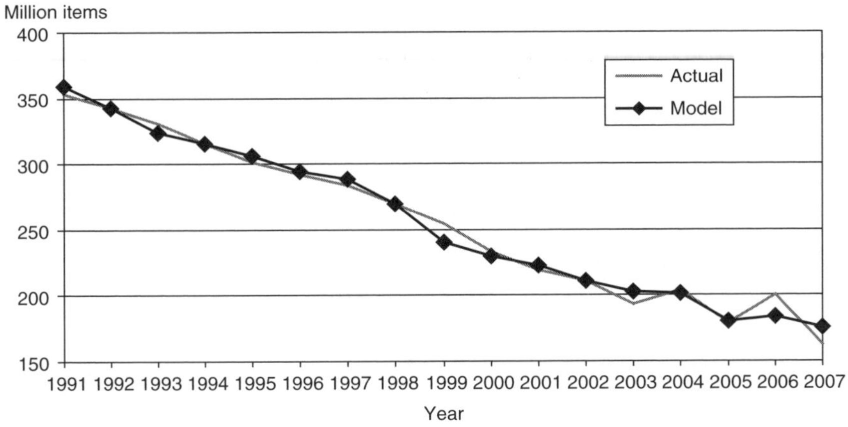

Figure 7.3 The B2B letter demand model

sitivity. Looked at from an international perspective, it would seem that letter services demand in the B2B sector in Finland is more price-sensitive than in many other countries (Harding, 2005; Feve et al., 2006). The threat of substitution most certainly increases sensitivity as far as the prices of services are concerned.

The annual volumes predicted by the model are presented in Figure 7.3. From this it can be seen that the total degree of explanation is excellent, and also that it is possible to model the alternations of recent years in letter volumes fairly accurately.

The letter substitution factor in the B2B model has a fundamental significance, even though the absolute value of its coefficient is small. Because the possibilities of using e-mail in communication between companies have not developed consistently, noticeably different periods of letter substitution can be elucidated. The degree of substitution is outlined in Figure 7.4. The degree of substitution is a ratio between actual and theoretical letter volumes (realised + substituted); that is, it describes how great a proportion of the theoretical letter volume has not been realised. If the degree of substitution is 1, then there has been no substitution; if the degree is 0.6, about 40 per cent of the theoretical letter volume has been substituted.

At the commencement of the 1990s there was still little letter substitution in the B2B sector. At that time there was a deep economic recession in Finland. When the slump was over, a period of fast economic growth occurred and, at the same time, a period of extremely rapid substitution in letter communication between companies. At the turn of the millennium there was a period of slack economic activity, accompanied by the disappointment brought by the overheating caused by the boom in technology, which was then followed by a period of slow substitution. This period ended in 2002, after which there has been no substitution in the B2B sector in Finland. Something exceptional is needed for substitution to once again get on to a speedy path, such as new or older user-friendly technological innovations or different work processes that are able to benefit from recent technological advances more fully. Further, new user groups taking advantage of existing electronic processes could change this course of development. For example, small or

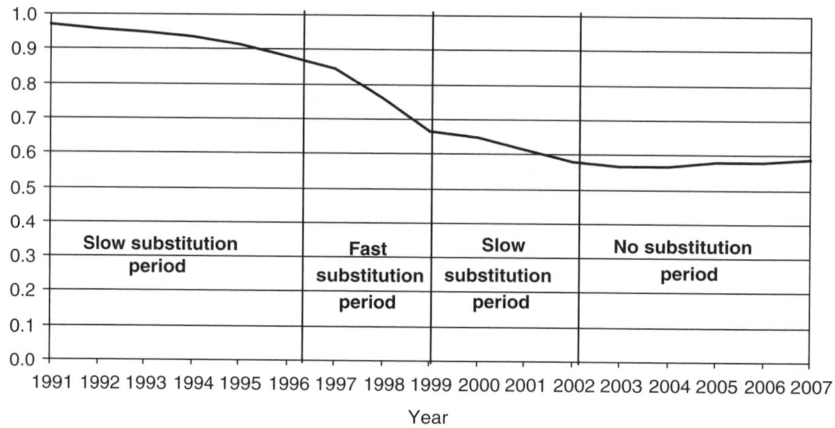

Figure 7.4 The degree of substitution for B2B letters

medium-sized companies and consumers could be enticed or bulldozed to use the electronic, rather than the paper, invoice. This will be the probable course of development in Finland in the coming years.

By studying the factors that affect the letter services demand of big companies, a study in Austria on the relationship between the growth of company's turnover and its correlation with substitution reached the same conclusion as this research (Koppe and Bosch, 2006). At a time when company turnover can grow rapidly, the demand for letter services in companies can remain small on account of accelerating substitution. Because substitution can vary periodically, it is possible that by gathering cross-sectional material during a period of slow substitution, a conclusion will be drawn, on the basis of calculated data, that there is no substitution and therefore wrong conclusions will be drawn. In order to get a total picture of quantitative substitution, a time series analysis is required.

4.2 B2C Letters

The volume of B2C letters in Finland has grown just as steadily as the B2B volume has decreased. Furthermore, in recent years the development of the letter volume has began to show signs of drifting up and down, which would appear to be the result of a one year delayed dependency on B2B letter volume. The volume of letters sent to private households by companies begins to grow one year after favourable market conditions have accelerated the growth of new businesses and, as a result, the volume of B2B letters. The same would appear to be true in the opposite case: if the state of the economy deteriorates, the volume of letters sent to consumers will fall in comparison with the B2B letter volume, with a delay.

The penetration of personal e-mail at home has grown appreciably in the wake of the popularity of e-mail at work. This has, understandably, reduced the possibility of e-mail substituting letters in the B2C sector. Another fundamental obstacle to the progression of substitution in this sector concerns the capacity of companies to send an e-mail instead of a letter, because companies do not have information on the e-mail addresses of their consumer customers. There is nothing similar to a telephone directory or a corresponding database with consumers' e-mail addresses. Companies must maintain these themselves, which is expensive and troublesome. What is more, the intense competition between operators in Finland has led to a situation in which consumers' e-mail addresses change so often that address registers are soon out of date. A third reason for the infrequent use of e-mail in communication between companies and consumers is the communication culture: before transmitting important information by e-mail, companies must know the e-mail behaviour of their customers, at least far as ensuring that the message will eventually be received by this means.

The structure of the estimated model for the B2C sector is effectively the same as for the B2B sector, although its content is quite different:

$$q_t^{B2C} = 1402.90 * T_t^{1.16} * S_t^{-0.11} * (P_t^{B2C})^{-1.38} * e^{0.00011 * G_t^{B2C}} * \varepsilon_t \tag{7.10}$$

Variable	Coefficient	t-value
Constant	1402.90	3.30
T_t	1.16	7.85
S_t	−0.11	−2.26
P_t^{B2C}	−1.38	−3.47
G_t^{B2C}	0.00011	0.09

Parameter	Value
T	1991–2007
R^2	0.99
s	0.025
Durbin-Watson statistic	2.25

The B2C model also satisfies statistical criteria extremely well. The correlation between B2B and B2C letter volumes and their temporal dependency has already been described. On the one hand, the letter volume received by consumers increases with economic growth, and on the other hand rapid economic fluctuations cause a negative correlation. This is a good example of the phenomenon that during an economic upturn business activities recover and this injection of expansion is reflected, after a delay, in the letter volume sent to households. Of course, the basic trend in B2C volume is due to the trend in GDP. Figure 7.5 shows how the prediction of volume compares with actual demand.

There are two surprising outcomes from this model: price elasticity and the substitution factor. For the first time in Finland, an over-elastic coefficient is achieved for letter services, −1.38. Previously, no demand model of its own for B2C sector letters had been calculated, but on the basis of many models estimated over the course of a number of decades, the following alteration in price elasticity of first class letters in particular can be seen: demand is accelerating towards a price that is over-elastic. With slight exaggeration

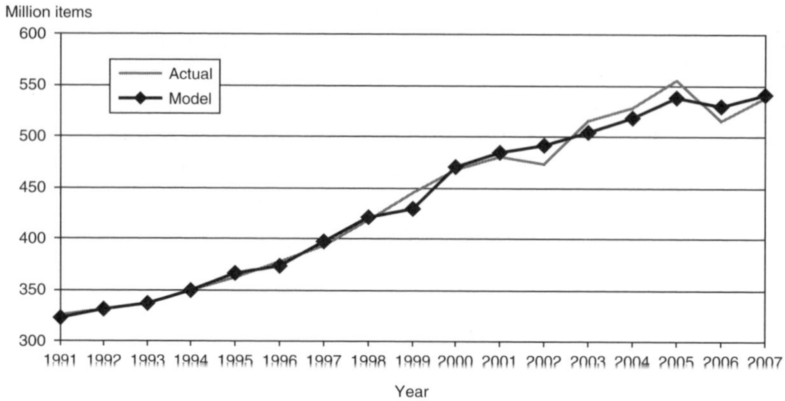

Figure 7.5 The B2C letter demand model

it can be said that, based on data from the 1960s, price elasticity for the first class letter was −0.3 (Soininvaara, 1974), based on data for the 1970s, −0.4 (Mäkinen et al., 1980), for the 1980s, −0.5 (Nikali, 2004) and for the 1990s, −0.7 (Nikali, 2004), while now based on data for the 2000s, an over-elastic state is reached −1.4 (Nikali, 2004). Obviously, comparison is complicated by the fact that a corresponding model has not been estimated earlier. Interestingly, the B2C sector includes first and second class letters alike and the absolute value of price elasticity for B2C sector estimated is now considerably higher than the elasticity for second class letters estimated by earlier models.

An international comparison shows that there are price elasticities of letter services that agree with these results, and over-elastic coefficients have been estimated for parcels too (De Rycke et al., 2001; Feve et al., 2006). A comparison of these models is, however, complicated by the fact that the models in question are aggregated demand models, not based on different sender and recipient sectors. The only demand model for B2C letter services to be found in the literature is based on data from several countries and the results show that the demand for letter services in this sector is very price sensitive, which supports the present findings (Harding, 2006). However, the estimated price elasticity coefficient in the B2C sector turns out to be a surprise in so far as the estimated values for price elasticities are usually lower in dynamic demand models based on time series than in those estimated in cross-section demand models based on individual customer data (Feve et al., 2006).

As previously mentioned, another surprise in the results is the small size of the substitution coefficient. This result actually means that letter demand in the B2C sector has not, so far, been substituted by electronic communication channels, even in Finland. In another sense, however, this result is not such a surprise. It was mentioned above that at present electronic channels for B2C targeted communication are not available except for the telephone, and in many cases the telephone cannot compensate for certain letter services such as, for example, the sending of documents. How much, then, of the price elasticity that has been achieved is influenced by the fact that compensating channels are not on offer is a moot question. Nevertheless, it can be said that this fact sensitises companies to consider alternative courses of action and, therefore, also the significance of the price of letter services.

The results of several studies showing that the substitution of letter services used by companies is not of any considerable size are to be found in the literature. In view of the results now available this should cause no astonishment, since almost all studies lump the B2B and B2C sectors together, and the developments of substitution in these are very different. Substitution in the B2C sector has not yet actually taken place and this proportion of the letter volume sent by companies is significantly greater than the letter volume in the B2B sector, where a large amount has already been transferred to electronic networks. Furthermore, because in the B2B sector substitution changes with time, revealing the real substitution effect is challenging and requires a diverse amount of data as a basis for constructing models.

4.3 Letters Sent by Consumers

The volume of letters sent by consumers continued to increase in Finland until the year 1999, after which volumes began to decrease. Since 2000, totals have fallen annually. The speed of the decrease has certainly varied during this period, the past four years showing a marked downward trend, on average over −9 per cent a year.

The consumers' option of using e-mail at home has coincided well with the number of letters they send – conversely, of course. In the 1990s the home use of e-mail was still somewhat infrequent. Not until 2000 did penetration reach 25 per cent, which began to be significant for letter mail. Although the likelihood at that time of two consumers coincidentally being able to communicate through e-mail was below 10 per cent, its importance as a communication channel began to become more emphasised. Those who had e-mail access of their own knew each other and were also generally more active than others as letter senders, and so were more alert to replacing the letter with an e-mail message. Since the turn of the millennium, the penetration of e-mail has continued to grow annually and the swift spread of broadband among Finnish households has proved to add considerable momentum.

The following equation as a demand and substitution model for consumer letters has been constructed:

$$q_t^C = 0.030 * T_t^{1.89} * S_t^{-0.17} * (P_t^C)^{-0.0043} * e^{-0.032 * G_t^C} * \varepsilon_t \tag{7.11}$$

Variable	Coefficient	*t*-value
Constant	0.030	4.33
T_t	1.89	6.64
S_t	−0.17	−3.12
P_t^C	−0.0043	−0.05
G_t^C	−0.032	−23.89

Parameter	Value
T	1991–2007
R^2	0.98
s	0.034
Durbin-Watson statistic	1.91

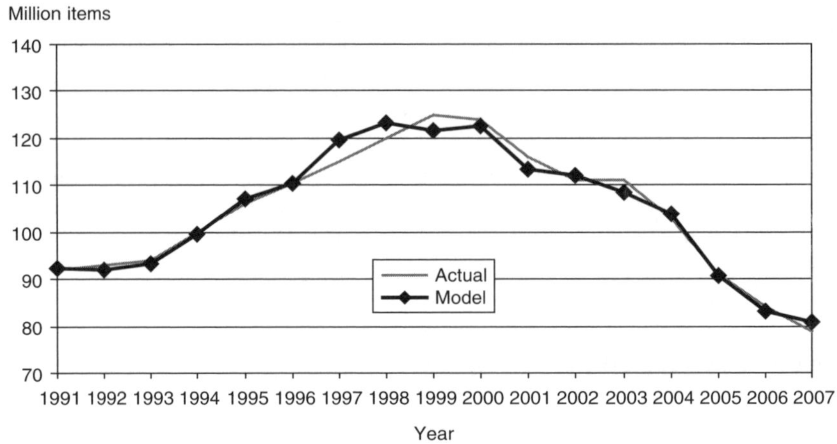

Figure 7.6 The demand model for letters sent by consumers

Statistically, that model has good explanatory power (see Figure 7.6). Consumer use of letter services drives economic expansion more powerfully than does the number of letters that companies send. Further, of the three models in this research, the business cycle effects are the strongest in this model. When the models calculated for all three sectors and the effects of the economic indicators in these are examined, the results are quite logical: market conditions drive the B2B sector and causal relationships are directly proportional, the B2C sector describes the consumer's relationships with the companies and this is driven by economic expansion and by business cycles, but inversely proportional, and the effects of the economy and the business cycle in the C sector are unidirectional, yet clearly stronger than in the B2C sector.

The marginal price elasticity in the letter services used by consumers is a surprise. There is no comparable data from earlier research in Finland. When consumers are asked what factors are important in their choice of different channels of communication, the price of the service occupies third place on the list (Elkelä et al., 2001a). This is preceded by reliability and data security of communication. This supports the conclusion that consumers are no longer as price sensitive. On average, a Finnish person sends 1.5 letters a month, which means an expenditure of only one euro a month. Viewed from this standpoint, the existence of low price elasticity can be understood. Small price elasticity is as a result uniform with estimated second class letter demand and substitution models (Nikali, 1997, 2004). And the reasons can also be the same: a cheaper letter alternative does not exist, other than a second class letter for companies and a first class letter for consumers. If the price is an obstacle there are two alternatives: to leave the letter unsent or to use electronic channels. The policy change in the use of letter services by companies in Finland has been observed as taking place first of all by transferring from first class to second class letters, and then to the use of electronic channels, which gives support to the results now obtained from consumer demand models (Nikali, 1997, 2004). Results from models estimated on the basis of panel data from a number of countries demonstrate that letter services in the C2C sector are not price sensitive and evidence of substitution is to be found, which lends support to the results of this research (Harding, 2006).

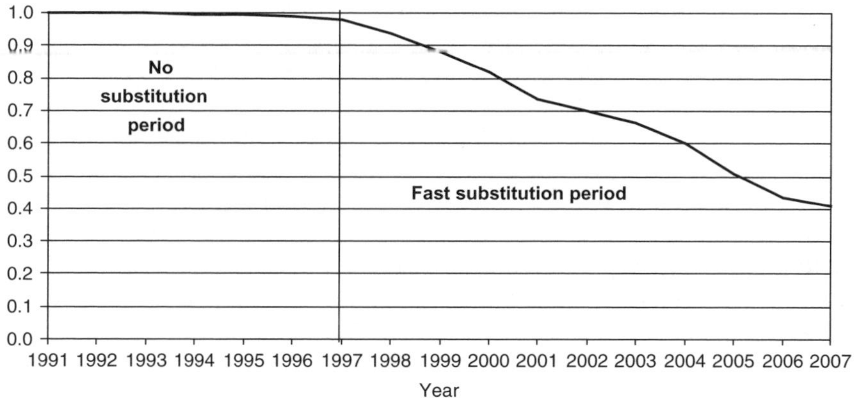

Figure 7.7 The degree of substitution for letters sent by consumers

The development of substitution of letters sent by consumers is illustrated in Figure 7.7. This shows that a period of rapid substitution began at the end of the 1990s. The correlation between substitution and letter pricing for consumers' mailing practices is interesting. Letter prices for consumers have risen, and have done so quite steadily throughout the period under review, but the price factor cannot explain why volume changed from continual growth to a trend-style fall at the turn of the millennium, and at the very time that e-mail penetration in domestic households had reached a critical level.

In comparing the results in all three sectors, it would appear that substitution has gone farthest in the communication behaviour of consumers, even though the penetration of new electronic channels in households is less than at the workplace. The explanation as to why substitution is the most advanced in households is that activities at home are simpler than at work, where processes such as bookkeeping, invoicing and so on must be taken into consideration. Attention must also be paid to the business processes of a company in receiving messages in B2B communication; for example, an invoice cannot be transferred to an electronic network unless the company receiving the invoice approves the transaction and is able to accept it. Then again, as stated earlier regarding B2C communication, companies do not know their consumers' e-mail addresses, and the cultural environment for receiving messages, which prevents the substitution of letters. Among consumers the change in the form of communication is the easiest. Messages are generally such that they can also easily be sent electronically. It is enough to know the e-mail address, and consumers normally send their messages to those they know.

5. CONCLUSIONS

A number of studies on letter services demand have been conducted in Finland. This is the first time demand has been modelled in the sender and receiver sectors. A systematic research program studying the structure of letter communication, which has taken 17 years, has made this possible. Particular attention has been paid to the possibilities for replacing letters through the use of electronic channels and to the measurement of the effect of this substitution in the models that have now been constructed. Because improving the possibilities for using electronic channels happens at different speeds in different sectors, the value of this study is concentrated on precisely the perspective of substitution in different sectors.

The literature contains numerous results from substitution studies, in which it has been stated that there is little substitution, and that it does not threaten the future of letter services. Nevertheless, models that do not take the temporal perspective of substitution and variation in development over time among different groups of letter services users into consideration may lead to misleading conclusions. In order for substitution to be modelled, it must be possible to analyse the possibilities for use and usability of electronic communication channels that replace letters, from the viewpoint of both the sender and the receiver. Therefore, a sector focused approach is required. Because the speed of substitution can change during different time periods, as has now been observed in the B2B sector, a temporal perspective should be added to the sector-focused approach. The use of cross-sectional data only explains the situation at a given point in time, and therefore does not give a complete picture of the development of substitution.

If the significance of substitution is analysed only on the basis of changes in total letter volume, the effect of substitution can be significantly underestimated. Total letter volume can still be increasing even while substitution is alarmingly fast in certain user groups, such as the B2B and consumer sectors in Finland. Concurrently, in other user groups – for example, B2C in Finland – substitution is still non-actual and therefore the letter volume is mainly increasing in this sector, and this keeps the total volume growing. Annual fluctuations in total volume, up and down, are an indication of this type of development.

In the light of the results of this research, the most imminent threat to the future of letter services is related to substitution and, specifically, substitution in the B2C sector. How companies use letters in communicating with consumers will determine the whole future of letter communication. If electronic channels are applicable from a company's point of view and are more cost-effective than letters, they will be chosen as the cheapest mode of operation. For the long term, this will be a greater threat to delivery operators than delivery market liberalisation, which will affect not only Finland but the entire developed world.

NOTE

1. In this study, letter volume includes domestic first class (delivery in one day) and second class (delivery in three days) letters, but not addressed and unaddressed advertising letters.

REFERENCES

Critelli, Michael (2005), 'The global mailstream: separating myths from realities', presented at the IPC Shareholders Meeting, Brussels, January.

De Rycke, Marc, Sarah Marcy and Jean-Pierre Florens (2001), 'Mail use by firms', in M.A. Crew and P.R. Kleindorfer (eds), *Future Directions in Postal Reform*, Boston MA: Kluwer Academic Publishers, pp. 213–32.

Elkelä, Kari (2007), *Channel preferences for receiving consumer advertising, Part 1. Choices and rejections of 13 most important channels*, Helsinki: Finland Post Corp., Research Publications 23/2007.
Elkelä, Kari, Katri Jakosuo and Heikki Nikali (2001a), *Kotitalouksien viestinvälitystarpeet 2001*, Helsinki: Finland Post Corp., Research Publications 19/2001.
Elkelä, Kari, Katri Jakosuo and Heikki Nikali (2001b), *Organisaatioiden viestinvälitystarpeet 2001*, Helsinki: Finland Post Corp., Research Publications 20/2001.
Feve, Frederique, Jean-Pierre Florens and Sophie Richard (2006), 'Microeconomic demand modelling for price elasticities', in M.A. Crew and P.R. Kleindorfer (eds), *Liberalization of the Postal and Delivery Sector*, Cheltenham, UK and Northampton, MA, USA: Edward Elgar, pp. 357–68.
FiCom (2007), *Statistic review: broadband*, May.
Harding, Mathew (2005), 'Mail demand models', a Pitney Bowes Background Paper for the project *Electronic Substitution for Mail: Models and Results; Myth and Reality*, www.postinsight.pb.com.
Harding, Mathew (2006), 'A panel data study of mail demand in advanced economies', presented at Rutgers 14th Conference on Postal and Delivery Economies, Bern, June.
Jimenez, Luis (2006), 'The new mailstream: convergence of mail and new technologies', presented at Post-Expo 2006, Amsterdam, October.
Jimenez, Luis, Anna Owsiany and Chrystal Szeto (2006), 'Scenarios of mail receipt patterns across generations', in M.A. Crew and P.R. Kleindorfer (eds), *Liberalization of the Postal and Delivery Sector*, Cheltenham, UK and Northampton, MA, USA: Edward Elgar, pp. 293–306.
Koppe, Peter and Christian Bosch (2006), 'Microanalyses of mail demand drivers for large business customers', in M.A. Crew and P.R. Kleindorfer (eds), *Liberalization of the Postal and Delivery Sector*, Cheltenham, UK and Northampton, MA, USA: Edward Elgar, pp. 307–25.
Ministry of Transport and Communications Finland (MoTC) (2006), *Prices of Mobile Calls in 2006, International Comparison*, Helsinki: Publications of the Ministry of Transport and Communications 33/2006.
Ministry of Transport and Communications Finland (MoTC) (2007), *Price Level of Telecommunications Charges in 2006*, Helsinki: Publications of the Ministry of Transport and Communications 17/2007.
Mäkinen, Mirja and Heikki Nikali (1980), *Jousto- ja suhdannemallit*, Helsinki: General Directorate of Posts and Telecommunication, Economic Department, The Research and Statistics Bureau, Memorandum 3/80.
Nader, Fouad H. (2004), 'Mail trends', a Pitney Bowes Background Paper for the project *Electronic Substitution for Mail: Models and Results; Myth and Reality*, www.postinsight.pb.com.
Nader, Fouad H. (2005), 'Business-to-business mail', a Pitney Bowes Background Paper for the project *Electronic Substitution for Mail: Models and Results; Myth and Reality*, www.postinsight.pb.com.
Nader, Fouad H. and Luis A. Jimenez (2005), Substitution Patterns, a Pitney Bowes Background Paper for the project *Electronic Substitution for Mail: Models and Results; Myth and Reality*, www.postinsight.pb.com.
Nikali, Heikki (1986), *Postiliikenteen tariffijoustot*, Helsinki: General Directorate of Posts and Telecommunication, Economic Department, The Research and Statistics Bureau, Memorandum 3/86.
Nikali, Heikki (1992), *Postiliikenteen kysyntä vuosina 1971–1991*, Helsinki: Posts and Telecommunication of Finland, Econometric Research Unit, Research Publications 9/92.
Nikali, Heikki (1997), 'Demand models for letter mail and its substitutes: results from Finland', in M.A. Crew and P.R. Kleindorfer (eds), *Managing Change in the Postal and Delivery Industries*, Boston MA: Kluwer Academic Publishers, pp. 133–61.
Nikali, Heikki (1998), *The Substitution of Letter Mail in Targeted Communication*, Helsinki: Finland Post Ltd, Quality and Business Development, Research Publications 27/1998.
Nikali, Heikki (2002), *Paperiviestinnän markkina-analyysi ja ennuste vuoteen 2010*, Helsinki: Finland Post Corp. Research Publications 1/2002.
Nikali, Heikki (2004), 'Demand models for letter mail in the competitive targeted communication market', in B.S. Sahay (ed), *Emerging Issues in Supply Chain Management*, New Delhi: Macmillan.
Nikali, Heikki and Aulikki Heino (2007), *Content Survey for Letter Communication 2006*, Helsinki: Finland Post Corp., Research Publications 17/2007.

Soinivaara, Osmo (1974), *Tutkimus tariffien vaikutuksesta kotimaiseen kirjeliikenteeseen*, Helsinki: Administration of Post and Telegraphs, Econometric Research Institute of Post and Telegraph Office.
Statistics Finland (2007a), Juha Nurmela, Timo Sirkiä and Vesa Muttilainen: *Suomalaiset tietoyhteiskunnassa 2006*, Reviews 1/2007, Helsinki, Multiprint.
Statistics Finland (2007b), *Consumer barometer*, February.
Teräsvirta, Timo (1966), *Tariffinmuutosimpulssin vaikutuksesta postimaksumerkkitulojen volyymiin*, Helsinki: Administration of Post and Telegraphs, Econometric Research Institute of Post and Telegraph Office.

8. Empirical analysis of service quality in Japan's small package market*

Shoji Maruyama

1. INTRODUCTION

Postal operators in industrialized countries are nowadays facing accelerating competitive pressure with private operators, in addition to the shifting of mail demand to electronic communication. Noteworthy policy decisions were coincidentally made in EU and the United States in 2006. In November, a proposal for amending the current Postal Directive (97/67/EC) was announced by the EU Commission, indicating that exclusive or special rights will not be granted to national postal operators, with the ultimate objective of creating a Europe-wide internal postal market by 2009. In late December, with the passage of the Postal Accountability and Enhancement Act (P.L.109-435) in the US, rate-and-weight based reserved areas will also be defined in US postal services, similar to the situation in most European countries. In these areas and countries, however, the fundamental components of the Universal Service Obligation (USO), which describes the minimum service standards to be provided by the postal operator as required by a national regulatory authority, were little modified, notwithstanding the significant progress in competition in recent decades.

In Japan, postal reform is scheduled to take place in 2007, four years after the establishment of Japan Post Corporation. Japan Post will be privatized and restructured into one stock-holding company and four business subsidiaries: mail delivery, post office network, postal bank, and postal life insurance companies. Japan's postal reform also redefines the scope of USO with the implementation of privatization. As a result of this reform, parcel services will be provided in Japan as a freight business rather than as a postal product, which means that parcel USO will not be imposed on any operators. This policy decision was made in light of the evaluation that service quality improvement due to the progress of competition in the small package market is so widespread that universal parcel delivery will be considered to be guaranteed without mandating USO in this business area.

This chapter aims to provide a forward-looking perspective for possible USO debates by conducting a demand analysis of the small package market in Japan based on two recent questionnaire surveys targeted at individual customers. The chapter also examines the implications of the analyses of the package market for the future letter-mail market, under the assumption that package delivery by a few dominant operators has the possibility of being harmonized with the letter-mail market structure after full liberalization. The current small package market in Japan is characterized by demand for a high level of service quality as a result of continuous competition, with customers being able to choose a specific operator that they expect will provide the service qualities they desire. A quantitative analysis of the relevant factors influencing customers' choice is expected to reveal their potential needs in the future competitive mail market. In the next section, questionnaire surveys in terms of service quality focusing on the small package market will be briefly presented, following by a model construction and estimation focused on choice behaviors of customers. In Section 3, the implications of the present chapter for the future USO debate in Japan are examined from the perspective of substituting the discipline of the competitive market for regulation of quality of service. Section 4 concludes the discussion.

2. SERVICE QUALITY IN JAPAN'S PACKAGE MARKET

2.1 Service Quality in the Postal Market

This chapter aims to analyze quantitatively choice of and switching among operators by individual customers, followed by a review from questionnaire surveys concerning needs and requests by customers for service quality attributes of small package delivery, which is composed of parcel products provided by the postal operator (Japan Post) and package services by private operators.[1] Individual customers will be targeted for a series of follow-up analyses, since the USO is considered to be fundamentally formulated to protect these customers' basic requirements.

Service quality in the postal market has been continuously discussed from the viewpoint of welfare analyses and USO at the previous Rutgers postal conferences and in the relevant literature. In Elsenbast (1997), four service quality factors comprising German customers' preferences for mail delivery were applied to conduct a conjoint analysis: mode of delivery, frequency of delivery, density of postal outlets, and speed of delivery. Estimation of the utility (part-worth) of these factors revealed that such service as delivery to the house on working days and next-day delivery were highly evaluated by customers. In Reay (2002), who conducted a welfare analysis incorporating a service quality index, willingness-to-pay demand functions were formulated, determined by the factor of volume consumed and the achievement rate of next-day delivery as a proxy for service quality. Ambrosini et al. (2006) discuss the possibility for international comparison of USO, in which service quality is defined in a broad sense as being comprised of some factors such as delivery and collection, transit times, accessibility, and doorstep delivery. They present a three-dimensional 'box' concept to determine the burden of USO constraints to be derived from the quality evaluation in addition to the scope of products and price controls.

2.2 Service Quality in the Small Package Market in Japan

A significant degree of competition has been observed in Japan's small package market, which has driven Japan Post to have only a less than 10 percent market share in recent years. Package delivery by private operators initially started in 1976, and it expanded to handle a volume of more than three billion items, with dozens of operators. This market swelling resulted from the introduction of new products and services such as COD (cash on delivery), delivery for iced, chilled, and temperature-controlled handling, and next-day delivery by air freighters. These characteristics of private packages imply that they could produce additional demand by introducing products and services reflecting or advancing customer requests by achieving service quality improvement.[2] These service qualities will be incorporated in a demand analysis targeted at Japan's small package market in the following sections. Basic information needed for the empirical analysis reported here was collected from questionnaire surveys conducted by Japan Post, targeted at nationwide individual customers. The first survey, of 4000 samples, was collected by cooperation with Nikkei Research Co. in 2002, and the second one, of 1800 samples, was with Survey Research Center Co. in 2006. We can examine customers' changing needs and requests by comparing the results of these two surveys.[3]

Four factors comprising quality of service concerning small package delivery will be taken into account hereafter: (1) access to post offices or collection points such as 'convenience retail stores'; (2) frequency of delivery; (3) speed of delivery; and (4) the package delivery rate. The graph part of Figure 8.1 shows the evaluation scores that represent the degree of importance for customers with regard to each quality factor when they intend to send a small package. To calculate the score, four points are associated with the answer 'this factor is the most important among four quality factors for me', three points with 'this factor is the second', two points with 'this factor is the third', and one point with 'this factor is the fourth', which can be expected to yield outcomes where each factor scores very highly when it is regarded as more important in choosing an operator. The table part of Figure 8.1 indicates changes of the scores regarding four factors compared with the previous survey.

According to the graph part of Figure 8.1, it can be implied that four quality factors – namely, speed and rate of delivery – can be distinctly categorized as two 'more important factors', compared to the other two factors: access to post offices or collection

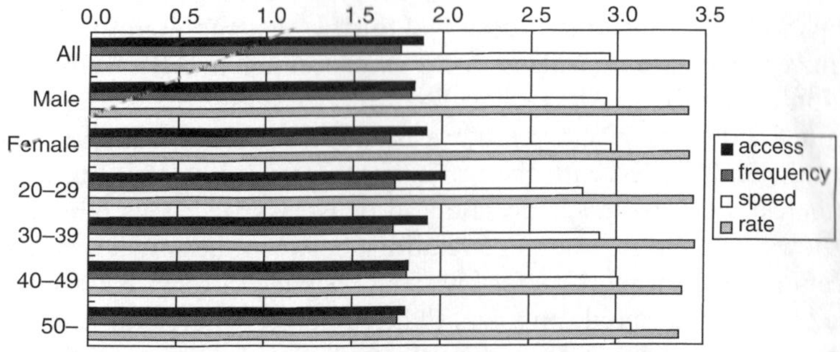

	access	frequency	speed	rate
All	–0.4	–0.0	+0.1	+0.3
Male	–0.5	+0.0	+0.0	+0.4
Female	–0.4	+0.0	+0.1	+0.3
Age 20–29	–0.2	–0.1	+0.0	+0.3
30–39	–0.5	+0.0	+0.2	+0.2
40–49	–0.6	+0.0	+0.1	+0.3
50–	–0.5	+0.1	+0.1	+0.4

Figure 8.1 Evaluation scores in small package services

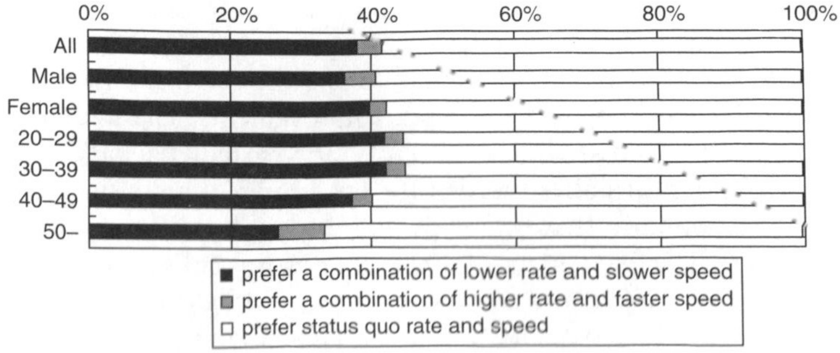

Figure 8.2 Relative evaluation between two service qualities

points and frequency of delivery. The degree of importance for the package rate and access to collection points has a decreasing tendency according to the increasing age of the customers, while in contrast the score for delivery speed is increasing. Compared with scores from four years ago, shown in the table part of Figure 8.1, increasing evaluation for rate and decreasing for access can be observed in all categories by gender and age. This outcome is likely to be derived from widespread free carrier pickup options and an aggressive marketing strategy of collection at convenience stores, where individual customers can pick their packages up in a timely fashion. This environmental transformation for small package services over four years has produced more rate-oriented customers.

The relative degrees of importance among the four service qualities observed in Figure 8.1, however, have a shortcoming in calculating the score in the sense that the differences in the evaluation scores among the quality attribute do not necessarily correspond to a precise quantitative impact in actual customer demand. Moreover, an improvement in one service quality attribute may be achieved via deterioration in another service attribute when technical efficiency is assumed for the relevant operator. In this case, both the welfare increases stemming from a service improvement and the welfare decrease from a deterioration combined must be considered in evaluating the welfare gained by customers. Figure 8.2 depicts such a relative evaluation for service quality attributes when they are hypothetically faced with the tradeoff situation with regard to requests for two quality attributes: the small package rate and delivery speed. Customers' evaluation in Figure 8.2 shows asymmetric reference relations between these two services in the sense that 40 percent of all customers prefer lowering package rates with a decreasing delivery speed, while on the other hand, only less than 10 percent prefer raising the rate with an increasing speed. The tendency to prefer a lower rate to a faster speed can be observed especially in females and the younger generations.

More than 50 percent of individual customers in the survey were found to have perceived quality improvements in the small package service in the past four or five years. igure 8.3 shows requests for the package service, distinguishing between customers who ognize quality improvements and those that don't recognize them. The package rate is to be a primary concern among customers, following the installation of collection and a speedup for delivery. The difference between the two categories of customers gard to the recognition of service improvements is noteworthy, implying that

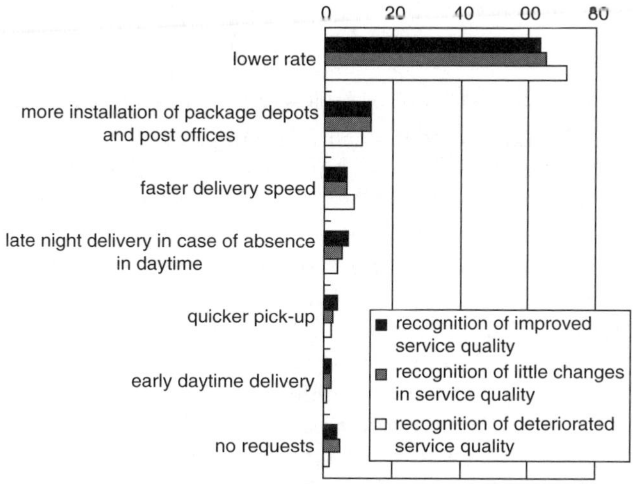

Figure 8.3 Requests to small package services

customers' requests and needs have the characteristics of demanding higher service quality no matter how much they are satisfied with past quality improvements.

2.3 The Model

In this section, models for explaining customer behaviors in selecting a particular delivery operator will be formulated, with a focus on analyzing the demand structure in the package market. When they are able to choose a favorite consignee from amongst those with significant differences in their service qualities, customers tend to decide on a specific operator with reference to their evaluation standards, as shown in Figure 8.1. The Logit model or the Probit model is frequently applied in such binary choice problems, in which dependent variables represent the probability of choosing the relevant operator in the following analysis. The dependent variable, Y_i, cannot be estimated by an ordinary least squares (OLS) method, since the estimated value is restricted to lying between 1 (meaning the choice of the operator) and 0 (otherwise).

A binary choice problem can be formulated by assuming a hypothetical variable, Y_i^*, which is an indicator or 'potential variable' representing a cutoff value of overall quality and leading to choice or non-choice, as captured in the choice variable Y_i which assumes the value of 1 (choice) or 0 (non-choice) as in the following equations (for a detailed discussion of the model structure for binary choice problems, see Maddala, 1992; Maki and Miyauchi, 1997)

$$Y_i^* = \beta_1 + \beta_2 * X_i + e_i, \quad i = 1, 2, \ldots, N,$$

where $Y_i = 1\ (Y_i^* \geq 0)$, $Y_i = 0\ (Y_i^* < 0)$.

Focusing on the probability of Y_i to be one, and assuming that the function F is a specific cumulative distribution function of e_i, with Prob(choice) + Prob(non-choice) = 1, we have

$$\text{Prob}\,(Y_i = 1) = \text{Prob}\,(e_i \geq -\beta_1 - \beta_2 * X_i)$$
$$= 1 - F(-\beta_1 - \beta_2 * X_i) = F(\beta_1 + \beta_2 * X_i).$$

A Probit model corresponds to the case where F is the cumulative standard normal distribution function, and a Logit model when F is a logistic distribution function, in both of which relevant coefficients can be estimated by applying the Maximum Likelihood method. Estimation by these two models would yield similar coefficients in terms of signature conditions, although the values estimated by a Logit model are greater than those estimated by a Probit model. The choice between these two models is usually determined by the degree of estimation suitability (see Maddala, 1992).

Service operators' selection models were estimated by Probit models in Rycke et al. (2000), which was targeted at 1200 French business units for sending second-class mail. The estimation results show that the probability of using the mail would increase positively as the number of staff as a proxy for business scale increased and negatively as in urban areas, which implies that customer and area characteristics significantly affected mail demand.[4] Hereafter, binary choice models will be formulated with regard to Japan's small package market to analyze the selection behavior of operators by individual customers, in which the applied dependent and independent variables are as follows:

A. *Dependent variables*. Dummy variables to represent binary choice of relevant operators (1, choice; 0, otherwise). Two major operators (operators A and B) among several delivery companies providing both BtoC and CtoC small package services will be applied for the estimations, although the names of the two operators will be treated anonymously for marketing reasons.
B. *Independent variables*. Next, five independent factors are specified to represent the basic factors that are assumed to account for determining the probability of choosing the relevant operators:

   1. Nine customer attribute factors: a gender dummy (1 if female), an age dummy, a job category dummy (1 if independent workers[5]), a ratio of working family members, the amount of salary, three residence areas dummies (1 if in urban areas, 1 if in medium-sized cities, and 1 if in rural areas, respectively).
   2. Three evaluation factors regarding quality of service: a dummy variable to be 1 if the customer highly evaluates access in choosing a delivery operator, 1 if the customer highly evaluates delivery speed, and 1 if the customer highly evaluates small package rates.
   3. Two recognition factors regarding the level of small package rates for both operators: a dummy variable to be 1 if the customer considers that the rate offered by operator A is high, 1 if the customer considers the rate offered by operator B is high.
   4. Two recognition factors regarding marketing achievement in service quality: a dummy variable to be 1 if the customer considers that the service quality of operator A has improved, and 1 if the customer considers that the service quality of operator B has improved.
   5. One competition factor: a dummy variable to be 0 if the customer responded to 2002 survey and 1 if he or she responded to the 2006 survey.

Information on these factors could be derived from both the 2002 and the 2006 surveys, with the exception of factors (3) and (4) regarding small package rates and service quality. We therefore used these two surveys for everything except factors (3) and (4), which were determined solely from the 2006 survey. The descriptive statistics of independent variables collected from the 2002 and 2006 surveys are shown in Table 8.1 (the dependent variable to represent the number choosing the relevant operators will not be presented for marketing reasons). The sample size was 3192 when data from both surveys was pooled, and 1724 if only the 2006 survey was applied.

The combination of independent variables tested included the following model specifications in estimating the probability of choice between small package operators A and B:

1. *Model 0*: attribute factors only.
2. *Model 1*: attribute and evaluation factors regarding quality of service.
3. *Model 2*: attribute factors and evaluation factors regarding quality of service, and recognition factors regarding both the level of small package rates and marketing achievement in service quality.
4. *Model 3*: attribute factors and evaluation factors regarding quality of service, and competition factors.

Whereas all available attribute variables for customer characteristics will be applied in model 0, in other model estimations only statistically significant variables, as measured at 10 percent confidence levels in model 0, will be included. While model 0 and 1 only cover customers' selection behaviors from the 2006 survey, the estimation results from models 2 and 3 enable us to analyze the effect of improvement in service quality developed from progress in competition. The signature condition of coefficients is expected to be positive in the probability of choosing operator A in model 2 with regard to the improvement in its own service quality and increasing recognition of the competitor's rate as being high. In model 3, the time dummy variable corresponds to a proxy for progress in competition and change in service quality. The coefficient of the competition factor in this model is expected to be positive if the operators could achieve service improvement in the competitive market, and subsequently attracted more new customers.

The model estimation results for the selection of package delivery operators are shown in Table 8.2, in which Logit models were applied rather than Probit models due to their better fitness for estimations.[6] Estimation performance in terms of McFadden's standards and estimation suitability would be accepted overall (McFadden R^2 score 0.18, suitability of fitness rate 70 percent at best). The former is referred to as the log-likelihood test, derived from comparing the log-likelihood between unrestricted and restricted models. The latter is the ratio of correct estimation (selection or otherwise) by the models, in which the test is conducted as follows: the theory data will be set to 1 (selection) if the simulated estimation in the model is equal to or greater than 0.5, the theory data will be set to 0 (non-selection) if the simulated estimation in the model is less than 0.5, and these outcomes will be compared to actual behaviors, with the suitability of the fitness rate then being the ratio of correct forecasting.

Coefficients in binary choice models should be interpreted carefully in the sense that the coefficients in the estimation equations shown in Table 8.2 represent no elasticity of each

Table 8.1 Descriptive statistics

(a) 2006 survey

	Customer attributes								
	Female	Age	Ind. work	Work ratio	Family	Salary	Urban	Mid-city	Rural
Average	0.531	39.490	0.164	0.538	3.487	665	0.213	0.403	0.218
Maximum	1.000	59.000	1.000	1.000	10.000	1500	1.000	1.000	1.000
Minimum	0.000	0.000	0.000	0.000	0.000	0	0.000	0.000	0.000
Std Dev.	0.499	9.189	0.370	0.264	1.311	377	0.410	0.491	0.413

	Evaluation factors concerning service quality			Recognition factors concerning service quality			
	Access	Speed	Rate	High A	High B	Impr. A	Impr. B
Average	0.629	0.253	0.144	0.585	0.703	0.398	0.581
Maximum	1.000	1.000	1.000	1.000	1.000	1.000	1.000
Minimum	0.000	0.000	0.000	0.000	0.000	0.000	0.000
Std Dev.	0.483	0.435	0.352	0.493	0.457	0.490	0.494

(b) 2002 survey

	Customer attributes								
	Female	Age	Ind. work	Work ratio	Family	Salary	Urban	Mid-city	Rural
Average	0.537	46.747	0.155	0.519	3.539	689	0.243	0.429	0.194
Maximum	1.000	69.000	1.000	1.000	9.000	1500	1.000	1.000	1.000
Minimum	0.000	20.000	0.000	0.000	1.000	0	0.000	0.000	0.000
Std Dev.	0.498	13.519	0.362	0.316	1.512	437	0.429	0.495	0.396

	Evaluation factors concerning service quality		
	Access	Speed	Rate
Average	0.650	0.135	0.311
Maximum	1.000	1.000	1.000
Minimum	0.000	0.000	0.000
Std Dev.	0.477	0.341	0.463

Note: Questions regarding improvement of service quality were not surveyed in 2002.11

Table 8.2 Estimation results for selection

(a) Operator A

	Model 0		Model 1		Model 2		Model 3	
	Coefficient	z-statistic	Coefficient	z-statistic	Coefficient	z-statistic	Coefficient	z-statistic
Constant	0.1777	0.5413	0.4598	1.4923	0.5891	1.7815	−0.3013	−1.3143
Female	−0.2850	−2.8083	−0.2794	−2.4749	−0.2288	−1.9832	−0.1690	−2.0815
Age	0.0082	1.4617	0.0048	0.7596	0.0040	0.6266	0.0058	1.6265
Independent work	−0.3254	−2.3735	−0.3449	−2.3228	−0.3723	−2.4711	−0.1548	−1.4186
Ratio of working	−0.0531	−0.2601						
Family member	−0.0683	−1.6606	−0.0584	−1.3810	−0.0586	−1.3604	−0.0095	−0.3249
Annual salary	0.0003	2.1853	0.0002	0.9850	0.0001	0.8809	0.0003	2.8389
Urban areas	−0.0874	−0.5401						
Medium cities	−0.0903	−0.6323						
Rural areas	−0.0084	−0.0528						
Access-oriented			0.3047	2.6762	0.3464	2.9914	0.6236	7.4661
Speed-oriented			1.3496	7.5330	1.3324	7.3549	1.5680	13.3646
Rate-oriented			−2.2710	−15.4004	−2.1925	−14.6324	−1.9313	−16.9996
High B rate					0.1285	0.9187		
High A rate					−0.4287	−2.8371		
Improve B qos					−0.5305	−4.4079		
Improve A qos					0.4876	4.1207	0.0704	0.8211
Time								
Observations	1724		1724		1724		3192	
Log-likelihood	−1176		−991		−970		−1842	
McFadden R^2	0.0105		0.1658		0.1838		0.1486	
Fitness (%)	55.34		70.24		71.06		69.24	

Table 8.2 (continued)

(b) Operator B

	Model 0		Model 1		Model 2		Model 3	
	Coefficient	z-statistic	Coefficient	z-statistic	Coefficient	z-statistic	Coefficient	z-statistic
Constant	0.0003	0.0007	−0.6509	−2.0598	−0.8797	−2.5519	−0.3018	−1.2201
Female	0.4217	3.9632	0.4255	3.6454	0.3516	2.9150	0.3029	3.4018
Age	−0.0145	−2.4663	−0.0112	−1.7322	−0.0111	−1.6692	−0.0163	−4.0779
Independent work	0.0417	0.2863	−0.0303	−0.1940	−0.0007	−0.0043	−0.1114	−0.9058
Ratio of working	−0.2357	−1.1052						
Family member	−0.0292	−0.6765	−0.0471	−1.0669	−0.0467	−1.0227	−0.0107	−0.3366
Annual salary	−0.0003	−1.7654	−0.0001	−0.9152	−0.0001	−0.8822	−0.0003	−2.4500
Urban areas	0.2388	1.4084						
Medium cities	0.1376	0.9120						
Rural areas	0.0857	0.5095						
Access-oriented			0.1480	1.2411	0.1057	0.8622	−0.2031	−2.2241
Speed-oriented			−1.2157	−6.5404	−1.2084	−6.3103	−1.8121	−12.3052
Rate-oriented			2.0371	15.4774	1.9272	14.1665	1.7451	16.1316
High B rate					−0.3197	−2.2513		
High A rate					0.7304	4.5726		
Improve B qos					0.7784	6.2002		
Improve A qos					−0.6180	−5.0028		
Time							0.2522	2.6929
Observations	1724		1724		1724		3192	
Log-likelihood	−1099		−949		−1119		−1607	
McFadden R^2	0.0179		0.1520		0.1894		0.1579	
Fitness (%)	64.39		73.96		76.10		76.69	

Notes:
z-statistics are asymptotical t-statistics.
Urban areas, Tokyo metropolitan areas and 13 ordinance-designated cities; medium cities, cities with a population of more than 50 000 (other than urban areas); rural areas, country areas.

independent variable to the selection probability. To acquire this information, marginal effects should be calculated, although this effect has a shortcoming in that it fluctuates with the levels of each independent variable. Signature conditions of coefficients and criteria for significance (z-statistics) can be examined as in the results of OLS estimation.

Asymmetric estimation results in terms of the significance of coefficients such as the customer attribute factors gender, age and salary can be observed between the selection behavior of operators A and B, while the ratio of working family and residence areas did not commonly show significant effects (model 0). It is noteworthy that no significant impacts of residential areas are shown, since both operators have already completed a nationwide delivery network offering universal collection and delivery, including sparsely populated areas, and their accessibility likely has indifferent competitiveness in its appeal to individual customers. In model 1, adding evaluating factors for service quality, the difference between the choice of the two operators becomes more apparent: the probability of choosing operator A increases with more customers who highly evaluate speed of delivery, while it decreases for those who highly evaluate package rates. Interestingly, the signature conditions for operator B are completely opposite to those for operator A.

In model 2, where recognition factors regarding the package rates and service quality of the two operators were added to model 1, the probability of being chosen as the favorite operator is expected to decrease when a customer recognizes higher rates offered by the operator and improved quality of service provided by competitors. The estimation results for both operators' selection behavior satisfy these expected signature conditions, except that the recognition of higher rates in operator B's service insignificantly affects operator A's selection behavior. These estimation results imply the importance of recognition factors for service quality improvement and package rates for influencing selection behavior by customers. The estimation results of model 3, where a proxy variable for the progress of competition and for service quality improvement was included, can be compared with those of model 1. Different estimation outcomes for this proxy variable were obtained between selection behavior for operators A and B (positively significant for only operator B), which implies that operator B acquired relatively more customers from other competitors than operator A, and that customers could readily switch their favorite operator as a consequence of comparing the service quality provided by multiple providers.[7]

3. POSTAL USO AND SERVICE QUALITY

3.1 The Small Package and Letter-mail Market

Individual customers' selection and switching between operators in the small package market can be expected to present important implications for the demand structure for the future letter-mail market, especially in such countries as Japan, where non-correspondence mail, such as magazines, catalogues, leaflets and most direct mail, are already delivered by private networks, bypassing the postal network as for small packages (Maruyama, 2006). Despite these already competitive market conditions, additional deregulation policy for private entry in the remaining correspondence products, such as personal communications, and financial bills and statements, is currently under discussion in a study group in the regulatory authority (the Ministry of Internal Affairs and

Communications, MIC).[8] A future possible full market opening policy, as may be introduced in the European Union countries, will enable Japan's private operators to enter the entire postal market by themselves, without depending on access to the postal operator's downstream delivery network. In this liberalization scenario, head-to-head competition in the mail market between private and incumbent operators will be realized as in the current small package delivery sector.

The postal operator, which has offered the postal service with a long history as a Universal Service Provider (USP), and the private delivery companies, which have accomplished an efficient nationwide delivery network making use of the latest Information Technology (IT), will provide differentiated mail products in terms of service quality and package rates due to the distinctions between their cost structures and network efficiencies. Customers will have a tendency to choose a favorite operator according to their own evaluation standards concerning service quality: frequency of collection and delivery, speed of delivery, access to collection points, service rates, and other factors. In choosing an operator, not only the levels or improvements in service quality offered by current operators but also those of competitive operators will be taken into account. In the preceding analysis, however, the Universal Service Obligation (USO), which is only imposed on postal operators, has not been explicitly incorporated. It should be noted that the postal operator has no flexibility to degrade its service quality below the standards determined by the USO, while the private operators have no such operational restrictions. The diversification and sophistication of customer requirements due to progress of competition among operators will be also apparent in the future liberalized mail market. In this situation, the postal operator will have no option to allow any service quality to deteriorate below USO in the business areas that are facing less competition with private operators. These possibilities will force a reconsideration of the significant role of requirements regarding minimal service standards and the USO in future letter-mail markets.

3.2 USO Redesign in Japan

In Japan, the enactment of the Correspondence Delivery Law in 2003 made it possible for private operators to legally enter the whole postal market in addition to the already liberalized non-correspondence and small package delivery sectors. The debates concerning the implementation of Japan Post privatization reform in 2007 are also raising questions concerning the role and necessity of the postal USO.

Japan's postal USO for the new mail company after 2007 postal reform will be modified in some business areas compared with current standards. Notably, the parcel service (ordinary and booklet parcels, but not international parcels and EMS) will be treated as a general freight business rather than a postal service,[9] which indicates that operators will no longer be burdened with obligations to provide universal small package (parcel) delivery after 2007, while in European countries up to ten (in many countries, 20) kilogram parcels must be provided as a USO product in affordable, nationwide, non-discriminated conditions. This policy implementation originated from a market assessment that nationwide package delivery will be preserved without mandating any operators to impose on parcel USO, since in Japan a significant degree of competition has been achieved with the evolution of private delivery, and service quality in small package delivery is expected to be maintained at higher levels with ongoing continuous competition.

Rate authorization by the Ministry of Communications (MIC) for ordinal postal products will be transformed from the current approval-based system to a notification-based system, aimed at granting more business flexibility to the postal operator. This new regulation, however, does not guarantee a sufficient degree of freedom for the mail company, since the standard rate for a minimal weight is not permitted to be priced above the predetermined current rate (80 JPY) stipulated in the ministerial ordinance. With regard to also ensuring accessibility to the postal service, the post office network company, a sister company of the mail delivery company, will be obliged to install and maintain national post office outlets. The mail company, unlike the other two financial group companies – the postal (Yucho) bank and postal (Kampo) insurance – is mandated to consign its counter business, including mail acceptance and stamp sales, exclusively to this network company. This associated constraint may give rise to an additional burden for the mail company.[10] In addition to this consignment obligation, the other requirements regarding collection and delivery (frequency and speed) will not be reduced after privatization at all, in spite of possible changes in customer needs due to the progress of the private mail business.[11]

Japan Post is currently requested by the ordinance relating to the Postal Services Law to provide mail services for the blind and for evacuated citizens suffering as a result of natural disasters free of charge, without receiving any compensation from governmental organizations. While after the 2007 privatization the mail company will still be obliged to provide these social services, it can be expected to partly be compensated by the newly organized 'local and social contribution fund' under the conditions of satisfying specific business environments approved by the MIC. One of these characteristics is that the fund is composed from dividends and profits of two financial units' stocks, rather than from contributions from competitive delivery operators, as proposed for some European countries. Based on a series of deliberations in the legislative body (the Diet), however, a restriction has been imposed concerning the funding mechanism, under which the postal operator will be authorized to exploit the fund only when the overall postal business has incurred a net financial loss. This implies that the fund cannot be wholly expected to function as an effective policy for preserving USO as a whole.

The possible welfare changes due to a series of USO modifications for the mail company, therefore, cannot be predicted precisely, since the effect of realistic enforcement, especially concerning consignment to the post office network company and the compensation fund mechanism, is still unclear. The challenging task of how to ensure postal USO after privatization will need more discussion in Japan, since customer demands that they should benefit from competition were not sufficiently incorporated in the debate surrounding postal reform and USO redesign, except for the exemption of the parcel business from USO coverage.[12] For profit-maximizing companies, including the new privatized postal operator, this exemption is unlikely to cause a deterioration in their competitive service quality, since such a marketing strategy would cause customers to switch immediately to other rival operators. With the progress of liberalization, and also assuming the privatization of public corporations, the necessity for imposing a minimal service quality on any operator should be re-examined in light of the discipline of the competitive market environment, to assure such service quality without regulation.

4. CONCLUSIONS

Throughout this chapter, the significance of service quality and USO have been discussed in the context of the fierce competition that most former monopolistic postal operators are now facing due to market entry by private-sector companies under a policy of liberalization. A demand analysis was made of the small package market in Japan, a market that is dominated by a very small number of delivery operators, including the postal operator. This market structure with strong competition, including competition in service quality attributes, might possibly be a forerunner of the future liberalized lettermail market, especially in Japan, where delivery bypass for non-correspondence items has already been established by private operators. The results of two questionnaire surveys targeted at individual customers showed that they have a tendency to demand more quality improvements no matter how much service levels have already been improved as a result of ongoing competition among operators. The factors inducing individual customers to select a particular service provider or to switch between providers were estimated by Logit models with several independent variables, such as customer attributes, evaluation and recognition of service qualities, and competition factors. The estimation results showed that customers tend to choose their favorite operators on the basis of the expectation that they will receive the service quality for which the operator's brand is characterized. In addition to such characteristics of the demand structure, customers could well switch to another operator without significant difficulty if they recognize service improvements by a competing operator that correspond better to their service quality preferences than those of their existing provider.

In Japan, the parcel USO will be removed from the new postal operator that will be established as a part of the postal reform. In the future, the parcel service will be provided through the competitive market, and small package operators can expect to face significant quality competition, as a decline in service quality will definitely cause customers to switch to other competitors. Some features of regulatory policy, however, such as cross-subsidies between the mail company's profitable and uneconomic delivery businesses, may burden it with almost the same obligations as those of the former public entity, although the new private company is intended to seek to maximize profits. These policy debates and decisions may also be relevant for USPs in other countries, especially if they face competition with emerging private operators. USO as a minimal service standard in the former monopoly environment should be re-examined from the viewpoint of ensuring reasonable obligations for the postal operator under the new business circumstances arising from liberalization.

NOTES

* The contents of this chapter are solely the personal views of the author and do not represent official opinions by Japan Post. I thank Norma Nieto for valuable comments and suggestions as a discussant at the conference.

1. Both public and private parcel products are characterized as a maximum weight of 30 kilograms, free pick-up by phone or web request, a free track and trace service, and next-day to three days delivery throughout the nation; these are sent by both individual and business customers.
2. In Maruyama (2007), it was shown that most of the fluctuations in the private package market could be explained by its own past fluctuations, contrary to the postal parcel market, whose fluctuation was also

influenced by fluctuations in the macroeconomic environment by estimating VAR models for the private and public parcel volume.

3. While the coverage of the questionnaire of the first survey was mainly restricted to only mail and parcels, the second survey targeted not only postal mail and parcels but also private packages.
4. When the choice option in the model is multiple rather than binary, Logit models are generally modified to Multinomial Logit models. Ida and Kuroda (2006) have analyzed such models for households' selection behavior of broadband (BB) service providers in Japan, by estimating Multinomial Logit models (ML) and also Nested Logit models (NL).
5. The independent workers dummy variable was incorporated in the estimation models by assuming that the selection behavior of delivery operators between independent and office workers would be different, since the former will likely request service quality satisfying not only personal but also business demand.
6. For the series of model estimations, Eviews version 5.1 (QMS) was applied.
7. The insignificance estimation for the relevant competition variable for operator A could be caused by decision factors other than service quality. Brand loyalty and switching cost issues can be possible factors in their decision making. See Burns et al. (2002) for a theoretical discussion about the impact of brand loyalty upon customers' switching behavior in the mail market.
8. The study group will present its final report in mid-2008. Documents and discussion overviews from past meetings can be obtained via the website of the MIC (only in Japanese) see http://www.soumu.go.jp/yusei/seido_minaoshi/index.html
9. The privatized mail company will provide parcel products under the regulation of the Ministry of Land, Infrastructure and Transport (MLIT), which is different from the regulatory authority of the mail business, MIC.
10. The newly established post office network company will have imposed upon it the obligation to maintain the post offices at the level before privatization (24 600 offices). The financial services offered by the Postal Bank business in remote areas can be subsidized in part by a local and social contribution fund, which will be discussed in this section.
11. The current Postal Law stipulates that mail items should be delivered to each doorstep within three days after posting; principally, once a day and six days a week. These operational requirements, including nationwide installation of more than 180 000 street letter boxes, were not modified in the new Postal Law in line with privatization.
12. In addition to the aforementioned restrictions to the postal service, the lack of business expansion can also be an obstacle to the preservation of USO in the sense that the starting of new businesses, such as international express and logistics operations, is strictly governed by the regulatory authority (MIC) and related organizations (the Postal Privatization Committee) for at least ten years after the 2007 privatization.

REFERENCES

Ambrosini, X., F. Boldron and B. Roy (2006), 'Universal service obligations in the postal sector: economic learnings from cross-country comparisons', in M.A. Crew and P.R. Kleindorfer (eds), *Progress toward Liberalization of the Postal and Delivery Sector*, New York: Springer, pp. 23–38.

Burns, P., I. Carslake and G. Houpis (2002), 'Brand loyalty and limited entry in postal markets', in M.A. Crew and P.R. Kleindorfer (eds), *Postal and Delivery Services: Delivering on Competition*, Boston, MA: Kluwer Academic Publishers, pp. 71–92.

Elsenbast, W. (1997), 'Do we have the right standards for universal service?' in U. Stumpf and M. Plum (eds), *Diffusion of New Regulatory Approaches in the Postal Sector*, Bad Honnef: WIK.

Ida, T. and T. Kuroda (2006), 'Discrete choice analysis of demand for broadband in Japan', *Journal of Regulatory Economics*, **29** (1), 5–22.

Maddala, G.S. (1992), *Introduction to Econometrics*, Englewood Cliffs, NJ: Prentice-Hall.

Maki, A. and T. Miyauchi (1997), *Application of Econometrics* II, Tokyo: Taga Publishing (in Japanese).

Maruyama, S. (2006), 'Competition structure and future postal reform in Japan', in M.A. Crew and P.R. Kleindorfer (eds), *Progress toward Liberalization of the Postal and Delivery Sector*, New York: Springer.

Maruyama, S. (2007), 'Empirical analysis of express services provided by different ownership', *Journal of the Japan Logistics Society*, **15**, June (in Japanese), pp. 73–80.

Reay, I. (2002), 'The welfare economics of universal service standards and service quality', in

M.A. Crew and P.R. Kleindorfer (eds), *Postal and Delivery Services: Pricing, Productivity, Regulation and Strategy*, Boston, MA: Kluwer Academic Publishers, pp. 107–26.

Rycke, M., S. Marcy and J.-P. Florens (2000), 'Mail's use by firm', in M.A. Crew and P.R. Kleindorfer (eds), *Future Directions in Postal Reform*, Boston, MA: Kluwer Academic Publishers, pp. 213–31.

WIK-Consult (2006), 'Main developments in the postal sector (2004–2006)', EU Commission; http://ec.europa.eu/internal_market/post/studies_en.htm

PART III

Pricing under Entry

9. Access, bypass and productivity gains in competitive postal markets

Francis Bloch and Axel Gautier

1. INTRODUCTION

In the European Union, Full Market Opening (FMO) of postal markets is now scheduled for January 1, 2011 (and January 1, 2013 for new members). FMO allows competitors of the incumbent postal operator to enter all the segments of the postal markets, including mail delivery. FMO might be a threat for the financing of the Universal Service Obligation (USO) imposed on the incumbent postal operator, particularly if the entrant bypasses the incumbent's delivery network.

In the postal sector, competition started long before FMO. However, with a few exceptions, competition was limited to the upstream segments of the market (collection and sorting) through the use of worksharing agreements. Worksharing or access means that a competitor can perform all the upstream operations of the postal value chain and buy access to the incumbent's PO delivery network at a discounted price (compared to the letter price). FMO means that in addition to the access solution that will continue to be available, the competitors also have the option to deliver mail with their own delivery network (bypass).

In this chapter, we are interested in the consequences of FMO on the behavior of the incumbent PO. As mentioned, FMO means that the entrant can bypass the incumbent's delivery network and build up its own. Bypass can be detrimental for both the incumbent's profit – with a negative impact on its ability to finance the USO – and welfare (Crew and Kleindorfer, 2005; De Donder, 2006; Bloch and Gautier, 2007). Our interest lies in the strategies that the incumbent can develop to prevent (inefficient) bypass by the entrant. In particular, we concentrate on the pricing and on the investment strategies undertaken by the incumbent (or the regulator) to deter bypass.

In this chapter, we will consider how the incumbent's strategies will be modified by the threat of bypass by the entrant. To this end, we construct a model where an incumbent PO competes in postal markets with a profit-maximizing entrant. The entrant chooses its letter price and the delivery method – access or bypass – that leads to the highest profit. As a starting point of our analysis, we consider the prices and investment level that apply when competition is limited to the upstream segments of the market. These pre-FMO prices are either set by a welfare-maximizing regulator or by a profit-maximizing firm. We show that, facing the threat of entry, the incumbent PO may change its price structure and may also strategically invest in its delivery network.

By changing its prices, the incumbent can strategically deter bypass by making this option less profitable for the entrant. To do so, the incumbent manipulates both its letter and access prices.[1] The two instruments affect differently the incentives to bypass. For the entrant, the access price is the cost of outsourcing delivery. Therefore a change in the access price amounts to a change in production cost. To deter bypass, the incumbent can thus lower its access price to make the access option relatively more profitable for the entrant.

A change in the letter price changes the volume of mails carried by the entrant. The lower the incumbent's letter price, the lower the demand faced by the entrant. And the magnitude of this effect depends on the cross-price elasticity of the demands. But this holds true under both access and bypass. So, how can the incumbent deter bypass by changing its letter price? Suppose that a given price change has the same impact on the entrant's mailing volume under access and bypass. Then, the impact of a price change on its profit depends on the price cost margin in the two cases. If the unit margin is highest under bypass, a price cut by the incumbent leads to a higher profit decrease with bypass. Therefore, decreasing the letter price makes the access option more attractive. Conversely, if the unit margin is highest under access, the incumbent will deter bypass by increasing its letter price; that is, by reducing the entrant's volume. In this chapter, we show that the incumbent PO must reduce both the access and the delivery prices to prevent bypass. However, constraining the entrant to choose access is costly in terms of foregone profit and welfare, since the incumbent departs from pre-FMO prices, which are assumed to be efficient.

Next, we introduce the possibility for the incumbent PO to increase the productivity of its delivery activity by restructuring it. For example, it could reorganize its delivery network or invest to expand automated sorting. The incentives to undertake these kinds of investment depend on the expected gains that are obviously affected by the delivery method chosen by the entrant. We can decompose the benefit of the investment into a direct and a strategic component. The size of the investment depends on the magnitude of these two components. The direct effect is linked to the mail volume processed by the incumbent. With a larger mail volume, the gains from reducing by a given amount the unit delivery cost are larger. Therefore the direct effect is linked to number of letters delivered by the incumbent, including those pre-sorted by the entrant and posted at an access point. Regarding the direct incentive only, the incumbent invests more under access than under bypass, since the latter implies a (possibly drastic) reduction in the number of postal items delivered. The strategic effect is linked to the impact of the investment on the competitor's behavior (for a related analysis, see Fundenberg and Tirole, 1984). In this context, the only change in behavior that the incumbent can expect from the entrant is a change of delivery method. Because of these strategic incentives, the incumbent PO may invest more to deter bypass. Hence, the investment together with its pricing decisions will be used by the incumbent to deter bypass by the entrant.

We show that it is not when the two firms are engaged in so-called facility-based competition that the incentives to invest are the highest. The incumbent firm has the highest incentive to invest when its investment can modify the delivery decision of the entrant. Hence, we will observe the highest investment levels for the firms that try to deter their competitor from engaging in facility-based competition.

The chapter is organized as follows: we present the basic ingredients of the model in Section 2. We derive the post-FMO price changes in Section 3. Section 4 considers the investment incentives and Section 5 concludes.

2. MODEL

The incumbent PO, denoted hereafter firm 1, offers two products: an E2E letter at price p_1 and access to its delivery network at price a. The entrant, firm 2, offers only an E2E letter at price p_2. Consumers view the two E2E letter products as imperfect substitutes. For example, the entrant may have a lower frequency of collection or delivery and/or a lower geographical coverage.

The demand for the E2E letter offered by firm $i = 1,2$ is denoted $x_i(p_1, p_2)$. These demand functions have the standard properties. The entrant has two options for mail delivery. It can either buy access at unit price a or it can set up its own delivery network. In the case that it chooses the access option, the demand for access is $x_2(p_1, p_2)$. In the case that it chooses to bypass, there is no demand for access and the incumbent sells only an E2E letter to consumers. This means that consumer direct access is not considered in this model.

We decompose the postal value chain into two composite activities: upstream activities (collection, transport, sorting) and delivery (distribution). The constant unit cost of all the upstream activities is denoted by c_i for firm i. Delivery involves two types of cost: a fixed cost and a constant per-unit cost. The fixed costs are denoted by F_1 and F_2, the per-unit cost d_1 and d_2. The entrant can avoid these delivery costs if it chooses to buy access from the incumbent. In addition, universal service obligations imposed on the incumbent operator involve a fixed cost F.

Firms compete in prices. We suppose that the incumbent is price leader. This means that the entrant decides on its price p_2 and on its delivery method after observing the letter and the access prices set by the incumbent. The entrant chooses the price and the delivery option that maximize its profits.[2] The prices of the incumbent are either set by the firm in order to maximize its profits or by a postal regulator that seeks to maximize welfare.

In the regulated case, the regulator can decentralize the welfare-maximizing prices by imposing a global price cap on the incumbent (Billette de Villemeur et al., 2003). The main difference between regulated and unregulated prices is the price levels and not the price structure. From now on, we adopt the convention that the incumbent and not the regulator sets the prices in order to maximize its profit (in the absence of a price cap) or to maximize welfare.

3. PRICING

3.1 Pre-FMO Pricing

Consider the pre-FMO situation where the entrant does not have the possibility to bypass the incumbent's delivery network. The game played by the incumbent and the entrant is a two-stage game. At a first stage, the incumbent sets its retail (stamp) price $\hat{p}_1$ and its access price $\hat{a}$. At a second stage, after observing these prices, the entrant sets its retail (stamp) price $\hat{p}_2(\hat{p}_1, \hat{a})$.

In this chapter, we leave aside the exact description of the optimal prices. This work has been done elsewhere by Laffont and Tirole (1994) or Crew and Kleindorfer (1992), Bloch and Gautier (2007) and Billette de Villemeur et al. (2007) for the postal sector. For our argument, it is sufficient to consider the maximization problems faced by the two firms.[3] The entrant chooses its price

$$\hat{p}_2^A(\hat{p}_1,\hat{a}) = \arg\max_{p_2} \Pi_2^A \equiv (p_2 - c_2 - \hat{a})x_2(\hat{p}_1, p_2).$$

We let Z^A denote the objective of the incumbent, where Z^A equals profit in the absence of a price cap and welfare otherwise. The optimal prices $\hat{p}_1$ and $\hat{a}$ are the solutions of

$$\frac{\partial Z^A}{\partial p_1} + \frac{\partial Z^A}{\partial \hat{p}_2}\frac{\partial \hat{p}_2}{\partial p_1} = 0,$$

$$\frac{\partial Z^A}{\partial a} + \frac{\partial Z^A}{\partial \hat{p}_2}\frac{\partial \hat{p}_2}{\partial a} = 0.$$

In particular, we note that the incumbent chooses its stamp and access prices taking into account their effects on the optimal choice of the entrant.

3.2 Post-FMO Pricing

FMO means that the entrant has the possibility of bypassing the incumbent's delivery network. Under FMO, the game played by the incumbent and the entrant becomes a three-stage game. First, as before, the incumbent sets its prices. Second, the entrant decides on its delivery method – access or bypass. And, third, the entrant sets its retail price.

Consider the last stage of this game. In case of access, the entrant chooses the price $\hat{p}_2^A$. In case of bypass, its optimal price is found by solving

$$\hat{p}_2^B(\hat{p}_1,d_2) = \arg\max_{p_2} \Pi_2^B \equiv (p_2 - c_2 - d_2)x_2(\hat{p}_1, p_2) - F_2.$$

The optimal delivery choice of the entrant at the second stage of the game is easily found. If $\Pi_2^B > \Pi_2^A$, the entrant will choose to bypass. If $\Pi_2^B < \Pi_2^A$, it will choose access, and if $\Pi_2^B = \Pi_2^A$, it will be indifferent between the two delivery methods. Obviously, the parameters of the delivery function of the entrant only affect profit under bypass. Hence, comparing the profit levels in the two cases, we can easily establish the following:

Proposition 1: At any prices (p_1, a), there exists a cut-off level for the entrant's marginal delivery cost $\tilde{d}_2$ such that (1) the entrant prefers bypass for $d_2 < \tilde{d}_2$ and access otherwise, (2) $\tilde{d}_2 < a$ and (3) the value of $\tilde{d}_2$ decreases with the fixed cost F_2.

PROOF: At given prices (p_1,a), the profit Π_2^B decreases in d_2. The profit Π_2^A is independent of d_2. Therefore, there exists a level $\tilde{d}_2$ such that $\Pi_2^B = \Pi_2^A$.

For $d_2=a$, $\Pi_2^B - \Pi_2^A = -F_2$. Hence, $\tilde{d}_2$ is clearly smaller that the access price level. ∎

In a liberalized market, the entrant has two available technologies for mail delivery: a constant return to scale one – access – available at price $\hat{a}$ and an increasing return to scale one – bypass – characterized by a fixed cost F_2 and a constant unit cost d_2.[4] Because of the fixed cost, the entrant does not choose the technology with the lowest marginal cost.

That is, for $d_2 \in [\tilde{d}_2, \hat{a}]$, the marginal delivery cost is lower under bypass but, because of the fixed cost, the highest profit is achieved if the entrant buys access.

Proposition 1 clarifies the conditions on the parameters of the model under which access or bypass is likely to occur. We now return to the first stage of the model, keeping the delivery costs d_2 and F_2 fixed, and computing the optimal choice of the incumbent.

3.3 Access, Bypass and Constrained Access

Formally, our model is similar to the classical model of entry barriers, where the incumbent chooses a price in order to block, deter or accommodate entry of a competitor (Tirole, 1988, Chapter 8). The model differs from the classical model in two respects: (i) the choice of the entrant is not whether to enter or not, but whether to bypass or use the delivery technology of the incumbent; and (ii) accordingly, the incumbent chooses two instruments rather than one, namely both an access price a and a delivery price p_1.

By analogy with the model of entry barriers, we can distinguish three regimes:

1. *Access (blocked bypass):* By setting its optimal delivery and access prices, the incumbent prevents bypass.
2. *Constrained access (deterred bypass):* The incumbent distorts its delivery and access prices in order to force the entrant to choose access.
3. *Bypass (accommodated bypass):* The incumbent prefers to let the entrant set up its own delivery network, and chooses its optimal prices anticipating bypass.

As in the model of entry barriers, some remarks are in order. First, the choice of the incumbent depends crucially on the 'entry' (F_2) and delivery (d_2) costs of the entrant. The higher these costs, the less likely the entrant is to choose bypass. Hence, when entry and delivery costs are high enough, bypass is always blocked. When they are very low, the incumbent prefers to accommodate bypass, and chooses its optimal prices accordingly. Constrained access appears only for intermediate values of the entry and delivery costs. Second, the analysis is conducted under the assumption that the incumbent can commit to its access and delivery prices. Absent this commitment, the incumbent would be unable to influence the entrant's decision, and the analysis would be markedly different: the incumbent and entrant would both choose Bertrand equilibrium prices.

3.4 Constrained Access

We now focus attention on the regime of strategic bypass deterrence, when the incumbent chooses its delivery and access prices in order to force the entrant to choose access. To do that, the incumbent must ensure that the following constraint is satisfied:

$$(\hat{p}_2^B(p_1,d_2) - c_2 - d_2)x_2(p_1,\hat{p}_2^B(p_1,d_2)) - F_2 \leq (\hat{p}_2^A(p_1,a) - c_2 - a)x_2(p_1,\hat{p}_2^A(p_1,a)). \quad (9.1)$$

This equation shows that the incumbent can use either of his two instruments (access or delivery price) to prevent bypass. Clearly, at the optimal delivery price, the incumbent needs to *reduce* its access price (with respect to the optimal access price) in order to deter bypass. Similarly, at the optimal access price (which satisfies $\hat{a} > d_2$, since the entrant prefers bypass at the optimal pre-FMO prices), the incumbent needs to *reduce* the delivery price, in order to lower mail volume, thereby reducing the mail volume of the entrant, and the relative advantage of bypass over access.

The previous heuristic argument shows that, if the incumbent sets either instrument at the optimal pre-FMO level, it will necessarily choose to lower the other price with respect to the optimal pre-FMO level. Hence, one expects that, in the constrained access regime, the full opening of the postal markets will induce a decrease in the delivery price of the PO or the access price charged to the entrant. What if the incumbent can now independently vary the two prices?

Formally, the optimal delivery and access prices in the constrained access regime will be chosen by the incumbent in order to maximize its objective function Z^A subject to the constrained access constraint (9.1). If we denote by μ the Lagrange multiplier of this constraint, the first-order conditions of the profit/welfare-maximization problem read as follows:

$$\frac{\partial Z^A}{\partial p_1} + \frac{\partial Z^A}{\partial \hat{p}_2}\frac{\partial \hat{p}_2}{\partial p_1} + \mu\left((\hat{p}_2^A - c_2 - a)\frac{\partial x_2(p_1, \hat{p}_2^A)}{\partial \hat{p}_2}\frac{\partial \hat{p}_2^A}{\partial p_1} - (\hat{p}_2^B - c_2 - d_2)\frac{\partial x_2(p_1, \hat{p}_2^B)}{\partial \hat{p}_2}\frac{\partial \hat{p}_2^B}{\partial p_1}\right) = 0,$$

$$\frac{\partial Z^A}{\partial a} + \frac{\partial Z^A}{\partial \hat{p}_2}\frac{\partial \hat{p}_2}{\partial a} + \mu\left(-x_2(p_1, \hat{p}_2^A) + (\hat{p}_2^A - c_2 - a)\frac{\partial x_2(p_1, \hat{p}_2^A)}{\partial \hat{p}_2}\frac{\partial \hat{p}_2}{\partial a}\right) = 0.$$

Let $\bar{p}_1$ and $\bar{a}$ be the solutions to this problem. We can establish the following:

Proposition 2: To deter bypass, (1) the access price must be lowered, $\bar{a} \leq \hat{a}$, and (2) the incumbent's letter price must be decreased, $\bar{p}_1 \leq \hat{p}_1$.

PROOF: If at prices $(\hat{p}_1,\hat{a})$, the constraint (9.1) is slack, $\mu = 0$ and bypass can be prevented with the pre-FMO prices (blocked bypass case). Otherwise, if the prices $(\hat{p}_1,\hat{a})$ induce bypass, prices must be changed and (9.1) is binding ($\mu > 0$).

1. The term

$$\left(- x_2(p_1, \hat{p}_2^A) + (\hat{p}_2^A - c_2 - a)\frac{\partial x_2(p_1, \hat{p}_2^A)}{\partial \hat{p}_2}\frac{\partial \hat{p}_2}{\partial a}\right)$$

is negative. Hence, when the constraint is binding $\mu > 0$, the access price is below its optimal level $\hat{a}$.

2. If $\mu > 0$, we have $a > d_2$ (see Proposition 1). This implies that the term

$$\left((\hat{p}_2^A - c_2 - a)\frac{\partial x_2(p_1, \hat{p}_2^A)}{\partial \hat{p}_2}\frac{\partial \hat{p}_2^A}{\partial p_1} - (\hat{p}_2^B - c_2 - d_2)\frac{\partial x_2(p_1, \hat{p}_2^B)}{\partial \hat{p}_2}\frac{\partial \hat{p}_2^B}{\partial p_1}\right)$$

is negative. Hence, when $\mu > 0$, the price $\bar{p}_1$ must be lower than $\hat{p}_1$. ■

Hence, in general, in order to prevent bypass, both the delivery and access prices will be adjusted downwards. The access price is reduced to increase the margin of the entrant and make access more attractive. The delivery price is lowered in order to reduce the mail volume carried by the entrant, again making bypass less attractive.

We now analyze how changes in the delivery and entry cost of the entrant affect the optimal value of the incumbent's objective.

Proposition 3: In the constrained access regime, when the costs of the entrant, F_2 and d_2, increase, the optimal value of the incumbent's objective increases. Furthermore, either the delivery or the access price of the incumbent must go up.

PROOF: The second part of the proposition is easily proved, by looking at constraint (9.1). If F_2 increases and a and p_1 both decrease, the difference between access and bypass must strictly increase – contradicting the equality of constraint (9.1). Similarly, when the delivery cost d_2 increases, one of the two optimal prices of the incumbent prices must go up. This holds true as long as (9.1) is binding. Prices will increase with the cost of the entrant up to their pre-FMO level. Once they reach that level, the constraint (9.1) is slack and we switch from the constrained access case to the access (blocked bypass) case.

For the first part of the proposition, notice that an increase in the entry or delivery costs relaxes constraint (9.1): any pair of prices $(\bar{p}_1, \bar{a})$ that was feasible under the old parameter values will remain feasible under the new values. Hence, the objective of the incumbent can never decrease, and will in fact generally increase, as the set of prices for which bypass is dominated by access will be strictly enlarged when F_2 and d_2 increase. ■

We thus conclude that the objective of the incumbent under the constrained access regime is a strictly increasing function of the delivery and entry costs of the entrant. When these values are high enough to guarantee that the entrant prefers to access the incumbent's network, blocked bypass is obtained. Furthermore, as in the classical model of barriers to entry, bypass deterrence will become more and more costly as the entry and delivery costs of the entrant go down. For low values of F_2 and d_2, the PO will prefer to accommodate bypass and let the entrant build its own delivery network.

4. INVESTMENT

In this section, we introduce the possibility for the incumbent firm to invest in a cost-reducing delivery technology before it fixes its prices. Consider that, before fixing its prices, the incumbent can undertake a costly investment that reduces its unit delivery cost d_1. Precisely, we consider that by investing an amount $\phi(e)$, the incumbent PO reduces its marginal delivery cost by an amount e. The function $\phi(e)$ is increasing and convex in e and the incumbent decides on the investment size e.

Increasing the productivity of the delivery network is a key challenge for postal operators in the perspective of FMO.[5] The recent PWC report (2006) recognizes that there is a significant potential for productivity growth in European PO and list some initiatives that can be put in place in order to increase efficiency (p. 62). Among those, the following recover the above idea of investments that reduce the variable cost of delivery: sorting automation and/or rationalization of transport and sorting networks, centralized sorting centers, walk sequencing and/or walk route optimization. The size of these investments can be considerable; For example, the Austrian Post invested €200 million in the reduction (from 39 to six) and the automation of its sorting centers.

If the competitor chooses access, the profit of the incumbent is equal to $\Pi_1^A = (p_1 - c_1 - d_1)x_1(p_1, \hat{p}_2^A) + (a - d_1)x_2(p_1, \hat{p}_2^A) - F_1 - F$ and if the competitor chooses to bypass profit is $\Pi_1^B = (p_1 - c_1 - d_1)x_1(p_1, \hat{p}_2^B) - F_1 - F$. Let $\hat{\Pi}_1^K$ be the value of the profit of firm 1 under access ($k = A$) and bypass ($k = B$) evaluated at the optimal prices. In the absence of a price cap, the investment level is determined by maximizing $\hat{\Pi}_1^K - \phi(e)$ with respect to e. In the accommodated and blocked bypass cases, the optimal value of e is found by solving $\partial(\hat{\Pi}_1^K - \phi(e))/\partial e = 0$. Taking the total derivative with respect to e and using the envelope theorem, the optimal investment level in the access and bypass cases are:

$$e^A = \phi^{-1}(x_1 + x_2) \quad \text{If the entrant chooses access}$$

$$e^B = \phi^{-1}(x_1) \quad \text{If the entrant bypasses}$$

This means that in the situations in which the incumbent accommodates bypass or access, the optimal investment size is directly linked to the volume of mail processed, including the mail of the competitors that are pre-sorted and posted at an access point. So mail volume is a key determinant of investment. The larger the volume, the higher is the profit increase for a given reduction in the per-unit delivery cost. We will refer to *direct incentives* as the investment incentives linked to the mail volume.

Given the observed price elasticities and displacement ratios in the postal sector, it is likely that the investment level would be higher when the entrant chooses the access option than when it chooses to bypass since in the latter case, the incumbent loses the volume x_2, which reduces the incentives for investment.

Next, consider the situations where, after FMO, the incumbent blocks bypass. In the constrained access region, the incumbent will manipulate its delivery and access prices to prevent bypass. This distortion will clearly affect the incentives to invest in a technology to reduce delivery cost. In fact, we now have the following. The derivative of $\Pi_1^A - \phi(e)$, evaluated at the optimal prices $(\bar{p}_1, \bar{a})$, with respect to e is written as follows:

$$\phi'(e) = x_1 + x_2 + \left(\frac{\partial \Pi_1^A}{\partial p_1} + \frac{\partial \Pi_1^A}{\partial p_2}\frac{\partial p_2}{\partial p_1}\right)\frac{\partial p_1}{\partial d_1} + \left(\frac{\partial \Pi_1^A}{\partial a} + \frac{\partial \Pi_1^A}{\partial p_2}\frac{\partial p_2}{\partial a}\right)\frac{\partial a}{\partial d_1}.$$

Given the constraint (9.1) faced by the incumbent, the derivatives

$$\left(\frac{\partial \Pi_1^A}{\partial p_1} + \frac{\partial \Pi_1^A}{\partial p_2}\frac{\partial p_2}{\partial p_1}\right)$$

and

$$\left(\frac{\partial \Pi_1^A}{\partial a} + \frac{\partial \Pi_1^A}{\partial p_2}\frac{\partial p_2}{\partial a}\right)$$

are no longer equal to zero. In fact, applying the same reasoning as above, we can easily show that these derivatives are strictly positive (see Proposition 2). Hence, there are two additional terms that increase the level of investment in the constrained access case. We will refer to these additional terms as the *strategic incentives* for investment.

In the constrained access case, there is still a direct incentive for investment, which is linked to the mail volume. But, there is in addition a strategic incentive. It captures the impact of the investment on the induced behavior of the entrant. The strategic incentives capture the impact of decreasing d_1 on the distortions in prices that the incumbent applies to deter bypass.

To understand this, notice that in order to prevent bypass, the incumbent reduces its access price a. If the incumbent reduces its delivery cost d_1, then the optimal pre-FMO access price also decreases. Hence, investing in the delivery network reduces the optimal access price and thus constitutes an alternative way to prevent bypass.[6] The incumbent also changes its letter price in the constrained access region. We know that a lower delivery cost implies a lower delivery price p_1. Hence, as it is optimal to reduce delivery price to deter bypass, investing in a delivery network makes the letter price reduction less costly. It therefore fosters the investment incentives.

On the other hand, if the incumbent chooses to accommodate bypass, incentives to invest decline sharply, because the incumbent now only faces a direct effect on its own mail volume, x_1. Hence, we expect to observe an abrupt, discontinuous, decrease in the level of investment when the entry and delivery costs of the entrant are so low as to prevent the incumbent from deterring bypass. But this also shows that the incumbent can use investments in productivity gains in order to affect the delivery regimes. When delivery costs d_1 go down, the incumbent's incentives to maintain access and prevent bypass increase, so that the incumbent may have an extra incentive to invest, in order to switch from a regime of accommodated bypass to a regime of constrained access.

If a price cap is imposed on the incumbent PO, the investment will depend on the same components: the strategic and the direct incentives. However, the investment level will not be the same, since the mail volume is changed when a price cap is imposed. In general, a quantitative analysis of the investment levels for a welfare-maximizing (or price-cap constrained) firm requires a detailed analysis of the demand functions. This is beyond the scope of this chapter.

Up to now, we only considered investments that reduce the marginal cost of delivery. Investments that aim at reducing the fixed cost of delivery and/or the financial burden of the USO would also prove useful to deter bypass. Decreasing the scope of the USO and the associated cost would do the same.[7] If the incumbent reduces its fixed costs, it can charge a lower mark-up over its costs to break even. Hence, these types of investment contribute to reduce the price p_1 and a, and therefore they are also useful to prevent inefficient bypass.

5. CONCLUDING REMARKS

In this chapter, we have shown that the incumbent PO may strategically deter bypass by modifying its price structure. By changing the access price, it manages to influence the cost of the entrant and by changing its letter price, it manages to modify the mail volume carried by the entrant. And both the mail volume and the cost determine the decision to bypass or not. We also consider the possibility for the incumbent of engaging in a costly restructuring of its delivery activity. We identify the incentives to undertake such an investment and we show that they are directly related to the mail volume distributed by the incumbent. Hence, it is when the entrant remains a monopolist in the delivery activity that the direct incentives are the strongest.

There is also a strategic motive for investment. In regions of the parameters for which the incumbent optimally deters bypass, a reduction of the delivery cost reduces the price distortion between the optimal price of the incumbent and its actual price. Hence, investing *ex ante* in a cost-reducing investment makes it cheaper for the incumbent to deter bypass. This suggests that the incentives to invest in cost-reducing technologies may not be highest when the incumbent and the entrant are engaged in facility-based competition (accommodated bypass), but when the incumbent strategically distorts its delivery and access prices in order to deter bypass (deterred bypass). Hence, POs may be compelled to invest massively in cost-reducing technologies before FMO, in order to induce their competitors to choose access over bypass. In order to better understand the strategic effects of cost-reducing investments, it would be necessary to study in detail the actual patterns of investment by postal operators in Europe in anticipation of the full opening of the postal market.

NOTES

1. In Bloch and Gautier (2007), the entrant is competitive and chooses the cheapest option for mail delivery. Therefore the letter price does not influence the delivery decision and the only possible way to deter bypass is to make access less costly than bypass; that is, to reduce the access price.
2. Other models of the mail sector typically assume that the entrant behaves as a competitive fringe and sets its price at marginal cost. This assumption of competitive fringe seems extreme. We consider here another extreme assumption – von Stackelberg leadership – where the entrant chooses its follower price in order to maximize profits. The reality of competition between the PO and the entrant lies probably somewhere between these two extreme assumptions.
3. We will assume that the second-order conditions hold for all maximization problems, namely that the entrant's profit, Π_2, is concave in p_2 and the incumbent's objective, Z^A, is concave in a and p_1.
4. In Bloch and Gautier (2007), we assumed F_2 to be zero. In this case, the entrant can choose between two constant returns to scale technologies for mail delivery. Clearly, it chooses the cheapest one: access for $d_2 \geq a$ and bypass otherwise.
5. Increasing the productivity of the incumbent PO is a way to finance (at least partially) the USO in a competitive postal market. Cremer et al. (2002) is an early model showing the relationship between productivity improvements and the ability of the incumbent to meet its universal service obligations after FMO.
6. Preventing bypass by changing the price requires that the incumbent PO is able to commit on its price. There is no problem of this kind for the investment.
7. Crew and Kleindorfer (2006) show that reducing the scope of the USO (reducing counter density) is optimal under FMO for a regulator that wants to avoid subsidies.

REFERENCES

Billette de Villemeur, Etienne, Helmut Cremer, Bernard Roy and Joëlle Toledano (2003), 'Optimal pricing and price-cap regulation in the postal sector', *Journal of Regulatory Economics*, **24**(1), 49–62.

Billette de Villemeur, Etienne, Helmut Cremer, Bernard Roy and Joëlle Toledano (2007), 'Worksharing, access and bypass: the structure of prices in the postal sector', *Journal of Regulatory Economics*, **32**(1), 67–85.

Bloch, Francis and Axel Gautier (2007), 'Access pricing and entry in the postal sector', *Review of Network Economics*, forthcoming.

Cremer, Helmut, Philippe De Donder and Frank Rodriguez (2002), 'Funding the USO under liberalisation: an analysis of the postal market', in Michael A. Crew and Paul R. Kleindorfer (eds), *Postal and Delivery Services: Pricing, Productivity, Regulation and Strategy*, Boston, MA: Kluwer Academic Publishers, pp. 31–53.

Crew, Michael A. and Paul R. Kleindorfer (eds) (1992), *The Economics of Postal Services*, Boston, MA: Kluwer Academic Publishers.

Crew, Michael A. and Paul R. Kleindorfer (2005), 'Competition, universal service and the graveyard spiral', in Michael A. Crew and Paul R. Kleindorfer (eds), *Regulatory and Economics Changes in the Postal and Delivery Sector*, Boston, MA: Kluwer Academic Publishers, pp. 1–30.

Crew, Michael A. and Paul R. Kleindorfer (2006), 'Approaches to USO under entry', in Michael A. Crew and Paul R. Kleindorfer (eds), *Liberalization of the Postal and Delivery Sector*, Cheltenham, UK and Northampton MA, USA: Edward Elgar, pp. 1–18.

De Donder, Philippe (2006), 'Access pricing in the postal sector: theory and simulations', *Review of Industrial Organization*, **28**(3), 307–26.

Fundenberg, Drew and Jean Tirole (1984), 'The fat-cat effect, the puppy-dog ploy and the lean and hungry look', *American Economic Review*, **74**(2), 361–6.

Laffont, Jean-Jacques and Jean Tirole (1994), 'Access pricing and competition', *European Economic Review*, **38**(9), 1673–710.

Pricewaterhouse Coopers (2006), 'The impact on universal service of the full market accomplishment of the Postal Internal Market in 2009', Report to the European Commission.

Tirole, Jean (1988), *The Theory of Industrial Organization*, Cambridge, MA and London: The MIT Press.

10. Pricing in competitive two-sided mail markets*

Christian Jaag and Urs Trinkner

1. INTRODUCTION

Postal letters are a means of communication between two parties with at least one of them having a positive willingness to pay. Postal operators offer a service that exploits this willingness to pay. Interestingly, virtually all postal operators apply a pre-paid mechanism that goes back on Rowland Hill's proposal of charging only the sender-side of the market instead of the receivers too. This involves the potential for senders to bill the postage onward to the receivers, which varies between the various classes of mail and is essentially determined by the bargaining position between the two communicating parties. Postage for advertising mail remains on the sender side, while postage in commercial relationships is usually – directly or indirectly – passed on to the receivers. For example, Swiss banks increasingly bill postage for bank statements directly to their clients (i.e., the receivers).[1]

The fact that mail consists of two parties communicating with each other over a choice of platforms (postal operators) makes the postal market potentially two-sided. If this two-sided market is served by only one operator (the current situation in most countries), the designated postal operator has the necessary bargaining power to choose the pricing mechanism of its choice (sender pays, receiver pays, or a mix between the two). In a second step, senders and receivers are able to reallocate postage by various means, such as billing surcharges as in the case of bank statements mentioned above. In competitive markets, two effects could potentially lead to different optimal pricing principles: (a) the historical operator loses its market power on the sender side because of competing networks, and (b) receivers get bargaining power in terms of whom to give the right to operate their P.O. box. The latter effect could in principle yield a situation where large receivers prefer P.O. boxes over mail boxes as the former gives them the possibility to exact better service or pricing arrangements, based on their size, and to allow access to their address exclusively to a specific operator.

In our contribution, we analyze whether the traditional pricing concept (the sender pays principle) remains dominant in competitive postal markets. We divide the competitive postal market into a processing and delivery part, where a postal operator faces two kinds of customers: senders in the former and receivers in the latter part of the market. Based on the contributions by Laffont et al. (1998), Rochet and Tirole (2003), Armstrong (2006), and Panzar (2006), we develop a theoretical model with consumers' platform choice between two operators competing in linear upstream and two-part downstream prices and being interconnected by a symmetric access regime to P.O. boxes. Thereby, we extend the analysis of a delivery flat rate by Felisberto et al. (2006) and Friedli et al. (2006) to a competitive environment and assess optimum pricing schemes in market equilibrium.

The chapter is structured as follows. Section 2 discusses the background on the theory of two-sided markets and its relevance for postal markets. Section 3 presents the model outline. Section 4 provides a rough calibration of the model and presents the derived optimal pricing structure for the two-sided P.O. box market. We conclude in Section 5.

2. BACKGROUND ON TWO-SIDED MARKETS

In two-sided markets, platforms enable the interaction of two or more groups of agents, where the surplus of one group of agents depends on the number of users connected to the platform on the other side (Armstrong, 2006). Real-world examples of such two-sided markets with multiple platforms include many internet applications, the credit card industry, radio or television broadcasting, peer-to-peer networks, computer operating systems, or telecommunication networks. A precise *definition of a two-sided market* is given by Rochet and Tirole (2005) and depends mainly on its pricing properties:

> Consider a platform charging per-interaction charges α_B and α_S to the buyer and the seller sides. The Market for interactions between the two sides is one-sided if the volume V of transactions realized on the platform depends only on the aggregate price level $\alpha = \alpha_B + \alpha_S$, i.e. is insensitive to reallocations of this price between the buyer and the seller. If by contrast V varies with α_B while α is kept constant, the market is said to be two-sided.

Hence, postal services would not satisfy the definition of two-sided markets, if mail demand remained the same in case postage was charged to receivers instead of senders.

Two-sided markets are linked closely to *network externalities*.[2] Rochet and Tirole (2003) note, 'many if not most markets with network externalities are two-sided'. Armstrong (2006) even includes (cross-) network externalities in his definition of two-sided markets: the number of subscribers of one group increases the surplus of the other one. Consequently, for virtually any (two-sided) platform, attaining the critical mass on both sides of the market is the core of the business with pricing being one of the most crucial success factors to overcome the chicken-and-egg problem involved when setting up a new platform. From this point of view, two-sided markets can be seen as the subset of markets with network externalities, where the allocation of prices among the various groups of agents affects the degree of exploitation of those externalities. This, in turn, is the case if the platforms pricing policy cannot be offset by private redistribution between the various groups of agents. In postal markets, for example, where postage predominantly is prepaid by the senders, often receivers finally pay the postage, as senders bill it onwards (e.g., distance selling). Hence, it is not *a priori* clear if the postal market is two-sided.

2.1 Pricing Structures in Two-sided Markets

In two-sided markets, we often observe pricing structures in which one side (one group of agents) heavily cross-subsidizes the other side of the market. Internet search engines provide their core business (searching the Internet) free, radio and TV channels are

Table 10.1 Overview of pricing structures in two-sided markets

	Credit card	Search engine	Electronic document viewing	Mobile	Direct mail
Side 1: Originator	Payer (buyer)	Searcher	Reader	Caller	Sender (advertiser)
Pricing	*Small or zero* subscriber fee, *fringes* with use	*Free*	*Free* (zero license charge for Adobe Reader)	Per minute, subscriber fee	Per-piece charge
Platform (Examples)	American Express, Visa, MasterCard	Google, Yahoo!	Adobe Writer and Reader	Mobile networks	Postal operators
Side 2: Enabler	Payee (seller)	Content provider / advertiser	Content providers	Receiver	Receiver
Pricing	Subscriber fee, % of transaction amount	Price per hit	Licensing costs	Mostly *free*, subscriber fee	*Free*

free of charge, and credit card holders even get fringe benefits for the frequent use of their card. Table 10.1 provides an overview of pricing structures in selected two-sided industries.

At a first glance, the cross-subsidization is astonishing, as both sides in each of those markets derive a positive utility of the platform and thus in principle would have a positive willingness to pay. Yet, those pricing policies persist even in mature markets, and it appears dominant in competitive two-sided markets not to exploit the willingness to pay on one side of the market.

In general, cross-subsidization aims at establishing a consumer base that as a whole can be made available to a group of individual commercial agents aiming to sell products to this consumer base. Thus, most two-sided markets are in effect intermediaries that derive their economic value by reducing transaction costs or information asymmetries (mostly between sellers and potential buyers). To get the critical mass and resolving the typical chicken-and-egg problem, the dominant strategy appears to heavily cross-subsidize one group of agents either directly (low, zero, or even negative price) or indirectly through tying a valuable product (free Internet query, free radio broadcasting) with a product establishing negative network externalities (advertisement).

Very close to the latter interpretation and related to the formal resolution of two-sided market models, two-sided markets can be seen as ordinary markets with the product being the provision of a client base that exhibits acquiring expenses equaling the loss on a second product offered to that client base. Thereby, acquiring takes place indirectly by offering a valuable, subsidized service (free Internet query). In most of the cases, this valuable product inhibits substantial economies of scale (and only indirect network externalities over the other side of the market) which in turn reduce acquiring cost per client, whereas the marginal indirect revenue remains constant. Consequently, two-sided markets are heavily concentrated.

2.2 The Two-sidedness of the Postal Market

We now turn to the important question whether postal markets are two-sided markets according to the definition of Rochet and Tirole (2005) cited above. Today, in most postal markets it is secured that any address is connected to the postal network by means of the 'Universal Service Obligation' that obliges at least one postal network to provide 'universal access' for universal services such as letters and parcels and to deliver that service to any address throughout the country. Thus, by regulation, network externalities are secured. Additionally, universal providers are – for example, in Switzerland – by law not allowed to charge the receivers for connecting them to the network. Even New Zealand, where the postal market is fully liberalized for a decade and Universal Service was reduced to its basics, forbids in its 'deed of understanding' with New Zealand Post a 'rural delivery fee' aimed at residents in remote areas. Those universal service definitions indicate that senders exhibit a positive network externality if everybody is connected to the postal network.

However, it is not yet clear whether total demand is affected by a change in the pricing structure; for example, if postage was to be paid by receivers too, as was the case before the reform of Rowland Hill. History on the reform of Rowland Hill reveals that demand virtually exploded after the change in the price structure towards 'sender pays it all'. Thus, we have a first indication of the two-sidedness of the postal market.

Research by Felisberto et al. (2006) on the receiver pays principle in the postal sector analyzes the effects of the introduction of a delivery flat rate, where receivers are given the choice between free P.O. box delivery and costly last mile doorstep delivery (in the form of a yearly flat rate).[3] This would enable a monopolistic platform to reduce senders' tariffs. By exclusion of a rebalancing between the two groups of agents behind the scenes and by assumption that P.O. box switchers originate the same amount of mail as before, positive demand effects were found.

More recent research by Friedli et al. (2006) on the delivery flat rate indicates that up to 35 percent of the customers switching to P.O. box delivery would no longer empty their mailboxes. This would cause a significant drop in mail volumes. This survey points towards the presence of two-sidedness in the postal market.

A similar argument is the following. If the receiver was about to pay, the sender has no guarantee that the receiver has accepted the mail (for example, paying postage for accepting unwanted direct mailings). Receivers would most probably reject unwanted mail, which in turn postal operators would send back to the senders by charging them accordingly. This would reduce response rates clearly and reduce the amount of direct mail sent, as observed in Chile.

A contrary argument might be that most senders of transactional mail bill their postage onwards to the receivers. Thereby, single-piece tariffs instead of (lower) business customer tariffs are charged. Thus, receivers' perceived cost might reduce if postal operators were to bill the postage directly to them (a positive demand effect).

We conclude that there exists substantial evidence that postal markets indeed are two-sided. This was first recognized by Panzar (2006). Our main contribution to the literature is the formalization of a competitive two-sided postal market, which we calibrate to yield robust results on optimal pricing strategies.

3. THE TWO-SIDED POSTAL MARKET MODEL

Our two-sided postal market model consists of two groups of agents, namely senders and receivers of mail, and two platforms (postal operators) linking the senders and the receivers. Senders choose over whom to hand over their mail to, whereas receivers have the possibility to grant special delivery rights to one of the two operators.[4] The assumption of special rights involves the necessity of interconnection of the two operators; in order to offer end-to-end service to her sender, a postal operator needs access to the other's delivery network. Otherwise, one operator would not be able to reach P.O. box addresses operated by the other one. We are primarily interested in how different interconnection rates affect the platforms' pricing strategies, thus we treat access prices as exogenous and provide sensitivity analysis in Section 4. For simplicity reasons, we assume reciprocal access pricing.

Thus, there are two sides in the postal market: upstream, postal operators compete for sending customers; downstream, they compete for receiving customers. We follow Laffont et al. (1998) in the modeling of network competition and link the postal upstream market on the sender's side to a downstream market for local delivery monopolies.

In our model, total mail demand is a function of the sum of the sender's price p_u and the receiver's price p_d per item. Total volume is determined by the sender primarily, but we assume that through private redistribution (as observed in practice) the receiver influences the sender's communication channel and vice versa. We include the possibility that the operators' optimal behavior leads to an interdependence of these prices and a delivery flat rate, such that total volume is sensitive to reallocations of the total price. Hence, the model qualifies as a two-sided market (with multihoming). Figure 10.1 provides a graphical representation of the model outline.

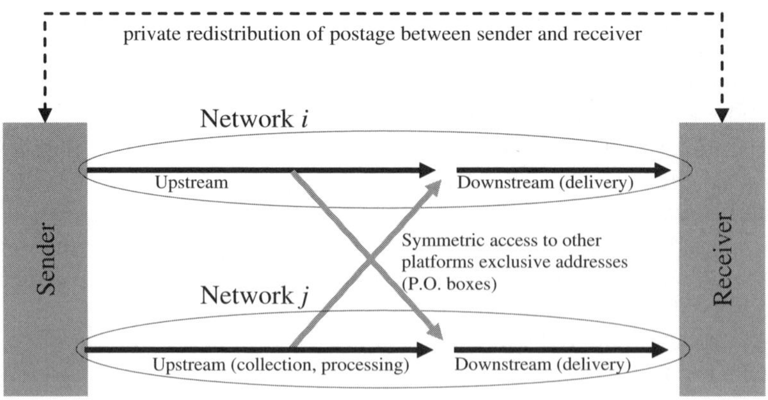

Figure 10.1 Model outline

As opposed to, for example, the telecommunications market, the two user bases (senders, receivers) are not necessarily linked together: a subscriber for delivery services with one operator does not predetermine the operator choice when sending a letter (P.O. box holders can still send the mail with other carriers). However, downstream market share affects both cost structure and downstream income, which determines competitive behavior upstream.

In both parts of the market, consumers can chose between two competing networks i and j, which are differentiated *à la* Hotelling. Given income y, constant utility v from subscription to the network, and mail consumption q, a consumer (sender/receiver) located at x and joining network i has utility

$$U = y + v - t_m|x - x_i| + u(q).$$

We assume that consumers are uniformly distributed over the interval [0,1] and the two networks are located at the extremes. t_m is a market-specific parameter for the substitutability of the two competing networks and determines the degree of disutility a sender perceives from the network offering services that do not exactly meet the sender's preference x. Thus, a consumer located at $x = 0.5$ is just about equally dissatisfied by the two operators i and j located at $x_i = 0$ and $x_j = 1$ and finds herself indifferent. Following Laffont, et al. (1998), we define quantity-dependent sender utility $u_u(q)$ by

$$u_u(q) = \beta^{\frac{1}{\eta}} \frac{q^{1-\frac{1}{\eta}}}{1 - \frac{1}{\eta}}.$$

We allow for *redistribution* of tariffs between senders and receivers by specifying the total quantity as a function both of the senders price p_u *and* the receivers price p_d. If, for example, a bank client orders the monthly bank statement knowing that the postage will be charged on her bank account, receivers generate the mail, and the sender's price still affects mail volumes although they do not actually pay for it. Similarly, if the client were charged a reception fee, this would again affect the sender's demand. Hence, the sender's utility maximization yields the total demand:

$$q = \beta \cdot (p_{u,i} + \zeta p_{d,i})^{-\eta}$$

with constant price elasticity of demand $-\eta$. ζ reflects to what *degree* customers can redistribute postage by means of private negotiation and hence, to what degree senders take into account the receiver's price. With ζ close to zero, senders' demand is independent of the receiver's price (resulting from the lack of negotiation between senders and receivers). $\zeta = 1$ yields a situation where the mail originating party maximizes over the aggregate *variable* price level, irrespective of the tariff structure. However, the market still qualifies the two-sided markets property as long as the fixed downstream reception fee P_d is nonzero (referred to in the literature as 'delivery flat rate'). For $P_d = 0$ and $\zeta = 1$, senders and receivers would be able to redistribute (pass through) charges behind the scene completely to the very same level irrespective of the operators' pricing strategies.

The total cost for end-to-end postal service consists of a fixed part f_m in both the upstream ($m = u$) and downstream markets ($m = d$) and quantity-dependent variable cost c_m:

$$C = f_u + f_d + q \cdot (c_u + c_d).$$

The operators' profit functions are then given by

$$\pi_i = \max_{p_{u,i}, p_{d,i}, P_{d,i}} \left\{ \begin{array}{l} \alpha_{u,i}\alpha_{d,i}[(p_{u,i} + p_{d,i} - c_{u,i} - c_{d,i})q(p_{u,i} + \zeta p_{d,i}) - f_u - f_d + P_{d,i}] \\ + \alpha_{u,i}(1 - \alpha_{d,i})[(p_{u,i} - a - c_{u,i})q(p_{u,i} + \zeta p_{d,j}) - f_u] \\ + (1 - \alpha_{u,j})\alpha_{d,i}[(p_{d,i} + a - c_{d,i})q(p_{u,j} + \zeta p_{d,i}) - f_d + P_{d,i}] \end{array} \right\}, \quad (10.1)$$

where $\alpha_{m,i}$ is the market share of operator i in market m. Hence, a postal operator's profit consists of three parts. The first part is due to letters she processes end-to-end. The second and the third ones relate to mails that originate in the own network and that are delivered through the other operator's network, and vice versa.

To solve the model, we derive the competitive outcome in the two sides of the postal market consecutively. Thereby, the model is solved backwards in order to find subgame perfect equilibrium. In a first step, we analyze upstream competition in nondiscriminatory linear tariffs, where the two networks compete for senders and yield optimal prices and market share in the upstream market as a function of equilibrium downstream prices and market shares. In a second step, we derive optimal two-part pricing structures[5] of the downstream market; that is, competition for P.O. box subscribers.

We focus on parameter constellations, in which there exist unique and symmetric equilibria in both the upstream and downstream markets (cf., Laffont et al., 1998, propositions 1 and 7).

3.1 Upstream Competition in Nondiscriminatory Linear Tariffs

We start our analysis with upstream competition, where postal operators compete for quantity. At that stage, downstream prices p_d^*, P_d^* and market shares α_d^* are given from downstream competition and are symmetric. Under the assumption of uniform and nondiscriminatory pricing (i.e., the postal operator is not able to discriminate mail by destination), the sender's net surplus in the upstream market is

$$v_u(p_u, p_d^*) = \max_{q_u} \left\{ u_u(q) - (p_u + \zeta p_d^*)q \right\} = \beta \frac{(p_u + \zeta p_d^*)^{-(\eta - 1)}}{\eta - 1}.$$

Operator i's market share is therefore

$$\alpha_{u,i} = \alpha_{u,i}(p_{u,i}, p_{u,j}) \equiv \frac{1}{2} + \sigma_u[v_u(p_{u,i}, p_d^*) - v_u(p_{u,j}, p_d^*)],$$

where $\sigma_u \equiv 1/2t_u$ is an index of substitutability resulting from the differentiated location of the senders and the operators.

In symmetric equilibrium, we have $\alpha_{d,i}^* = \alpha_{u,i}^* = 0.5$, $p_{u,i}^* = p_{u,j}^* = p_u^*$, and $p_{d,i}^* = p_{d,j}^* = p_d^*$. The first-order condition of (10.1) with respect to p_u is

$$\frac{1}{4}[(p_u+p_d^*-c_u-c_d)q'+q]+\frac{1}{2}\frac{\partial\alpha_{u,i}}{\partial p_u}[(p_u+p_d^*-c_u-c_d)q(p_u,p_d^*)-f_u-f_d+P_{d,i}^*]$$

$$+\frac{1}{4}[(p_u-a-c_u)q'+q]+\frac{1}{2}\frac{\partial\alpha_{u,i}}{\partial p_u}[(p_u-a-c_u)q(p_u,p_d^*)-f_u]$$

$$+\frac{1}{4}[(p_d^*+a-c_d)q'+q]-\frac{1}{2}\frac{\partial\alpha_{u,i}}{\partial p_u}[(p_d^*+a-c_d)q(p_u,p_d^*)-f_u]=0.$$

Note that a unit increase in price lowers market share by σ_u times quantity per customer: $\partial\alpha_{u,i}/\partial p_{u,i}=-\sigma_u q$ and a unit loss of market share leads to the loss of the per-customer profit. In analogy to equation (8) in Laffont et al. (1998), the first-order condition can be rewritten as

$$\frac{p_u^*-\kappa}{p_u^*}=\frac{1}{\eta}[1-2\sigma_u\pi(p_u^*,p_d^*,P_d^*)],$$

where $\kappa=c_u+\frac{a+c_d-p_d^*}{2}$ is perceived direct marginal cost and

$$\pi(p_u,p_d,P_d)=\frac{1}{2}[(p_u+p_d-c_u-c_d)q(p_u,p_d)-f_u-f_d+P_d]$$

is the per-customer profit when the two networks charge identical prices.

3.2 Downstream Competition in Two-part Tariffs

In upstream competition, downstream prices p_d^*, P_d^* and market shares α_d^* have been taken as given. They are determined in downstream competition, where postal operators compete for market share. Again, differentiation is *à la* Hotelling. Thereby, operators can build local monopolies, which strengthen their market power upstream. Receiver net surplus from chosen network i is

$$w_{d,i}=v_{d,0}+v_d(p_{d,i})-P_{d,i}.$$

Receiver surplus net of per-piece price $p_{d,i}$ is, by analogy to the above, denoted by v_d. We introduce the term $v_{d,0}$ to assure that $w_{d,i}>0$; that is, that every receiver is interested in joining one of the two delivery networks. Since a fraction ζ of this price is passed on to senders, we have

$$v_d(p_{d,i})=u_d(q)-(1-\zeta)p_{d,i}q,$$

such that operator i's market share is

$$\alpha_{d,i}\equiv\frac{1}{2}+\sigma_d[w_{d,i}-w_{d,j}]\quad\text{with } \sigma_d\equiv\frac{1}{2t_d}.$$

The model allows for any functional form of $u_d(q)$. For simplicity, we choose it such that

$$v_d'(p_{d,i})=-q.$$

Then, the first-order condition to (10.1) with respect to $p_{d,i}$ yields

$$p_{d,i} = c_{d,i} - (1 - \alpha_{u,i})a - \alpha_{u,i}(p_{u,i} - c_{u,i})$$

or, in a symmetric equilibrium,

$$p_{d,i} = c_{d,i} - \frac{1}{2}a - \frac{1}{2}(p_{u,i} - c_{u,i}).$$

Hence, the networks' optimal downstream usage fee equals perceived marginal cost. Downstream market share is unaffected by it. However, the symmetric equilibrium subscriber fee determines the size of the downstream user base. It is given by

$$P_{d,i} = -\frac{d\pi_i}{d\alpha_{d,i}} + \frac{1}{2\sigma_d}$$

and therefore equal to the net marginal cost of adding a subscriber to the downstream network plus the Hotelling markup.

Each unit loss of downstream market share implies a profit loss of

$$\frac{d\pi_i}{d\alpha_{d,i}} = (p_d - c_d)q(p_u, p_d) - f_d + P_d,$$

which is the per-customer downstream profit when the two networks charge identical prices.

4. SIMULATION RESULTS AND DISCUSSION

Our main goal is to derive optimal pricing structures in liberalized postal markets, where potentially all involved parties (senders, receivers, and operators) can exert their bargaining power. Senders have the choice over competing operators; receivers can exclusively attribute a postal operator as their delivery partner of choice; and operators can establish a consumer base on one side of the market and sell it to the other one.

A calibration of the model enables us to compute numerically the operators' optimal pricing strategies as a function of the reciprocal interconnection rate. We calibrate the model to correspond roughly to the size and the characteristics of the Swiss letter market. The number of receivers is equal to 4 million households and businesses. The current volume of addressed letters is 2.8 billion at an average price of CHF0.75 with price elasticity $\eta = 0.27$.[6] Utility parameter β is calibrated to 650 to represent the Swiss letter market with approximately 700 letters per year and receiver. Total cost is CHF2 billion.[7] With roughly 50 percent delivery cost, of which 50 percent is fixed and a fraction of fixed cost of 30 percent in collection and processing, we calibrate f_u, c_u, f_d, and c_d accordingly. Moreover, we set $\sigma_u = \sigma_d = 0.2$.

The following observations and results apply for the calibration as above. Other calibrations might yield different optimal pricing strategies. Note that Switzerland exhibits a very high postal scale.[8] Moreover, given the rough calibration and the stylized model, the results are only indicative.

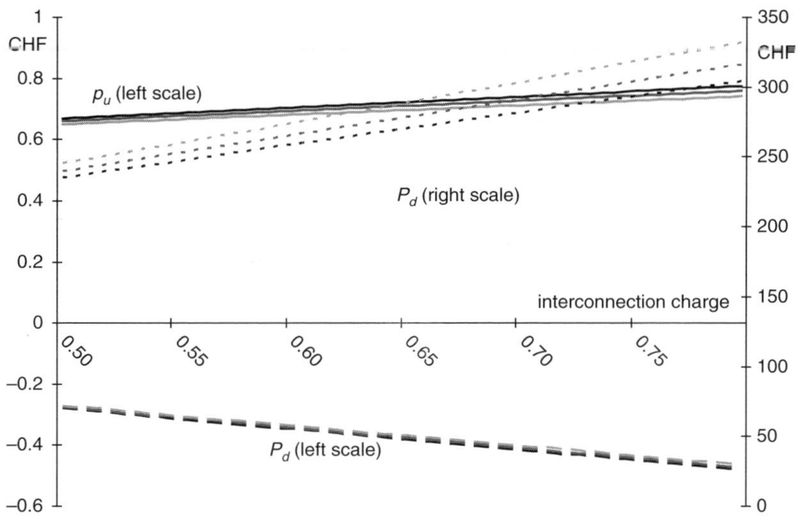

Figure 10.2 Optimal pricing structure depending on interconnection rate

Figure 10.2 displays the optimal pricing strategies depending on the exogenously set access price. We ran simulations with various values of ζ. Black lines are computed with $\zeta = 0.25$, dark gray lines with $\zeta = 0.5$ and light gray lines with $\zeta = 0.75$.

Observation 1 – optimal pricing structure: The results partly replicate the pricing structure as observed in the completely liberalized postal market of New Zealand, where market participants agreed on symmetric access prices to P.O. boxes. Given a similar regulatory regime, as set out in the model, we find an optimal pricing strategy in two-sided postal markets as follows. If the interconnection rate is about CHF0.6, charge your key receivers a yearly delivery flat rate between CHF250 and CHF300. In turn, for every mail piece you deliver now exclusively, you *pay* (not charge!) your client (the receiver) about CHF0.3 per mail piece (i.e., p_d is negative). On the sender side, you charge about CHF0.7 per piece. In such a setting, given upstream and downstream variable costs and before considering fixed costs, net profits on end-to-end services are about break even, whereas upstream services incur a loss ($p_u - a < c_u$) and downstream products are profitable ($a + p_d > c_d$).

The results indicate that competition in two-sided postal markets forces operators to strongly cross-subsidize large receivers.

Figures 10.3 and 10.4 show the effect of an increase of the interconnection rate on operators' profit per customer and mail volumes.

Observation 2 – effect of interconnection charge: Increasing interconnection rates make the downstream business more attractive (higher earnings for downstream operators) and result in fiercer downstream competition. This forces the operators to give their subscribers higher per piece incentives (more negative p_d), which are funded by higher stamp prices. In part, operators can recover higher incentives by higher subscriber fees too. Note that the receivers' incentives grow faster than the stamp price due to the increased

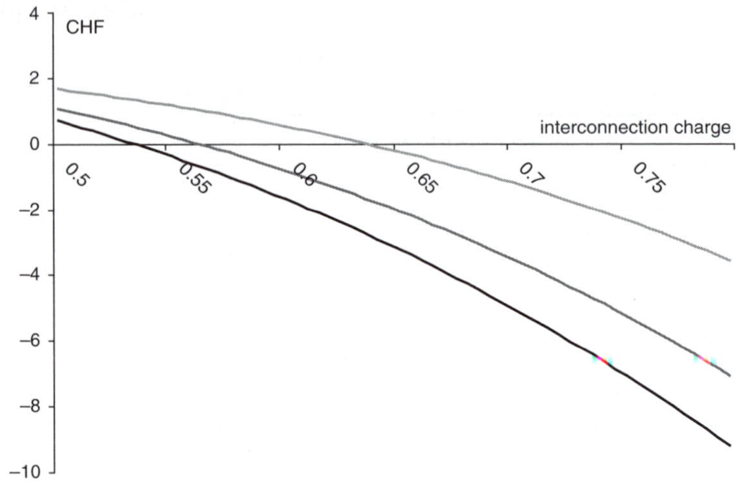

Figure 10.3 *Postal operator profit per customer*

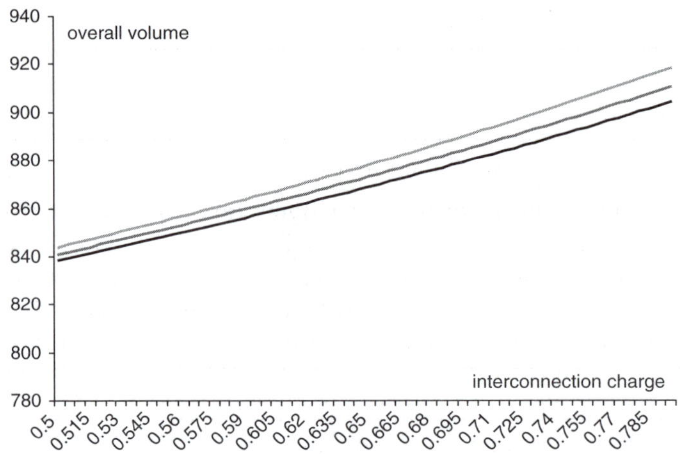

Figure 10.4 *Mail volumes*

relative importance of downstream market shares (which are the basis for downstream profits). Interestingly, the receivers' average price ($p_d + P_d/q$) becomes negative for high interconnection rates; that is, they become increasingly subsidized and make a profit by being connected to the postal network.[9] Importantly, this redistribution comes at the cost of the networks, not at the cost of the senders, as the latter benefit from the receivers' better bargaining position by means of private rebalancing, which yields a lower price level $p_u + p_d$ and thus higher mail volumes q.

Thus, if we can exclude tacit collusion, high interconnection rates make the industry unattractive, as receivers enjoy increased bargaining power by means of regulation.

Observation 3 – effect of private redistribution: A higher value of ζ enables senders and receivers better to offset pricing structures by means of private redistribution. Recapitulate that at the extreme ($\zeta = 1$) complete pass-through of per piece prices takes place such that mail volumes $q(p)$ depend just on the sum of the two variable prices $p = p_u + p_d$. Hence, the mail-originating side includes total marginal postage in its calculations.

Since the downstream price p_d is negative, such redistribution leads to a participation of senders in downstream incentives, which decreases their perceived costs and thereby increases volumes (cf., Figure 10.4) and profits (cf., Figure 10.3). Put differently, if receivers are able to exert their market power not only towards the operators, but also towards the senders (a lower value of ζ), we can expect negative demand effects and a significant drop of industry profits.

5. SUMMARY AND CONCLUSIONS

Practical evidence from postal markets suggests that mail markets are two-sided. Hence, postal operators are platforms that enable communication and transactions between two parties – senders/mailers on one side, and receivers/recipients on the other. This two-sidedness raises two main issues, network effects and pricing.

Network effects are present in most two-sided markets, and probably in postal markets too. Thus, we can expect the value of a postal network to increase the more customers are connected to it. We presume that the notion of ubiquitous access and delivery, which lies at the core of the Universal Service Obligation, is to be seen in this context. We do not include network effects directly in our model (although indirect network effects between the upstream and downstream market are present), as we are primarily interested in the pricing implications of the two-sidedness of the postal market.

In terms of pricing, the two-sidedness makes things more complicated. Standard results of economic theory (related to one-sided markets) might fail in two-sided markets. Wright (2004) spells out 'eight fallacies that arise from using one-sided logic in two-sided markets' and concludes that 'the results may be very different from the normal marginal cost pricing familiar in one-sided markets'. In our model, the interconnection of the two sides (upstream and downstream) of the mail market yields interesting pricing considerations, which are a challenge for pricing departments as well as for regulators and competition authorities. In posts, recipients traditionally have been served by monopoly platforms that charged the senders and served receivers free of charge. This still holds true in virtually any industrialized country. For example, Swiss recipients get home delivery and P.O. boxes free of charge, the latter having the advantage of early morning delivery.

How do things change in liberalized two-sided mail markets? Will receivers remain subsidized? Our results indicate that in liberalized markets, key receivers will likely be subsidized even more. Depending on P.O. box regulations, the optimal strategy of postal operators towards receivers will be to offer them a costly P.O. box while paying them money for every mail piece delivered to this P.O. box. Thereby, large receivers will succeed in capitalizing on their address. Such pricing would have harmful effects on overall mail volumes unless senders participate accordingly (which is unlikely for the case of direct mail). We conclude that it is quite risky for postal operators to introduce receivers' pricing or incentives. This result may not hold for value-added services. The results raise the more general question of who should pay for postal services from a welfare point of view. Jaag (2007b) proposes a model and framework to address such issues.

The current common regulatory view states that P.O. boxes are monopolistic bottlenecks with a consequent need for regulation. This is somewhat astonishing, as there are no sunk costs related to P.O. box provision.[10] Our two-sided model suggests that we can expect competition for P.O. boxes, as observed in New Zealand, and that operators have a common interest for low access prices. Hence, in terms of P.O. box regulations, our results contradict the common view. We leave it for further research to assess whether this holds also true for models with asymmetric equilibria. However, as Panzar (2006) points out, the two-sidedness of the postal market makes access regulation to P.O. boxes a rather complex task and cost-based pricing rules rather inappropriate.

NOTES

* The views expressed are those of the authors and do not necessarily reflect the opinion of the institutions they are affiliated with.

1. Often, the official single-piece tariff is billed instead of the reduced business rates.
2. Network externalities arise if the utility that a given user derives from joining a network depends upon the number of other users who are in the same network. *Positive* network externalities are present if a customers' utility of a good or service is an increasing function of the number of other users.
3. Jaag (2007) discusses the welfare effects associated with the consumers' choice between costly doorstep delivery and free delivery to a P.O. box.
4. In most countries, receivers have the choice between a free doorstep delivery and (sometimes costly) P.O. box. It is important to note that as soon as a P.O. box is chosen, the P.O. box operator obtains the exclusive rights for final delivery into the P.O. box. In this view, the assumption could reflect the subset of mail destined to P.O. boxes, or a regulation where every household appoints the operator of her choice as its exclusive delivery carrier.
5. That is, the pricing for P.O. boxes consists of a fixed and a variable part, where both parts, can be positive (receiver pays), negative (receiver obtains), or zero (no money flow in either direction).
6. For a discussion of demand parameters, see Trinkner and Grossmann (2006).
7. For a discussion of the cost structure of the Swiss mail market, see Dietl et al. (2005) and Jaag (2007a).
8. See also PWC (2006).
9. Recipients are therefore interested in joining a network that relaxes the previously introduced assumption of a value of $v_{d,0}$ such that $w_{d,i} > 0$.
10. Note that considerable sunk costs are a precondition for the presence of monopolistic bottlenecks.

REFERENCES

Armstrong, Mark (2006), 'Competition in two-sided markets', *RAND Journal of Economics*, **37**(3), 668–91.

Dietl, Helmut M., Urs Trinkner and Reto Bleisch (2005), 'Liberalization and regulation of the Swiss letter market', in M.A. Crew and P.R. Kleindorfer (eds), *Regulatory and Economic Challenges in the Postal and Delivery Sector*, Boston, MA: Kluwer Academic Publishers, pp. 53–72.

Felisberto, Càtia, Beat Friedli, Matthias Finger, Daniel Krähenbühl and Urs Trinkner (2006), 'Pricing the last mile in the postal sector', in M.A. Crew and P.R. Kleindorfer (eds), *Progress Toward Liberalization of the Postal and Delivery Sector*, New York: Springer.

Friedli, Beat, Christian Jaag, Daniel Krähenbühl, Ole Bach Nielsen, Søren Michael Pihl and Urs Trinkner (2006), 'Consumer preferences and last mile pricing in the postal sector', in M.A. Crew and P.R. Kleindorfer (eds), *Liberalization of the Postal and Delivery Sector*, Cheltenham, UK and Northampton, MA, USA: Edward Elgar.

Jaag, Christian (2007a), 'Liberalization of the Swiss letter market and the viability of universal service obligations', *Swiss Journal of Economics and Statistics*, **143**(3), 263–84.
Jaag, Christian (2007b), 'Who should pay for postal services? Tax payers vs. senders vs. receivers', Presented at the 1st GPREN Postal Research Conference.
Laffont, Jean-Jacques, Patrick Rey and Jean Tirole (1998), 'Network competition: I. overview and nondiscriminatory pricing', *RAND Journal of Economics*, **29**(1), 1–37.
Panzar, John C. (2006), 'PO box access: competition issues in a two-sided postal market', Presented in Toulouse at the 4th IDEI/La Poste Conference on Regulation, Competition and Universal Service in the Postal Sector.
PricewaterhouseCoopers (2006), 'Evaluating the impact of a full market opening on Swiss post', study commissioned by Swiss Post.
Rochet, Jean-Charles and Jean Tirole (2003), 'Platform competition in two-sided markets', *Journal of the European Economic Association*, **1**, 990–1029.
Rochet, Jean-Charles and Jean Tirole (2005), 'Two-sided markets: a progress report', mimeo, IDEI University of Toulouse.
Trinkner, Urs and Martin Grossmann (2006), 'Forecasting Swiss mail demand', in M.A. Crew and P.R. Kleindorfer (eds), *Progress Toward Liberalization of the Postal and Delivery Sector*, New York: Springer.
Wright, Julian (2004), 'One-sided logic in two-sided markets', *Review of Network Economics*, **3**(1), 42–63.

11. Pricing, welfare and organisational constraints for postal operators*

Philippe De Donder, Helmuth Cremer, Paul Dudley and Frank Rodriguez

1. INTRODUCTION

National postal operators providing universal service typically are integrated operators where all stages of production up to and including the sale of postal services to final customers are contained within a single company. In some countries, a number of business units may have been created within such companies, and there may also be reporting arrangements for accounting and performance purposes for these business units. Based on precedents from other network industries, the organisational structures of national postal operators are likely to come under increased regulatory review in the future to assess whether an alternative to current structures may be in the public interest, not least because of the opening up of postal markets to competition, which in some countries has led to full liberalisation. Changes in organisational structures have been seen by regulators in other sectors as a way to encourage competition and increase the transparency of pricing and contractual arrangements of national operators.

This represents an area which to date has not been considered explicitly by the postal economics literature, although a number of related areas, such as the working of price controls, the analysis of the effects of market liberalisation and the pricing of access to postal networks, have been explored (Crew and Kleindorfer, 2006; De Donder, 2006; De Donder et al., 2006). Our chapter begins to examine some of the pricing and welfare economic questions raised by this area. In particular, we develop a formal economic model to understand how postal prices, volumes, profits and associated economic welfare differ under alternative sets of objective functions and constraints, particularly in respect of the transfer prices for intermediate services. We develop cases where a national postal operator (PO) is developed as two parts: a mail network operator (MNO) and a retail business (RB). Explicit objective functions and constraints are formed for the regulation of the MNO and RB, with the MNO being seen as a provider of intermediate mail services to the RB and also entrants in the market.

We consider three cases. In the first, we model a PO that offers access to entrants. The PO is regulated with a Global Price Cap (GPC) price control and alternatively under an equiproportional mark-up (EPMU) on marginal costs. In the second, we consider a GPC for the RB with prices for intermediate services, including access, regulated as a mark-up on marginal costs and charged by the MNO to the RB. In the third, we model a regulation of the single-piece price only, with prices for the MNO's intermediate services, including access, regulated as an EPMU on marginal costs. Hence the second and third cases consider an organisational structure where there are transfer prices operated by the MNO that are set by reference to an EPMU rule. Our primary focus throughout the chapter is on the pricing and associated welfare economic implications of these cases and, in particular, differences between them. To this end, we calibrate our model with stylised data to help illustrate and gain intuition from the formal results of the model.[1]

The remaining sections of the chapter are as follows. In Section 2 we outline the main elements of our model and in Section 3 we discuss in more detail the objective functions and regulatory framework we consider. Section 4 briefly outlines the calibration of the model, while Section 5 summarises the main results from the cases examined. We conclude by drawing out implications from our results.

2. THE MODEL

The model we study here is based on De Donder et al. (2006), to which we add a mail network operator (MNO). There are two postal operators: the retail business (RB, denoted by a superscript I) and a number of entrants (superscript E) acting as a competitive fringe. The RB offers two products (single-piece mail and bulk mail) to two delivery areas (urban and rural). Single-piece mail is sold at a uniform price, denoted by q, without distinction of the delivery area, thus meeting the requirement under universal service for a uniformly priced service which is available to all final customers. We denote the demand function for single-piece mail delivered to area $i = U,R$ by $x_i(q)$.

Entrants offer a bulk mail product for urban and rural delivery. Both bulk mail products (the one offered by the RB and by entrants) are imperfect substitutes in any given area. The demand in one area does not depend on the price charged for delivery to the other area. The demand function for RB bulk mail delivered in area $i = U,R$ is denoted by $y_i^I(p_i^I,p_i^E)$, with p_i^I as the RB price and p_i^E as an entrant's price, and with $\partial y_i^I(.)/\partial p_i^I < 0$ and $\partial y_i^I(.)/\partial p_i^E > 0$. Similarly, the demand for entrants' bulk mail product is given by $y_i^E(p_i^I,p_i^E)$, with $\partial y_i^E(.)/\partial p_i^E < 0$ and $\partial y_i^E(.)/\partial p_i^I > 0$. Bulk mail sold by the RB may be subject to a uniform pricing constraint or not, the latter implying de-averaged prices. Note also that the demands for the RB's two products are independent of one another and in the model could be viewed equivalently as being offered by two distinct providers, one for the single-piece product and a second for the bulk mail product. The demand functions come from the maximisation of net consumer surplus, with gross consumer surplus given by $V_i(x_i)$ for single-piece mail sent to area i and $U_i(y_i^I,y_i^E)$ for bulk mail sent to area i. As is standard in this literature, we use surplus as a measure of welfare for firms buying mail products.

The postal activity is divided in two segments: the upstream segment is composed of collection, sorting and transportation, while the downstream segment is delivery. Products sold to final customers can be thought of as combinations of these activities or operator services. These activities are performed by a MNO. In this sense, the MNO produces intermediate services which require an agent (the RB or an entrant) to assemble and sell these combinations to final customers although, in principle, the MNO also could sell postal service directly to final customers. In providing these intermediate services, the MNO incurs also a fixed cost, F, for its network, which is structured so as to be able to meet the requirement for the provision of a universal postal service. Each segment of volume variable activity has a constant marginal cost. Upstream MNO marginal costs are c_{sp} for the single-piece good and c_b for the bulk mail product, with $c_{sp} > c_b$. Downstream MNO marginal costs are d_i for delivery of any item (single-piece mail or bulk mail) to area $i = U,R$. We assume that $d_R > d_U$. Similarly for entrants, we have that rural delivery of bulk mail, d_R^E, is more expensive than urban delivery, d_U^E.

The MNO sells upstream and downstream services to the RB as well as downstream services to entrants.[2] It sells upstream services at a unit price of c'_{sp} to the RB for single-piece mail, and c'_b for RB bulk mail. It sells downstream services at a price of a_i for single-piece mail and for USO bulk mail delivered to area $i = U,R$. Downstream charges to entrants are a_i^E in the case of delivery to area i. Entrants can choose whether to deliver themselves or to access the MNO delivery network on each area. An entrant will choose the cheaper way such that it uses access to the MNO delivery network in area $i = U,R$ if $d_i^E > a_i^E$ and to bypass otherwise. The price of entrants as a competitive fringe is then

$$p_i^E = c^E + \min(a_i^E, d_i^E), \quad i = U, R.$$

Finally, we impose throughout the chapter that

$$q - p_i^j \geq c_{sp} - c_b, \quad j = I, E, i = U, R, \tag{11.1}$$

which is a necessary condition for the demand for bulk mail to be positive. We report in the Appendix the profit functions of the MNO and RB.

3. THE REGULATORY FRAMEWORK AND OBJECTIVE FUNCTIONS

3.1 Case A: MNO and RB in Single Entity (the PO) which Maximises Welfare

In case A, the MNO and RB belong to a single entity, the PO, and the objective functions and constraints are set at the level of the PO overall. In effect, the MNO and RB are divisions of the PO, which also offers access to entrants. Here we assume that the PO maximises welfare under a break-even constraint or, equivalently, that it maximises profit subject to an optimally set price cap. We use the fact that entrants' profit $\Pi^E = 0$, because entrants act as a competitive fringe. Then, for case A, assuming access and de-averaged PO bulk mail prices, the PO can be represented as solving the following problem:

$$\text{PO } Max_{q,p_i^I,a_i^E} \; W = \sum_{i=U,R} V_i(x_i) + \sum_{i=U,R} U_i(y_i^I, y_i^E)$$
$$- (x_U + x_R)q - p_U^I y_U^I - p_R^I y_R^I - p_U^E y_U^E - p_R^E y_R^E + \Pi^{PO}$$
$$\text{s.t. } \Pi^{PO} \geq 0 \text{ [associated Lagrange multiplier: } \lambda], \tag{11.2}$$

where the PO's profit Π^{PO} is as defined in the Appendix. First order conditions for this problem yield Ramsey formulas for q, p_i^I and a_i^E that are also reported in the Appendix.

We report in Section 5.1 results when all prices are set according to an EPMU mark-up, m (see the Appendix).

3.2 Case B: PO Maximises Welfare and the MNO and RB are Both Required to Break Even

The structure from case A is developed in case B, where the objective function remains welfare maximisation by the PO overall but under the additional condition that the MNO and RB are both required to break even. Setting these accounting constraints implies that formal transfer prices are charged by the MNO to the RB and affect the ability of both to achieve their objectives. The transfer prices then enter the optimisation program such that for case B, and again assuming access and de-averaged RB bulk mail prices, the PO can be represented as solving:

$$\text{PO } Max_{q,p_i^I,a_i^E,a_i,c_b',c_{sp}'} \quad W = \sum_{i=U,R} V_i(x_i) + \sum_{i=U,R} U_i(y_i^I, y_i^E)$$

$$- (x_U + x_R)q - p_U^I y_U^I - p_R^I y_R^I - p_U^E y_U^E - p_R^E y_R^E$$

$$+ \Pi^{MNO} + \Pi^I$$

$$\text{s.}t.\, \Pi^{MNO} \geq 0 \;\; [\text{associated Lagrange multiplier:}\lambda]$$

$$\Pi^I \geq 0 \;\; [\text{associated Lagrange multiplier:}\mu], \quad (11.3)$$

where Π^{MNO} and Π^I are as defined in the Appendix, which also contains first order conditions for a_i, c_b', c_{sp}' and a_n and Ramsey formulas for q,p_i^I and a_i^E for this case. We obtain that, at the optimum, the PO uses internal transfer prices a_i, c_b', c_{sp}' so as to equalise the values of the Lagrange multipliers of the two profit constraints in equation (11.3) ($\lambda = \mu$). In that case, the optimisation problems (11.2) and (11.3) become equivalent, with the same optimal values for the retail prices q,p_i^I and a_i^E.

Rather than letting the PO set the prices charged by the MNO for intermediate services, we then assume that the regulator imposes an EPMU rule, with the same proportional[3] mark-up m applied for all the intermediate services sold to the RB. Formally, we use the following set of constraints:

$$c_{sp}' = c_{sp}(1+m), \quad c_b' = c_b(1+m), \quad a_U = d_U(1+m), \quad a_R = d_R(1+m),$$

where the value of m is set by the regulator. In Section 5 we consider numerical results from the model, which show that there is a value of m that causes case B to yield the same welfare outcome as case A.[4] In practice, there is likely to be sufficient uncertainty over the parameter values within the model that this optimal value is unlikely to be identified. A value of m different to that yielding the same outcomes as case A results in a different set of prices for intermediate services, including access, and final goods and a lower welfare outcome in case B compared with case A (see the Appendix).

3.3 Case C: MNO and RB are both Required to Break Even, the RB Maximises Profit and a Price Cap is Set for Single-piece Product

In our third case, case C, the MNO again sets prices for the intermediate services it produces and sells to the RB and entrants and, as in case B, we assume that the regulator requires that it set these prices using an EPMU rule with mark-up, m. However, instead of the GPC control in case B, the regulator is now assumed to set a cap only on the single-piece universal service product, $\overline{q}$. We consider two variants. In the first one, the RB continues to sell both goods, such that it also is regulated directly through $\overline{q}$. In the second one, the RB sells only the bulk mail product, so that the MNO sells the single-piece product and is regulated through two instruments, m and $\overline{q}$. In this second variant, the RB is not regulated directly and only, as in the case of entrants, through the effect of m and $\overline{q}$ on the MNO's prices for intermediate services.

In both variants, the regulator sets the values of m and $\overline{q}$ such that:

1. Intermediate prices are given by the EPMU rule with mark-up, m:

$$c'_{sp} = c_{sp}(1 + m), c'_b = c_b(1 + m),$$
$$a_I^E = a_i = d_i(1 + m), \quad i = U, R.$$

2. The single-piece mail price is capped at $\overline{q}$.
3. The RB and the MNO both break-even: $\Pi^I = 0$ and $\Pi^{MNO} = 0$.
4. The RB sets profit-maximising bulk mail prices:

$$\text{RB } max_{p^I_U, p^I_R} \Pi^I.$$

The two variants differ according to which operator sells the single-piece mail product, thus satisfying the USO. The profit functions when the single-piece mail is sold by the MNO are given at the end of the Appendix.

4. CALIBRATION

Our calibration assumptions are the same as in De Donder et al. (2006). We start from the hypothetical situation where the PO does not face any entrants and posts a price of €0.50 for the single-piece product and €0.40 for its bulk mail product. Total quantities sold at those prices are, respectively, 2 billion and 8 billion items. We assume that 80 per cent of all mail flows are urban while 20 per cent are rural and that the direct price elasticities of these two goods are −0.2 for single-piece mail and −0.4 for bulk mail (the same elasticity in urban and rural markets). Finally, we calibrate linear demands based on these quantities, prices and elasticities. We need further information to calibrate the demand functions for bulk mail products when the market is opened to competition. We use two types of information: the extent of entry for different price configurations and the substitutability between the two bulk mail products for consumers. We assume that entrants would capture 10 per cent of the total market for bulk mail if both bulk mail products had the same price and 50 per cent of the market if entrants were to offer a 20 per cent price discount over the PO. As for substitution between those products, we assume that the displacement ratio $-(\partial y_i^I/\partial p_i^F)/(\partial y_i^F/\partial p_i^F)$ is set at 0.75 in both areas, which means that three quarters of the quantities sold by entrants are displaced from the PO, while one quarter represents additional volumes sold in the sector.[5]

The PO unit upstream cost, c_{sp}, is €0.18 for single-piece mail and €0.12 for bulk mail, c_b. The PO urban delivery cost (for all kinds of mail), d_U, is €0.11 in the urban area and €0.16 in the rural area, d_R. The fixed cost F equals €1.68 billion, so that the PO breaks even in the hypothetical monopoly situation (including a normal rate of profit, F equals 40 per cent of revenue of €4.2 billion). An entrant's collection cost, c^E, is set at €0.15, its delivery cost at €0.15 in the urban area, d_U^E, and €0.36 in the rural area, d_R^E. An entrant does not face any fixed cost, but we assume that this results in higher variable collection and delivery costs than the PO.[6]

5. NUMERICAL RESULTS

5.1 Case A: PO Maximises Welfare

We report our main results for case A in Table 11.1, which contains four simulations given by whether, first, entry is only through access or can also be through bypass; and, secondly, whether all prices are second-best welfare-maximising (Ramsey) or set on a EPMU basis. The results can be viewed as a benchmark against which to compare prices, volumes and economic welfare under alternative objective functions and regulatory constraints in cases B and C.[7]

In Table 11.1, consider first the case where entry is only through access. Then, in the welfare-maximising case with Ramsey prices, the mark-up over marginal cost is higher for the goods for which the demand elasticity with respect to price is lower (single-piece mail compared with bulk mail). The value of the Lagrange multiplier (λ in equation (11.2)) is low, which means that the PO's budget constraint is not costly, at the margin, in terms of society's welfare. Due to lower bulk mail prices and entry to this market, total market volume at 10.401 billion items is above the value of 10 billion used to calibrate the model.[8] Table 11.1 also reports results when all prices charged by the PO incorporate the same EPMU, m, such that the PO breaks even; this value of m is 0.747.[9] Compared with the Ramsey situation, the single-piece price is lower while the PO bulk mail prices are higher. Consumers of the single-piece good benefit from this move, at the expense of the bulk mail consumers. Total welfare decreases as we move away from the Ramsey optimal prices, but the decline is small and total volumes are higher.

Observe that, in these two cases, the optimal urban access charge paid by the entrant is larger than entrants' delivery cost (set at €0.15). This means that, if the option of bypass is available to entrants, it will occur in the urban (but not rural) area. We cover this situation in the remaining columns of Table 11.1. Compared to the no-bypass case, Ramsey prices are higher for single-piece mail, rural PO bulk mail and for entrants' access to the rural area. The equilibrium urban bulk mail price for the PO is lower, because an entrant's corresponding price is lower with bypass. The value of the Lagrange multiplier more than doubles, showing that the PO budget constraint is much more costly (at the margin) when bypass is available. Total welfare in the economy decreases, and although total volume in

Table 11.1 Prices, volume and welfare where MNO and RB in single entity, PO (case A)[1]

	Entry only through access		Entry through access and bypass	
	Welfare maximising	EPMU	Welfare maximising	EPMU
EPMU factor	–	0.747	–	0.881
Prices, €				
PO, single piece	0.608	0.524	0.853	0.564
PO, bulk mail urban	0.359	0.402	0.287	0.433
PO, bulk mail rural	0.424	0.464[4]	0.538	0.504
PO, access urban	0.210	0.192	–	–
PO, access rural	0.269	0.280	0.357	0.301
Entrants, urban	0.360	0.342	0.300	0.300
Entrants, rural	0.419	0.430	0.507	0.451
Volumes, billion items				
PO, single piece	1.914	1.981	1.718	1.949
PO, bulk mail urban	5.909	4.194	6.221	2.107
PO, bulk mail rural	1.526	1.315	1.370	1.191
Entrants, urban	0.922	2.838	1.142	5.350
Entrants, rural	0.130	0.333	0.116	0.421
PO, total single piece and bulk mail[2]	9.349	7.490	9.309	5.247
Total entrants	1.052	3.171	1.258	5.771
Total market	10.401	10.661	10.567	11.018
PO Profit, € billion	0	0	0	–0.411
Welfare, € billion	6.526	6.448	6.407	5.852[3]
Lambda	0.148	–	0.347	–

Notes:

1 Calibration values are set out in Section 4.

2 PO access mail equals entrant volumes under simulation where entry is only through access and entrant rural volume under simulations where entry can also be through bypass.

3 Assumes cost of public funds of 0.3 to cover PO deficit.

4 Set at maximum of single piece price less €0.06.

the market increases the welfare decreases for single-piece mail users more than offset gains to bulk mail consumers. Looking at the results for the EPMU simulation, we find that no value of the mark-up allows the PO to break even. We then report the value of the mark-up that minimises the PO loss. The loss-minimising mark-up is 88 per cent, and the minimum PO loss is just over €400 million. This mark-up is higher than in the no-bypass case. Although the total market is significantly larger at over 11 billion items, the sum of consumer surplus and PO loss is much lower than without bypass. We report the value of the welfare level when the cost of public funds to cover the PO deficit is set exogenously at 0.3.

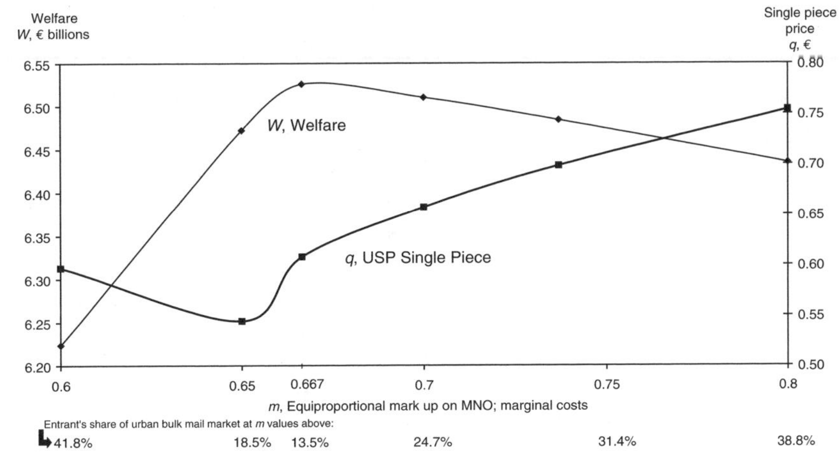

Figure 11.1 Welfare, prices and market shares for case B where entry is only through access

5.2 Case B: MNO Prices at EPMU, RB Maximises Welfare and Both Required to Break Even

We summarise in Figure 11.1 some key results for case B when entry is only through access. As explained in Section 3.2, an EPMU mark-up, m, is applied to internal transfer prices charged by the MNO to the RB, while final prices are set at their welfare-maximising levels compatible with both the MNO and the RB breaking even. In addition to recording values of m along the horizontal axis, Figure 11.1 reports the level of welfare on the left-hand axis and the prices of the single-piece product on the right-hand axis. The level of entry is recorded (through the entrants' share of the total market) under the values of m.

As explained in Section 3.2, adding EPMU constraints to the optimisation program (11.3) need not change the results compared to program (11.2) in case A. The main difference between imposing these constraints or not is that, without EPMU, there are many different internal prices that allow the PO to set the final prices at their Ramsey level as obtained from equation (11.2) in case A, while with EPMU there is a single value of m that allows this. As Figure 11.1 shows, this optimal value of m is about 67 per cent. Increasing m above this value in turn increases the intermediate prices to the RB, with the RB posting a higher single-piece mail price q in order to break even. For low values of m, the constraint on the difference between q and p_U^I (see equation (11.1)) becomes binding and q (together with p_U^I) decreases with m. Consequently, total welfare is first increasing and then decreasing in m. For low values of m, both single-piece consumers and bulk mail customers benefit from an increase in m while, for larger of values, the main effect of an increase in m is distributional: single-piece consumer surplus decreases while bulk mail customer surplus increases.

We have considered case B also, where entry through bypass is possible. The directional nature of the results is similar to those recorded in Figure 11.1 for the access-only case, although there is no set of RB prices that result in break-even individually for both the MNO and the RB.[10]

5.3 Case C: MNO Prices at EPMU, RB Maximises Profit and Both Required to Break Even Subject to a Price Cap on Single-piece Product

To compare the results of the case C set of objective functions and constraints with that of case B, we seek outcomes in case C where both the RB and the MNO break even. The regulator here has two instruments: the EPMU, m, for the MNO and a price cap that applies only to the single-piece product, $\overline{q}$. As noted in Section 3.3, it is possible in principle in case C for the single-piece product to be sold by either the MNO or the RB. Where entry is only through access, the selling of the single-piece product through either agent leads to similar outcomes, at least at the calibration values used for the numerical analysis. However, where entry can also be through bypass, the sale of the single-piece product through the MNO appears to produce a set of results that better meet the objective that both the MNO and RB should break even, and we report results for this case in Table 11.2. This allows a comparison with the results for cases A and B.

Table 11.2 reports results for three simulations. In all of them the break-even constraints are met by both the MNO and RB individually. The first set of results is for a situation where entry is only through access and is for the pair $(m,\overline{q})$ that maximises economic welfare. Here, the regulator would need to set a low value of the price cap ($\overline{q}$ = €0.503) and a relatively high mark-up (m = 0.798) to achieve this outcome. The overall level of welfare is lower than in cases A and B (at €6.351 billion compared with €6.526 billion). Although the single-piece price is lower in case C, the main difference between the cases is associated with the profit-maximising level of RB's bulk mail prices in the urban area, which are well above those in case A. Entry through access is significantly higher as a result, although the difference in total market volume between cases A and C is quite small (at 10.621 billion instead of 10.401 billion items).

The two remaining columns in Table 11.2 report results of simulations where entry is possible through bypass, which at these parameter values only occurs in the urban area. In both of these simulations, unlike case B, the MNO and the RB both satisfy the break-even constraint individually.[11] The first of these columns reports results for the pair $(m,\overline{q})$ that maximises economic welfare. To achieve this the regulator would need to set a high value of the price cap ($\overline{q}$ = €1.205 compared with q = €0.608 in case A) and a low EPMU (m = 0.386). While neither entrants nor the RB are regulated directly, overall outcomes in the market are clearly dependent on the value of m set by the regulator. At the same time, the value of m set by the regulator itself needs to take account of its effect on the prices of entrants and the RB for the solution values in the bulk mail market in turn depend on the MNO's prices and hence on the value of m. As in the case of entry only through access, the RB's profit-maximising prices are higher than in case A (it makes a profit of €0.321 billion) and entry is significantly higher, although the entrants' rural bulk mail continues to be delivered by the MNO in addition to all of the RB's bulk mail and the single-piece product. Welfare is significantly reduced compared with the simulation of entry through access and more so compared with case A.

If the regulator wished to set a lower price cap for single-piece mail, it would be able to do so and still set a pair $(m,\overline{q})$ that allowed break-even for the MNO (and RB). The final column of Table 11.2 reports the lowest price cap it could set and still allow the MNO to break even ($\overline{q}$ = 1.060). If it were to set a lower value than this, there would not be a value of the EPMU m that would allow the MNO to break even. Note that this case results in

Table 11.2 Prices, volume and welfare, case C [1,2]

	Entry only through access	Entry through access and bypass	
	Welfare maximising	Welfare maximising	Lowest single piece price for MNO to break even
EPMU factor	0.798	0.386	0.672
Prices, €			
MNO, single piece	0.503	1.205	1.060
RB, bulk mail urban	0.443[4]	0.413	0.446
RB, bulk mail rural	0.443[4]	0.448	0.552
MNO, access urban	0.198	–	–
MNO, access rural	0.288	0.222	0.268
Entrants, urban	0.348	0.300	0.300
Entrants, rural	0.438	0.372	0.418
Volumes, billion items			
MNO, single piece	1.998	1.436	1.552
RB, bulk mail urban	3.206	2.659	1.732
RB, bulk mail rural	1.530	0.710	0.598
Entrants, urban	3.798	4.786	5.734
Entrants, rural	0.089	1.094	1.118
MNO + RB, total[3]	6.734	4.805	3.882
Total entrants	3.887	5.880	6.852
Total market	10.621	10.685	10.734
PO Profit, € billion			
MNO	0	0	0
RB	0	0.321	0.157
Welfare, € billion	6.351	5.843	5.680

Notes:

1 MNO prices at EPMU, RB maximises profit and both required to break even subject to a price cap on a single-piece product. Variant: MNO sells a single-piece product.

2 Calibration values are set out in Section 4.

3 PO access mail equals entrant volumes under simulation where entry is only through access and entrant rural volume under simulations where entry can also be through bypass.

4 Set at maximum of single piece price less €0.06.

a much lower level of welfare. The use of the MNO's delivery network in the urban area is much reduced and the RB's bulk mail prices remain high. Thus, for the present calibration, there is only limited flexibility available to meet the fixed costs of the USO through revenues from bulk mail products rather than through single-piece mail.

It is possible that greater amounts of switching away from RB's bulk mail product could occur than at the calibration values used in Table 11.2. To test for this, we performed a sensitivity analysis with greater displacement due to entry such that nine tenths of the quantities sold by entrants were displaced from RB, rather than three quarters as in the base case. For the access-only case, in addition to more traffic switching to entrants, all retail prices rise, which causes volumes and welfare to decline compared with the results in Table 11.2.[12] Where urban bypass is possible, the welfare-maximising outcome results in higher single-piece but lower RB bulk mail prices. Market volumes are lower, with a small decline in welfare.[13] Finally, the minimum value of the single-piece price with the MNO breaking even is higher when the displacement ratio increases, and although the RB bulk mail prices are lower, the welfare gains enjoyed by bulk mail users are less than the loss in single-piece mail user surplus and the RB's profit, so that welfare decreases.[14] Overall, the results from this sensitivity are broadly in line with those in Table 11.2 and the conclusions are similar to those from the base case.

6. CONCLUSIONS

In this chapter we have considered the structure of optimal pricing under various objective functions and organisational constraints that might be associated with or imposed on a national postal operator (PO). These constraints refer to different regulatory rules for pricing of intermediate services, including access, and end-to-end or final products of a mail network operator (MNO) and retail business (RB) that may comprise the PO or be distinct companies. We have developed a formal model to analyse associated pricing and welfare economic issues and gained further insights through the calibration of the model with stylised data. We focus on the directional and qualitative nature of the numerical results rather than their details, since the latter clearly depend on the specific parameterisation of calibration values.

Our first conclusion is that it is objectives and constraints that primarily determine outcomes with regard to pricing and associated economic welfare rather than the organisational structure of whether the MNO and RB are in the same company or not. If a Global Price Cap (GPC) applies for the RB and there is no bypass, within the numerical examples provided, it is possible to obtain both break-even and welfare-maximising outcomes whether or not there is an EPMU rule applied to the set of prices for intermediate services. As a corollary, if the EPMU rule is not set at the appropriate level (which is much more likely, given the uncertainties that would attend setting it properly), then break-even occurs, but not at the welfare-maximising level.

Our second conclusion is that, within the numerical examples, if the GPC is not set optimally across all end-to-end prices and instead a price cap is set only for the single-piece price, then different organisational structures can affect the outcome. However, with careful selection of structural constraints, it may be possible to reach a break-even position for both the MNO and RB. Doing so requires that the mark-up be set at the appropriate level, but structural constraints can also lead to significantly reduced welfare.

More generally, as regulatory constraints increase and move away from optimal GPC, it becomes more difficult to identify optimal or even sustainable values for key instruments. There is then a key issue of compatibility between constraints. For example, in case B (where a GPC was imposed on the PO together with two separate profit constraints on the MNO and the RB) it was not possible to find a solution under bypass, within the numerical examples, that allowed both the MNO and the RB to break even individually. Similarly, in case C (where the regulator set the EPMU factor and the single-piece mail price cap while the RB set profit-maximising bulk mail prices) the ability of the MNO to satisfy its break-even constraint depended on a consistent setting of the mark-up, m, and the price cap on the single-piece price product, $\bar{q}$, and the impact of m on the bulk mail market, which was not regulated directly. Only high values of $\bar{q}$ led to a feasible solution and an attempt to lower that price too far would lead to losses for the MNO. In all these examples, there is a significant amount of uncertainty regarding the effect of constraints on market behaviour and outcomes, which adds to the difficulty of ensuring compatibility.

In practice, it would be challenging to set fully consistent constraints, given the level of uncertainty over the parameter values for demand and cost. It may not matter much that such constraints fail to meet this requirement if the effect of moving from such values is modest and regions around these solutions are flat. However, where this is not the case, which may be, for example, because of significant changes in the underlying demand for postal products or the extent of or options for entry to the market, then the issue of risk management becomes important. This can then require other mechanisms and instruments to offset any inconsistency in the setting of constraints in a changing environment and perhaps also to determine a sustainable solution in the first place.

Our focus in the chapter has been on the application of our model to pricing and welfare issues associated with specific sets of objectives, constraints and organisational structures. There may be other factors than pricing and welfare that are significant with regard to these issues, such as transactions costs in the planning or operations between various divisions (here the MNO and RB), which may impact materially on the conclusions from our model. Similarly, it is clearly possible to consider a wider range of possibilities which either relax some constraints and/or tighten others and compare and contrast such alternatives. We believe that our model provides a useful starting point for considering such factors and developments.

NOTES

* The analysis contained in this chapter reflects the views of the authors and may not necessarily be those of Royal Mail Group.

1. We note that the chapter develops a setting with complete information: all cost and demand characteristics, as well as objectives of postal operators, are fully observable by all. We abstract from incentive considerations when considering the consequences of different organisational structures. We also do not model costs associated with organisational governance. Finally, we do not include in our modelling any transaction costs between the MNO and the RB. Such costs could be significant in size. The presence of such transactions costs would be an additional factor affecting regulatory prescription of organisational structure (for example, regarding the MNO and RB). This potentially is an important area but is outside the scope of the current chapter.
2. In principle, the MNO could sell upstream services to entrants but in our model we consider the much more significant case of its selling only downstream services to the entrant. Similarly, it could sell intermediate services to two distinct providers if the RB's single-piece and bulk mail product were offered by two different companies to final consumers.
3. With a proportional mark-up, each activity would contribute to the funding of the fixed cost in proportion to the revenue it generates. Alternatively, using the same absolute (rather than proportional) mark-up would entail that each activity contributes to the funding of the fixed cost in proportion to its volume.
4. In other words, one degree of freedom – the setting of the value of m – is enough to transfer revenue between the MNO and the RB in order to equalise the values of the two Lagrange multipliers λ and μ in equation (11.3).
5. See De Donder (2006) for an analysis and discussion of the displacement ratio.
6. We are capturing any entrants' fixed costs and capital payments to investors as a markup on marginal costs, so that the indicated collection and delivery costs reflect this markup. Thus, even though entrants' labor costs could be below those of the PO, the result is that entrants' marked up (average or unit) costs are higher than the marginal costs of delivery of the PO.

7. The pattern of the results in Table 11.1 is similar to that reported in De Donder et al. (2006).
8. The 10 billion value corresponds to a monopoly case that is not reported here separately, but that is similar to that in De Donder et al. (2006).
9. Note this differs from the mark-up of 0.667 implied by the calibration value ratio of the fixed cost to marginal costs due to the effect of entry on volumes and the constraint at (Equation 11.1) that the rural bulk mail price be at least the upstream marginal cost difference of €0.06 below the single-piece price.
10. For the calibration values used in the model, it is possible to secure break-even overall for this case by relaxing the requirement that both the MNO and RB break even individually (i.e. by allowing RB to make a profit greater than or equal to the loss of the MNO).
11. Note that in case C it is also not possible to satisfy the break-even constraints for the MNO and the RB individually if the single-piece product is sold through the RB. This is because the MNO profit constraint is more difficult to satisfy than the RB's (mainly because the MNO faces a fixed cost while the RB does not) so that transferring the contributions to profit generated by the single-piece mail product from the RB to the MNO helps the MNO to break even.
12. Here, single piece price, $q = €0.553$; EPMU factor, $m = 0.950$; entrant volumes = 5.129 billion items; total market volume = 9.718 billion items; welfare = €6.021 billion.
13. Single piece price, $q = €1.240$; EPMU factor, $m = 0.352$; entrant volumes = 4.849 billion items; total market volume = 9.844 billion items; welfare = €5.837 billion.
14. Single piece price, $q = €1.107$; EPMU factor, $m = 0.665$; entrant volumes = 6.072 billion items; total market volume = 9.738 billion items; welfare = €5.615 billion.

REFERENCES

Crew, M.A. and P.R. Kleindorfer (2006), 'The welfare effects of entry and strategies for maintaining the USO in the postal sector', in M.A. Crew and P.R. Kleindorfer (eds), *Progress toward Liberalisation of the Postal Delivery Sector*, New York, Springer, pp. 3–22.

De Donder, P. (2006), 'Access pricing in the postal sector: theory and simulations', *Review of Industrial Organisation*, **28**(3), 307–26.

De Donder, P., H. Cremer, P. Dudley and F. Rodriguez (2006), 'A welfare analysis of price controls with end-to-end mail and access services', in M.A. Crew and P.R. Kleindorfer (eds), *Liberalisation of the Postal and Delivery Sector*, Cheltenham, UK and Northampton, MA, USA: Edward Elgar, pp. 227–48.

APPENDIX

Profit Functions of Three Postal Entities

The RB's profit is given by

$$\Pi^I = (q - c'_{sp} - a_U)x_U(q) + (q - c'_{sp} - a_U)x_R(q) + (p^I_U - c'_b - a_U)y^I_U(p^I_U, p^E_U) + (p^I_R - c'_b - a_R)y^I_R(p^I_R, p^E_R).$$

The MNO's profit is

$$\begin{aligned}\Pi^{MNO} = {} & (c'_{sp} - c_{sp})[x_U(q) + x_R(q)] + (a_U - d_U)x_U(q) + (a_R - d_R)x_R(q) \\ & + (c'_b - c_b)[y^I_U(p^I_U, p^E_U) + y^I_R(p^I_R, p^E_R)] \\ & + (a_U - d_U)y^I_U(p^I_U, p^E_U) + (a_U - d_R)y^I_R(p^I_R, p^E_R) \\ & + (a^E_U - d_U)y^E_U(p^I_U, p^E_U) + (a^E_R - d_R)y^I_R(p^I_R, p^E_R) - F\end{aligned}$$

in the case of entrant's access. In the case of bypass in area i, the corresponding term in the last line disappears.

The PO's profit is the sum of Π^{MNO} and Π^I, and is given by

$$\begin{aligned}\Pi^{PO} = {} & (q - c_{sp} - d_U)x_U(q) + (q - c_{sp} - d_R)x_R(q) \\ & + (p^I_U - c_b - d_U)y^I_U(p^I_U, p^E_U) + (p^I_R - c_b - d_R)y^I_R(p^I_R, p^E_R) \\ & + (a^E_U - d_U)y^E_U(p^I_U, p^E_U) + (a^E_R - d_R)y^I_R(p^I_R, p^E_R) - F\end{aligned}$$

in the case of entrant access. In the case of bypass in area i, the corresponding term in the last line disappears.

A.1 First order conditions and Ramsey formulas

Case A The first order conditions are well known and give the following Ramsey formulas:

1. For q:

$$q = c_{sp} + d_U \frac{\partial x_U/\partial q}{\partial(x_U + x_R)/\partial q} + d_R \frac{\partial x_R/\partial q}{\partial(x_U + x_R)/\partial q} + \frac{\lambda}{1+\lambda}\frac{q}{\varepsilon_x},$$

where

$$\varepsilon_x = -q\frac{\partial(x_U + x_R)/\partial q}{x_U + x_R}$$

is the direct price elasticity of demand for single-piece mail.

2. For p_i^I:

$$p_i^I = c_b + d_i + (a_i^E - d_i)\sigma_{y_i^I} + \frac{\lambda}{1+\lambda}\frac{p_i^I}{\varepsilon_{y_i^I}}, \tag{11.A.1}$$

where

$$\sigma_{y_i^I} = -\frac{\partial y_i^E/\partial p_i^I}{\partial y_i^I/\partial p_i^I}$$

is the displacement ratio between bulk mail products following changes in the RB bulk mail price and

$$\varepsilon_{y_i^I} = -p_i^I \frac{\partial y_i^I/\partial p_i^I}{y_i^I}$$

is the direct price elasticity of demand for RB bulk mail.

3. For a_i^E:

$$a_i^E = d_i + (p_i^I - c_b - d_i)\sigma_{y_i^E} + \frac{\lambda}{1+\lambda}\frac{p_i^E}{\varepsilon_{y_i^E}}, \tag{11.A.2}$$

where

$$\sigma_{y_i^E} = -\frac{\partial y_i^I/\partial p_i^E}{\partial y_i^E/\partial p_i^E}$$

is the displacement ratio between bulk mail products following changes in the entrant's bulk mail price and

$$\varepsilon_{y^E_i} = -p_i^E \frac{\partial y_i^E/\partial p_i^E}{y_i^E}$$

is the direct price elasticity of demand for entrant's bulk mail. The scenarios with bypass and/or with uniform RB bulk mail prices ($p_U^I = p_R^I$) can be derived in a similar way.

Alternatively, we also study the EPMU setting where all prices exhibit the same mark-up factor m:

$$q = (c_{sp} + \alpha d_U + (1-\alpha)d_R)(1+m),$$

$$p_U^I = (1+m)(c_b + d_U),\ p_R^I = (1+m)(c_b + d_R),$$

$$a_U^E = d_U(1+m),\ a_R^E = d_R(1+m)$$

where α is the proportion of single-piece mail sold in the urban area and where m is chosen so that the PO breaks even ($\Pi^{PO} = 0$).

Case B The first order conditions for final prices and access charges to the entrant are as follows:

1. For q:

$$q = c_{sp} + d_U \frac{\partial x_U/\partial q}{\partial(x_U + x_R)/\partial q} + d_R \frac{\partial x_R/\partial q}{\partial(x_U + x_R)/\partial q} + \frac{\lambda}{1+\lambda}\frac{q}{\varepsilon_x}. \tag{11.A.3}$$

idem the previous section (but λ denotes a Lagrange multiplier on a different constraint, so its value will differ at equilibrium).

2. For p_i^I:

$$p_i^I = c_b' + a_i + (a_i^E - d_i)\sigma_{y_i^I} - \frac{1+\lambda}{1+\mu}(c_b' + a_i - c_b - d_i) + \frac{\mu}{1+\mu}\frac{p_i^I}{\varepsilon_{y_i^I}}. \tag{11.A.4}$$

Observe that (11.A.4) reduces to (11.A.1) when $\mu = \lambda$.

3. For a_i^E:

$$a_i^E = d_i + \left[c_b' + a_i - c_b - d_i + \frac{1+\mu}{1+\lambda}(p_i^I - c_b' - a_i)\right]\sigma_{y_i^E} + \frac{\lambda}{1+\lambda}\frac{p_i^E}{\varepsilon_{y_i^E}}. \tag{11.A.5}$$

Observe that (11.A.5) reduces to (11.A.2) when $\mu = \lambda$.

We obtain the following FOCs for a_i, c_b' and c_{sp}':

4. For a_i:

$$(1+\lambda)y_i^I - (1+\mu)y_i^I$$

5. For c_b':

$$(1+\lambda)(y_U^I + y_R^I) - (1+\mu)(y_U^I + y_R^I)$$

6. For c_{sp}':

$$(1+\lambda)(x_U + x_R) - (1+\mu)(x_U + x_R)$$

The meaning of these last three FOCs is as follows. The prices for a_i, c_b' and c_{sp}' are purely transfer prices: they are used to transfer revenue between the RB and MNO and do not necessarily affect the final prices of the postal operators. From (11.3), the welfare cost of the two constraints is minimised when the Lagrange multipliers of the two profit constraints are equalised ($\lambda = \mu$), which means that we revert to case A. Where this is not the case in general, there will be a difference between case A and case B.

Case C In the variant where the single-piece mail is sold by the MNO rather than by the RB, profit functions become:

$$\Pi^I = (p_U^I - c_b' - a_U)y_U^I(p_U^I, p_U^E) + (p_R^I - c_b' - a_R)y_R^I(p_R^I, p_R^E).$$

and

$$
\begin{aligned}
\Pi^{MNO} = {} & (q - c_{sp} - d_U)x_U(q) + (q - c_{sp} - d_R)x_R(q) \\
& + (c_b' - c_b)[y_U^I(p_U^I, p_U^E) + y_R^I(p_R^I, p_R^E)] \\
& + (a_U - d_U)y_U^I(p_U^I, p_U^E) + (a_U - d_R)y_R^I(p_R^I, p_R^E) \\
& + (a_U^E - d_U)y_U^E(p_U^I, p_U^E) + (a_R^E - d_R)y_R^I(p_R^I, p_R^E) - F
\end{aligned}
$$

in the case of entrant access. In the case of bypass in area i, the corresponding term in the last line disappears.

12. National postal strategies after a full postal market opening

Gonzales d'Alcantara and Axel Gautier

1. INTRODUCTION

In October 2006 the European Commission presented to the European Parliament and the Council of Ministers a proposal for a Directive[1] modifying Directive 97/67/CE[2] and 2002/39/EC[3] to open fully the postal market in the European Union by January 1, 2009. In a vote on the proposal and amendments on July 11, 2007, the European Parliament modified this proposal with a few additional conditions, but postponing the date to 2011–13 (with most of the EU-15 members subject to the 2011 date and new members and countries like Greece and Luxembourg facing special conditions subject to the 2013 date). This proposal requires Full Postal Market Opening (FMO) in all EU member states and the obligation for all member states to provide a Universal Postal Service, including postal delivery every day, to every address and at an affordable price. The proposal foresees the possibility that losses for a National Postal Operator (PO) as a result of its Universal Service Obligation (USO) may need to be financed by various means, including a state subsidy.

Let us assume that this Directive is also accepted by the European Parliament and that, within this context, all member states have to specify a well-defined USO, a corresponding financing mechanism and regulatory constraints. Such specifics will result from a national decision process involving three national players: the Incumbent (I) or historical Universal Service Provider (USP), an Entrant and a National Policy Maker (Regulator). We assume that the Regulator has the power to determine both USO and Regulatory constraints on the USP, within the setup defined by the FMO, and has the budgetary capacity to pay USO related subsidies, either directly or through a competition fund, needed by the USP to reach balanced accounts.

In the postal sector, a main driver of delivery costs is the density of delivery points. Boldron et al. (2006) estimate the cost of delivery on the basis of population density, the Grouping Index (the ratio between the number of delivery points and the number of stop points) and the mail volume. Boldron et al. undertook their analysis at a rather detailed level, based on relatively small delivery areas, and their results exhibit large variations in delivery costs across and within countries. The approach adopted in this present chapter extends their analysis and shows how, why and to what extent different cost structures at the delivery route level (referred to below as route-cost profiles) are likely to give rise to different dynamics of Market Entry under FMO.

We assume a duopoly between the Incumbent and an Entrant, and we show that different route-cost structures have very different consequences under FMO. For example, if unit delivery costs were the same for all routes, the USP would have little difficulty fending off an Entrant of roughly the same efficiency level. However, if the USP has some urban routes that are low cost and many rural routes that are high cost, then FMO can be expected to give rise to cream skimming by the Entrant (E), as analyzed by many previous authors (see, e.g., Crew and Kleindorfer (2005) and d'Alcantara and Amerlynck (2006) for a discussion of earlier contributions). While these two examples of route-cost structures do not exhaust the interesting possibilities, they do point to the central role of postal route-cost structures in predicting the outcome of FMO. The main point of our analysis here is to summarize the consequences of FMO in varying environments as captured in different route-cost profiles. We do this both theoretically, through a general duopoly model, and for five illustrative cases that are derived in part from empirical literature on existing national operators in the EU, as summarized by Boldron et al. (2006).

In the duopoly modeled here between an Entrant and the USP, the USP must serve all addresses while E is free to cover a limited portion of the territory. The model is a pure bypass model: E builds up its own delivery network and does not buy access from the USP. Firms compete with a single product ('average mail') that the USP must sell at a uniform price.

Our results show a large diversity of outcomes after FMO. We first consider three different distributions of the route costs keeping the total cost constant (as well as the pre-FMO break-even tariff). Depending on the distribution of costs, E coverage of market ranges from 3.5 percent (Homogenous route-cost profile) of the addresses to 45.4 percent (Dual route-cost profile). These differences are solely the result of different structures for the route costs within the stylized countries analyzed.

In the Homogenous route-cost profile, the universal service can be sustained without any safeguarding measures and, if prices are regulated, the price increase is rather limited. In the Dual route-cost profile, the rise in the USP unit cost (due to entry) is such that the USO cannot be sustained without state subsidies, even if the USP has complete freedom to set its price (except for the uniform price constraint that is part of the USO). In an intermediate case (Homogenous route-cost profile), the USP makes losses after FMO if prices are set at the welfare-maximizing level. These losses resulting from the USO under FMO can be financed by state subsidies, by a pay-or-play mechanism or by removing price regulation.

We then consider two configurations where most of the routes are in a low-cost (urban) area and in a high-cost (rural) area, respectively. In the Dense Stop Point route profile, E covers most of the addresses without threatening the financial stability of the USP and the viability of the USO. In the Non-Dense Stop Point route profile, E picks only the most profitable routes and, despite a limited geographical coverage, the USO cannot be sustained without subsidies. Taken together, these results show that different country configurations lead to different outcomes after FMO and that different solutions for USO financing are also dictated by different route-cost profiles.

This chapter is organized as follows. Section 2 contains a brief description of the model, details of which may be found in the technical appendix. In Section 3, we provide details of the calibration of our simulation model, whose results are presented in Section 4. Section 5 concludes.

2. THE MODEL

2.1 A Summary of the Model

We consider two firms: the Incumbent PO (I) and an Entrant (E). The two firms compete for an average mail product. The model is a pure bypass model: firm E builds up its own delivery network and is engaged in facility-based competition with I. A USO is imposed by the Regulator on I. The USO constraints include a geographically uniform tariff, the obligation to serve all the customers and other obligations such as frequency of delivery, that impose costs on the PO. E is not subject to the same constraints and is not required to cover the whole territory. There is no possibility of access in this model. This means that E cannot achieve universal coverage by buying access to I's delivery network for the addresses that it does not cover. While the assumption of no access may seem extreme, it allows a clean representation of the results of route-cost profiles and accords with the business models of several existing markets (e.g., Sweden) where competitors begin their entry by serving specific regions, choosing their customers to be those that only are interested in delivery in the areas served by these competitors. Note that customers in our model can use the services of both E and I, sorting their mail out according to the delivery route coverage of these two service providers.

We decompose the postal value chain in two main activities: upstream activities and delivery. Upstream activities include mail collection, mail transport and sorting. Upstream activities are operated under constant returns to scale. Delivery is an increasing returns to scale activity and it involves both fixed and variable costs. In this model, we consider a fixed delivery cost per address.

There are N addresses in the country. We rank these addresses according to their fixed delivery cost. In the graphs below, the address on the left has the lowest fixed delivery cost, while the address on the right has the highest. The main driver of the fixed delivery costs is the Delivery Stop Point Density. This means that if E and I can have a different delivery cost per address, the ranking of addresses according to their cost is the same because they both depend on the observed height of the buildings, quantified using the Grouping Index.

We define a demand per address that is the number of mail items sent to address n. We make the assumption that this demand only depends on prices. This means in particular that (1) the demand is independent of the receiver's location. (2) The demand addressed to E does not depend on its market coverage – that is, there is no network effect – and (3) given that I is subject to a uniform tariff constraint, E serves first the addresses with the lowest delivery cost.

According to the bypass decision of E, some addresses are served by two firms while others are served only by I. If E does not cover the whole territory, a sender that uses E's mail service must pre-sort its mailing in order to consign to E only the mailing with a covered address.[4]

The welfare is the sum of the total consumer surplus net of the senders' expenses and the firms' profits. In case the profit of the USP is negative, subsidies must be paid and their net cost must be subtracted from welfare. Subsidies have a shadow cost, meaning that transferring one euro to the USP reduces the welfare by more then one euro.

2.2 A Four-stage Process

In a first stage, we consider that a monopoly situation prevails before FMO and we search for the price that maximizes welfare while guaranteeing that the USP manages to cover the costs of the USO with its profits. In a second stage, we evaluate the consequences of FMO when the USP continues to sell its product at the pre-FMO price. E invests in an alternative Postal Distribution Network with a freely chosen frequency of delivery and freely chosen distribution zones; that is, E is not bound by any universal coverage constraint. The firms then compete for mail volumes posted to a limited number of addresses. Given that the demand is independent of the location, E covers first the low-cost addresses. As a matter of fact, the region covered by E is such that E realizes a zero margin on the last-covered address. Because delivery exhibits increasing returns to scale and density, the entry of a competitor increases the unit cost of delivery for the USP by eroding its volumes. The consequence is that the USP is unable to finance universal coverage at a uniform price with the pre-FMO tariff. In this case, the Regulator must pay a subsidy to the USP, as authorized by the proposed European Postal Directive.

In a third stage, we analyze the possibility that the Regulator prefers to reduce or eliminate the subsidy of stage 2 by allowing the USP to set its tariff freely. This also leads to changes in price and market coverage of E, which is assumed to be a price follower in a von Stackelberg price game. Finally, we consider a fourth stage where the Regulator imposes a price cap on the USP. The price cap results from welfare optimization by the Regulator and may still leave the need for subsidies to attain break-even operations.

It is necessary to note a number of limitations of the model presented. The USO constraints imposed on the USP, as defined by the Commission Proposal, include a geographically uniform tariff, the obligation to serve all the customers and obligations in term of frequency of delivery. We assume that uniformity applies for the standard average letter mail to which we restrict our analysis here. Assuming uniform tariffs for a single product is neither general nor realistic. In practice, uniform tariffs will be imposed only on single piece letter mail, not on bulk mail, but bulk mail does use the same delivery network as single piece letter mail. This aspect is not considered here and has to be taken into account when assessing the final results and calibrations. Finally, the model is a pure bypass model and we therefore neglect the possibility that competition remains limited to the upstream segments of the market with competitors buying mail delivery to I. So our model can only explain one form of competition (bypass) and neglects the other (access or worksharing). In countries where E has a limited coverage of the addresses because the delivery costs per addresses are high, our model predicts little competition after FMO. In reality, in these countries competition can be substantial but limited to the upstream market segments.[5] Taking this possibility into account would give us a clearer picture of market situations after FMO, but would obviously lead to a more complicated model.

3. MODEL CALIBRATION

3.1 Parameter Values

We calibrate our model and generate numerical results to evaluate quantitatively the extent of entry and the consequences of FMO on welfare. For our numerical exercise, we derive a system of linear demand equations from the maximization of the utility of a representative sender defined as:

$$U(x_I, x_E) = \alpha_I x_I + \alpha_E x_E - \beta_I \frac{x_I^2}{2} - \beta_E \frac{x_E^2}{2} - \delta x_I x_E,$$

where x_I and x_E are the number of postal items sent to address n with I and E, respectively.

We use the following elements to calibrate the demand functions: (1) we consider that a monopoly USP faces a demand of 200 postal items per household if it charges a price of €0.40 and (2) at this price/mailing volume, the elasticity of the monopoly demand is −0.4. When the two firms compete, we assume that (3) the displacement ratio is equal to 0.9, meaning that 90 percent of the mails proceeded by E were previously carried by the USP, (4) at identical prices, the mail volume per address carried by E is equal to 20 percent of the Incumbent's volume and (5) with a 20 percent price discount, E has a mailing volume per address equal to that of I. The parameters used to calibrate this model are similar to the ones used by De Donder et al. (2006). The hypothetical country we consider has a population of 2 million households with an average household size of 2.5 persons.

Households and companies – which means addresses – are grouped into routes that are ranked according to their fixed cost of delivery. We generate upstream and downstream costs for two postal regions with extreme postal densities: a 'most dense stop point' (urban) region and a 'most non-dense stop point' (rural) one. These regions differ according to the number of delivery points per stop (Grouping Index) and the distance between two stops in each route. Consequently, the delivery method differs in the two regions. We generate values for the delivery costs using the best practice cost model developed in d'Alcantara and Amerlynck (2006), with hypothetical country data defined above and factor costs equal to the average across European Union Countries in euros for 2005. Best technology includes different distribution modes in the two types of areas: by foot 90 percent, by bicycle 9 percent and by car 1 percent in the 'most dense stop point' (urban) area; by foot 1 percent, by bicycle 9 percent and by car 90 percent in the 'most non-dense stop point' (rural) area. The 'most dense' region has a Grouping index of 15, which corresponds to a reasonable higher limit for this index (Boldron et al., 2006). The 'most non-dense stop point' region has a Grouping Index of 1. Our resulting unit cost estimates are given in Table 12.1.

Reported on an annual basis, the delivery cost of one address in the postal 'most dense' region is equal to €9 (€0.045 per unit) and it increases to €67 (€0.335 per unit) in the postal 'most non-dense' region. These costs are considered to be fixed; that is, independent of the mailing volume. The estimated variable costs is equal to €0.185 per letter and it is independent of the delivery point.

We consider that E is more cost effective than the USP. In particular, both the fixed cost per address and the variable cost per mail are assumed to be equal to 80 percent of USP's

Table 12.1 Unit costs derived using the best practice cost model

Configuration of Stop Points	Non-Dense	Dense
USP unit cost	0.520	0.230
Upstream unit cost USP	0.185	0.185
Delivery unit cost USP Urban	–	0.045
Delivery unit cost USP Rural	0.335	–

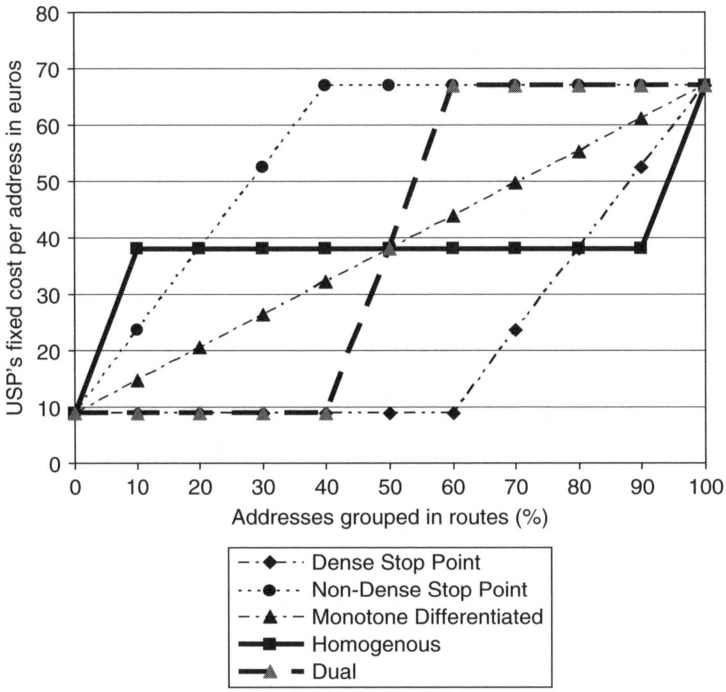

Figure 12.1 Five typical USP fixed cost curves per address

cost. A lower frequency of delivery could explain such a cost differential, but so could labor cost differentials between E and I.

3.2 Typical Country Configurations

We then generate the five possible route-cost profiles representing five typical country configurations shown in Figure 12.1. For the case of the *Monotone Differentiated route-cost profile*, the delivery cost per address is monotonically and linearly increasing from the lowest value to the highest value corresponding to addresses located in Stop Points with decreasing density. For a *Dual route-cost profile*, 40 percent of the addresses are located in Stop Points with a constant high density, and 40 percent are located in Stop

Points with a constant low density. The remaining addresses have a delivery cost that is monotonically increasing between these extreme values. In the case of a *Homogenous route-cost profile*, 80 percent of the addresses have a delivery cost equal to the average cost between rural and urban cost. The remaining costs per address are monotonically increasing from the lowest value to the average and from the average to the highest. The three configurations introduced are symmetric, meaning that the average delivery cost per address is €38 and hence, the total fixed cost for the USP is identical. The two next configurations are non-symmetric. In the case of the *Dense Stop Point route-cost profile*, 60 percent of the addresses are in a constant high postal density zone, while for the *Non-Dense Stop Point route-cost profile*, 60 percent of the addresses are in a constant low postal density zone. In both cases, for the remaining addresses, the delivery cost is monotonically increasing up to the highest value and starting from the lowest value, respectively. These two route-cost profiles result in a lower and a higher total delivery cost than the other three configurations, respectively. The distributions of fixed cost per address within the national population of postal destinations are represented in Figure 12.1.

4. SIMULATION RESULTS

For each of the five route-cost profiles, we generated four different sets of prices and other market results. The first scenario considered refers to the situation where the USP operates as a monopolist. In this monopoly case, the USP price is regulated and set at the break-even point. The second set of results corresponds to the situation where the market is opened to competition and where the USP continues to apply the pre-FMO price. Then, we adapt the prices to competition and we present the unregulated USP prices that maximize the firm's profit and the regulated USP prices that maximize the welfare. For each configuration, we report the prices (p_I, p_E), the market coverage of E, (n), the mail volume per address in the one-operator (x_I^M) and the duopoly zones (x_I^D, x_E^D), the profits and welfare and the subsidy to the USP. Subsidies are evaluated at a shadow cost of 0.3, meaning that transferring one euro to the USP reduces welfare by 1.3 euros.

4.1 General Overview

The five typical country configurations generate different outcomes after FMO. To mention a few striking figures, we observe that the market coverage of E is extremely limited in the Homogenous route case (no more than 10 percent), while it is substantial in the Dual (at least 45 percent) and the Dense Stop Point route case (at least 65 percent). If prices are capped after FMO, consumers do not face high price increases, since the highest is limited to 4 eurocents. In one case (the Non-Dense Stop Point route), the price even decreases after FMO. The reason for that decrease in price is the misalignment between prices and costs for the low-costs addresses where the firms compete. Despite a limited price increase, the USO financing is threatened in three route configurations. In the Dual and the Dense Stop Point route cases, it is not possible to maintain the USO without subsidies. And these subsidies could be quite high (up to €10.57 per address). In the Monotone Differentiated route case, the regulator has more options to finance the

USO after FMO. We show that a pay-or-play mechanism, the removal of price regulation or state subsidies can all be used to finance the USO with different welfare impact.

4.2 Graphical Analysis

The five typical country configurations can also be overviewed in a graphical way. Figures 12.2–12.6 show unit cost curves before FMO corresponding to the five route-cost profiles. These figures should be interpreted exactly like Figure 12.1 except that fixed cost per address is replaced by unit costs per address and that the uniform USP price of the average product can be shown in the same figure. At a given price, E captures a fraction of the mails sent to the covered addresses. This results in a per-address profit for E. E covers all

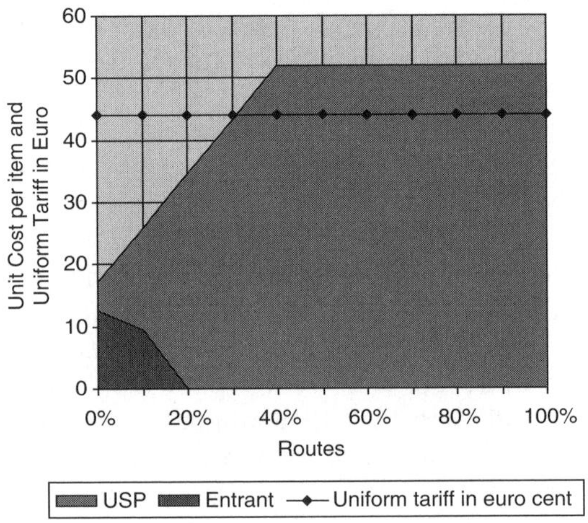

Figure 12.2 Non-Dense Stop Point routes

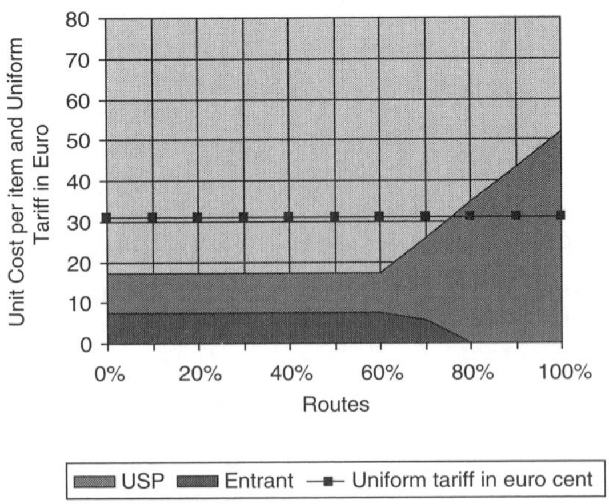

Figure 12.3 Dense Stop Point routes

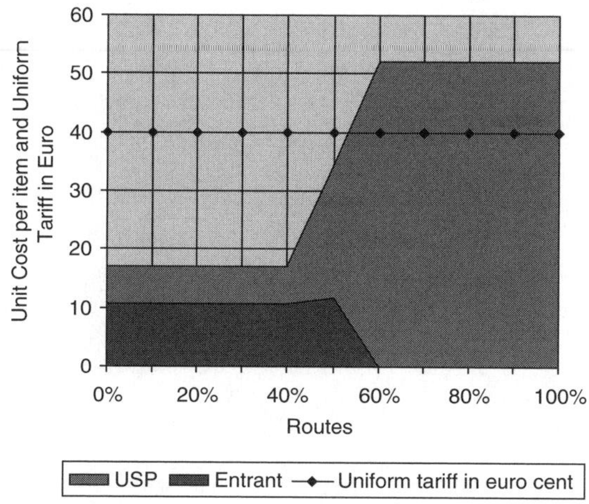

Figure 12.4 Dual routes

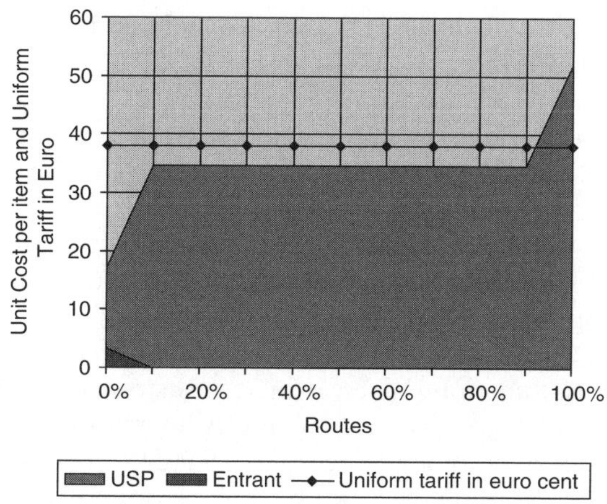

Figure 12.5 Homogeneous routes

the addresses for which the fixed delivery cost is smaller than the per-address profit. Clearly the two main determinants of market coverage by E are (1) the price charged by the USP who affects the per-address profit and (2) the distribution of the fixed cost per address. These two factors explain the observed differences in market coverage and in the mail volume of E.

The uniform price set by the USP at the first stage of the process and the final results of market coverage for Es obtained in the fourth stage, with FMO under welfare-maximizing prices, are shown on each figure. The dark areas at the bottom left-hand side of these figures correspond to the mail volume share of E within his coverage. The size of his coverage, in percent, is given by the extreme right-hand side point of this dark area at the bottom of the figure.

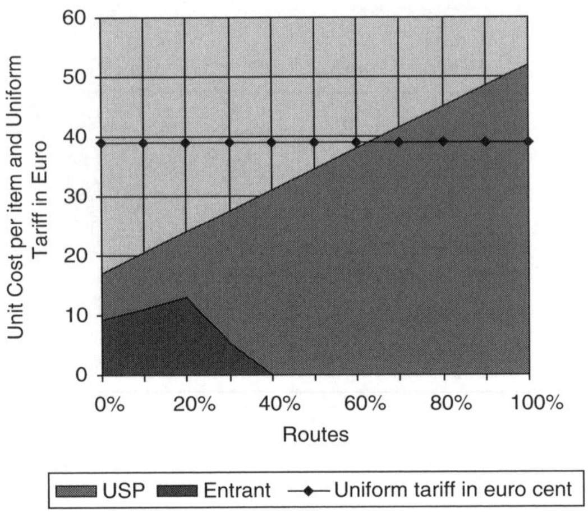

Figure 12.6 Monotone Differentiated routes

4.3 Symmetric Country Configurations: Monotone Differentiated, Dual and Homogenous Route Profiles

It is interesting to start our analysis with these three symmetric cases, because these three route-cost profiles have the same total delivery cost. Hence, the price charged by a regulated monopoly USP is the same (€0.37) and so is welfare.

But FMO has different consequences in these three country configurations. In the case of FMO with constant USP price, the market coverage of E ranges from 3 percent of the addresses in the Homogenous route-cost profile (Table 12.4) to 43.5 percent in the Dual route-cost profile (Table 12.3). The market coverage of E depends on the shape of the delivery cost per address function. When it increases steeply (Homogenous route-cost profile), the coverage is limited. With a smoothly increasing function, the coverage becomes more substantial and in the limit case of a flat delivery cost per address function (Dual and Dense Stop Point route-cost profile), E coverage is extremely important, since it consists of the flat zone and a fraction of the routes with increasing cost.

In all the cases, with unchanged prices, the entry of a new firm results in losses for the USP, losses that must be compensated with subsidies. In the dual route case, where E has a high market coverage, the subsidies is more than €8 per address.

Consider the optimal reaction after FMO. From the following tables, we see that in all configurations, both the unregulated and the regulated prices increase compared to the monopoly situation. This means that tariffs of E and of the Incumbent are strategic complements: when the tariff of I increases, the tariff of E follows by increasing as well. Consequently, the price charged by E and its market coverage increase too. But the magnitude of the price increase depends on the configuration. In all cases, the optimal price increase does not exceed €0.03. But, this limited price increase imposes the condition that to finance the universal coverage by I, the Regulator intervenes in USO financing through subsidies. This holds true except in the Homogenous route case, where E's market coverage is limited and the USP manages to break even at regulated prices after FMO.

Table 12.2 Monotone Differentiated route-cost profile: total fixed cost to USP: €76 million

	Monopoly USP	FMO with constant USP price	FMO, profit-maximizing prices	FMO, welfare-maximizing prices
p_I	0.37	0.37	0.43	0.39
p_E	–	0.27	0.32	0.30
x_I^M	206	206	193	200
x_I^D	–	100	79	98
x_E^D	–	117	127	113
n	–	351 601 (17.5%)	653 664 (32.6%)	472 004 (23.5%)
Π_I (€ million)	0	−6.82	1.03	−1.19
Π_E (€ million)	0	1.43	4.95	2.58
Welfare (€ million)	212	204	199	204
Subsidy (€ million)	0	6.82	0	1.19

Table 12.3 Dual route-cost profile: total fixed cost to USP: €76 million

	Monopoly USP	FMO with constant USP price	FMO, profit-maximizing prices	FMO, welfare-maximizing prices
p_I	0.37	0.37	0.45	0.40
p_E	–	0.28	0.31	0.29
x_I^M	206	206	188	198
x_I^D	–	100	52	78
x_E^D	–	117	151	132
n	–	870 320 (43.5%)	960 832 (48%)	908 685 (45.4%)
Π_I (€ million)	0	−16.90	−9.24	−11.57
Π_E (€ million)	0	6.81	16.42	10.77
Welfare (€ million)	212	187	185	189
Subsidy (€ million)	0	16.9	9.24	11.57

Table 12.4 Homogenous route-cost profile: total fixed cost to USP: €76 million

	Monopoly USP	FMO with constant USP price	FMO, profit-maximizing prices	FMO, welfare-maximizing prices
p_I	0.37	0.37	0.48	0.375
p_E	–	0.28	0.29	0.28
x_I^M	206	206	182	205
x_I^D	–	100	34	98
x_E^D	–	117	164	118
n	–	70 320 (3%)	200 000 (10%)	74 403 (3.5%)
Π_I (€ million)	0	−1.36	25.5	0
Π_E (€ million)	0	0.28	2.32	0.32
Welfare (€ million)	212	210	197	211
Subsidy (€ million)	0	1.36	0	0

Table 12.5 Total mail volume after FMO, in millions of items

Mail volume	Monotone Differentiated	Dual	Homogenous
USP	353.07	287.72	402.51
Entrant	53.53 (13.2%)	120.78 (29.6%)	8.84 (2.2%)
Total	406.60	408.51	411.36

Table 12.6 The average cost of the USP in the monopoly case and after FMO

Monopoly USP	Monotone Differentiated	Dual	Homogenous
0.37	0.40	0.44	0.37

Now compare these regulated prices with the prices that the USP would have charged in the absence of regulation. Price increases are limited by the fact that higher prices imply higher market share and higher market coverage by E. For example, in the Homogenous route case any further price increase would increase the market coverage from 10 percent to 90 percent of the addresses. The reaction of E explains why we observe different price differentials between regulated and non-regulated prices. Welfare consequences of relaxing regulatory price restrictions are also different, and particularly important in the Homogenous route case where a large price increase is imposed on captive customers.

In the Dual route-cost case, the market coverage of E is close to 50 percent. Moreover, with regulated prices, it is in this configuration that E has the highest market share in the duopoly region. Consequently, in this configuration, the mail volume of the Incumbent falls considerably, as illustrated in Table 12.5.

This fall in volume increases the average cost of the mail (Table 12.6). This holds true in all configurations, with the specificity that in the Dual route case, it is impossible to find a price that would guarantee a non-negative profit for E. The important decline in I's mailing volume – E carries a third of all mails while it covers less than a half of the territory – and the associated rise in the average cost is such that there no longer exists a price such that I breaks even. This impossibility to find a price for the USP compatible with a non-negative positive profit is referred to as a graveyard spiral (Crew and Kleindorfer, 2005). As illustrated in these three examples, the need for subsidies after FMO potentially depends on the route-cost country configuration.

4.4 Non-Symmetric Distributions: Dense and Non-Dense Stop Point Route-cost Profiles

In the Dense Stop Point route-cost case, the country is mainly urban and the total delivery cost and the average cost in the monopoly case (€0.27) are the lowest. Conversely, in the Non-Dense Stop Point route-cost case, the average cost for a monopoly USP (€0.49) and the total cost are the highest.

In the Non-Dense Stop Point route-cost case, a majority of addresses are located in the high-cost rural zone. Consequently, to cover the fixed cost of delivery – which is the highest of all configurations – a monopoly USP must set a high letter price. At first, it

Table 12.7 Non-Dense Stop Point route-cost profile: total fixed cost to USP: €110.8 million

	Monopoly USP	FMO with constant USP price	FMO, profit-maximizing prices	FMO, welfare-maximizing prices
p_I	0.49	0.49	0.50	0.44
p_E	–	0.33	0.33	0.31
x_I^M	182	182	180	190
x_I^D	–	33	29	57
x_E^D	–	165	168	148
n	–	402 276 (20%)	424 350 (21%)	300 732 (15%)
Π_I (€ million)	0	−18.20	−18.81	−21.41
Π_E (€ million)	0	4.7	5.22	2.62
Welfare (€ million)	165	135	133	138
Subsidy (€ million)	0	18.2	18.81	17.36

Table 12.8 Dense Stop Point route-cost profile: total fixed cost to USP: €41.2 million

	Monopoly USP	FMO with constant USP price	FMO, profit-maximizing prices	FMO, welfare-maximizing prices
p_I	0.27	0.27	0.39	0.31
p_E	–	0.23	0.28	0.24
x_I^M	224	224	188	217
x_I^D	–	152	83	129
x_E^D	–	79	130	98
n	–	1 211 830 (65%)	1 405 130 (70%)	1 262 730 (65%)
Π_I (€ million)	0	−7.98	8.19	0
Π_E (€ million)	0	0.82	15.49	4.47
Welfare (€ million)	252	239	240	247
Subsidy (€ million)	0	7.98	0	0

seems that this configuration would deter E to invest in a large delivery network. But this is countervailed by the high price charged by I. A high price allows E to capture a large mail volume and to realize a high margin on its sales. Hence, E could have a large profit per address and the market coverage is substantial.

After FMO, the Regulator faces the following dilemma: either it increases the price – which further increases the mail unit cost because E reacts by extending its market coverage – or it decreases the price and the mail unit cost. In our numerical simulations, we found that the optimal regulatory response is a slight price decrease, which has a consequent impact on E's market coverage.

In the Dense Stop Point route-cost case, a majority of the addresses are located in the low-cost urban zone. At first, it seems that this configuration is the most favorable to E because the delivery costs are low. But, this uniformity in delivery conditions implies that the monopoly price necessary to break even is low. Therefore, E has a low margin on its

Table 12.9 Total mail volume after FMO, in millions of items

Mail volume	Dense Stop Point route-cost	Non-Dense Stop Point route-cost
USP	322.87	340
Entrant	123.74 (27.7%)	44.5 (11.57%)
Total	446.62	384.51

Table 12.10 Results for FMO under welfare-maximizing prices

	Tariff, USP (€)	Coverage, E (%)	Subsidy per address (€)	Subsidy per Entrants' profit
Non-dense Stop Point route-cost	0.44	15.0	10.57	6.6
Dual route-cost situation	0.40	45.4	5.79	1.1
Monotone differentiated route-cost	0.39	23.5	0.60	0.5
Homogenous route-cost situation	0.38	3.5	0.00	0
Dense Stop Point route-cost	0.31	65.0	0.00	0

sales, and its mail volume is limited too. A low profit per address generates large scale entry only if the margin is high enough to cover the urban delivery cost. If this is the case, the market coverage of E is at least the urban zone (60 percent of the addresses). In the Dense Stop Point route-cost case, the entry decision is dependent on the mail demand configuration and on the possibility to achieve a sufficient margin to cover the fixed delivery cost in the urban region. This is hampered by the low price charged by I.

Mail volumes and market shares in the Dense and Non-Dense Stop Point route-cost cases are given in Table 12.9. Despite the highest coverage in the Dense Stop Point route-cost profile, the market share of E is not the highest of all cases, because I's low price makes mail capture more difficult.

4.5 USO Financing after FMO

Let us compare the results for our route-cost profiles in the fourth and final stage with FMO under welfare-maximizing prices. In Table 12.10 we have ordered the results for five route-cost profiles starting with the highest USP tariff results. We compare USP tariffs, entrant's coverage, the subsidy per address to be paid by the regulator and the ratio between this subsidy and E's profit.

It appears that high prices are associated with high subsidies. High prices and high subsidies mean that in these configurations, the cost of maintaining the USO is the greatest in a competitive market. Subsidy per address is the highest in the Dual and the Non-Dense Stop Point route-cost profiles, though the market coverage by E differs. These two configurations have in common that a high fraction of the addresses are located in the rural region. In the monopoly case, the USO financing is possible through high cross-subsidies from the low-cost addresses to the high-cost ones. After FMO, these subsidies are no longer possible because E captures a large fraction of the mail sent to the low-cost addresses. Mail capture is facilitated by the relatively high prices charged in these two configurations. In these two configurations, we clearly observe cream-skimming of the market by E. E captures a large fraction of the mail in the profitable region and leaves the non-profitable zones to I. Clearly, USO financing is a major concern in this case.

In the Dense Stop Point and the Homogenous route-cost cases, no subsidy must be paid to the USP after FMO, even at welfare-maximizing prices. But the mechanism at play is different. In the Dense Stop Point route-cost case, the market coverage of E is substantial but its market share is limited due to low pricing by the USP (see Figure 12.3). This low pricing is feasible because there are few high-cost addresses that must be subsidized (unlike the Dual route-cost case). In the Homogenous route-cost case, the market coverage of E is extremely limited. There are few profitable addresses for E and E captures only 2.2 percent of the total mail volume (Table 12.5). Such a limited lost volume can easily be compensated with a slight price increase.

We finally report the ratio between the USO Subsidy and E's profit. If this ratio has the value one, this means that the amount of subsidy to be paid by the Regulator corresponds to the amount of E's profit. With a ratio of one or below, the Regulator can, instead of paying subsidies, establish a pay-or-play mechanism where E is required to contribute to the USO financing unless it satisfies the obligations itself (as is the case in Finland today[6]). With a ratio above one, a pay-or-play mechanism alone cannot be used to sustain the USO. Notice that, because subsidies are evaluated at a shadow cost of 0.3, the welfare would be higher with a pay-or-play financing than with state subsidies.

5. CONCLUDING REMARKS

With all the limitations of our model in mind – the use of a single average product model may be the greatest – we can conclude from this set of calibrations that, assuming FMO at the EU level, the results of the market outcomes will differ widely according to national configurations of delivery route-costs. This means that both the requirements for a national USP subsidy and the likely FMO bypass coverage of Es need to be studied in light of national route-cost configurations. When the Regulator chooses a price cap to maximize national welfare, we find that the largest coverage by E appears in the 'Dense Stop Point' and Homogenous route-cost situations and the smallest coverage in the Homogenous route-cost cases. We can also conclude no subsidy is due by the Regulator in the 'Dense Stop Point' and the Homogenous route-cost cases and the Subsidy per address is highest in the 'Non-dense Stop Point' and Dual route-cost cases. Finally we can conclude that subsidies, where necessary or desirable, could be financed out of E's profits in the Dual route-cost and Monotone Differentiated route-cost cases. In these instances, the pay-or-play mechanism could be used as a way of financing the Universal Postal Service.

Another set of calibrations should be made to explore the sensitivity of the results to various assumptions such as the displacement ratio, the shadow cost of subsidies, the relative cost effectiveness of E with respect to the USP and other inputs to this model.

Because different market outcomes are observed in our five typical configurations, our model calls for empirical research about the observed route-cost profiles in EU member countries. Such research, together with extensions of the present model, should lead to greater insights about the consequences of FMO on POs and on the extent of competition likely to be established in various postal markets.

NOTES

1. http://eur-lex.europa.eu/LexUriServ/site/en/com/2006/com2006_0594en01.pdf based on the study by the EC to be found in http://eur-lex.europa.eu/LexUriServ/site/en/com/2006/com2006_0596en01.pdf
2. http://eur-lex.europa.eu/LexUriServ/LexUriServ.do?uri=CELEX:31997L0067:EN:HTML
3. http://eur-lex.europa.eu/LexUriServ/site/en/oj/2002/l_176/l_17620020705en00210025.pdf
4. If this operation is cheap enough for the sender, it could justify that the demand addressed to the Entrant is independent of its market coverage.
5. Bloch and Gautier (Chapter 9, this volume) show that high delivery costs mean that the Entrant is likely to choose the access option for mail delivery.
6. But the payment required is so high that up to now, no competitor has entered the market (PricewaterhouseCoopers, 2006).

REFERENCES

Boldron, F., D. Joram, L. Martin and B. Roy (2006), 'From size of the box to the costs of universal service obligation: a cross-country comparison', in M.A. Crew and P.R. Kleindorfer (eds), *Liberalization of the Postal and Delivery Sector*, Cheltenham, UK and Northampton, MA, USA: Edward Elgar, pp. 37–52.

Crew, M. and P. Kleindorfer (2005), 'Competition, universal service and the graveyard spiral', in M.A. Crew and P.R. Kleindorfer (eds), *Regulatory and Economic Changes in the Postal and Delivery Sector*, Kluwer Academic Publishers, pp. 1–30.

d'Alcantara, G. and B. Amerlynck (2006), 'Profitability of the universal postal service provider in a free market with economies of scale in collect and delivery', in M.A. Crew and P.R. Kleindorfer (eds), *Progress toward Liberalization of the Postal and Delivery Sector*, Springer; annex on http://www.alcantara.be/belgium/Antwerp.htm

De Donder, P., H. Cremer, P. Dudley and F. Rodriguez (2006), 'A welfare analysis of price controls with end-to-end mail and access services', in M.A. Crew and P.R. Kleindorfer (eds), *Liberalization of the Postal and Delivery Sector*, Cheltenham, UK and Northampton, MA, USA: Edward Elgar, pp. 227–47.

PricewaterhouseCoopers (2006), 'The impact on universal service of the full market accomplishment of the Postal Internal Market in 2009', report to the European Commission; http://ec.europa.eu/internal_market/post/doc/studies/2006-impact-report_en.pdf

APPENDIX

Model Structure

A.1 General assumptions and notation

The model is a pure bypass model. Firm I (the incumbent) serves all addresses and firm E (entrant) is not bounded to universal coverage. Firms compete in price. The price game is a von Stackelberg price game where firm I decides first on its price.

A.1.1 Cost We denote by c_k the sum of all variable costs per mail proceeded by firm $k=I,E$. This cost includes the cost of all upstream activities and the variable cost of delivery. Delivery to address n implies a fixed delivery cost. We rank the N addresses according to their fixed delivery cost. A function $F_I(n)$ represents the fixed delivery cost of I for delivery at address n. The function $F_I(n)$ is such that $\partial F_I(n)/\partial n \geq 0$. The total delivery cost for I who must serve all addresses is $\bar{F}_I = \int_0^N F_I(\tau)\,\mathrm{d}\tau$. E is characterized by a fixed delivery cost per address $F_E(n)$. We assume that $\partial F_E(n)/\partial n \geq 0$; that is, the fixed cost may differ between E and I but the ranking of addresses does not, because the ranking depends on delivery point density. The total fixed delivery cost for an Entrant who serves only the n^* cheapest addresses is $\int_0^{n^*} F_E(\tau)\,\mathrm{d}\tau$.

A.1.2 Demand The demand for mail addressed to the receiver in n is derived from the utility of a representative sender. Denote by $U(x_I,x_E)$ the utility of a sender that sends x_I and x_E mails to address n. We derive inverse demand functions by solving $\max_{x_I,x_E} U(x_I,x_E) - p_I x_I - p_E x_E$. If an address n is only served by firm I, the corresponding monopoly inverse demand function is found by solving $\max_{x_I} U(x_I,0) - p_I x_I$. From these inverse demand functions, we define:

Monopoly demand: $x_I^M(p_I)$,
Duopoly demands: $x_I^D(p_I,p_E)$ and $x_E^D(p_I,p_E)$.

We assume that the products sold by firms I and E are imperfect substitutes.

A.1.3 Profit When E covers the n cheapest addresses, the profits of the firms are as follows:

$$\Pi_I = (N-n)(p_I - c_I)x_I^M + n(p_I - c_I)x_I^D - \bar{F}_I, \tag{12.A1}$$

$$\Pi_E = n(p_E - c_E)x_E - \int_0^n F_E(\tau)\mathrm{d}\tau \tag{12.A2}$$

E is the second mover in the price game. If firm I charges a price p_I, the profit-maximizing price $p_E^*(p_I)$ and the optimal coverage $n^*(p_I)$ are found by solving the following equations:

$$\frac{\partial \Pi_E}{\partial p_E} = (p_E^* - c_E)\frac{\partial x_E}{\partial p_E} + x_E = 0, \tag{12.A3}$$

$$\frac{\partial \Pi_E}{\partial n} = (p_E^* - c_E)x_E - F_E(n^*) = 0. \tag{12.A4}$$

The price charged by E maximizes the per-address profit and the area covered consists of all addresses for which the per-address profit is larger than the fixed delivery cost. We will assume that prices are strategic complements:[1] $\mathrm{d}p_E^*/\mathrm{d}p_I > 0$. This implies that an increase in p_I increases the market coverage of E.

A.1.4 Welfare The welfare is the sum of the consumer surplus and the firm's profit minus the subsidies. Subsidies have a shadow cost of λ, meaning that transferring one euro to the USP reduces the welfare by $1 + \lambda$ euros. The welfare is as follows:

$$W = (N - n^*)U(x_I^M, 0) + n^*U(x_I^D, x_E^D) - c_I((N - n^*)x_I^M + n^*x_I^D) - c_E n^* x_E^D$$
$$-\bar{F}_I - \int_0^{n^*} F_E(\tau)\mathrm{d}\tau - (1 + \lambda)S,$$

where $S = \text{Max}[0, -\Pi_I]$ and p_E^* and n^* are given by (12.A3) and (12.A4).

A.2 The four stages

A.2.1 Monopoly USP At an initial stage, the market is not yet open to competition and firm I operates as a monopolist. We assume that before FMO, the regulator imposes a price $\bar{p}_I$ that maximizes the welfare while guaranteeing a non-negative profit for firm I. The efficient price is the solution of: $\max_{p_I} W$ subject to $\Pi_I = 0$ and $n^* = 0$.

A.2.2 FMO with pre-FMO prices In a second stage, the market is open to competition but the Regulator continues to impose the pre-FMO price $\bar{p}_I$. The price charged by E and its coverage are $p_E^*(\bar{p}_I)$ and $n^*(\bar{p}_I)$ (see equations (12.A3) and (12.A4)). Since firm I realizes a zero-profit at price $\bar{p}_I$, $S > 0$ (equivalently, $\Pi_I < 0$) after FMO.

A.2.3 FMO with profit-maximizing prices In a third stage, the regulator allows firm I to set its price freely. Anticipating the reaction of E at price p_I, I determines its price by solving the following equations:

$$\max_{p_I} \Pi_I = n^*(p_I - c_I)x_I^D + (N - n^*)(p_I - c_I)x_I^M - \bar{F}_I.$$

The first-order conditions read as follows:

$$\frac{\partial \Pi_I}{\partial p_I} = n^*\left[(p_I - c_I)\left(\frac{\partial x_I^D}{\partial p_I} + \frac{\partial x_I^D}{\partial p_E}\frac{\partial p_E}{\partial p_I}\right) + x_I^D\right] + (N - n^*)\left[(p_I - c_I)\frac{\partial x_I^M}{\partial p_I} + x_I^M\right]$$
$$+ \frac{\partial n^*}{\partial p_I}[(p_I - c_I)(x_I^D - x_I^M)] = 0. \tag{12.A5}$$

The first two terms are a linear combination of the profit-maximizing conditions under duopoly and monopoly. The weights given to these two conditions depend on the market coverage of E. If we ignore the last term, we can show that the optimal price lies in between the optimal duopoly price,[2] found by solving

$$(p_I - c_I)\left(\frac{\partial x_I^D}{\partial p_I} + \frac{\partial x_I^D}{\partial p_E}\frac{\partial p_E}{\partial p_I}\right) + x_I^D = 0$$

and the optimal monopoly price,[3] found by solving

$$(p_I - c_I)\frac{\partial x_I^M}{\partial p_I} + x_I^M = 0.$$

And clearly, the larger is E's market coverage, the closer is the price to the duopoly price. But there is a third term in the first-order condition that captures the fact that a change in price will induce E to change its market coverage. In particular, if I raises its price, the per-address profit of E increases and so does the market coverage.

Since $x_I^D < x_I^M$, this third term is negative and therefore it contributes to reduce the price charged by a profit-maximizing incumbent. In other words, the optimal price for I will be lower *once it takes into account the impact of its pricing decision on the area covered by E.*

But how important is this effect? To capture that, we must turn back to the equation giving the optimal value of n^*. Rewriting (12.A4), we have $n^* = F_E^{-1}((p_E^* - c_E)x_E)$, where F_E^{-1} is the inverse of F_E. F_E^{-1} is an increasing function of p_I, meaning that any price increase by the USP leads to a higher coverage by E. This seriously limits the possibility for the USP to raise its price in a competitive market. The flatter $F_E(n)$, the larger the increase in market coverage by E following a price increase. Clearly the distribution of the fixed cost, described by the function $F_E(n)$, has a central importance in determining the evolution of prices after FMO.

A.2.4 FMO with welfare-maximizing price In the last stage, the regulator imposes a welfare-maximizing price to I. This price is the solution of $\max_{p_I} W$, taking into account the impact of p_I on the price and the coverage of E. The first-order conditions read as follows:

$$\frac{\partial W}{\partial p_I} = n^*\left[\frac{\partial W}{\partial x_I^D}\left(\frac{\partial x_I^D}{\partial p_I} + \frac{\partial x_I^D}{\partial p_E}\frac{\partial p_E}{\partial p_I}\right)\right] + (N - n^*)\left[\frac{\partial W}{\partial x_I^M}\frac{\partial x_I^M}{\partial p_I}\right] + \frac{\partial W}{\partial n^*}\frac{\partial n^*}{\partial p_I} = 0. \quad (12.A6)$$

Equation (12.A6) is similar to (12.A5). This first-order condition is a linear combination of the one that applies in stage 1 when the USP is a monopolist and the one that would apply in the duopoly case. There is, in addition, a third term that captures the impact of the USP price on E's coverage. If the welfare under duopoly is higher than the welfare under monopoly, this third term is positive and, it will contribute to increase the price and the market coverage. If the welfare is higher when the USP remains a monopolist, this third term is negative and it will contribute to decrease the price and E's coverage.

NOTES

1. The linear demand functions used in the calibration exercise satisfied that assumption.
2. The price that firm I would have charged if $n^* = N$.
3. The price that firm I would have charged if $n^* = 0$.

PART IV

Regulation

13. Postcodes in competitive postal markets: is there a case for regulation?

Alex Dieke and Sonja Schölermann

1. INTRODUCTION

In most countries, postcodes had been developed by postal administrations (incumbent postal operators) long before postal markets were exposed to competition. Postcodes were – and continue to be – largely regarded as internal operational systems and their designs reflect the operational necessities of the incumbent postal operator. However, postcode systems exhibit significant spillovers (external effects). For example, changing postcodes cause transaction costs for anybody that uses them, including senders and receivers. In addition, they affect many users outside the postal sector that, for example, use postcodes to specify unique addresses for automobile navigation systems. In competitive postal markets, alternative delivery services use the public postcode systems as well since the postcode is typically part of the address on any postal item.

When telecommunications markets were liberalized, responsibility for numbering (allocating access line numbers) was typically handed over to sector regulators. Independent numbering was regarded a prerequisite for competition in the local loop. Inspired by this (possible) analogy to telecommunications markets, this chapter investigates whether operation of the postcode system gives incumbents the opportunity to discriminate its competitors.

In October 2006, the European Commission has presented a proposal for a new Postal Directive, which stipulates that

> Whenever necessary to protect the interest of users and/or to promote effective competition, and in the light of national conditions, Member States shall ensure that transparent and non-discriminatory access conditions are available to the following elements of postal infrastructure or services: *postcode system*, address database, post office boxes, collection and delivery boxes, information on change of address, redirection service, return to sender service (Commission of the European Communities, 2006; emphasis added).

Against this background, the chapter discusses whether or not there is a need for regulating public postcode systems. For that purpose, we investigate two potential causes for regulation: (i) whether – or to what extent – postcodes can be considered as public goods; and (ii) whether opportunities for anti-competitive conduct result from the incumbent's control over the postcode system.

Section 2 of the chapter analyzes postcode systems from the perspective of public goods theory and discusses whether external effects provide arguments for regulating postcode systems. Section 3 discusses opportunities for anti-competitive conduct by incumbent operators that control national postcode systems; based on the case study of Germany. If such opportunities exist, some form of regulatory control over postcodes may be necessary. Section 4 concludes.

2. POSTCODES IN THE THEORY OF PUBLIC GOODS

This section examines postcodes from the perspective of the theory of public goods. After a short introduction to the theory, postcodes are analyzed from the points of view of senders and receivers. The objective of this section is to assess whether or not postcode systems exhibit characteristics of public goods and whether this provides reasons for regulatory measures.

2.1 A Sketch of the Theory of Public Goods

The theory of public goods uses two criteria to classify goods: rivalry and excludability.[1] Rivalry describes the degree to which a good can or cannot be jointly consumed by several users at the same time. A good is non-rivalrous if individuals can jointly consume it and do not interfere with each other in consumption. In contrast, a good is rivalrous if it can be consumed by one individual only.

Excludability describes whether individuals can be excluded from consuming a good. Most goods are excludable since, for example, they can be locked or hidden away. A good is non-excludable if it is impossible to stop other individuals from using the good (e.g., fresh air). The combination of excludability and rivalry yields four categories of goods which are shown in Table 13.1.

In reality, pure public goods rarely exist. Generally accepted examples for public goods are national defense or air purity (absence of air pollution). More common phenomena than public goods are 'club goods' and 'common pool resources'. It is feasible to exclude individuals from the consumption of club goods, but rivalry among them does not occur (e.g., television broadcasting or the use of a private golf course). Yet rivalry occurs when individuals are using common pool resources where exclusion is not possible (under current legislation). Examples for common pool resources include offshore fishing resources or public roads.

Public good theory is often used to justify regulatory intervention (government action). The basic conclusion is that free markets produce efficient outcomes only for private goods. The excludability of other users means that each individual buys exactly the amount of the good he or she wants to consume. Since consumption exhibits no externalities on other con-

Table 13.1 Public and private goods

	Excludable	Non-excludable
Rivalrous	Private good	Common pool resource
Non-rivalrous	Club good	Public good

Source: Microeconomic textbooks, e.g. Grossekettler (2003).

sumers, the free market leads to a social optimum. The provision of public goods is complicated by the free rider problem: as individuals cannot be excluded, they benefit not only from the quantities of the public good they buy themselves, but also from those paid for by other users. If a public good were provided in an unregulated market, users would conceal their true preferences for consumption and benefit from the consumption of other users instead. Hoping for others to buy what they want, everybody will end up with having less of the public good than the society is initially willing to pay for. A free market for public goods will lead to suboptimal results: there will be too little of the good (or too poor quality).

It is widely accepted that regulation (some form of social decision-making) is necessary to ensure that a socially optimal amount of a public good is available.[2] The case for regulation is less straightforward for club goods and common pool resources: the literature provides clear indications that there is a risk for market failure for these goods, but careful cost–benefit analysis is needed in order to assess whether regulation is beneficial in a social perspective.

2.2 Postcodes from Senders' and Receivers' Points of View

This section discusses whether postcode systems exhibit characteristics of public goods. It therefore discusses whether consumers can be excluded from 'consuming' postcodes and whether there is rivalry in the use of postcodes.

The first important question is: 'Who is the consumer of a postcode system?' Clearly, both senders and receivers are affected by postcode systems. However, senders and receivers have different expectations and needs towards the 'good' postcode system. Therefore, good characteristics of postcodes are different for senders and receivers. Consequently, we test for the two criteria 'excludability' and 'rivalry' separately for the two groups. In addition, we found that good characteristics are different for 'geographic postcodes' on the one hand and 'non-geographic postcodes' on the other hand. Geographic postcodes relate to a specific area; that is, the standard type of postcodes. By contrast, non-geographic postcodes relate to receivers (addressees), but do not necessarily have a clear geographic meaning. Examples of non-geographic postcodes are those used for post office boxes, individual postcodes attributed to large business customers or temporary postcodes that postal operators offer advertisers as reply addresses for advertising campaigns.

2.2.1 Senders' perspective

Theoretically, senders could be excluded from 'consuming postcodes' if they were kept secret. In practice, however, a postal operator will necessarily publish a postcode system since it is in his own interest that senders use correct postcodes. Indeed, geographic postcodes can only work if they are public. Similarly, exclusion of senders might be possible for those postcodes which have been changed or added after the last publication of the postcode system. Practically, though, a postal operator cannot be interested in excluding senders from using postcodes since this would lead to more misaddressed mail, which in turn causes operational trouble and raises cost for the operator. In practice, it seems impossible (or grossly irrational) to exclude senders from using a postcode system (both geographic and non-geographic postcodes).

There is no rivalry between different senders that use the same postcode (for addressing a letter). When using a postcode, senders do not diminish each other's benefit and may use all kinds of postcodes without abrasion or deterioration. The quality of the postcode

Table 13.2 Are postcodes public goods?

	Type of postcode	Excludable?	Rivalrous?	Conclusion
Senders' perspective	Geographic	No	No	Public good
	Non-geographic	No	No	Public good
Receivers' perspective	Geographic	No	Some	Public good
	P.O. box	Yes	Some	Club good
	Large business	Yes	Yes	Private good
	Ad campaign	Yes	Yes	Private good

system does not decrease when it is used more. Thus, there is no rivalry from the senders' perspective – for neither geographic nor non-geographic postcodes. Nor can senders be excluded. From the senders' perspective, consequently, the postcode system is a public good (see Table 13.2).

2.2.2 Receivers' perspective

Each residential receiver living in the territory of a country has an address that is assigned a postcode (geographic postcode). Since every address is assigned a postcode, it is impossible to exclude a receiver from using this geographic postcode.[3]

Rivalry among receivers depends on the exact design of the postcode system. For example, if a system was designed in such a way that each building was assigned a specific postcode, while at the same time the postcode system was a system with very limited free resources (e.g., a three- or four-digit-system), receivers might well be rivals for postcodes. Practically, however, postcode systems typically leave free resources and adapt the design of the system periodically to the number of postcodes needed (e.g., by using more digits or introducing alpha-numeric systems). In Germany, the postcode system is designed so that large numbers of receivers can share the same postcode without interfering with each other's consumption.[4] Even where postcodes are assigned to single buildings, several inhabitants of the same building can share a postcode effectively without rivalry.

2.2.3 Are postcodes public goods?

For geographic postcodes, we conclude that they are non-excludable and – in practice – non-rivalrous from the receivers' perspective. Therefore, geographic postcodes must be considered as public goods.

Non-geographic postcodes are generally excludable from the receivers' perspective: the organization that administers the postcode system (typically the incumbent operator) could easily refuse granting a non-geographic postcode to anybody seeking such postcode. For these non-geographic postcodes, there is some rivalry from the receivers' perspective. For example, a postcode granted to one firm for an ad campaign cannot be used by another firm (meaningfully). Similarly, once a postcode has been assigned to one business (as a complete address), it cannot be assigned to other users any more. For postcodes that relate to post office boxes, rivalry is only weak since several P.O. boxes can share the same postcode. As in practice there is a limit to the number of P.O. boxes at one location, we consider postcodes for post office boxes to be club goods. Other non-geographic postcodes, however, are private goods from the receivers' perspective.

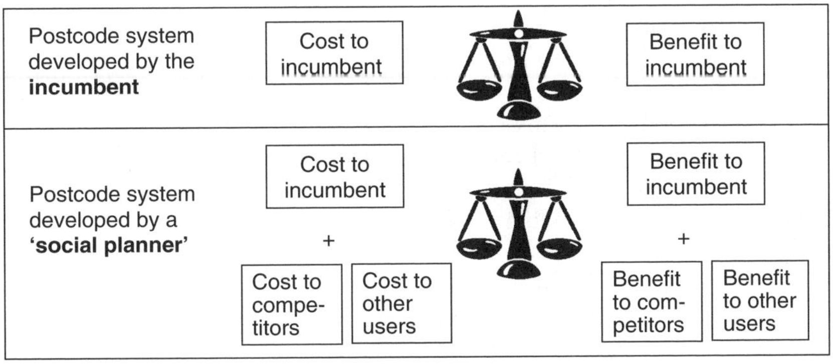

Figure 13.1 Relevant considerations for a socially optimal postcode system

To conclude, large parts of the postcode system can be classified as public goods. In particular, geographic postcodes are classified as public goods from both the senders' and the receivers' perspectives. We see this result as an indication that market failure seems likely for geographic postcodes and this area is therefore possibly susceptible for regulation. By contrast, public good theory offers less indication that any regulation should be necessary for non-geographic postcodes.

2.3 Does Private Supply of Postcode Systems Lead to Market Failure?

The public good characteristics of large parts of the postcode system could easily lead to the conclusion that it should be regulated in some way. The critical question in this context is whether the current postcode systems are efficient from a social perspective, taking into account costs and benefits of all users of a postcode system (see Figure 13.1).

Where an incumbent manages the postcode system independently, he will optimize the system according to his costs and benefits stemming from the postcode system. Therefore, the postcode system will not be socially optimal if other groups of users have different expectations and needs towards the postcode system than the incumbent operator. In light of the costs related to regulation, we would deem regulation necessary only if the social needs were significantly different from those of the incumbent operator.

2.3.1 Costs to the incumbent and total costs to society

The total costs of the postcode system stem from two sources: on the one hand, from development and introduction of the system; on the other hand, from the maintenance and ongoing changes of postcodes.

In the first case, costs for developing and introducing postcodes have been predominantly borne by the incumbent (postal administration). In addition, all holders of postal addresses incurred transaction costs at the time when the postcodes were introduced. More efficient sorting and conveyance and thus lower cost for the production of postal services were the major benefit for the incumbent – and the key objective for introducing postcodes.

Second, the incumbent regularly incurs costs for maintaining the postcode system and making changes to it. Typically, postcodes change where new residential areas arise, and when postcodes are changed for existing addresses significant transaction costs for postal users (and other users) occur. For example, businesses and households need to memorize their new postcode, reprint business cards and inform all regular business contacts about the new address etc.[5] When making ongoing changes to the postcode system, absent regulation, the incumbent has little incentive to consider the cost incurred by other users.

2.3.2 Benefits to the incumbent and total benefits to society

When designing postcode systems, postal operators mainly aimed at improving the efficiency of mail processing and related costs. A social optimum needs to consider, in addition, benefits for other users of the postcode system. Practically, though, the incumbent's optimization will differ from a social one only if the individual interests of the incumbent differ strongly from those of other users.

Competitors (i.e., other postal operators than the incumbent) mainly expect the postcode system to allow for unique identification of addresses. They share this need with the incumbent. In addition, an operator would wish that the structure of the postcode system reflects the network of sorting centers and transport routes. Current postcodes systems generally are tied to the network infrastructure of the incumbent – but not those of competitors. Yet, this only seems to be a problem if competitors process mail volumes at least as large as those of the incumbent. With lower volumes, entrants will need less sorting centers and thus less granular sorting. As long as entrants' volumes are lower than those of the incumbent, entrants are able to merge several postcode areas for their operational procedures (sorting and transport).

Other postal users are senders and receivers of postal items. Their basic interest is to identify addresses uniquely via the postcode system when sending postal items. In addition, users will prefer less complex postcodes as they are easier to memorize (e.g., prefer less digits over more digits). Non-postal users (e.g., market research companies, GIS suppliers) have similar needs: unique identification and ease of use. All these users thus require nothing more than a logical, coherent nationwide system.

Overall, our assessment is that the requirements of other users do not differ substantially from those of the incumbent. Of course, the postcode system is not designed to fit other users' requirements exactly. In principle, it may have been possible to generate even higher social benefits if the postcode system were more adapted to the needs of other users. However, changing existing postcodes would cause high costs that outweigh eventual extra benefits for competitors or other users.

2.3.3 Market failure?

Overall, postal and non-postal users of the postcode system would not want a significantly different postcode system. Their needs towards postcodes are essentially similar to those of the incumbent. At the stage of introduction of postcodes, therefore, market failure of a considerable extent seems very unlikely. It must be noted that the incumbent bears a major share of the total social cost of introducing a postcode system and also accounts for a significant share of the social benefits. It is due the dominant role of the incumbent with respect to both costs and benefits of the postcode systems that postcode systems can develop even in an unregulated market. This is in contrast to many public goods that are not provided at all without social decision-making, or only in miniscule quantities.

For changes to existing postcodes, however, cost implications for other users (than the incumbent) can be very relevant and should be taken into account before changing a postcode. In an unregulated situation, there is a risk that the incumbent may not limit changes of geographic postcodes to those that are strictly needed from a social perspective. In order to address this possible market failure, participation of affected parties seems an appropriate solution.[6] There are different options for such participation. In Sweden, changes of geographic postcodes need to be agreed by a 'Postcode Council'. The council is composed of representatives from the incumbent and other postal operators (effectively, CityMail and one association of private operators), the postal national regulatory authority and local land registry offices. This procedure, in Sweden, runs smoothly and does not seem very costly, as there are very few changes to geographic postcodes (about ten a year) and there is little controversy about the changes. A more light-handed approach would be to oblige the incumbent to consider the interest of all affected parties when changing a geographic postcode – but make no prescriptions as regards the procedure for this consideration. We cannot give a general recommendation about the appropriate form of participation. Different options may be suitable for different countries, depending on the degree of controversy to be expected. Absent a relevant number of complaints from users, competitors, or local authorities, however, complex consultation procedures appear overly prescriptive. In any case, clear procedures should be established for dealing with postcodes-related complaints. In the EU, a practicable solution would be to extend (or clarify) the NRA's competence for arbitration and resolution of complaints related to changes of postcodes.

3. POSTCODES AND POSSIBLE RISKS TO COMPETITION: THE GERMAN CASE

In addition to possible arguments from public goods theory, regulation of postcodes would be needed if an incumbent that operates the postcode system had the opportunity to discriminate against its competitors. This section discusses three potential factors that could be risks to competition: (i) incumbents could hold up information about changes in the postcode system; (ii) incumbents could entirely deny competitors information on non-geographic postcodes (geographic postcodes are public by nature); or (iii) competitors cannot 'issue' own postcodes to large business customers. Based on discussions with market participants in Germany, we discuss whether or not these three factors are relevant problems for competition.[7] However, we assume that the relevance (or irrelevance) would be similar for other countries.

3.1 Risk 1: Slow or Ineffective Information about Postcode Changes

Competitors and mailers need up-to-date information about postcodes to correctly address and deliver postal items. Thus, competitors are interested in being informed immediately about postcode changes. Delay in receiving such information means extra cost for both mailers and competitors.

In Germany, incumbent Deutsche Post AG (DPAG) offers three possible ways to access changes of the postcode system.[8] First, DPAG publishes a CD-ROM with postcode information quarterly. Complete information about changes of postcodes is not available more frequently. Second, there is an Internet research option on DPAG's website. The

Internet research facilitates only searches for single postcodes or addresses. This access option is meant for household users rather than large mailers and competitive postal operators. Third, competitors can look up changed addresses in an address database operated by DPAG (fees determined by the German postal regulator Bundesnetzagentur).[9]

The current publication practice of DPAG generally seems to work well and there is no systematic obstruction of competitors. However, the access to postcode information is not optimized to the needs of competitors. According to Bundesnetzagentur, there were very few complaints from competitors about delayed information on new postcode areas. Slow information about changes of postcodes thus appears as a relevant, though not very urgent, problem.

3.2 Risk 2: Incumbent Entirely Denies Competitors' Information on Non-geographic Postcodes

Geographic postcodes are necessarily public, since they must be known to senders and receivers. For non-geographic postcodes, however, the delivery address is agreed in a contract between incumbent and receiver and may therefore (theoretically) only be known to these two parties.

In Germany, there is no obligation for DPAG to inform about changes of postcodes transparently. In practice, however, Deutsche Post AG publishes postcode information for non-geographic postcodes in the three manners described above. An exception is that holders of non-geographic postcodes can object to publication of their delivery address for privacy reasons. In this case, postcodes (and addresses) of these receivers are available neither to senders nor to other postal operators. If a competitor receives a letter addressed to such a non-geographic postcode for delivery, there is no way to get information about the delivery address. The operator will have to hand over the letter to DPAG (and pay postage).

A particular case of non-geographic postcodes in Germany, that are problematic for competitors, are those with a 'fake destination'. The actual delivery address for these postcodes is outside the area indicated by the first two digits of the postcodes. This service is typically used by firms that are widely known to be located in a certain city but have their mail department (or service provider for mailroom management) in a different area. For example, a bank located in Frankfurt may want its postcode to start with '60xxx' (for Frankfurt) but want its mail to be physically delivered to a subsidiary in some distant low-cost area. Without information about proper delivery addresses, it is impossible for competitors to deliver mail addressed to such non-geographic postcodes. While there are no indications that Deutsche Post currently behaves in such obstructive manner against its competitors, the possibility exists.

3.3 Risk 3: Competitors Cannot 'Issue' Own Postcodes to Business Customers

As a service to receivers of mail – and to reduce their own delivery cost – incumbents offer post office boxes (to smaller firms) and direct postcodes (to larger firms – see the French CEDEX system). In Germany, entrants in the postal market do not have the opportunity to offer such services to their customers. By contrast, Swedish regulation allows competitors of Sweden Post to operate post office boxes and to issue specific postcodes to their customers (PTS, 2000).

Facilitating customized delivery options for business customers, and therefore issuing postcodes, however, does not directly affect the end-to-end delivery business. An end-to-end operator does not need to grant postcodes to its customers in order to provide delivery services. As long as there is transparent information about the delivery address related to a postcode, there will not be more or less competition in the delivery market if competitors operate own postcodes for their customers. Consequently, a requirement for access to postcodes (to assign their end-customers) is not necessary to ensure fair competition in the delivery market.[10]

In Germany, there are currently no operators that call for the right to assign postcodes themselves. Consequently, this does not appear a very relevant problem. Low usage of regulated postcodes in Sweden, too, indicates that there may not be an important need for regulated access to postcodes that competitors can assign to their customers.

3.4 Summary Evaluation of the Possible Risks

Access to information on postcode addresses as well as timely information about changes to the postcode system is crucial to new entrants and other users of postcode systems. Where incumbents operate the postcode system entirely unconditioned by regulation, they may be tempted to hold up or deny information to competitors in order to achieve competitive advantages. In Germany, the only country where we have examined this question in detail, the incumbent does provide a fair amount of information on postcodes as well as on postcode and address changes. Therefore, potential competition risks arising from postcode systems do not seem to be urgently relevant.

In many countries, incumbents operate their postcode systems without clear rules about the extent of information to be provided to new entrants as well as to the public. Sweden and the UK are notable exceptions, where legislative provisions on access to postcode information exist. For all liberalized postal markets, we suggest that the rights to information about postcodes should be clarified by legislation or regulatory decree.

4. CONCLUSIONS

Our first conclusion is that incumbents – given their current dominant market positions – are best placed to operate and administer the postcode system of a country. Potential risks to competition that result from the incumbent's responsibility for operating the postcode system do not appear to justify transferring this responsibility to the regulator.

Second, we conclude that incumbents should be obliged to provide the public with transparent and up-to-date information about all postcodes: geographic and non-geographic ones.[11] Where privacy rules do not allow publication of postcode addresses in a country (e.g., for a postcode assigned to a firm that does not want its address to be published), regulation should ensure that all postal operators have access to the addresses related to these postcodes.

Third, no additional regulation – in excess of transparent information – is necessary for non-geographic postcodes.

Fourth, changes of geographic postcodes affect the interests of various stakeholders: private households and businesses (as postal users), competitive postal operators, municipalities, and many other non-postal users; for example, website operators, list brokers, governmental administrations and so on (all of which use geographic postcodes to identify addresses, shops, customers, or citizens). Therefore, the postal regulator should have competence for resolving complaints about postcode changes. The Swedish example suggests that additional consultation procedures can work effectively and can be relatively inexpensive, but it is not clear that such procedures are necessary and appropriate in other countries.

NOTES

1. See, for example, Musgrave et al. (1990).
2. While there should be a collective/regulatory decision for the amount of the public good, the good need not necessarily be produced by the government (or a public operator).
3. The situation may be somewhat different for the case of houses built without permission. This, however, is rather a problem of general housing regulation/regional planning and appears unrelated to our subject.
4. See Kuhlmann (1992).
5. In addition, municipalities may be affected by changes of geographic postcodes as many regard the postcodes as a part of their municipal identity. In fact, a substantial fraction of complaints received by German postal regulator Bundesnetzagentur are from municipalities (as mentioned by Bundesnetzagentur staff in discussions with the authors).
6. In two European countries, there is some regulatory oversight over changes of postcodes: In Sweden, any change to the postcode requires consultation of the postal operators, land registry offices, and other public administrations (see PTS, 2000). In the UK, ballots and specific information rules are included in Royal Mail's licence (see Postal Services Commission, 2004).
7. See Dieke and Schölermann (2006) for a more comprehensive discussion of the German case.
8. All these options are technically 'access to address changes' but include postcode information. In all cases, information about postcode changes is not available for such households that have 'opted out'; that is, have objected to their address being forwarded. For households that object to forwarding of their address, competitive postal operators cannot access the new address or new postcodes by any means.
9. While there is a legal requirement for DPAG to provide access to address changes, it is not clear that this includes access to postcodes. In German legislation, postcodes are not a necessary element of an address.
10. The postcode system also impacts the provision of services downstream to the conveyance of postal items, especially operation of post office box facilities and the handling of incoming mail for receivers. Competition in this downstream market could be promoted by giving competitors the opportunity to assign postcodes to their customers.
11. Of course, such requirements should be limited to those incumbents that operate public postcodes systems. Whether or not incumbents should be forced to introduce postcodes in countries where no postcodes exist today is a different question.

REFERENCES

Commission of the European Communities (2006), 'Proposal for a Directive of the European Parliament and of the Council amending Directive 97/67/EC concerning the full accomplishment of the internal market of Community postal services', COM(2006) 594 final.

Dieke, A. and S. Schölermann (2006), 'Wettbewerbspolitische Bedeutung des Postleitzahlensystems', WIK Discussion Paper No. 276, Bad Honnef.

Grossekettler, H. (2003), Öffentliche Finanzen, in D. Bender et al. (eds), *Vahlens Kompendium der Wirtschaftstheorie und-Politik*, 8th edn, Munich: Vahlen, vol. **1**, pp. 561–717.

Kuhlmann, R. (1992), 'Die neue gesamtdeutsche Postleitzahl', *Postpraxis*, **43**(7), 146–55.

Musgrave, R.A., P.B. Musgrave and L. Kullmer (1990), *Die öffentlichen Finanzen in Theorie und Praxis*, 5th edn, Tübingen: UTB Siebeck.

Postal Services Commission (2004), 'Review of Royal Mail's licence condition 20 – postcode address file code of practice. A decision document', March.

PTS (2000), 'Definition of the postal infrastructure in Sweden', August.

14. Negotiated volume discounts in a regulated post*

Matthew H. Robinson, Margaret M. Cigno and J.P. Klingenberg

1. INTRODUCTION

In 2002, the US Postal Service (USPS) proposed to implement a ground-breaking deal with Capital One Services, Inc., then the largest user of First-Class Mail® in the United States. This negotiated service agreement (NSA), as it was termed, represented a significant departure from the tariff rate structure that has historically been employed for domestic rates. For the first time, volume-based discounts were offered to encourage growth in First-Class marketing mail. The agreement consisted of two main features. The first feature was a cost-based proposal to provide Capital One with electronic notifications when its First-Class solicitations were found to be undeliverable, in lieu of physical return of such pieces.[1] The second feature was a schedule of discounts designed as declining blocks, whereby Capital One would pay lower marginal rates as its First-Class volume achieved certain volume thresholds. The duration of the agreement was three years.

After review by the Postal Rate Commission (PRC),[2] the agreement was approved with the addition of a constraint that the total amount of discounts from the declining block provision could not exceed the estimated savings from the cost reduction provision. Four more customized agreements have since been approved and implemented, as has a one-year extension of the Capital One agreement. In addition, two other agreements have been proposed.[3]

Volume discounts in regulated posts are becoming more common, partly as a means of stemming diversion to electronic alternatives. There is a risk that these agreements could result in net losses for the posts. For posts that have been privatized this may not be a significant concern, as shareholders bear the risk of losses and management is accountable to shareholders. However, USPS is a public enterprise that has historically operated with a break-even constraint, so any losses from volume discounts would be recovered through rates paid by non-participating mailers.[4]

This chapter will focus on analyzing the effects of volume-based discounts on the NSAs that have been implemented to date. Section 2 will attempt to estimate the net financial impact on USPS of the discounts, and discuss specific issues to each that complicate the analysis. Section 3 will examine the effects of changing circumstances on specific agreements. Section 4 will briefly discuss the limitations of various volume forecasting methods.

2. EVALUATION OF EXISTING DISCOUNTS

2.1 Background

When USPS filed the first NSA with the PRC in 2002, several issues received public attention. The Capital One NSA (as well as the Discover, Bank One, HSBC, and Washington Mutual NSAs) contained two monetary features: cost savings to USPS through electronic Undeliverable as Addressed (UAA) returns, and volume discounts for the mailer aimed at driving marketing mail growth and creating 'new' contribution to USPS.

The relatively non-controversial feature of the mailer foregoing physical returns in favor of electronic Address Correction Service (ACS) returns provided cost savings to USPS. When the NSAs with ACS return savings were filed, USPS was charging mailers for electronic returns of UAA mail, while providing physical returns as a bundled element of First-Class Mail.[5] To protect potentially sensitive customer information in statement mail, only the marketing mail was eligible for the electronic returns feature of the NSA.

The primary issue of controversy in the NSAs was related to the volume discounts, designed to create additional contribution. This contribution would come from new First-Class marketing mail, induced by volume discounts. A central concern was the ability of the USPS, in conjunction with the mailer, to accurately estimate future volumes under a given set of rates. The mailer provided USPS with estimates of volume it would send without the agreement (before rates volumes). These estimates were filed publicly with the PRC in the request for approval of the agreement. USPS and the mailer agreed to a schedule of declining block rates, whereby the mailer would receive increasing marginal discounts as it increased its volume of First-Class Mail. Based on this agreement, the mailer provided an after rates forecast predicting how much its volume would grow in response to the volume discounts. The reliability of these before rates and after rates forecasts has been a key issue for both interveners and for the Commission.

Predicting mailing patterns for long-term periods (over a year in advance) is considered difficult to do with accuracy. Direct mail marketing is driven by the expected profitability of each mailing; influenced by diverse factors ranging from interest rates to real wages. The difficulty of long-term forecasts will be discussed in greater detail in Section 3. In each NSA, the co-proponents of the NSA provided the volume forecasts. The Commission was concerned that inaccuracies in the forecasts could result in discounts being awarded to 'anyhow' volume; that is, volume that would have been mailed regardless of the discounts. Providing discounts for anyhow volumes in excess of new contribution from volume growth due to the discounts results in less contribution to the Service than would have been achieved without the NSA.

In its first recommended decision on an NSA, the Commission capped total discounts at the level of savings from the electronic ACS provision. This meant that in the worst case scenario where all discounted volume was anyhow volume, the Service would still break even on the NSA. The cap was met with heavy criticism from USPS and the mailer who claimed that limiting the discounts would prevent the NSA from reaching its full potential. The cap has also led to assertions that many potential NSA partners have abandoned the process for fear of having their discounts capped. A savings-based cap is particularly burdensome for mailers who may not easily be able to generate savings for the USPS.

When the Commission again used the ACS savings cap for the Bank One NSA in

MC2004-3, the USPS Board of Governors requested the Commission reconsider its decision, the circumstances of which will be discussed in more detail in Section 3.1. As part of its response to the request, the Commission developed a framework for designing NSAs that would not require a savings-based stop loss cap.[6]

2.2 Model Description

In the Commission's Decision in Response to the Reconsideration request in MC2004-3 (the Bank One NSA), a model to explain volume growth in response to NSA discounts and determine net contribution to the USPS was outlined.[7] The model works in the following manner. The price elasticity is used to draw a demand curve through the point defined by the after rates volume and the discounted rate. The before rates volume is estimated by moving back up the demand curve to the full rate. The net effect on contribution can then be estimated. In Figure 14.1, the shaded area marked as A represents the contribution from mail above the initial quantity, and the area marked as B represents the revenue lost to discounts on mail that would have been sent at the full rate.[8] In this example, A is greater than B, indicating a net increase in USPS contribution.

For this chapter, our analysis uses a range of econometrically devised elasticities[9] to construct demand curves for each of the NSAs for which periodic data reports have been submitted. Using the actual after rates volumes reported in the periodic data reports, we then move back up the demand curve to the full price rate and determine what the before rates volume would have been. We have termed the difference between the calculated before rates volume and the discount threshold as anyhow volume. Discounts paid to anyhow volume constitute leakage discounts, or revenue lost on discounts for mail that would have been sent without the NSA (area B in Figure 14.1). These discounts reduce the value of the NSA to USPS. Combining the leakage discounts with the new contribution[10] from the volume responsive to the discount (area A in Figure 14.1) gives the net

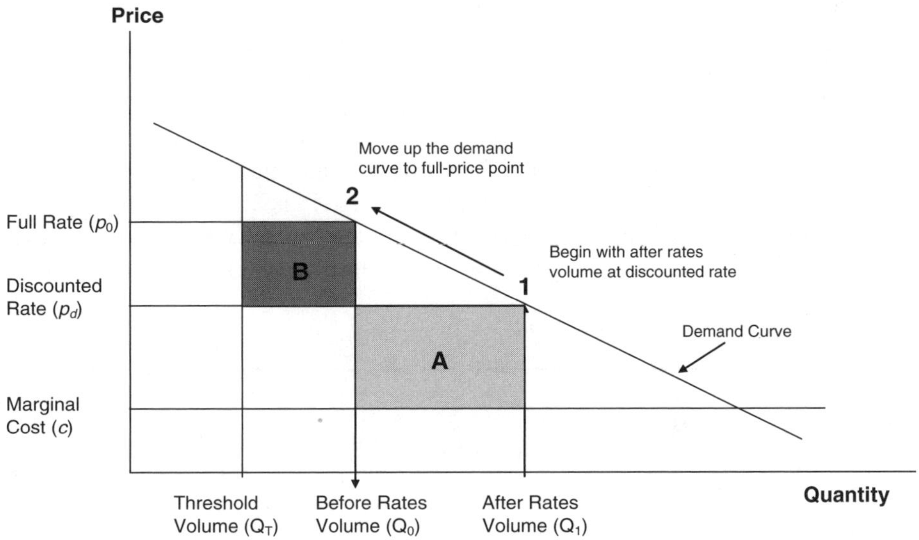

Figure 14.1 Contribution effects of volume discounts

contribution of the NSA discounts to USPS. Thus, the model provides an independent and empirical analysis of the range of profitability to USPS of either growth or an intra-class shift in volume due to NSA discounts.

The formula for calculating the before rates volume with the own price elasticity is as follows:

$$V_b = V_a \left[\frac{P_0}{P_d} \right]^{E_p}$$

Where V_a is the after rates volume, P_0 is the original price, P_d is the discounted price of the last mailed piece, and E_p is the own price elasticity.[11]

Since the NSA discounts have been intended to increase the use of First-Class Mail for advertising, it is likely that some volume that the mailers would have otherwise sent using Standard Mail (a lower-priced advertising class) would shift to First-Class in response to the discounts. To reflect the effects of this shift, we incorporate a discount elasticity that captures cross-price effects based on the average rate difference, or 'discount', between First-Class and Standard Mail. The formula for calculating the before rates volume with both own-price elasticity and the discount elasticity from Standard Regular mail is as follows:

$$V_b = V_a \left[\frac{P_0}{P_d} \right]^{E_p} \left[\frac{P_0 - P_S}{(P_d - P_S)} \right]^{E_C}$$

Where P_s is the price of Standard and E_c is the discount elasticity.

For this chapter, we evaluate the NSAs using three scenarios with different assumptions about the elasticity of the mailers' marketing mail. Table 14.1 shows the elasticities used in this chapter.

These elasticities represent subclass averages developed by the USPS in the most recent rate case.[12] While subclasses are typically understood to share common market characteristics, there is undoubtedly some degree of variation in elasticity among the mailers that make up each subclass. In the NSAs we are evaluating, the mail eligible for discounts is workshared First-Class Mail. Therefore, we use the average elasticity for that category of mail as the starting point for our analysis. However, the discounts are designed to leverage the mailers' use of First-Class for advertising, and our analysis assumes that it is the advertising mail that will respond to the discounts. Since workshared First-Class mail includes large volumes of mail that are unlikely to be very price-elastic (e.g., statements), we also utilize the elasticity of Standard Regular (an advertising subclass), which is about twice that of workshared

Table 14.1 Elasticities used in the model

	R2006-1 elasticities
First-Class workshared own price	−0.013
Standard Regular own price	−0.296
Average Standard Regular letter discount (relative to First-Class)	−0.111

Table 14.2 NSA data summary

		NSA data					
		Historical volume			Active NSA volume		
		Year −3	Year −2	Year −1	Year 1	Year 2	Year 3
Capital One	AR projected				757.5	744.4	713.6
	Actual	753.6	788.9	1137.9	843.0	811.7	704.6
	Discounts				$1.83	$2.57	
Discover	AR projected				169.0	174.0	174.0
	Actual	209.0	196.0	138.0	196.9	192.5	
	Discounts				$2.82	$2.65	
Bank One	AR projected				232.7	260.5	266.4
	Actual	103.9	270.6	207.8	261.9		
	Discounts				$8.81		
HSBC	AR projected				174.2	265.2	319.3
	Actual	107.7	95.7	95.7	24.6		
	Discounts				$_		

Notes: Marketing volumes in millions; Discounts in millions; Bank One forecasts are merger adjusted.

First-Class. We also incorporate the effects of shifts in volume from Standard Mail to First-Class in response to a reduction in the difference between the prices of the two classes.

Using these elasticities, and the model described above, this chapter will develop a range of possible net contribution to the USPS of NSAs thus far.[13] First, a review of some basic data from each NSA is helpful. The table above contains the volume (in millions of pieces) of First-Class marketing mail projected in the after rates forecast (AR Projected Volume) as well as the volume actually sent (Actual Volume). It also includes the discounts received (in millions of US$). Because the NSAs do not run concurrently, a standardized time label is used. Each NSA is filed with three years of historical data and will run for three years. Thus, years −3 to −1 contain historical volumes before the NSA, and years 1 to 3 contain volumes during the NSA.

2.3 Capital One

With three full years completed, the Capital One NSA provides the richest data for examination. The basis for the NSA was to retard the escalating shift by Capital One from First-Class marketing mail to Standard Mail by providing an incentive to continue mailing First-Class, for which mail pieces make a higher contribution to institutional costs.[14] Table 14.3 shows the breakdown of Capital One's mail volume (in millions of pieces).

The NSA began in 2004, and the First-Class to Standard shift, even with the NSA, is quite pronounced. The overall marketing mail dropped by over 133 million pieces, with First-Class declining by 295 million. In the first year of the agreement, Capital One

Table 14.3 Capital One historical volume

	Historical volume			Active NSA volume		
	Year −3	Year −2	Year −1	Year 1	Year 2	Year 3
FC marketing	753.6	788.9	1137.9	843.0	811.7	704.6
FC operational	338.6	470.6	582.9	553.3	493.7	496.4
Std marketing	538.2	980.4	896.3	1057.7	1084.7	1426.3

Table 14.4 Estimate of net contribution from discounts: Capital One

	FC workshared	FC with cross price	Std with discount
Year 1	200 220	2 740 705	5 595 563
Year 2	(669 161)	869 305	3 154 567
Year 3	–	–	–

received discounts totaling $1.83 million on 69 million pieces. In the second year of the agreement, Capital One received discounts of $2.57 million on 80 million pieces. In the third year, the discount threshold was not reached.

The difference between the projected First-Class marketing mail and the actual First-Class marketing mail is explained in the periodic data reports provided by USPS as an increase purely in response to the discounts for the first two years of the agreement. This explanation does not discuss the increase in Standard volume, nor does it attempt any empirical economic analysis.

Using the elasticities provided in Table 14.1 and the volume analysis model described above, we calculated a range of net contribution from the new Capital One volume. Our results are shown in Table 14.4.

The net contribution is the difference between the increase in contribution resulting from mail generated in response to the discounts and the contribution lost by providing discounts for mail that would have been mailed at full price. In year one the net contribution ranges from $0.2 million, assuming an elasticity equal to the own-price elasticity of First-Class workshared mail, to $5.6 million assuming an own-price elasticity equal to Standard Regular Mail and a discount elasticity between First-Class workshared and Standard Regular.[15] In year two the range is between negative $0.7 million and positive $3.2 million. While the true elasticity of Capital One is not known, we believe that it likely falls between the own-price elasticity of First-Class workshared and Standard Regular and that a First-Class/Standard discount elasticity applies. Consequently, according to our analysis it is likely that USPS had a net gain in contribution from the declining block rates. The savings from electronic returns generated by the agreement provided an additional benefit.

2.4 Discover

The next NSA implemented was with Discover, another financial institution. Filed with the PRC as MC2004-4, this agreement was the first functionally equivalent NSA; available to

Table 14.5 Discover historical volume

	Historical volume			Active NSA volume	
	Year −3	Year −2	Year −1	Year 1	Year 2
FC operational	309.0	333.0	313.0	300.4	300.3
FC marketing	209.0	196.0	138.0	196.9	192.5
Std marketing	591.1	499.8	483.8	471.6	692.4

Table 14.6 Estimate of net contribution from discounts: Discover

	FC workshared	FC with discount	Std with discount
Year 1	(2 154 692)	(1 071 760)	(300 966)
Year 2	(1 941 493)	(1 112 960)	(334 244)

co-proponents who were in similar mailing situations to Capital One. While Discover does not mail as much as Capital One, it still represents a significant portion of the mail stream. In addition, both firms use a mix of First-Class and Standard Mail to solicit new customers. The deal contained the same elements of the Capital One NSA: foregoing physical returns in favor of electronic ACS, and new First-Class solicitation mail driven by volume discounts.

Discover's volume history was more stable than Capital One's in the immediate period before implementation of the NSA. Its overall use of the mail, and its mix of Standard Mail and First-Class Mail, was more consistent than that of Capital One. Only two years of the NSA have been completed to date.[16]

The primary issue of contention with the Discover NSA was the fact that the volume threshold for discounts was below the before rates volume forecast provided by Discover. This meant that for the first time the Commission and the interveners had to consider leakage discounts a nearly unavoidable aspect of the deal made between the co-proponents. In the first year of the NSA, Discover received discounts on First-Class marketing mail that even USPS agrees would have been sent without any discounts. The leakage incorporated into the deal produces net losses with all elasticities considered in our analysis.

Discover responded to the NSA by sending an amount of First-Class marketing mail consistent with its historical pattern, raising questions about the efficacy of the discounts in inducing new mail volume. In the periodic data reports, USPS cites the decrease in Standard Mail and the increase in First-Class Mail as an indication that the deal is working better than expected at developing new First-Class contribution. However, the data suggest that while some mail may have been encouraged to remain in First-Class, a significant amount of the First-Class Mail was anyhow volume. The resulting leakage is very difficult for the Discover NSA to overcome with new contribution. Table 14.6 examines the range of net contribution from the Discover NSA estimated in the same manner as the Capital One case outlined above.

Our analysis shows that unlike Capital One, the Discover NSA discounts are likely to have resulted in negative contribution for USPS. Because of this, we performed additional analysis on the data whereby we used an iterative process to calculate the own-price elasticity assumption that would have resulted in breakeven contribution. Interestingly, our analysis found that the volume discount feature of the NSA breaks even for the USPS if Discover's marginal piece of First-Class marketing has an own-price elasticity of −0.362, just a little more elastic than the class-wide average for Standard Regular Mail.[17]

An important lesson from our analysis is that minimizing leakage volume is essential for volume discount agreements to be profitable for the post. In the Discover filing, the co-proponents estimated the before rates First-Class marketing volume at 156 million pieces and the after rates at 169 million,[18] with discounts starting at 105 million.[19] Using the assumption that the marginal piece has the elasticity of Standard Regular Mail, and is responsive to discount elasticity with Standard Mail, our analysis shows that an after rates volume of 169 million pieces of First-Class marketing mail corresponds to a before rates volume of 152 million pieces; remarkably close to the forecasted before rates volume. This suggests that, assuming the above elasticity, the 28 million piece discrepancy between the projected after rates marketing volume and the actual after rates marketing volume is likely due to economic factors other than the discount. Furthermore, based on the forecasts provided in the proposal, the model indicates the USPS would realize $1.7 million in contribution from new First-Class marketing mail but lose nearly $1.5 million in leakage discounts in the first year; a net gain in contribution of just $0.2 million.[20] Had the discount threshold been set at the estimated before rates volume, the USPS would have earned an additional $1.5 million.

2.5 Bank One/Chase

The third NSA to be implemented was with Bank One, again a financial institution. Due to a merger between Bank One and JP Morgan/Chase (Chase), this case presents unique problems that are discussed at further detail in Section 3.1. It is very difficult to distinguish historical volumes of the merged bank. In Table 14.7, no Chase volumes are included for the first year (year −3).

When the two companies merged, the provision in the NSA was for the discount threshold to increase by the volume of the new company in the previous year. The USPS appears to have had some difficulty in implementing this NSA. The full periodic data report concerning the Bank One discounts was filed late and contained incomplete data.[21] In this data report, the USPS states that the mailstreams of the merged institution were

Table 14.7 Bank One/Chase historical volume

	Historical volume			Active NSA volume
	Year −3	Year −2	Year −1	Year 1
FC operational	479.1	825.4	846.6	676.3
FC marketing	103.9	270.6	207.8	261.9
Std marketing	967.0	1606.1	1232.1	2391.0

Notes: Chase volumes are included for 2002 and 2003; Chase FC marketing and std volumes are 95% estimates from interrogatory OCA/BOC-T1-18; The Postal Service estimates that Bank One and Chase integrated mailstreams halfway through year 1.

Table 14.8 Comparison of projected and actual Bank One/Chase volumes

	Bank One	Chase	Merged	
	1/2 of year 2 Projection	1/2 of year 2 Projection	Columns (1) + (2) Projection	October 1 to March 30 Actual
	(1)	(2)	(3)	(4)
FC operational	253.3	190.3	443.6	444.3
FC marketing	81.7	48.6	130.3	238.4
Std marketing	468.4	200.0	668.4	1922.5

integrated halfway through the year (October 1, 2005). The 2005 volume of 'heritage' Chase volume was reported by USPS to be 373 million pieces, and the threshold was increased based on this volume, per the merger provision in the NSA. In the Chase comments concerning the Commission reconsideration, Chase states that the 2005 volume of First-Class Mail was 574 million pieces, and that mailstream integration occurred on January 2, 2006. This discrepancy appears as if it may be similar to the difficulty that Washington Mutual and USPS had reconciling volume figures.[22] Furthermore, the cap will be increased by only 373 million pieces for each year of the Chase NSA. If Chase is correct in its estimate of 574 million pieces of heritage volume, the difference represents 201 million pieces of anyhow volume that will receive discounts. In fact, if the thresholds were incorrectly adjusted then further leakage occurred in a manner for which our model cannot accurately account.

Table 14.8 combines the data from the first two data reports. Using the data from the first data report, which contained only heritage Bank One volumes, combined with the full year data report, which contained between ½ year (USPS estimate of integration date) and ¼ year (Chase declaration of integration date) of integrated volumes, we can separate volumes under the NSA before and after integration. The first two columns represent one half of the after rates projection provided by the co-proponents in the NSA filing. Column three combines these projections to estimate a half-year of volume for the combined company. Column four is actual merged volume for the second half of year 2, calculated using the periodic data reports.

A comparison of the projected (column 3) and actual (column 4) volumes for the merged company suggests that something dramatic and unexpected happened when the two banks merged. The post-integration merged company sent nearly 2 billion pieces of Standard Mail in the six months directly following the merger. This is far in excess of the projections. Since Standard Mail is not eligible for the negotiated discounts, it seems likely that the high volume was due to non-price factors. Therefore it is also likely that the variance of First-Class marketing mail volume from the projection is at least partly due to non-price factors. This is discussed further in Section 3.1

While something anomalous occurred with the volumes, the USPS considered the result both reasonable and profitable. The full year data report states that USPS realized $7.5 million of new contribution as a result of the NSA.[23] After the discount threshold was modified to account for the volume of the new bank, the deal remained in place. The significant losses estimated by the model are presented in Table 14.9

Table 14.9 Estimate of net contribution from discounts: Chase

	FC workshared	FC with discount	Std with discount
Year 1	(7 671 150)	(6 389 294)	(5 063 731)

An elasticity-based analysis of the Chase NSA is quite striking. The USPS lost between \$5.1 and \$7.7 million under the elasticity estimates used in the analysis. Given the discrepancy between the USPS and Chase over the heritage Chase volume, it is likely that the Chase leakage is greater than that of other NSAs. In order for the net financial position of the USPS to have improved due to the volume discounts given in the first year of the Bank One NSA, the marginal piece of marketing mail would need to have had an own-price elasticity of over −0.983.[24]

2.6 Summary

Table 14.10 summarizes all of the model values for the NSAs that have provided periodic data reports at this time. The final row contains a range of possible net contributions to the USPS from NSAs to date. The overall value of the NSAs under an assumption that all the participants' marketing mail had own-price elasticities equal to Standard Mail as well as cross-price elasticity with the price of Standard Mail is positive, in spite of losses from all but one of the mailers receiving discounts. Under both other elasticity assumptions, the net results from volume discounts are negative. These results illuminate the risks to USPS, and perhaps other posts, of entering into volume discount agreements, particularly when the own-price elasticity of the mailer is not known.

Under the Postal Reorganization Act (PRA), the USPS operated under a break-even constraint. Therefore, any losses from unprofitable volume discounts would ultimately be recovered by charging higher rates to non-participating mailers. To protect against this, the PRC placed significant restrictions on NSAs. However, the implementation of the Postal Accountability and Enhancement Act (PAEA) will remove the break-even constraint and replace it with a price-cap mechanism.

This has important implications for the regulation of NSAs. First, losses from unprofitable agreements will not automatically be recovered through increased rates on non-participants. Second, the USPS will be permitted to generate a net profit. However, these changes alone will not place the USPS in the same situation as competitive, private companies for whom regulation of negotiated rates would be unnecessary and counter-productive.

For USPS products that face little meaningful competition, the potential for harm to the competitors of mailers who are offered NSAs still exists.[25] Also, the ability for the USPS to generate net profits does not, in the absence of a shareholder or residual claimant, assure that it will behave as a profit maximizer. At this time it is not known what incentives will be put in place as a result of the new law to encourage profit-maximizing behavior by USPS management.

Finally, the price cap will be imposed at the class level, which potentially could allow the USPS to use NSA discounts to offset larger increases on mail in the same class that is not sent under an NSA. This could occur whether or not the NSAs were profitable. To

Table 14.10 Estimate of net contribution from discounts

		FC workshared	FC with cross price	Std with discount
Capital One	Year 1	200 220	2 740 705	5 595 563
	Year 2	(669 161)	869 305	3 154 567
	Year 3	–	–	–
Chase	Year 1	(7 671 150)	(6 389 294)	(5 063 731)
Discover	Year 1	(2 154 692)	(1 071 760)	(300 966)
	Year 2	(1 941 493)	(1 112 960)	(334 244)
HSBC	Year 1	–	–	–
Total		(12 236 276)	(4 964 004)	3 051 188

protect those mailers who may be too small to justify incurring the transaction costs of an NSA, it may be desirable to exclude discounts awarded to NSA mailers from the test of compliance with the rate cap.

3. VOLUME DISCOUNTS IN CHANGING CIRCUMSTANCES

Some of the NSAs filed with the Commission included aspects that were uniquely challenging. A review of these unusual situations illuminates the problems that can arise in trying to evaluate volume discounts when economic and business conditions change. The merger of Bank One and JP Morgan/Chase shortly after the filing of the agreement and the withdrawal of the request for the Washington Mutual NSA provide two examples of the potential effects of changing circumstances.

3.1 Bank One/Chase

Less than two weeks after the filing of the Bank One NSA, Bank One and JP Morgan/Chase (Chase) merged. In anticipation of the merger, the agreement included enhanced provisions to adjust the discount structure by increasing the volume thresholds for discounts to account for the additional volume of Chase.[26] The merger provisions were structured to allow the merged entity (which retained the Chase name) to receive discounts on only the 'heritage Bank One' volume until it chose to integrate the volume of the merger partner ('heritage Chase').[27] This rendered the analysis of the financial impact of the agreement provided by USPS obsolete almost as soon as it was filed. The bank-wide impact of the merger combined with the timing of the integration made it impossible for the USPS to generate a reliable post-merger financial analysis.

In its initial response to discovery, USPS took the position that it was not possible to estimate the effects of the merger on the value of the agreement. In order to facilitate settlement discussions, USPS provided an estimate of the financial effects under a hypothetical scenario that assumed integration of Chase's volumes would occur in January 2005. The analysis also assumed that, without the NSA, heritage Chase marketing volume would adopt the same proportional mix of First-Class and Standard Mail as the heritage

Bank One. The combination of these assumptions, and Chase's heavy use of First-Class for its marketing mail, led to aggressive projections of both growth and savings, and the analysis put forth by USPS suggested that the merger would increase the three-year value of the agreement from $11.6 million to $20.3 million.[28]

As a condition for recommending approval, the Commission added a provision to the agreement that limited the discounts to the level at which they would not exceed the estimated savings from electronic returns of undeliverable mail. After implementing the agreement, Chase and USPS requested that the Commission reconsider the addition of the discount cap. In its pleadings to the Commission, Chase argued that the cap would severely limit the potential benefits of the NSA, because it was responding to the incentives so aggressively that it was likely to exhaust the maximum allowed discounts before the end of the first year. Because the mailer-provided forecasts indicated that the cap would not be reached during the entire three-year term of the NSA, this raised concerns that the re-branding of heritage Bank One credit cards as Chase might potentially lead to the awarding of discounts to heritage Chase mail before integration and the attendant adjustment of thresholds.

In later comments, Chase attempted to assuage these concerns by explaining that in the last year before integration (2005), about 574 million pieces of First-Class Mail were sent under heritage Chase permits.[29] Since the forecast volume was only 419 million, it was unlikely that Chase had shifted heritage Chase volume to heritage Bank One permits in order to receive unjustified discounts. This logic is reasonable; however, it raises a different possible explanation for the higher than expected volume of heritage Bank One mail. A post-merger, re-branded but pre-integration Chase presents a situation akin to a controlled experiment. Heritage Chase and heritage Bank One credit card solicitations were sent out concurrently by the same company operating in the same market environment, and one (heritage Bank One) was eligible for volume discounts while the other (heritage Chase) was not. Yet both experienced large increases in First-Class marketing mail volume. If discounts were not available for heritage Chase volumes before integration, one can conclude that the massive heritage Chase volume increase was due to non-price factors. It seems very likely that the same non-price factors that caused the increase in heritage Chase volume also caused some of the increase in heritage Bank One volume.

In approving each NSA to date (including the Bank One NSA), the Commission included a requirement that the USPS file annual data collection reports that include an evaluation of the impact on contribution. However, the most recent Bank One report[30] states that '[t]he occurrence of the merger precludes any reliable evaluation of the impact on contribution [.]' This means that two years into a three-year agreement, the USPS cannot reliably determine the extent of its success or failure. This presents a significant obstacle to evaluating the desirability of extending the Bank One agreement or offering similarly designed agreements to other mailers. It also greatly reduces the value of the provision in the agreement that allows USPS to unilaterally withdraw if it determines that continuing would not be in its best interest. The existence of the unilateral withdrawal provision was cited by parties opposing the imposition of the savings-based stop-loss cap, because the USPS could terminate the agreement if it began to lose money. However, if USPS is unable to determine whether or not it is losing money, the ability to terminate is not especially useful.

Finally, while this chapter focuses on examining the volume discount aspect of NSAs, the Bank One data collection report indicates that much of the anticipated savings from avoiding the costs of physically returning undeliverable mail has not occurred. The Commission approved the agreement with the expectation that USPS would realize about $7.6 million in savings over three years, $6.1 million of which would come from not having to physically return flat-sized mail pieces. This figure was estimated based on an assumption that Bank One would continue to make use of flat-sized First-Class marketing mail at levels similar to those it had in the past.[31] Because flats are relatively expensive to handle, avoiding the physical return of even a few would bring large benefits. However, USPS reports that Chase has discontinued its use of flat-sized First-Class marketing mail, and therefore 80 percent of the expected first-year savings did not materialize.

3.2 Washington Mutual

The proposed NSA with Washington Mutual was structured to be very similar to previous agreements, except that the savings from avoided physical return costs were excluded from the expected value to the USPS. Thus, the reliability of the mailer-provided forecasts was again a central issue during the discovery process. The first-year (2006) volume forecast coincided with the litigation period, which led to requests for comparisons between the year one forecast and the actual volume as that year progressed.

In late July 2006, Washington Mutual indicated that volume through the first three months was trending very close to the forecast, within 10 to 20 million of a before rates forecast of 450 million pieces.[32] Later in the year, however, the situation had apparently changed. Attempting to respond to a similar request for actual year-to-date volume in November, USPS and Washington Mutual were unable to reconcile discrepancies between their estimates. Washington Mutual believed that it had sent more volume than USPS records indicated. Washington Mutual explained that it had increased its volume of First-Class marketing mail because it was achieving better than expected response rates. This success caused it to increase its marketing budget and direct more of the budget to First-Class Mail. It pointed out that '[t]his highlights the difficulty in precisely forecasting mail volumes given the competitive nature of our business.' The changed circumstances led USPS to withdraw its request for the NSA.

The conclusions that can be drawn from these events are mixed. While the discovery process was able to bring to light information that prevented the implementation of an agreement that 'would not be in [Washington Mutual's and USPS's] common best interests,'[33] the events seem to suggest that mail volume for some individual mailers is very sensitive to ordinary changes in business conditions. Designing volume discount schedules that will continue to benefit both USPS and the mailer when these types of changes occur is difficult.

4. DETERMINING AN APPROPRIATE VOLUME FORECASTING METHOD

As can be seen from the analysis in Section 2, model results are highly dependent on the elasticity that is used. We modeled volume using elasticity assumptions that have passed rate-case scrutiny: the own-price elasticity for First-Class workshared mail; the own-price elasticity for Standard Regular Mail, and the discount elasticity of First-Class and

Standard Mail. The method employed to develop these elasticity estimates dates back to docket number R80-1.

This method has proved successful in forecasting volume at the subclass level. However, it produces an average elasticity of all rate categories in the subclass. Necessarily, the true elasticity will be higher than the average for some mailers and lower than the average for other mailers. Consequently, using the average elasticity of a subclass to forecast the volume of an individual firm is not ideal. It may be possible to develop elasticities for subsets of mail, such as First-Class advertising, providing the appropriate data is available. As the number of negotiated discount agreements increase, more data should become available.

To date, parties to NSAs have relied on volume forecasts that arise from marketing budgets. Marketing decisions are driven by many factors other than the price of the chosen advertising medium. These factors include, but are not limited to, response rates, overall economic conditions, company profits, and strategic marketing decisions. These factors fluctuate continually and are not easily quantified. Marketing campaign volumes are determined by reviewing all of these factors. In the Bank One case, Buc described the process as follows:

> For a particular marketing campaign, the firm must estimate (1) the probability of response for each individual on the list ('response rate') and (2) the present value of the stream of profits over the duration of that individual's relationship with the firm (the 'lifetime expected value'). By multiplying the response rate by the lifetime expected value, the firm can determine the expected value of the mailing for each individual. The expected value can then be compared with the costs of producing the marketing material and the postage charges (totaling 'costs per piece') to determine whether the economic benefit from a mailing is positive.[34]

The profitability of marketing campaigns under different discount scenarios can then be calculated and volumes forecast.

The primary problem with relying on volumes forecast in this manner is the asymmetry of available data. Mailers are reluctant to share the value of their customers because the data is commercially sensitive. This leaves the USPS with no way to independently verify volume forecasts during negotiations or to determine the extent of anyhow volume after the discounts are put into place. Until this asymmetry is overcome, the USPS will not be able to ensure that it is not losing money on these agreements.

5. CONCLUSIONS

Many in the postal community want fewer restrictions on negotiated discounts, and the commission has received criticism for the stop-loss caps added to NSAs to reduce risks to the USPS. There is valid and influential economic theory that speaks to the potential value of volume discounts. However, our analysis demonstrates the potential for losses to result from inaccurate forecasts. Capping discounts at the level of cost savings limits the loss in contribution but it does little to encourage additional volume.

Using a volume estimation model similar to the one outlined in the Commission's Recommended Decision in MC2004–3 can result in volume discount agreements that are beneficial to both the mailers and the post. Close and constant monitoring of each negotiated discount is critical to realizing its maximum potential value. Knowledge gained from careful analysis should allow improvements in subsequent agreements.

The newly passed legislation may allow the USPS more flexibility to implement agreements, but it also recognizes that future deals incorporating volume discounts must improve the net financial position of the USPS. While the USPS will be permitted to earn a net profit, the lack of a residual claimant means that the incentive to maximize profit cannot be assumed. Furthermore, the price cap must be carefully implemented if non-participating mailers are to be insulated from financing the discounts of NSA mailers.

NOTES

* The views expressed in this chapter are those of the authors and do not necessarily represent the opinions of the US Postal Regulatory Commission.

1. First-Class Mail is currently entitled to forwarding and return service at no additional charge.
2. In December 2006, the commission was restructured as the Postal Regulatory Commission under the Postal Accountability and Enhancement Act (PAEA) of 2006.
3. The USPS withdrew one of these agreements, with Washington Mutual, before the PRC completed its review, and the other, with Bank of America, is currently under review. The proposed NSA with Bank of America does not include volume-based declining block discounts, but instead provides performance-based incentives. At the time of this writing, the Bank of America NSA is being actively litigated before the PRC, and further discussion of it falls outside the scope of this chapter.
4. The passage of the PAEA in 2006 removed the break-even constraint, introducing a rate cap and permitting the USPS to make a profit. The implications of the new law for NSAs are discussed further in Section 2.6.
5. In R2006-1 the USPS proposed, and the Commission approved, an option to receive the first two ACS notices per address free of charge for First-Class Mail.
6. The framework and model were developed in consultation with Ted Pearsall and others.
7. The framework and model are described in Docket No. MC2004-3, Opinion and Further Recommended Decision, pp. 21–38.
8. The demand curve in the figure is drawn as a straight line to simplify the graphical presentation. The model assumes a constant elasticity.
9. Elasticities have been provided by the USPS in every rate case under the PRA of 1970.
10. New contribution is the difference between the new revenue and the new costs. Our analysis uses the unit costs provided in the periodic data reports. For pieces converting from Standard Mail to First-Class Mail, the difference in unit contribution between these two classes is used.
11. Since Docket No. R80-1, the USPS has been using log–log or constant-elasticity demand equations to estimate elasticities and forecast volumes. The constant-elasticity demand equation evaluated at the initial (undiscounted) price p_0, assuming all other variables, such as income and population, held constant, is: $Q_0 = ap_0^e$; where Q_0 is the initial quantity (or before rates volume), and e is the constant own-price elasticity of demand. Similarly, the constant-elasticity demand equation evaluated at the discounted rate p_d is $Q_1 = ap_d^e$; where Q_1 is the new quantity (or after rates volume). The ratio of Q_0/Q_1 can be expressed as

$$\frac{Q_0}{Q_1} = \frac{ap_0^e}{ap_d^e} = \frac{p_0^e}{p_d^e} = \left(\frac{p_0}{p_d}\right)^e.$$

Therefore,

$$Q_0 = Q_1\left(\frac{p_0}{p_d}\right)^e.$$

12. Docket No. R2006-1, USPS-T-7, pp. 73 and 114.
13. A Technical Appendix providing a detailed example of the calculations is available on The Commission's website at www.prc.gov.
14. At the time of the proposal, the per-piece contribution from First-Class letter mail was approximately 8 cents higher than that of Standard Mail.

15. The \$5.6 million is calculated using inputs from the required periodic data reports:

After rates marketing volume = 843 million
Marginal revenue = 0.292; Discounted revenue = 0.257; Standard revenue = 0.177
Own price elasticity = 0.296; Discount elasticity = 0.111
Discount threshold volumes: Tier 1 = 773.8; Tier 2 = 823.8
Tier 1 discount = 0.03; Tier 2 discount = 0.035
Contribution: Tier 1 = 0.141; Tier 2 = 0.136; Standard = 0.0914

Thus:

Before rates volume $= 843 \times (0.292/0.257)^{-0.296} \times ((0.292 - 0.177)/(0.257 - 0.177))^{-0.111} = 779.7$
Leakage $= (779.7 - 773.8) \times 0.03 = \$0.2$
Contribution $= ((823.8 - 779.7) \times 0.141) + ((843 - 823.8) \times 0.136) = \$8.8$
Net new contribution $= \$8.8 - \$0.2 = \$8.6$

Because some of the new First-Class marketing mail is volume that has shifted from Standard Mail, the loss in Standard contribution from these pieces must be subtracted from the new contribution. This loss is calculated as follows:

Before rates volume using elasticity discount alone $= 843 \times ((0.292 - 0.177)/(0.257 - 0.177))^{-0.111} = 809.8$
Loss in contribution $= (843 - 809.8) \times 0.0914 = \$3$
Net contribution $= \$8.6 - \$3 = \$5.6$

A technical appendix including a more detailed description of the calculations is available at www.prc.gov.
16. Due to the filing in the middle of 2004, there is a gap in the volume data available.
17. The existence of ACS savings makes the deal profitable regardless.
18. See Docket No. MC2004-4, USPS-T-1, Appendix A.
19. These numbers assume the discounts are only aimed at Marketing mail; the large base of operational mail means that the discounts started at a volume of 405 million pieces of total FC mail in the first year of the agreement.
20. In the initial proposal the co-proponents expected any gain in contribution to come primarily from the ACS savings feature.
21. A half-year data report was filed at the beginning of 2006, before the mailstream of the merged companies had integrated. This data report provides insight into a possible result of the NSA had the institutions not merged.
22. The Washington Mutual NSA is discussed further in Section 3.2.
23. This result is calculated in the Excel file attached to the data report. The report elsewhere states that a reliable estimate of the financial impact of the agreement cannot be calculated due to the merger.
24. As well as a discount elasticity with Standard Mail of −0.111.
25. While to date no competitor has alleged that harm would result from a proposed NSA in any PRC proceeding, the PRC has indicated that it would take allegations of competitive harm into consideration.
26. Previous NSAs included merger and acquisition provisions, but the Bank One agreement expanded on them.
27. Chase was required to provide 90 days notice before the date of integration, and provide evidence to the USPS that mail preparation requirements stipulated in the agreement were met by the 'heritage Chase' mail.
28. In short, this occurred because heritage Chase First-Class marketing volumes before integration would force increases in the threshold volumes to qualify for discounts. The assumption that, absent the NSA, most of the heritage Chase volume would shift to Standard resulted in an estimate of virtually no post-integration leakage.
29. In the USPS data report on the first full year of the NSA, it reported that Chase's 2005 First-Class volume was 373 million pieces. This 200 million piece discrepancy is discussed in Section 2.5.
30. The report, due January 29, 2007, was filed on April 12, 2007 and covered the first year of the agreement (April 1, 2005 to March 31, 2006).
31. While limiting the maximum number of flats eligible for discounts, the NSA was not designed to discourage Bank One from continuing to use flats at levels consistent with its history.
32. Docket No. MC2006-3, Transcript Vol. 2 at 245.
33. Docket No. MC2006-3, United States Postal Service Notice of Withdrawal of Request for Recommended Decision on Negotiated Service Agreement with Washington Mutual, December 8, 2006.
34. Docket No. MC2004-3, Direct Testimony of Lawrence C. Buc on behalf of Bank One Corporation, p. 3.

BIBLIOGRAPHY

Ayub, Ali, Jessica A. Dauer and Michael K. Plunkett (2006), 'Pricing for the true value of mail: the credit card example', presented at the 13th Conference on Postal and Delivery Economics, Antwerp.

Levy, David M., Joy M. Leong, Lawrence G. Buc and Michael K. Plunkett (2006), 'Benefit–cost regulation of negotiated service agreements', in Michael A. Crew and Paul R. Kleindorfer (eds), *Progress Toward Liberalization of the Postal and Delivery Sector*, New York: Springer.

Panzar, John C. and J. Gregory Sidak (2006), 'When does an optional tariff not lead to a Pareto improvement? The ambiguous effects of self-selecting nonlinear pricing when demand is interdependent or firms do not maximize profit', *Journal of Competition Law and Economics*, **2**(2), 285–99.

US Postal Rate Commission (2003), Opinion and Recommended Decision, Docket No. MC2002-2 (available at www.prc.gov).

US Postal Rate Commission (2006), Opinion and Further Recommended Decision, Docket No. MC2004-3 (available at www.prc.gov).

US Postal Service (2005), Data Collection Report for Sept. 01, 2003 to Sept. 30, 2004, Docket No. MC2002-2 (available at www.prc.gov).

US Postal Service (2006a), Data Collection Report Capital One NSA October 2005 – September 2005, Docket No. MC2002-2 (available at www.prc.gov).

US Postal Service (2006b), Data Collection Report JP Morgan Chase (Bank One) NSA April 2005 – September 2005, Docket No. MC2004-3 (available at www.prc.gov).

US Postal Service (2006c), First Data Collection Report, Docket No. MC2004-4 (available at www.prc.gov).

15. Development of competition in EU postal markets: the influence of the regulatory framework on the pattern of competition

Patrick de Bas and Nick van der Lijn

1. INTRODUCTION

Dietl and Waller (2002) were one of the first to pay explicit attention to the potential business models of entrants in the postal market. In their paper, seven potential business models of entrants were identified. In the paper, a first assessment was made of the business models that will be profitable, the reaction of the incumbent to emerging competition, the likely services that will be offered, and the resulting price levels of these services. This assessment is primarily based on the economics of postal service provision and disregards the influence of the regulatory framework on the viability of the business models.

In this chapter, we assess to what extent the business models of entrants described by Dietl and Waller (2002) can be observed in practice. Moreover, we examine to what extent the viability of the business models, and hence the pattern of competition, is influenced by the regulatory regime. Looking forward, we assess whether it is likely that the pattern of competition in EU postal markets will converge over time.

In our analysis, we focus our attention on some of the main EU postal markets (Germany, the Netherlands, Spain and the UK). These countries have been selected because they are relative frontrunners in the liberalisation process in the EU and because there are marked differences in the chosen paths to liberalise the postal markets in these countries.

The results of our analysis are to a large extent based on the opinions expressed in dozens of interviews with postal sector stakeholders conducted during previous studies (ECORYS, 2005a, b, 2007) and while preparing this chapter and reflect our own value judgements.

In Section 2 we review the business models of entrants of Dietl and Waller (2002). The current regulatory framework of the countries reviewed and a description of the business models currently observed in these countries is given in Section 3. In this section we also discuss the interaction between the observed business models and the regulatory framework. Section 4 concludes.

2. BUSINESS MODELS OF ENTRANTS IN THE POSTAL MARKET

Dietl and Waller (2002) identify the following seven potential business models of entrants in EU postal markets: Local mail services, Networked local mail services, Document exchanges, Mass mail provider, Spot operator, Consolidator, and National full-service provider. In addition to these seven models, Dietl and Waller (2002) also mention activities in niche markets as part of the possible strategy for some of the types of operators listed above. We consider activities in niche markets as a possible stand-alone strategy; for example, the provision of nationwide delivery services in niche markets. Below, we provide the descriptions of these models as introduced by Dietl and Waller (2002), followed by the definition we use for niche services.

2.1 Local Mail Services

Local mail services focus on a single city or agglomeration. They have low entry costs because they concentrate on (business) mail within city limits. The accessible market is about 30 per cent. Customers include local authorities, utilities, banks, medical insurance companies and the legal sector, all of which have a high proportion of local mail. Local mail services primarily compete on quality, customer orientation and flexibility. They cannot compete on price because their delivery volumes are too small to challenge larger competitors. To increase their delivery volumes, local mail services would have to expand geographically.

2.2 Networked Local Mail Services

Interregional networks exchange mail between mainly independent local mail services. The network itself provides only sorting and transportation. Customer relations, collection and delivery remain in the hands of local mail services. Interregional collaboration enables local operators to expand their customer base and to enhance market penetration. Market coverage of networked local operators increases from 30 per cent to about 80 per cent. The higher market volume reduces the unit delivery costs of the local operators. If networked local operators can combine these scale effects with labour and process cost advantages, they might actually be able to offer lower prices than the incumbent.

2.3 Document Exchange

Document exchanges focus on customer groups with close mutual relationships. Customers pay a monthly or yearly fee to exchange mail at the provider's locations. Document exchanges only sort and transport the mail between different locations. Cost advantages result from the large volumes participants exchange between each other. However, market potential is thus limited.

2.4 Mass Mail Provider

The mass mail service focuses on computer-generated mass mailings. It competes on price. Typically, mass mail services reduce their distribution costs by delivering mail only on two or three days per week in a given area. The lower delivering frequency allows mass mailers to serve a given area with only half or a third of the personnel required by traditional postal services, who usually deliver mail six days a week.

Mass mail services are able to capture between 40 per cent and 50 per cent of the market segments, which do not require daily distribution.[1] They concentrate on relatively few customers with large volumes. Serving smaller customers would endanger their business model and cost advantage.

2.5 Spot Operator

A spot operator does not run a regular network. Instead, it hires workers only for the few occasions when it distributes action mailings such as mail order catalogues. The spot operator's strength is its ability to handle large fluctuations and its low cost position. Spot operators cannot compete with mass mail services for regular mailings because of lower quality and few cost advantages only.

2.6 Consolidator

Consolidators act like arbitrageurs or intermediaries. Their business model is based on the fact that other operators charge different prices among customer groups. For instance, most operators will charge small customers higher prices in the future than large customers. Consolidators exploit these price differences by aggregating the mail of small customers and then injecting it into the network of regular operators at rates for larger accounts. Alternatively, consolidators can benefit from the fact that the sum of their own costs of performing selected activities (e.g. collection and sorting) and the access charges for injecting mail into the network of other providers is lower than a competitor's total end-to-end (E2E) costs. Consolidators introduce competition into market segments, which are usually not targeted by entrants (e.g. small businesses and households). This business model works on a local as well as on a national level. Note that Dietl and Waller do not consider other business models that are based on access agreements for final mile delivery.[2]

2.7 National Full-service Provider

A national full-service provider tries to outperform the incumbent by offering superior quality in a broad range of services. The higher quality enables the national full-service provider to charge a premium price. This strategy is only profitable in countries where the incumbent suffers from low quality. The high quality standard of the incumbents prevents the entry of new national full-service providers in most European countries. However, in less developed countries this business model is a viable strategy.

2.8 Niche Services

In addition to the business models identified by Dietl and Waller (2002), we consider it useful to also regard the provision of niche services as a potential business model of entrants in the postal market. We define niche services as services focused on specific products, such as heavy mail items or valuable mail items (credit cards, passports etc.) and/or specific delivery points, such as nationwide delivery to P.O. Boxes.

3. THE REGULATORY FRAMEWORK AND DEVELOPMENT OF COMPETITION IN FOUR EU COUNTRIES

In this section we describe the development of the regulatory framework and the development of competition in Germany, the Netherlands, Spain and the UK. Regarding the regulatory framework, we focus on those aspects that we have identified in ECORYS (2005a) as having the largest impact on the development of competition: the reserved area and network access arrangements, the VAT regime and the mandate of the regulator.

3.1 Germany

3.1.1 The reserved area and network access arrangements

The reserved area has been gradually reduced in line with the EC postal directives. Currently, the reserved area consists of the conveyance of domestic mail items weighing less than 50 grams and priced lower than 2.5 times the stamp prices, with the exception of higher-quality and value-added services for this group of mail items, which are not part of the reserved area (Art. 51, German Postal Law). Since 1998, various licences can be obtained for offering postal services, including licence D for 'high quality and value-added services'. Full liberalisation of the German postal market is anticipated as of 1 January 2008.

In Germany, dominant postal operators are obliged to grant competitors access to parts of its network (Art. 28, German Postal Law). Access should be granted at rates considered reasonable and competitive by the National Regulatory Authority (NRA), *Bundesnetzagentur*. In its price-cap regime the NRA adopted the principle that the price for access to the network of Deutsche Post, the only postal operator considered to have a dominant position, should be set at the retail price for the postal service in question minus the avoided costs by Deutsche Post. According to information obtained from *Bundesnetzagentur*, the maximum price difference between the public tariff and the access tariff for items of correspondence is between 18 per cent (the highest scale of discount for injecting mail at the outgoing sorting centres) and 21 per cent (injecting mail to incoming sorting centres; Art. 28, German Postal Law).

From the wording of the Postal Act, however, it is not clearly stated whether or not competitors of the incumbent have the right to consolidate mail items weighing less than the weight and price limits described in the exclusive licence of Deutsche Post and are entitled to rebates. For a number of years, this lack of clarity effectively barred consolidators from access at the discounted tariffs that Deutsche Post offered to large customers.

The European Commission ruled, in its decision from 20 October 2004, that Germany, by extending the exclusive rights of Deutsche Post to the collection of mail and mail preparation services, had not transposed the postal directives properly into national law. This was taken up by the Federal Cartel Office (*Bundeskartellamt*), which, in its decision of 11 February 2005, ordered Deutsche Post to stop discriminating against competitors with regard to the consolidation of mail, granting competitors the same access conditions as large customers. Both the German government and Deutsche Post refused to accept the respective decisions and went to the law courts. Following a provisional approval of the decision by administrative courts in April 2005, many consolidators have reached access agreements with Deutsche Post under the terms determined by the NRA.

3.1.2 The VAT regime

Currently, Deutsche Post has a VAT exemption with regard to all services under the universal service obligation. In practice no VAT exemption exists for bulk parcel delivery (i.e. all parcels that are not over-the-counter parcels). The European Commission started infringement procedures with regard to the VAT exemption of Deutsche Post and the distorting effect that this has on the development of competition. No conclusion has yet been reached. It is acknowledged by the German government that the current VAT exemption of Deutsche Post is distorting competition. Irrespective of the outcomes of the infringement procedures, the German Ministry of Economics and Labour expects that the VAT issue will be settled before the anticipated full liberalisation of the German postal market per 1 January 2008 (personal communication).

3.1.3 The mandate of the regulator

The position of the postal regulator is *de jure* strong but, according to stakeholders in the German postal market, *de facto* rather weak.[3] The NRA has the power to grant and withdraw licences, to settle disputes between postal operators regarding services provided and to act on the abuse of a dominant position. In addition, the NRA can request data from postal operators, set rates for the universal service provider and enforce rulings (levy fines and seek judicial order; WIK-Consult, 2006, p. 120).

3.1.4 The development of competition

Around 2000 licences have been granted to German companies, of which more than 75 per cent are D-licences. The combined market share of competitors in mail volume increased from 3.7 per cent in 2003 to 5.3 per cent in 2004. End of 2005, the market share of all competitors for licensed postal services is about 6.6 per cent in items and 6.9 per cent in terms of revenue. In the part of the market that is licensed, but open to competition, the market shares are 27.4 per cent and 16.8 per cent, respectively. More than half of the revenues of competitors are generated through the provision of services under the D-licence (*Bundesnetzagentur*, personal communication).

Most of the licensees are small companies, with local or regional focus. The small *local mail service* providers are usually local entrants that are active in express and courier services, or local delivery organisations of unaddressed mail, moving into the addressed mail market. On a regional scale regional press distributors, who have expanded into mail services, are active. In addition, some local mail service providers have expanded their business to other geographical areas, leading to *networked local mail services*. One example is Citipost, that started as a local mail service provider in Hannover and now has 11 branches in different cities (see www.citipost.de). Also, PIN AG started with local mail services in Berlin and gradually expanded through cooperation with others towards a network approaching national coverage. We estimate that currently PIN AG's delivery network covers about 75 per cent of households. PIN AG is aiming to have a nationwide delivery network at the time of full market opening in January 2008.

To offer *document exchange services* in Germany, one needs a C-licence. Although quite a number of these C-licences have been granted, the total revenue of competitor postal operators in this market is still very small, roughly €1 million (*Bundesnetzagentur*, 2006, p. 16).

One of the main competitors of Deutsche Post, TNT Post AG, started its business by providing *mass mail services*. With 36.5 per cent of the total German mail market consisting of direct mail, entering this market allowed TNT to capture a large volume of mail items, thus reducing its average costs per item (ECORYS, 2005a, p. 113). Currently, the TNT Post network has about 90 per cent coverage and TNT Post is aiming to have 100 per cent coverage by the time of full market opening expected in January 2008.

The NRA reports that the operations of *consolidators*, after many consolidators have reached access agreements with DPAG in April 2005 under the terms determined by the NRA (see above), have gained momentum since mid-2005. According to *Bundesnetzagentur*, mail volumes handled by consolidators increased from 30 million in the whole of 2005 to 60 million mail items in the first quarter of 2006 (personal communication). We are not aware of any competitors that focus on *niche services*, other than on the delivery of value-added services under a D-licence.

3.1.5 Interaction between regulation and development of competition

The possibility to deliver value-added mail products in Germany has given rise to the entry of many local and regional players. Mainly publishers (of magazines, newspapers), unaddressed mail deliverers, former internal postal departments of large companies that were outsourced, and unemployed citizens making greenfield investments have entered the German postal market. The spread between access tariffs and retail prices are small enough for competitors to have an incentive to build own E2E networks. Currently, two organisations, TNT Post and PIN AG, are eager to establish a nationwide delivery network through taking over local and regional players and through cooperation agreements. The development of nationwide delivery networks appears to be facilitated through the existence of (small) local and regional mail service providers. The activities of consolidators are still rather limited, but growing strongly after the legal position was (at least temporarily) clarified and more favourable agreements could be closed with the incumbent.

3.2 The Netherlands

3.2.1 The reserved area and network access arrangements

In the Netherlands, the market for the delivery of printed matter was liberalised at the end of the 1980s. There have been disputes about the definition of addressed printed matter and ultimately it has been decided that direct mail (with specific name and address information, but with identical content of the mail message itself) should be considered printed matter and hence open to competition. The further gradual reduction of the reserved area (in particular, for the delivery of items of correspondence) has been in line with the postal directives. Currently, the reserved area consists of the conveyance of domestic mail items weighing less than 50 grams (and priced lower than 2.5 times the stamp prices), with the exception of outgoing cross-border mail (Art. 2b, Dutch Postal Act). Full liberalisation is anticipated in 1 January 2008. There is negotiated third-party access, with prices agreed on a retail-minus basis. The spread between the access tariffs and the retail rates is not publicly available.

3.2.2 The VAT regime

The incumbent TNT is exempt from charging VAT on universal services. As the delivery of addressed printed matter (and of unaddressed mail) is not part of the universal service, both TNT and its competitors have to charge VAT for these services. The new Postal Act foresees the limitation of the universal service to the conveyance of single item mail.[4] As the VAT exemption of TNT will continue to be linked to the universal service, all operators will have to charge VAT on bulk mail services. Hence, with regard to charging VAT, there will be a level playing field for the largest part of the postal market.

3.2.3 The mandate of the regulator

Postal sector regulation is carried out by the Ministry of Economic Affairs and the postal sector regulator OPTA. The position of OPTA is fairly strong, but resources are currently rather limited. In addition, OPTA does not have powers to set rates for the USP, cancel unlawful rates and neither has the authority to require the USP to provide downstream access (WIK-Consult, 2006, p. 120). The policy maker, the Ministry of Economic Affairs, does have a number of powers, including, *inter alia*, setting (guidelines on) postal rates and preventing of unfair competition (Art. 5, Dutch Postal Act).

3.2.4 The development of competition

The competition in the Netherlands has seen a strong development in the recent years. The combined market shares of Sandd and Selekt Mail has risen in the period 2001–6 from 0.3 per cent to 11.2 per cent of the total addressed mail market (including the reserved services) in terms of volume (RBB Economics, 2007, p. 53).

There is a small group of companies providing *local or regional mail services*.[5] These operators usually have started between 1990 and 1995, a few years after 1988, the year when the delivery of printed matter was liberalised in the Netherlands. The average local operator delivers twice a week and covers a delivery area of 100 000 to 200 000 households. In addition, there are a fair amount of institutions offering work to mentally challenged persons (in Dutch, *sociale werkplaatsen*) that are engaged in small-scale local mail delivery as well.

In the last few years, the first group of local operators have seen an increase in their delivery volumes, with Sandd and to a lesser extent Selekt Mail (see below) using these operators for building a nationwide delivery network.[6] Currently, however, the mail volumes are slowly declining again as a result of the decline in mail volumes caused by e-substitution. The expected future liberalisation of the mail market will have a slightly positive effect on the expected mail volumes, as the local operators then can, and probably will, also target individual consumer mail.

An example of a company in the Netherlands that has a number of characteristics of *networked local mail services* is Businesspost.[7] Linking local delivery networks, Businesspost managed to build a nationwide delivery network. However, unlike in the definition of Dietl and Waller (2002), marketing and customer relations were primarily undertaken at the central level. Moreover, Businesspost clearly focused on bulk mail products and competes on price, offering mail services at lower price levels than the incumbent, TNT. Hence, it is more appropriate to regard Businesspost as a *mass mail provider*.

Two other *mass mail providers*, Sandd and Selekt Mail, are by far the two largest competitors of the Dutch national postal operator TNT. Sandd and Selekt Mail are focusing on the B2C segment and have managed to develop an E2E delivery network with 100 per cent national coverage. Sandd and Selekt Mail operate a low-cost E2E business model focusing on pre-sorted bulk mail (mainly addressed direct mail, periodicals and sponsored magazines) with two deliveries per week achieved with a flexible work force. Both operators intend to deliver low-weight transactional mail as well, as soon as the reserved area in the Netherlands is abolished (anticipated per 1 January 2008 as in Germany). Sandd has plans to target the market for consumer post in the near future (*Financieel Dagblad*, 2 February 2007).

It should be mentioned that Sandd and Selekt Mail actually operate a hybrid model of providing mass mail services with their own delivery network on the one hand, while on the other hand part of the delivery is undertaken through cooperating with a number of local and regional mail service providers.

An important example of a *consolidator* in the Netherlands is Euro Mail. Established in 1989, Euro Mail provides pre-postal activities, such as preparation of mailings, printing, packaging and pre-sorting activities. Delivery was initially fully done through PTT Post. Currently, Euro Mail Group works with three different competing postal operators with national coverage in the Netherlands (TNT, Sandd and Selekt Mail Nederland) for its mail deliveries. In 2004 Euro Mail Group realised a turnover of €17 million with handling of circa 40 million mail items.

MailMerge, recently acquired by Deutsche Post, and initially also Business Post focus on the delivery of addressed printed matter to almost all P.O. Box locations in the Netherlands. Unlike in some other cases, the P.O. Box in the Netherlands is a physical box, located in the post office, that can be accessed by third parties. Within the typology of business models used in this chapter, we consider the type of business model used a *niche services* model.

3.2.5 Interaction between regulation and development of competition

The liberalisation of the delivery of addressed printed matter in the Netherlands has given rise to a variety of new entrants. The Postal Directive in 1997 (97/67/EC), providing the perspective of a fully liberalised market in the medium term, seems to have triggered the entry of competitors with the ambition to develop nationwide delivery networks. In particular, after 2000, competition intensified with the entry and development of Sandd and Selekt Mail in the Dutch postal market. What further contributed to the development of competition in this market segment is that with regard to VAT there is a level playing field.

It appears that the liberalisation of the delivery of addressed printed matter allowed new entrants to develop interesting business propositions for specific clients: the network and service requirements for the delivery of addressed printed matter are rather similar to the network and service requirements for the delivery of bulk transaction mail – in particular, for predictable mail streams – meaning that these business models are a good stepping stone towards offering services on the entire mail market after fully opening the postal market to competition.[8]

3.3 Spain

3.3.1 The reserved area and network access arrangements

In Spain, domestic intra-city mail is not part of the reserved area and direct mail delivery has always been open to competition. The delivery of items of correspondence with a weight level of less than 50 grams and priced lower than two and a half times the basic tariff is still reserved for inter-city mail and cross-border mail (Art. 18, Spanish Postal Act). The delivery of value-added services and document exchange is liberalised in line with the postal directives.

Currently, there are no specific access regulations in Spain, but commercial negotiations to use the network of Correos y Telégrafos are possible under the condition that the access conditions are non-discriminatory and transparent. In practice, large customers qualify for special commercial agreements in cases where the number of items handed over to Correos y Telégrafos fulfils certain requirements. Furthermore, small private postal operators have worksharing agreements with the universal service provider.

Over recent years, several complaints from competitors have been issued to the Spanish competition authority. Disputes mainly concentrate on the contract arrangements of voluntary access and pricing issues. Competitors have complained about lengthy discussions regarding the terms and conditions with Correos y Telégrafos. This year, the terms and conditions have still been subject to negotiation, although Correos y Telégrafos, under pressure from the competition authority, has guaranteed that the prices for its largest competitors in comparison with competitors will cover the real cost of service.

Despite these developments, the Spanish government has recently approved plans which will allow domestic and foreign competitors access to the network of Correos y Telégrafos on a more regulated basis. The government passed a royal decree on 11 November 2006, after which Correos and its competitors started negotiations with Spain's Ministerio de Fomento (Ministry of Development) concerning the conditions and fees for the use of the infrastructure of Correos y Telégrafos (*El Pais*, 10 November 2006). According to a press release of the Ministerio de Fomento on 10 November 2006, five months after the approval of the royal decree, the first reference access contract should be in place. The conditions of this reference contract will be binding in case Correos y Telégrafos and a private postal operator do not reach an agreement two months after starting negotiations. Currently, it is unclear which access issues will actually be solved and if change in address notifications and the redirection of mail will be covered under the conditions.

3.3.2 The VAT regime

Since 1 January 2006, Correos is only exempt from charging VAT for the reserved services (mainly inter-city mail and cross-border mail below 50 grams).

3.3.3 The mandate of the regulator

In Spain, there is no separate independent regulatory authority, but the regulatory tasks and the legislative tasks are separated in the government organisation. According to stakeholders interviewed, the position of the postal regulator is both *de jure* and *de facto* rather weak.

3.3.4 The development of competition

The early liberalisation of domestic intra-city mail has led to the creation of many local mail operators. The competitors are mainly active in intra-city mail, direct mail, parcel delivery, logistics and express. The emergence of competitor postal operators is generally considered to be related to the relatively low service and quality level that the national postal operator, Correos y Telégrafos (in short, Correos), was able to offer in practice. This performance has improved in recent years as a result of large investments in the infrastructure of the network and a further automation of the logistic process (ECORYS, 2005a, p. 86). Only one major competitor on a national level exists, Unipost. The estimated market shares for 2006 in addressed mail delivery are 92–93 per cent for the national postal operator Correos, 7–8 per cent for Unipost and less than 1 per cent for other operators (Deloitte, 2006, p. 74).

Around 200 *local mail service* operators are active in addressed mail delivery. Some provide a regional service through collaboration with other operators, creating a networked local mail services provider.

The main example of *networked local mail services* is Entrega en Mano (part of Unipost, see below). Founded in 1988, it currently acts as a coordinator for more than 200 distribution points.

Unipost (based in Barcelona) comprises of a network of the 19 main private postal operators in Spain. In 2001, Unipost was formed and it started to integrate and consolidate local and regional postal operators into one national network. Some postal operators have merged into Unipost: other operators work under their own name but are part of the Unipost: network and others (around 170 operators) act as a franchise. The most important operators that are part of Unipost are Suresa CIT, Post Express, Urbandisa, Entrega en Mano and Hermanos. Unipost reported 70 per cent national coverage in 2004 and has an ambition to reach 100 per cent national coverage in 2009. Deutsche Post acquired a stake of 38 per cent in Unipost in 2004.

Unipost provides the following postal services: (a) collection, sorting, transport and delivery of addressed inter-city mail above 50 grams, direct mail and addressed intra-city mail, (b) delivery of inbound international mail above 50 grams received from Deutsche Post World Net, and (c) collection of outbound international mail above 50 grams further processed via DHL Global Mail. In addition, Unipost provides the service of planning and implementation of direct marketing campaigns for their main clients.

Judging from the description provided above, one can say that the business model of Unipost combines elements of a *networked local mail services provider* with elements of a *mass mail provider*, with the potential of expanding into a *national full-service provider*.

3.3.5 Interaction between regulation and development of competition

The existence of many local mail operators in Spain can be attributed to the early liberalisation of domestic intra-city mail in combination with the low service and quality level of the national postal operator, Correos. The perspective of full liberalisation acted as a stimulus to combine forces and, in the case of Unipost, to build a nationwide delivery network. More than in the other countries discussed in this chapter, the local mail services providers form the backbone of the business model used by new entrants.

3.4 The United Kingdom

3.4.1 The reserved area and network access arrangements

The full liberalisation on 1 January 2006 was preceded with the opening up of the UK letter mail market to competition for bulk mail services and the general limitation of the reserved area to 100 grams in January 2003. A licence is required for offering postal services.

A mandatory access regime was initiated in 2001. Third parties can negotiate access with Royal Mail and the principles of non-discrimination and transparency are applied. If no access agreement can be reached, either party can request the UK postal sector regulator Postcomm to determine the access terms.

UK Mail was the first to start access negotiations with Royal Mail in spring 2003 and the first to conclude an access agreement in spring 2004. Postcomm subsequently regulated the minimum headroom between access products and their analogous (bulk) retail products as a (minimum) percentage price difference as part of the 2006–10 Price Control. The minimum headroom varies per access product and is around 21 per cent of the access prices for the main access products.[9] The difference between the public (single item) tariff and the access tariff (inward sorting facility) is approximately 54 per cent (WIK-Consult, 2006, p. 145).

3.4.2 The VAT regime

Royal Mail is currently exempt from having to charge VAT for services supplied to customers, whereas competitors are required to charge VAT at the full rate of 17.5 per cent. A specific consequence of Royal Mail's VAT exemption is that various large customers that are also VAT exempt (mainly large financial institutions) have opted for a downstream access agreement with Royal Mail, the so-called *customer direct access* (CDA). Part of the upstream services needed to prepare the mail for downstream access is generally undertaken by one of the access operators, who act as an agent rather than formally submitting the mail to Royal Mail for final delivery (customers with CDA tend to do the pre-sorting themselves).

3.4.3 The mandate of the regulator

The position of the postal regulator is strong. The regulator has a full set of powers, ranging from information gathering (obtaining data from the USP and competitors, including making use of the USP's accounting system and being able to order new data studies) to enforcement (cancelling unlawful rates, setting new rates, levy fines, forcing the USP to grant downstream access; WIK-Consult, 2006, p. 120).

3.4.4 The development of competition

At the end of 2006, there were 18 licensed competitors. Most competitors have entered the market from 2004 onwards using third-party access, focusing on collection and presorting of bulk mail of business customers for final sorting and delivery by Royal Mail. According to information obtained from Postcomm, access volumes rapidly increased to around 11 per cent of total addressed mail items in the period April 2006 to December 2006.

One aspect of the very detailed access agreement between UK Mail and Royal Mail is that additional charges may apply (above the access price) if the postings over a certain period do not fulfil the so-called *national geographical profile requirement*.[10] As a result of the applied principle of transparency and non-discrimination, the access agreement with UK Mail was subsequently used as the basis for access agreements with a variety of other postal operators and (large) customers.

Over the course of 2004, another type of access agreement was negotiated – based on de-averaged zonal prices.[11] This access agreement became the second standard access agreement – as of January 2007 four access operators and three large customers have concluded *zonal access agreements* with Royal Mail.

Around ten competitors are active in addressed mail delivery, but they only have a very small combined market share. In the year 2005/6, the market share in terms of volume of E2E delivery by competitor postal operators was 0.2 per cent of the licensed area (items weighing less than 350 grams and costing less than £1), although a substantially higher volume was carried by those operators outside the licensed area.[12]

Unlike in Germany or Spain, in the UK no *local E2E delivery networks* focusing on B2C (bulk) letter mail have been developed to date. Before 2003, the development of these local delivery networks was not an option given the scope of the reserved area. With the liberalisation of the delivery of bulk mail (batches of 4000 identical mail items or more) in January 2003, the opportunities for local E2E delivery were substantially enhanced.

In our opinion, the main reason why no local networks were developed subsequently is that the possibility of downstream access (as stipulated in Royal Mail's licence since 2001) and the access negotiations that started between UK Mail and Royal Mail in spring 2003 together created a temporary 'regulatory uncertainty', which effectively resulted in a standstill with regard to the development of local (and national) B2C E2E delivery networks.[13]

With the conclusion of various access agreements in the last couple of years and the full liberalisation of the UK postal market in January 2006, this period of regulatory uncertainty has come to an end. However, currently the development of local E2E competition is also generally regarded sceptically by postal operators, mainly because of the low mail volumes that can be effectively targeted, competition from access operators in addition to competition from Royal Mail and difficulties to combine own delivery with using access.

The main supplier of *document exchange services* is DX Network Services, providing a closed private mailbox network of 4500 collection–delivery points dedicated to the secure movement of business documents, parcels and pouches. In addition DX Network Services provides delivery services for pre-sorted mail and parcels.

As (access) competition for pre-sorted bulk mail is intensifying and margins are under pressure, it is unlikely that business models focusing exclusively on offering pre-sorted bulk mail services through access will be able to survive in the market. Rather, there is a clear need to combine this model with offering *consolidation services* for unsorted business mail. Given the higher retail prices for unsorted business mail products of Royal Mail, the margins for consolidation services can be considerably higher than for pre-sorted bulk mail. Currently, both TNT Post and UK Mail are offering to handle the unsorted mail of their large bulk mail customers and are actively marketing consolidation services to smaller mailers, offering consolidation services for unsorted mailings of at least 250 mail items per day.[14]

There are no competitors pursuing a *national full-service providers* model.

One of the major *niche services provider* is Special Mail Services (SMS). SMS provides a door-to-door nationwide delivery service for security sensitive and valuable items of mail.

3.4.5 Interaction between regulation and development of competition

Until 2003, the relatively large reserved area acted as a barrier to the development of competition. The liberalisation of the delivery of bulk mail and the general limitation of the reserved area to mail items below 100 grams in January 2003, in principle, opened the path for competition. However, the temporary 'regulatory uncertainty' that resulted from the access negotiations between UK Mail and Royal Mail and the need to establish a position as an access competitor first (to secure mail volumes and to build up customer relations), put effectively a hold on the development of local and national E2E delivery networks.

In various instances, TNT Post has expressed its ambition to establish an E2E delivery network covering the largest part of the UK. DHL Global Mail has been investigating this option as well, whereas UK Mail has consistently said that it does not plan to develop its own network. In a number of aspects however, establishing a nationwide delivery network in the UK is more challenging than in Germany, the Netherlands or Spain. National E2E delivery networks have to be developed from scratch in the UK, as there are no local and regional delivery networks of any importance. In addition, the inequality in the VAT status of operators is distorting the development of competition by encouraging (VAT-exempt) customers to switch to customer direct access rather than to E2E services. Competition is relatively intense, with competition from access operators in addition to competition from Royal Mail. The access prices can be perceived as low from several perspectives (see the text box below) and low access prices worsen the business case of an E2E entrant: a prerequisite for E2E competition to become successful is that it proves possible to operate a business model with lower delivery costs per item than the downstream access prices. Finally, the access conditions make combining own delivery with using access unattractive.

On the positive side, as a potential launch path to E2E competition, the current downstream access agreements enable acquiring mail volumes through access before actually starting delivery through a parallel delivery network. High headroom and low access prices are conducive to the development of access competition and to potential E2E competitors acquiring substantial mail volumes before starting delivering themselves. However, low access prices are acting as a barrier to the development of E2E competition.

LOW ACCESS PRICES IN THE UK

The current downstream access prices can be perceived as low from several perspectives. From a cost perspective, Royal Mail is claiming that it is making a loss on its access products and that retail customers (Mailsort 2) are in fact cross-subsidising access customers. From an entry perspective, the initial access prices agreed between Royal Mail and UK Mail was referenced as too low by TNT UK at the time. From an international perspective, the access prices in the UK are low as they are cost based and not established on a retail-minus basis as in Germany, the Netherlands or Spain – the latter methodology providing a contribution to 'fixed' upstream costs that the access mail does not actually incur.

4. CONCLUSION

Developments within the postal markets in Germany, the Netherlands, Spain and the UK show that there is a clear interaction between the developments in the regulatory environment and the development of competition. The business models of the entrants are to a large extent based on the possibilities that are on offer in the regulatory framework in these respective countries.

Competitor postal operators have pursued various strategies and apply different business models to realise their strategies. All these different business models have in common that they differ markedly from the business model of the national postal operator, and that the size of the networks that they have developed is substantially smaller than the network of the national postal operators. In none of the countries that we have investigated are entrants following a full-service strategy.

Whether or not entrants build an E2E delivery network seems to depend on the access regime. In this respect, the actual terms and conditions for access seem to be more important than whether or not access has been regulated. The access prices in the Netherlands and Spain are negotiated or, in the case of Germany, regulated at a retail-minus basis, and are much less favourable in the UK, where they have been negotiated but reflect the underlying cost structure of Royal Mail.[15] Moreover, many practical problems have made access unattractive for entrants in Germany, the Netherlands and Spain.

The market shares of E2E competitors, and in particular of E2E competitors focusing on B2C mail, have grown substantially in Germany, the Netherlands and Spain, reaching an estimated market share of 8–12 per cent in addressed mail delivery in 2006. This growth in market share has taken place despite the fact that part of the addressed mail market is reserved for the incumbent and that, in particular in Germany and the Netherlands, competitors have to compete with very large and efficient incumbents.

4.1 Convergence of Business Models?

Given the dynamics it seems that, at least in Germany, the Netherlands and Spain, some convergence of the business models applied by competitors is to be expected once these postal markets have been fully liberalised. Competition will mainly arise from a small number of competitors, with nationwide delivery networks focusing on B2C mail streams. The business model is likely to resemble a mass mail services provider making use of cooperation agreements with local and regional mail deliveries to a smaller or larger extent. Moreover, the services provided will not be restricted to computerised pre-sorted bulk mailings, but will include smaller unsorted mail batches as well.

In addition to these competitors, consolidators will be able to gain in importance once they have a choice between a small number of E2E competitors rather than having to deal with an incumbent-monopolist only. Dependent on the local situation and the chosen liberalisation path, a variety of local operators and niche services providers will also be active on the market. Spot operators and full service providers seem less likely to emerge in a liberalised market.

According to the authors, it is most likely that the chosen access regime will have a dominant impact on the pattern of competition in the UK. Rather than acting as a launch path to E2E competition, it seems more likely that competitors will continue to use a business model based on an access agreement with Royal Mail for final mile delivery. As observed in Section 3, the low access prices, other access conditions (in particular, the penalties for not meeting the national geographical profile) and the VAT exemption of Royal Mail are favouring access competition over E2E competition. Having said this, it may prove possible for TNT Post (or another competitor) to establish a competing E2E delivery network with a business model resembling the business model of the main competitors in the other countries discussed, but this competitor has to compete in an environment that in a number of aspects significantly differs from the environment in Germany, the Netherlands or Spain.

NOTES

1. This percentage is likely to increase over time as a result of substitution from high-cost/high-QoS products to lower-cost/lower-QoS products.
2. In ECORYS (2005a, section 6.5.3), three reasons or purposes for arranging access are mentioned. First, access can be sought as a matter of last resort: a competitor postal operator that is operating a delivery network that is not (yet) fully covering all customers may want to hand over part of the mail of their customers to the national postal operator for final delivery. Second, access can be sought by mail consolidators who primarily realise their business case because of the price discrimination of the national postal operator between small and large customers (cf. the definition of Dietl and Waller, 2002). Third, access for final mile delivery can be sought by companies that position themselves as postal operators and want to deliver services in a smaller or larger part of the value chain. These operators tend to focus on large customers.
3. Conclusion based on interviews with stakeholders. See also the interview with Pieter Kunz, chairman of European Mail Networks (TNT) in Document Manager, *Deutsche Post kiest steevast juridisch machtsmiddel*, Year 9, issue 2, March 2007, pp. 32–5.
4. The new Act still needs the approval of the Senate.
5. Direct communication with a number of local mail services providers in the yellow pages and other address book lists.
6. In the initial stages of developing the company, Sandd cooperated with the *sociale werkplaatsen* as well. Later on, Sandd developed its own delivery network in the regions concerned.
7. The current situation of Businesspost is unclear. One of the main drivers behind the organisations has left. Whether the remaining organisation will be able to continue to provide postal services is unknown yet.
8. See ECORYS (2005a, table 5.1) for an overview of the network and service requirements for different postal products. Analysing the similarities and differences of the network and service requirements, one can conclude that the economies of scope of combining the delivery of bulk transaction mail with addressed direct mail are higher than the economies of scope of combining the delivery of bulk transaction mail with addressed catalogues and particularly higher than if combined with unaddressed mail delivery (where the economies of scope are lowest of the three postal products referred to).
9. See Postcomm, Royal Mail's Price and Service Quality Review 2006–2010 – License Modifications Proposals, March 2006.
10. See also *Condition 9 Access Services for Inward Mail Centres User Guide*, www.royalmailwholesale.com.
11. As downstream access arrangements are not part of Royal Mail's universal service obligation, Royal Mail is not obliged to charge a geographically uniform price.
12. Postcomm (2006, pp. 14 and 48). For example, the mailroom services by TNT Post (66 million items per annum) fall outside the licensed area.
13. This point of view is supported in interviews we conducted with competitors of Royal Mail. As long as the exact terms of access (prices, conditions, products) were unknown, it was not possible to establish whether there was a business case for setting up an E2E network for B2C (bulk) letter mail. Given the substantial investments needed to establish such a network and the considerable risks involved, these investment decisions were postponed until the access conditions, and in particular the access prices, were determined.
14. Consolidation services can (in principle) also be offered without targeting pre-sorted bulk mail as well, most likely combined with other upstream services such as client and market definition (value-added services to support the effective targeting of direct marketing campaigns), mail preparation and printing. Currently, this is not an attractive business model given the restrictions of that the access agreements pose: it is easier to fulfil all requirements when combined with tendering pre-sorted bulk mail.

15. The prime difference between cost plus and retail-minus access tariffs is that in the former tariff no compensation is included for the fixed costs of the network of the access provider (the incumbent) upstream of the point of access.

REFERENCES

Bundesnetzagentur (2006), *Ninth Market Study in the Field of Licensed Postal Item*, April. http://www.bundesnetzagentur.de/media/archive/7256.pdf

Dietl, Helmut M. and Peter Waller (2002), 'Competing with Mr. Postman, Business strategies, Industry structure, and competitive prices in liberalized letter markets', *Schmalenbach Business Review*, **54**, 148–70.

Deloitte (2006), 'Memoria del sector postal español 2004', study for the Ministry of Public Works (ES), DG Regulation of postal services, Madrid, July 2006. http://www.fomento.es/MFOM/LANG_CASTELLANO/DIRECCIONES_GENERALES/SERVICIOS_POSTALES/ESTUDIOS/ MEMORIA/2004/

ECORYS (2005a), 'Development of competition in the European postal sector', study for the European Commission, DG Internal Market, Rotterdam, 2005. http://ec.europa.eu/internal_market/post/doc/studies/2005-ecorys-final_en.pdf

ECORYS (2005b), 'Barriers to competition in the German and UK postal market, Does *de jure* liberalisation lead to *de facto* liberalisation?', study for the Ministry of Economic Affairs (NL), Rotterdam, 2005. http://english.ecorys.nl/dmdocuments/ECORYS-Barriers%20to%20competition%20in%20the%20German%20and%20UK%20postal%20market.pdf

ECORYS (2007), 'Prospects for competition in the UK postal market', (unpublished) study for the UK postal regulator (Postcomm), Rotterdam, 2007.

Postcomm (2006), *2006 Competitive Market Review*, http://www.psc.gov.uk/postcomm/live/competition/competitive-market-reviews/Competitive_Market_Review_2006_revised.pdf

RBB Economics (2007), *Postmarktmonitor – Openbare Versie*, March. http://www.opta.nl/download/RBB%5FPostmarktmonitor%5Fopenbaar%2Epdf

WIK-Consult (2006), *Main Developments in the Postal Sector (2004–2006)*, study for the European Commission, May 2006. http://europa.eu.int/comm/internal_market/post/studies_en.htm

16. An incentive regime for quality of service of universal service providers in the postal sector*

Luis Correia da Silva, Leonardo Mautino, Paul Dudley and Elizabeth Payling

1. INTRODUCTION

In recent years service quality has taken on prominence in regulated industries where regulatory authorities have been concerned with avoiding quality degradation, and with creating the right incentives for regulated companies to deliver optimal levels of quality. In principle, the optimal level of quality of service is set when the incremental cost of providing that quality of service is equal to the incremental willingness to pay and therefore the incremental charge for that service. At levels of service below this, the incremental willingness to pay may exceed the incremental cost; the converse may be the case above this equilibrium. This approach can then be used to determine the appropriate level of investment for quality of service (Reay, 1993).

In a free market the quality of service can act as a product characteristic, in addition to price, with which to compare the offerings of alternative providers, provided that the measures of quality of service are themselves comparable. Customers have the option of alternative providers and thereby can choose their preferred offering of price and service.[1] The provider may be expected to benefit in terms of sales from improvements in service quality and, conversely, lose out in terms of sales from deterioration in service quality. In these circumstances, the market creates the incentive to compete on price and service.

In the presence of market imperfections or insufficient competition, there is a role for regulation to induce optimal price and quality outcomes. Market imperfections may arise, for example, if there is insufficient comparable information between service providers on their service quality. Insufficient competition may lead the incumbent postal operator to have caps placed on its prices which, if not extended to include incentives for service quality, may lead the provider to lower quality in order to reduce costs and enhance profit (Joskow, 2006). Further, if the price caps do not allow for the recovery of returns on investment to enhance service quality, they may lead to under-investment (Sappington, 2005).

The theoretical literature on service quality incentives for regulated and unregulated industries is extensive. Sappington (2005) provides a detailed review of the economic literature on the design of service quality regulation in public utilities, and concludes that service quality regulation entails many complications and subtleties that do not arise in price regulation. This is particularly true of the postal industry. In the context of the postal sector, the issue of quality of service has received some attention in the academic literature,[2] although there are only a few studies focusing on how incentive regulation should be implemented in practice.

In practice, price caps are set on specific groups of assumptions, primarily of cash costs, an allowed level of return or cash profit, and levels of service. The level of profit will match the allowed profit if circumstances turn out as those expected at the time of setting the control, in which case the profit acts as a reward to the business and shareholder. However, the regulatory incentives would need to ensure that the level of profit changes if, for example, the achieved level of service differed from that expected when the control was set. A deterioration in the service level would be expected to lead to a reduction in the return or profit and, conversely, an improvement in the service level would be expected to lead to an increase in the return or profit.

There is an extensive and growing literature in postal economics investigating global price-cap (GPC) regulation. This literature has considered some alternative price-cap structures to GPC and found cases where the universal service provider (USP) is no longer able to break even (i.e. no longer recovers the return assumed in the fixed component of such models in the presence of competition) (De Donder et al., 2006). These analyses assume a known demand function and therefore predictable demand outcome. In practice, this is an area of considerable uncertainty (see Cazals et al., Chapter 5 this volume) which is further affected by potential changes in service quality, and leads to the need to test structures and their recovery of the return under alternative volume (and service quality) scenarios.

A capital asset pricing model (CAPM) approach can be used by postal regulators to set the return needed for the business where, for example, the investment is required to satisfy the market investor principle. CAPM is applied normally to profit-maximising firms interacting in an efficient capital market rather than a publicly owned enterprise.[3] However, CAPM was used recently by the UK postal regulator (Postcomm, 2005) using information from market comparators. Using the CAPM framework, the price control structure is shown, in this chapter, to affect the financial risk to the USP, as expressed by the expected return. Further, having determined a structure that is optimal within CAPM, in the sense of minimising the required profit allowance when setting the control (assuming there is a market set of prices that would make such profit), this chapter considers the financial risks relating to quality of service and how regulators may address these in practice in such a regulatory environment.

The CAPM assumptions are typically based on an expected profit level within a symmetric, (perhaps) normal, distribution of alternative profit level. However, particular market circumstances or regulatory intervention may lead to asymmetric distributions of the alternative outcomes and affect the expected level of return.

This chapter is concerned with some of the practical implications for the postal industry when designing a regulatory framework for quality of service, assuming a CAPM framework and with a particular focus on addressing risk. Section 2 considers three core components of regulatory intervention in service quality: measurability, setting targets and scope. Section 3 considers a framework for assessing the risk to investment returns arising from service quality. Section 4 examines practical ways in which the regulatory mechanisms can reduce risk to investment returns. Section 5 concludes.

2. REGULATORY INTERVENTION

There are three core components of any regulatory intervention in service quality. Firstly, there is the need to be able to measure service quality performance. Secondly, there is the need to have a target or standard against which that performance is measured. Thirdly, the products and services that are to have an incentive regime for service quality need to be identified.

2.1 Measure

The mechanisms available to provide incentives for the regulated business within the price control fall under two broad categories. Firstly, prices can be allowed to increase or decrease for the regulated business depending on the level of service. This may be addressed either directly through the prices themselves allowed under the control (this would take the form of a factor for quality added to the price- or revenue-cap formula) or indirectly through the level of compensation offered to all users of a service. Secondly, costs can be imposed on the regulated business for a decrease in the level of service or for individual service failures. This may be administered through a fine or compensation to individual users.[4]

These mechanisms rely on the level of service quality being measurable. Measurability is important, as difficulties in obtaining accurate measures of service standards can have implications for the effectiveness of the regulatory regime.[5] For example, the proportion of mail conveyed within a transit time from collection to delivery is often used as a measure for the majority of standard product performance. Overall service levels can be robustly measured by statistical surveys based on sampling of test items and can therefore be used to apply mechanisms involving all service users (e.g. automatic compensation to account customers and price-cap adjustments). However, while statistically robust in assessing overall levels of performance, such measures may not reflect individual actual or perceived experience. This can affect assessments of willingness to pay for different service levels, as perception tends to lag measured performance.

The application of fines takes measurability to another level of granularity. Fines do not directly benefit the customer, but provide further means of penalising the provider (Balogh et al., 2006) that require detailed understanding of the circumstances under which they apply and whether such circumstances have occurred. This can increase uncertainty, particularly as the process for determining culpability can be protracted and the financial consequences of a breach unknown, and therefore exposure to the expected return on investment, where the application of those penalties is not clearly set out.

Other aspects of performance, such as overall levels of loss and damage arising due to the postal operator's fault, are particularly difficult to measure in any accurate and meaningful way using statistical surveys. One recourse is to deal with these aspects of performance using compensation for service failure in relation to individual items or events.[6] Such compensation schemes or arrangements may be made through primary legislation, the operator's licence, operator contracts with customers or on a voluntary basis.

2.2 Setting Targets

The setting of the target level or standard for quality of service requires an assessment of the willingness to pay and cost of incremental changes to service quality.[7] In the absence of this information, setting targets may be based on actual historical performance levels or a perception of what those target levels should be, possibly based on benchmarking or market research.

If the desired target levels exceed the historical levels or if actual performance is unknown then there is a substantial risk that the target levels may not be attained in practice without significant cost or redesign of the postal network. The postal operator may then be unable to achieve these levels within other constraints such as price and service specification and the performance regime will not incentivise appropriate levels of service quality. Establishing actual performance, as measured by the chosen measurement methodology, and understanding of the reasons for substantial differences between actual performance and the desired target are therefore crucial precursors to setting an appropriate target in practice.

Figure 16.1 shows the performance of some European postal operators' next-day delivery services against their regulatory target for single-piece priority mail. Targets range from 80 per cent to 95 per cent, averaging at 90 per cent. 2005 performance ranged from 69 per cent to 98 per cent, averaging at 89 per cent. Overall there is only weak correlation between target and performance, though for some countries the performance is close to target.

There have been several studies into the willingness to pay for service quality.[8] These studies are often based on seeking to reveal customer preferences through consumer

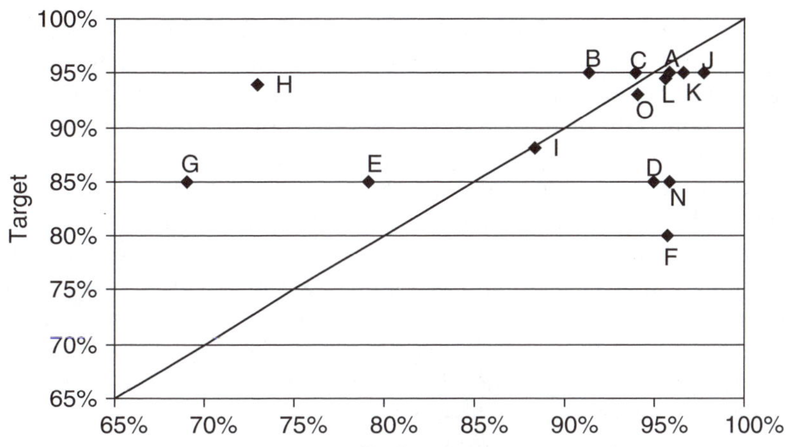

Note: A, Austria; B, Belgium; C, Denmark; D, Finland; E, France; F, Germany; G, Greece; H, Ireland; I, Italy; J, Luxembourg; K, Netherlands; L, Portugal; N, Sweden; O, UK.

Sources: Operators' websites (F, K, O), accounts (C, E, I, J, L, N) or regulator (A, B, H, G).

Figure 16.1 Comparison of service quality performance and targets in 2005 for next-day services across Europe

surveys and preferences when given choices of a range of options. Without careful design, when asked if customers want to pay more for a service above the expected or target level there is a tendency to say 'no', and when asked if customers want to pay less for a service below the expected or target level there is a tendency to say 'yes'. In addition, problems may arise if the customers are not aware of, or do not believe, the current service levels. Hence the design of the studies becomes critical to revealing true preferences.

A study by Accent and RAND Europe (2005) sought to address this issue directly by establishing for the customers within the survey a clear understanding of what the existing service quality was and then providing choices to reveal preference. The study, which examined ten products with varying service specifications, revealed several products where customers were willing to pay more for enhancements in service performance, and found that for most products there was no willingness to pay or need to alter the price for small changes in performance. These findings are consistent both with the basic structure of prices applied by postal operators across the world in charging more for a one-day service than for a two- or three-day service and consistent with the observations of willingness to pay in other UK sectors.

In respect of analysis of the cost of quality of service changes, research has been more limited.[9] There may be several reasons for this. For example, any estimate of the cost of quality of a change depends on both the existing network and the change envisaged, and is therefore specific to both that network and the change. In addition, the scale of change may be limited by legal obligations placed on the service provider through primary legislation and licence (such as the number of days of delivery in the week).[10]

2.3 Scope

Several aspects of the scope of regulatory intervention for service quality have already been touched upon. For example, where there is a free market, sufficient competition and limited imperfections in the market, there may be no role for regulatory intervention.

Where there is competition and significant market imperfections there may be scope for regulatory intervention – for example, in the consistency with which service quality measures apply across providers. Several issues of measurement arise when the end-to-end service is fulfilled by more than one provider, including the different means of measuring the service performance within the parts of the service and the presentation and treatment of mail at their interfaces. Hence competition raises several issues over the standard measurement of service quality and the transparency and comparability of service quality between providers. This may, in part, be overcome by technology that facilitates the tracking of mail through different pipelines.[11] This then forms part of the consideration as to whether the incremental cost is matched by the willingness to pay an incremental price.

Where there is insufficient competition, the regulator needs to consider the price and quality service framework for the regulated business. Further, where the regulated business undertakes the provision of the universal service, the requirements under the European Postal Directive and country-specific primary legislation act as constraints on that framework.

To these guidelines, the licence of the regulated business may overlay additional definitions and requirements. For example, it may define the products that fulfil the activities as part of the universal service obligation, and the prices and expected service standards thereof. Within the broad remit of the European Postal Directive and state primary legislation, there remains a considerable degree of discretion as to what constitutes the universal service obligation to be fulfilled by the regulated business. A reduction in the requirements set within the licence may assist in ensuring the provision of the universal service (Crew and Kleindorfer, 2006). Hence these requirements are a precursor to forming a view of other aspects of regulatory intervention in respect of allowed costs and price caps.

3. THE RISKS TO THE REGULATED BUSINESS

There are risks to an investor that are inherent within the postal sector and reflect the characteristics that make it different to other sectors. As an example, service quality can change the demand within its service offering (a product mix effect) and in terms of the total mail passing through its network relative to that of its competitors. An investor may be able to diversify its portfolio between providers to reduce this risk. However, if the universal service obligation is non-transferable, it may not be possible for the investor to diversify its portfolio away from the USP in the event of a downturn in service quality – for example, where there is state ownership of both incumbent and the universal service obligation. There then may be added uncertainty of penalties if the application of penalties is poorly defined.

Against these risks, the regulator has to determine a level to cap prices and the regulated business has to ensure that it earns sufficient return to undertake investments to improve productivity and service quality in order to remain competitive. The risk of a business is typically reflected in the cost of capital, the cost of raising debt and equity to facilitate investment and change within the business. The weighted average cost of capital (WACC) of the CAPM is a standard means through which regulatory authorities seek to assess the cost of capital used in setting the price control,[12] and was used recently by the UK postal regulator. The WACC weights the expected debt and equity costs by the proportion of debt and equity relevant for the business. The equity costs comprise a risk-free rate plus a generic equity premium and multiplier (or beta value) that reflects the principal non-diversifiable risks.

The CAPM provides a useful framework in which to start to assess the risks of service quality (Kraus and Litzenberger, 1976). The CAPM makes several important assumptions; for example, it assumes that investors can diversify their portfolio of assets so that it is only the risks that are correlated with overall market risk that should be of concern to investors – as measured by the beta value in the CAPM.[13] In contrast, the alpha value reflects risks that are specific to the company and therefore are assumed to be diversifiable within an investor's portfolio. The WACC for regulated business i is as follows:

$$\text{WACC}_i = (1 - g_i) \times r_{ei} + g_i \times r_{di},$$

where g_i is the gearing level (net debt/total value), r_{di} is the return required on debt investments, and r_{ei} is the return required on equity investments, such that

$$r_{ei} = r_f + (\alpha_{ai} + \beta_{ai}) \times \text{ERP}_t/(1 - g),$$

where r_f is the risk-free rate, β_{ai} and α_{ai} are asset beta and alpha respectively (relating to the principal and supplementary company-specific risk), and ERP_i is the equity risk premium. While β_{ai} typically assumes a symmetric distribution, α_{ai} can take a value from a non-symmetric distribution. It is within this framework that we consider the risk of service quality.

3.1 CAPM Beta Risk

On the supply side, change to service quality may affect specific parts of the network and therefore affect the products in different ways. This depends on the degree to which the products use the affected parts of that network and the extent to which scarce resources are allocated between different products. Where there is technology improvement, this may improve service performance, and where there is an adverse effect, it may have a detrimental impact on the performance. Hence changes to the service quality can affect products in different ways and therefore, on the demand side, the relative demand for those services.

If the actual service performance achieved is generally low at the outset, then any improvement in the general level of service performance may cause customers to recognise that a greater proportion of mail is reaching its destination more quickly and switch to lower-priced services with longer specified transit times. The converse may be the case where an incumbent has a high level of performance that deteriorates (Reay, 1993). The altered flows of mail then change the overall incremental costs of the provider.

Further, where there is competition, customers not only have the choice of switching between services of the incumbent, but also switching to alternative providers for some or all of the service. With a price-per-item charge, this affects the recovery of fixed costs.

The effect that changes in demand have on the returns of the regulated business with some fixed costs may be made by reference to the way in which the variance for the distribution of alternative levels of return changes in response to unanticipated and permanent changes in demand under different structures of the price control. Under a pure revenue control, demand changes cause costs to change but revenues to remain the same; in this instance an increase in demand worsens the cash position. Under a pure price control, revenues change by the full price and costs by the marginal cost; in this instance, an increase in demand improves the cash position if the prices exceed marginal cost. Between these two cases is a scenario where a change in demand has no impact on the cash position of the business. This occurs when the structure of the control has a fixed component of revenue that recovers the fixed costs and a variable component that recovers the marginal costs. This may be referred to as an 'optimal' structure.

Within the CAPM, this reduction in the variance for the distribution of alternative levels of return results in a low beta value. For simplicity, the regulated business is assumed to have this structure for a single product with a long-run marginal cost of 0.6 and the fixed costs as a portion of total costs at 0.4. The change in risk premium can be calculated for an unpredicted and permanent change in economic growth when the fixed revenue as a proportion of total revenue is 0.3 at the forecast level of volume. For illustration it is assumed that for a 1 per cent growth in GDP there is a 1 per cent increase in mail volumes, assuming volume : economic growth elasticity of 1. A 1 per cent increase in mail volume raises costs by 0.6 per cent and revenue by 0.7 per cent. Assuming costs of

€5 billion, the 1 per cent increase in mail volume would result in an increase in profit of about €5 million. The unpredicted and permanent change in GDP could happen at any time within the price control period, which is assumed to be five years. If it happens at the start of the period, the present value of five years of additional annual profit of €5 million discounted using a discount factor of about 10 per cent is about €20 million. If it happens at the end of the period, the value is zero. Hence, the average value for the period is €10 million. Assuming that the asset value of the regulated business is €3 billion, the additional €10 million in profit would increase the long-term return by 0.33 per cent. For a business valued at €5 billion, the additional €10 million in profit would increase the long-term return by 0.20 per cent.

There is a strong statistical relationship between changes in the stock market index and GDP. For illustration, the FTSE All-share index was regressed on successive lags of the growth rate in GDP for a data series comprising quarterly observations from 1980 onwards in nominal terms. It showed that a change of 1 per cent in GDP is consistent with a 2.3 per cent change in the value of the market. Only contemporaneous changes in GDP have a significant impact on the movement of the FTSE All-share index. The correlation between the return to the regulated business and the FTSE All-share index is then 0.14. The beta value for a control with no fixed revenue would then be about 0.6 (i.e. 4×0.14) higher than for an optimal control for which 40 per cent of revenue is fixed.

This has some important implications for the regulatory framework for quality of service. Firstly, it indicates that unanticipated and permanent changes within the market caused by quality of service and affecting market demand present a risk to the regulated business. Secondly, it indicates that these risks can lead to a higher beta value and WACC if not addressed appropriately through the structure of the control. Thirdly, it indicates that where there are multiple services, prices and fixed costs and the potential for switching arising from changes in service quality, there could be a structure that has a fixed revenue component and variable components that reflect the various incremental costs of the services that will minimise the WACC estimate of the CAPM. In practice, this would be tested through alternative projections of volumes over the price control period, and in some circumstances (and as shown in the literature), there may be no pricing solution where the fixed costs and assumed return within those costs is no longer made by the USP.

3.2 CAPM Alpha Risk

While the beta value within the CAPM approach may be a useful starting position, it may not fully reflect the risks of the USP in the postal sector and its provision of the universal service. The traditional CAPM approach assumes that the investor can fully diversify its portfolio of assets. This is an important assumption within the context of the postal sector where the incumbent fulfils the obligation of a universal service and is a government-owned entity. For this assumption to be valid within a price control period, it would require the obligation for the provision of the universal service to be fully transferable between operators. As entrants entered the postal market and the investor diversified its asset portfolio into those businesses, there is the potential for the incumbent to have under-investment and not be able to provide the universal service. At that point the obligation of the provision of the universal service would need to be fully transferable to the other operators. If this were not the case, then the assumption that investors can diversify their asset portfolio and support the obligation of the provision of the universal service would not necessarily be met.

Again, this has some important implications for the regulatory framework for quality of service. The CAPM approach refers to the risks of the business and industry by reference to an alpha value, but does not include them in the traditional estimation of the WACC.

In practice, the alpha risks can take several forms. As quality of service within the postal service requires significant labour input, disruption to the service can lead to a fall in volume and actual revenues falling below allowed revenues. Even if this shortfall in one year leads to higher prices to recover it in the subsequent year, this may not necessarily be achieved if the mail transfers to other media or competitors, or if there is further disruption to the service. Alternatively, the implementation of major transformation change that adversely affects quality in the short term may lead not only to loss of revenue for the regulated business but also to a reduction in allowed revenue, and greater compensation to large users, payments to individuals and fines, dependent on the regulatory regime.

The alpha risks skew or move the distribution of risk adversely, with the effect of reducing the expected rate of return below the required rate set within the control. As such, the CAPM beta measure of risk can understate that faced by the incumbent in an environment where there is under-investment and the obligation for the provision of the universal service is not fully transferable. Within CAPM, this leads to consideration of an increment to the WACC to act as an additional incentive to investors in the presence of such risks.

In many respects, these quality-of-service considerations bring the issue of the financing of the USP, as expressed by many papers of postal economics over the years, closer to hand. Clearly, the financing of the USP requires careful consideration when setting the regulatory incentives within a price control.

4. REGULATORY INCENTIVES

The potential for underestimating the required return on investment through inappropriate quality of service incentives is recognised in the literature (Weisman, 2005). There are several means by which the regulatory regime, having identified realistic service targets (as discussed earlier), can recognise the alpha risks in ways that do not just lead to a potentially significant increase in the estimated WACC identified above.

4.1 Insurance

The regulated business can look at ways to insure against the alpha risk. As an example, it may issue some form of shares for take-up by employees on preferential terms so that the performance of the business is linked to the employee's capital value. This approach was used at the time of flotation on the stock market of the regulated industries, including by some companies in the postal sector, and, though not floated, is being mirrored in Royal Mail.

4.2 Exceptions

The regulatory regime can identify circumstances in which various service quality penalties are not applied. As an example, there may be exemption from penalties, expressed in terms of compensation payments or reduced prices, if the cause of the deterioration in service quality arises from industrial action and in the presence of reasonable responses to maintain service quality by the regulated business. Such an approach requires definitions and measurements of the impact of industrial action, as well as reasonable responses.[14] This approach has been used for some of the regulated businesses in the UK, particularly in the years following the flotation.

4.3 Financial Exposure Limit

The extent of the financial exposure of adverse regulatory impacts through prices, compensation or fines can be limited to within reasonable and estimated bounds. As the beta value within the CAPM reflects the principal non-diversifiable risk premium on equity, assuming that the regulatory authority has some duties of ensuring the financial viability of the regulated business, the level of financial exposure arising from deterioration in service could be limited to ensure debt coverage and some equity return.

There is some evidence that this has been followed in practice. The percentage of the maximum financial penalties (excluding individual compensation payments) for service failure relative to the proportion of allowed profit related to equity within the WACC for several regulated businesses are shown in Table 16.1. These percentages were typically well below 100 per cent. The main exception is Railtrack (which went into

Table 16.1 Level of exposure relative to the return on equity for downturns in service performance in UK regulated companies

Sector	Year	Revenue exposure (%)[1]	Profit exposure (%)[2]	Return on equity exposure (%)[3]
Air traffic control	2003	2	15	25
Air traffic control	2006	6	42	65
BAA (London airports)	2003	2	3	4
Electricity distribution	2005	4	14	21
Network Rail		Uncapped	Uncapped	141
Postal services	2006	5	150	215
Water companies	5 years	1	3	21

Notes:

1 Revenue exposure measures the ratio between maximum penalties for failing service standards (excluding individual compensation payments and fines) and the allowed revenues.

2 Profit exposure measures the ratio between maximum penalties and the allowed profits (defined as regulatory asset base × WACC).

3 Return on equity exposure measures the ratio between maximum penalties and the equity component of the allowed profit.

Sources: See CAA (2002), CAA (2003a or b), CAA (2005), Ofgem (2001), Ofgem (2003), Ofgem (2004), ORR (2003), Ofwat (2004) and Postcomm (2005).

Table 16.2 Inclusion of incentives for outperformance of service quality

Country	Sector	Outperformance incentive
UK	Electricity distribution (2005–10)	✓
	Postal services (2006–10)	×
	BAA London airports (2003–8)	×
	Water (2005–10)	✓
	Air traffic control (2000–5)	✓
	Air traffic control (2006–10)	✓
	Network Rail (2004–9)	✓
Ireland	Electricity supply and distribution (2006–10)	✓
Belgium	Postal services (2005–10)	✓
Italy	Electricity supply	✓
Portugal	Electricity supply	✓

Sources: See Ofwat (2002), Commission for Energy Regulation (2006), Council of European Energy Regulators (2005) and Moniteur Belge (2005).

administration 2001 after the Hatfield derailment and became Network Rail) and Royal Mail (2006–10).[15]

4.4 Incentive Structure

The adverse impact on alpha risks can be offset in part through changes to the allowed prices within the structure of the regime for service quality. Examples include the potential to include allowance for greater returns for outperformance of quality targets; and a window of change to service quality around the target in which there is no change to the price-cap entitlements of the regulated business (Balogh et al., 2006).

The inclusion of incentive properties for outperformance has been acknowledged in the literature (Holt, 2005) and has been applied in practice, as shown in Table 16.2. Most UK regulators have recognised the need for this incentive. The two main exceptions where penalties only for underperformance apply are BAA London airports (2003–8) and Royal Mail (2006–10);[16] in addition, the controls for BT and gas distribution have applied no adjustment whatsoever for service quality. Some regulators outside of the UK have also supported the adoption of this incentive within the price control. In most of these cases, the scale of penalty for a decrement in service quality exceeds the reward for the equivalent increment.[17]

Revealed-preference studies can inform what outperformance incentive could apply and the band in which no adjustment applies by reference to revealed preference of the willingness to pay. For example, Accent and RAND Europe (2005) found symmetry in the willingness to pay more for increments of service quality relative to the existing level (and pay less for decrements of service quality) for first-class (priority) services and second-class (non-priority) stamped mail and parcels. They found this to be less prevalent for other second- and third-class services. In addition, they found the band in which there was no change to the willingness to pay to exceed one percentage point either side of the transit service quality measure for the third-class service.

4.5 Compensation Scheme Design

Compensation schemes are widely used for regulated industries to provide incentives for service performance, as shown in Table 16.3. In some cases, operators are required to compensate automatically when they know a service failure has occurred; in other cases, the customer must make a claim. Payments for some schemes are linked to the customer's expenditure (e.g. refund of rail fares). Other schemes offer flat-rate payments, but these may be capped in relation to the customer's annual expenditure (e.g. total drought payments).

Compensation paid to customers for postal service failures as part of a regulatory or statutory regime generally relates to loss of, or damage or delay to, an individual item. However, the nature and accessibility of universal postal services means that, unlike compensation schemes in other regulated industries, there may be little or no evidence that a problem has occurred or that it has been caused by the operator. Technology has been developed to enable customers to track express or valuable mail, which typically has higher levels of available compensation, and may be used to establish, among others, the evidence of loss or delay of a particular item for delivery.[18] However, such systems are not feasible or cost-effective for ordinary mail; therefore, it is difficult to determine whether loss or delay has occurred. Similarly, assessments of mail damage need to consider the extent to which damage has been caused by inadequate packaging and whether damage has occurred outside the postal network.

A second key difference between the postal service and other regulated industries is that compensation payments for individual failures are usually small in relation to the total expenditure on the service provided. For typical social customers using universal service products, this is much less likely to be the case, given that across the EU the average non-business mailer spends about €25–€30 on postage (WIK-Consult, 2006).[19]

Table 16.3 Compensation schemes as part of service regime

Country	Sector	Automatic compensation	Claims-based compensation
EU	Air travel	✓	✓
UK	Electricity distribution	✓	✓
	Gas distribution	✓	✗
	Electricity suppliers	✓	✓
	Gas suppliers	✓	✓
	Postal services – USP	✓†	✓
	Postal services – other	✗	✗
	Water and sewerage companies	✓	✓
	Telecoms (BT)	✓	✓
	Train operating companies	✗	✓
	London Underground	✗	✓

Note: † Bulk mail only.

Source: Conditions of service and customer charters.

The postal regulatory regime should therefore permit decisions about compensation payment levels and claim handling procedures that balance the considerations of genuine claimants against the risks to the operator of paying out large amounts in compensation, particularly in respect of unwarranted or even fraudulent claims.

5. CONCLUSION

The requirement to meet service quality standards increases risk to the regulated business. This risk may be expressed within a CAPM framework as an alpha risk in addition to the standard beta risk used to estimate the expected or allowed return for the business when setting the price control and its allowed revenues. Consistent with the existing literature, which indicates that inappropriate incentive regimes can lead to under-investment, failure to account for the alpha risks in the setting of the regulated business's allowance may lead it to under-invest.

Alpha risks are present in the postal sector where the universal service is non-transferable and the investor is not able to diversify its investment portfolio. This is the case for government-owned public enterprises (or postal operators). This leads to the need to consider the inclusion of an additional premium for the alpha when estimating the WACC for the incumbent regulated business. This premium may be reduced if alternative means within the incentive regime are adopted to mitigate the alpha risk. These alternatives are relevant to the postal sector in setting an appropriate incentive regime for service quality.

NOTES

* Luis Correia da Silva and Leonardo Mautino from Oxera, Elizabeth Payling and Paul Dudley from Royal Mail Group. The analysis contained in this chapter reflects the views of the authors and may not necessarily be those of Royal Mail Group or Oxera.

1. The provider may re-bundle its offering in many ways, including the offer of compensation for failure to meet specific service levels, and as a means of linking price and service level.
2. Reay (1993) considers an approach based on market research to decide on appropriate levels of investments to improve service quality within the service structure and the constraints of providing universal services under a regulated monopoly. Reay (2002) looks at how to incorporate standard and service quality into a welfare economics analysis. Cremer et al. (1997) investigate the impact of imposing minimum quality standards on welfare. Calzada (2005) investigates the impact on welfare of quality standards on the incumbents and entrants. Bourguignon and Cazenave (2006) analyse the consequences of introducing regulation of the universal service with minimum quality standards on the operators and on competition.
3. See, for example; Brealey and Myers (2001), and Kolbe et al. (1993).
4. For an explanation of alternative mechanism for quality regulation see, for example, Rovizzi and Thompson (1995) and Holt (2005).
5. See, for example, Sappington (2005).
6. Individual compensation payments may also be used in addition to overall measurement and setting targets. Examples for regulated UK industries include compensation for delayed mail, rail journey delays and cancellation, and unplanned interruptions to the water supply, all of which have service targets and individual compensation.
7. See, for example, Waddams Price et al. (2002).
8. See, for example, Swinand and Jones (2006).
9. See, for example, Swinand (2004) and Reay (1993).
10. Part 1, Section 4 of the Postal Services Act 2000 requires that 'at least one delivery of relevant postal packets is made every working day to the home or premises of every individual or other person in the

United Kingdom' and 'at least one collection of relevant postal packets is made every working day from each access point'. It also requires 'a registered post service'. In this instance, 'working days' is defined as referring to six days a week.

11. For example, radio frequency identification (RFID) tagging.
12. See, for example, Brealey and Myers (2001) and Kolbe et al. (1993).
13. CAPM is applied normally to profit-maximising firms interacting in an efficient capital market rather than a publicly owned enterprise.
14. A further example may arise in circumstances where there is a general requirement to make individual compensation payments for loss of, and damage to, mail items for exemption when there is not reasonable evidence of loss of, or damage to, the items involved, coupled with reasonable proof that the item was posted with the operator. Such an approach again requires definitions of what constitutes 'loss' and 'damage', as well as 'reasonable evidence' and 'reasonable proof of posting'.
15. This is coupled with a retail compensation scheme for ordinary mail making individual payments of up to €15 for delayed items and about €50 for lost and damaged items; and the potential for fines of up to 10 per cent of turnover if performance falls 5 per cent or 0.5 per cent below target.
16. However, the Civil Aviation Authority, the UK aviation regulator, has recently recommended to the UK Competition Commission the introduction of a bonus element to reward improving performance across London Gatwick and Heathrow Airports for the control period 2008–13 (CAA, 2007). See also Ofgem (2001), Ofgem (2003) and Ofcom (2004).
17. An exception is air traffic control (2006–10), where the penalty and reward are symmetric.
18. There is also scope to insure for loss or damage of a particular item, and involve a premium charge to cover the additional costs involved in the special handling of, and additional compensation payable for, these items. These registered and insured service offerings enable customers with higher willingness to pay to purchase a higher-priced service to enable them to assess the service quality received for themselves and thereby better understand the offerings of alternative providers.
19. For example, in the UK, a customer can claim up to about €15 for a delayed item and up to about €50 for a lost or damaged item. The average UK household spends under €50 per annum on postage.

REFERENCES

Accent and RAND Europe (2005), 'Pricing quality of service', www.royalmailgroup.com

Balogh, T., R. Moriarty, P. Smith, R. Doherty and I. Leigh (2006), 'The economic implications of quality of service regulation in a liberalized postal market', in M. Crew and P. Kleindorfer (eds), *Progress toward Liberalization of the Postal and Delivery Sector*, Boston, MA: Kluwer Academic Publishers, chapter 12, pp. 193–208.

Brealey, R. and S. Myers (2001), *Principles of Corporate Finance*, 6th edn, New York, London: McGraw-Hill.

Bourguignon, H. and T. Cazenave (2006), 'Universal service, quality constraint and competition', mimeo.

CAA (2002), '"NATS" application to re-open the Eurocontrol charge control', Consultation on CAA's Preliminary Conclusions, May.

CAA (2003a), 'Economic regulation of BAA London Airports (Heathrow, Gatwick and Stansted) 2003–2008', CAA Decision, February.

CAA (2003b), 'Economic regulation of Heathrow and Gatwick London Airports: service quality: statement of standards and rebates', May.

CAA (2005), 'NATS price control review 2006–2010: CAA's firm proposals', May.

CAA (2007), 'CAA recommendations to the Competition Commission for Heathrow and Gatwick Airports', March.

Calzada, J. (2005), 'Universal service obligations in the postal sector: endogenous quality and coverage', mimeo.

Commission for Energy Regulation (2006), 'Quality of service incentive mechanisms during the 2006–2010 price control period for ESP PES & ESB DSO', Response and Decision Document, O6/107, Dublin.

Council of European Energy Regulators (2006), 'Third benchmarking report on quality of electricity supply', December.

Cremer, H., M. De Rycke and A. Grimaud (1997), 'Service quality, competition and regulatory policies in the postal sector', *Journal of Regulatory Economics*, **11**, 5–19.
Crew, M. and P. Kleindorfer (2006), 'Approaches to the USO under Entry', in M. Crew and P. Kleindorfer (eds), *Liberalization of the Postal and Delivery Sector*, Cheltenham, UK and Northampton, MA: Edward Elgar, pp. 1–18.
De Donder, P., H. Cremer, P. Dudley and F. Rodriguez (2006), 'A welfare analysis of price controls with end-to-end mail and access services', in M. Crew and P. Kleindorfer (eds), *Liberalization of the Postal and Delivery Sector*, Cheltenham, UK and Northampton, MA: Edward Elgar, pp. 53–72.
Holt, L. (2005), 'Utility service quality – telecommunications, electricity, water', *Utilities Policy*, **13**, 189–200.
Joskow, P. (2006), 'Incentive regulation in theory and practice: electricity distribution and transmission networks', mimeo, MIT.
Kolbe, A., W. Tye and S. Myers (1993), *Regulatory Risk: Economic Principles and Applications to Natural Gas Pipelines and Other Industries*, Topics in Regulatory Economics and Policy series, no. 14, Boston, MA: Kluwer Academic Publishers.
Kraus, A. and R. Litzenberger (1976), 'Skewness preference and the valuation of risk assets', *Journal of Finance*, **314**, 1085–1100.
Moniteur Belge (2005), '4eme Contrat de Gestion entre "Etat et La Poste S.A. de Droit Public" ', December.
Ofcom (2004), 'A statement on providing quality of service information to consumers'.
Ofgem (2001), 'Review of Transco's price control from 2002: final proposals', September.
Ofgem (2003), 'Separation of Transco's distribution price control: final proposals', June.
Ofgem (2004a), 'Electricity distribution price control review: final proposals', 265/04, November.
Ofgem (2004b), 'Electricity distribution price control review: impact assessment', 265b/04, November.
Oftel (1992), 'The regulation of BT's prices: a consultative document', January.
Ofwat (2002), 'Linking service levels to prices', February.
Ofwat (2004), 'Future water and sewage charges 2005–10'.
ORR (2003), 'Access charges review 2003: final conclusions', December.
Postcomm (2005), '2006 Royal Mail price and service quality review: final proposals', December.
Reay, I. (1993), 'Models of reliability in postal services', in M. Crew and P. Kleindorfer (eds), *Regulation and the Nature of Postal and Delivery Services*, Boston, MA: Kluwer Academic Publishers, chapter 16, pp. 291–99.
Reay, I. (2002), 'The welfare economics of universal service standards and service quality', in M. Crew and P. Kleindorfer (eds), *Postal and Delivery Services. Pricing, Productivity, Regulation and Strategy*, Boston, MA: Kluwer Academic Publishers, chapter 6, pp. 107–26.
Rovizzi, L. and Thompson, D. (1995), 'The regulation of product quality in the public utilities', in J. Kay and C.P. Mayer (eds), *The Regulatory Challenge*, Oxford: Oxford University Press, pp. 336–57.
Sappington, D. (2005), 'Regulating service quality: a survey', *Journal of Regulatory Economics*, **27**(2), 123–54.
Swinand, G. (2004), 'A production model of service quality at An Post', in M. Crew and P. Kleindorfer (eds), *Competitive Transformation of the Postal and Delivery Sector*, Boston, MA: Kluwer Academic Publishers, chapter 14, pp. 269–86.
Swinand, G. and S. Jones (2006), 'Estimation of consumers' willingness-to-pay for quality of service in post', in M. Crew and P. Kleindorfer (eds), *Progress toward Liberalization of the Postal and Delivery Sector*, Boston, MA: Kluwer Academic Publishers, chapter 13, pp. 209–26.
Waddams Price, C., B. Brigham and L. Fitzgerald (2002), 'Service quality in regulated monopolies', CCR Working Paper 02-4, University of East Anglia.
Weisman, D. (2005), 'Price regulation and quality', *Information Economics and Policy*, **17**(2), 165–74.
WIK-Consult (2006), 'Main developments in the postal sector (2004–2006)', Bad Honnef.

PART V

Postal Reform

17. The Postal Accountability and Enhancement Act: some consequences

Robert A.F. Reisner, Lawrence G. Buc and James Pierce Myers

On December 20, 2006, President George W. Bush signed into law the Postal Accountability and Enhancement Act of 2006 (PAEA, or Act).[1] This signing marked the culmination of a 12-year effort to reform the statutory charter for the United States Postal Service (USPS). This chapter discusses what the new law seeks to accomplish and how we will know whether it succeeded.

This chapter focuses on legislative changes and regulatory developments in the US, but the implications of this subject have global significance. USPS has a significant share of the world's mail, and has played an important role in postal history, serving as a model for reform when it was introduced in 1970. The fundamental changes that PAEA has brought to the US operating and regulatory model are of interest throughout the postal world.

What is more, even today, as privatization and deregulation have been advanced by some as the *new* postal model, questions remain – How far? How fast? The new USPS model presents a clear alternative to the trends toward privatization that have been seen in Europe in the past decade. The global postal industry will follow future developments in the US and will want to know whether the new US postal reform law was a success. This chapter offers some initial considerations in this coming discussion.

By any standard, the journey to postal reform in the US has been a struggle. From the first congressional hearing in 1995, we identified 38 legislative hearings and six different versions of comprehensive postal reform bills. At the end of this process, Congress defined a markedly different direction with its reform or 'liberalization' of the postal sector than that seen in Europe and elsewhere, particularly with respect to the maintenance of the postal monopoly.[2]

In the end, Congress and the President settled on continuation of the Universal Service Obligation (USO) and public ownership of USPS with a continued, albeit slightly relaxed, letter mail monopoly that remains fixed in law.[3] They agreed that they should not, or perhaps could not, prescribe the fine details of a 'modern regulatory system' for the US. They chose instead to delegate this responsibility to the Postal Regulatory Commission (PRC) created by PAEA to replace the Postal Rate Commission, the former regulatory body, providing in the law a framework within which the PRC would operate. The law also requires the PRC to review the system in ten years (2016), and empowers the PRC at that time to revise the system as necessary.

The lawmakers 'required' the new system, at least for its first ten years, to be a price-cap regime. They did so despite ongoing debate over the efficacy of such a system in guiding a public-sector institution: 'Without privatization and changed labor relations, reforms envisioned in [postal reform], or almost any other adoption of price cap regulation would do little or nothing to improve the status quo.'[4] However, counterposed against this price-cap 'requirement', lawmakers interwove nine 'objectives' that the PRC is directed to achieve, and 14 'factors' it must take into account in doing so. These objectives and factors are sometimes contradictory but rather consistently restate the provisions of prior US law under the cost-of-service system that was in effect for more than three decades.[5]

The US PRC is now in the midst of proceedings to fulfill its responsibility to design the modern system which necessarily requires it to address the requirements, objectives, and factors of the new law. The PRC is writing rules to 'establish . . . a modern system for regulating rates and classes for market dominant products' and 'to bound Postal Service [USPS] discretion in setting rates for competitive postal products.'[6] This is a daunting task, which for the most part must be completed no later than June 20, 2008.

From the requirements, objectives, and factors stated in the Act, and the statements and official documents surrounding its creation (the 'legislative history'), we identify six core goals of the new law.[7] Section 1 describes those goals. Section 2 discusses how to determine whether on not these goals are being achieved by the new regulatory system. Section 3 discusses the implications of the emerging regulatory developments for the future of the US postal sector by exploring the issues that are likely to arise for USPS management and the new regulator.

The history of the Act suggests that six core goals – (1) Long-Term Financial Stability, (2) Price Stability, (3) Efficiency (Productivity), (4) Service Quality and Performance, (5) Fair Competition, and (6) Preservation of Quality, Universal Service at Affordable Rates – comprise the heart of the new law.

1. THE PAEA: WHAT IT WAS MEANT TO ACCOMPLISH

1.1 Long-Term Financial Stability

In January 1995 John M. McHugh, a second-term United States Congressman from Watertown, New York, became Chairman of the Congressional subcommittee with responsibility for oversight of USPS.[8] Later that year he began a series of hearings into the state of USPS. He found an organization that faced considerable financial uncertainty and service failures. What's more, USPS CEO, US Postmaster General Marvin Runyon, had recently decried his situation, claiming the need for the ability to control 'people, products, and prices' in a high-profile speech intended to communicate with the new Republican led, reform-minded Congress. According to the Postmaster General, it took longer to change a price than it did to have a baby. Others stressed the need for Congressional direction. The Chairman of the Postal Rate Commission, Edward Gleiman, described the situation:

> Now as for the Postal Service, it is at a crossroads with no signpost. As it did 25 years ago, Congress should provide direction. A major public policy question needs to be answered. And unless Congress Acts, I fear that by default, it will be answered by Postal Service managers. The question is both simple and complicated. It is this, what do we want, and what can we reasonably expect from our Postal Service? Do we want the Postal Service to limit its focus to its historical mission, the reliable, prompt delivery of hard copy mail, or do we want it to attempt to compete in new technologies and enter fields heretofore foreign to it?[9]

In 2001, the US Government Accountability Office (GAO) placed USPS on its 'High Risk List.'[10] Perhaps the most eloquent description of the plight of the USPS came in 2002 from US Senator Fred Thompson, who observed succinctly that '[i]t is obvious the ox is in the ditch, big time.'[11]

Proponents of the PAEA expect that the Act will result in the financial stability that was so sharply missing in the late 1990s.[12] By resolving the uncertainty regarding USPS retirement obligations in the USPS's favor, the PAEA puts USPS in a much better financial position, thus ensuring a viable post that will provide universal service at affordable rates.[13] The PAEA also seeks to provide stability by preserving the statutory letter mail monopoly, while limiting USPS's focus to its core function of providing postal services, separating USPS into two distinct lines of business ('market dominant' and 'competitive'), and strengthening unfair competition provisions to protect private market participants.[14] 'In establishing the postal regulatory structure in the bill, the Committee has attempted to balance the Postal Service's [USPS's] need for additional flexibility with the mailing community and the public's need for increased financial transparency and established safeguards to protect against unreasonable use of the Postal Service's statutorily granted monopoly.'[15] 'The new system will, for the most part, continue the ratemaking factors found in . . . [the then current] law while providing increased flexibility, predictability, incentives for efficiency, and long-term financial stability.'[16]

1.2 Price Stability

The PAEA also provides important stability, and perhaps more importantly predictability, for the mailing industry by establishing a rate-cap system that will ensure that rate increases for 'market dominant' products are tied to the Consumer Price Index for All Urban Consumers (CPI). Market dominant products include First-Class Mail, Periodicals (magazines, newsletters, and newspapers), Standard Mail (largely advertising mail such as catalogs) and some other services. Market dominant products comprise the vast majority of current USPS mail volume. While USPS analysts have stated that since the last postal reorganization in 1970[17] postal rate increases have largely tracked inflation (measured on a per-piece basis), rate increases during those three and one-half decades have been sporadic and often large (if the content of the mailstream is held constant to make comparisons of like services).

The Act requires the PRC to establish a system that will 'create predictability and stability.'[18] If price stability is achieved, it will largely be the result of an annual limitation on the percentage changes in rates (including fees) in any given year; that is, a rate cap.[19] The annual limitation is equal to the percentage change in the Consumer Price Index for All Urban Consumers ('CPI') unadjusted for seasonal variation. Based upon years of debate, it is fair to say that no feature of the Act is more important to the mailing community.

1.3 Efficiency (Productivity)

As seen in the objectives and the factors contained in PAEA, the primary objective of the Act, at least its first stated, is 'to maximize incentives to reduce costs and increase efficiency.'[20] A debate is ongoing as to how the PRC should proceed to achieve this objective.[21] This debate centers on whether the PRC should require the USPS to follow principles that would shift work to the most efficient provider of service (the principles of Efficient Component Pricing) as a means to achieve a ratemaking system that lowers the total postal sector costs, thereby increasing efficiency. Under the PAEA, the PRC is directed to design a system that will 'reduce costs and increase efficiency.'[22] There can be no doubt that efficiency is an important goal. The postal committees in both houses of Congress made this clear:

> Under the new system, the Postal Regulatory Commission will have the flexibility to design a system that will improve efficiency and control costs. The details of such a system have been left to the Commission so that this regulatory body will be able to respond to changes in mail volume, technologies, and other factors.[23]

1.4 Service Quality and Performance

The Act emphasizes the importance of service standards, service performance measurement, and the use of technology such as Intelligent Mail™ to support improved service, enhance mail value, and enable transparency. The Act's objectives and factors include the maintenance of 'high quality service standards,' 'the need for the Postal Service to provide high quality, affordable postal services,' and 'the value to the Postal Service and postal users of promoting intelligent mail . . .'[24]

Lawmakers devoted significant portions of the Act to the issue of 'service.' The Act requires USPS to establish service standards for the vast majority of its products including First-Class Mail, Periodicals, and Standard Mail.[25] The Act spells out in fine detail the objectives the service standards are supposed to achieve, and eight statutory factors that must be taken into account in setting the standards.[26] Section 302 of the Act requires USPS to submit a detailed plan for meeting the established service standards. Under the law, all of this must be completed no later than June 2008. Thereafter, the Act requires USPS to report annually to the PRC about service, and entitles mailers to file formal complaints of service failures with the PRC.[27] The importance of service for US lawmakers was noted in the Senate Report:

> The service standards established by the [Postal] Regulatory Commission should also serve as a benchmark for measuring the Postal Service's performance. The Postal Service should strive to exceed the standards set by the [Postal] Regulatory Commission, but the [Postal] Regulatory Commission should regularly measure the Postal Service's performance to ensure that these standards are met. The [Postal] Regulatory Commission is required to inform Congress in the annual reports required of them under section 204 of the bill whenever the Postal Service has failed to meet any existing service standards. The Committee expects the Postal Service to provide the [Postal] Regulatory Commission with the data the [Postal] Regulatory Commission believes necessary to determine whether or not service standards are being met.[28]

1.5 Fair Competition

The PAEA strives to ensure 'a level playing field' in those markets in which USPS has competed and will continue to compete; that is, its 'competitive products', which include Express Mail, Priority Mail, bulk parcel post, and bulk international mail.[29] In response to concerns expressed by competitors, Congress in the PAEA sought to 'level the playing field' for USPS and its competitors by removing certain 'governmental advantages.' For example, under the Act USPS must pay tax on its income from competitive products,[30] 'unfair competition' is prohibited,[31] and anti-trust laws are made applicable to its 'competitive' activities.[32] Section 703 of the Act requires the US Federal Trade Commission to prepare a report on laws that apply differently to USPS and private companies and to make recommendations for bringing these legal differences to an end.

At the same time, USPS has to comply with numerous requirements that do not apply to its competitors. For example, USPS will have to comply with new accounting rules to be defined in the regulatory process,[33] receive PRC approval before it can introduce new products,[34] and have its contract rates reviewed by the PRC.[35] Perhaps most importantly, to prevent cross-subsidy, the Act requires the PRC to 'ensure that all competitive products collectively cover what the Commission determines to be an appropriate share of the institutional costs of the Postal Service [USPS].'[36] In sum, there are substantial reasons to be concerned that the new regulatory framework that seeks to level the playing field between USPS and the private sector, will have imposed significant new limits on future USPS competitive flexibility and to be cautious about future developments.

At the time of the last comprehensive postal reform in the United States, the Postal Reform Act of 1970,[37] USPS and one private carrier each held roughly half of the market volume. Today, USPS competitive products comprise only 14 percent of the parcel delivery market, far less than the 57 percent share held by United Parcel Service and Federal Express' 21 percent share. Measured as a percentage of revenue in this market, USPS's share is even smaller.[38]

As one party commented recently to the PRC:

> Only time will tell if Congress struck the appropriate balance in 'leveling the playing field' on which the Postal Service competes with private sector enterprises. PSA suggests that there is no reason to fear that the Postal Service will advance significantly in competitive markets to the detriment of private competitors. There is, however, a substantial possibility it could fail if the Commission inadvertently injures its competitive position.[39]

1.6 Preservation of Quality, Universal Service at Affordable Rates

Throughout the 12-year consideration of postal reform legislation, continuation of the USO was never in doubt. The US political climate ensured it would be maintained as reflected in the title of the report of the Commission appointed by President Bush to study USPS: 'Making the Tough Choices to Preserve Universal Service.'[40] The Act retains the statutory requirement that the 'Postal Service shall receive, transmit, and deliver throughout the United States' and that 'it shall provide prompt, reliable, and efficient services to patrons in all areas and shall render postal services to all communities.'[41] Under the reform law it must continue to provide 'universal service.' The Postmaster General has made clear his view that 'quality, universal service at affordable rates' is the 'ultimate goal'[42] even as he has stated that the model for providing such service is broken.[43]

The USO and the maintenance of the postal monopoly will be under regular review. Section 702 of the Act requires the PRC, no later than December 2008, 'to submit a report to the President and Congress on universal postal service and the postal monopoly in the United States,' including the monopoly on the delivery of mail and on access to mailboxes, and to include any recommended changes to universal service and the postal monopoly.

The new US postal reform law contains many other changes to the traditional US operating and regulatory models, but the blur of changes, large and small, will only tend to diffuse attention of policymakers and others. This discussion has sought to present a 'critical few' goals of reform to help focus discussion on the essential core and to understand whether the law succeeds in attaining its most important goals.

2. HOW WILL WE KNOW WHETHER THE LAW HAS SUCCEEDED?

The PAEA requires the PRC to review the system it establishes for regulating the rates for market dominant products after the system has been in place for ten years. The review will examine whether the system is meeting the objectives and factors of the Act.[44] However, mailers, USPS employees and management, and the PRC will have to address the question of whether Postal Reform has accomplished its intended goals long before this scheduled review. An informed and reasoned exploration will be aided by setting forth objective, quantifiable outcomes and specifying metrics to determine whether or not the objectives are being met. Below, we explore outcomes and metrics for evaluating achievement of the six goals discussed in Section 1.

2.1 Long-Term Financial Stability

As described above, there was widespread recognition during the 1990s that USPS was not financially stable. Issues that were raised included large off-balance-sheet obligations for retiree pensions and health benefits as well as the issue of the balance sheet itself in the view of many outside the service. In its opinion and recommendation in Docket No. R94-1, an omnibus postal rate case, the Postal Rate Commission noted that according to USPS's own witness, 'if USPS were a private firm, it would be a financial disaster':[45]

> [2085] Because of the chronic stream of operating losses and the consequent erosion of its equity, the Service has failed to meet the financial goals expected of it. Instead of operating like a business, it is dependent on its ability to borrow in order to fund $9.425 billion of cumulative losses. In the world of private industry cumulative losses and the negative equity of the magnitude the Postal Service has incurred would spell financial disaster. It would result in the inability to borrow, the loss of suppliers, who would fear a company in such financial straits would not be able to make payments, the loss of business contracts due to the inability, real or perceived, to complete jobs, and the severe restriction of capital projects. Severe equity erosion would eventually lead to a state of bankruptcy. According to the Postal Service's own witness Ward, if the Postal Service were a conventional business operation, it would be bankrupt. Tr. 5/2396. The Service would not have been able to survive without the $15 billion line of credit afforded it by statute. It is only because the U.S. taxpayers ultimately stand responsible for its debt, that the Postal Service, with its large negative equity, is able to borrow at all.

While the off-balance-sheet obligations for pension benefits had been remedied by the time of the reform enactment, the PAEA was intended also to remedy both the retiree health benefits obligation and the balance sheet itself.

The PAEA puts USPS in a more stable financial position by freeing up substantial funds to pay down USPS's unfunded retiree health benefit obligation, estimated to be approximately $50 billion at the end of FY 2006.[46]

The PAEA frees up these funds in two ways. First, section 804 of the PAEA repeals the requirement that USPS place approximately $3 billion per year in savings resulting from previous USPS pension reform legislation into an escrow account. Second, section 802 transfers the responsibility for paying the Civil Service Retirement System (CSRS) costs of USPS employees related to their military service to the US Treasury. These actions produced a surplus in USPS's CSRS account and eliminated the need for USPS to make any future contributions to the CSRS fund.

The PAEA did not return the freed-up funds to USPS but instead required they be dedicated to pay down the unfunded retiree health obligation. To do this, section 802 requires the surplus in the CSRS fund to be transferred into a newly created Postal Service Retiree Health Benefits Fund. Section 803 requires USPS to make fixed pre-funding payments ranging from $5.4 to $5.8 billion into this fund each year from 2007 to 2016. Progress against the full funding of this obligation will be tracked through annual reports from the Office of Personnel Management.[47]

Before reform, USPS balance sheet also posed a serious issue. With the break-even cost of service regime required by the former law, there was no opportunity to build a sound balance sheet by allowing for retained earnings. The Act also severs the traditional link between rates and costs. The reform law thus provides the opportunity for improved financial stability and performance, allowing USPS to accumulate retained earnings.

On an ongoing basis, there are many metrics that might be used to judge financial stability. Assessing this goal against a small number of key measures will permit the entire community of mailers, postal operators, regulators and other interested parties to have clearer performance visibility.

By examining the immediate post-reform balance sheet and then the balance sheet each quarter going forward (available in the USPS Quarterly Financial Report), the financial health of USPS will be visible by tracking the retained earnings figures. If retained earnings are growing substantially, the Service will be financially stable. Short-term fluctuations may occur, but overall growth of retained earnings will be a telling indicator. The balance sheet for the first quarter of FY 2007 shows retained earnings since reorganization of $510 million, and this is a baseline against which future retained earnings should be tracked.

Cash reserves and debt levels are two other measures of financial stability and both of these can also be tracked in the USPS Quarterly Financial Report. These metrics will depend upon costs and revenues, which are also available in this report.

2.2 Price Stability

The PAEA seeks to provide price stability for mailers by setting an annual limitation on price increases for the market dominant classes of mail. These increases are capped by the Consumer Price Index (CPI), thus breaking the former link between postal rates and USPS costs.

USPS, however, is allowed an exception, the ability to file an 'exigent case' to impose price increases that exceed the price cap due to either extraordinary or exceptional circumstances under certain restrictions. As the first and most important measure of performance, the PAEA will be a success if the Service is able to live within the cap. If USPS files an exigent case seeking to increase prices beyond levels permitted by the cap, the reasons for seeking an exception will be examined closely and will offer another perspective on the ability of the new regulatory system to provide price stability.[48]

A second measure of interest would be offered if post-reform (PAEA) average annual increases are smaller than pre-reform increases, by class, for market dominant products. Predictability alone will be valuable to the mailing community and would be a valuable contribution for PAEA to make. But if post-reform rates are increasing faster than pre-reform, many will question whether the law has been successful.

2.3 Efficiency (Productivity)

The PAEA was clearly meant to encourage improvement in the efficiency of USPS: in fact, the first objective is '[t]o maximize incentives to reduce cost and increase efficiency.'[49] But the definition of efficiency has historically been a subject of intense discussion at USPS. We define efficiency in two different high level measures: (1) getting more with less, and (2) minimizing end-to-end costs in the mailing sector.

The first measure of efficiency – getting more with less – concerns the inputs and the outputs of USPS. Typically, it is measured at USPS by comparing the levels of the inputs and outputs to produce a measure called Total Factor Productivity (TFP).

The simplest metric would be to continue to track TFP and to measure whether the compound average growth rate has increased or decreased in the post-reform era. However, as productivity in the overall US economy changes over time, it may also be important to benchmark the Service's productivity against that of the entire US economy or even analogous sub-parts of the US economy in addition to tracking comparisons within the postal industry alone. Changes in TFP would thus be compared with changes in multi-factor productivity for the entire economy to gain perspective on changes in USPS TFP.

The third measure of efficiency – minimizing end-to-end costs in the entire mailing community – is important as well. End-to-end costs (the costs incurred by USPS and by USPS customers taken together) can be measured by examining future PRC consideration of worksharing discounts. These are discounts for which mailers receive discounts for performing some of the upstream work of the Service (generally replacing USPS sorting or transportation workload). Worksharing discounts promote efficiency if they are set at the costs avoided for the worksharing activity. When they are, the total costs incurred represent the lowest combined costs.

The PAEA generally prohibits worksharing discounts that exceed avoided costs except under special circumstances. To assure compliance with this part of the law, USPS is required to provide cost data to show that the discounts do not in fact exceed the avoided costs. These same USPS cost data to be considered in future PRC proceedings can be used to judge the success of the law in achieving least total costs.

2.4 Service Quality and Performance

Another goal of the PAEA was to ensure sustained service quality and to that end, the Act requires that service standards be developed for all products. Many participants in the reform debate noted that the goals of price stability and cost reduction should not be achieved through a strategy of lowering service levels. Given the old adage 'what gets measured gets improved,' the Act's requirement for service measurement must be intended to achieve more reliable mail delivery. Pre-reform metrics are not widely available since the Service currently only publishes measures of performance for First-Class Mail. One question that the PRC will soon face is whether to direct USPS to publish trend data that was previously held privately. In the post-reform world it will be possible to track post-reform service over time with the development of service standards for market dominant products by publishing service tracking information.

2.5 Fair Competition

As described above, USPS's market share in its competitive products business has declined dramatically from the time of the last comprehensive postal reform in the United States. The PAEA was intended to let USPS compete in this market, to the extent that it could, on a level playing field. One implicit assumption was that the structure of the existing law had rendered USPS less than competitive because of, for example, the regulatory burden that it faced in offering new products and changing prices. Assuming that the PRC will set a level playing field, there are two metrics for the success of the law to enable new USPS agility in the competitive marketplace. The first is the total volume of competitive products delivered over time. And the second is USPS's market share. Yet, since there will be many factors that shape future postal markets, these measures will have to be considered in the context of a broad-scale market assessment to understand the meaning of potential volume and market share changes.

2.6 Preservation of Quality, Universal Service at Affordable Rates

As described previously, preserving universal service is an important goal of reform. And the universal service mission of USPS encompasses multiple dimensions: the products to be offered, the service standards by which USPS service will be judged, the access points offered to mailers and competitors, the number of delivery points and frequency of delivery and price of services. Assessments of service and price have been discussed above. This remaining discussion concerns products, access and delivery points served by the universal service provider.

USPS already reports the number of its delivery points and the number of its retail outlets. Legal and regulatory restrictions require public discussion of any proposed changes in these commitments. Access points and restrictions are also subject to regulatory oversight.

The new law will require that the regulator and the mailing community review all of the interrelated dimensions of universal service. Section 702 of the PAEA requires the PRC to study universal service as a whole and to report on it no later than December of 2008. That report must consider the 'cost' of Universal Service as well as its benefits. At that time, there will be a need for USPS and for the entire mailing community to discuss the implications of this report: Who should be carrying the costs? How might they be managed and alleviated? This undoubtedly will be one of the most controversial debates resulting from enactment of the PAEA and will be a critical point for setting standards by which to judge its success. There are multiple models globally for specifying the requirements and limitations of universal service obligations. The coming debate over the 2008 report will be a critical time for USPS and for the US mailing community to define the balance between public service obligations and the business model of the future USPS.

3. CONSIDERATIONS FOR THE FUTURE OF THE REFORMED USPS

PAEA was fashioned to encourage a light-handed regulatory approach. By creating a new price-cap framework, the new law redesigned the role that will be played by the PRC. USPS will be permitted to set prices for postal services within the limits of the cap and the PRC (the regulator) will play a new role in judging the effect of USPS actions and in hearing complaints. However, the simplicity of the pricing concept may be confounded by the complexity of another dimension of US postal pricing, the workshare discounts granted to compensate mailers for sharing the burden of processing or transporting the mail.

The reform law sustains the principle of granting workshare discounts structured according to Efficient Component Pricing (ECP). Yet while urging the new PRC to sustain its historic role of supporting the principle that work should be done where it can be performed most efficiently – whether inside the traditional USPS or through worksharing – the need to judge postal *and* mailer costs in order to design the discounts will pose future challenges for the PRC. The future PRC must engage in some, but not all, of its traditional role of reviewing postal costs and in doing so must strike a delicate balance.

USPS must similarly be balanced in exercising new pricing freedoms that reduce the obligation to connect the price of postal services with costs. USPS will need to balance a number of variables. How much 'work' will USPS require the mailers to perform to attain the discounts? How will discounts have to shift in the future as new automation is introduced? What will USPS strategy be for attaining end-to-end operating efficiency? These and other questions will create a new dialogue between the operator and the regulator in the US.

In seeking perspective on the nature of the emerging redesigned regulatory process under the new law, there are two important points that should be recognized. First, the new law represents a complex realignment of traditional roles. Both with respect to regulation of pricing and service, the roles of the US operator and regulator will change. While pricing decisions are now more in the hands of USPS, the regulator has a significant new role in overseeing service. Even if the PRC limits itself to a philosophy of encouraging transparency but limiting its intervention into the complex system of postal operations, at least initially, the new law creates a complaints process that may make this moderate approach difficult to sustain. When a future service related complaint is filed by a mailer the long-term success of the new law will be tested by the need to balance a philosophy of limited intervention and the need to assert regulatory responsibility.

The subject of management communications will also test this need to be moderate and balanced in exercising regulatory authority. The complex new law will require the PRC to play a role in many new arenas such as the regulation of service quality, and to communicate with USPS managers and policymakers in new and unprecedented ways. When the role of the PRC was limited to review of complex postal pricing proposals, communications were limited to a small community familiar with the terms of the regulatory dialogue. But the future PRC will be required to make judgments about service that will have broad implications for the national USPS operating system and its communications will cast a broader net reaching far deeper into USPS.

A traditional regulator might seek to play the limited role of rule-maker and umpire. But the core of the new law gives the regulator more responsibility than that. The new law incorporates the responsibilities under the 1993 Government Planning and Results Act (GPRA). This 1993 law that required USPS to publish Five-Year Strategic Plans every three years, Annual Performance Plans and Annual Performance Reports, formerly limited the review process to the oversight responsibility of Congress. The former Postal *Rate* Commission did not have a role in reviewing these performance reports. However, the new PRC (Postal *Regulatory* Commission) is going to have to take responsibility for both process and outcomes, as it will play a role in guiding and adjusting performance reporting over time. If 'what you measure is what you can improve' as the quality management movement learned in the 1990s, then the Commission will play an important future role in shaping the service that it is regulating through its power to define reporting requirements.

Each of these observations relates to the new roles that the PAEA gives to the PRC and the new regulatory process that it creates. They suggest that both the USPS and the PRC will have a major role in permitting the reform law to succeed. A new collaboration that is largely unknown to the litigious US postal ratemaking process will have to be created to enable the new shared responsibilities for the success of reform. Achieving a new era of collaboration and partnership in which both the post and the regulator take responsibility for the impact of their actions on the future mailing industry will be important.

The need for collaboration is reinforced by a second important point of perspective, anticipation of the future mail marketplace. None of the postal reforms that we have discussed here will take place in a vacuum. At the same time that these changes are being implemented, the entire mailing industry will continue to transform as the dynamics of the internet market continue to emerge.

In recent years, for the first time, the volume of Standard Mail exceeded the volume of First-Class Mail. Many forecasts expect these trends to continue as transactions become increasingly electronic and fewer bill payments are carried in the mail. Irrespective of the future of any electronic substitution, a second, equally important trend will be the growth of competition from traditional sources that are built on services that are based on more sophisticated technology platforms (e.g., track and trace systems). These services will continue to shape the future mail and parcel marketplace. There will be many implications for USPS in this continuing market shift, not the least of which is that a 'mix change' that results from carrying higher proportions of lower contribution mail changes the balance between work and reward.

In the final analysis, there might be multiple scenarios for the future of regulation of USPS. In one scenario, the regulatory process could become burdensome and limit USPS in taking advantage of favorable trends in the mailing marketplace. But perhaps a more likely scenario will be one in which the market trends are adverse. Here, even successful implementation of the objectives of the reform law would take place in a mail market that puts increasing negative pressure on the traditional postal model. Even successful implementation of the new law in a downward-trending mail market could render a negative verdict on the reform law and on the performance of postal management and the regulator. Market trends are likely to be challenging even if the law works well. Finding the right balance of regulation and collaboration will be essential to ensuring a vigorous future for both the mailing industry and the post.

The experience of the US mailing community under the new postal reform law will offer important lessons for regulatory practice and for the international mailing community. After a dozen years of debate over postal reform, the Congress decided to take a number of conservative steps. The new law did not seek to privatize the USPS or to free it from regulatory constraints entirely. The law also affirmed continuation of the traditional US commitment to universal postal service. But the vehicle for achieving these traditional goals will be a regulatory process that will be redesigned in coming years and it will be important to begin early in creating a clear framework for judging its success and for permitting the multiple stakeholders in the mailing community to review the success of US postal reform.

NOTES

1. Pub. L. No. 109-435, 120 Stat. 3198 (December 20, 2006). The PAEA amends numerous sections of title 39 of the United States Code.
2. 'The proposed price and weight limits for the postal monopoly, six times the first-class stamp price and 12 and a half ounces, remain significantly more protective of the Postal Service than postal monopoly limits enacted in other industrialized nations that have concluded smaller monopolies will promote greater efficiency without jeopardizing universal service.' H.R. Rep. No. 109-66, 109th Cong., 1st Sess., Part 1 (April 28, 2005) (2005 House Report) at 57. During the reform debate, three legislative 'committee reports' were produced that explained different versions of postal reform legislation (H.R. 22 (109th Cong., 1st Session)) see 2005 House Report; (S. 2468, (108th Cong., 2nd Session)) see S. Rep. No. 108-318, (108th Cong., 2nd Session) (August 25, 2004) 2004 Senate Report; and (H.R. 22, (108th Cong. 1st Session)) see H.R. Rep. No. 108-672, (108th Cong., (2nd Session, Part 1) (September 8, 2004) 2004 House Report)). These reports are helpful in understanding the concerns addressed by the lawmakers.
3. See note 2, *supra*. The scope of the monopoly will remain fixed unless changed by law, a decidedly difficult task in the United States. See 39 U.S.C. §601.
4. Hearings on H.R. 22 before the Subcommittee on the Postal Service, Committee on Government Reform and Oversight, US House of Representatives (April 16, 1997) at 102. The wisdom of a price-cap regime was strongly questioned in legislative hearings before the US Congress. *Idem* at 30 et. seq. (statements of John Kwoka, Kenneth Rose, Joel Popkin, Gregory Sidak, Paul Kleindorfer, and Michael Crew).
5. See 39 U.S.C. §§3622(b) and (c). For the 'factors' under prior law, see former 39 U.S.C. §3622.
6. PRC Order No. 2, 72 Fed. Reg. 5230 (February 5, 2007).
7. Indisputably, the Act has more than six goals and we address here six we believe are core. Other observers, of course, might add to or subtract from this list.
8. Subcommittee on the Postal Service, Committee on Government Reform and Oversight, US House of Representatives, 104th Congress.
9. Hearings before the Subcommittee on the Postal Service, Committee on Government Reform and Oversight, US House of Representatives, 104th Congress at 83. Some postal managers of course debated whether it was so unreasonable for them, as public officials, to seek to guide the Service at such a crossroads while agreeing with Commissioner Gleiman that the Internet revolution did indeed represent a crossroads for posts throughout the world.
10. See GAO-07-310, *High Risk Series: An Update*, p. 9 (January 2007) (observing that in 2001 the Government Accountability Office had designated the Postal Service as a 'high risk' because its financial outlook had deteriorated substantially). Shortly after passage of the PAEA, the GAO removed the Postal Service from its list. Ibid.
11. *The Financial Outlook of the U.S. Postal Service*, Hearing before the Committee on Governmental Affairs, United States Senate, 107th Cong. 1st Sess. (May 15, 2001) at 18.
12. By the time of enactment of the law, Postal Transformation under Postmaster General Jack Potter plus reform of the postal retirement system had already substantially revised the short-term financial outlook.

But proponents of the law argued that these factors adjusting the traditional organization are short-term fixes and that the reform law addressed longer-term structural issues.

13. In 2002, the Government recognized that the Postal Service had been 'over funding' its accrued retirement obligation. The Postal Civil Service Retirement System Funding Act of 2003, Public Law 108-18 (approved April 23, 2003), corrected this situation temporarily releasing more the $10 billion in future Postal Service payment obligations over the period from 2003 to 2005. This permitted the Postal Service to forego rate increases during this period. Nevertheless, early this year, the current Postmaster General noted that the Postal Service business model was still 'broken.' ('The business model is, was, and is broken. And, we have had some good success in the last couple of years. But, it masks the fact that the underlying premise upon which this model was built, which is that growth and volume combined with rate increases at the rate of inflation will finance universal service to a growing population. That model, simply stated, has broken.') Postmaster General John E. Potter, remarks at the American University School of Public Affairs' Forum on Postal Reform, March 1, 2007, transcript at 24. The PAEA also sets aside payments for prepayment of healthcare liability.
14. See, e.g., 39 U.S.C. §§404a, 409, 3633.
15. 2005 Senate Report at 19.
16. 2005 House Report at 46.
17. The Postal Reorganization Act of 1970 ('PRA'), see Pub. L. No. 91-375, 84 Stat. 719.
18. 39 U.S.C. §3622(b)(2).
19. 'The system for regulating rates and classes for market-dominant products shall (A) include an annual limitation on the percentage changes in rates to be set by the PRC that will be equal to the change in the Consumer Price Index . . . .' 39 U.S.C. §3622(d)(1)(A).
20. 39 U.S.C. §3622(b)(1).
21. Docket No. RM 2007-1, Advanced Notice of Proposed Rulemaking before the US PRC, available at www.prc.gov.
22. 39 U.S.C. §3622(b)(1).
23. 2005 House Report at 48. See also 2004 Senate Report at 32–3 ('S. 2468 requires the new PRC to develop – with appropriate input from the postal community – a new, highly streamlined, rate-setting process. This new process should apply rigorous standards to rate-setting, but at the same time, give postal officials the ability to manage and lead. The process should also proactively encourage the Postal Service to improve productivity and efficiency and not rely solely on rate increases to secure its fiscal health.')
24. 39 U.S.C. §§3622(b)(3), (c)(12), (c)(13).
25. 39 U.S.C. §3691(a).
26. 39 U.S.C. §3691(b), (c).
27. 39 U.C.C. §S3652, 3662.
28. 2004 Senate Report at 23.
29. 39 U.S.C. §3631(a).
30. 39 U.S.C. §3634.
31. 39 U.S.C. §404a.
32. 39 U.S.C. §409(d).
33. 39 U.S.C. 2011.
34. 39 U.S.C. §3641–2.
35. 39 U.S.C. §3622(b).
36. 39 U.S.C. §3633(a).
37. Public Law 91-375, 84 Stat. 719.
38. See Comments of the Parcel Shippers Association before the PRC, Docket No. RM2007-1 (April 6, 2006), available at www.prc.gov.
39. *Idem* at 3.
40. The President's Commission on the US Postal Service, 'Embracing the future: making the tough choices to preserve universal mail service' (July 31, 2003).
41. 39 U.S.C. §101(a), 403(a).
42. *Remarks of Postmaster General/CEO John E. Potter before the National Postal Forum* (Washington, DC, March 26, 2007); see also statement of Postmaster General/CEO John E. Potter before the Subcommittee on Federal Workforce, Postal Service, and the District of Columbia of the Committee on Oversight and Government Reform, US House of Representatives (April 17, 2007). ('While the pace of change will continue, our nation is fortunate that so many have recognized, understood, and acted to preserve affordable, universal postal services for the people and businesses of America.')
43. 'That model, simply stated, has broken.' Postmaster General John E. Potter, remarks at the American University School of Public Affair's Forum on Postal Reform, March 1, 2007, transcript at 24.
44. 39 U.S.C. §3622(d)(3).
45. PRC Op. R94-1, ¶2085 (November 30, 1994).

46. Congressional Budget Office Cost Estimate for S. 662, The Postal Accountability and Enhancement Act (July 1, 2005).
47. 5 U.S.C. §8905a.
48. In their April 6 letter to Chairman Blair, Senators Collins and Carper state that their intent was to limit the use of exigent cases to the most extreme kinds of emergencies such as a terrorist attack.
49. 39 U.S.C. §3622(b)(1).

18. The proper scope of the rules on abuse of dominant position in a liberalized postal services market

Richard Eccles and Pauline Kuipers*

1. INTRODUCTION

The European postal services sector once again stands on the threshold of significant further liberalization. In October 2006, the European Commission published, on the website of the Directorate General for the Internal Market, a proposal for a further Directive amending Directive 97/67, on the internal market for Community postal services.[1] This new Proposal is described as 'concerning the full accomplishment of the internal market of Community postal services'. It proposes full liberalisation – the abolition by member states of all special and exclusive rights granted to postal operators – by 31 December 2008; that is, with effect from 1 January 2009.

Separately, the Directorate General for Competition is in the middle of an in-depth review of competition policy on the application of Article 82 of the EC Treaty; that is, the rules on abuse of a dominant position. It published, in December 2005, a discussion paper on the application of Article 82 to exclusionary abuses, including, in particular, predatory pricing, loyalty discounting, tying and refusals to supply. The substance of the Commission's review involves increased economic realism in its proposals for future application of Article 82 EC. It also discusses important issues for dominant companies such as, for example, their ability to reduce prices selectively to 'meet the competition'.

The discussion paper is expected to be followed by draft Commission guidelines on the application of Article 82 EC, codifying the Commission's approach to various types of abuses of dominant position. The forthcoming draft guidelines are expected also to cover exploitative abuses such as excessive or discriminatory pricing.

Meanwhile, case law continues to develop both at European Court and national court level. For example, the present rules on discriminatory discounts have recently been reinforced by the judgment of the European Court of Justice ('ECJ') in March 2007, in *British Airways plc v Commission*.[2] The trends in the case law will influence the outcome of the Commission's Article 82 review.

These developments will carry implications for dominant incumbent operators in the postal sector, just as in other sectors of the economy. At the same time, the application of competition law in the postal services sector must take into account the developing

* The authors are partners in Bird & Bird, in London and The Hague respectively.

economic conditions of the sector, the steadily reducing levels of regulatory protection given to incumbent postal operators and the emergence of competition to incumbent postal operators. This chapter will review the implications of these developments for the position of such incumbent operators under the competition rules on abuse of dominant position.

2. THE BACKGROUND TO THE EUROPEAN COMMISSION'S FURTHER LIBERALISATION PROPOSAL

The Commission's proposed amending directive for full liberalisation of the internal market for postal services is accompanied by a report from the Commission to the European Council and Parliament,[3] which is supported by a Commission Staff Working Document.[4] This report, whilst emphasising the importance of postal services and infrastructure as an important input into many key sectors such as e-commerce, publishing, mail-order retailing, insurance, banking and advertising, also emphasises that there are a number of drivers for change within the postal sector. The five most important of these are stated to be changing customer demand, organisational change, market opening, automation/new technologies and electronic substitution.

The EU report highlights various trends including the fact that the postal services sector is increasingly focused on the business-to-consumer (B2C) segment of, in particular, letter post. Over 87.5 per cent of letter post items (EU wide) are sent by businesses and 62 per cent of volume (up from 60.5 per cent in 2004) are B2C letters. The growth rates of direct mail (addressed and unaddressed) are substantially higher than those for traditional letter mail. The report states that developments in the wider communications market are resulting in a number of new products and services based around, for example, home shopping and hybrid mail, such as the digital transmission of an electronic document for remote printing and mailing. Real competition in postal services is now emerging, although meaningful competition has yet to develop in many member states. The report adds that the postal sector needs to follow the pace of change in the wider communications market and the Postal Service Directive needs to continue to reflect these changes. There is 'broad agreement that postal services do not constitute natural monopolies'. The report states that consequently new and more efficient uses of resources over time can be brought about in the postal sector by increasing competition.

Most importantly, note that the Commission's report states that competition is not an end in itself. Rather, competition is stated to be 'a means to promote innovation, investment and consumer welfare'. Since these considerations are driving the sector-specific regulation and liberalisation measure, they should, in our view, also be the guiding principles of the application of competition law in the postal services sector.

With regard to the new rules in relation to the reserved area, the Commission Staff Working Document (para 3.2) reviews the progress to date and reports that at present all member states have limited their reserved areas in accordance with the Postal Directive. The reserved area is the largest barrier to the completion of the Internal Market, as the provision of letters up to 50 g (that accounts for the majority of all postal items) may still be monopolised. So far, Finland, Sweden and the United Kingdom have already abolished the reserved area, while Germany and the Netherlands intend to abolish their reserved areas entirely by 2008. Several other member states have opened up the market of direct mail and other mail streams in advance of the 2009 target date. It must be observed that it is far from clear whether the Commission's objective and timescale for full liberalisation will be accepted by the member states, or if accepted, whether in all cases it will be implemented on time.

3. THE CONTENT OF THE COMMISSION'S LIBERALISATION PROPOSAL

As already mentioned, the Commission's Proposal will require member states to achieve full liberalisation of the postal services sector as from 1 January 2009, by abolishing any remaining or exclusive or special rights for the establishment and provision of postal services. The Proposal contains a number of consequential amendments to reflect the removal of the reserved sector. It also contains further amendments as follows:

1. The obligation to ensure that prices for universal services are costs-orientated, so as to stimulate efficiency gains, is strengthened. Interestingly, the Commission states that translation differences resulted in this requirement being weaker than intended, in some member states.[5] The right, but not the obligation, of member states to stipulate a geographically uniform tariff for universal services, is retained (Amended Article 12(b)).
2. There is a strengthening of the obligation on universal service providers to offer, to customers, the same special tariffs as are offered to bulk mailers or consolidators of mail, applying the principles of transparency and non-discrimination.
3. The current prohibition on cross-subsidisation of universal services outside the reserved sector out of revenue from services in the reserved sector is deleted rather than being modified following the (proposed) abolition of the reserved sector.
4. A new Article 11(a) is inserted requiring member states to ensure the availability of transparent and non-discriminatory access to the following facilities that are ancillary or related to postal infrastructure or services: the postcode system, address databases, post office boxes, collection and delivery boxes, information on change of address, redirection services and return to sender services. However, recital 22 of the proposed Directive makes clear that this access right applies to postal operators providing similar services to the universal service, and the Commission's accompanying Explanatory Memorandum states that the requirement on member states is limited to that of adopting an informed decision on the need and extent for regulation, the choice of regulatory instrument and any eventual compensation that might be required.
5. Under the proposed Article 4, member states are to be given more flexibility in designating how the universal service is to be performed. They will be able to determine the most efficient and appropriate mechanism to guarantee the universal service subject to the principles of objectivity, transparency, proportionality and least market distortion. The Commission's Explanatory Memorandum states that this might involve leaving its provision to market forces or using public tendering procedures for specific services or regions.
6. An express requirement was introduced to the effect that member states that retain ownership or control of postal operators shall ensure effective structural separation

of the regulatory functions from activities associated with ownership or control. This follows from the European Commission's condemnation of France for failure to ensure separation of regulatory and operational activities in relation to *La Poste*[6] of France (Article 22(1)). The national regulatory authorities may also be charged with ensuring compliance with the competition rules and all relevant national authorities, including the competition authorities, must co-operate within the field of the Directive (Article 22(2) and Recital 30).

The Commission's Explanatory Memorandum accompanying the proposed Directive emphasises the need to provide sufficient freedom to universal service providers to adapt to competition as well as ensuring adequate monitoring of the conduct of the likely dominant operator, to safeguard effective competition. In particular, it states that the mandatory provision of uniform tariffs in a fully competitive environment may lead to increasing costs for and risks to the viability of certain services, as the universal service provider will risk losing profitable business in those areas subject to competitive pressure (section 3.2.2, second paragraph). The Explanatory Memorandum goes on to state that member states should limit regulatory intervention to ensure the financially viable provision of the universal service and should allow universal service providers the necessary flexibility to react to competition, so as to limit any risks to the financial equilibrium of the universal service (section 3.2.2, third paragraph). Rather, it is stated, member states should limit tariff uniformity to single-piece tariff items that are mostly used by consumers and small enterprises. These statements can be interpreted as going beyond the right already given to universal service providers (in Article 12, third and fourth indents) to conclude non-discriminatory individual agreements on prices with customers. To that extent, they set out an important principle, of allowing incumbent universal service providers to avoid loss of profitable business to competitors ('cream-skimming') as a result of being required to offer all services (for example, in more remote rural areas) under the constraints of a uniform tariff.

This approach also partly explains the deletion of the requirement on member states to monitor cross-subsidies whilst, at the same time, maintaining substantially the same rules as at present on transparency of accounts and allocations of common costs, but as between universal service and non-universal service operations (Article 14).

The Commission's report stresses the particular importance and role of national regulatory authorities (hereinafter referred as 'NRAs') and the need for them to become more active in reviewing the separation of accounts, cost allocation and monitoring prices of universal services by conducting investigations into the major areas of tariff policy, including special tariffs, terminal dues and cross-subsidies. In this context, the collection of information, including financial information, is of particular importance.

The importance of structural separation of the regulatory and universal service operations at national level was emphasised in the European Commission's decision in the application of Article 86(1) combined with Article 82 concerning *La Poste* of France (above) 'on the lack of exhaustive and independent scrutiny of the scales of charges and technical conditions applied by *La Poste* to mail-preparation firms for access to its reserved services'. The Commission decided, following the reasoning of the ECJ in *GB-Inno-BM*,[7] that the French government had allowed a situation to persist in which the public undertaking *La Poste* was faced with a risk of conflict of interest as the monopoly provider of basic postal services, in relation to determining the terms of access to its reserved services and especially its postal network, because of its activities as a competitor on the upstream market for mail-preparation services. In such circumstances, it was the responsibility of the State to ensure an effective monitoring system so as to re-establish effective competition on the upstream market by ensuring that the drawing up of technical specifications and the monitoring of their application would be carried out by a body that is independent of *La Poste* as the relevant public undertaking. French legislation gave *La Poste* the power to set its own technical and financial conditions for access by mail-preparing firms to its network, including, for example, conditions as to volume and standard presentation of the mail produced. These conditions were subject to only partial scrutiny by the relevant French public authority, which was not sufficiently independent and neutral in relation to *La Poste*. This European Commission decision was subsequently followed by a similar decision of the Commission under Article 86 EC against a provision of the German Postal Act, in October 2004, which is discussed in Section 6.

4. REMOVAL OF PROHIBITION ON CROSS-SUBSIDIES

The proposed removal from Article 12 of the prohibition on cross-subsidies appears to be an appropriate deregulatory measure by way of partial quid pro quo for full liberalisation. This move is consistent with the judgment of the European Court of First Instance in *UPS v Commission*,[8] which ruled that the alleged use by *Deutsche Post* of profits from the reserved sector to finance acquisitions of interests in undertakings were not abusive *per se*, but could infringe Article 82 if such cross-subsidies were closely linked to other abusive behaviour such as predatory pricing, excessive pricing or price discrimination.

The objective set by Article 12 of the Directive was that cross-subsidisation of universal services outside the reserved sector using revenues from services in the reserved sector shall be prohibited except to the extent to which it is shown to be strictly necessary in order to fulfil specific universal service obligations imposed in the competitive area.

The EC competition law approach to cross-subsidisation has in any event allowed cross-subsidisation from monopoly areas to competitive areas within the universal service, to the extent necessary to ensure that the universal service is provided in conditions of financial equilibrium, without giving rise to unfair pricing; for example, predatory pricing in the competitive area of activities. In its decision concerning State aid for *Deutsche Post AG*,[9] the European Commission observed (in its preliminary notice inviting comments) that revenues from reserved services, in particular the letter post monopoly, can be used to finance a parcel service within the universal service to the extent that this allows the postal operator to provide universal parcel services under financially balanced conditions, and provided that the universal parcel service costs are not over-compensated.

By contrast, cross-subsidisation cannot be allowed where it directly results in abusive pricing practices in the competitive area of activities. However, the abuse can be said to exist in the resulting unfair prices in the competitive area, rather than in the cross-subsidy itself. The main examples of the European Commission's intervention against the result of such cross-subsidy are the following two cases against *Deutsche Post*. In the above *State*

Aid case, the Commission found that the cross-subsidy carried out by *Deutsche Post* (involving €552 million received from the state to finance its public service mission) was used to finance price-undercutting in the parcel sector between 1994 and 1998.

In its Article 82 decision of 20th March 2001 against *Deutsche Post*, for abuse of dominant position in the German mail-order parcel delivery market,[10] the Commission laid down a rule for measuring cross-subsidies between reserved area and competitive activities in the postal sector to determine whether predatory prices result in the competitive area: the prices for the competitive businesses must cover at least the incremental costs incurred in the competitive activities (the costs that would be avoided if such activities were discontinued), in this case a mail-order parcels service. These incremental costs comprised the additional costs incurred solely as a result of providing the service. It was necessary to distinguish common fixed costs, which were not incurred solely as a result of such service, but the Commission did include an appropriate proportion of common variable costs that were attributable to the mail-order parcels service. For this purpose, the Commission assessed the attributable costs and whether or not they would be saved if the mail-order parcel service were discontinued, by reference to each of the following activities: collection, sorting, long-distance transport, regional and local transport, and delivery. Deutsche Post was found not to have covered the incremental costs of its mail-order parcels delivery service, over a period of five years (from 1990 to 1995). This, the Commission concluded, prevented competition by deterring entry by other competitors generally; the Commission did not identify a particular competitor that was targeted. These prices resulted from fidelity rebates; the Commission found that from 1974 until October 2000, Deutsche Post gave substantial discounts to its large mail-order customers in return for all or a sizeable proportion of their mail-order parcel business. Deutsche Post was required to transfer its non-reserved parcel services business to a separate new company, and to ensure that any inputs from the reserved-sector business would be at market prices, and that all inputs that it supplies to the new company would also be supplied to competitors at the same prices and conditions.

As regards the substantive rules on predatory pricing, the ECFI confirmed the existing case law, albeit in a 'new economy' sector (Internet access services), in its judgment of 30 January 2007 in *France Telecom S.A., formerly Wanadoo Interactive S.A. v Commission.*[11] This is that, essentially, a strategy of predation will be presumed where the dominant undertaking fails to recover its variable costs, whilst the existence of a plan to eliminate competition must be proved where it covers variable costs but its prices are below average total costs. The intention to eliminate competition must be established on the basis of sound and consistent evidence, by reference to the *Tetra Pak* case.[12] The Commission established that Wanadoo had a dominant position and was unable to cover its variable costs prior to August 2001 and was unable to recover its full costs between that date and October 2002, for which period the Commission had provided solid and consistent evidence of a plan of predation by Wanadoo. The ECFI also confirmed the Commission's statement that it is not necessary to prove recoupment of losses as a precondition to making a finding of predatory pricing.

In conclusion, postal operators should avoid conduct amounting to excessive pricing or predatory pricing, and also discriminatory pricing that clearly has a material adverse effect on competition (this will be discussed further below), whether or not such conduct results from cross-subsidisation. However, cross-subsidies in themselves should not be treated as being contrary to the competition rules even if carried out by a dominant postal operator, by reference not only to the Commission's approach in its Proposed Amending Directive but also by reference to the ECJ's decision in *UPS v Commission*.

The Commission's proposed amendment to the Postal Services Directive both supports this analysis and also demonstrates that sector regulation pursuant to the Directive serves a different purpose to the application of competition law in the sector. The proposed abolition of the reserved sector as from 1 January 2009 results in the removal of the current regulatory restriction on cross-subsidies (under which, they can at present only be allowed from the reserved sector activities to the extent necessary to support the maintenance of the universal services). However, the proposed retention of the rules requiring transparency of accounts and cost-allocation under Article 14 of the Directive, in modified form, will provide a regulatory platform for observing for purposes of the general competition rules, where cross-subsidies may take place as between the universal service and non-universal service activities. Insofar as the universal service area may equate in practice to the market or markets in which the postal services operator is in a dominant position, regulatory obligations may serve to enable national authorities, including competition authorities, to identify where cross-subsidies from a dominant to a competitive area of activity are taking place, in order to be able to take action where this results in unfair or anti-competitive pricing in the competitive area.

5. DISCOUNTING BY DOMINANT OPERATORS

Discounting for larger-scale purchasers is commonplace across industry. However, discounting with anti-competitive objectives or effects is a key area of scrutiny for possible abuse of dominant position contrary to Article 82 EC. This area is highly controversial and is the focus of a considerable amount of detailed economic debate, in the Commission's Discussion Paper on exclusionary abuses. Past Commission decisions – for example, *Michelin*[13] and *Michelin II*[14] – have been criticised as being overly formalistic. The Commission is earnestly seeking to address the need for an economically realistic analysis, in its Discussion Paper, though many practitioners still consider the Commission's model to be impractical.

The question of whether discounts are abusive depends on a number of factors, but above all on the question of whether the discounts are loyalty-enhancing in relation to the customer, either directly or indirectly. The issues have recently been reinforced by the judgement of the ECJ in *British Airways plc v Commission* of March 2007.[15] This case concerned British Airways' discount arrangements for remunerating travel agents for purchases of British Airways' tickets. The ECJ applied a two-step approach in holding that in order to decide whether a discount is abusive, it must first be determined whether the discount has an exclusionary effect (i.e. an effect disadvantageous to the competition), and if so, whether it can be counterbalanced by advantages in terms of efficiency that benefit consumers.

The key factors of the finding of abuse that was upheld by the ECJ included the following. First, British Airways' scheme imposed individualised sales targets that were dependent on the growth in turnover in BA tickets by the travel agents over a specified period. The individualised nature of the sales objectives for each agent was considered to have an exclusionary effect. Second, the discount or bonus was based on the whole turnover achieved from sales of BA tickets during the relevant period, and not just the increase in turnover above the target level. The retroactive nature of the discount arrangement increased the pressure on the agent to remain loyal to BA and resulted in a strong incentive to the agent not to switch to competing airlines. Third, due to BA's dominant market position, other airlines were not in a position to offer the same advantages as BA; the other airlines would have to be able to offer a disproportionately higher rebate, which would have been uneconomic for them, in order to regain business from BA. Therefore the fact that BA's discounts were based on the overall turnover from its products would in practice take precedence in the purchasing decisions of travel agents and thus have an exclusionary effect.

The possibility of individualised, turnover, growth-related discounts being discriminatory was addressed by Postcomm in its 2005 decision under the non-discrimination condition of Royal Mail's licence: *Investigation into Royal Mail Catalogue and Advertising Mail Promotion Scheme, Postcomm Decision dated 20 January 2005*.[16] The investigation concerned a trial promotion undertaken by Royal Mail with 12 catalogue mailing customers during July and August 2003, with the aim of verifying whether it was feasible to launch a wider catalogue and advertising market promotion with a view to growing the overall catalogue mailing market. Postcomm questioned whether a policy of granting of discounts to customers by reference to their incremental mailings, as opposed to the absolute volume of their mailings, could ever be implemented by a company with the dominance of Royal Mail, in a way that is acceptable in practice. However, Postcomm did not reach any conclusion, stating rather that it would be disproportionate to prohibit Royal Mail from seeking to introduce schemes intended to develop incremental mailings. Postcomm considered that the evidence in this case indicated that growing the overall postal market was not the only aim of the promotions and that Royal Mail had not taken adequate safeguards to ensure that, in practice, account handlers only applied the available discounts to altogether new mailings, as opposed to using the discounts to grant incentives to customers to switch mailings from a competitor of Royal Mail.

Further, the French Competition Council condemned *La Poste* in November 2004 for proposing tying rebates bundling services in competition. La Poste was reproached for two types of practices: first, the application of a 'global tying rebate' for purchases of all products open to competition – La Poste granted its clients rebates on the basis of the total turnover achieved on the services opened to competition (non-addressed mail, catalogues, B2B packages), thus inciting them (by using its wide range of products) to concentrate their purchases with La Poste – and second, the application of a 'target rebate' whereby La Poste granted rebates based on the increase of the customer's purchases from one year to the other.[17] Therefore, La Poste was condemned for the loyalty-effect of its tying rebates, and also the loyalty-effect of individualised rebates based on yearly growth on the customer's purchases from La Poste.

Based on the case law, it is possible to extract and summarise certain key principles that should be followed notwithstanding the uncertainty that exists in this area of competition law. As a general rule, the following can be stated. First, rebates that are linked to exclusive purchasing or are conditional on the customer purchasing all or most of the requirements from the dominant undertaking are likely to be abusive: *Hoffmann La Roche*.[18]

Second, volume-related discounts that are closely related to the customer's actual total requirements for the relevant reference period, are likely to be abusive: the European Commission's decision in *Irish Sugar* (1997).[19] Third, retroactive rebates (i.e. rebates on all purchases, not just those above a specified threshold) may be abusive even if they are standardised for all customers: the European Commission's decision in *Michelin II* (2002) (see above). Fourth, rebate schemes requiring the customer to exceed individualised thresholds – for example, by reference to its purchase levels in previous reference periods – are likely to be considered abusive especially if they are retroactive – that is, for all purchases, not just incremental purchases (*Michelin II* and *British Airways v Commission*) (see above) – and especially if the individualised sales targets are based on total sales over a relatively long reference period.

In conclusion, any discount scheme to be granted by a dominant postal operator should be carefully assessed for compliance with the competition rules, on a case-by-case basis. The case law experience shows that such postal operators should exercise particular caution in relation to discount schemes based on incremental growth in a customer's purchases, especially if the discount is calculated with reference to all purchases and not just those above a threshold or target. Moreover, individualised purchase thresholds or targets should generally be avoided as a basis for granting rebates, especially rebates on all rather than just incremental purchases. Clearly also, rebates schemes based on exclusive purchasing, or (directly or indirectly) purchasing all or most of the customer's requirements, should be avoided. However, in our view, there should be a presumption in favour of allowing postal operators to offer discounts on standardised terms provided that they cover their average total costs, especially where these apply only to incremental purchases, even if there is no direct evidence of costs savings or economies of scale to the postal operator. This would allow postal operators the flexibility to adopt pricing structures that meet the needs and expectations of their customers, in line with normal commercial practice in many product and service sectors. This is provided, of course, that there is no evidence that such discount structures are used as a disguised means of foreclosing competition or restricting the ability of other postal operators to compete.

6. DISCRIMINATION ISSUES

In most member states of the EU, the incumbent postal services operator is under a regulatory obligation of non-discrimination. In many cases, competition law principles will be relevant (either directly or indirectly) in defining the scope of such a non-discrimination obligation. Considerations of legal certainty and efficiency of regulation require, in our view, that the concept of non-discrimination be interpreted co-terminously in both competition law and regulatory context.

The terms agreed with different parties can only be discriminatory if they are differentiated in relation to equivalent transactions, or if the same terms are applied notwithstanding materially different circumstances. In assessing the equivalence of different transactions, all relevant aspects of the transaction as a whole need to be taken into account.

This is shown, for example, in certain decisions by the Commission under the EC Merger Control Regulation (Regulation 4064/89 now replaced by Regulation 139/2004) in the postal services sector. In two cases, *Case No. IV/M.102 – TNT/Canada Post, DBF Post Dienst, La Poste, PIT Poste & Sweden Post*, and *Case No. IV/M.1168 – DHL/Deutsche Post*, the Commission imposed requirements on the relevant postal operator to provide services to third parties on similar terms and conditions to those offered to the joint venture company the subject of the investigation in each case, to the extent that the transactions were equivalent. For this purpose, the terms of the undertakings given by the relevant postal operators required that account be taken of the following factors: volume, range and frequency of service to be performed, the area and density of geographical coverage, financial compensation, liability and payment terms, and length of contract.

It would therefore be inconsistent with this established case law if, in assessing differential prices offered by a postal operator to different customers for the provision of, for example, bulk mail services within the liberalised area of the universal service, a competition regulator did not take into account an equally diverse range of factors. The regulator should weigh up all relevant terms of the service offering and the circumstances in which it is provided in order to see whether the contract terms taken as a whole are equivalent in one case to another.

The competition case law of the ECJ, and also in the national courts of some member states, is increasingly reflecting the position that price discrimination carried out by dominant companies is not in itself an abuse of dominant position, and should only be regarded as abusive if clear anti-competitive effects can be demonstrated through foreclosure of competition or immaterial impediment to another undertaking's ability to compete. For example, in *GSK v Commission*[20] (an Article 81 case), the European Court of First Instance's judgment in September 2006 included an observation that the differential prices charged by GSK in Spain to exporter wholesalers and to wholesalers for resale and domestic use within Spain, and the distinct characteristics of the two types of sale and customer markets, meant that the differential prices to wholesalers within Spain would not constitute discriminatory pricing for the purposes of Article 82(c) EC. Further, in February 2007 the English Court of Appeal handed down a judgment in *Attheraces v British Horseracing Board*[21] to the effect that quite different prices charged in equivalent transactions for different licensees of data (concerning horse-racing) did not place either licensee at a competitive disadvantage and therefore did not amount to discriminatory pricing contrary to Article 82. Although the licensee that charged the higher price was less profitable that it otherwise would have been, its ability to compete was not affected. The Court of Appeal observed that this was not a case where the licensor was seeking to leverage an advantage for itself into a downstream market. Also, account should be taken of the fact that each licensee's onward market may be significantly different and that differential pricing may therefore legitimately reflect the distinct value of the licensed products to each licensee. The Court of Appeal concluded that the only basis on which discrimination could be found would be if the prices charged were excessive and that discrimination between customers distorted competition between them, which was not shown to have been the case.

The European Commission announced, in 2004, details of a decision finding that the German postal law was contrary to EC competition law in that it induced Deutsche Post to abuse its dominant position by discriminating against commercial mail-preparation firms, by denying them discounts off the normal postal tariff that were granted to direct bulk mailers in otherwise equivalent circumstances.

The European Commission concluded[22] that the relevant provisions, which prevented commercial mail-preparation firms from earning discounts for handing over pre-sorted letter post at Deutsche Post's sorting offices, were discriminatory against such mail-preparation firms. Individual large users (senders) were allowed to feed self-prepared mail directly into sorting offices and receive volume-related discounts, whilst postal consolidators or intermediaries were prevented from obtaining comparable discounts for mail preparation. Germany and Deutsche Post have appeals pending with the European Court of First Instance, claiming that the Commission's decision infringes Article 82 of the EC Treaty and the Postal Directive.[23] However, the Commission's infringement decision can clearly be seen to be based on the foreclosure effects of the discrimination involved in withholding discounts from competitors (mail-preparation firms) that were granted in equivalent circumstances to direct customers, because this could be expected to make it unreasonably difficult for the mail-preparation firms to act as consolidators as a source of upstream competition to Deutsche Post. The withholding of the rebates was therefore not only discriminatory, in the Commission's view, but also could be said to have a material adverse effect on the mail-preparation firms' ability to compete.

In the European Commission's cross-border mail decision against *Deutsche Post* in July 2001,[24] Deutsche Post was held to have wrongly intercepted, surcharged and delayed incoming international mail from the UK, which it erroneously classified as international remail, circumventing the national postal monopoly.[25] Since the mail in question was found to be normal cross-border mail, Deutsche Post's actions had discriminated between customers and involved an unlawful refusal to supply delivery services (i.e. a refusal to supply unless the surcharge was paid), and the resulting price was excessive, thereby restricting competition in the German market for incoming international mail and in the UK for international mail bound for Germany.

The European Commission also adopted a decision[26] that the Belgian incumbent postal operator, *La Poste*, had abused its dominant position by refusing rebates on its reserved-sector mail service to customers who refused to subscribe to La Poste's business mail service launched at the beginning of 2000 to compete with a document exchange service offered by the complainant, Hays Management Services SA, both of which services were supplied to insurance companies and insurance brokers in Belgium. La Poste's business-to-business mail service offered overnight delivery and time-certain pick-up and delivery; it fell outside the reserved area and La Poste's conduct signified an attempt to leverage its dominance in the reserved area to exclude competition in this competitive sector. A fine of €2.5 million was imposed.

This tying by La Poste of its basic letter mail service, in which it was in a dominant position, with its competitive business mail document exchange service, also involved discrimination between those purchasers of its letter mail services who did or did not also purchase the document exchange service. Such tying and the inherent discrimination had the effect of diverting business away from an alternative services provider in a competitive area and could, therefore, be seen to materially impede competition in the competitive document exchange market.

In all of these cases, the price discrimination can be seen to have involved leveraging by a dominant operator of its market power into a neighbouring or downstream market, or as otherwise significantly impeding competition in the market in which the effects of the discrimination where realised. In other cases, in our view, dominant postal operators should be permitted to price-discriminate (or at least make offers that 'meet' the competition), where this is consistent with the provision of the universal service under financially stable conditions. Indeed, this appears to be allowed for by the Commission in its Explanatory Memorandum, where it encourages member states to give universal service providers the necessary flexibility to react to competition, thus limiting possible risks to the financial equilibrium of the universal service. Otherwise, under a geographically uniform tariff requirement for the universal service, not only would discrimination be mandated insofar as the same price is charged for equivalent services irrespective of the highly variable costs of delivery (for example, as between dense urban areas and remote rural areas), but the resulting competitive pressures could impose risks on the financial viability of universal service provision (see Section 3.2.2 of the Explanatory Memorandum and Section 2 above).

In an increasingly liberalised European postal services environment, a rigid application of rules against price discrimination could be inconsistent with the fundamental objectives of ensuring universal service provisions in conditions of economic equilibrium, especially where maximum prices are limited by the uniform tariff. In our view, such economic policy considerations provide justification for selective price cutting by an incumbent postal operator in response to bulk mailers, provided that such a response to new entry is carried out on a consistent basis, which is proportionate in financial terms to the individual competitive threat involved and to the need for financial equilibrium, so as to ensure the maintenance of sufficient revenue to enable sustained fulfilment of the universal service, subject to the uniform tariff. By way of example, the ECJ allowed Deutsche Post to discriminate in the charges imposed for delivery of international mail from the Netherlands and alleged e-mail posted in the Netherlands, so as in the latter case to charge the higher internal (as opposed to cross-border) postal charges (after allowing for any contribution received from the postal operator of the sending country).[27] The ECJ concluded that it was justified for the purposes of 'the performance, in economically-balanced conditions, of the task of general interest entrusted to Deutsche Post'[28] to treat such cross-border mail as internal mail (provided that allowance was made for the terminal dues paid by the Dutch postal operator). The ECJ stated that postal services of member states cannot simultaneously bear the costs entailed in the performance of the service of general economic interest (delivery of international mail) and the loss of income resulting from the fact that bulk mailings may be posted in a different member state to the one in which the sender and addressees are resident.[29] The ECJ upheld and allowed an element of price discrimination as a proportionate response to a competitive threat which, if unchecked, could have undermined fulfilment of the universal service obligation.

In the long-running Swedish *CityMail* case, concerning the incumbent's Posten's two-zone discount system (for urban and rural areas respectively), which was introduced in response to the competitive threat from CityMail, the Swedish Market Court ultimately allowed Posten's zonal price differentiation once Posten was able to provide improved data justifying the two-zone price system on a costs basis. In reaching its decision on the objectively acceptable grounds for the two-zone price scheme, the Market Court acknowledged that dominant companies may take reasonable measures to meet competition but may not adopt pricing strategies solely for the purpose of eliminating competition.[30]

Further, in our view, postal operators should be allowed to rely on the 'meeting competition' defence; that is, to make selective price cuts as a proportionate response to a genuine competitive threat, where the dominant operator may otherwise lose its customer. For example, the Commission allowed the meeting competition case in this way in *Digital*.[31] Digital had offered selective price cuts targeted at the business of third-party maintainers, which were found to be one of the various abuses of Digital's dominant position in the supply of hardware maintenance services for Digital computer systems. The Commission accepted an undertaking from Digital not to offer non-standard price reductions to meet competition, except only where such price reductions would be granted only on individual component services (and not on the complete hardware service package) and would only be granted as a proportionate response to competition and not so as to foreclose or distort competition. Therefore, Digital was in effect permitted to make selective price cuts in relation to individual existing customers as a proportionate response to the competition, to meet but not undercut competitors' prices on individual but not bundled service offerings. This decision can be regarded as granting dominant undertakings an appropriate degree of leeway in taking reasonable steps to safeguard their competitive position in the face of price competition. However, it allows the dominant operator only to take measures in reaction to such competition, and it is not a basis for a proactive selective price reduction policy by a dominant undertaking.

In the European Commission's 'Discussion paper on the application of Article 82 to exclusionary abuses', the Commission states (paras 81–3) that the 'meeting competition defence' can provide objective justification for pricing that might otherwise be abusive, where the dominant company's response (i.e. a response as opposed to a new initiative) is proportionate and indispensable (i.e. the legitimate aim cannot be achieved to a similar extent by any less anti-competitive alternatives and that the conduct is limited to the minimum necessary duration), and provided also that the dominant company's price is not reduced below average avoidable costs. On this basis, the meeting competition defence should only be allowed in the postal or other sectors, where the dominant operator is taking defensive action as a reasonable commercial operator, in defence to a genuine commercial threat, and is not using selective price cuts to divert business away from competing operators so as to impede the competitive process.

Furthermore, in our view selective discounts should be allowed by dominant postal operators where these serve to grow the market. Selective price cuts might be appropriate in relation to product sectors in which there is greater price stability or which themselves tend to produce greater volumes of follow-on mail which, in turn, can contribute to efficiencies and economies of scale, even if they may, superficially, appear to be discriminatory. An example of this may be the direct mail field, where postal communications are competing with other advertising media such as television, radio, magazines and other communications technologies, including the Internet. Indeed, this was acknowledged by the European Commission in its report to the Council and the Parliament on the application of the Postal Directive (explained above) to the effect that developments in the wider communications market need to be taken into account. In granting selective price cuts in the direct mail field so as to increase the overall level of business, discounting by a dominant postal operator could even contribute, ultimately, to an ability to limit future price increases generally. It may also be noted that the UK Office of Fair Trading stated, in its guidelines on *Assessment of Individual Agreements and Conduct*,[32] that 'in general, price discrimination will not be an abuse if it leads to a higher level of output in the relevant market(s) than could be achieved if all customers were charged to the same price' (para 3.9).

We would agree that selective or discriminatory pricing should be disallowed where it serves as part of a strategy to exclude competition or to leverage the dominant postal operator's market power into a downstream or neighbouring area, or if such a strategy is used as a means of significantly impeding or excluding competition. However, in our view discounts and selective pricing should be permitted where used by a postal operator as a reasonable form of defence against commercial threats or market developments, and further where they are not used in a predatory manner, are not used systematically to divert customers away from a competitor for a particular type of service to the dominant operator, and are not used so as to tie two different types of products or services together (so as to give a joint incentive to the customer to obtain both services from the dominant operator).

This is especially the case, in our view, where selective discounting is used in a genuine way to grow the overall postal market; this might be possible if discounts are granted, for example, to direct mail as compared with other forms of bulk mail, insofar as direct mail can result in significant volumes of follow-on mail and therefore result in efficiencies for the dominant postal operator.

7. PRICING OF ACCESS TO THE POSTAL SERVICES NETWORK

The Commission Staff Working Document states in paragraph 3.4 that member states have different policies on whether dominant operators are obliged to provide access to third parties. As far as specific facilities are concerned, it is worth noting the roles of National Regulatory Authorities in ensuring that any such access barriers are removed. The progress to date is reported as follows. Seven member states have granted the NRA authority to require downstream access to third parties. Seven member states (Germany, Denmark, France, Hungary, Portugal, Slovenia and the United Kingdom) have granted the NRA authority to require downstream access to the public postal network under the appropriate circumstances. Three NRAs (Germany, Denmark and Portugal) report that they have used this authority to encourage access. Two others (Italy and Lithuania) indicated that once the universal service provider has granted access to one customer, they have required the universal service provider to give downstream access to all customers on a non-discriminatory basis.

In the amended EC Directive 97/67, the revised Article 12 states that where universal service providers apply special tariffs for bulk mailers or consolidators of mail, the universal service provider must:

1. First, apply the principles of transparency and non-discrimination regarding the tariffs.
2. Second, ensure that the tariffs 'take account of the avoided costs, as compared to the standard service covering the complete range of features offered for the clearance,

> transport, sorting and the delivery of individual postal items'. This clearly supports the use of the 'retail-minus' principle. The retail-minus principle involves charging the normal final price for full processing and delivery by the incumbent postal operator, minus the cost of the upstream operations that the party seeking access (and therefore not the incumbent) has carried out.

However, the same provision also states that the proposed tariffs shall apply equally (without discrimination) both as between different third parties and also as between third parties and universal service providers supplying equivalent services. This latter requirement appears to presume an operational separation of the upstream and downstream parts of a postal operator's postal conveyance operations, yet the Postal Services Directive does not require any such operational separation. Indeed, most postal operators are single vertically integrated entities. In reality, therefore, the minimum obligation required to be laid down by member states pursuant to the Directive is an obligation on the postal network operator to grant equivalent terms of access to bulk mail customers dealing directly with the postal operator, and to postal competitors or consolidators who collect mail from their customers in order to obtain downstream access to the postal operator's network.

This was the issue in the case explained above, concerning *Deutsche Post AG and the German Postal Law.* The Commission concluded that the Postal Law induced Deutsche Post to grant discounts to bulk mailers for pre-sorted mail that was fed directly into Deutsche Post's sorting centres, but prohibited Deutsche Post from granting equivalent discounts to mail-preparation firms acting as consolidators. For this reason, the German Postal Law was found to infringe Article 86(1) combined with Article 82 of the EC Treaty, and not to be justified on the basis of Article 86(2). The German government and Deutsche Post have appealed against the Commission's decision to the European Court of First Instance (as already mentioned). The Commission's conclusion, however, was that mail-preparation services (including pre-sorting of mail and its transportation from the mailer's premises to the access point to Deutsche Post's network) did not fall within the reserved area, and that the provision of mail-preparation services was, therefore, subject to the EU competition rules. In any event, the amended Article 12 of the Postal Services Directive, which was required to be implemented by member states from 31 December 2002, now clearly requires equivalent terms of access between bulk mailer customers and mail consolidators notwithstanding the reserved area, which continues to exist at least until 31 December 2008.

The further important issue raised by Article 12 of the Postal Services Directive is the terms on which access is to be granted, in particular, taking into account the avoided costs or 'retail-minus' principle. This issue has been the scope of considerable debate in the UK. Royal Mail's licence requires Royal Mail (condition 9, para 2) to grant downstream network access to all users. Royal Mail has concluded various network access agreements, the first of which, with UK Mail, was, in essence, a test case, in March 2004. Agreement was reached voluntarily between Royal Mail and UK Mail, and was followed by similar agreements by Royal Mail with TPG Post UK Limited and Deutsche Post in April 2004. Postcomm published its Observations on the *Royal Mail – UK Mail* agreement in March 2004, stating that the price of access was based on the cost of the downstream sorting, transportation and delivery services, and not on the retail-minus principle, which was the basis favoured by Royal Mail. However, this was merely an observation of Postcomm on a voluntary agreement reached by the parties, and Postcomm's conclusions, therefore, have no specific legal effect.

It should be noted that, generally, competition authorities and tribunals can be expected to take a cautious approach to allowing the use of retail-minus pricing. The UK Competition Appeal Tribunal stated in a recent judgment, *Albion Water Limited v Water Services Regulation Authority*,[33] that careful scrutiny of retail-minus pricing is required with reference to the facts of each individual case (paras 728 and 739). The Tribunal rejected the use of the retail-minus pricing for the granting of access to a regional water network where the price used as the 'retail' element of the retail-minus calculation was not shown to have been reasonably related to costs, and the evidence strongly suggested that the price was excessive (para 761). However, in the postal services sector, taking into account the reference to the avoided costs principle in Article 12 of Directive 97/67 (as amended), the application of the avoided costs or retail-minus principle cannot be excluded, at least if there is no clear evidence that the relevant retail price is excessive in relation to costs.

As a result of the amended Postal Services Directive, the European Commission's approach in the *Deutsche Post and the German Postal Law* case and Postcomm's observations on Royal Mail's network access agreement, it is possible to venture the following conclusions:

1. The essential regulatory requirement is for postal operators to treat consolidators (i.e. competitors) in the same way as direct mailer customers in granting access, and in particular discounts for worksharing arrangements, pursuant to Article 12 of the Postal Services Directive.
2. Prior to full liberalisation, the granting of preferential or discounted terms for pre-sorted mail to mail-preparation firms or consolidators does not fall within the reserved sector and is therefore covered by the EC competition law requirement of non-discrimination on the part of the dominant undertaking. In any event, at least as from the amendment of the Postal Services Directive by Directive 2002/39, there is an express EU regulatory requirement for the provision of such equivalent terms as between consolidators and competitors and direct customers.
3. There is no fundamental requirement under the Directive to grant access to postal networks as such, as opposed to the requirement of non-discriminatory access. As a result, contrary to the position in other regulated network industries, the access pricing obligation is not a cost-plus obligation but a retail-minus obligation by reference to the avoided costs of the upstream collection and sortation operations, as is made clear in the amended Article 12 of the Postal Services Directive.
4. It is reasonable for postal network operators to implement a proportionate differentiation in the terms or prices offered for network access, so as to reflect the differential costs of the downstream delivery operation, with reference to the following: first, the geographical profile of the mail to be delivered; second, the relative costs affected by the position in the mail conveyance chain at which the mail is to be entered into the network operator's mailstream; and/or third, other irregular requirements of the party seeking network access in respect of the mail to be deposited with the network operator.

The specific obligations required under the Postal Services Directive to be imposed by member states leave it open to question whether an incumbent postal services operator should ever properly be accused of margin squeezing in relation to network access, provided that it complies with the requirement to offer the same discounts to upstream competitors as it does to direct customers under worksharing arrangements, applying the avoided costs (or retail-minus) principle. There is no further obligation under the Directive (present or proposed) to grant access on a cost-orientated basis so as to allow a margin to competitors of bulk purchasers of an input or network capacity. Therefore, in order for an incumbent postal operator to be accused of margin squeezing in relation to network access, national regulatory measures of a stricter nature would have to be applied, or competition law would have to be invoked in order for such action to be taken effectively. However, in a situation where the EU regulatory measure stipulates a specific basis for network access terms, it would in our view not be appropriate for national regulatory measures to go significantly further; nor would it be appropriate, in the interests of the harmonised approach across Europe, for competition law to be applied in a way that results in significantly harsher treatment of the incumbent than the regime required by the EU Directive. In any event, where there is scope for interpretation of the scope and extent of the national regulatory measure, as is perhaps the position in the UK with regard to condition 9 of Royal Mail's licence, then the correct approach should now be to refer back to the content of the Postal Services Directive as determining the scope of the national regulations or obligations on network access.

8. CONCLUSIONS

The removal of the reserved sector under the Postal Services Directive and the consequential amendments to the Directive as from 1 January 2009 will expand the scope for application of competition law in the postal sector. The extent to which competition law, as opposed to sector-specific regulation, will be applied, will depend upon such questions as the nature of the sector regulatory measures in place and also on the question of whether the sector regulator holds powers under competition legislation, or not. In any event, we consider it important, as a general objective, in the interests of legal certainty and harmonisation across Europe, that:

1. Competition regulatory obligations under sector-specific regulation – for example, regarding non-discrimination – should be interpreted and applied consistently with competition law under Article 82 EC and equivalent national legislation.
2. National regulatory provisions regarding matters covered by the Postal Services Directive – for example, with regard to the grant of access to postal networks – should as far as possible be interpreted in accordance with the specific provisions of the Postal Services Directive, thereby to limit the scope of obligations on incumbent postal operators.

The Commission's report to the Council and the European Parliament correctly states that the promotion of competition is not an end in itself. Against this background, the application of postal regulatory measures and of competition law in the postal sector on the lines suggested above will serve to safeguard the fulfilment of the continuing objective of ensuring universal service provision under economically stable conditions.

NOTES

1. Directive 97/67/EC of the European Parliament and the Council of 15 December 1997 on common rules for the development of the internal market of Community postal services and the improvement of quality of service; amended by Directive 2002/39/EC of the European Parliament and of the Council of 10 June 2002 amending Directive 97/67/EC with regard to the further opening to competition of Community postal services.
2. Case C-95/04P, judgment of 15 March 2007.
3. Report from the Commission to the European Parliament and the Council on the application of the Postal Directive (Directive 97/67/EC as amended by Directive 2002/39/EC) COM (2006) 595 final; http://ec.europa.eu/comm/competition/antitrust/art82/hearing.html
4. The Commission Staff Working Document 18.10.2006 is the latest report and provides a comprehensive assessment of the Postal Directive in member states and the application of key elements of the Directive, as well as detailed market trends (including economic, technical, social, employment and quality of services aspects).
5. This is stated by the Commission in its Explanatory Memorandum concerning its Proposal, in Section 3.2.2 (opening paragraph), though no details are given of the particular differences of interpretation or the relevant language versions involved.
6. Decision of 23 October 2001, OJ (2002) L120/19.
7. Case C-18/88, *GB-Inno-BM* (1991), ECR I-5941.
8. Case T-175/99, *UPS Europe v Commission*, judgment of 20 March 2002.
9. Commission Decision of 19 June 2002 on measures implemented by the Federal Republic of Germany for Deutsche Post AG, OJ (2002) L247/27.
10. Case COMP/35 141, *Deutsche Post AG*, OJ 2001 L125/27.
11. Case T-340/03, judgment of 30 January 2007.
12. Case T-83/91, *Tetra Pak v Commission.*
13. Case IV/29.491, OJ (1981) L353/33; Case 322/81, *Michelin NV v Commission* [1983] ECR 3461.
14. Commission decision of 20 June 2001 (COMP/E-2/36.04/PO-Michelin); Case T-203/01 – *Michelin v Commission* CFI (Third Chamber), 30 September 2003.
15. Case C-95/04P – *British Airways plc v Commission* ECJ (Third Chamber), 15 March 2007.
16. 'Investigation into Royal Mail's catalogue and advertising mail promotion scheme'; Decision of the Postal Services Commission 20 January 2005; http://www.psc.gov.uk/postcomm/live/policy-and-consultations/documents-by-date/2005/12492Decision.pdf
17. Decision 04-D-65 of 30 November 2004 (http://www.conseil-concurrence.fr/pdf/avis/04d65.pdf).
18. *F Hoffmann La Roche & Co AG v Commission of the European Communities* (85/76) (1979) ECR 461 (ECJ).
19. Commission Decision of 14 May 1997 (IV/34.621, 35.059/F-3 – Irish Sugar plc) (97/624/EC).
20. Case T-168/01 – *Glaxo Wellcome plc v Commission* (2006); CFI (Fourth Chamber: Extended Composition), 27 September 2006.
21. [2007] EWCACiv38.
22. European Commission press release IP/04/1254, 20 October 2004. The decision is not yet published in the Official Journal, but the draft is available on the Commission's website: http://europa.eu.int/comm/competition/antitrust/cases/decisions/38745/en.pdf
23. Case T-490/04, *Germany v Commission* and Case T-493/04, *Deutsche Post AG v Commission*, OJ (2005) C 31/29.
24. Case COMP/C-1/36.915 – *Deutsche Post AG – Interception of cross-border mail*, OJ 2001 L331/40.
25. If genuine international remail had been involved, Deutsche Post may have relied on the ECJ ruling in Joined Cases C-147 and 148/97, *Deutsche Post v GZS and Citicorp*, ECR (2000) I-827.
26. Case COMP/37.859 – *De Post – La Poste*, OJ 2002 L 61/32.
27. *Deutsche Post v GZS and Citicorp*, Joined Cases C-147 and 148/97.
28. Ibid., para 52.
29. Ibid., paras 51 and 54.
30. Competition Authority cases Dnr. 1074/96 and 1142/96, both appealed to the City Court of Stockholm A8-151-96 and A8-7-97, Decision 1998-03-11, and finally to the Market Court, MD1998:15; Other relevant Competition Authority decisions include Dnr. 1129/96,1143/96 and 1324/96.

31. Commission press release IP/97/868.
32. OFT 414, September 1999.
33. Case No. 1046/2/4/04, [2006] CAT 23, judgment dated 6 October 2006.

BIBLIOGRAPHY

Eccles, Richard and Pauline Kuipers (2006), 'Postal services regulation in Europe', in M.A. Crew and P.R. Kleindorfer (eds), *Progress towards Liberalisation of the Postal and Delivery Sector*, New York: Springer Verlag, pp. 321–40.

19. Licensing regimes in the postal sector: the impact of the recent EC proposal for a third Postal Directive*

Joost Vantomme and Alessandra Fratini

1. INTRODUCTION

The purpose of this chapter is to review the European licensing regimes for the postal sector within an evolving legal framework. Licensing requirements and related regulations have always been regarded under competition law as constituting potential barriers to entry. Indeed, on the one hand, licensing requirements such as territorial restrictions, mandatory standards or legal requirements can be viewed as affecting the market's normal functioning by unnecessarily deterring or delaying entry. However, on the other hand, these requirements can be considered as being necessary on public service grounds to ensure the affordability, reliability and efficiency of a service of general interest.

The current Postal Directive[1] authorizes Member States to set up authorization procedures, including individual licenses, provided that they do not go beyond what is necessary to ensure universal service provision. Its implementation has led to a wide range of licensing regimes at national level. The recent proposal for a third Postal Directive ('the Proposed Directive')[2] suggests further harmonization of the divergences to reduce unjustified and burdensome barriers to the free movement of postal services (often referred to in EU jargon as 'removing barriers to the internal market').

Section 2 will be devoted to summarizing the current licensing systems, as provided by EU law and implemented by Member States into their national legislation, combined with an overview of the changes that would be made to this system by the Proposed Directive. In Section 3, we will assess the existing licensing regimes under the proportionality principle, a broad requirement under EU law. The main conclusions are highlighted in Section 4.

2. AN OVERVIEW OF LICENSING MECHANISMS IN THE EU

2.1 Licensing under the Current Postal Directive and the Proposed Directive

Under the general notion of 'authorization'[3] in the Postal Directive, the intensity of permitted regulatory controls may differ according to whether the postal service concerned falls within or outside the universal service. A Member State may legislate and impose 'general conditions',[4] for postal activities outside the scope of universal service, and 'individual licenses'[5] for activities falling within the scope of universal service. A Member State may also refrain altogether from establishing authorization procedures, but where it chooses to establish them, licensing procedures shall be 'transparent, non-discriminatory, proportionate and based on objective criteria'.[6]

For services falling outside the scope of the universal service, the scope for regulatory intervention in the form of licensing is circumscribed. An *ex-ante* authorization system may only be introduced where a Member State considers that there is a need for regulatory control to comply with 'essential requirements'. These essential requirements are defined in the Directive and purposely concern public interest objectives of a non-economic nature; that is, confidentiality of correspondence, security of the network as regards the transport of dangerous goods and, where justified, data protection, environmental protection and regional planning. Data protection may include personal data protection, the confidentiality of information transmitted or stored and the protection of privacy.[7]

For services falling within the universal service, Member States enjoy more flexibility in designing an *ex-ante* licensing system based on individual licenses. Conditions may be introduced to the extent necessary to guarantee compliance with the essential requirements and to safeguard universal service. In particular, the conditions in individual licenses may (1) *where appropriate*, impose universal service obligations, (2) *if necessary*, impose requirements concerning quality, availability and performance of the relevant services, (3) impose the obligation not to infringe the exclusive rights granted to the universal service provider for reserved postal services, and (4) require a financial payment to a universal service compensation fund, where established.

Member States have discretion to assess the 'appropriateness' and 'necessity' of conditions related to the quality, availability and performance of the services. Although the Member States might be guided in doing so by principles drawn by the case law of the European Court of Justice ('ECJ') and the European Commission's practice, one must admit that the wording of the legislative text lacks certainty, as even the scope of and the difference among conditions encompassed by the first and the second indent remain unclear. Hence, it is no surprise that Member States have in practice set up a variety of assorted and at times rather inconsistent conditions, as is shown by the individual country practices outlined in the following paragraphs.

The Proposed Directive leaves untouched the principle of individual licenses and general authorizations, together with the permissible conditions,[8] depending whether or not the postal service falls within the scope of universal service. Member States may in fact continue to use authorizations and individual licenses whenever justified and proportionate to the objective pursued. However, the Proposed Directive provides for an amendment to Article 9 (2) and introduces the following list of prohibited conditions, drawn from practical experience and sector studies:

1. *Limiting the number of licensees*. According to the Commission, while this measure is used in other network industries where duplication of infrastructure is not economically, physically or socially desirable, this is not applicable to the postal sector.
2. *The concurrent requirement to (a) contribute to a sharing mechanism for universal services costs and (b) the imposition of universal service or quality obligations for the same quality, availability and performance requirements*. The universal service obligations

spread the economic costs burden of the service on those companies designated to provide universal service, while the compensation fund imposes a levy on all companies in the sector to finance the uneconomic cost incurred by one company. Hence, imposing both obligations on the same company is unjustified.

3. *Duplicate conditions that are applicable to undertakings by virtue of other, non sector-specific, national legislation.* In the Commission's view, this would limit unnecessary administrative costs on postal service providers.
4. *Disproportionate or unjustified technical or operational conditions.* The Commission takes the view, by way of illustration of what constitutes a justified condition that any conditions aimed at, for instance, protecting the confidentiality of mail, or facilitating the return of wrongly delivered mail, would continue to be acceptable.

These prohibitions on types of restrictive licensing conditions do not apply to designated universal service provider(s), which may be subject to a different type of regulation as they may have to meet different objectives or operate under a distinct legal basis, such as one for government ownership.

2.2 Licensing Regulations in Some Member States

Based on the 2006 overview prepared by WIK-Consult,[9] the Commission highlighted in its third Application Report that 13 Member States have issued individual licenses for all universal services including parcel services (Belgium, Cyprus, Estonia, Finland, Spain, Greece, Hungary, Italy, Latvia, Luxembourg, Lithuania, Malta and Portugal). However, the largest Member States and several smaller Member States, accounting for more than three quarters of the Community's letter post by volume, apply less burdensome procedures. For example, Germany, France, Poland, Sweden and the UK require licenses for some or all letter post services within the universal service area; in five other Member States (Austria, Denmark, Ireland, Slovenia and Slovakia), a general authorization procedure has been implemented and in two other Member States (the Czech Republic and the Netherlands) no authorization procedures are applied at all. The following is a short overview of selected existing licensing systems, highlighting their respective scope and specificities.

2.2.1 Bulgaria[10]

A license is required for any service falling within the scope of universal service. The total duration of the license may not exceed 35 years. The license can be denied in certain circumstances, including the following: (i) security – the presence of circumstances that endanger the country's security or defense; (ii) financial – lack of evidence of sufficient financial potential resources for performing the universal postal service (bank guarantee, fixed assets liquidity, etc.); and (iii) quality – the technology described does not meet the high quality performance standards set by the country for the postal service in question.[11] Furthermore, the license contains requirements for the provision of postal security, as well as conditions for the supervision and control exercised by competent government bodies. The requirements also pertain to environment protection and employee health and safety protection in the course of performing the activities. The licensed operator is to keep an analytical accounting. Price regulation is very strict and applies to the designated universal service provider as well as to other licensed operators.

2.2.2 Finland[12]

Universal postal services can only be provided under a license issued by the government. The license is issued for 20 years. The delivery of newspapers and periodicals, unaddressed mail, courier services and postal parcels falling outside of the scope of universal service are not subject to licensing. The license framework in Finland can be regarded as a 'pay and play' system in a fully liberalized market. All postal service providers must comply with the following obligations: (1) concerning reception, transmission and seizure of items of correspondence, service to a customer can only be refused in a limited set of circumstances – for example, dangerous goods; (2) concerning the obligation to distribute post at least every working day, derogations are only possible in a limited number of cases; (3) the privacy of confidential messages must be ensured and secrecy and language rights respected; (4) the annual publication of information on the quality of services, including the number of complaints and their handling, must be guaranteed; (5) the quality standard of universal services must be respected; (6) agreements must be concluded between the postal undertakings on service delivery and quality standards (multi-operator environment); and (7) the financial capacities to fulfill the above-mentioned obligations must be demonstrated.

If necessary in order to guarantee universal service and if the imposition of the obligation is not unreasonable from the point of view of the postal undertaking, the regulator may impose on a licensed operator a universal service obligation for another region or for universal postal services other than those that the undertaking has requested in its licensing application. A separate piece of tax legislation[13] obliges license holders to pay a fee to the State (and not to Finland Post Corporation) based on the turnover of the company. The percentage is calculated by dividing the population density (number of inhabitants per square kilometer of the land area) in the concession area at the end of the previous calendar year by the figure of 50 and rounding off the resulting amount to the nearest whole number. The percentage may not be greater than 20. The fee is not collected in a concession area where population density is less than 250 inhabitants per square kilometer of the land area.[14]

2.2.3 France[15]

Individual licenses are required for delivering items of correspondence falling within the scope of universal service. Express and courier services are not subject to a license obligation. Operators who are not established in France but are contractually bound to customers established in France need a license for international outbound services. The regulator grants licenses for a ten-year period and the following conditions are attached to licenses: (1) to put in place the necessary procedures and methods of operation to ensure continued service if the company enters bankruptcy; (2) to affix a sign or logo on the postal items, identifying the postal operator; (3) employees providing distribution services must carry a professional employee identification card and a sign or logo identifying the postal operator 'in order to guarantee the calm in the private rooms where they enter into'; (4) operational procedures to guarantee confidentiality, integrity, data protection and privacy must be established; (5) customers must be provided with information related to the commercial offer and complaint handling (free of charge); and (6) a sector collective convention (a labor union agreement) must be concluded.

If one or more of the above conditions is not fulfilled, the license shall not be granted, or shall be withdrawn. The license can also be refused or withdrawn in case the applicant/licensee proves to be incapable of fulfilling its obligations linked to its postal obligations on technical, economic or financial grounds. A mandatory contribution to a universal service compensation fund, if activated, is limited to licensed operators and is based on a percentage of their turnover in the universal service area.

2.2.4 Germany[16]

The German licensing system is much more detailed than most others and its scope seems to go further than services falling within the scope of universal service. Indeed, as long as reserved postal activities remain assigned to Deutsche Post AG ('DPAG'), a detailed licensing regime will continue to apply for the following services that are rendered on a profit basis: (1) conveyance of letters (including direct mail) or addressed catalogues (outside the reserved area), (2) conveyance of letters through a document exchange service, (3) conveyance of letters collected on the sender's behalf from the sender and taken to the nearest DPAG acceptance point or another within the same community,[17] (4) conveyance of letters collected on the addressee's behalf from DPAG's PO boxes and delivered to the addressee, and (5) conveyance of letters destined for other countries and of letters from other countries.

Licenses do not contain a minimum duration period. Most of these licenses fall under the 'D-license', the so-called services providing higher quality than those provided under universal service. There has been extensive case law on this issue and the regulator considers the following services to fall in the higher quality service category: (i) same-day delivery service, (ii) overnight delivery service, (iii) time-certain delivery service, (iv) tracking and tracing service and (v) integrated mail logistics service.

Licensing conditions for D-licenses are related to, first, the availability of the production inputs for setting up and operations necessary to exercise license rights. Second, it concerns reliability, implying that the applicant can comply with legal provisions. Third, it concerns specialized knowledge, meaning the applicant has the necessary knowledge, experience and skills of the persons engaged in the exercise of license rights. Moreover, if facts warrant the regulator's assumption that public safety would be endangered by the start-up of an activity subject to license, or that the applicant fails to a significant extent to meet the basic labor conditions common in the licensed sector, the license will not be granted.

2.2.5 Hungary[18]

Operators providing services within the scope of universal service are subject to a licensing requirement. The applicable legislation does not address license duration – neither setting a minimum nor a maximum period.

Prerequisites for obtaining a license pertain to personnel qualifications and assets. The personnel-related qualifications refer to academic and/or professional training as well as conditions designed to avoid any potential conflict of interests. The assets-related conditions are aimed at ensuring the financial security necessary for the provision of postal services. The applicant needs to guarantee that he has the suitable real estate, premises, vehicle fleet and technical equipment required for the collection, clearance, transmission and delivery of postal items, and financial collateral of a magnitude specified by the regulator. The obligation to have financial collateral is set to protect the consumers' interest, since the collateral can be used only to cover any damage caused by the licensed operator.

The general terms and conditions of customer contracts are to be approved by the regulator. Furthermore, the legislation requires that 'the postal and other related services are to be comparable with one another with regard to the quality requirements prescribed by law and undertaken by the licensee. They have to contain the content-related elements defined in regulation (e.g. definitions, service levels, prices & discounts, limitation and suspension of services, . . .)', the aim being to have general terms and conditions designed in a transparent and user-friendly manner.

Finally, it is interesting to note that the licensee's services must cover a sufficient portion of the national territory as strictly defined in the regulation.[19]

2.2.6 The United Kingdom[20]

With the opening of the market on January 1, 2006, a new license system entered into force that encompasses most types of mail weighing less than 350 grams and costing less than £1 to post. Carriage of catalogues, books, newspapers, periodicals, unaddressed items, outbound international mail, courier, express and other services of more than £1 per item are not subject to a licensing requirement. The licensing regime is the product of an extensive public-sector consultation exercise and is designed to make the multi-operator market work effectively, and balance the need to encourage new entrants to the mail market with the regulator's responsibilities to protect customer interests. Companies applying for licenses must meet the following minimum obligations: (1) *conveyance and delivery* (operators must convey and deliver letters and report on their performance compared to their contract obligations), (2) *mail integrity* (operators must have sound arrangements, appropriate for their business, for protecting mail and delivering it safely), and (3) *guarantees* (applicants must be able to show how mail left in their system will be delivered in the event of their company exiting the postal market).

Postcomm has issued two Codes of Practice, one requiring licensees to ensure the safety and security of the mail they handle (mail integrity) and the other dealing with operational issues, including handling wrongly addressed and misdelivered mail (common operational procedures). Licensees are required by the Codes to sign up to a default agreement that has effect in the absence of bilateral arrangements, for managing these issues between operators. Postcomm makes checks on these issues and conducts criminal record checks before granting a license. The license is granted for ten years. Postcomm is able to initiate criminal or civil proceedings against unlicensed operators.

Royal Mail's license conditions include provisions that do not apply to other licensees; for example, pricing and quality of service obligations. Finally, all licenses have a national geographic scope, but there is no territorial coverage obligation.

2.2.7 Malta[21]

The regulator issues licenses for services falling within the scope of universal service and enjoys discretionary powers as to the relevant license conditions and contents. Article 9.3 of the Postal Services Act reads in fact: 'An individual license granted under this Act may include – (a) such conditions (whether relating to the postal services to which the individual license relates or otherwise) as appear to the Authority to be requisite or expedient having regard to the duties of the Authority and to the international obligations of Malta'.

By way of example, it is worth mentioning some conditions that were attached to the license issued on March 30, 2007 to Premiere One Limited. First, the licensee shall establish and operate adequate systems for measuring and recording its performance in achieving its contract standards and for recording, analyzing and responding to customer complaints. Second, the licensee shall develop a mail integrity procedure to be approved by the regulator (containing matters such as selection, vetting, training, provision of incentives to and disciplining of personnel and the security of buildings and vehicles). Finally, the licensee shall keep an independently audited analytical accounting with a separation of the following service groups: (i) non-reserved services within universal service, (ii) any other service related to conveyance of postal items, and (iii) any other service not comprising the conveyance of postal items.

3. LICENSING AND THE PROPORTIONALITY PRINCIPLE

3.1 The EC Principle of Proportionality

As mentioned earlier, Article 9 of the current Directive is rather vague as regards conditions that might be attached to the granting of licenses by using wording such as 'if appropriate' and 'if necessary'. The precise significance of such terminology is unclear. Actually, guidance might be found in a review of the application and enforcement of the EC proportionality principle by the European Commission and the EC courts. We proceed with such a review in this section.

The establishment of authorization regimes falls within the Member States' discretion. However, the procedures, obligations and requirements established by the national licensing systems, to the extent that they are likely to hinder the exercise of the Community freedom and rights to provide services, are subject to a strict evaluation under the EC principle of proportionality. That is, any regulatory restrictions (requirements and conditions) shall be appropriate to guarantee the achievement of the intended objective and not exceed what is necessary in order to attain that objective ('less restrictive alternative' test).[22]

Member States in fact are entitled, on the basis of derogations contained in the EC Treaty,[23] to enact or maintain in force restrictive national measures that might interfere with the Community freedoms, provided that their justification complies with general EC law principles. Proportionality is one of these EC principles.

The notion of proportionality goes back to ancient times. It found only limited expression in the Treaty of Rome,[24] but it has been developed by the ECJ as a fundamental principle derived from the rule of law.[25] The ECJ has required that 'the individual should not have his freedom of action limited beyond the degree necessary in the public interest'.[26]

One of the most often quoted definitions of proportionality in Community law was the one given by the ECJ in its 1983 judgment in the *Fromançais* case.[27] According to this definition: 'in order to establish whether a provision of Community law is consonant with the principle of proportionality it is necessary to establish, in the first place, whether the means it employs to achieve the aim corresponds to the importance of the aim and, in the second place, whether they are necessary for its achievement'.

Later on,[28] the ECJ elaborated on the definition, including the sub-principle of suitability: 'the principle of proportionality (. . .) requires that measures adopted by Community institutions do not exceed the limits of what is appropriate and necessary in order to attain the objectives legitimately pursued by the legislation in question; when there is a choice between several appropriate measures recourse must be had to the least onerous, and disadvantages caused are not to be disproportionate to the aims pursued'.

Thus, the concept of proportionality entails some concept of balance and of a proper relationship between means and ends. In addition, it provides a criterion whereby the intensity of a specific action can be measured. Where proportionality is invoked in order to challenge the compatibility with Community law of national measures affecting one of the fundamental freedoms (e.g., freedom to provide services and freedom of establishment), the ECJ is called upon to balance a Community *vis-à-vis* a national interest. In this case, the principle is applied as a market integration mechanism that is based, at least in most cases, on the notion of 'necessity' exemplified by the 'less restrictive alternative' test. Therefore, licensing requirements that affect the fundamental freedoms of the EC Treaty will be found incompatible with Community law unless these are necessary to achieve a legitimate aim and provided that this aim cannot be achieved by other measures that are less restrictive of Community interests.

3.2 The Impact of the Proportionality Principle on Current Licensing Practices

The above country overview shows a significant variation in the level of detail in national regulatory frameworks (e.g., from very detailed in Bulgaria, Germany, Hungary and the UK to less detailed in France and Malta) and as to the set of applicable conditions. It is not always clear whether such conditions legitimately fall under the imprecise concepts of 'safeguarding universal service' or 'requirements concerning the quality, availability and performance' (Article 9 (2) of the Postal Directive).

The most problematic conditions appear to be those that are allegedly necessary to safeguard universal service and are vaguely defined by the Postal Directive: these shall pass the proportionality test. To facilitate the analysis, we have grouped the existing conditions and appraised their proportionality.

3.2.1 Conditions linked to universal service / quality of service

Some of the conditions linked to quality of the service obviously do not raise any doubts with respect to their legitimacy, as the Directive itself expressly mentions them. These include the obligation to have contract terms specifying the promised or agreed quality levels (e.g., standard levels for $D + x$ deliveries expressed in percentages delivered on time or agreed levels as specified in dedicated service level agreements) or the obligation to publish such performance in annual reports or through other media. Other examples of unproblematic conditions relate to the setting up of customer complaint procedures and the publication of complaint handling results and to the rules to be respected in a multi-operator environment, such as for wrongly addressed and wrongly delivered mail.

Similarly, conditions with respect to carrier identification on the mail items appear to be justified on quality grounds (e.g., customer information in a multi-operator environment).[29]

By contrast, some other criteria – for example, those required in Malta linked to the selection, vetting, training, provision of incentives to and disciplining of personnel and the security of buildings and vehicles – seem to go beyond the balanced solution mandated by the proportionality criterion. These requirements can hardly be justified on the ground of safeguarding the universal service.

Furthermore, it remains to be seen whether *ex-ante* regulatory approval of customer contract terms meets the proportionality test. For example, under Hungarian law, contract terms are subject to such approval and Bulgarian law requires that contract terms be previously discussed and coordinated with the regulator. It might be argued that these requirements exceed the limits of what is appropriate and necessary in order to attain the objectives legitimately pursued by the legislation in question.

3.2.2 Conditions linked to availability and performance

As to the conditions concerning availability and performance of services, it is worth mentioning, first, the Finnish licensing system. This imposes service obligations in terms of frequency of delivery (items of correspondence shall be distributed by all postal operators at least every working day). It also establishes a strong incentive (if not an absolute requirement) to reach a sufficient level of territorial coverage[30] to avoid a burdensome taxation on revenue (up to 20 percent). Hungary also establishes minimum coverage obligations, however, without a sanctioning mechanism based on taxation. The difference between the Finnish and the Hungarian systems is that the former allows a 'play territory up to the choice of the candidate' whereas the latter imposes an *ex-ante* minimum 'play territory to cover'. Both systems aim at preventing cream skimming and sharing the burden of the net cost of the universal service among market players. It is arguable whether the Finnish model goes beyond the aim pursued. The absence of competitors in the Finnish addressed letter mail segment might be a result of the design of the tax mechanism.

Instead, conditions linked to a minimum territorial 'play' remain justifiable in case of objective economical parameters,[31] such as the size of the country, mail volumes per capita, the urbanization ratio, and so on.

In general, criteria upon which regulatory authorities rely when considering whether to grant licenses are particularly vague and leave a fair margin of discretion in their hands. The commonly used language contains generic wording such as 'maintain technical and human resources suitable for fulfillment of the obligations inherent to this activity' or 'evidence of sufficient financial potential for performing the postal service (bank guarantee, fixed assets liquidity, . . .)', 'the technology described has to provide a high quality of the performance of the postal service' or 'the applicant should be in possession of the efficiency, reliability or specialized knowledge required to exercise the license rights'.

Furthermore, some Member States allow their regulatory authority to attach further unspecified license conditions. A good example is the discretionary power found in the Maltese Postal Act, previously mentioned: 'an individual license granted under this Act may include such conditions (whether relating to the postal services to which the individual license relates or otherwise) as appear to the Authority to be requisite or expedient having regard to the duties of the Authority and to the international obligations of Malta'. The proportionality of these measures appears to be open to challenge.

As to the conditions linked to accounting, most systems require a separation between licensed services and other services (e.g., Finland, Malta). It is our opinion that such requirements are proportional to the pursued aim; that is, the identification of a calculation basis for a compensation mechanism.

Finally, it is worth noting that Ecorys analyzed the licensing systems in Germany, UK and the Netherlands.[32] They concluded that the various license requirements in the countries under review do not constitute entry barriers, but are burdens that must be and can be overcome by new entrants marshalling their own efforts.

4. CONCLUSIONS

We examined the various licensing regimes in view of the proportionality criterion. Our analysis did not cover the barrier to entry aspect: the concept of entry barriers indeed plays an important role in a wide variety of competition matters because it is vital to the analysis of market power. The effects of entry barriers on competition and the issues they raise for policy makers require a separate study and will be something for future research.

As with the current Directive, the Proposed Directive fails to shed new light on the existing vague terms and remove their ambiguity. It remains unclear what the difference is between the expressions 'where appropriate' and 'if necessary' in Article 9 (2). Furthermore, it seems that the Proposed Directive allows Member States to enact licensing systems including 'universal service obligations' and 'service conditions concerning quality, availability and performance'. The exact scope and difference between these two sets of conditions calls for clarification to avert legal uncertainty.

Thus, at first sight, one may argue that the Proposed Directive reaffirms the status quo. However, recall that the Proposed Directive, at least in the version adopted by the European Commission on 18 October 2006, is meant to be applied in a fully opened market, where no place is left for reserved areas. Consequently, a broader category of services would be open for licensing. Not only the number but certainly also the types of licenses will increase. Licensing may become the real battlefront, the core issue of the EC internal postal market, as it constitutes a key tool for regulating market entry in a given market.

Today, the lack of certainty gives rise to a large range of licensing systems. In the future, it is reasonable to expect that the continued lack of certainty and stability will trigger litigation at both the national and the EC level. Clarification in this respect would be to the benefit of Member States and stakeholders alike. This clarification might be achieved through enhanced cooperation between regulators in order to share best practices and to promote harmonization of regulatory practices in the internal market. The existing Postal Directive Committee and the CERP (Committee of European Postal Regulators) can provide relevant input for the shaping of an appropriate soft-law instrument such as a Commission notice. In this respect, the Proposed Directive contains a provision (new Article 22) encouraging mutual assistance to facilitate application of the Directive.

The analysis of the existing regimes confirms that there is room for further clarification efforts as to the scope of services for which licensing regimes can be introduced or maintained. The wording 'services which are within the scope of the universal service' in the Postal Directive results in divergent interpretations. National legislation should provide clear boundaries for licensable services, and hence for services that either are or are not within the universal area. Some Member States already provide guidance on this, thereby placing express and courier services outside the scope of universal service. Germany has experienced litigation on whether a service should be considered as having higher quality than the universal service. Linked to this area of uncertainty is the need to clearly indicate what part of the postal value chain the license requirements pertain to (collection, transportation, sorting, distribution, mail consolidation, etc.).

Furthermore, it is our view that licensing regimes should contain explicit language to justify any requirement imposed in connection with essential requirements and the safeguard of universal service. Proper justification could be drawn from the array of policy options such as the need to increase competition, enhance consumer protection, maintain a high-quality universal service provision and ensure a social level playing field.[33]

NOTES

* This chapter only binds its authors and does not necessarily express the views of De Post NV – La Poste SA or Fratini Vergano (Brussels). Special thanks to Vanig Kasparian for review and comment on the draft text. The chapter has been finalized in June 2007 and does not take into account changes in the Proposed Directive following the ongoing co-decision procedure.

1. Directive 97/67/EC of the European Parliament and Council of 15 December 1997 on common rules for the development of the internal market of Community postal services and the improvement of quality of service (OJ L 15, 21.1.1998, p. 14), as amended by Directive 2002/39 of the European Parliament and of the Council of 10 June 2002 amending Directive 97/67/EC with regard to the further opening to competition of Community postal services (OJ L 176, 5.7.2002, p. 21).
2. Proposal for a Directive of the European Parliament and of the Council amending Directive 97/67/EC concerning the full accomplishment of the internal market of Community postal services COM (2006) 594 final.
3. Article 2 (14) of the Postal Directive: '(. . .) any permission setting out rights and obligations specific to the postal sector and allowing undertakings to provide postal services and, where applicable, to establish and/or operate postal networks for the provision of such services, in the form of a "general authorization" or individual license.'
4. Ibidem: '(. . .) authorization, regardless of whether it is regulated by a 'class license` or under general law and regardless of whether such regulation requires registration or declaration procedures, which does not require the undertaking concerned to obtain an explicit decision by the national regulatory authority before exercising the rights stemming from the authorization.'
5. Ibidem: 'authorization which is granted by a national regulatory authority and which gives an undertaking specific rights, or which subjects that undertaking's operations to specific obligations supplementing the general authorization where applicable, where the undertaking is not entitled to exercise the rights concerned until it has received the decision by the national regulatory authority.'
6. Article 9 (3) of the Postal Directive. The Commission Competition Notice further recalls that 'obligations should, as a general rule, be enforced within the framework of class licenses and declaration procedures by which operators of postal services supply their name, legal form, title and address as well as a short description of the services they offer to the public. Individual licensing should only be applied for specific postal services, where it is demonstrated that less restrictive procedures cannot ensure those objectives. Member States may be invited, on a case-by-case basis, to notify the measures they adopt to the Commission to enable it to assess their proportionality [. . .]. Member States should, in that event, ensure that the conditions set out in those procedures are transparent, objective, and without discriminatory effect, and that there is an efficient procedure of appealing to the courts against any refusal'.
7. Article 2 (19) of the Postal Directive.
8. Explanatory memorandum to the Proposed Directive, pp. 6–7.
9. SeeWIK-Consult (2006).
10. Law on postal services, prom. SG. 64/4 Aug 2000 as subsequently amended later on.
11. The Bulgarian legislation requires a description from the applicant concerning delivery times, measures for observing the confidentiality and reliability of postal services and a sketch showing the location of the places of access to the post network, the number thereof being in accordance with the consumers' needs. However, concrete guidance as to these requirements is not present in the regulatory framework.
12. Postal Services Act (313/2001, amendments up to 153/2005 included).
13. Act no. 708/1997 on the Fee Collected for Securing the Provision of Postal Services on Sparsely Populated Areas.

14. If one applies the density of the Netherlands to Finland, there should be a population of 148 million instead of 5 million.
15. Code des postes et des communications électroniques, Articles L. 3, L. 5-1, R. 1-2-1 to R. 1-2-8, décret no 2006-507 du 3 mai 2006; arrêté du 3 mai 2006, pris en application de l'article R. 1-2-6 du code des postes et des communications électroniques.
16. The Postal Act (PostG) published in *Federal Law Gazette*, 1997, Part I, p. 3294ff., entered into force on 1 January 1998. as amended by three Acts (*Federal Law Gazette*, 2001, Part I, p. 2271, *Federal Law Gazette*, 2002, Part I, p. 572 and *Federal Law Gazette*, 2002, Part I, p. 3218ff.).
17. Within the framework of incidental service contracts, it is also permissible to collect letters from several senders, pre-sorting them and then delivering them to DPAG letter mail centers (commercial consolidators need to file a partial service access application with DPAG).
18. Article 7 of Act 101 of 2003 on the post; government decree no. 68/2004 (IV. 15.) Korm. on the conditions of entry to the market of postal service providers. By virtue of the authorization granted in Article 53 (1) *b*) of Act 101 of 2003 on the Post.
19. That is, one of the following geographical areas: one or more municipalities other than cities; at least one county, with the exception of Pest County; Pest County plus at least one more county; Budapest and at least two counties (with the exception of Pest County) together; the whole country.
20. Postal Services Act 2000 (section 11), Code of Practice of Common Operational Procedures. Note that Postcomm is considering a review of the current licensing system.
21. Postal Services Act (Cap 254 of the Laws of Malta).
22. Case C-154/89, *Commission/France*, §15; Case C-198/89, *Commission/Greece*, §19.
23. For example, Articles 30, 39(3), 46 and 55 EC Treaty. The Court has ruled that all exceptions permitted by the above Treaty provisions must comply with the principle of proportionality. See, for example, Case 104/75, *De Peijper*, Case 36/75, *Rutili* and Case 203/80, *Casati*.
24. See now Article 5(3) EC. The case law has held that, among others, the following provisions incorporate proportionality standard: Articles 34(2), 134, 284 and those providing the derogations to the fundamental freedoms; that is, Articles 30, 39(3), 46, 55 EC.
25. Case 4/73, *Nodl/Commission*.
26. Case 11/70, *Internationale Handelsgesellschaft/Einfuhr und Vorratsstelle Getreide*.
27. Case 66/82, *Fromançais*. This definition was also used in Case C-118/89, *Lingenfelser* and Case C-155/89, *Philipp Bros*.
28. Case C-331/88, *Fedesa*; Cases C-133/93, 300/93 and 362/93, *Crispotoni*.
29. The license regulation in France requires the employees who distribute mail to wear a sign or logo identifying the postal operator 'in order to guarantee the calm in the private rooms where they enter into'.
30. The area needed to avoid taxation is, for example, Helsinki plus a couple of city centers.
31. A comprehensive overview of exogeneous parameters can be found in the study of PricewaterhouseCoopers (2006).
32. Ecorys (2005).
33. From the country analysis, it appears that currently only two national licensing schemes include conditions related to the social/employment environment. France imposes a national collective convention for employees and the German regulator can refuse a license if 'facts warrant the assumption that the applicant fails to a not inconsiderable extent to meet the basic working conditions common in the licensed sector'.

BIBLIOGRAPHY

Boston Consulting Group (2005), *Level Playing Field Indicator for Addressed Mail Markets in the Netherlands, Germany and the UK*, the Netherlands.

Copenhagen Economics (2005), *Economic Assessments of the Barriers to the Internal Market for Services: Final Report*, study for the European Commission, DG Internal Market, Copenhagen.

Craig, P. and G. De Búrca (2003), *EU Law – Text, Cases, and Materials*, Oxford: Oxford University Press.

de Bijl, P., P. van Damme and P. Larouche (2003), *Towards a Liberalised Postal Market*, Tilburg Law and Economics Center, the Netherlands.

Draganic, I. (quarterly 4/2006), *State Aid or Compensation for Extra Costs: Tuning the Test of Proportionality in EC Competition Law*, European State Aid Law, Berlin.

Ecorys (2005a), *Barriers to Competition in the German and UK Postal Market*, the Netherlands, p. 14.

Ecorys (2005b), *Study on the Development of Competition in the European Postal Sector*, the Netherlands.
Emiliou, N. (1996), *The Principle of Proportionality in European Law – a Comparative Study*, London: Kluwer Law International.
European Commission (2002), *Report on the State of the Internal Market for Services*, presented under the first stage of the Internal Market Strategy for Services, COM/2002/0441, Brussels.
European Commission (2006a), *Public Consultation on the Future of Postal Services*, http://ec.europa.eu/internal_market/post/consultations_en.htm, Brussels.
European Commission (2006b), *Report to the Council and the European Parliament on the Application of the Postal Directive*, third application report, COM/2006/595 final, Brussels.
High Level Group chaired by D. Mandelkern (2001), *Mandelkern Group on Better Regulation: Final Report*, study for European Council, Brussels.
Moriarity, R. and P. Smith (2005), 'Barriers to entry in post and regulatory responses', in M. Crew and P. Kleindorfer (eds), *Regulatory and Economic Challenges in the Postal and Delivery Sector*, Boston, MA: Kluwer Academic Publishers.
NERA Economic Consulting (2006), *Review of Boston Consulting Group Analysis of Entry Barriers to National Postal Markets Using 'Level Playing Field' Indicator*, London.
PricewaterhouseCoopers (2006), *The impact on Universal Service of the Full Market Accomplishment of the Postal Internal Market in 2009, Brussels.*
Tridimas, T. (2006), *The General Principles of EU Law*, Oxford: Oxford University Press.
WIK-Consult (2005), *Study on the Evolution of the Regulatory Model for European Postal Services*, Bad-Honnef.
WIK-Consult (2006), *Main developments in the postal sector* (2004–2006), pp. 69–77.

20. Waiting for 'Rowland Hill' – elements of reform of postal services in Sub-Saharan Africa*

José Ansón and Joëlle Toledano

1. INTRODUCTION

Mail communication in Sub-Saharan Africa (SSA) struggles to maintain even its current extremely low level. While only 3.4 postal items per capita are exchanged on average in SSA (2004), receivers must pay an annual fee equivalent to 56 stamps for receiving mail through the exclusive P.O. Box delivery system chosen by most SSA countries.

Once structural factors such as literacy and the youth of the population were taken into account, no statistically significant relationship was found between the level of mail and income per capita in low income countries in one of our recent studies (Ansón et al., 2006). The purpose of this research is to shed light on the determinants that hinder postal development in SSA.

A survey of postal delivery in SSA (Ansón and Toledano, 2007) was organized so as to get detailed insights on the organization of postal delivery that could ease the understanding of postal markets in SSA. Economic theory – two-sided markets theories (e.g., Rochet and Tirole, 2003; Armstrong, 2006), and a dynamic panel econometric estimation *à la* Arellano and Bond (1991) – supports the insights arising from the survey.

It is puzzling to notice that while network infrastructure is steadily expanding in SSA (Estache and Goicoechea, 2005), postal communication and networks are not so doing. It is somewhat puzzling that the postal infrastructure barely benefits from increasing access to other infrastructure services, such as water, telecommunications, electricity or transportation.

The chapter shows that the value of postal services in SSA is reduced for utilities and other firms in the segment of businesses-to-customers (B2C) communication, due to actual recipients' costs and low quality of service. Designated postal operators are failing to develop B2C mail services since most potential addressees cannot afford the charge for renting a P.O. Box, which in turn prevents the development of positive indirect network externalities on postal traffics. It is then econometrically shown that a move towards free delivery should be undertaken, since sufficiently positive club effects could enable the compensation of the loss of P.O. Box revenue by a large enough traffic increase, provided that a sufficiently high quality of service is ensured.

The chapter is organized as follows. Section 2 covers the main results of the survey in three blocks: the delivery network, the pricing of postal and delivery services, and the trust in the designated postal operators. Then Section 3 presents a two-sided markets economic analysis of SSA postal markets. A dynamic panel econometric estimation showing a strong consistency with the survey results and the two-sided markets analysis follows in Section 4. Section 5 concludes. A Technical Appendix provides more details of the dynamic panel econometric estimation.

2. SURVEY OF POSTAL DELIVERY IN SUB-SAHARAN AFRICA

2.1 Organization of the Survey

The survey (Ansón and Toledano, 2007) was organized during winter 2006, so that information was gathered in four areas: the geography of the country; the delivery network with respect to its organization and costs; the prices of postal services relative to basic goods; and the postal market environment, with a focus on big mailers and the level of competition.

As for geography, questions were raised at four hierarchical layers: the most populated city of the country, the second most populated city of the country, the third most populated city of the country, and the rest of the country; that is, less populated cities and rural areas.

Various dimensions of the delivery network were covered. The purpose was to get a better knowledge of the level of access offered to postal services as well as the organization of the networks and its relevant costs.

A questionnaire was built to serve as a basis for personal interviews of Sub-Saharan postal administrations. Interviews were conducted either by phone or directly. Responses were analyzed and categorized to provide a view of the best, worst and median (average) case for each issue. Countries' comments, reactions and suggestions were acknowledged. Further anecdotal evidence was gathered by the authors through three field missions in Benin, Malawi and Niger.

2.2 Coverage of the Survey

Twenty-six out of a total of 47 SSA countries participated in the survey, and provided first-hand information about the organization of their postal delivery system. A vast majority of them (21 of the 26) belong to the group of least developed countries using the United Nations ECOSOC definition. Twenty-five countries are also classified as low-income countries by the World Bank.

The gross domestic product (GDP) per capita reaches an average of US$667 within the group of participating countries. In terms of economic production, the surveyed countries account for 72 percent of the overall GDP of SSA countries. The population is, on average, 17.3 million inhabitants per surveyed country, and the country's land area average is 641 000 square kilometers. Our sample represents 64 percent of the overall population of SSA countries.

In terms of postal specific indicators, the countries participating in the survey account for 91 percent of the total domestic mail volumes in SSA countries.

2.2.1 A focus on low-income countries

The Universal Postal Union's postal statistics for the low-income SSA countries in the sample show a traffic per capita varying from 0.01 to 2.9 domestic letters per capita. One must understand that the average share of literate adults in the population is only 33 percent. This in turn represents the average share of potential postal users in low-income SSA countries. Once we take into account each country's literacy rate, the volumes per potential postal user vary from 0.02 to 5.9 domestic letters.

In terms of network coverage, the number of inhabitants per post office ranges from 25 433 to 421 340 in our sample of low-income SSA countries, for an average of 93 000 (the distribution of this statistic being skewed to the left).

2.3 Results: the Postal Delivery Network

The delivery network has been studied at four geographical levels as shown by summary Table 20.1: the most populated city of a SSA country where 9.3 percent of the population lives at the median, the second most populated city where 2.5 percent of the population lives at the median, the third most populated city where 1.2 percent of the population lives at the median, and the rest of country where 82.5 percent of the population lives at the median. The geographical layer named as 'Rest of the country' encompasses small and medium-sized cities as well as rural areas.

Table 20.1 The postal delivery network

	Most populated city	Second most populated city	Third most populated city	Rest of the country (smaller cities and rural)
Median share of the population living in	9.3% (2.9–22.3%)	2.5% (0.3–8.1%)	1.2% (0.2–5.1%)	82.5% (73.3–95.4%)
Median number of inhabitants per P.O. Box in	67.4 (8.5–281.4)	107.2 (12.8–2 046)	136.2 (15.2–849.6)	1554.9 (11.5–14 378.3)
Median share of total P.O. Boxes placed in	53.1% (14.6–83.6%)	6.7% (1.2–26.1%)	3.5% (1.5–12.1%)	32.0% (10.7–78.7%)
Median number of inhabitants per post in	100 000 (23 250–186 065)	77 077 (3 979–800 000)	57 500 (3 518–666 666)	151 222 (13 574–604 551)
Median share of total post offices placed in	10.1% (2.2–74.0%)	2.9% (0.5–21.7%)	1.9% (0.2–14.7%)	80.8% (23.0–95.0%)
Median number of inhabitants per postman	79 730 (5 440–244 171)	176 580 (1 968–365 533)	70 000 (1 568–515 723)	n/a
Posts/private MO operators	0.24	0.42	0.72	6.45

Note: Minimum and maximum values are indicated between parentheses below the median values for 25 low-income SSA countries.

Data source: UPU 2006 Survey of Postal Delivery in SSA.

When one examines the geographical distribution of the postal delivery network, one can notice that access to postal delivery, in terms of reception, tends to be low, and is geographically unbalanced. This is because, out of 26 SSA countries, 24 countries have chosen to mostly deliver into P.O. Boxes. Only two have free home delivery as their main delivery mode; only 32 percent of the countries offer partial home delivery; and when home delivery exists, the median number of inhabitants per postman varies from 70 000 to 176 580 across the four geographical levels (most populated city, second most populated city, third most populated city, and the rest of the country). So there is low delivery coverage of the population in terms of letter-post reception, with 50 percent of SSA countries above 297 inhabitants per P.O. Box.

Furthermore, P.O. Boxes, which must be rented for receiving mail, are not distributed proportionally to the population of the various cities and regions in most SSA countries. More than half of the total P.O. Boxes of a country are concentrated in the most populated city at the median. The median number of inhabitants per P.O. Box ranges from 67.4 in the most populated city, with a median share of total population of 9.3 percent, to 1554.9 in smaller cities and rural areas where, at the median, 82.5 percent of the population lives. The econometric study of Section 3 will examine why the expansion of the delivery network through P.O. Boxes has not helped develop postal traffic in SSA over time.

Unlike P.O. Boxes, post offices and counters are distributed proportionally to the population of the various cities and regions in most SSA countries: at the median, 13 percent of the country's population actually living in the three main cities benefits from 14.9 percent of total post offices, while 82.5 percent of the country's population living in smaller cites and rural areas can access 80.2 percent of total post offices. This is a remarkably well-distributed network with respect to the access to counters. However, access could still be further improved, since the median number of inhabitants per post office ranges between 57 500 and 100 000 in the three most populated cities and up to 151 222 in smaller cities and rural areas. Eventually, compared to private networks such as money order transfer networks (MO operators), the postal network offers a much denser access in less populated cities (i.e., beyond the three most populated cities of a country) and rural areas (see the last line in Table 20.1).

2.4 Results: Pricing of Basic Postal and Delivery Services

Table 20.2 provides a summary of the survey results for the pricing of postal services in SSA. Prices for postal service can be compared to prices of basic goods and services, such as one kilogram of bread, of rice, or of meat, or one minute of mobile telephony (i.e., air time). The comparisons lead to the conclusion that the price for sending a first weight step letter is usually very affordable in SSA. At the median, it corresponds to the price paid for 0.21 kg of bread, 0.33 kg of rice, and 0.10 kg of meat, respectively, and exactly one minute of cellular phone call.

However, renting a P.O. Box is much less affordable. P.O. Box prices were compared to the price for sending a letter as well as to the aforementioned basic goods and services. At the median, the P.O. Box annual rental fee is equivalent to sending 56.3 letters or buying 13.3 kg of bread, 19.7 kg of rice, or 6.2 kg of meat. It costs almost the equivalent of one hour of mobile telephony. When one takes into account SSA's citizens' habits of consuming goods and services that have a very low cost per unit purchased, due to their severe

Table 20.2 The pricing of postal and delivery services

	Median service price relative to bread price (1 kg)	Median service price relative to rice price (1 kg)	Median service price relative to meat price (1 kg)	Median service price relative to air time price (one-minute call)	Median service price relative to the price for sending a letter by the post
Sending a first weight step letter	0.21 (0.04–1.75)	0.33 (0.07–1.25)	0.10 (0.01–1.00)	1.00 (0.27–7.14)	1.00
Renting a P.O. Box (annual fee)	13.3 (2.5–73.9)	19.7 (4.3–80.3)	6.2 (0.7–50.0)	57.3 (32.1–275.0)	56.3 (19.3–334.6)
Exchanging one letter (i.e., sender + addressee overall charge)	0.54 (0.07–8.14)	0.69 (0.12–11.01)	0.25 (0.02–2.75)	1.76 (0.52–23.67)	–
Receiving a 'self-delivered' letter (e.g., a utility bill)	0	0	0	0	0
Competitor's price for sending a letter (i.e., at the charge of the sender)	1.11 (0.11–6.06)	3.33 (0.11–5.61)	1.00 (0.05–1.16)	8.75 (1.33–25.00)	7.5 (1.0–50.0)
Competitor's price for receiving a letter (i.e., at the charge of the addressee)	0	0	0	0	0

Note: Minimum and maximum values are indicated between parentheses below the median values for 25 low-income SSA countries.

Data source: UPU 2006 Survey of Postal Delivery in SSA.

short-run financial constraints, the usual requirement of paying P.O. Box rental fees by means of a single yearly payment further reduces the affordability of accessing postal delivery services.

Once the overall transaction price is computed for a mail exchange, the apparent affordability of the letter-post is very much reduced. For example, the cost for a domestic letter exchange is equivalent to 0.54 kg of bread instead of 0.21 kg paid by the sender only, once both prices for sending and receiving a letter-post item are taken into account together. So the affordability of letter-post services is more apparent than real in SSA.

Interestingly, designated postal operators' competitors in the domestic letter-post market never charge the addressee but only the sender in SSA. Likewise, firms delivering their own mail to customers never charge the addressee for delivering items. Competitors' prices are, however, much higher for sending a letter than the designated postal operators' rates. At the median in SSA, the competitors charge the sender 7.5 times as much as the designated postal operator.

2.5 Results: Trust in Designated Postal Operators

The survey indirectly assessed the postal customers' trust in SSA designated postal operators. Self-delivery, illegal competition, and higher competitors' prices could provide signals of public distrust towards the designated postal operator.

As far as utilities are concerned, seven out of ten utility companies deliver their mail themselves in SSA: this is the case for 87 percent of the electricity companies, 86 percent of the water companies, and 33 percent of the telecommunications companies. Utilities' firms also collect payment for their bills in 94 percent of the cases. As far as the financial sector is concerned, 24 percent of the banks do not contract the designated postal operators to deliver their mail.

Illegal competition was found in all countries participating to the survey. In terms of pricing, as already shown before, 50 percent of the competitors, either legal or not, charge more than 7.5 times the price of the designated postal operator.

All these results tend to suggest that clients do not fully trust designated postal operators in SSA countries. The econometric results of Section 4 are fully consistent with these survey results.

3. TWO-SIDED MARKETS ANALYSIS AND CLUB EFFECTS: AN APPLICATION TO POSTAL DELIVERY NETWORKS IN SSA

It is worth highlighting the fact that pricing of postal services is an old debate in many countries. For a long time, addressees were charged for the mail they received according to the distance covered by mail from the origin to the destination. This was true for most European and North American countries, until Rowland Hill's reform in Great Britain introduced the principle of a delivery free of charge for the addressee in the first half of the 19th century (e.g., Crew and Kleindorfer, 1991). Generalized in 1840, the Penny Post faced lower and lower financial losses year after year, until the service became profitable in 1852. The reform was extensively followed by other countries; the sender became the only party to be charged for any exchange of letters. However, the issue of knowing who pays for a mail exchange has been periodically opened and discussed in a number of countries that have adopted free delivery – yet so far none of them has decided to come back to a model where the addressee is either charged for usage or access. Exceptions are to be found in SSA, where several countries gave up free delivery and established a paying P.O. Box delivery mode.

Besides postal history, economic theory also brings important insights to this debate. Although very recent and in continuous development, two-sided markets economic theories can help shed light on the current underlying mechanisms behind the functioning of today's SSA postal markets.

The main result of the two-sided markets literature (e.g., Rochet and Tirole, 2003; Armstrong, 2006) is that each side participating in a common exchange platform (herein the postal communication platform) is not charged according to the costs it respectively triggers. There could be a number of reasons why one side of the platform could be charged in a different manner. If one side is more sensitive to price variations than another, it could then well be that the side with the highest price-elasticity is charged relatively less compared to the other, or even not at all. It could also well be that if one side triggers a positive externality on the participation of the other – that is, attracts the participation of the other – then again, this side would benefit from relatively lower prices. Following the same logic and approach, one could also wonder whether reducing transaction costs could be another reason for charging one side while not charging the other.

On SSA postal markets, too little is known with respect to the two sides' reactions to price variations (i.e., the reaction of senders to the stamp price and of the addressee to the P.O. Box rental fee). Therefore little can be said with respect to the impact of price-elasticity on two-sided pricing. Yet it is worth noticing that almost all studies estimating price-elasticity for sending mail on monopolistic postal markets in ICs have not only found values lower than one, but very often much lower than one (Fève et al., 2006). Furthermore, while receiving mail into a P.O. Box, and thus renting it, is a choice in ICs (e.g., for a firm willing to be delivered earlier or to benefit from other value-added services), this is not the case in SSA, where renting a P.O. Box is a *de facto* obligation to receive letter-post items. So reactions to price variations could be very different on ICs and SSAs' postal markets in this regard.

While only very little can be said in terms of price-elasticity, this is not so in terms of inter-group externalities and transactions costs on SSA postal markets. Regarding inter-group externalities, the development of postal B2C communication requires a very high number of addressees to be reachable. One must keep in mind that B2C is the segment with the best prospects in terms of postal traffic growth for SSA countries. Businesses, and particularly utilities in SSA, need to be able to communicate with an increasing number of customers. They need to reach more citizens in order to help their markets grow. When these customers are not reachable through the designated postal operators, they do not hesitate to organize their own delivery network for reaching them – and they are able to do so, as the results of the survey show. The fact that these businesses are ready to bear extra costs for organizing delivery is also probably indicative of a low sensitivity to price variations for sending letter-post items to their customers, provided that the quality of service is high enough. This is likely to be untrue for the business-to-business (B2B) postal market segment: B2B is less likely to be sharply impacted by inter-group externalities due to the 'closed club' communication between businesses.

With respect to transactions costs, a large number of addressees in SSA are facing very tight budget constraints in the short run, which in turn prevent them from renting a P.O. Box. The lack of human resources for managing complex pricing schemes probably further increases the real impact of the actual transactions costs on SSA postal markets.

So examining whether the addressee could be free of any charge for receiving mail is both consistent with the expected inter-group externalities related to the development of the B2C segment and the reduction of transactions costs for citizens with highly constrained budgets.

Should inter-group externalities be developed and transactions costs reduced, one would expect postal traffic to increase due to the potential for indirect network externalities in SSA, which are also referred to as club effects. This issue did not attract much attention in the postal economics literature developed for industrialized countries (ICs), because all potential addressees are covered by postal delivery services in the developed world. Therefore, giving access to delivery to a potential addressee is considered as granted in ICs. As highlighted by the survey, this is not the case in SSA. Only a very limited share of the potential addressees is reachable by the letter-post, and thus makes the postal network less attractive at use. In SSA, there is little doubt that significant potential exists for the development of club effects through a much larger access of citizens to postal delivery. Section 4 econometrically estimates these club effects, and shows how they could in turn sustain a move towards free delivery.

3.1 Designated Postal Operators and Competitors in SSA: Two Opposite Pricing Strategies Leading to Postal Exclusion

The survey results particularly outline the different pricing strategies respectively applied by the designated postal operators, and their competitors. Interestingly, the literature on competition on two-sided markets provides theoretical foundations for the existence of this kind of market equilibrium (e.g., Rochet and Tirole, 2003; Armstrong, 2006). Most notably, these models point out the possible negative welfare effect that could be triggered by this competitive equilibrium.

The reality of the SSA postal markets turns out to reflect these theoretical propositions very well. On the one hand, the designated postal operators usually charge any addressee for receiving a letter-post item by asking a relatively high fee for renting a P.O. Box, while sending an item remains affordable. On the other hand, the designated postal operators' competitors never charge the addressee for delivering an item, but apply very high rates to the sender. This corresponds to a situation where one of the operators supplies postal services applying a high access charge to the delivery network (i.e. the designated public operator through the P.O. Box rental), whilst the others pursue the opposite strategy of charging relatively high transactions fees for the usage of the delivery network (e.g., the bus company transporting letter-post items). In practice, customers who cannot access a P.O. Box are thus receiving their letters, flats, packets, and parcels through the networks of designated postal operators' competitors, or are using other more informal delivery channels.

The end result of the current state of competition in SSA postal markets is that a large share of the population in SSA is excluded from the mail communication markets, either because they cannot afford the P.O. Box supplied by the designated postal operator or due to the very high tariff the sender must pay to competitors. Unlike in industrialized countries, with very few exceptions, universal service cannot be actually supplied in the current market conditions of SSA countries.

4. FREE DELIVERY AND CLUB EFFECTS

From the economic analysis insights provided in Section 3, it follows that freeing the addressee of any charge for receiving mail would reduce transactions costs, and further foster the development of the inter-group externalities necessary for a sustainable growth of B2C postal traffic. Yet an empirical question remains open: Would the development of a club effect have a large enough quantitative impact on postal traffic to sustain a move towards free delivery in SSA? Or in other words, would revenue streams generated by the increased postal traffic compensate for the revenue loss resulting if P.O. Boxes, or other delivery points, were offered for free?

In order to tackle this concern, the possible effect of greater access to delivery on the volumes of mail must be assessed. To do so, the evolution of domestic and international incoming letter-post traffic in response to an increased access to the delivery network through P.O. Boxes is modeled using the dynamic panel approach of Arellano and Bond (1991). The details of the econometric analysis implementation, as well as complementary results, are provided in the Technical Appendix. The most important econometric estimation results regarding the dynamics that network externalities trigger on postal traffic development over time are directly provided in the following paragraphs.

The short- and long-run effects of an increase in the number of delivery points – that is, P.O. Boxes in most of SSA – on postal traffic development are computed using an unbalanced panel of 32 SSA countries over a 26-year time period (1980–2005). In order to enable a better assessment of the club effect dynamics, the cumulated and marginal effects of an increase in P.O. Boxes on the volumes of mail are computed over five periods using the econometric results provided in the Technical Appendix. Figure 20.1 presents the results for domestic mail: the dashed line represents the cumulative effects of one new P.O. Box on total domestic mail volumes, and the plain line traces its marginal effects.

Except for the first period, short- and long-run effects are statistically significant for domestic mail. As shown in Figure 20.1, statistically significant marginal effects vary from a marginal increase of 70 domestic letter-post items in the short run due to a marginal P.O. Box to a marginal decrease of 227 domestic letter-post items in the medium term and the long run. Relatively similar results are found in the long run for international incoming mail, as shown in the Appendix.

As for the pricing of postal services, the econometric results help shed light on the logic applied for setting the prices that the sender and the addressee are, respectively, paying for an exchange of mail in SSA. Figure 20.2 compares the time-varying marginal effect of a supplementary P.O. Box on total domestic volumes over five years to the current SSA median annual price for renting a P.O. Box in terms of first weight step letters. In other words, it thus compares the real increase in terms of letters due to one more P.O. Box to the current real price of a P.O. Box in terms of letters. The interest of this exercise is the following: should the increase in domestic mail volumes due to one more P.O. Box be

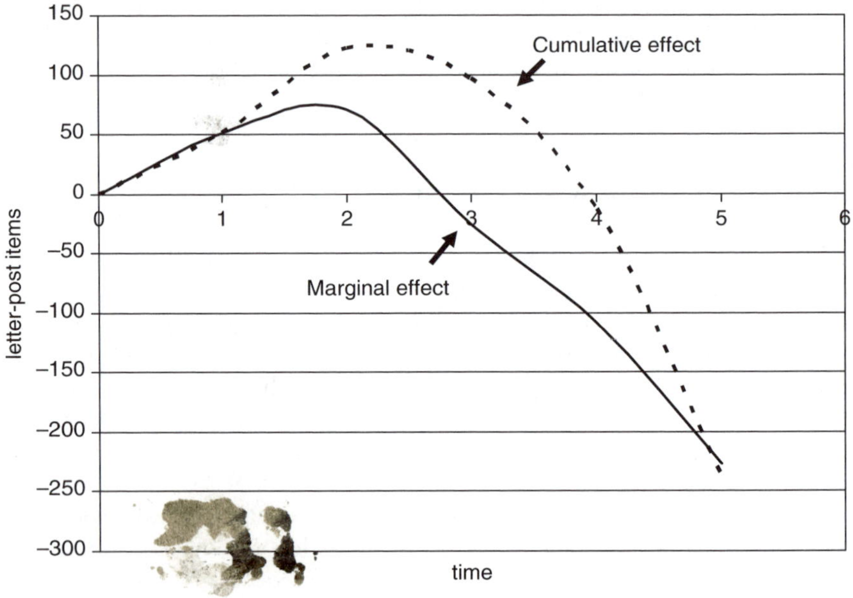

Figure 20.1 *GMM estimation* à la *Arellano and Bond of the cumulative and marginal effects of a P.O. Box on total domestic mail volumes over five periods*

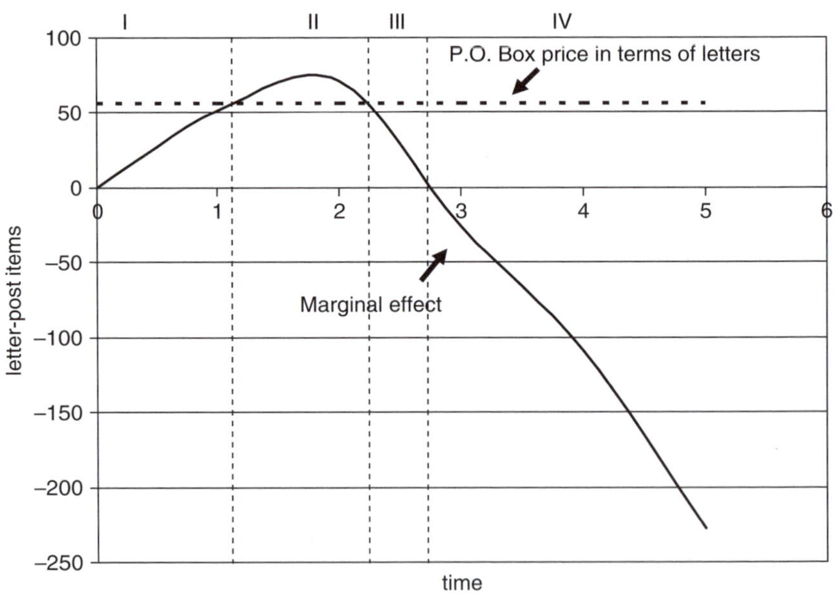

Figure 20.2 *The real price of P.O.Boxes versus real marginal variations in mail volumes*

higher than the current price equivalent of this P.O. Box in terms of letters, then this one more delivery P.O. Box could be offered for free. The club effect would thus enable a move towards free delivery.

As obtained in the 2006 survey of postal delivery in SSA presented at Section 2, the current median price for renting a P.O. Box is the equivalent of 56 first weight step letters (or 56 stamps, if one assumes one stamp for a basic letter). Four different phases can thus be noticed in Figure 20.2; in phase I, the marginal effect of one more P.O. Box in terms of total letters exchanged is lower than the current price, in terms of letters, asked for renting this supplementary P.O. Box; in phase II, the marginal effect of one more P.O. Box in terms of total letters exchanged is higher than the current price for renting a Box; in phase III, the marginal effect of a P.O. Box in terms of letters is again lower than the current price for renting a Box, as was already the case in phase I; eventually, in phase IV, not only is the marginal effect of a P.O. Box on the domestic traffic lower than the current rental fee of a P.O. Box in terms of letters, but the marginal effect of a P.O. Box increase has now become negative.

In two-sided markets such as the postal market, the transactions costs triggered by charging both the sender and the addressee in a context of people on severely constrained budgets, as in SSA, are very likely to limit the number of participants in the postal platform (i.e. the senders and the addressees in our case). So in order to foster participation in the postal communication platform and in postal traffic development in SSA, could those transactions costs be reduced by charging only one side: the sender? Should it be so, inter-group externalities could further feed B2C traffic increases.

The four phases in Figure 20.2 help answer this question. Since the marginal effect of a P.O. Box in terms of letter-post traffic increase in phase II is higher than the current real price of a supplementary P.O. Box in terms of letters, the real price for renting a P.O. Box could be set to zero: marginal free delivery could arise in this phase. This is not the case in phase I, and financial support by the government may be needed in this transition phase where statistically significant positive club effects do not appear. Unfortunately, phases III and IV very quickly emerge. In phase III, the increase in traffic no longer covers the current real price of a P.O. Box, which jeopardizes any move towards free delivery. In phase IV, the situation is even worse, since the marginal decrease in postal traffic is likely to be compensated by an increase of P.O. Box real prices, closing a vicious circle where expanding access to delivery into initially paying P.O. Boxes eventually leads to even more expensive delivery for addressees compared to the initial situation. Anecdotal evidence tends to confirm this analysis, with losses in postal volumes compensated by P.O. Box price increases. Therefore, a sustainable introduction of free delivery – that is, a time-consistent affordable pricing policy – requires phases III and IV to be avoided, so that the benefits of positive club effects could be harvested in freeing the addressee of any charge for receipt of mail.

How could phases III and IV be avoided? Answering this question requires us to understand what is likely to trigger the puzzling negative club effects in the long run, as depicted in the above three figures. What is the rationale for an increase in access to delivery to lead to lower levels of postal traffic than initially?

Research often focuses on network positive externalities; negative network externalities are barely considered. In SSA postal context, however, the possible existence of negative network externalities makes great sense at some point. Although an increase in the number of P.O. Boxes fosters the overall development of domestic letter-post in the short run by attracting more and more senders – for example, utilities and banks – this can also quickly create bottlenecks in the postal process due to insufficient quality of service (e.g., if the postal process cannot absorb the increasing volumes of mail). Those bottlenecks then trigger negative boomerang effects on postal volumes in the medium term and the long run. These boomerang effects are even stronger for the public postal operator, since unsatisfied customers have more and more access to unlicensed competitors, and do not hesitate to organize their own self-delivery networks. Furthermore, the principle of using a P.O. Box as a delivery technology could also represent a bottleneck in itself should the P.O. Box be shared among many people, or should the recipient ignore, as is usually the case, that mail was delivered to his P.O. Box. The quality of service provided by a P.O. Box delivery system will also suffer from these weaknesses.

Our econometric results on potential negative externalities are, for instance, consistent with the current low utilization of the designated postal operators by most utilities companies in SSA, as revealed by the survey. In spite of higher and higher access to utilities for SSA's citizens, the increase in P.O. Boxes provided by many designated postal operators has not proven to be a sensible solution for answering utilities' needs in terms of the delivery of bills, and thus they retain this key segment of postal traffic, with self-delivery of bills by utilities companies remaining the dominant mode of bill delivery. With negative indirect network externalities on postal volumes in the long run, the current prospects for B2C traffic development by most of the current designated postal operators in SSA are not good.

The above results strongly suggest that, in terms of policy timing, a reform providing for significant increases in access to free delivery first requires a sufficiently dimensioned network in terms of size in order to allow increasing traffic volumes to be processed smoothly over the postal chain and enable a high enough quality of service. Otherwise, the short-run benefits of an increase in terms of access to delivery would be quickly overturned in the medium term and the long run due to severe bottlenecks. This also implies that it is preferable to have management accountability for revenue and volume development targeting a five- rather than a two-year period, in order to provide managers with incentives which are aligned on the right time-horizon.

5. CONCLUSION

The survey of postal delivery in SSA (Ansón and Toledano, 2007) provides important insights into the organization of SSA postal markets: P.O. Boxes are used as the main mode for delivery, which is not free of charge for the recipient. Large mailers such as utilities companies are unsatisfied with the service offered by the actual designated postal operators, and tend to organize their own delivery networks.

The chapter suggests that any reform approach should consist of implementing delivery free of charge for the recipient. Interestingly, this approach is already apparent in Rowland Hill's famous reform pamphlet of 1837, as discussed in Crew and Kleindorfer (1991). Previously to Hill's proposal, both senders and recipients were charged for any exchange of mail, usually according to the distance covered from the origin to the destination. Importantly, Hill also noted that there would be significant costs associated with final free delivery in certain areas. He therefore argued that his original Penny Post proposal apply only for 'post town to post town'; that is, for free delivery to some central location (e.g., the post office) in each town. Final distribution (which he referred to as 'secondary distribution') was to be left in the hands of local districts.

Rowland Hill's proposal has nevertheless been progressively extended beyond its original scope, and home delivery free of charge for the recipient became universal over the years in Great Britain, as well as in other industrializing countries in the 19th century.

Like the reform proposed by Rowland Hill in the 19th century in Great Britain, a reform of postal delivery in SSA towards delivery free of charge for the recipient could dramatically change the evolution of their postal markets. While Rowland Hill justified his reform proposal in terms of costs, this chapter shows that postal service can be viewed as a club good, where externalities suggest cross-subsidization of recipients by senders, namely free delivery. Once a well-enough dimensioned postal network offering a good quality of service is provided, the value of postal services increases in the absence of recipients' costs.

In order to remedy the problems that poor quality and high recipient cost have in reducing the value of postal service in SSA, as shown in this chapter, any reform approach consistent with Rowland Hill's revolution should implement free delivery, although the detailed implementation of it must be worked out, and may vary according to the geographical areas to be served. In this regard, little can be learnt from the Rowland Hill experience in terms of detailed reform implementation in Great Britain, since the geography and organization of the economy may well be different between Great Britain in the 19th century and SSA countries today. Yet one could easily have the sense that today's value of postal service is higher the nearer it is to the final recipient, due to B2C postal delivery demand such as billing.

Adapting Rowland Hill's revolution to SSA countries conditions today may consist of allowing a controlled expansion of free delivery, with control on quality so that congestion does not undermine the value of the service as volume increases in response to price decreases for recipients. The biggest challenge for adapting Rowland Hill's proposal is probably the choice of delivery points. While a more centralized delivery system, such as delivery into satellite free P.O. Boxes (e.g., the recent experience in Israel), could dramatically reduce delivery costs, this offering would also represent a step back for B2C large mailers and recipients, which are already provided with home bill delivery in most SSA largest cities. There is thus a tradeoff between the cost saved by centralized delivery points and the value of postal services in terms of delivery proximity. This tradeoff requires further local studies in order to achieve a balanced solution where maintaining the value of postal services does not trigger unbearable costs, but also where controlling costs does not jeopardize the present and future value of postal services, where B2C senders' needs must be fulfilled. Mixed solutions with free home delivery in the largest cities and low-cost areas, and satellite free P.O. Boxes delivery in the high-cost and rural areas, could also be assessed.

NOTE

* The views expressed here are those of the authors and should not be attributed to the institutions to which they are affiliated. We are grateful to Michael Crew and Paul Kleindorfer for very helpful suggestions during

the revision process. We are also grateful to the Universal Postal Union's staff for all comments and suggestions during the writing of this article, particularly to Edouard Dayan, Won-Ja Lee, Claude Defoundoux, Nathalie Chemineau, Laurent Boncoungou, Nils Clotteau, Ricardo Guilherme, and Matthieu Boillat.

REFERENCES

Ansón, J. and J. Toledano (2007), 'Survey of postal delivery in Sub-Saharan Africa: final report', mimeo, Bern: Universal Postal Union.

Ansón, J., R. Cuadra, A. Lindares, G. Ronderos and J. Toledano (2006), 'First steps towards new postal economics models for developing countries: learning from the Latin American experience', in Michael A. Crew and Paul R. Kleindorfer (eds), *Liberalization of the Postal and Delivery Sector*, Cheltenham, UK and Northampton, MA, USA: Edward Elgar, pp. 217–36.

Arellano, M. and S. Bond (1991), 'Some tests of specification for panel data: Monte Carlo evidence and an application to employment equations', *Review of Economic Studies*, **58**, 277–97.

Armstrong, M. (2006), 'Competition in two-sided markets', *RAND Journal of Economics*, **37**(3), 668–91.

Crew, Michael A. and Paul R. Kleindorfer (1991), 'Rowland Hill's contribution as an economist', in Michael A. Crew and Paul R. Kleindorfer (eds), *Competition and Innovation in Postal Services*, Boston, MA: Kluwer Academic Publishers, pp. 1–11.

Estache, A. and M.A. Goicoechea (2005), 'A research database on infrastructure economic performance', World Bank Policy Working Paper 3643.

Fève, F., J.-P. Florens and S. Richard (2006), 'Microeconomic demand modelling for price elasticities', in Michael A. Crew and Paul R. Kleindorfer (eds), *Liberalization of the Postal and Delivery Sector*, Cheltenham, UK and Northampton, MA, USA: Edward Elgar, pp. 357–68.

Rochet, J.-C. and J. Tirole (2003), 'Platform competition in two-sided market', *Journal of the European Economic Association*, **1**(4), 990–1029.

Universal Postal Union (1980–2005), Postal Statistics, Bern.

TECHNICAL APPENDIX

This is the first time in postal economics that the Arellano and Bond (1991) GMM dynamic panel econometric estimation method has been applied. This enables us to track the cumulated and marginal effects of variations in the number of P.O. Boxes and post offices on traffic over five years after a change. The numbers of P.O. Boxes and post offices are treated as endogenous covariates in the econometric estimation.

Domestic and international incoming traffics, respectively denoted n and w, are modeled by means of a dynamic econometric setting *à la* Arellano and Bond (1991). That is,

$$n_{it}=an_{i,t-1}+\mathbf{x}_{it}\boldsymbol{b}+v_i+e_{it}, \quad i=1,\ldots,31, \quad t\in 1980,\ldots,2005, \qquad (20A.1)$$

$$w_{it}=cw_{i,t-1}+\mathbf{y}_{it}\boldsymbol{d}+u_i+\varepsilon_{it}, \quad i=1,\ldots,32, \quad t\in 1980,\ldots,2005. \qquad (20A.2)$$

$\mathbf{x}_{it}$ and $\mathbf{y}_{it}$ are vectors of covariates, which include the number of P.O. Boxes p_{it} and post offices o_{it} in the domestic mail equation (20A.1) but only P.O. Boxes p_{it} in the international incoming mail equation (20A.2); a and c are parameters to be estimated, $\boldsymbol{b}$ and $\boldsymbol{d}$ are vectors of coefficients to be estimated, v_i and u_i the random effects that are independent and identically distributed over the panels, and e_{it} and ε_{it} the error terms. Index i represents countries and t years.

In order to use the Arellano and Bond (1991) dynamic panel-data estimator, the first differences for equations (20A.1) and (20A.2) are derived. This implies that any time-invariant fixed effect is removed: so are time-invariant measurement errors and omitted variables effects. The generalized method-of-moments can then be applied. No second-order autocorrelation in the first-differenced idiosyncratic errors is assumed. This assumption will be tested below following Arellano and Bond's seminal paper (1991).

P.O. Boxes p_{it} and post offices o_{it} are suspected to be endogenous (e.g. P.O. Boxes may depend upon their rental fees and postal rates) in that $E[p_{it}\, e_{it}] \neq 0$, $E[o_{it}\, e_{it}] \neq 0$ for $s \leq t$ but $E[p_{it}\, e_{it}] = 0$, $E[o_{it}\, e_{it}] = 0$ for $s > t$ in equation (20A.1), and $E[p_{it}\, \varepsilon_{it}] \neq 0$ for $s \leq t$ but $E[p_{it}\, \varepsilon_{it}] = 0$ for $s > t$ in equation (20A.2). Therefore, on top of the country population h_{it}, levels of the endogenous variables p_{it} and o_{it} lagged up to five periods serve as instruments.

Econometric estimations results are presented in Table 20.3. First, the statistical validity of the econometric model must be checked. The Arellano and Bond (1991) underlying assumption of no second-order autocorrelation in the first-differenced idiosyncratic errors is met, as shown by the values for the AR(1) and AR(2) tests. The Sargan test of overidentifying restrictions also confirms a sound choice of instruments. Once the validity of the econometric model is confirmed by AR(1), AR(2), and the Sargan tests, the results can be interpreted.

For international incoming mail, short-run effects are not statistically significant. As shown in Figure 20.3, statistically significant marginal effects in response to a supplementary P.O. Box vary from a marginal decrease of 78 international incoming letter-post items in the third period ('medium term') to a marginal decrease of 169 international incoming letter-post items in the fifth period ('long run').

Unlike domestic letter-post, where a few senders are trying to reach many addressees at a time (e.g., B2C), international letter-post incoming to SSA is more likely to consist of

Table 20.3 Dynamic unbalanced panel econometric estimation results

	Domestic mail (1)	International mail (2)
Lagged one domestic mail	0.3773** (0.0243)	
Lagged one international mail		0.7635** (0.0310)
P.O. Boxes		
First difference	92.34* (36.98)	98.58** (25.03)
Lagged one	−41.36 (47.46)	−52.78 (33.50)
Lagged two	70.81 (49.52)	−7.39 (30.98)
Lagged three	−25.65 (48.25)	−78.03** (15.20)
Lagged four	−108.65* (42.54)	15.34 (9.85)
Lagged five	−227.18** (34.18)	−169.58** (18.70)
Post offices		
First difference	3 007.27 (10 761.90)	
Lagged one	−17 258.30 (13 510.89)	
Lagged two	−4 063.78 (12 943.89)	
Lagged three	−5 221.55 (13 388.12)	
Lagged four	2 586.37 (13 951.50)	
Lagged five	−2 128.64 (11 813.25)	
Constant	84 711.64 (146 680.50)	
Observations	269	266
Sargan test	463.63	313.14
AR(1) test	−3.01	−7.07
AR(2) test	0.31	0.44

Note: ** and *, respectively, denotes 1% and 5% statistical significance levels; standard errors between parentheses below coefficients.

Data source: UPU Postal Statistics.

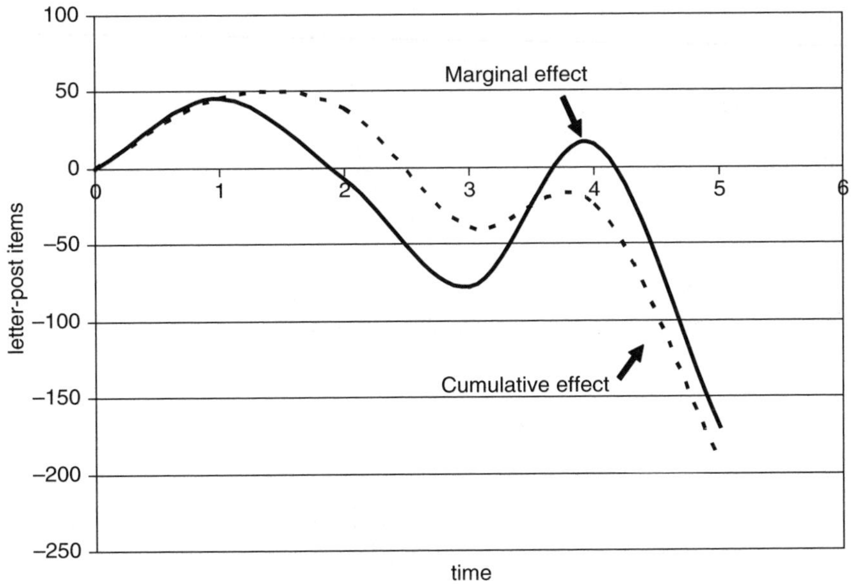

Figure 20.3 *GMM estimation* à la *Arellano and Bond of the cumulative and marginal effects of a P.O. Box on international incoming mail over five periods*

many foreign senders trying to reach rather few addressees at a time. So there is a less obvious case for the development of a positive club effect. Yet the bottlenecks triggered by the higher network attractiveness for domestic purposes following an increase in the number of P.O. Boxes also affect negatively the evolution of international mail exchanges in the long run. This is an *a priori* unexpected perverse effect of expanding access to mail delivery in SSA under the current conditions.

PART VI

Accounting and Cost

21. Are there economies of scale in mail processing? Getting the answers from a large-but-dirty sample*

Lawrence Fenster, Diane Monaco, Edward S. Pearsall and Spyros Xenakis

1. INTRODUCTION

In this chapter we present econometric evidence that United States Postal Service (USPS) mail processing plants are mostly operated at levels where the returns to density and scale are decreasing. The evidence is derived from production functions fit as stochastic switching regressions to large panel samples of pieces, work hours, capital usage, delivery points, delivery units and other plant-level information mostly drawn from USPS's Management Operating Data System (MODS). Decreasing returns were found for production functions defined for every aggregate of pieces handled by shape, for pieces fed in most single automated, mechanical and manual processes, and when piece-handlings were divided into inbound and outbound sub-streams.

Samples drawn from MODS are problematic because they exhibit anomalies at frequencies suggesting that they are a dirty mix of good observations and occasional reporting mistakes. Our econometrics employs a Maximum Likelihood (ML) estimator for fitting a two-regime stochastic switching regression model as first proposed by Quandt (1972). The motivation for this approach is that the good observations are generated by the production function, while the bad observations are the result of data collection failures consistent with a different regime.

Our estimates indicate that mail processing is primarily an industrial process rather than a network support activity. Returns to scale typically exceed returns to density. This result is anomalous for an activity like transportation that directly supports a distribution network, but it is readily explained for an industrial process as the effect of production smoothing. USPS plants serving larger and more diverse segments of the network apparently benefit from longer continuous flows of mail through the plants.

Our results also show that scale is only one of many statistically significant determinants of productivity among USPS processing plants. Other determinants include the types of delivery points served by a plant, the composition of the mail stream passing through the plant, the ratio of originating to destinating mail in a plant's service area, the configuration of related equipment/processes and the skill profile of a plant's work force.

2. MAIL PROCESSING

USPS plants process mail in separate outgoing and incoming streams for letters and cards, flats, parcels and Priority Mail.[1] Outgoing mail is cancelled, barcoded and sorted for transportation to other processing centers or for insertion into the local incoming stream. Incoming mail is sorted at least to the carrier-route level. Most incoming letter mail is further sorted to the delivery sequence on the routes. Workshared mail is inserted at various points in the processing streams. Processing of letters and flats, and some processing of parcels and Priority Mail, is now largely done with automated and/or mechanized equipment that is specialized by shape. Manual processing is reserved for pieces that either cannot be fed to automated equipment or have been rejected by the automated processes.

Mail processing is typically viewed as a network support activity; first, because sorting the mail is essential for moving it along the USPS network and, second, because processing plants are located at hubs of the network and serve as transshipment points. In testimony before the US Postal Regulatory Commission (PRC), the principal USPS witness compared mail processing to transportation along the network (Bozzo, 2006).

However, there is an alternative way to view mail processing that describes the activity as a conventional industrial process. In this alternative view, mail processing plants are like generating plants on an electrical network. A generating plant is certainly affected by activity on the network, but its output is solely measured by the power it produces. The number of customers or the geographic area served by the electrical network are not considered outputs of the plant. A similar view of mail processing would confine the measures of a plant's output to the volumes and shapes of mail processed. The levels of network variables, such as the number of delivery points and the number of delivery units served by the plant, may have important effects on a plant's productivity, but are not included among the plant's outputs. This view conforms well to the cost model used by USPS and the PRC in postal rate proceedings. The cost model treats mail processing costs as separable by shape with a single driver – piece handlings.

The distinction between mail processing as a network activity and as an industrial process is important because the two views lead to divergent predictions of the effects of expanding the network on the productivity of a plant.

When treated as additions to output, more delivery points and delivery units would lead to a decrease in the volume of mail that is processed by a fixed work force and complement of equipment at a plant. This happens when additional runs are needed to sort to more divisions. Then, more piece handlings are required to sort a given volume of mail. Expanding the network may also disproportionately increase the setup and teardown times for processing runs, especially with automated equipment. For example, more bins would have to be set up and cleared at the beginning and end of each run to sort the same volume of mail.

Both of these effects are likely to be small. The processing schemes used by USPS plants all involve fixed integer numbers of passes through the machines. For example, delivery sequence sorting of letters is mostly done in two passes through the Distribution Bar Code Sorting (DBCS) machines. New delivery points or delivery units are usually accommodated by increasing the number of utilized bins rather than by increasing the number of passes and piece handlings. Adding bins increases setup and teardown time.

But this time is only a small fraction, typically less than 10 percent, of the total time for a processing run.

When mail processing is viewed as an industrial process whose output cannot be stored, the network output variables indirectly represent the limitations on continuous operations imposed by a plant's schedule of arrivals and dispatches. The productivity of electric generating plants improves when the plants are connected to larger networks by the expansion of power grids. Productivity improves because the plants can generate electricity at efficient levels over longer continuous periods of time. Mail processing is also done most efficiently in plants where the various processes can be conducted almost continuously with few interruptions. When production is interrupted, the inevitable result is a decline in productivity due to the temporary forced idleness of both labor and capital.

USPS plants serving larger and more diverse segments of the network are often the beneficiaries of smoother flows of mail through the plant. Mail processing can be more efficient in these plants because the various processes can be conducted in longer uninterrupted runs. A plant serving a small number of delivery points and delivery units will find it hard to schedule arrivals and dispatches to create a continuous flow of pieces through the plant. As the number of delivery points and delivery units grows, it becomes possible (up to a point) to smooth the schedule so that the same volumes pass through the plant over longer uninterrupted periods of time. This can be done by deferring the processing of incoming mail to delivery units that are nearby and to routes, such as suburban residential routes, where deliveries are made later in the day.

Mail processing has aspects of both a network support activity and an industrial process, so the controlling aspect must be ascertained empirically.

3. RETURNS TO DENSITY AND SCALE

For distribution networks it is customary to distinguish between returns to density, which describe the effects of changing inputs proportionately with the network fixed, and returns to scale, which describe the effects with the network variable. Returns to density and scale as defined for the USPS network directly relate to current issues of costing and plant consolidation.

Returns to density and scale in mail processing have been investigated for more than 30 years, with conflicting results. In specific density/scale studies and in studies that have attempted to develop cost-based rates in USPS postal rate proceedings before the PRC, both increasing and decreasing returns have been found.[2]

Beginning in 1997, USPS has presented econometric studies in five successive rate proceedings to support the contention that mail processing labor variabilities are less than 100 percent (US Postal Rate Commission, 1998, 2001, 2002, 2006; US Postal Regulatory Commission, 2007). This evidence has been rejected by the PRC, which continues to use variabilities close to 100 percent based on an assumption that work hours vary mostly in proportion to volumes processed.

Labor variability is defined as the derived demand elasticity of labor with respect to pieces fed or handled in various processing operations. The importance of the variability estimates for US rate-setting is that they are used to derive the marginal costs of processing, which form part of the per unit attributable costs of the various subclasses of mail.

These unit attributable costs have been legislated as rate floors for most subclasses. Marginal costs are also essential components of the Ramsey pricing formulas for welfare-maximizing rates. However, the PRC does not rely upon the formulas for recommending rates.

Variabilities are not the same thing as returns to density or scale, but the concepts are closely related. Variabilities of less than 100 percent are likely to accompany increasing returns to density; decreasing returns to density signal that variabilities exceed 100 percent.

In 2006, USPS sought PRC approval of the models and methods of analysis used in ongoing studies of possible restructurings of its network (US Postal Rate Commission, 2006). The cost functions for these models describe marginal costs for mail processing that decline in steps to approximate the same less-than-100-percent variabilities rejected by the PRC in rate proceedings. The importance of the variability estimates for the USPS network studies is that the declining marginal cost functions will drive the results towards restructurings that consolidate processing plants. This occurs because the cost of processing a given volume of mail, as predicted by the USPS's cost functions, always decreases when consolidation leaves the network with fewer but larger plants.

4. THE MODS DATA

We derive process- and shape-level economies of density and scale from restricted translog production functions fit to panel samples aggregated from MODS.[3] The samples consist of quarterly observations from GFY 1999 to GFY 2005 of man-hours (HRS), total pieces fed (TPF), total pieces handled (TPH) and first-handled pieces (FHP) for various manual and machine-specific operations by shape (letters, flats and parcels) at up to 368 USPS processing plants. The MODS data has been supplemented by capital indices (QICAP) derived from USPS equipment registries and facility records, and by other plant statistics drawn from USPS records by Bozzo, including the numbers of various kinds of delivery points (DP) and delivery units (DU) served by the plant. The MODS data have also been matched to volume statistics from other USPS sources for the areas served. Altogether, the data set includes several alternative measures of processing outputs, matching observations for work hours, capital services and network coverage, and enough information to fashion controls for mail flow composition, plant and process configuration, labor force composition and the distribution of delivery points by type to support econometric modeling of production functions by shape and by process.

In releasing the MODS data, USPS has followed the practice of not providing any information that could be used to specifically identify individual plants. This makes it impossible to supplement the MODS observations with information that could be used to fashion a complete and unambiguous set of controls for exogenous factors affecting processing productivities. Among the factors for which we have no direct controls are the quality of the local postal labor force, the geographic dimensions and demographic characteristics of a plant's service area, the proximity of the delivery units served by the plant, the condition of the local ground transportation system, the plant's air and ground connections, the smoothness (or lack of smoothness) of the plant's arrival and dispatch schedules, the age of the plant, its classification by type, its square foot area, number of floors and other salient physical characteristics. These are major omissions. Nevertheless, the basic MODS observations of piece handlings and work hours have been supplemented by Bozzo with enough plant-level information to allow us to define variables that indirectly control for most of the major factors that exogenously affect productivity.

The MODS data includes work hours and labor costs for several broad Labor Distribution Code (LDC) categories from which nominal labor rates may be derived. However, these nominal rates cannot be converted to real rates, because a local wage or cost-of-living index cannot be associated with the plants without identifying them. The MODS data also contains no information whatsoever that might be used to derive real rental rates for the different categories of equipment and other capital used in the plants. These omissions are not important for fitting production functions, but are serious handicaps when the MODS data are used to fit cost functions or derived demand functions.[4]

Panel samples drawn from MODS are large but known to be dirty because of the methods used to collect the data. MODS is a real-time USPS reporting system with weak quality controls at the point of collection and no mechanism for identifying and recovering missing observations. The missing observations are indistinguishable from observations that are truly zero-valued. The MODS data are collected by work shift and aggregated in stages by week, accounting period and postal quarter, with missing observations treated as zero values at each stage. HRS is subject to various kinds of clocking errors made by employees that mis-assign work hours to processes. QICAP is derived from USPS equipment inventory registries. The major difficulty with these records is that equipment changes are sometimes registered at times that do not correspond exactly to when the equipment actually entered or left service. The other explanatory variables in the data set appear to be much less likely to contain major errors than HRS and QICAP. However, it is still possible that errors in the other variables may cause some of the data to be bad.

Large-but-dirty samples are an increasingly common result of self-collection schemes using electronic equipment. The amount of data that can be collected cheaply by these schemes is often enormous. MODS is typical. The samples we have extracted often contain over 8000 observations. Unfortunately, the practice that makes self-collection cheap is an absence of review and verification as the data are collected. Inevitably, the samples produced by such schemes contain bad observations because self-collection is prone to occasional undetected malfunctions.[5]

The observations of HRS, TPF (or TPH) and FHP for the various processes all contain apparent errors and anomalies that have been described and documented in recent PRC Decisions (US Postal Rate Commission, 1998, 2001, 2002, 2006). The anomalies mostly consist of unrealistic extreme values for TPF/HRS, occasional incompatible values for TPF, TPH and FHP, and missing values for either HRS or TPF (or TPH) but not both. The anomalies are more frequent for processes that are starting up or shutting down at a plant. The patterns suggest that the bad data in the samples are the result of intermittent reporting mistakes.

Bozzo (2006) and Roberts (2006) have attempted to deal with the dirty data by using screens to delete the grossly erroneous observations and, in some cases, by applying an Instrumental Variables (IV) estimator. Both approaches require auxiliary assumptions and non-sample information. Bozzo's screens remove observations from the samples used to fit his equations at frequencies that range from about 0.7 percent to over 20.0 percent. The screens cannot identify and remove all of the bad data in the samples without also non-randomly deleting good data.[6] This risks creating selection biases in the screened sample. Nevertheless, the screens (but not the IV estimator) are compatible with an assumption that the bad data are intermittent. We have not screened the MODS data for our work except to remove observations when the information needed to construct the variables of the production function is incomplete.

5. THE STOCHASTIC SWITCHING REGRESSION MODEL

Our research employs a Maximum Likelihood (ML) estimator to fit two-regime linear stochastic switching regressions with exogenous fixed-probability independent switching.[7] The ML estimator relies only on sample information. The estimates are consistent, asymptotically normal with a known variance–covariance matrix, and asymptotically efficient under general regularity conditions as described in standard statistics and econometrics texts (Wilkes, 1962; Maddala, 1977; Judge et al., 1985).

Linear stochastic switching regressions are a natural choice for modeling large-but-dirty samples that contain an unknown mix of 'bad' and 'good' observations. Bad observations are defined as observations that are not generated by the same linear equation with the same standard error as the more numerous good observations. Ordinary Least Squares (OLS) estimates of the production functions will be inconsistent when the good and bad equations are different if any bad data remains after screening or if the screens non-randomly remove any good data. However, the ML estimator for the stochastic switching model makes it unnecessary to identify and delete bad observations from the sample. Instead, the ML estimates allow us to compute a set of conditional probabilities, one for each observation in the sample, that correspond to the Bayesian posterior probabilities that the observations are bad (or good).

Many of the kinds of problems that are known to cause OLS estimates to be inconsistent may be viewed as the result of samples generated by an observationally equivalent linear model. In Pearsall (2007) it is shown that outliers, replaced observations and errors-in-variables can all be treated as dirty data from an observationally equivalent linear model. The essential aspect of the bad observations for the ML estimator is that they are intermittent in the sample.

In our applications the good observations are assumed to be generated by the translog production function whose parameters and standard error correctly describe the normal operation of USPS processing plants. The bad observations are assumed to be generated by a different linear equation with the same form and variables.

The ML estimator yields estimates for the coefficients and standard errors of the equations for both the bad and good observations, and an estimate of the frequency of the bad data. The estimates were computed using a special-purpose algorithm embedded as a macro in a set of Lotus 1-2-3 worksheets.[8] The algorithm uses the first-order conditions for a maximum of the log-likelihood function within an iterative process to simplify and speed the calculation of the estimates. The method for computing the asymptotic variance–covariance matrix is described in Judge et al. (1985) and Maddala (1976). The conditional probabilities have been computed and are used to estimate sample means for the good observations in the MODS samples. The sample means and the parameter estimates from the good equations are used together to calculate elasticities.

6. THE PRODUCTION FUNCTIONS

Shape-level production functions were fit for letter, flat and parcel sorting operations and for letter cancellation operations. Process-level production functions were fit for automated, mechanized and manual sorting and cancellation operations. Separate production functions were also fit for the inbound and outbound components of the letter and flats sorting operations both by shape and by process.

The processes are identified by the equipment they use:

1. Letter Sorting: Mail Processing Bar Code Sorters (MPBCS), Distribution Bar Code Sorters (DBCS), Optical Character Readers (OCR) and Manual Letter Sorting.
2. Flats Sorting: Flats Sorting Machine 881 (FSM 881), Flats Sorting Machine 1000 (FSM 1000), Automated Flats Sorting Machine (AFSM 100) and Manual Flats Sorting.
3. Cancellation: Advanced Facer Canceller Machine (AFCS) and Non-AFCS Cancellation.
4. Parcels Sorting: Small Parcel Bar Code Sorter Other that Priority Mail (SPBS Other), Small Parcel Bar Code Sorter Priority Mail (SPBS Priority), Manual Parcels Other than Priority Mail and Priority Mail.

The same general equation form was used for the production functions for the shape-level and process-level models. The fitted equations are translogs with respect to the labor and capital inputs and measures of the network served by the plant. The translog was chosen because it is a general form that imposes few structural restrictions on the shape of the fitted production functions. In addition, the equations include sets of other controls to account for exogenous factors affecting the productivity of the plants. These factors are the season of the year, a productivity trend, the distribution of delivery points by type, the composition of the mail stream for the applicable shape, the ratio of originating to destinating mail volume for the shape, the availability of equipment and processes at the plant, and the skill profile of the plant's labor force.

The dependent variables of the regression equations are natural logarithms of pieces fed or handled as follows:

ln(FHP) – the aggregate of first-handled pieces for the shape-level sorting operations;
ln(TPH) – total pieces handled for shape-level cancellations;
ln(TPF) – total pieces fed for automated and mechanized sorting processes; and
ln(TPH) – for manual sorting and cancellation processes.

The MODS data are aggregated to postal quarters of unequal length so weekly averages of the pieces handled (FHP, TPF and TPH), work hours (HRS), and the capital services indices (QICAP) were calculated and used in the regressions. The data for work hours in MODS exactly match the data for piece handlings, but the capital indices constructed by Bozzo match only approximately.[9] Two measures of the size of the distribution network assigned to the plants are used in the production functions. These are the total number of delivery points (DP) in the plant's service area, and the total number of delivery units (DU) assigned to the plant.

The translog component of the production function is as follows:

$$\alpha + \beta_l \ln(\text{HRS}) + \beta_k \ln(\text{QICAP}) + \beta_p \ln(\text{DP}) + \beta_u \ln(\text{DU})$$
$$+ \ln(\text{HRS})\,[\beta_{ll} \ln(\text{HRS}) + \beta_{lk} \ln(\text{QICAP}) + \beta_{lp} \ln(\text{DP}) + \beta_{lu} \ln(\text{DU})]$$
$$+ \ln(\text{QICAP})\,[\beta_{kk} \ln(\text{QICAP}) + \beta_{kp} \ln(\text{DP}) + \beta_{ku} \ln(\text{DU})]$$
$$+ \ln(\text{DP})\,[\beta_{pp} \ln(\text{DP}) + \beta_{pu} \ln(\text{DU})] + \beta_{uu} \ln(\text{DU}) \ln(\text{DU}).$$

We have defined sets of additional control variables for most of the information that has been matched to the MODS data. The added controls are as follows:

1. *Dummy variables for postal quarters 1, 2 and 3*. These controls represent systematic seasonal variations in productivities due to changes in address quality, work force composition, arrival/dispatch schedules, and so on.
2. *An annual trend*. The mid-quarter time in years from the beginning of the first quarter of GFY 1999. This variable captures the effects of gradual progressive changes in productivity associated with the adaptation of improved technology and changes in the education or training of the work force.
3. *Delivery point shares*. The fraction of DP consisting of various types of delivery points: CURB – city kerb delivery points, NDCBU – city box units, CENT – city central delivery points, OTHER – other city delivery points, RB – rural boxes, HCT – highway contract delivery points, and POBOX – possible P.O. Box deliveries. All except the share for OTHER are included in every equation.
4. *Mail subclass and worksharing shares*. The shares of originating, destinating or total volume by selected subclasses and worksharing categories for the mail shape (letters, flats or parcels) for the territories served by each plant. Shares of total mail for the shapes by Revenue, Pieces and Weight (RPW) category have been computed from USPS volumes passing through the plants. The shares are included in the production functions except for the share of single-piece first-class letters and flats, and the combined share of first-class and priority parcels to account for the effects of the composition of the mail stream on productivity.
5. *ln(origin/destination)*. The natural logarithm of the ratio of originating to destinating volume for the mail shape. The ratio is computed from volume data rather than from piece handlings, to avoid including the equation error in the calculation of the ratio.
6. *Shape dummy variables*. Shape dummy variables for parcels, Priority Mail and/or cancellation were included in many of the equations. These dummies are set to one in plant/quarters for which TPH for all processes involving these shapes are zero. The shape dummies are included in the production functions as a means of identifying the type of processing plant.
7. *Process dummy variables*. Process dummy variables were defined for all of the automated and mechanized machine types. These dummies are set to one for a process under the following two conditions: (1) the plant handles mail of the associated shape, and (2) TPH is zero for the machine type in the plant/quarter. These variables identify the machine types that are missing or inactive in each plant/quarter. The production functions include those process dummy variables that are appropriate for the shape of mail, but omit the dummy for the process itself. The process dummies represent the equipment configuration at the plant for the shape.

8. *Labor skill shares*. The MODS data has been supplemented with plant-level work hours in five LDC categories: Automated letters sorting, Mechanized flats sorting, Mechanized parcels sorting, Manual sorting and Allied labor. This data was used to compute work force shares. Two of these share variables are included in each of the equations to represent the skill distribution of the plant's work force.

7. ESTIMATES OF RETURNS TO DENSITY AND SCALE

We calculate returns to density and scale by summing output elasticities with respect to HRS, QICAP, DP and DU. For our translog production functions these elasticities are linear functions of ln(HRS), ln(QICAP), ln(DP) and ln(DU) that employ the ML estimates of the coefficients for the good equations. The following formulas express returns to density and scale as elasticities of FHP, TPF or TPH with respect to proportionate changes in the input and network variables:

Returns to density: $E_l + E_k = \partial \ln(\text{FHP})/\partial \ln(\text{HRS}) + \partial \ln(\text{FHP})/\partial \ln(\text{QICAP})$.

Returns to scale:[10] $\dfrac{E_l + E_k}{1 - E_p - E_u} = \dfrac{\partial \ln(\text{FHP})/\partial \ln(\text{HRS}) + \partial \ln(\text{FHP})/\partial \ln(\text{QICAP})}{1 - \partial \ln(\text{FHP})/\partial \ln(\text{DP}) - \partial \ln(\text{FHP})/\partial \ln(\text{DU})}$.

For the process-level equations, TPF or TPH appear in the formulas in place of FHP. The elasticities in the formulas are derived from the coefficients of the translog production functions as follows:

$$
\begin{aligned}
E_l &= \beta_l + 2.0\beta_{ll} \ln(\text{HRS}) + \beta_{lk} \ln(\text{QICAP}) + \beta_{lp} \ln(\text{DP}) + \beta_{lu} \ln(\text{DU}),\\
E_k &= \beta_k + \beta_{lk} \ln(\text{HRS}) + 2.0\, \beta_{kk} \ln(\text{QICAP}) + \beta_{kp} \ln(\text{DP}) + \beta_{ku} \ln(\text{DU}),\\
E_p &= \beta_p + \beta_{lp} \ln(\text{HRS}) + \beta_{kp} \ln(\text{QICAP}) + 2.0\, \beta_{pp} \ln(\text{DP}) + \beta_{pu} \ln(\text{DU}),\\
E_u &= \beta_u + \beta_{lu} \ln(\text{HRS}) + \beta_{ku} \ln(\text{QICAP}) + \beta_{pu} \ln(\text{DP}) + 2.0\, \beta_{uu} \ln(\text{DU}).
\end{aligned}
$$

We can see from the formulas that returns to density and scale at a plant will depend somewhat on the levels of HRS, QICAP, DP and DU during the quarter.

Table 21.1 displays returns to density and scale computed using the sample means for ln(HRS), ln(QICAP), ln(DP) and ln(DU) for the good data in the samples. Increasing returns to density and scale correspond to estimates in Table 21.1 that are greater than one; constant returns correspond to estimates that are equal to one; and, decreasing returns to density and scale correspond to estimates that are less than one. Also shown in Table 21.1 are *t*-values for large sample one-tail tests under the null hypothesis that returns to density and scale are constant. The formula for returns to density is a linear function of the estimated parameters of the translog equations, so its standard deviations can be calculated in the usual way from the asymptotic variance–covariance matrix of the ML estimates.[11] For returns to scale the *t*-values are computed with DP and DU treated as controls. The *t*-values are the differences of the estimates from one divided by their asymptotic standard deviations.

Estimates are shown in Table 21.1 for all of the shape- and process-level production functions that we have fit to samples drawn from MODS. Most of our estimated returns

Table 21.1 Returns to density and scale

Mail shape or process	Returns to density		Returns to scale		Plants ≥ 1		Labor variabilities (%)		
	Estimate	*t*-value	Estimate	*t*-value	Density (%)	Scale (%)	Capital fixed	Fixed input proportions	Expansion path
Shape (first handled pieces, all processes)									
All letters	0.7350	48.114	0.9051	20.537	0.33	15.00	196.35	136.06	103.82
Letters inbound	0.6924	49.096	0.9193	13.901	0.33	14.97	204.63	144.44	105.20
Letters outbound	0.5608	91.469	0.8198	22.743	0.00	5.64	249.72	178.32	143.86
All flats	0.7032	42.561	0.8485	23.892	0.04	1.50	157.86	142.20	147.92
Flats inbound	0.6448	49.349	0.8256	26.406	0.00	0.60	171.78	155.10	139.49
Flats outbound	0.5936	62.087	0.9013	7.261	0.04	13.24	177.58	168.48	172.79
All cancellation	0.3829	93.442	0.9144	6.717	0.00	43.63	566.35	261.15	231.77
All parcels and Priority Mail	0.8128	19.655	0.9307	5.958	0.87	16.85	125.61	123.04	115.80
Letter sorting process (total pieces fed or handled)									
MPBCS total	0.8889	11.747	0.8897	9.588	4.77	10.64	136.10	112.50	104.99
MPBCS inbound	0.8512	18.067	0.8720	10.929	7.50	8.19	132.73	117.49	106.53
MPBCS outbound	0.7744	26.380	0.8908	4.295	9.87	25.43	133.16	129.13	132.07
DBCS total	0.8023	42.418	0.9394	13.797	0.41	14.77	178.84	124.64	233.47
DBCS inbound	0.7648	47.083	0.9238	15.421	1.11	13.86	189.36	130.76	259.87
DBCS outbound	0.6246	78.923	1.0302	−2.736	0.00	62.91	176.37	160.11	193.17
OCR total	0.7285	38.357	0.9429	6.271	2.64	31.22	202.99	137.27	93.89
OCR inbound	0.5677	54.748	0.8432	8.113	0.32	0.59	221.30	176.14	129.43
OCR outbound	0.6508	59.036	0.9361	5.524	2.01	43.38	208.63	153.65	111.11
Manual letters total	0.7377	29.199	0.8024	21.524	0.00	0.00	140.53	135.55	136.34
Manual letters inbound	0.7045	28.175	0.8171	15.052	0.00	0.11	146.59	141.95	141.43
Manual letters outbound	0.6750	29.960	0.8336	12.664	0.04	0.31	164.04	148.14	155.39

Flat sorting process (total pieces fed or handled)									
FSM881 total	0.8741	14.234	0.9292	6.845	4.74	8.80	131.80	114.40	106.40
FSM881 inbound	0.8469	17.228	0.9068	8.432	0.47	3.88	131.69	118.08	112.44
FSM881 outbound	0.8864	13.982	0.9775	1.364	8.98	38.54	120.19	112.81	112.64
FSM1000 total	1.0581	−5.678	0.9296	8.055	68.65	24.74	126.90	94.51	68.18
FSM1000 inbound	0.9553	4.659	0.9263	7.165	37.69	30.01	147.45	104.68	64.74
FSM1000 outbound	0.8354	21.477	0.8863	8.386	5.01	31.53	131.43	119.70	104.37
AFSM100 total	0.8551	23.169	0.9151	14.416	0.29	0.43	124.92	116.95	112.18
AFSM100 inbound	0.8508	20.049	0.9126	11.704	0.81	1.05	127.84	117.53	111.41
AFSM100 outbound	0.6947	40.311	0.9290	3.948	0.14	27.46	126.22	143.95	127.92
Manual flats total	0.9397	6.035	0.8472	15.265	0.00	2.64	109.02	106.42	106.56
Manual flats inbound	0.9225	7.869	0.8500	14.937	7.40	2.44	109.03	108.40	107.71
Manual flats outbound	0.9747	1.401	0.8338	8.848	38.50	0.11	114.44	102.59	104.58
Cancellation process (total pieces handled)									
AFCS total	0.4607	75.787	1.0461	−3.797	0.23	67.07	452.91	217.07	209.49
Non-AFCS	0.2882	50.283	0.5799	12.769	0.00	0.01	440.19	347.04	340.68
Parcels process (total pieces fed or handled)									
SPBS total	0.7875	25.110	0.9695	2.992	0.48	31.84	139.61	126.98	121.28
SPBS other	0.7984	24.730	0.9886	1.020	0.00	42.18	138.57	125.25	119.65
SPBS Priority Mail	0.8162	10.420	1.1882	−4.877	6.76	66.32	122.08	122.52	121.83
Manual parcels	0.5047	19.862	0.4852	17.897	0.06	0.00	204.61	198.13	204.72
Priority Mail	0.8094	8.909	0.8772	4.649	3.57	12.14	120.96	123.54	125.48

to density and scale are less than one at confidence levels that exceed 99 percent. In fact, the majority of the t-values are so high that there is virtually no chance that returns to either density or scale could actually exceed one for any of the shapes and most of the processes at an average USPS mail processing plant.

It is also unlikely that many of the individual plants operate at levels that leave increasing returns. We have calculated returns to density and scale for each plant/quarter in the MODS samples. These have been used to compute the percentages of the plant/quarters for which the returns to density and scale exceed one as weighted averages for the good data using the conditional probabilities. These percentages are displayed for every shape and process in Table 21.1. Only a few exceed 50 percent; most are very small numbers. The USPS processing network as currently configured presents few opportunities to increase productivity by consolidating processing plants to exploit increasing returns to scale.

It is usually the case in Table 21.1 that returns to scale exceed returns to density for a shape or process. This occurs because our econometrics has yielded estimates of E_p and E_u that are mostly positive and statistically significant. The explanation for this result is that ln(DP) and ln(DU) may serve as either output measures, controls or some combination of the two in the production functions. As output measures for a network service activity, we would expect their elasticities to be negative. As controls for an industrial process, the elasticities are more likely to be positive, because ln(DP) and ln(DU) indirectly represent the limitations on continuous operations imposed by the schedule of arrivals and dispatches from the plant. Clearly, our results are best explained by the view that mail processing is primarily an industrial process.

8. LABOR VARIABILITIES

The variabilities that are used to attribute USPS postal costs are the elasiticites of the inputs for various cost categories with respect to single drivers that serve as intermediate output proxies. Mail-processing labor is one of the cost categories and its driver is piece handlings. Therefore, the mail-processing labor variability, ε_l, for a shape is d ln(HRS)/d ln(FHP), and for a process is d ln(HRS)/d ln(TPF). The conventional microeconomic definition for ε_l is that it is the elasticity of the derived demand for labor with respect to output.

The most direct econometric approach to estimating ε_l is to fit the derived demand for labor as a function of piece handlings, relative prices and various controls, and then extract the elasticity from the estimates. This is the route taken by Bozzo (2006), Roberts (2006), Neels (2006) and all others who have submitted econometric estimates of mail-processing labor variabilities derived from the MODS data in postal rate proceedings since 1997.

An alternative approach is to derive the variabilities from econometric estimates of production functions by making one of many possible assumptions about the way that inputs would be adjusted within a processing plant to deal with changes in output. Labor variabilities for three such assumptions are shown in Table 21.1. The assumptions are as follows:

1. *Capital fixed.* Labor variability is derived under the assumption that HRS is variable but QICAP is fixed. This assumption best describes the operation of USPS mail-processing plants in the very short run: $\varepsilon_l = 1/E_l$.

2. *Fixed input proportions.* Labor variability is derived under the assumption that HRS/QICAP is fixed; that is, HRS and QICAP respond proportionately to changes in FHP or TPF. The variabilities of labor and capital are the same: $\varepsilon_l = \varepsilon_k$. This assumption corresponds to the way that USPS and the PRC use the labor variabilities in postal cost accounting. ε_l is regarded as a constant and is applied to both labor costs and the associated mail-processing equipment cost categories. The practice is called 'piggy backing'. The assumption can be defended as an approximation to USPS operating plans in the intermediate run. USPS does not rethink the way that it equips and staffs its processing plants every time postal volumes change. Instead, USPS rescales the existing levels of labor and equipment to handle such changes without altering the input proportions. Reevaluations of the proportions are likely to occur much less frequently and to be initiated by changes in equipment technology and relative factor prices rather than volumes: $\varepsilon_l = 1/(E_l + E_k)$.
3. *Expansion path.* Labor variability is derived under the assumption that HRS and QICAP are maintained in an economically efficient combination at the relative factor prices implied by the first-order conditions for minimizing cost under the production function. This assumption corresponds to a long-run equilibrium in which both HRS and QICAP are variable and USPS optimally adjusts the input levels at its plants. Under this assumption, HRS and QICAP move in tandem along an expansion path that is determined by a fixed ratio of factor prices. The variability of labor, ε_l, the variability of capital, ε_k, and the elasticity of a Lagrange multiplier, $\varepsilon_\lambda = d\ \ln(\lambda)/d\ \ln(\text{FHP})$, are calculated by solving a system of three simultaneous linear equations:

$$(2.0\beta_{ll} - E_l)\varepsilon_l + \beta_{lk}\varepsilon_k + E_l\varepsilon_\lambda = 0,$$
$$\beta_{lk}\varepsilon_l + (2.0\beta_{kk} - E_k)\varepsilon_k + E_k\varepsilon_\lambda = 0,$$
$$E_l\varepsilon_l + E_k\varepsilon_k = 1.$$[12]

All but four of the mail-processing labor variabilities in Table 21.1 exceed 100 percent, as would be expected for production functions exhibiting decreasing returns to density. There is also a general tendency for the variabilities to progress from highest to lowest in order from short to long run. However, the long-run expansion path variabilities still remain mostly above 100 percent.

9. THE FITS OF THE SWITCHING REGRESSIONS

There are large differences in labor and capital productivity among the mail-processing plants covered by MODS. These differences occur with every shape of mail and for every process. At first glance, they seem hard to explain. The plants all use the same types of processing machines and other equipment. They are organized and staffed following the same USPS guidelines. And, they are all managed according to the same practices and standards. Our ML estimates of the translog production functions largely solve this puzzle. Selections of shape-level and process-level ML estimation results for the stochastic switching regressions are provided in Tables 21.2 and 21.3.

Table 21.2 Selected shape level maximum likelihood regressions

Equation	All letters		All flats		All cancellation		All parcels and Priority Mail	
Dependent variable	ln(FHP) total sorting		ln(FHP) total sorting		ln(TPH)		ln(FHP) total sorting	
Capital index	QIAHE		QIMHE		QIAFCS + QICANC		QIMHE	
Goodness of fit	Good eq'n	Bad eq'n	Good eq'n	Bad eq'n	Good eq'n	Bad eq'n	Good eq'n	Bad eq'n
Adjusted R-square	0.9789	0.8282	0.9747	0.9282	0.9553	0.8331	0.9382	0.7833
Standard deviation of error	0.1241	0.6049	0.1363	0.3249	0.1736	0.7546	0.2757	0.8180
Number of observations	8435	136	6686	1887	7994	325	7013	1440
	Percent	t-value	Percent	t-value	Percent	t-value	Percent	t-value
Bad data	1.59	9.548	22.01	20.854	3.90	12.285	17.03	22.718
	Good equation		Good equation		Good equation		Good equation	
Control variable	Coefficient	t-value	Coefficient	t-value	Coefficient	t-value	Coefficient	t-value
Intercept	11.9023	24.279	11.9291	13.631	2.6502	3.208	0.3044	0.197
Quarter 1	0.0364	9.236	0.1266	21.275	0.0232	4.068	0.0237	2.111
Quarter 2	0.0484	12.047	0.0077	1.325	0.1932	33.079	0.0015	0.134
Quarter 3	0.0352	9.061	0.0927	15.933	0.0658	11.519	0.0322	2.948
Annual trend	0.0168	17.109	0.0220	11.907	−0.0294	−19.292	0.0260	10.324
CURB share	0.0752	2.944	0.1867	4.731	−0.1021	−2.552	0.4421	5.704
NDCBU share	0.6542	17.443	0.4963	9.366	0.4186	7.295	0.1058	1.008
CENT share	−0.3432	−14.929	0.0742	1.744	0.2231	5.535	−0.3847	−4.923
RB share	−0.0040	−0.260	−0.0798	−3.633	−0.1023	−4.516	−0.2238	−5.356
HCT share	0.2146	2.885	0.1403	1.360	0.2616	2.574	1.1493	6.396
POBOX share	−0.3615	−11.358	−0.3621	−7.451	−1.1180	−22.465	−0.1377	−1.632
1st Presort share	0.0225	0.909	−0.4121	−2.421	−0.3060	−14.483		
Std CR share	0.1630	3.235	0.0115	0.274	−0.2228	−4.444		
Std Presort share	0.1342	5.290	0.0402	0.784	−0.1423	−5.808	−0.3036	−4.276
Periodicals share			0.0806	1.107			−0.1471	−1.875
Parcel Post share							−0.3041	−3.025

BPM share							−0.3388	−3.726
Media Mail share							0.4828	3.786
ln (origin/ destination)	0.0632	19.351	0.0521	13.603	0.1582	23.425	0.0642	8.155
No parcels	0.0164	1.507	0.0201	0.900	−0.0334	−2.952		
No Priority Mail					0.0234	4.316	−0.1108	−8.206
No cancellation	0.0737	9.150	−0.0040	−0.288			0.1912	7.413
No MPBCS	−0.0097	−2.313			0.0190	3.316		
No DBCS	−0.5929	−22.193						
No OCR	−0.0839	−12.139			−0.0606	−6.252		
No AFCS	−0.0395	−5.839			−0.1377	−11.445		
No FSM881			0.0893	13.744				
No FSM1000			0.0548	9.592				
No AFSM100			−0.1554	−22.636				
No SPBS Other							−0.0586	−4.509
No SPBS Priority							−0.0448	−3.822
Auto labor share	0.4738	12.606	1.1305	16.951	0.5768	8.843		
Mechanized labor share							−1.6617	−9.741
Manual labor share								
Other labor share	0.5404	21.429	0.9862	25.492	0.0445	1.112	−0.0570	−0.854
Elasticity at mean	Estimate	*t*-value	Estimate	*t*-value	Estimate	*t*-value	Estimate	*t*-value
Labor hours	0.5093	93.398	0.6335	86.894	0.1766	38.936	0.7961	96.575
Capital index	0.2257	36.766	0.0698	16.444	0.2063	38.681	0.0166	2.213
Delivery points	0.1237	18.871	0.1106	11.776	0.4649	50.450	0.0772	5.101
Delivery units	0.0643	13.537	0.0605	8.234	0.1163	16.358	0.0495	3.602

Table 21.3 Selected process level maximum likelihood regressions

Equation	DBCS total		Manual letters total		AFSM100 total		SPBS Other	
Dependent variable	ln(TPF)		ln(TPH)		ln(TPF)		ln(TPF)	
Capital index	QIDBCS		QIPSE		QIAFSM		QIMHE residual	
Goodness of fit	Good eq'n	Bad eq'n	Good eq'n	Bad eq'n	Good eq'n	Bad eq'n	Good eq'n	Bad eq'n
Adjusted R-square	0.9790	0.8276	0.9299	0.8235	0.9802	0.9741	0.9422	0.8019
Standard deviation of error	0.1306	0.5805	0.2398	0.4390	0.0906	0.1102	0.2457	0.8568
Number of observations	8215	305	7353	1134	2776	395	5345	209
	Percent	*t*-value	Percent	*t*-value	Percent	*t*-value	Percent	*t*-value
Bad data	3.58	10.618	5.82	10.007	12.46	7.763	3.76	9.150
Control variable	Coefficient	*t*-value	Coefficient	*t*-value	Coefficient	*t*-value	Coefficient	*t*-value
Intercept	2.7142	4.870	8.7399	7.667	3.0581	3.508	2.0618	1.196
Quarter 1	0.0291	6.756	0.0511	6.171	0.0667	11.507	0.0634	6.136
Quarter 2	0.0576	13.180	0.0213	2.521	0.0077	1.367	0.0164	1.603
Quarter 3	0.0267	6.242	0.0480	5.921	0.0408	7.235	0.0447	4.482
Annual trend	0.0300	28.790	−0.0206	−8.902	0.0344	11.813	0.0022	0.884
CURB share	0.2117	6.969	0.0995	1.793	0.0537	1.453	−0.0335	−0.456
NDCBU share	0.7591	18.393	0.9695	13.647	0.1921	4.228	0.0452	0.494
CENT share	0.1352	5.110	−0.3596	−6.572	0.0995	2.842	−0.4440	−5.142
RB share	0.0688	4.196	−0.1919	−6.353	−0.0312	−1.548	−0.2489	−6.511
HCT share	−0.3942	−5.415	−0.1941	−1.377	0.0955	0.786	−0.7973	−4.281
POBOX share	−0.2627	−7.441	−0.3929	−5.853	−0.0697	−1.196	0.2407	2.623
1st Presort share	0.1799	6.820	0.2526	4.901	−0.2474	−1.516		
Std CR share	0.0838	1.448	0.1436	1.273	−0.1471	−3.236		
Std Presort share	0.1955	6.997	0.2774	4.693	−0.0225	−0.396	−0.4769	−7.152
Periodicals share					−0.1401	−1.698	−0.5710	−7.649
Parcel Post share							−0.3242	−3.415
BPM share							−0.4608	−4.828
Media Mail share							−0.0527	−0.382

ln (origin/ destination)	0.0490	13.178	−0.0026	−0.340	0.0191	4.279	0.0832	11.487
No parcels	0.0166	1.807	−0.0825	−2.551	−0.0232	−1.742		
No Priority Mail	−0.0162	−3.985			−0.0159	−2.581	0.1071	9.204
No cancellation	0.0098	1.059	0.0325	1.820	0.0132	0.774	0.1420	4.598
No MPBCS	0.0179	3.958	−0.0424	−4.835				
No DBCS			−0.4981	−11.278				
No OCR	−0.0835	−10.686	−0.0645	−4.514				
No AFCS	−0.0923	−12.533	−0.1015	−6.946				
No FSM881					0.0205	2.428		
No FSM1000					−0.0186	−3.231		
No AFSM100								
No SPBS Other								
No SPBS Priority							0.0805	8.771
Auto labor share	−0.6830	−15.335			0.0616	0.903		
Mechanized labor share							−0.9772	−6.372
Manual labor share			0.7966	15.661				
Other labor share	−0.1292	−4.741	0.3897	7.028	0.4499	9.987	0.2836	4.133
Elasticity at mean	Estimate	*t*-value	Estimate	*t*-value	Estimate	*t*-value	Estimate	*t*-value
Labor hours	0.5592	121.408	0.7116	81.054	0.8005	123.490	0.7216	88.336
Capital index	0.2432	52.354	0.0262	3.745	0.0546	10.098	0.0767	14.391
Delivery points	0.0958	15.678	0.0287	2.166	0.0749	8.652	0.2142	15.150
Delivery units	0.0502	10.066	0.0519	5.333	−0.0094	−1.227	−0.0218	−1.601

One of the explanations to be found in the tables is that there can be a lot of bad data in the MODS samples. The percentage of bad data found by the ML estimator ranges from about 1.5 percent (letters) to over 20 percent (flats). The high *t*-values for these percentages mean that there is little chance that the MODS samples could actually be clean. Much of the bad data consists of observations of extreme values for FHP (or TPF), HRS or QICAP. Such observations are assigned high conditional probabilities of being bad by the ML estimator. Observations with high conditional probabilities also appear mostly in runs and clusters associated with single plants.

Our translog model fits the MODS samples quite well despite the bad data. The standard deviation of the errors and adjusted *R*-squares for the good and bad equations have been corrected for degrees of freedom as is customary for an OLS regression. The *R*-squares for the good equations are mostly in the neighborhood of 0.89 to 0.98. The *R*-squares for the bad equations are somewhat lower, but still high enough to show in every case that the bad data is explained well by a distinct linear regime. The standard errors of the good equations are also all less than the standard errors for the bad equations. This accords well with the kinds of dirty samples analyzed in Pearsall (2007). Notice, however, that the standard errors for the good and bad equations for the AFSM 100s in Table 21.3 are almost identical. This has happened because many of the observations given high conditional probabilities of being bad correspond to periods when the new AFSM 100s were first installed in the plants. The bad equation is actually a fit of the production function for a startup regime.

Coefficient estimates and *t*-values are shown for the good equations in Tables 21.2 and 21.3. Many of the *t*-values in every equation are far above (absolutely) the critical values for two-tailed tests at the 95 and 99 percent confidence levels. The reason for this high precision in the good data estimates is that the MODS samples are so large that the ML estimator can accurately separate the effects of the good and bad data. The overall conclusions to be drawn from the estimates are, first, that the variables and controls included in the production functions as explanatory variables are statistically effective, and, second, that a two-regime stochastic switching regression is a good model of the flawed data generation process that produced the dirty MODS samples.

10. OTHER DETERMINANTS OF PRODUCTIVITY

Returns to density and scale are only one of many statistically significant determinants of productivity. There are high *t*-values for one or more of the variables in every group of controls in almost every equation. This is somewhat surprising, since many of the controls are no better than indirect proxies for plant characteristics that USPS will not disclose. This means that there are often multiple explanations for the signs and magnitudes of the coefficient estimates. Nevertheless, the estimates exhibit patterns that support several hypotheses regarding the determinants of mail-processing productivity besides returns to density and scale.

There is a seasonal pattern to productivity. USPS processing plants are less productive during postal quarter 4 (July to September) than at other times of the year. Most regular employees take their annual vacations during this quarter. The drop in productivity could also be explained by seasonal variations in weight and other hedonic properties of the average piece.

Productivity for most shapes and processes exhibits a highly significant autonomous trend. For automated and mechanized processes the trend is usually positive; for manual processes it is negative. These patterns could be the result of frequent minor upgrades to processing equipment and a deterioration of labor skills as manual sorting is slowly phased out. The increasing use of automated processes could also be leaving more difficult residues of pieces to be processed by hand.

The delivery point shares are proportions of DP, a variable that indirectly controls for arrival and dispatch schedule effects on productivity. The coefficient estimates for the delivery point shares follow a distinct pattern confirming that schedule effects are among the most important determinants of productivity. City central deliveries (CENT) and P.O. boxes (POBOX) are made early in the day, while other deliveries are often made later. Deliveries to rural boxes (RB) take longer than city and suburban deliveries, so the mail must be available to rural carriers at delivery units early in the day. A plant with high percentages of CENT, RB and POBOX delivery points in its service territory is likely to have a more difficult schedule for dispatching processed incoming mail to its delivery units. This explains the evident tendency for the coefficients of these shares to have a negative sign. On the other hand, mail delivered to central box units (NDCBU) is usually delivery point sorted only to the box unit. Such mail requires fewer handlings and appears to be somewhat easier to process than other mail. The estimated coefficients for the NDCBU share of delivery points are mostly positive numbers.

For the shape-level production functions in Table 21.2 we would expect presorted mail to increase productivity because it requires fewer piece handlings to process. For the process-level functions in Table 21.3 we would also expect presorted mail to increase productivity, but for a different reason. Presorted mail conforms to a higher standard of address hygiene than other mail. This should make this mail easier to process using automated equipment. These effects seem to be present in the coefficients for letters, flats, cancellations and the processes for letters and flats, except for the AFSM 100. For parcels, the coefficients of the subclass and worksharing shares probably are a reflection of the effect on processing of differences in the average sizes and weights of parcels in the categories. First-class parcels, priority parcels and media mail all tend to be smaller and lighter than other kinds of parcels.

Outgoing (originating) mail usually requires less processing than incoming (destinating) mail because it is sorted to fewer divisions. The coefficients of ln(origin/destination) in Table 21.2 are all positive and highly significant. However, this cannot be the only effect represented by the variable 'ln(origin/destination)'. The coefficient is also positive and significant in most of the shape-level equations that distinguish between incoming and outgoing pieces, and in most of the non-manual process-level equations with ln(TPF) as the output variable, including those shown in Table 21.3. The positive coefficients in these other equations show that a higher proportion of outgoing (originating) mail for a shape makes all of the automated and mechanized processes for the shape more productive. It is not really clear why this occurs. It may be that large mailers, whose mail is generally easier to process, prefer to submit their mailings at the more productive plants, or that USPS caters to large mailers by making the plants they use more productive.

The shape dummy variables for parcels, priority and cancellations were included to indirectly identify the type of plant. Significant coefficients with both positive and negative values can be found frequently among our estimates of these coefficients, so the type of plant is an important determinant of productivity.

The process dummy variables in each of the production functions identify the equipment present in the plant that pertains to the associated mail shape. Most of the estimated coefficients for these dummy variables turn out to be statistically significant at very high levels, including all of those shown in Tables 21.2 and 21.3. The presence or absence of complementary shape-specific equipment appears to be the single most important determinant of productivity at USPS processing plants.

The coefficients of the process dummies often display a distinctive pattern. The largest negative coefficient is frequently associated with the most modern automated type of equipment. The coefficients then grow smaller absolutely as they progress through the equipment types, and sometimes turn positive as the oldest and least automated types are reached. We can observe this pattern in many of the fits shown in the tables. For example, the coefficient for the variable 'No DBCS' is negative and is the largest absolutely in the equations for 'All Letters' and 'Manual Letters'. Next in order are the negative coefficients for 'No OCR' and 'No AFCS'. The coefficient for 'No MPBS', the oldest of the letter-processing machines, is still negative but is smaller than the others.

The labor skill shares are the least satisfactory of the controls included in the equations. They are included because the MODS data offer no other choice for representing the skill levels of a plant's labor force. The shares actually represent work assignments that may or may not be based on skills. The coefficient estimates are usually significant, but difficult to interpret as evidence of the effects of specific labor skills on productivity.

The elasticities of FHP (or TPF) with respect to HRS, QICAP, DP and DU have been computed from the formulas given earlier and are displayed at the bottom of Table 21.2 and Table 21.3 for the selected production functions.[13] All of the estimated elasticities for labor, E_l, are greater than zero, but less than one as would be expected for an input subject to diminishing returns. The elasticities for capital, E_k, are also in the zero-to-one range with a few process-level exceptions, of which only one (AFSM 100 Outbound) is statistically significant. The capital elasticities are typically much smaller than the labor elasticities, especially for the manual processes. All cancellations and cancellation using the AFCSs are an important exception in which the labor and capital elasticities are almost equal. As we have already noted, the estimates of E_p and E_u in Tables 21.2 and 21.3 are mostly positive and statistically significant.

11. CONCLUSION

Our stochastic switching models' ML estimates supply a statistically robust answer to the question in our title. USPS mail processing is commonly conducted in its plants at volume levels that are sufficiently high to encounter decreasing returns to density and scale. We have found generally decreasing returns for plant-level aggregates of pieces handled by shape, for pieces fed in single processes, and for most inbound and outbound sub-streams of the mail.

The finding that the average plant operates in the region of decreasing returns to density translates under several assumptions into average variabilities for labor in mail processing that exceed 100 percent. Therefore, the use of variabilities that are less than 100 percent in USPS cost accounting will lead to under-estimates of the marginal costs and attributable costs of processing the mail.

The finding that individual processing plants mostly operate in the region of decreasing returns to scale means that simply consolidating plants is not likely to be an effective strategy for restructuring the USPS network with the object of increasing aggregate productivity. Most plant consolidations will actually decrease the volume that can be processed by the same equipment and labor force in the consolidated plants.

Finally, there are strong indications in our estimates that factors other than scale are chiefly responsible for the large observable differences in average productivities among USPS plants. Perhaps the most interesting of these indications is the indirect evidence we have found that productivity is affected by a plant's ability to schedule arrivals and dispatches to smooth mail flows through its processing operations.

NOTES

* The views expressed in this chapter are those of the authors and do not necessarily represent the opinions of the US Postal Regulatory Commission.

1. For a more detailed description of USPS mail processing, see Bozzo (2006, pp. 11–33).
2. In the cost studies increasing returns are evidenced by decreasing marginal costs and vice versa. Merewitz (1971), Gupta (1982), Strack (1986), Moriarty et al. (2006), Cohen and Chu (1997), Roberts (2006), and Neels (2006), have all found decreasing returns at some level of mail processing and/or overall postal operations. On the other hand, studies by Panzar (1984), Kleindorfer (1987), Norsworthy et al. (1991), Bradley and Colvin (1999), Bozzo (2006), Wells (1987), and Rogerson and Takis (1993) have found increasing returns.
3. See Bozzo (2006). The samples were constructed by combining three separate worksheets found in Library References sponsored by Bozzo for the R2006-1 omnibus rate proceeding. The Library References accompanied his direct testimony on behalf of USPS and his responses to interrogatories and requests for data from United Parcel Service and the PRC's Office of the Consumer Advocate.
4. Bozzo (2006) and Roberts (2006) fit derived demand functions for labor to the MODS data under the assumption that capital is fixed. This is clearly not a desirable underlying assumption for a study of returns to density and scale. Bozzo and Roberts' models also explicitly rely on an assumption that USPS mail processing is both economically and technologically efficient. Fitting production functions, as we have done, enlists only the assumption that processing is technologically efficient.
5. There is an element of moral hazard in the MODS self-collection system that may cause malfunctions. The MODS reports are used by USPS's higher management partly to assess the performance of the plants.
6. See, especially, Neels (2006) on the specific defects in the screens proposed by Bozzo (2006).
7. The ML estimator is described in detail in a manuscript that is available from one of the authors. See Pearsall (2007). ML estimation of stochastic switching models was first proposed by Quandt (1972) and extended by Goldfeld and Quandt (1973), Maddala and Nelson (1975), Quandt and Ramsey (1978), Hartley (1978), and Hamilton (1989). Exogenous switching regression models have been widely applied and have been particularly useful in econometric studies of markets in disequilibrium. ML estimation is the method of choice for fitting stochastic switching models with exogenous fixed-probability independent switching. It is the method described in Judge et al. (1985) and implemented in statistical software such as LIMDEP and SAS.
8. Several of these worksheets are available at www.prc.gov.
9. Our practice was to choose the capital equipment index that most closely matched the shape or process for each equation. Manual processes were fit using the capital index for postal support equipment (QIPSE). The capital index for SPBS was calculated as a residual by subtracting all other mechanized process indices from the index for total mechanized processing equipment (QIMPE). The capital service indices for the incoming and outgoing equations were pre-multiplied by the proportions of incoming and outgoing work hours.
10. The derivation of the formula for returns to scale is as follows:

$t^k y = f(t^k P, t^k U, tL, tK)$ the production function with y = FHP, TPF (or TPH), P = DP, U = DU, L = HRS and K = QICAP; k is the measure of returns to scale and t is a scale factor such that t=1 gives an input/output combination on the production function.

$kt^{k-1}y = kt^{k-1}f_p P + kt^{k-1}f_u U + f_l L + f_k K$ differentiate through with respect to t. f_p, f_u, f_l and f_k are the partials of f with respect to P, U, L and K.

$ky = kf_pP + kf_uU + f_lL + f_kK$ the equation must hold at $t = 1$.
$k = (f_lL + f_kK)/(y - f_pP - f_uU)$ solve for k.
$k = (f_lL/y + f_kK/y)/(1 - f_pP/y - f_uU/y)$ divide the numerator and denominator by y.
$k = (E_l + E_k)/(1 - E_p - E_u)$ substitute the elasticities in the formula for k.

A measure of returns to scale that treats DP and DU as controls is $E_l + E_k + E_p + E_u$. Statistical tests under the null hypothesis (H_0) that returns to scale equal one yield identical results for this measure and for the measure with DP and DU treated as outputs. However, $E_l + E_k + E_p + E_u$ is linear in the parameter estimates of the translog production function, so its standard deviation can be computed readily from the variance–covariance matrix of the estimates. The t-values for returns to scale shown in Table 21.1 are computed for $H_0: E_l + E_k + E_p + E_u = 1$.

11. The calculation of the asymptotic variance–covariance matrix follows Maddala (1977, pp. 176–81) and Judge et al. (1985, pp. 177–80). Standard deviations are calculated for linear combinations of the model parameters. A complete description is in Pearsall (2007).
12. These equations are derived from the first-order conditions for a cost minimization with the translog production function as a constraint and the price ratio P_k/P_l held constant. The translog production function can be reduced to the terms involving ln(HRS) and ln(QICAP) for this derivation:

$$\ln(\text{FHP}) = [\beta_l + \beta_{lp}\ln(\text{DP}) + \beta_{lu}\ln(\text{DU})]\ln(\text{HRS}) + [\beta_k + \beta_{kp}\ln(\text{DP}) + \beta_{ku}\ln(\text{DU})]\ln(\text{QICAP}) + \beta_{ll}\ln(\text{HRS})^2 + \beta_{lk}\ln(\text{HRS})\ln(\text{QICAP}) + \beta_{kk}\ln(\text{QICAP})^2 + \text{other terms.}$$

Using the elasticities for HRS and QICAP, the first-order conditions are as follows:

$\text{HRS} + \lambda E_l = 0$, $(P_k/P_l)\text{QICAP} + \lambda E_k = 0$, and the translog production function.

With ln(HRS), ln(QICAP), λ and ln(FHP) as variables, we take total differentials of the first-order conditions with P_k/P_l held fixed:

$$\text{HRS d}\ln(\text{HRS}) + E_l\text{d}\lambda + \lambda[2.0\beta_{ll}\text{d}\ln(\text{HRS}) + \beta_{lk}\text{d}\ln(\text{QICAP})] = 0$$
$$(P_k/P_l)\text{QICAP}\ln(\text{QICAP}) + E_k\text{d}\lambda + \lambda[\beta_{lk}\text{d}\ln(\text{HRS}) + 2.0\beta_{kk}\text{d}\ln(\text{QICAP})] = 0$$
$$E_l\text{d}\ln(\text{HRS}) + E_k\text{d}\ln(\text{QICAP}) = \text{d}\ln(\text{FHP}).$$

Next, we substitute for HRS and (P_k/P_l)QICAP from the first-order conditions and divide the first two differentials by λ. After rearranging terms, the differentials become:

$$(2.0\beta_{ll} - E_l)\text{d}\ln(\text{HRS}) + \beta_{lk}\text{d}\ln(\text{QICAP}) + E_l(\text{d}\lambda/\lambda) = 0,$$
$$\beta_{lk}\text{d}\ln(\text{HRS}) + (2.0\beta_{kk} - E_k)\text{d}\ln(\text{QICAP}) + E_k(\text{d}\lambda/\lambda) = 0,$$
$$E_l\text{d}\ln(\text{HRS}) + E_k\text{d}\ln(\text{QICAP}) = \text{d}\ln(\text{FHP}).$$

We divide all three differentials through by d ln (FHP). The equations in the text result from the substitutions $\varepsilon_l = \text{d}\ln(\text{HRS})/\text{d}\ln(\text{FHP})$, $\varepsilon_k = \text{d}\ln(\text{QICAP})/\text{d}\ln(\text{FHP})$, and $\varepsilon_\lambda = \text{d}\ln(\lambda)/d\ln(\text{FHP}) = (\text{d}\lambda/\lambda)/\text{d}\ln(\text{FHP})$.
13. The 14 'beta' coefficients of the translog segments of the production functions do not have individual economic meanings. However, these coefficients collectively determine the elasticities. The calculations used the sample means of ln(HRS), ln(QICAP), ln(DP) and ln(DU) for the good data. Standard deviations were derived from the asymptotic variance–covariance matrices for the ML estimator and used to compute the t-values for the elasticities.

REFERENCES

Bozzo, A.T. (2006), Direct Testimony (USPS-T-12), sponsored Library References and Responses to Interrogatories, PRC Docket No. R2006-1.

Bradley, M.D. and J. Colvin (1999), 'Productivity and technical change in a public service enterprise,' in M.A. Crew and P.R. Kleindorfer (eds), *Emerging Competition in Postal and Delivery Services*, Boston, MA: Kluwer Academic Publishers, pp. 75–88.

Cohen, R.H. and E. Chu (1997), 'A measure of scale economies in postal services,' in M.A. Crew and P.R. Kleindorfer (eds), *Managing Change in the Postal and Delivery Industries*, Boston, MA: Kluwer Academic Publishers, pp. 115–32.

Goldfeld, S.M. and R.E. Quandt (1973), 'A Markov model for switching regressions', *Journal of Econometrics*, **1**, 3–16.

Gupta, S.N. (1982), 'Production and cost functions of the United States Postal Service', Ph.D. dissertation, The George Washington University.

Hamilton, J.D. (1989), 'A new approach to the economic analysis of non-stationary time series and the business cycle', *Econometrica*, **57**, 357–84.

Hartley, M. (1978), 'Comment' (on Quandt and Ramsey), *Journal of the American Statistical Association*, **73**, 738–41.

Judge, G.G., W.E. Griffiths, R.C. Hill, H. Lutkepohl and T.-C. Lee (1985), *The Theory and Practice of Econometrics*, New York: John Wiley and Sons, pp. 177–80, 806.

Kleindorfer, P.R. (1987), Direct Testimony (USPS-T-4), PRC Docket No. R87-1.

Maddala, G.S. (1977), *Econometrics*, New York: McGraw-Hill, pp. 176–81.

Maddala, G.S. and F.D. Nelson (1975), 'Switching regression models with exogenous and endogenous switching', *American Statistical Association Proceedings of Business and Economics Statistics Section*, pp. 423–6.

Merewitz, L. (1971), 'Costs and returns to scale in U.S. post offices,' *Journal of the American Statistical Association*, **66**, 504–9.

Moriarty, R., S. Yorke, G. Harman, J. Cubbin, M. Meschi and P. Smith (2006), 'Economics analysis of the efficiency of Royal Mail units and the implications for regulatory policy', in M.A. Crew and P.R. Kleindorfer (eds), *Liberalization of the Postal and Delivery Sector*, Cheltenham, UK and Northampton, MA, USA, Edward Elgar, pp. 165–82.

Neels, K. (2006), Direct Testimony (UPS-T-2), Docket No. R2006-1.

Norsworthy, J.R., S.-L. Jang and W.-M. Shi (1991), 'Productivity and cost measurement for the United States Postal Service: variations among regions', in M.A. Crew and P.R. Kleindorfer (eds), *Competition and Innovation in Postal Services*, Boston, MA: Kluwer Academic, pp. 141–72.

Panzar, J.C. (1984), Rebuttal Testimony on Behalf of ANPA, PRC Docket No. R84-1.

Pearsall, E.S. (2007), 'A dirty data estimator', manuscript available at www.prc.com.

Quandt, R.E. (1972), 'A new approach to estimating switching regressions', *Journal of the American Statistical Association*, **67**, 306–10.

Quandt, R.E. and J.M. Ramsey (1978), 'Estimating mixtures of normal distributions and switching regressions', *Journal of the American Statistical Association*, **73**, 730–8.

Roberts, M. (2006), Direct Testimony (OCA-T-1), Docket No. R2006-1.

Rogerson, C. and W. Takis (1993), 'Economies of scale and scope and competition in postal services', in M.A. Crew and P.R. Kleindorfer (eds), *Regulation and the Nature of Postal and Delivery Services*, Boston, MA: Kluwer Academic Publishers, pp. 109–27.

Strack, W.D. (1986), 'Returns to scale and economies of scope in large mail processing facilities,' Rate Research Division, Office of Rates, USPS.

US Postal Rate Commission (1998, 2001, 2002 and 2006), Postal Rate and Fee Changes, Opinion and Recommended Decision, Cost Attribution Section and Appendices F and I, Docket Nos. R97-1, R2000-1, R2001-1 and R2005-1.

US Postal Rate Commission (2006), Evolutionary Network Development Service Changes Advisory Opinion Concerning a Proposed Change in the Nature of Postal Services, Docket No. N2006-1

US Postal Regulatory Commission (2007), Postal Rate and Fee Changes, Opinion and Recommended Decision, Mail Processing Variability Section and Appendix J, Docket No. R2006-1.

Wells, F.J. (1987), Direct Testimony (USPS-T-5), PRC Docket No. R87-1.

Wilkes, S.S. (1962), *Mathematical Statistics*, New York: John Wiley and Sons, pp. 344–65.

22. The accounting implications of the EU's Third Postal Directive*

John Hearn

1. INTRODUCTION

This chapter considers the regulatory accounting requirements of the independent National Regulatory Authorities (NRAs) following the full accomplishment of the Internal Market for postal services within the European Union, in which a high-quality universal service will be obligatory (normally referred to as Full Market Opening or FMO).

The term 'regulatory accounting' is used throughout the chapter to describe the accounting methodology, principles and systems that Universal Service Providers (USPs) are required to use when maintaining their own internal management accounts and when supplying accounting information to the European Commission and NRAs. The accounting information extracted from these systems is referred to as the regulatory accounts.[1] Article 13 of the Telecoms Framework Directive (2002) uses the terms 'accounting separation and financial reports' to describe the same concepts.

The first part of the chapter highlights the need for NRAs to secure further improvements in the standard of regulatory accounting, including accounting principles, methodology, and frequency of preparation and audit. Several areas where the decisions taken can have significant impacts on the quality of regulatory accounting are examined, and the impact that granularity of accounting can have on unit costs is highlighted.

The second part of the chapter deals with the accounting implications of the functions of NRAs under the proposed Third Postal Directive (2006).[2] The implications for the accountant of obligations about price control, interoperability of postal networks, and the financing of Universal Service Obligations (USO) are considered in detail. On the USO issue, the chapter sets out a concise flow chart to structure the key decisions required by NRAs, and the discretion available to them, in making these in consonance with the proposed Third Postal Directive.

The chapter concludes with a summary of the main accounting issues to be considered.

2. REGULATORY ACCOUNTING REQUIREMENTS

The Third Postal Directive does not envisage any change to the requirement that USPs must maintain a regulatory accounting system under the oversight of their NRAs. Recital 26 to the proposed Third Postal Directive makes it clear, however, that this is only a transitional obligation.

The First Postal Directive (1997) made provision for USPs to be relieved of the obligation to maintain regulatory accounting systems in certain circumstances. The relevant NRA has to decide that three conditions are met: namely, no services are reserved to the USP; no operator has to contribute to a compensation fund to finance universal service provision; and the USP must not be in receipt of any state subvention, 'hidden or otherwise'. To date, no NRA has relieved its USP of this obligation.

The proposed Third Postal Directive (2006) requires NRAs to be satisfied, also, that 'competition in the market is fully effective' and that none of the mechanisms to finance universal service provision have been used. Even if a NRA were so inclined it will, in future, have to consult with the European Commission before taking any decision to relieve its USP of the obligation to maintain regulatory accounting. However, it is difficult to see on what basis NRAs might propose to relieve USPs of the obligation so long as NRAs will need regulatory accounts to inform decisions about compliance with tariff principles, and so on.

2.1 Accounting Principles

The First Postal Directive (1997) required all USPs to maintain accounting systems 'on the basis of consistently applied and objectively justifiable cost accounting principles'. CERP (2004) proposes these should be:

> Cost Causality – revenues and costs should be attributed in accordance with the activities which cause the revenue to be earned and the costs to be incurred.
>
> Objectivity – all allocation and apportionment basis should be performed on an objective basis and should not be intended to unduly benefit the USP.
>
> Consistency – where practical all allocation and apportionment basis' should be consistently applied from one year to the next.
>
> Transparency – methods of allocation/apportionment should be transparent and the revenues and costs should be clearly distinguishable from each other.

CERP (2004) also recognizes the need to exclude exceptional and non-recurring financial transactions from the regulatory accounting systems and of the need for reconciliation with the financial accounts.

2.2 Methodology

The current Postal Directive requires a three-stage approach to the process of attributing an organization's costs to the various products and services that it provides. First, whenever possible, costs must be classified as 'costs which can be directly assigned'. Second, 'common costs' must be analyzed into costs that can be directly or indirectly allocated to a particular service or services. Thirdly, the residual 'common costs' must be allocated on the basis of a 'general allocator'.[3]

A key factor in ensuring the accuracy of a USP's regulatory accounts is to allocate costs directly to specific products to the greatest extent possible. It is now clear that this granularity of accounting is crucial. For example, if costs are simply allocated to 'delivery' this will, of necessity, have to be treated as a common cost. However, if the activity 'delivery'

Table 22.1 Impact on unit costs of disaggregation of total costs

Product	Weighted volume	Disaggregated costs: Travel time	Calling time	Waiting time	Dealing with undeliverable items	Total cost (€ million)	Unit cost (cents)
Scenario 1: cost allocation of 'delivery' cost based on aggregated information							
Letters	412 944					36.9	8.93
Flats (reserved)	35 253					3.1	8.93
Flats (non reserved)	20 199					1.8	8.93
Packets (reserved)	11 710					1.0	8.93
Packets (non reserved)	32 260					2.9	8.93
Other	215 636					19.3	8.93
TOTAL	728 002					65.0	8.93
Scenario 2: cost allocation of 'delivery' cost based on disaggregated information							
Letters	412 944	25.3	7.7			33.1	8.01
Flats (reserved)	35 253	2.2	0.7			2.8	8.01
Flats (non reserved)	20 199	1.2	0.4	2.2		3.8	18.74
Packets (reserved)	11 710	0.7	0.2	1.3	1.0	3.2	27.58
Packets (non reserved)	32 260	2.0	0.6	3.5	2.9	8.9	27.58
Other	215 636	13.2				13.2	6.14
TOTAL	728 002	44.7	9.6	6.9	3.9	65.0	8.93

is disaggregated into its various components/activities, some of these costs can be directly allocated to specific products. Table 22.1 illustrates the potential impact of these two approaches on unit costs, using hypothetical figures. In both scenarios the 'weighted volumes' and the total cost are the same, but in the second scenario costs are disaggregated into the various activities, not all of which are relevant to all products. It will be noted that for some products the unit cost is reduced significantly and for others it is increased.

The allocation of indirect costs must be driven by the cost causality principle. In this connection, the use of appropriate cost drivers that reflect, for each cost category, the factor(s) that causes the particular cost to be incurred. CERP (2004) sets out an extensive list of cost drivers that might be appropriate when allocating the costs of various postal activities.

However, it is in allocating what the Postal Directives call 'common costs which cannot be directly or indirectly allocated to a particular service or services' that the greatest care needs to be taken. The European Commission envisaged that for telecoms the percentage of such costs should be no more than 10 percent.[4] However, publicly available information suggests that the level of common costs in the postal sector is significantly higher. For example, Postcomm (2004) report that Royal Mail's costing and contribution system only attributes 53 percent of total costs to specific services, which means that common costs represent 47 percent of total costs. USPS, interacting with its regulator, the Postal Rate Commission (PRC), has only managed to attribute 54 percent of total costs to specific services, which means that common costs represent 46 percent of USPS total costs – see USPS (2004).

From the point of view of complying with competition law in markets where there is effective competition, there is usually no requirement to allocate common costs in a specific way. The price charged for a product or service will often be determined by the market – that is, the value of the product or service to the customer rather than the cost of production – and this is quite acceptable. In these circumstances it is only necessary to ensure that the price charged is above marginal cost and that contributions – that is, Revenues less Direct and Indirect Costs – earned from all the products and services provided are, in aggregate, sufficient to cover the common costs and generate a Profit.

However, what would be unacceptable is a conscious decision to sell a service below cost with the intention of eliminating competitors or deterring entry – that is, predatory pricing – and therefore infringing Article 82 of the EC Treaty. According to the case law of the European Court of Justice (ECJ), pricing below average variable costs must be regarded as abusive. The principle was established in the AKZO case (1991), where the Court defined average variable costs as 'costs which vary depending on the quantities produced'.

The level of common costs in the postal sector, as already noted, is significant. This gives significant leeway for anti-competitive conduct, including predatory pricing. Postal Notice (1998) issued by the European Commission's Competition Directorate observes that USPs use

> . . . a single postal network to compete in a variety of markets. Price and service discrimination between or within classes of customers can easily be practised by operators running a universal postal network, given the significant overheads which cannot be fully and precisely assigned to any one service in particular. . . .

The basis on which common costs are allocated between services/products can have a significant impact on the relative unit costs of specific services/products. Hearn et al. (2007) exhibit a hypothetical example to illustrate the impact that the choice of allocator can have on unit cost calculations. The example is based on an operator with a significant level of common costs who provides two services – one a high-volume, low-cost service (such as letters) and the other a low-volume, high-cost service (such as parcels). Allocating common costs on the basis of total direct and indirect costs, rather than volume, reduces the unit cost of the high-volume, low-cost service in the example by 15 percent and increases the unit cost of the low-volume, high-cost service by 20 percent. The figures are hypothetical, but illustrate the impact that the choice of allocation method can have on unit costs.

The Postal Directives are very prescriptive as to how common costs should be allocated. Common costs 'shall be allocated on the basis of a general allocator computed by using the ratio of all expenses directly or indirectly assigned or allocated'. The concern, of course, is that USPs may allocate a disproportionate share of common costs to universal services. The Third Postal Directive does not change these rules. However, an amendment adopted by the European Parliament when it considered the European Commission's proposal requires that 'common costs, which are necessary for the provision of both universal services and non-universal services, shall not be entirely allocated to universal services; the same cost drivers must be applied to both universal services and non-universal services'. While this does not alter the principles to be applied, it does spell out in very clear and precise language that common costs used to provide both universal and non-universal services must be shared proportionately between the two groups of services.

This is not how a private company seeking to maximize profits would allocate costs, but within the EU most USPs remain state-owned companies with a public service remit, but are now free to exploit a postal network that no private company could afford to establish. As the Postal Notice (1998) points out in section 8(b)(vi):

> Price and service discrimination between or within classes of customers can easily be practised by operators running a universal postal network, given the significant overheads which cannot be fully and precisely assigned to any one service in particular. It is therefore extremely difficult to determine cross-subsidies within them, both between the different stages of the handling of postal items in the public postal network and between the reserved services and the services provided under conditions of competition.

Inappropriate cost allocation rules could lead to higher costs/prices for users of universal services, a larger net cost of universal service obligations, and/or reduced costs/prices for non-universal services, which may act as a barrier to market entry and product innovation. For example, Karlsson (2005) argues that because a commercially focused operator would probably provide deliveries on only two days a week, then only the cost of two deliveries per week should be shared between universal and commercial services. The entire cost of deliveries on the other three days should be allocated solely to the universal services. This could not possibly be accepted if the commercial services actually used the delivery network on five days a week.

NRAs must therefore be especially vigilant to ensure that USPs apply the prescribed rules when preparing regulatory accounts. WIK-Consult (2006) provided detailed analysis of regulatory accounting within the EU's postal sector that has led to the European Commission raising questions about the reliability of the costing systems employed.[5] This is an area where NRAs will have to devote considerable attention if postal markets are to function efficiently in the future.

2.3 Frequency of Preparation

The Postal Directives do not explicitly make provision for the preparation of regulatory accounts on a regular basis. Article 14(7) simply provides that 'On request, detailed accounting information arising from these systems shall be made available in confidence to the national regulatory authority and to the Commission.' However, from a practical and cost-saving point of view it is best if such information is provided in a predetermined format once a year. This would be consistent with the Fourth Council Directive 78/660/EEC 1978, which obliges Member States to enact laws that require all limited liability companies to prepare and publish annual 'financial' accounts in a prescribed form.

2.4 Audit

This is an aspect of regulatory accounting to which NRAs will have to give more detailed consideration in the future. Article 14(5) of the Postal Directives provides that:

> National regulatory authorities shall ensure that compliance with one of the cost accounting systems described in paragraphs 3 or 4 is verified by a competent body which is independent of the universal service provider. Member States shall ensure that a statement concerning compliance is published periodically.

This obligation is, of course, concerned with the application of the methodology prescribed by the Directives. NRAs are equally concerned with the actual accounting information produced by the accounting systems. CERP (2004) recommends:

> An independent auditor should audit cost accounts. The purpose of the audit is to enhance the quality, objectivity and credibility of the accounts. The following should therefore be considered; the scope of the audit, the skills required from the auditor, conformity and publication of the audit opinion.

USPs may prefer to use the same firm of accountants for the regulatory accounts as they use to produce their financial accounts. There are, however, significant differences in the range of the audit work to be undertaken and it is important to ensure that the auditor has the necessary skills to perform such audits and accepts that he has a duty of care to the NRA. These issues are explored in more detail in LECG (2006).

2.5 Transparency of Accounts

There is no obligation under the Postal Directives to publish regulatory accounts: indeed, Article 14(7) specifically requires detailed accounting information to be provided to the NRA and to the European Commission in confidence. However, the USPs in at least seven countries, including Britain and Ireland, publish a summary of their regulatory accounts.[6] The need for publication of regulatory accounts may become less of an issue once more USPs prepare their financial accounts in compliance with International Accounting Standards; in particular, IAS 14 Segment Reporting.[7]

3. ACCOUNTING IMPLICATIONS OF THE FUNCTIONS OF NRAs UNDER THE PROPOSED THIRD POSTAL DIRECTIVE

3.1 Scope of Regulatory Accounting

The uses to which regulatory accounting information might be put are not specifically set out in the Postal Directives. The following is a summary of the reasons why regulatory accounts are necessary, drawn from the relevant recitals in all three Postal Directives:

1. To adopt decisions related to the universal service.
2. To be used as an input when determining whether the universal service obligations imposed entail a net cost and represent an unfair financial burden for the USP.
3. To ensure that the tariffs applied to the universal service comply with the tariff principles set out in Article 12.
4. To ensure compliance with the terminal dues principles set out in Article 13.
5. To monitor fair market conditions until competition becomes effective.

It is appropriate to note also that the European Commission considers that the most appropriate way of ensuring that Community law with regard to competition is fully complied with is for Member States to require USPs to keep appropriate cost accounts.[8] The following sections summarize the principal provisions that impact on the regulatory accountant's work.

3.2 Price Control

WIK-Consult (2006) provides a detailed analysis that reveals that a wide range of instruments regarding price regulation have been adopted within the EU. It seems essential that each NRA should review the nature of the price control appropriate after FMO.

The current provisions with regard to the tariff principles applicable to services forming part of the provision of the universal service are retained subject to minor amendments. The most important is that the term 'cost oriented' will be substituted for 'geared to cost', bringing the postal sector objectives into line with the telecoms sector. There is also a new requirement that the price control procedures stimulate efficiency gains.[9]

There are four distinct interests that have to be taken into account in deciding what method is appropriate for a particular Member State:

1. The need to protect the consumer from excessive pricing.
2. The need to give the USP the opportunity to react quickly to competitive challenges.
3. The need to control predatory pricing and other cross-subsidies.
4. The availability of accurate regulatory accounting information of sufficient granularity.

This chapter is only concerned with the last issue; however, it must be noted that the need to protect consumers and identify anti-competitive behavior must always take precedence over an easy life for the accountant.

From the accountant's perspective, the easiest and most accurate accounting systems are those that apply on an *ex-post* basis and where services are grouped into 'baskets' of services defined on an operational basis. However, the utility of such systems is extremely limited. It is therefore necessary to consider some of the issues that arise in attempting to increase the utility of the price control system.

The first issue to be considered is the accounting demands of an *ex-ante* system rather than an *ex-post* system. This involves taking the latest regulatory accounts prepared on an *ex-post* basis and projecting them forward to produce forecasts for between one and five years ahead. It might be argued that company management regularly undertakes such exercises in terms of budgetary control and strategic planning. It must, however, be acknowledged that price control systems require a more rigorous approach to the accuracy of forecasts, and often the preparation of the forecasts on a more detailed basis for each service. When pricing decisions are made on the basis of forecast information, the accountant will need to make judgments about (i) the reasonableness of the base period – that is, the latest actual information available; (ii) the credibility of the assumptions made about future changes (Are they realistic or based on aspirations?); and (iii) the track record of the body making the forecasts (How accurate have previous forecasts been?).

Price-cap systems inevitably require the accountant to produce regulatory accounts for different baskets of services. However, rather than basing the baskets on operational design, the need is for baskets that are determined by the level of competition for the services concerned. This is an extremely difficult task for accountants when their services required for different 'baskets' may be identical from an operational/cost viewpoint but face different levels of competition.

Price control systems that involve the proposed price(s) for each specific service being examined by the NRA place significant demands on the accountant to allocate costs and revenue to a large number of services, some of which are very similar. From a practical viewpoint, a layered approach is probably the best way of dealing with these issues. The first step is to identify the revenues and costs attributable to the broad service categories – for example, letters, flats, packets, parcels, and registered – and the second to analyze, say, the letter group into specific products.

The proposed Third Postal Directive (2006) also requires the price control system to stimulate efficiency. However, it must be noted that this is not a requirement that prices should be fixed at those of an efficient operator, as this could in fact require operators to charge prices below their actual costs. This challenge for the regulatory accountant is to identify what scope the USP has to reduce costs in the short term, and to implement a price control that encourages the realization of those reductions.

Another issue that will arise for the regulatory accountant under the proposed Third Directive is the sensitive issue of uniform prices. Many operators have claimed that deliveries in some areas are extremely expensive, while deliveries in the larger cities are much cheaper, and that therefore it will be necessary to introduce zonal pricing to prevent 'cream skimming'. The accountant will require accurate accounting information to back up such claims.

WIK-Consult (2006) suggests that no NRA has conducted an analysis of the variation in delivery costs between zones. There is some information in the public domain that challenges the conventional wisdom. Postcomm (2007) provides details of the cost variation by zone, which suggests that Greater London is the most expensive delivery zone in the context of a proposal from Royal Mail to implement zonal pricing for certain bulk mail services. Earlier analysis by Bernard et al. (1999) using a combination of postal density (addresses per hour) and volume (pieces per address per annum) showed a somewhat wider range. This analysis does report, however, that 'in the U.S. the most sparsely populated areas do not correspond to the highest cost routes'.

In many countries the variation in costs between zones may be such that the transaction costs, to both service provider and customers, may make it unattractive to implement zonal pricing even for users posting large volumes of mail. In the case of wholesale (access) prices, including terminal dues, the need to prevent cream skimming and the larger volumes involved may necessitate zonal pricing irrespective of the transaction costs.

3.3 Interoperability of Postal Networks

Cross-border mail has historically been dealt with by granting operators in other countries access to the monopoly network in the country of destination. Until the latter half of the last century, this was done on a 'knock-for-knock' basis, but even today prices are rarely set on a fully cost-reflective basis.

The Second Postal Directive (2002) introduced a requirement relating to special tariffs. It is a crucial requirement relating to the price regulation of services for high-volume mailers and consolidators (other operators), particularly those that are able to produce mail by computerized methods, and which therefore requires minimal or no sorting by the postal operator.

Under the proposed Third Postal Directive, NRAs will be required to assess whether some elements of the postal infrastructure or certain services generally provided by USPs should be made accessible to other postal operators to promote effective competition and/or protect users. The right of Member States to adopt measures to ensure access to the postal network under conditions of transparency and non-discrimination to ensure the interoperability of postal networks is confirmed.[10]

The focus for the accountant is to ensure that these prices, which often will be calculated on a case-by-case basis, accurately reflect the avoided costs; that is, that they only cover the cost of the services provided and the appropriate share of common costs. To do this accurately, the accountant will need information about the volumes handled at each stage of the value chain. It will no longer suffice to say that there are 'X' million letters and assume that this is the divisor for each activity in the letter value chain when calculating unit costs.

3.4 Determining the Net Cost of Universal Service Obligations

The fundamental economic principle is quite clear. The net cost of universal service obligations involves establishing the difference between the net cost for a designated undertaking operating with the universal service obligations and the same undertaking operating without the universal service obligations. It is also necessary to take into account all other relevant elements, including any market benefits that accrue to an undertaking designated to provide universal service, the entitlement to a reasonable profit and to avoid paying for inefficient work practices. It is reasonable to assume that the Third Postal Directive will implicitly confirm this generally accepted approach as set out in papers such as those by NERA (1998) and Panzar (1999).

This section argues that the accountant's task of determining the net cost of providing the USO can best be tackled if the NRA makes its decisions on the key interrelated decisions about the scope of the USO, selection of the USP(s) and determination of costs in that order. In particular, it must be emphasized that the choice made about how to select the USP(s) can have a significant impact on the amount of work needed to be undertaken by the accountant and the accuracy of the end result.

In this regard, it should be noted that in some instances NRAs may have to work within the guidelines set for them by legislators; for example, in some Member States the scope of universal service may be determined by political decision rather than independent analysis of what the market requires.

The starting point for the work of the NRAs must be to establish the scope of universal service and any obligations of a non-commercial nature that may need to be imposed. The provision of a high-quality universal service is one of the cornerstones of European Union policy. Member States, however, have considerable discretion as to the nature of the universal service obligations to be imposed, and on which operators. It can be envisaged that there will continue to be a significant difference between Member States with regard to the scope of universal service. Table 3.2.3 of WIK-Consult (2006) shows that addressees in most of the larger Member States[11] receive deliveries of mail on six days a week, compared with the minimum of five deliveries a week set out in the Postal Directive that applies in most of the other Member States.[12] The delivery of newspapers, magazines, and periodicals is part of universal service in about half of the Member States, while there is considerable debate as to whether bulk mail services should form part of the universal service or not.

NRAs must bear in mind that it is essential to avoid requiring the provision of services and facilities that are obsolescent. On the other hand, they must not fail to mandate the provision of services that are required but that are not currently available to all users. A good example from the telecommunications sector is the failure to make provision for access to broadband services in remote areas.

The next step is to decide how these services and obligations should be provided. It is important at the outset to note that the postal sector is quite different in some respects from other regulated industries, and that problems and solutions relevant to those industries may not always be appropriate to the postal sector. For example, in the postal sector there is only one operator capable of providing universal service, as envisaged by the Postal Directives. Even in countries that have already liberalized their postal markets, it is clear that alternative end-to-end networks are not designed to provide service on a daily basis or for all types of mail (they tend to focus on the provision of services for 'industrialized' mail only). Furthermore, unlike the telecoms sector it will not be feasible in most cases to allocate different aspects of the universal service obligations to different operators.[13]

The proposed Third Postal Directive offers three options:

3.4.1 Option 1

Designate or license one or more operators to provide the universal service. In the majority of cases, the operators are owned by the state and it is therefore perhaps instinctive to follow this approach. However, this approach poses considerable difficulties for the accountant in determining the net cost of the USO.

The first step is for the NRA to establish whether there is a net cost for the USP(s) in providing universal service. This involves making assumptions about what the designated operator/concessionaire would do on a commercial basis relative to what the requirement is. It also involves measuring the benefits of ubiquity of coverage, an extensive daily delivery network that is not available to other operators and the value of its reputation built up in most cases over hundreds of years. These are intangible items that are not normally reflected in accounts and involve considerable judgment. They also leave much room for debate between all the parties involved.

It is quite clear that incumbent operators have significant advantages, such as name recognition, an established infrastructure, economies of scale, density and scope, ubiquity of geographical coverage and frequency of service provided; and as the ECJ has observed in the Chronopost case (2003), 'that network would never be created by a private undertaking'. However, quantifying these benefits precisely presents the accountant with a considerable challenge.

What is clear, however, is that the situation will differ considerably from country to country and that NRAs must be careful to ensure that decisions are based on data and circumstances relevant to the geographical area concerned. Accounting systems will need to be enhanced to correctly identify the costs of delivery in different parts of an operator's networks. However, the options that determine the net cost of universal service in a more objective manner will obviously be much more attractive from the accountant's perspective.

3.4.2 Option 2

Use public procurement policies to select a USP. As already noted, a limitation of this option in the postal sector is the lack of any credible tenderers, other than the incumbent operator. Furthermore, the cost of any successful bid would have to be met from state funds.

3.4.3 Option 3

Let the market decide what services it is willing to provide and then consider whether this is sufficient to meet user's requirements or whether it is necessary to secure the provision of additional services.

The benefits that accrue from the ubiquity of geographical coverage make it unlikely that any USP would propose to withdraw service from specific high-cost areas, although cost reduction measures such as a reduced number of deliveries may be proposed. As Cohen et al. (2002) observed, 'because the value of the network is positively correlated with the number of points served, few customers would think it worthwhile to trade a rate reduction of this small magnitude [4.1%] for the inability to reach 45 percent of the population'.

An advantage of this approach is that it determines in a straightforward and simple manner what the incumbent is able to provide on a commercial basis. As experience in Sweden demonstrates, it is probable that in most countries the incumbent operator will offer to provide all that is sensibly required. In so far as there is any shortfall, the challenge for the NRA will most probably be to find a niche operator prepared to provide services in a limited geographical area utilizing economies of scope from the provision of other services. Within this option, measures are obviously necessary to ensure that the offer of the incumbent operator is not understated.

If it is determined that universal service obligations represent a net cost, the final step is to determine whether these represent an unfair financial burden. This is a much more straightforward issue, taking into account the net cost and setting it against the resources of the company as a whole. The proposed Third Postal Directive sets out a number of options for financing universal service obligations in these circumstances, including creation of a compensation fund or direct state aid. Any other method compatible with the EC treaty is acceptable.

The process described above is summarized in Figure 22.1.

4. CONCLUSIONS

The full accomplishment of the Internal Market for postal services within the European Union, in which a high-quality universal service will be obligatory, will require further improvements in regulatory accounting.

This chapter has highlighted a number of key areas where regulatory accountants must be especially vigilant. These include the granularity at which costs are identified, the level of common costs and the way in which these costs are allocated between the various services using the postal network. The chapter has demonstrated that there is considerable scope for mis-allocation of costs between universal services and other services provided under full competition. It NRAs are not vigilant, this could lead to higher costs/prices for

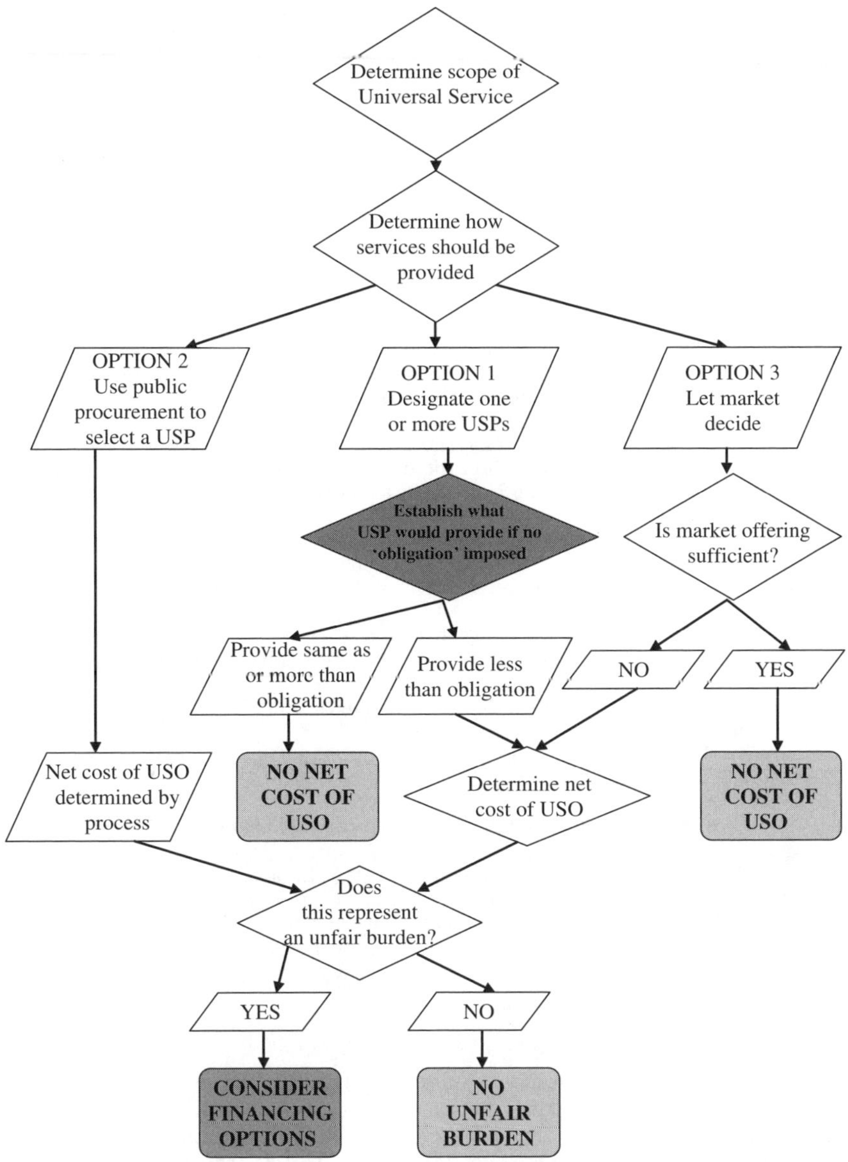

Figure 22.1 Net cost of Universal Service Obligations: decision tree for NRAs

users of universal services, a larger net cost of universal service obligations, and reduced costs/prices for non-universal services, creating a barrier to market entry and product innovation.

The responsibilities of NRAs for price control, charges relating to the interoperability of postal networks and the funding of universal service will require regulatory accountants to further enhance accounting systems and the quality of data. Choosing the right option in regard to these functions can make the task of the NRA considerably simpler.

It can also fundamentally affect the efficiency of the pricing and investment decisions by the USP and others that are based on the costs identified by the accounting system.

NOTES

* This chapter represents the personal views of the author and should not be taken to represent the policy of ComReg, CERP, or any other organisation. The author would like to thank the numerous individuals from Ireland, the United Kingdom, Belgium and the United States of America who have assisted in the preparation of this chapter by way of contributions, guidance, advice and constructive criticism. Responsibility for the content of this chapter and the views expressed therein rests with the author alone.

1. The precise words used in the First Postal Directive (Article 14(2)) are 'The unversal service providers shall keep separate accounts within their internal accounting systems at least for each of the services within the reserved sector on the one hand and for the non-reserved services on the other.' In the French language version the term used is 'analytical accounts', which translates literally as analytical accounts.
2. The European Commission proposed that its proposed Third Postal Directive should be implemented from 1 January 2009. The European Parliament has subsequently recommended that FMO should be deferred to 31 December 2010, or 31 December 2012 for specific countries with special problems. The precise accounting requirements are not the subject of significant debate irrespective of the operative date.
3. See Article 14(3) of the First Postal Directive (1997).
4. 'A well defined cost-allocation system will enable at least 90 percent of the costs to be allocated on the basis of direct or indirect cost-causation.' Commission Recommendation of 8 April 1998 on interconnection in a liberalized telecommunications market (Part 2 – Accounting separation and cost accounting) (98/322/EC).
5. See the Annex to the Third Application Report (2006), p. 30.
6. The other countries, according to WIK-Consult (2006), are Denmark, Hungary, Italy, Lithuania and Malta.
7. See Regulation (EC) No 1606/2002 of the European Parliament and of the Council of 19 July 2002 on the application of international accounting standards.
8. See Section 8 (b) (vi), 'Transparency of accounting', of the Postal Notice (1998).
9. See Article 1(14)(b) and Recital 24.
10. See Article 1(13) and Recital 22.
11. Germany, France, Britain, the Netherlands, Denmark, Italy (not mandatory) and Spain (urban areas only – not mandatory).
12. Exceptions are Malta and the urban areas of Estonia, Latvia, Lituania, and Slovenia.
13. For example, in the electronic communications sector it is entirely possible to give responsibility to one operator for the directory database and to another for payphones.

REFERENCES

AKZO Case (1991) Case C-62/86 AKZO v Commission [1991] ECR I-3359.

Annex to the Third Application Report (2006), Accompanying document to the *Report from the Commission to the European Parliament and the Council* on the application of the Postal Directive (Directive 97/67/EC as amended by Directive 2002/39/EC) {COM(2006) 595 final} SEC(2006) 1293.

Bernard, Stephane, Robert Cohen, Matthew Robinson, Bernard Roy, Jöelle Toledano, John Waller and Spyros Xenakis (1999), 'Delivery cost heterogenity and vulnerability to entry' In M.A. Crew and P.R. Kleindorfer (eds), *Postal and Delivery Services: Delivering on Competition*, Boston, MA: Kluwer Academic Publishers.

CERP (2004), 'Recommendation on best practices for cost accounting rules II', Document CERP PL 2004/2 Doc. 8E; www.cerpt-cerp.org

Chronopost case (2003), ECJ Judgment of 3 July 2003 – joined cases C-83/01 P, C-93/01 P and C-94/01 P ('Chronopost').

Cohen, Robert, Matthew Robinson, John Waller and Spyros Xenakis (2002), 'The cost of Universal Service in the U.S. and its impact on competition', Washington, DC, United States Postal Rate Commission.

First Postal Directive (1997): Directive 97/67/EC of the European Parliament and of the Council of 15 December 1997 on common rules for the development of the internal market of Community postal services and the improvement of quality of service.

Hearn, John, Robert H Cohen, Alex Kalevi Dieke, and Antonia Niederprüm (2007), 'Regulatory cost accounting in the postal sector', presented at the 10th WIK Königswinter Seminar on Postal Economics, 'Postal Markets between Monopoly and Competition', 12–14 February 2007; www.wik.org

Karlsson, Peter (2005), 'The costs of USO and the pricing of postal services – the experiences of Finland Post', presented at the 13th Conference on Postal and Delivery Economics, Antwerp, Belgium, 1–4 June 2005.

LECG (2006), 'Revised accounting direction and related issues report by LECG Ltd', ComReg document 06/55a, Commission for Communications Regulation, Dublin.

NERA (1998), 'Costing and financing of Universal Service Obligations in the postal sector in the European Union', Report for the European Commission, November 1998, Brussels and London.

Panzar, John C. (1999), 'A Methodology for measuring the cost of Universal Service Obligations', paper presented to IDEI Conference on Competition and Universal Service in the Postal Sector, University of Toulouse, March 1999.

Postal Notice (1998), Competition Notice: 98/C 39/02 Notice from the Commission on the application of the competition rules to the postal sector and on the assessment of certain State measures relating to postal services, OJ C 39, 06 February 1998.

Postcomm (2004), 'Royal Mail's proposal to introduce size based pricing: a consultation document', April, paragraph 4.45.

Postcomm (2007), Postcomm's Stakeholder letter dated 2 April 2007 at www.psc.gov.uk

Second Postal Directive (2002), Directive 2002/39/EC of the European Parliament and of the Council of 10 June 2002 amending Directive 97/67/EC with regard to the further opening to competition of Community postal services.

Telecoms Framework Directive (2002), Directive 2002/21/EC of the European Parliament and of the Council of 7 March 2002 on a common regulatory framework for electronic communications networks and services.

Third Postal Directive (2006), Proposal for a Directive of the European Parliament and of the Council amending Directive 97/67/EC concerning the full accomplishment of the internal market of Community postal services. COM (2006) 594 final.

USPS (2004), Cost and Revenue Analysis Report FY 2004, United States Postal Service.

WIK-Consult (2006), 'Main developments in the postal sector (2004–2006)', study for the European Commission, Brussels and Bad Honnef.

23. Tradeoffs in product costing: the statistical impact of cost pool formation decisions

Alan Robinson, Richard Waterman and David Rawnsley

1. INTRODUCTION

The accuracy of a product costing approach is often a compromise between the cost of data collection and analysis and the market and regulatory demands on a postal administration. As no postal administration has unlimited resources for product costing, identifying ways to reduce product costing expenses without significantly reducing accuracy of cost measurement would free up resources to work on costing issues that could use greater attention.

In an unregulated environment, costing efforts are driven by market demand to tailor products and prices for individual customers. Freeing resources could allow a postal administration to develop accurate product costs and profitability measures for more specialized products that appeal to small subsets of their customer base. In the increasingly competitive marketplace following postal liberalization, customers will expect that the postal supplier will bid for their business in the same manner that their other postal, transportation, and logistics suppliers do and these bids will likely include specific service and price parameters that reflect the demands that the customer places on the postal network. Finding more efficient ways to develop accurate product costs should be a priority for postal administrations following postal reform, as it would temper the demand for increased spending on product costing and the associated data collection and analysis efforts that a customer-tailored bidding process would require.

In a regulated environment, finding means to improve the efficiency of product costs also has significant benefits. In the short term, more efficient costing methods can reduce the burden that a regulator may place on a postal administration for product cost data. If a regulator must impose a specific costing method, understanding the cost effectiveness of various alternative costing methods may help the regulator, as well as the regulated postal administration, to identify a method to provide product cost information at the required level of accuracy at a lower cost. As postal reform has created new or refocused regulatory processes in nearly every country where it has been enacted, understanding the cost effectiveness of potential costing methods early in the process can prevent the imposition of expensive costing methods that provide no better results than less expensive alternatives. Attacking expensive costing methods before they are imposed is important, as changing methods is difficult once regulatory precedent becomes established.

In order to understand the tradeoffs between complexity and simplicity, or more expensive and less expensive product costing methods, we examine the consequences of creating a simpler cost modeling approach than the underlying reality that postal operations or economic theory would suggest. We use the cost modeling structure used by the United States Postal Service (USPS) to examine this tradeoff. The complexity of the USPS's model is determined by the number of cost groupings or cost pools that are analyzed independently. We specifically look at a world in which economic theory or postal operations define two distinct underlying cost pools and the consequences of replacing it with a single cost pool. To achieve this, we formulate a theoretical framework that allows us to investigate the consequences of incorrect cost pool formation on the bias and variance of product-level volume variable costs.

Our examination of this issue using the USPS's model also provides guidance for product costing at other postal administrations, as prior studies have noted that most if not all of the largest postal operators use similar product costing structures (Linx, 1999).[1] Most importantly, postal costing models in other administrations measure the similar types of economic costs (marginal or incremental costs); use complex models that incorporate numerous cost pools across the retail, pick-up, sortation, transportation and delivery operation that all postal administrations employ to provide mail service; and incorporate the use of data collected through corporate data systems, sampling of corporate data, and sampling-based data-collection systems designed specifically for product costing.

The chapter contains eight sections. Section 2 describes the USPS's cost model and approaches that could be used to develop distinct cost pools. Section 3 discusses the impact of cost estimation bias and precision on the usefulness of product cost estimates. Section 4 presents the structure of the simulation model and the scenarios that we evaluate. Section 5 presents the results of our simulation model. Section 6 presents an explanation of the results of the simulation model. Section 7 reviews how sensitive cost estimates are as the variance associated with cost elasticity varies, and finally, Section 8 presents our conclusions on cost pool formation, and identifies areas for further study.

2. THE VOLUME VARIABLE COST MODEL

The USPS's unit volume variable cost model is the method it uses to estimate product marginal costs. Under certain assumptions, it also provides a valuable input into the measurement of product incremental costs.[2]

In this model, the USPS measures volume variable costs (VVC) for a specified time period for each of its products 'i' based on the following two equations:[3]

$$VVC_i = \sum_j VVC_{ij}, \tag{23.1}$$

where

$$VVC_{ij} = Cost_j \times CostElasticity_j \times DistributionKeyShare_{ij}, \tag{23.2}$$

and

VVC_{ij}=the unit Volume Variable Cost of product 'i' in cost pool 'j'

$Cost_j$ = the general ledger costs associated with cost pool '*j*'
$CostElasticity_j$ = the elasticity of costs in cost pool '*j*' in relation to the cost driver for that cost pool, most often a measure of mail volume
$DistributionKeyShare_{ij}$ = the proportion of product '*i*' associated with the cost driver in cost pool relative to total volume of the cost driver of cost pool '*j*'

Costing analysts at the USPS, and at postal administrations using a similar approach, have substantial flexibility in defining the number of cost pools in this model. In general, they define the number of cost pools by answering three questions. First, is the cost elasticity (volume variability) believed to be different for the cost pool and can it be measured separately? Second, are the products using a cost pool believed to be distinct from similar cost pools, so that measured distribution key shares will be different? Third, can the specific costs associated with a cost pool be determined? Answers to the first two questions are based on an understanding of the underlying production economics and the postal operations used by different products. An answer to the third question depends on the USPS's ability to aggregate costs.

Three methods are used to separate costs into individual cost pools prior to analysis. First, accounting, budgeting and operating conventions allow costing analysts to group costs following cost groupings used for other purposes at the USPS. Accounting conventions divide costs based on how the input is paid for, such as different payment processes for employees than for purchased inputs, and for purchased input by the type of inputs. Budgeting conventions divide inputs into departments, regions, facilities and other management units. Operating conventions divide inputs into units that are used for measuring operating productivity. For example, a plant, which may be a single budgetary unit, is divided into operating units based on the operating function of the unit, the type of machine employed, and so forth. Accounting, budgeting and operating conventions allow for a nearly infinite number of cost pools for a large organization like the USPS.

Second, functional definitions of cost pools sum costs separated by accounting, budgeting and operating conventions to incorporate all costs associated with all production inputs to a unique production activity within the collection to delivery process. For example, a functional cost pool associated with machine sortation of mail would include sortation labor, equipment depreciation, equipment maintenance labor, equipment maintenance parts, and energy associated with the machine sortation. Functional definitions of costs can be broad or narrow. A broad definition would include all letter sortation activities and their cost inputs. More narrow definitions could separate functions between manual and machine functions, between activities performed on different machines, and between originating, destination, and carrier route sortation functions regardless of the type of sortation.

Third, theoretical conventions divide costs that were defined by either of the previous two methods into cost pools based on a theoretical model as to the relationship between costs and potential cost drivers. Theoretical conventions, by their nature, have the effect of increasing the number of costs pools beyond the number formed by accounting, operating, or budgetary conventions. For example, the accounting costs associated with city delivery carriers are divided into separate cost pools for activities that occur within an office and those that occur outside of the office, and activities outside of an office are divided into cost pools associated with the time getting to the route and time on the route.

Theoretical conventions require specially designed data collection systems to divide an accounting cost into the cost pools that are analyzed.

As additional cost pools increase the expense of analytical and data collection efforts associated with product costing, straightforward criteria are needed to ensure that the additional expense produces value in the costing process. As nearly all of the data elements in this model may come from the results of analyses that involve the estimation of statistical parameters, the statistical bias and variance characteristics of these parameter estimates provide information that can guide the creation of these criteria. The next section looks at the impact that statistical bias and variance has on cost estimation and the value of the information that they provide in this process. The simulation model then provides an illustration of how these bias and variance characteristics are traded-off when cost pools are aggregated.

3. THE IMPACT OF COSTING ERRORS (BIAS) AND UNCERTAINTY (VARIANCE)

The accuracy of cost estimates depends upon understanding both potential errors or bias and uncertainty or statistical variance. Both of these issues have different effects on the quality of the cost estimates.

Bias issues send the wrong signals to the postal administration as it attempts to evaluate the viability of products based on their profitability, and identify operating areas that require increased cost reduction focus in order to improve product profitability. In situations where product costs are used in the regulatory process to set prices, biased cost estimates have the potential of affecting overall welfare, total net revenue, price levels of individual or all products, and the level of outputs of individual or all products.[4]

If cost estimates that determine the price of a broadly offered product are biased, so will prices of products that are determined based on differences in costs from the biased cost estimates for the broadly offered products. Such derivative products are often defined by the type of work that the postal administration does not do, whether the customer has to spend resources to do the work or not, and often include products defined to meet the needs of individual customers.

Uncertainty or statistical variance errors have a different set of consequences. The value of statistical parameters with high statistical variance could differ greatly each time they are estimated. When costing models are re-calculated on a regular basis – for example annually – then product costs estimated with parameters with high statistical variance could change each year. As changing product costs result in changing understanding of product profitability, an annual change in product costs would result in an annual change in the understanding of product profitability. In an extreme example, a product could flip from a profit-making to a loss-making condition without any changes in the production processes, production inputs or costs of these estimates just because of the uncertainty associated with statistical parameters used in cost estimation. To the extent that management or regulatory decisions are made based on these profitability estimates, this uncertainty undermines confidence in the expected impact that decisions of management or regulators will have.

As the accuracy of cost estimates depends on both the bias and variance associated with cost estimates, choosing a level of accuracy involves assessing a tradeoff between the two. If concerns about the bias of results are paramount, then this can lead to an increasingly complex and expensive modeling process. The consequence of a complex modeling process can be increased variance or uncertainty about the cost estimates developed, and therefore increased difficulty in making consistent decisions based on product profitability on a year-to-year basis. Alternatively, if concerns about either the cost of product costing or the variance of results are paramount and the costing method is simplified, then biased estimates could result and management or a regulator's decisions could be steered in the wrong direction.

4. THE STRUCTURE OF THE SIMULATION MODEL

In order to investigate the impact of combining cost pools, we set up a two-cost-pool, two-product world. We work with the knowledge that the two-cost-pool world is the true world, and investigate the consequences of getting things wrong; that is, if we act as if there were only one cost pool.

The question of interest is how much this hurts the quality of the cost estimate, if at all. The non-obvious result is that in some situations aggregating the two cost pools into one provides for better statistical estimation of product volume variability than treating them separately.

A standard way of assessing the quality of a statistical estimate, $\hat{\theta}$, of some parameter θ's true value is through Mean Squared Error (*MSE*).[5] *MSE* can be written as

$$\begin{aligned} MSE\,(\hat{\theta}) &= E(\hat{\theta}-\theta)^2 \\ &= E\{\hat{\theta}-E(\hat{\theta})+E(\hat{\theta})-\theta\}^2 \\ &= E\{\hat{\theta}-E(\hat{\theta})\}^2+E\{E(\hat{\theta})-\theta\}^2 \\ &= Var(\hat{\theta})+Bias^2(\hat{\theta}). \end{aligned}$$

This simple formulation reveals why if practitioners only focus on one component of the *MSE*, they may well end up performing in a suboptimal way. The statistician who focuses purely on variance may pay a large price in bias, (a precise estimate of the wrong quantity is not helpful), whereas the economist who focuses on obtaining the perfect model – that is, removing bias – may pay a price in variance and end up with an imprecise estimate of the quantity of interest.

MSE provides a formal way to balance these competing objectives.

4.1 A Framework for Aggregating Cost Pools

We posit a simplified postal model that can be defined as a two-cost-pool world and analyze the impact on *VVC* estimates when it is incorrectly modeled as a world with only a single cost pool. To do this we find the one-cost-pool model that is 'closest' to the two-cost-pool world. This involves estimating both an 'incorrect' single cost elasticity and distribution key shares for the aggregated cost pool. We present the details

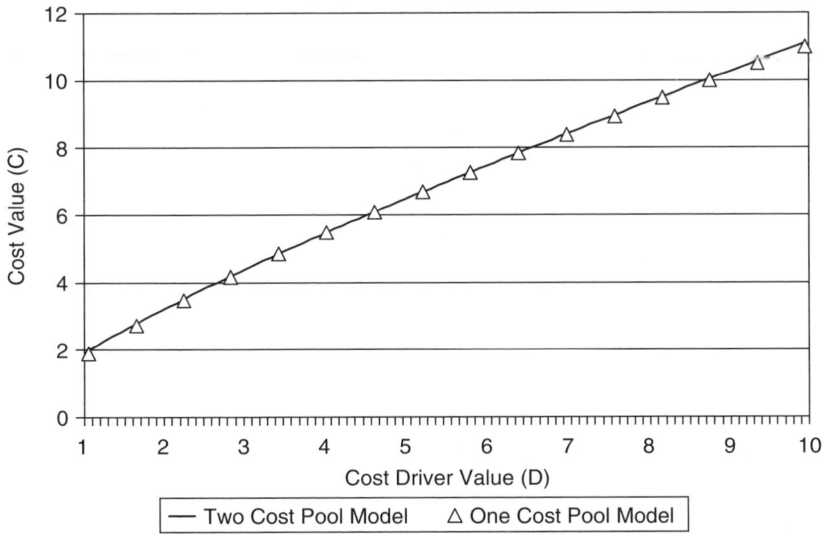

Note: Only one-sixth of the data points generated by the one cost pool model are illustrated so that the two cost pool model data can be seen.

Figure 23.1 A comparison of the cost functions of the 'true' two-cost-pool model with the best one-cost-pool model

of a formal framework for investigating the impact of aggregating cost pools in Appendix A.

In the USPS's cost estimation system, elasticities are typically estimated through econometric studies, and distribution key shares through statistical sampling systems. Consequently, when we use a simulation to investigate the aggregation effect, we use a normal distribution to capture the uncertainty in the elasticity estimate, and a multinomial distribution to mimic the uncertainty in the distribution key share estimates.

In the graph in Figure 23.1, the true cost function is displayed as a solid line. This true cost function includes two cost pools, with cost elasticities of 0.5 and 0.9 for the two cost pools. The one-cost-pool approximation is illustrated as a series of triangles, which lie nearly on top of the solid line. As illustrated, the depictions of the values generated by the two-cost-pool and one-cost-pool models are nearly indistinguishable. In the two models, when evaluated at the average value for the cost driver, D, which is equal to 5, the volume variable cost is 4.949 for the correct two-cost-pool model, whereas the volume variable cost from the incorrect one-cost-pool model is 4.947.

Given the similarity of the results, we conclude that even with substantially different 'true' cost elasticities associated with the two cost pools, using one cost pool could allow estimation of total volume variable cost accurately. So we will focus our attention on how the statistical properties of the distribution keys within each cost pool come into play.

In evaluating how the statistical properties of distribution keys affect the 'quality' of the model, we continue to use a simplified model by simulating a postal operation that has only two products. In adding distribution keys to the model, we add an additional stochastic component to reflect the fact that distribution keys are generated based on 'tallies' collected as part of a sampling effort.[6] In generating distribution keys shares for our simulation, we employ a multinomial distribution. This allows for a very flexible framework in our model, and allows us to examine a range of features relating to both cost elasticity and distribution key share.

Our simulations involve two scenarios that differ as to the method employed to vary the distribution key shares between the two products and the two cost pools, in order to illustrate a broader range of differences than might be expected in such a simple model.

In order to investigate the impact of using the wrong cost pool formulation (that is, using a single cost pool when two should be used), we use the ratio of the *MSE* for the volume variability estimates for Product 1. That is, we look at

$$\frac{MSE(VVC_{1CP})}{MSE(VVC_{2CP})}$$

where VVC_{1CP} represents volume variable cost estimated under the single cost pool model and VVC_{2CP} denotes estimation under the two-cost-pool approach. If this ratio is less than one, then combining the cost pools (even though it is wrong in some sense) provides for a better statistical estimate of the product-level volume variability than treating them separately.

In the simulation, we replace the elasticities and distribution keys with simulated values, but keep the accrued costs in the two cost pools as fixed. The rationale is that the accrued costs would typically be fixed numbers as appearing in a General Ledger, and we are just trying to capture the statistical uncertainty due to the estimation of the elasticities and distribution keys.

For both scenarios, we look at four elasticity assumptions: the first uses elasticities of 0.5 and 0.9, the second 0.6 and 0.8, the third has elasticities of 0.65 and 0.75 and the fourth sets them both at 0.7.

Each graphic displays the result of a simulation of 1000 iterations, run at each point on a range of distribution key values for each Product 1 within the first cost pool, designated as π_{11} and the proportion of tallies in each cost pool, designated as π^*. This lets us explore the sensitivity of the MSE ratio to the distribution key share values.

5. PRESENTATION OF THE RESULTS

In each of the graphs in this section, dark areas in the graph represent pairs of values for π^* and π_{11} for which combining the two cost pools into a single cost pool is preferred in the sense of having a lower *MSE*. Conversely, the light areas represent pairs of values for π^* and π_{11} for which keeping the two cost pools separate results in a lower *MSE*. More specifically, we plot a dark pixel when the *MSE* ratio is less than one, and a light one when it is greater than one.

5.1 The Asymmetry Scenario

In the asymmetry scenario we assume that the distribution key shares associated with Products 1 and 2 in Cost Pool 1 are inversely related to the distribution key shares in Cost Pool 2 as illustrated in Table 23.6, which is in Appendix B. We vary the proportion of tallies collected in Cost Pool 1 by varying the π^* parameter. Figure 23.2 includes four graphs generated by this scenario. All four graphs indicate that there are times when a single cost pool is preferable over two cost pools. This simple observation illustrates that even after adding the complexity of distribution keys to the model, combining cost pools can still be preferable.

In all four graphs, a single cost pool is generally preferred when π_{11} is near 0.5, meaning that the proportion of Products 1 and 2 are nearly equal. As can be expected then, a single cost pool results in a lower *MSE* than two cost pools, regardless of the proportion of tallies collected between the two cost pools.

In the three simulations that contained different elasticity parameters for the two cost pools, another area exists to the left of the center column where one cost pool is preferable to two. In all three graphs, the area reflects a condition in which the cost pool that has the lower price elasticity also has a lower proportion of the tallies collected. This area includes proportions of π_{11} below 0.5 through 0.25, the lowest value we included. We posit that the reason for this is that elasticities in our model drive the costs within each cost pool, and there are certain values of π^* for which the number of tallies collected is approximately proportional to costs, so that the combined distribution key share for the single cost pool model is correctly weighted.

Notice that as the elasticities get closer together, that is going from Figure 23.2(a) to Figure 23.2(d), the area for which aggregation is preferred decreases – the dark bands are getting thinner and the left-hand side's dark extension moves up. Again, this is likely because these are the values of π^* that generate tallies approximately proportional to costs. Finally, in Figure 23.2(d), the left-hand extension disappears, and is replaced with an area in the center of the graph that is a mixture of light and dark areas. This graph illustrates that when both the proportion of tallies between the two cost pools are near equal and proportion of tallies between the two products are near equal, then the *MSE* ratio is about equal to one, so in the simulation which method wins is a coin flip, and hence there is the 'noisy' area in the center of the graph.

5.2 The Perturbation Scenario

In the perturbation scenarios we continued to compare the results under four different assumptions about cost elasticity. Under each assumption we held the distribution key shares of Products 1 and 2 constant in Cost Pool 2, while we varied the distribution key shares of Products 1 and 2 in Cost Pool 1. The proportion of tallies used to estimate the distribution key shares (π^*) was varied as well. The results are contained in Figure 23.3 and are quite similar to the asymmetry scenario. In this scenario, just as in the asymmetry scenario, there are instances when one cost pool is preferred over two and a single cost pool is preferred in a wider range of the graph than before under all four assumptions about cost elasticity.

Just as in the asymmetry scenario, the perturbation scenario generates a vertical dark column in the center of the graph where one cost pool is preferred, but the column is wider than the column generated by the asymmetry scenario, because the second cost pool's distribution key share is no longer moving in the opposite direction. As would be expected, the center of this column is near the value of the distribution key share of Product 1 in Cost Pool 1 that is equal to the distribution key share of Product 2 in Cost Pool 2. The

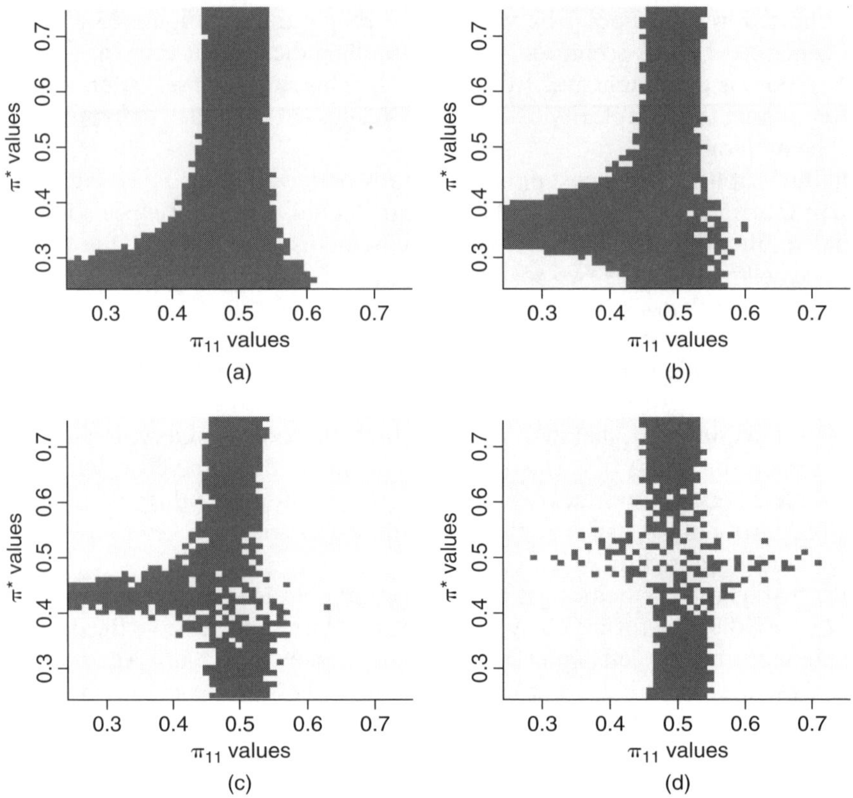

Figure 23.2 *The asymmetry scenario: (a) elasticity parameters of 0.5 and 0.9; (b) elasticity parameters of 0.6 and 0.8; (c) elasticity parameters of 0.65 and 0.75; (d) elasticity parameters of 0.7 and 0.7.*

width of this column suggests that the proportion of Product 1 in Cost Pool 1 can differ from the proportion in Cost Pool 2 to a significant extent before two cost pools need to be considered.

The existence of a horizontal dark area that crosses the vertical dark column suggests that there are instances in which the proportions of Product 1 in the two cost pools vary to a great extent and still one cost pool is preferable. The horizontal dark area where one cost pool is preferable is again wider than the horizontal area produced in the asymmetry scenario. The horizontal dark area appears on both sides of the vertical dark area, suggesting that conditions under which a single cost pool is preferred occur both when the proportion of Product 1 in Cost Pool 1 is both greater than and less than the proportion in Cost Pool 2.

The width, position, and consistency of the dark area vary among the charts in Figure 23.3. The width of the range of values under which one cost pool is preferable appears to grow between Figures 23.3(a) and 23.3(b). The wider range of values under which a single cost pool is preferred suggests that when cost elasticities between the two cost pools are closer in value, the range over which the proportion of the two products in the two cost pools can differ increases.

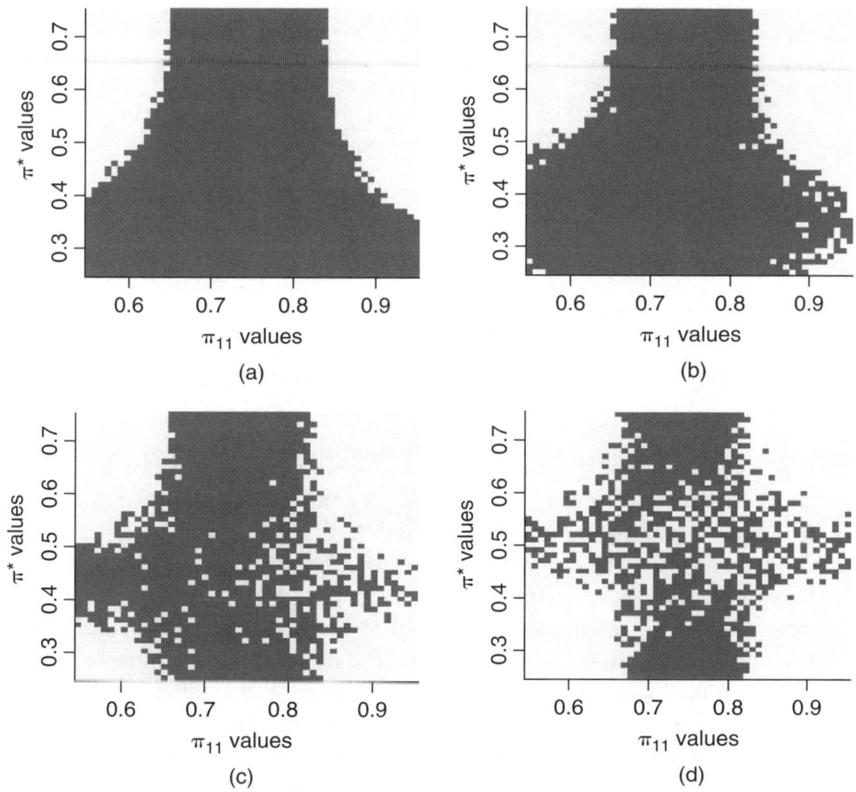

Figure 23.3 *The perturbation scenario: (a) elasticity parameters of 0.5 and 0.9; (b) elasticity parameters of 0.6 and 0.8; (c) elasticity parameters of 0.65 and 0.75; (d) elasticity parameters of 0.7 and 0.7.*

As in the asymmetry scenario, the horizontal area rises as the two cost elasticities become closer together. This suggests that a single cost pool becomes preferable over a wide range of differences in distribution key shares when tallies (as driven by π^*) are approximately proportional to costs.

Finally, when the cost elasticities are identical, the graph becomes less cohesive, with light and dark areas appearing to exist almost randomly over a broad range of the center of the graph. This suggests that when price elasticities are identical, or near identical the choice of one or two cost pools is moot. From the simulation perspective, the *MSE* ratio is about equal to one, and the graph becomes 'noisy'.

6. WHY COMBINING DOES NOT ALWAYS WORK

In this section we take a look at the perturbation scenario results when the two elasticities are both 0.7 and examine why aggregating works sometimes but not always. Specifically, we look at the variance and bias components of *MSE* and contrast them between the

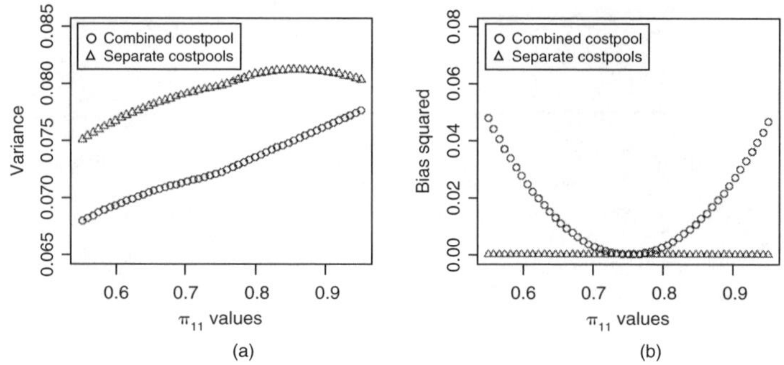

Figure 23.4 Variance (a) and bias (b) comparison elasticities = 0.7, and 0.7π = 0.25*

separate and combined cost pool approaches. We fix π^* at 0.25 (that is, looking at the bottom row of the grid in Figure 23.3(d)) and plot the variance and squared bias for the two approaches as π_{11} varies between 0.55 and 0.95.

What is apparent is that the combined cost pool approach always provides a lower variance for the volume variability estimate than the separate cost pools.

This is because we are getting the benefit of the lower elasticity variance in the combined approach. We note that the variance for the combined cost pools is an increasing function of π_{11} and is likely the result of the fact that $\pi_{11}$is a scaling factor in the volume variability equation, and as scale increases so does variance.

The bias picture shows that there is no bias in the volume variability estimate for the separate cost pools approach, which is to be expected because we are doing the 'right thing' – there are two cost pools and we are using two cost pools, so there will be no estimation bias. Not surprisingly, the bias due to aggregating the distribution key shares is largest when the two distribution keys are furthest apart, and is negligible as the distribution keys coincide (that is, at a value of $\pi_{11} = 0.75$, which is the fixed value of the distribution key in the second cost pool in the perturbation scenario).

So in summary we see a lower variance when we aggregate, but we pay a price in bias and as the distribution keys in the two cost pools diverge, so this bias penalty dominates the *MSE* calculation and aggregation no longer wins in the sense of having a lower *MSE*.

7. SENSITIVITY TO THE PRECISION OF ELASTICITY ESTIMATES

The entire analysis so far has set the coefficient of variation (*cv*) of the elasticity estimates within each cost pool at 10 per cent and the *cv* of the combined cost pool estimate at 7.07 percent. We now briefly examine the sensitivity of our results to this assumption by allowing the *cv* of the elasticity estimates to equal 20 percent, 10 percent and 5 percent. The *cv* of the elasticity estimate in the combined cost pools is always set at $1/\sqrt{2}$ times the *cv*'s in the individual cost pools.

What is revealed in Figures 23.5(a) through 23.5(c) (where the elasticity *cv* moves from 20 percent, to 10 percent to 5 percent) is that as the precision of the estimates of the elas-

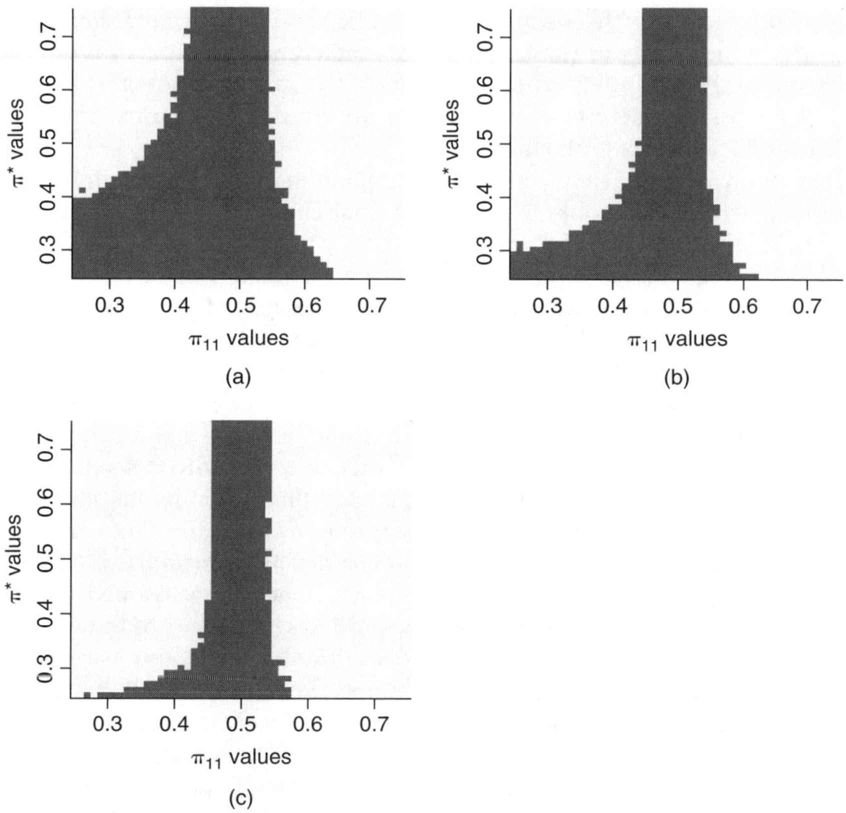

Figure 23.5 *Sensitivity to the elasticity* cv *in the asymmetry scenario with elasticities equal to 0.5 and 0.9 and* cv*'s equal to (a) 20 percent, (b) 10 percent and (c) 5 percent*

ticities increases (that is, their *cv* gets smaller), the bias dominates in the combined cost pool estimate's *MSE* and it makes less sense to combine. Conversely, when the precision is low, it makes more sense to combine the cost pools.

8. CONCLUSIONS

To the extent that regulators and managers have seen themselves judged on each repeated cost measurement decision independently of previous cost estimates, there is a myopic focus on the impact of bias in the cost estimation process, as changes in cost estimates from measurement to measurement have no consequences. However, if regulators and managers see that the future of a postal administration will require business relationships that incorporate consistency in service and pricing over time, then they will work to create a broader focus and pay more attention to the tradeoff between bias and uncertainty in estimating product costs.

The question of combining cost pools goes to the heart of the challenge of evaluating the tradeoff between bias and uncertainty and managing the cost of providing accurate estimates of product costs. If costing efforts can be simplified by combining cost pools without a loss in the quality of the cost estimates, then the overall cost of product costing could be reduced. If combining cost pools reduces the cost of conducting one part of a highly complex costing exercise, then resources are freed up for more profitable use to solve other product costing problems.

This chapter provides the first steps in an examination of the issue as to how to evaluate the development of cost pools. We believe that the chapter provides a solid framework for investigating the cost pool aggregation question. The framework is flexible enough to apply to a more realistic and complex description of postal operations than the two-product, two-cost-pool world we examined. Even for our illustrative world, we see that the tradeoffs between bias and uncertainty in designing cost estimation systems are not intuitive and require careful statistical analysis to understand.

The scenarios that we examined illustrate that there are conditions under which creating a single cost pool would be advantageous over one that uses multiple cost pools. Our scenarios included theoretical cost elasticities that were broadly different. As current empirical estimates of cost elasticities differ less than those used in our simulations, the advantage of combining cost pools would appear to be even greater. The results illustrate the importance of focusing both on issues of bias as well as uncertainty of cost estimates. The simulations suggest that a myopic focus on bias alone is unwarranted. The focus on bias has the most negative effect on low-volume products, as the *cv*'s of low-volume products in a model using numerous small cost pools will be large.

The chapter has three significant practical implications for the USPS as it moves into a changed costing environment. First, in the new environment, the USPS will likely have to present for regulatory review a more limited set of costs for broad categories of classes of mail for review. At the same time, it will have increasing freedom for developing and pricing individual products within those classes, creating the possibility that it will need to cost more low-volume products than ever before. If an examination of existing costing efforts focused on simplifying the process can provide cost estimates of equivalent quality at a lower cost, resources can be reallocated to meet the new demands for developing product costs for services tailored for individual or small groups of customers that the new regulatory scheme and pricing freedoms will create. Second, the chapter highlights the challenge faced by the USPS in developing consistent estimates of product costs when parameters in the cost equation have a large variance. Currently, the largest variance around cost estimates exists around estimates of the product costs of low-volume products. This chapter suggests that an examination of the tradeoff between bias and variance of cost estimates might recommend using more complex models for higher-volume products that are estimated using parameters that have low measured variance, and less complex models for products that are estimated using parameters that have high measured variance. Third, to the extent that simplification can produce cost estimates with lower variance and that are more stable over time, then the costing effort can improve the consistency of the business relationship between the USPS and its customers.

To the extent that any postal administration uses a cost modeling approach and data similar to what the USPS employs, the implications are identical. For these administrations, developing simulation models to evaluate the quality of their cost estimates could assist them in identifying cost-effective ways of improving their costing efforts.

This chapter does have significant limitations that provide directions for further research. First, the formulation we have used assumes that costs in each cost pool are a function of the cost elasticity. Separating the calculation of the magnitude of total accrued costs associated with a cost pool and the cost elasticities of the cost pool should be examined in further analysis.

Second, the simulations are driven by the assumption that when cost pools are aggregated, the *cv* of the combined elasticity estimate is improved. Further analyses would examine what happens with actual econometric data, though our assumption of a more precise elasticity estimate in the aggregated cost pool does seem reasonable and is supported by preliminary analyses.

Third, we did not investigate the possibility of combining cost pools for measuring cost elasticity while keeping them separate for distribution key share estimation. Such a hybrid approach may have advantages; especially if *a priori* the processes involve similar cost drivers but would involve significantly different mixes of products. For example, it may make sense to combine the elasticity estimation of letter mail sortation, across all machine and manual processes, while estimating distribution key shares separately for originating, terminating, and carrier route sortation of mail as the range of products handled by a process increases as the process gets closer to the delivery point.

Finally, we did not investigate how the combination of census and sampled data may affect product costing models that use multiple cost pools but use different methods for collecting product costing data or estimating the distribution keys and cost elasticities associated with individual cost pools. For example, costing models that use flow models to determine distribution keys or industrial engineering models to estimate cost elasticity may have different statistical properties in individual cost pools that need to be investigated.

NOTES

1. The 'Data Quality Study' included a number of technical reports on postal costing methods and supporting accounting systems. Technical Report #4 of this study reported the results of a survey of ten postal administrations regarding their product costing systems and identified similarities with the costing methods employed by the USPS. The origin of the Data Quality Study was as follows. The United States House of Representatives Committee on Government Reform, Subcommittee on the Postal Service (the Subcommittee) examined the Postal Service Rate Regulation Process in conjunction with its continuing deliberations on possible postal reform legislation. As part of this examination, the Subcommittee requested an independent review of the quality of data used in rate making. This request led to a joint agreement in early 1997 among the United States General Accounting Office (GAO), the Postal Rate Commission and USPS to undertake a detailed study of data quality used in postal regulation, which led to the publication on 16 April 1999 of the 'Data Quality Study'.
2. Crew and Kleindorfer (2000, pp. 154–5).
3. Many discussions of the postal service's cost models focus on *UVVC* = Unit volume variable costs. *UVVC* is equal to *VVC* of product *i* by dividing by the volume for product *i*.
4. Crew and Kleindorfer (2000).
5. Wolter (1985, p. 3).
6. Sampling systems are used to estimate the proportion of mail products handled by any cost pool because current data collection technology does not permit the collection of a census of mail. Advances in intelligent mail may allow for the possibility of collecting a census, but it may still be cost effective to continue to sample mail to determine the products handled by a cost pool.

REFERENCES

Crew, Michael A. and Paul R. Kleindorfer (2000), 'Cost estimation and economically efficient prices', in Michael A. Crew and Paul R. Kleindorfer (eds), *Current Directions in Postal Reform*, Boston, MA: Kluwer Academic Publishers, pp. 149–70.

Linx (1999), 'Technical Reports # 1–4' in *Data Quality Study*.

Waterman, Richard, Donald Rubin, Neal Thomas and Andrew Gelman (2000), 'Simulation modeling for cost estimation', in Michael A. Crew and Paul R. Kleindorfer (eds), *Current Directions in Postal Reform*, Boston, MA: Kluwer Academic Publishers, pp. 171–93.

Wolter, Kirk M. (1985), *Introduction to Variance Estimation*, New York, New York, Springer-Verlag.

APPENDIX A

Approximating Two Cost Pools with a Single Cost Pool

We use a simple cost equation for the *j*th cost pool:

$$C_j = \exp(\beta_{0j}) D_j^{\beta_{1j}},$$

where C_j is the cost in the *j*th cost pool, β_{0j} can be interpreted as a scaling factor, and β_{1j} is the elasticity of cost with respect to the cost driver D_j.

In our model we have two cost pools, denoted by *j* and *k*. We write the true cost across the two cost pools as

$$C_{j+k} = \exp(\beta_{0j}) D_j^{\beta_{1j}} + \exp(\beta_{0k}) D_k^{\beta_{1k}},$$

and consider what happens when we mistakenly treat this as a single cost pool using the cost function

$$\tilde{C} = \exp(\tilde{\beta}_0)(D_j + D_k)^{\tilde{\beta}_1}.$$

Our first question is for specified values of β_{1j} and β_{1k} how close is the approximating incorrect cost function. We choose to find values of $\tilde{\beta}_0$and $\tilde{\beta}_1$to make the incorrect cost function as 'close' as possible to the true one.

A definition of 'closeness' is needed. We choose to minimize the average absolute distance between the two cost curves, where the averaging is done with respect to a weighting function. Being close where most of the data would lie should be more important than at the extremes. To this end we find $\tilde{\beta}_0$ and $\tilde{\beta}_1$ such that they are the minimizers of the objective function

$$\int_0^{\infty} |C_{j+k}(\beta_{0j}, \beta_{1j}, \beta_{0k}, \beta_{1k}) - \tilde{C}(\tilde{\beta}_0, \tilde{\beta}_1)| dF(D; D^*, \sigma),$$

where F is the normal distribution function, with mean D^* and standard deviation σ.

The example illustrated in the body of the article sets $\beta_{0j} = \beta_{0k} = 0$ and the two elasticities as $\beta_{1j} = 0.5$ and $\beta_{1k} = 0.9$. Then, for $D^* = 5$ and $\sigma = 1$, the optimal values for $\tilde{\beta}_0$ and $\tilde{\beta}_1$ are 0.644 and 0.762, respectively.

APPENDIX B

Adding Distribution Keys to the Mix

In our simple world we think of distribution keys as the result of 'tallies' collected as part of a sampling effort and posit that the tallies come from a multinomial distribution where the level of effort put into estimating the tallies is governed by the size of the multinomial parameter '*n*', and the distribution key shares will be provided by the appropriately standardized multinomial probabilities.

Table 23.1 Multinomial probabilities (tally proportions)

	Cost Pool 1	Cost Pool 2
Product 1	π_{11}	π_{12}
Product 2	π_{21}	π_{22}

Note: $\pi_{11}+\pi_{12}+\pi_{21}+\pi_{22}=1$.

Table 23.2 Within-cost-pool distribution keys

	Cost Pool 1	Cost Pool 2
Product 1	$\frac{\pi_{11}}{\pi_{11}+\pi_{21}}$	$\frac{\pi_{12}}{\pi_{12}+\pi_{22}}$
Product 2	$\frac{\pi_{21}}{\pi_{11}+\pi_{21}}$	$\frac{\pi_{22}}{\pi_{12}+\pi_{22}}$

Table 23.3 Combined cost pool distribution keys

	Combined cost pool
Product 1	$\frac{\pi_{11}+\pi_{12}}{\pi_{11}+\pi_{12}+\pi_{21}+\pi_{22}}=\pi_{11}+\pi_{12}$
Product 2	$\frac{\pi_{21}+\pi_{22}}{\pi_{11}+\pi_{12}+\pi_{21}+\pi_{22}}=\pi_{21}+\pi_{22}$

Note: As $\pi_{11}+\pi_{12}+\pi_{21}+\pi_{22}=1$, Table 23.3 illustrates that the ratios in the combined cost pools can be simplified.

The setup is shown in Table 23.1.

The distribution keys in each cost pool are given in Table 23.2 and would give rise to a combined distribution key as shown in Table 23.3.

B.1 The distribution key asymmetry scenario

For this scenario, we reparameterize the multinomial with just two parameters, π_{11} and π^*, where π_{11} is the distribution key share of Product 1 in Cost Pool 1 and π^* controls how many tallies will be observed in each cost pool.

Our working parameterization for the asymmetry scenario is displayed in Table 23.4.

We will call π_{11} the 'asymmetry', parameter and $\pi^*$the 'cost pool tally weighting' parameter, and refer to the whole setup as the 'asymmetry scenario'.

For example, if we had $\pi_{11}=0.4$ and $\pi^* = 0.7$, we would have multinomial probabilities as displayed in Table 23.5.

The within-cost-pool distribution keys would be then calculated as in Table 23.6.

Table 23.4 Working parameterization for the multinomial

	Cost Pool 1	Cost Pool 2
Product 1	$\pi_{11}\pi^*$	$(1-\pi_{11})(1-\pi^*)$
Product 2	$(1-\pi_{11})\pi^*$	$\pi_{11}(1-\pi^*)$

Table 23.5 Example distribution keys using the working parameterization

	Cost Pool 1	Cost Pool 2
Product 1	$0.4 * 0.7 = 0.28$	$0.6 * 0.3 = 0.18$
Product 2	$0.6 * 0.7 = 0.42$	$0.4 * 0.3 = 0.12$

Table 23.6 Example within-cost-pool distribution keys

	Cost Pool 1	Cost Pool 2
Product 1	$\frac{0.28}{0.28+0.42} = 0.4$	$\frac{0.18}{0.18+0.12} = 0.6$
Product 2	$\frac{0.60}{0.28+0.42} = 0.6$	$\frac{0.12}{0.18+0.12} = 0.4$

Table 23.7 Combined cost pool distribution keys

	Combined cost pool
Product 1	$0.28 + 0.18 = 0.46$
Product 2	$0.42 + 0.12 = 0.54$

There is a special case here when the distribution keys are the same within each cost pool ($\pi_{11} = 0.5$), and in this case the distribution key in the combined cost pool will be identical to the individual cost pools.

The combined cost pool distribution key is shown in Table 23.7 and is closer to the distribution key share of Cost Pool 1 as there are more tallies in that cost pool, and so it gets more weight in the aggregation.

24. Data requirements for cost accounting in the mail communication system*

Leon A. Pintsov and Andrei Obrea

> The modern age has a false sense of superiority because of the great mass of data at its disposal. But the valid criterion of distinction is rather the extent to which man knows how to form and master the material at his command.
>
> J.W. Goethe (1749–1832)

1. INTRODUCTION

One of the fundamental challenges concerning governance and operations of modern postal enterprises is cost accounting. It is desirable to make the cost accounting process repeatable, verifiable and minimally expensive. The accuracy, reliability, verifiability and efficiency of the cost accounting depend on cost models and their associated data and conventions. Therefore, it is likely to be beneficial to identify all sources of data that can be brought to bear to improve reliability of data.

This chapter attempts to specify the objective (measurable) elements of data required for cost accounting and to identify the main system-wide sources of such data elements. Typically, an internal view of data related to costs is taken in which only data available from the postal operator itself is considered for cost accounting purposes. This chapter argues that, in fact, other parties, including the sender and receiver of mail, may provide very valuable additional sources of data of interest in estimating costs for direct and support services provided by postal operators. This topic is likely to become a central theme for strategy and regulation as liberalization drives price and value closer to cost. Interestingly, detailed data concerning actual cost accounting procedures employed by postal operators is sketchy, as shown in a NERA study of the European Market in 2004 (NERA, 2004). This chapter aims to contribute to this important theme using publicly available information from Royal Mail, Postcomm, the US Postal Service (USPS) and the Postal Regulatory Commission (PRC), in addition to academic publications.

2. THE MAIL COMMUNICATION SYSTEM

We take a system viewpoint that implies that all parties and processes involved in the mail communication system are considered as potential sources of useful information. With regard to the system organization and information itself, we adhere to the principle of 'information frugality'. This principle compels system designers to identify, collect and utilize every bit of useful information (system wide) that could be identified, collected and

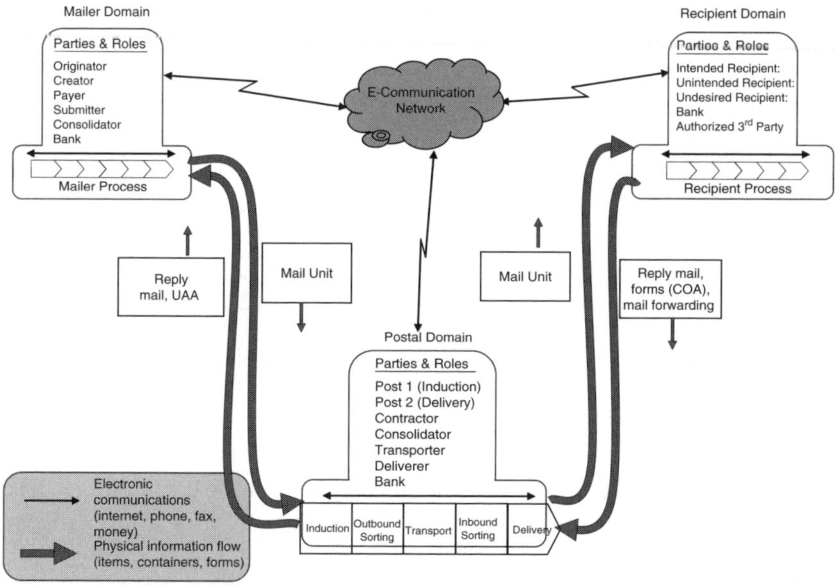

Figure 24.1 Mail communication system reference model

used economically (i.e. when the cost of having such a bit does not exceed its expected benefits). The application of information frugality to mail involves a system reference model depicted in Figure 24.1.

The model contains three major domains of the mail communication system, namely the mailer (sender), postal and recipient domains. Mailers (shown on the left side) and recipients (shown on the right side) are connected via the postal infrastructure that accepts processes and delivers mail items. Mailers and recipients are divided into several categories according to their legal status (party) and role; for example, originator, creator, payer, intended recipient, unintended recipient and so on. There is a multiplicity of mailer and recipient domains. The postal domain shown at the bottom also has various participants (parties) characterized by their roles. For definitions of the parties and roles see CEN TC 15523 and CEN TC 15524. All three domains employ processes for mail creation (mailers), mail acceptance or collection (posts), processing and delivery (posts) and mail receipt (recipients). Sometimes processes are also referred to as 'value chains', reflecting a viewpoint that each step in the process is designed to add value. These processes in turn could be combined into a single process that would contain all discreet activities taking place from the moment of mail unit content conception till the moment of the processing and disposition of this content in the recipient's domain. The arrows on the diagram exemplify paths from senders to recipients and back for mail units traveling through the postal infrastructure. One important and still significantly unexplored aspect of the mail communication system is electronic connectivity between parties and processes in all three domains, achieved through public or private electronic networks, depicted as the E-Communication Network in the central top portion of the diagram. Idealized mail communication could be viewed as an integrated system where all parties

Table 24.1 Postal cost distribution by function

Network function	USPS fixed cost (%)	USPS variable cost (%)	USPS contribution to total cost (%)	Royal Mail contribution to total cost (%)	Average cost (Europe) (%)
Delivery	52	48	36	36.7	50
Mail processing	4	96	34	23	15
Transportation	8	92	7	7.5	7
Window service	54	46	5	Collection 5.3	Collection 12
Other (G&A)	77	23	18	27.5	16
Total	37	63	100	100	100

and processes are enabled to exchange information via physical mail units (letters, flats, parcels, trays etc.) and electronic channels. The objective of this chapter is to explore how postal cost accounting could be improved assuming full connectivity (physical and electronic) between the mailer, postal and recipient domains. We illustrate the relative cost significance of different activities in the postal processing and delivery chain. Consider the following fixed/variable cost data broken down by network function from the USPS (fiscal year 1999, calculated using the PRC method; Cohen et al., 2002), the Royal Mail (LECG, 2006) and Europe in 2004 (European Commission, 2005) presented in Table 24.1.

As can be seen from Table 24.1, two major contributors to the total cost are mail delivery and mail processing costs, and they also constitute the bulk of the variable cost (70 percent for USPS and 60 percent for Royal Mail). Transportation cost is largely variable but insignificant, and could be easily incorporated into our analysis. On the other hand, cost ingredients of window services (collection services) and general administrative expenses (overhead) are generally unknown to mailers and largely fixed. It is for these reasons that in the remainder of the chapter we consider only delivery and mail processing costs.

3. POSTAL COST ACCOUNTING

There are multiple models for cost accounting, estimation and allocation, each with its own advantages and drawbacks (Bradley et al., 1993, 1997; Awerbuch and Preston, 2000; Bradley and Colvin, 2000; Crew and Kleindorfer, 2000; Panzar, 2001; Cohen et al., 2002; Crew and Kleindorfer, 2005; Gori et al., 2006; Roberts, 2006). There are also multiple dimensions to cost accounting; for example, accounting by product and by activity (process). The cost of processing and delivering a mail item is a function of the mail item (e.g. size, weight, information readability, level of presort), service (e.g. geography of induction and delivery points, timing aspects and information requirements) and network attributes (topology, IT infrastructure, administration).

We are interested in identifying input parameters to the cost function (in whatever way it has been chosen), values of which could be obtained from mailers independently of postal operators. More formally, cost of product (i) is a computable function of multiple variables $v_1, v_2, \ldots, v_k$ and (fixed) parameters $p_1, p_2, \ldots, p_n$:

$$\text{Cost } (i) = C_i\,(v_1, v_2, \ldots, v_k, p_1, p_2, \ldots, p_n)$$

Examples of variables are volumes and wages, while examples of parameters are productivity and the cost of equipment. Our question is: What are input sources for $v_1, v_2, \ldots, v_k, p_1, p_2, \ldots, p_n$ and which of the variables $v_1, v_2, \ldots, v_k$, are most significant ('cost-causative').

In activity-based accounting methods, the mail volume dependent cost of each product is calculated by computing cost components of a given product independently for each activity in the value chain [e.g., collection, mail processing (sorting), and delivery] and then adding up all these cost components for all activities involved in delivering the product (Bradley et al., 1993; LECG, 2006). In the remainder of this section, we shall give a brief overview of cost accounting data requirements in USPS and Royal Mail as they relate to marginal (volume variable costs) for mail processing and delivery operations.

3.1 USPS Cost Accounting

In this section, we provide a brief summary of the cost accounting procedures employed by the USPS. The discussion in this section is based on information obtained from the Cost and Revenue Analysis Report (CRA, 2005), an analysis published by Roberts (2006), and materials from PRC (PRC Docket 2006-1, 2006).

The USPS algorithm for computing the unit variable volume cost of a given product consists of four steps:

1. Costs are segregated into 19 segments that are further divided into well over 100 cost components depending on the segment. Some segments have more components than others.
2. Each cost component is associated with at least one cost driver, implying a causal relationship. Some components have multiple cost drivers. A volume variable cost pool is computed by using the relationship between the component's cost and its cost driver.
3. The volume variable cost pool is divided between different products to arrive at the share of the cost pool for each product.
4. The total volume variable cost for a product is computed by summing the volume variable costs for the product across all cost elements: 'Unit variable costs are found by dividing a product's total volume variable cost by its originating volume' (CRA, 2005).

Mail processing costs are concentrated in Cost Segments 2 and 3 (salaries, benefits and certain other costs of clerks, mail handlers, supervisor and technical personnel related to mail handling, equipment maintenance, technical, custodial and supply services at livery distribution centers, processing distribution centers, bulk mail centers, remote encoding centers, the majority of post offices and a few other types of facility). Cost segments 15 and 16 cover expenses for renting and leasing facilities, particularly for sorting centers and for mail processing equipment supplies and services, and are relatively small. Mail processing costs are almost entirely volume variable, which hardly requires any explanation.

The volume variable costs in Cost Segment 2 are distributed to different products (classes and subclasses of mail) in the same proportion as direct labor costs in Cost Segment 3. Therefore, computation of volume variable costs in Cost Segment 3 in essence defines the fundamentals of cost analysis for mail processing. Data that is used for this computation is collected in the Management Operating Data System (MODS). The MODS contains records of mail volumes and work hours for each operation during mail processing. In addition, the In-Office Cost System (IOCS) is used for computing certain cost drivers (keys) that are in turn used to assign volume variable costs to different products.

Mail volume or piece handling data is of particular interest. The USPS makes use of econometric techniques to compensate for measurement errors in significant mail volume variables. During automated mail sorting, MODS collects presumably accurate values for machine-counted variables such as Total Pieces Fed (TPF) and Total Piece Handled (TPH) in manual operations. On the other hand, the value of the variable 'First Handling Pieces' (FHP) is derived from the weight of inputted mail containers and is inherently error prone.

Roberts (2006) argues that the 'big advantage of the USPS framework' in computing mail processing marginal cost is the assumption of fixed proportionality between manual and automated input in producing a given level of output (sorted letters and flats). This assumption makes measurement of the mail volume in the processing facility unnecessary by substituting it with the measurement of cost drivers at each stage of production (at each activity), presumably because of the absence of reliable measures for mail volumes. His suggestion is 'to develop measures of mail volume in the (processing) plant'. The difference between the USPS approach and the approach advocated by Roberts lies in the definition of the plant output. In the USPS framework the output is a sum of the TPFs over all operations of which accurate count could be kept, while Roberts suggests the FPH count as a more suitable measure of output. He argues that the FHP is more appropriate based on theoretical grounds and also because FHP is exogenous to the plant. However, as we have already mentioned and as was correctly observed by Roberts, the FHP is inherently error prone due to the method of its derivation, which makes use of the weight and the pieces per pound conversion factor. Roberts's suggestion for fixing this is to use instrumental variables estimators, a standard statistical technique in regression analysis. Another problem with FHP as a measure of output is the fact that it treats all letters arriving at the plant as if they need the same level of sortation; that is, the FHP (as defined) is homogeneous with regard to the amount of processing that is required by different letters. In order to fix this problem, Roberts suggests the development of FHP counts 'for categories of mail that distinguish the amount of preparation the mailers have undertaken' (which implies presorting by mailers), but this runs into the problem of lacking relevant information in MODS. Note that MODS data is the only source of information considered by Roberts. Roberts analyzed the statistical significance of different factors in observed variations in FHP and notably found that 'the technology shifts (at the plant – LP/AO) are not important, but rather the seasonal *fluctuations in the activities of the mailers*, which generate the fluctuations in FHP, *are what dominates the data*' (cursive is ours). In his comments on mail volume data, he suggests that such data 'needs to be incorporated into empirical analysis'. In a rate case testimony (R2006, USPS-T-12) on behalf of the USPS, T. Bozzo provided a detailed analysis of Roberts's method and conclusions. His major argument (and a point of disagreement with Roberts) is that FHP is not a better measure of output than the TPF/TPH parameters, because FHP aggregates do not reflect differences in the depth of sort while TPF does. Fixing the FHPs as a measure of output by decomposing them using a set of cost-causing characteristics could add major inefficiency to the model (T. Bozzo, private communication, 2007). Both Roberts and Bozzo agree that the data captured in MODS is of poor quality. The Postal Regulatory Commission (PRC) recommendation (PRC Docket 2006-1) echoed this conclusion, as quoted below.

The PRC has been critical of USPS econometric models of mail processing labor demand variability (Docket R2006-1). The Commission found MODS data 'error-ridden' and characterizes it as a formidable obstacle to the accurate econometric estimation of mail processing costs. The Commission also believes that MODS data may be quite inaccurate due to insufficient quality controls and potential censorship and manipulation. PRC in its recommendation stated that 'if the system by which MODS piece handling data is collected is not reformed, or a comprehensive substitute measure of volume is not provided through the Intelligent Mail program, econometricians will have few alternatives but to continue to search for valid instruments. This search is not likely to bear fruit, however, unless a new category of data is made available for their use'.

Mail delivery costs are concentrated in Cost Segment 6 (salaries, benefits and other costs related to in-office work of city delivery carriers), Cost Segment 7 (salaries, benefits and other costs related to street [actual delivery] work of city delivery carriers) and in Cost Segment 10 (salaries, benefits and other costs related to the work of rural carriers). Cost Segment 6 covers primarily carrier walk sequencing and is roughly equivalent in size to Cost Segment 10 (between 5 and 6 billion dollars according to year 2005 estimates). Cost Segment 7 is almost equal in size to Cost Segments 6 and 10 combined. The cost in Cost Segment 6 is 80 percent volume variable, while the cost in Cost Segment 10 is only 50 percent variable. The cost in Cost Segment 7 is only 40 percent volume variable. The explanation of the proportions for the volume variable costs in the delivery cost segments is as follows. Because Cost Segment 6 mostly covers the cost of walk sequence sorting, the less mail there is to sort, the less is the amount of work to be performed. In Cost Segment 10 the overall cost is driven by 31 distinct cost drivers (based on a set of identified discreet activities carried out by rural carriers), of which only 16 activities require work hours proportionate to the volume. Cost Segment 7 accounts for a large amount of 'fixed' activities such as 'network travel' (unrelated to volume), collection activities, regular delivery (that is scheduled regardless of the volume of mail to be delivered) and delivery support that covers the unproductive time of traveling from and to the delivery office.

A desirable situation would materialize if the USPS had information concerning volume distribution for each delivery point in the network some time *before* actual mail arrival into the delivery destination offices. The questions are how much time before can realistically be expected, and whether this realistic expected time is sufficient for plant and delivery office management to constructively adjust their respective operations. In this chapter we are concerned only with the availability of forward-looking information, particularly from the cost accounting viewpoint.

3.2 Royal Mail Cost Accounting

In this section we give a brief summary of the cost accounting procedures employed by the Royal Mail (RM). Discussion in this section is based entirely on materials obtained from the LECG study (LECG, 2006) and from a paper by Moriarty et al. (2006) which provides a good summary of the voluminous LECG study. Unlike the case of the USPS, the LECG report used a more differentiated approach to the study of Mail Processing Centers and Delivery Offices costs. The main tool that was used in the study was internal benchmarking, using several econometric techniques based on the sample of data from 69 of the RM mail centers. The study identified more effective mail centers and delivery offices and the sources of their effectiveness in view of potential cost savings for less effective operations. We review cost functions and their variables employed by LECG in the cost analysis of mail centers and delivery offices. We are concerned with the quality and availability of the volume data.

In analysis of mail centers, RM uses volume and type of mail as a measure of output. More specifically, RM employs mail volume weighted by several characteristics, such as the mail class (first or second), the nature of processing (mechanized/manual), the mail type (letters, flats or packets), the type of sort performed (inward/outward/walk sorted to inward mail center) and the special delivery requirements. The total list of variables considered for econometric analysis by LECG included 29 variables, of which four were deemed not to have a material impact on cost. The remaining 25 variables could be divided into two categories, namely controllable or not controllable by management. The non-controllable category consisted of six variables that were essentially determined by the volume and composition of the center's incoming mail (and thus controlled by mailers' communication needs). This category included composition of incoming mail by the class, by the type (letters, flats and packets), by the amount and split between inward/outward sorted volumes, by the split between business and street letter box collection volumes, by the proportion of the mail that is local, neighboring or distant, and by the volume of special delivery mail. The controlled category included such variables as a split between mechanized and manual processes (which could be at least partially controlled by the management), labor requirements, overtime hours, physical characteristics of mail centers and the geographical areas they serve. Several of the controllable variables were difficult to quantify due to the lack of information. Nineteen most relevant variables were selected based on researchers' industry knowledge and statistical significance testing by regression analysis. Variables that were deemed to be controllable by the local management of mail centers were excluded from final regression. Finally, six 'explanatory' variables were selected for the estimation, which was performed using a basic Cobb–Douglas model. *Volume (presumably weighted volume) was the most significant variable* judging by the Student *t*-ratio, which is an intuitively obvious conclusion. The percentage of inward mail volume that comes from other mail centers was another significant variable. The size of the mail center (small or large) also was found to be important, as well as the percentage of the area served by the mail center that is qualified as 'urban'. The RM mail centers internal benchmarking study by LECG provided considerable insight into the overall quality of RM data, particularly with regard to mail volumes. RM believed that the data concerning disaggregated mail volume estimates should not be used due to its poor quality. RM suggested the use of 'weighted volume estimates' that are produced using sampling techniques and engineering studies. LECG remarks also that mail centers data that 'is sourced directly from mail centres managers are not audited' and may be subject to clerical errors, particularly with regard to inward mail volume data. RM believed that the outward volume data is accurate, since it is calculated by sampling outward mail at each mail center. However, LECG was unable to use the outward volume as 'a robust measure of sorted volume'. LECG study also mentions that 'for mail centre activities there is variation in the nature of the mail received (reflected in the weighted volume figures) and the extent of pre-sorting in incoming mail and sorting of outgoing mail', affecting the accuracy of the data. Not surprisingly, the data issues are quite similar to the issues experienced by the USPS. Finally, the RM method for counting the volume of mail 'tends to overstate the actual amount', due to several reasons, particularly volume-based incentives for management. To compensate, RM uses *estimated average revenues* for each product to arrive at more accurate 'revenue equated volumes'.

In an analysis of delivery cost drivers, RM initially identified 37 variables, of which two were deemed not to have a material impact on cost, and two others were already accounted for in the overall weighted volume variable (the key variable that is always included as a measure of output). Of the remaining 34 variables, eight have no value information. Using processes and criteria similar to those outlined above in consideration of the mail centers cost analysis, LECG selected 12 variables for inclusion in the final cost equation. The number of delivery points served by a delivery office and the *mail volume per delivery point* were the most significant determinants of the delivery office cost. The study indicated that 'the volume per delivery point is an important source of economies of density with a cost elasticity in the region of 0.65–0.67', meaning that a 10 percent increase in mail volume per delivery point causes a cost increase on average from 6.5 percent to 6.7 percent. In comparison, the number of delivery points has cost elasticity 1 and does not display any economies of density.

The LECG study of delivery cost provided considerable insight into the overall poor quality of RM cost data, particularly with regard to mail volumes. As with the mail centers, the data is not audited and there are possible incentives for delivery office managers to inflate mail volumes. The data was also subject to clerical error: 'RM data identified 240 delivery offices that had experienced year-on-year changes in volume in excess of ±15%'. The study emphasized the importance of accurate data concerning volumes, particularly for the estimation of delivery cost.

3.3 A Summary of Cost Accounting Data Analysis

Analysis of cost accounting (exemplified by the USPS and RM mail processing and delivery costs) reveals that the most difficult problems are associated with the collection of various measures of volume (traffic) processed by mail sorting plants (mail centers) and delivery offices. Specifically, it appears that effective cost accounting requires knowledge of volumes of different mail products apportioned by activities that take place during processing and delivery of mail. With regard to data collection for cost accounting purposes, postal operators have traditionally relied on such methods as engineering studies, sampling surveys and econometric techniques. It appears that the quality of data (particularly various volume estimates) used for cost accounting purposes by USPS and Royal Mail is poor, and there is no obvious and effective way to improve it.

We were unable to find any estimates of the postal costs (relative or absolute) associated with internal collection and maintenance of data required for cost accounting, but given the sheer size and scope of the operations it must be substantial. These 'data' costs fall into the category of transaction costs (or, more precisely, into a specific category of transaction costs known as 'coordination costs') and as such should be minimized. We believe that data from mailers or their agents (e.g. consolidators) could prove to be a very useful additional source of information. The next section provides description and analysis of such data.

4. MAILER-GENERATED DATA

Discussion of postal cost accounting practices reveals several significant shortcomings that largely result from the lack of reliable and accurate data on volumes. We now outline potential remedies that can be applied using system-wide data.

Between 80 percent and 90 percent of the total mail in the industrialized world is business-generated mail. Moreover, most businesses that use mail regularly and efficiently create the bulk of their mail volume using computer-driven equipment. Mail production and finishing equipment comes in many forms and varieties, and ranges from large mainframe computers for address and content data generation and processing and high-speed mail assembly systems (inserters) to medium and small mailing and franking machines, characterized by lower productivity and lesser functionality. In many instances, mail is created in small enterprises and offices by using standard office equipment (e.g. personal computers, and office and label printers). The majority of the mail in the industrialized world is directly computer generated or assisted in its generation by computers. This implies that mail generation systems (when properly designed) could collect all sorts of relevant data concerning the mail that they either produce entirely or whose production they aid. Importantly, the relevant data could in most cases be collected without significant cost, since computers have a pleasant habit of keeping track of what they are doing as a part of their normal operation. Furthermore, once collected, the data could be communicated for processing and interpretation without incremental cost, since (at least in comparison with other costs discussed in this chapter) the Internet is free. Thus, the mail communication system has a significantly untapped source of valuable information, namely computer-assisted mail generators. In the next section, we shall review what data relevant to cost accounting is available to mailers and how it can be collected, formatted, aggregated, processed and communicated to postal operators or their designated agents.

4.1 What Do Mailers Know?

Mail items (units) as communication objects have intrinsic physical and informational characteristics, also referred to as attributes. Attributes have names and values. We are interested in intrinsic attributes of mail items that influence the cost of their processing. In addition to mail item intrinsic attributes, the processing cost is also influenced by the type of the service required. The service is also referred to as a postal product. The postal product can, in turn, be defined from an informational viewpoint as a collection of attributes. We view the pair {mail item, product} as a unit that (together with postal network structural information) determines the cost of processing and delivery

The physical attributes of a mail item are summarized in the following table:

Mail item physical attributes	**Dimensions**	**Weight**	**Cover material characteristics**	**Content**
	W × L × T Type: machinable or non-machinable		Type (e.g. paper or plastic) color, spectral response etc.	(e.g. fragile, perishable etc., defining restrictions of handling)

Note that the mail-processing marginal cost for a given mail item – product pair depends on the qualification of the mail item (for the purpose of sorting) as an 'automated' or a 'manual' piece (Roberts, 2006). The automated category includes items that could be automatically fed into (mechanical machineability) and read (informational machineability) by postal sorting equipment. According to postal statistics, up to 95 percent of business-generated mail is machine readable. Thus, the mail item physical attributes that are known to the mailer and presented in the 'Dimension' column of the table above determine in practical terms whether a given item is 'automated' or 'manual'. This means that mailer-generated data could be effectively used as clean input data for computing the mail-processing marginal cost.

The informational attributes of a mail item are exemplified in the following table:

Mail item informational attributes	**Origination address**	**Destination address**	**Special markings**
			For value-added services, payment verification or automated processing (e.g. various bar codes containing postage, destination postal code or unique identifier)

Knowledge of the attributes of a postal product is shared by the mailer and the postal operator. These are informational attributes exemplified in the following table:

Postal product attributes	**Delivery time**	**Special information requirements**	**Special handling or exception processing requirements**
	For example, defined by a date when the item is expected to be delivered	For example, tracking and tracing requirements	For example, registered processing, insurance etc.

The classification of product attributes given in the table is sufficient for illustrative purposes, although postal product attributes can be greatly extended and further formalized.

When mail items are combined into a group (typically containing at least hundreds of items and known as a mailing submission or mailing), there are additional attributes, which we will refer to as 'submission attributes':

Submission attributes	**Induction point or area**	**Induction time**	**Group and containerization attributes**
	Typically identified by a postal code	For example, defined by a period of time	For example, level of presort and containerization

The mail item physical attributes could be divided into several categories determined by attributes that are relevant for automated mail sorting, transportation and delivery [for example, machinable letter mail (up to certain dimensions, e.g. with a thickness less than ¼ inch), machinable flats etc.]. Similarly, submission attributes – for example, group attributes – could be codified into levels such as mail center level sort, delivery office sort, walk sort or walk sequence sort.[1]

For each {mail item–product} pair, all four sets of attributes are known to mailers before induction. Data derived from these sets can be aggregated into a data structure summarized and exemplified in Table 24.2, where the row (segment number '*n*') represents a cluster and contains information defining a homogeneous subset of mail items from a mailing submission:

The granularity and presence of the different parameters presented in Table 24.2 are controllable by postal data requirements. For example, some data elements (e.g. physical characteristics such as color and spectral response, which could affect the machine readability of information) could be omitted, while some other data elements could be added or extended (for example, the information describing postal code distribution in segment 1 of Table 24.2 can be further divided into five- or nine-digit zip code areas). The contribution from a given mailer to mail flows between different facilities in the network (for example, flows of mail between sorting plants identified by three-digit zip codes) can be deduced from the information stored in Table 24.2. If data contained in Table 24.2 are available from all mailers, then all mail flows for each postal product could be computed by aggregation of homogeneous segments of the data, using any suitable aggregation criteria. Thus, data elements that are critically important for postal cost accounting (e.g. volumes of different mail products) can be computed by aggregating data from mailers.

How practical is this concept and, realistically, what data can be obtained from mailers? The answer depends on the mail distribution from different classes of mailers. The traditional rule of thumb that 20 percent of mailers generate 80 percent of the mail applies. In reality, mail generation in the industrialized world is probably far more concentrated when a few hundred mailers (from 200 to 1000, depending on the country) produce close to 40 percent of all business mail. Adding a few more thousands to these few hundreds will cover the next 30 percent of the business mail. For large mailers, a significant portion of the required data can be collected from information systems even prior to physical mail production.

According to some estimates, 'correspondence' mail, which is produced by medium- and small-size mailers, constitutes about 30 percent of business mail. For this type of

Table 24.2 Clustered mailing submission data

Segment number or code	Physical attributes	Informational attributes	Product attributes	Submission attributes	Volume
n	*Size:* 4 × 9.5 × 0.25" *Weight:* 0.5 ounce *Cover material color:* white machineable	*Origination address:* Pitney Bowes, 35 Waterview Drive, Shelton CT 06484, USA *Destination address:* Los Angeles BMC ZIP Code 091 *Special markings:* Metered mail 11 digit Postnet code	*Delivery time:* June 1, 2007	*Induction point:* Springfield BMC Zip Code 021 *Induction time*: May 27, 2007 *Grouping and containerization:* Presort five-digit ZIP code *Containers*: labeled trays	10 000 items

mail, the values of some critical attributes (e.g. the destination address) are not easily available at the time of mail production. This means that data from this class of mailers can describe only the total number of mail pieces for each class of products without detailed mail flows. In several countries, many of the mailers in this category submit their mail first to consolidators, in order to benefit from worksharing discounts. Consolidators scan mail in order to capture and process address information for sorting purposes. Thus consolidators can compile the information contained in Table 24.2.

T. Bozzo (private communication, 2007) correctly pointed out that knowledge of mail flows computed from mailers' sources is in itself insufficient for postal cost accounting, since mailers have no information concerning where and when and in what way their mail will be processed. This means that for effective use, data from mailers should be augmented with information about the sort plans and transportation activities of postal operators. Data obtainable from mailers could be then used as a supplementary source of the accounting raw data (the traffic between network terminals segregated by products). It also could be used as a check for data computed by postal operators using econometric or sampling means. In either case, knowledge of the proportion of the total mail volume about which information is obtainable from mailers is critical. This proportion can be computed with reasonable certainty from postal and mailer sources.

4.2 The Statement of Mailing Submission (SMS)

The SMS is a formal mechanism for collecting and communicating mailer-generated information. The SMS is standardized in Europe (CEN/TS 15523, 2006), and it defines the content of a message that is typically implemented as an XML structure. Figure 24.2 depicts the structure of the SMS content and the attributes of mail items contained in a mailing submission as defined in the SMS standard.

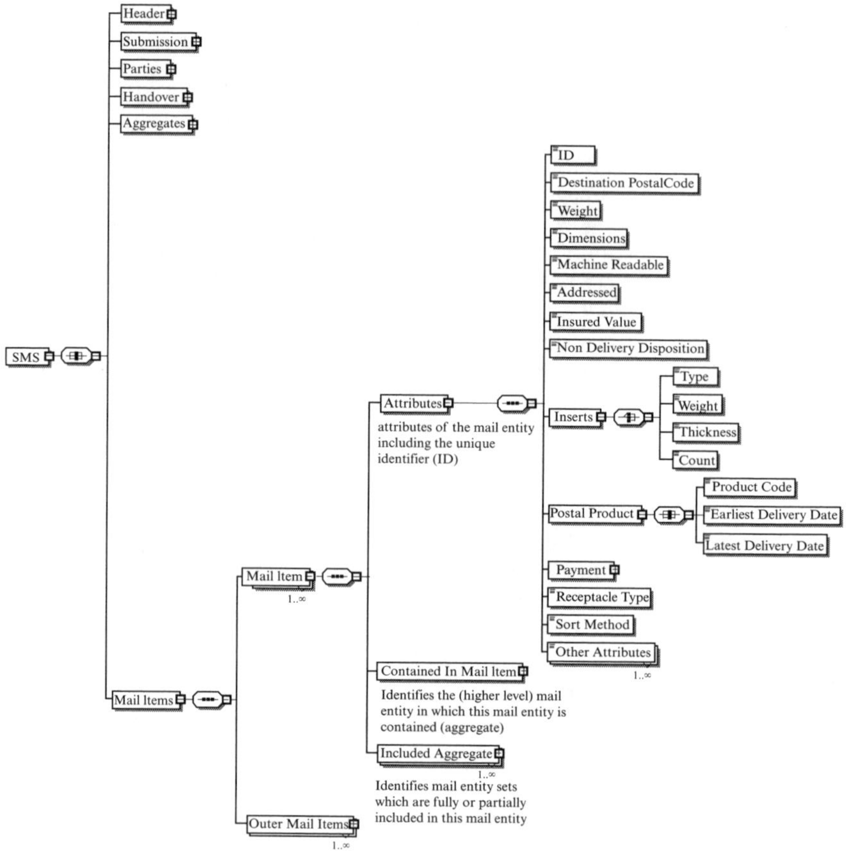

Figure 24.2 The structure and elements of SMS

The SMS message has a tree structure and is organized hierarchically into six sections, several layers deep. In the SMS message, each section is represented by an XML element. The main information content of the SMS is carried by mail item attributes. Some of the attributes in the diagram are self-explanatory. Others are defined in Table 24.3.

The SMS is an open standard extendable to include additional attributes as they become useful. A review of the SMS structure makes it clear that the SMS as defined by the existing standard (CEN/TS 15523, 2006) contains all of the attributes discussed in Section 4.1 for all mail items in the submission.

5. CONCLUSION

Analysis of USPS and Royal Mail published information concerning their postal cost accounting practices demonstrates that they both suffer from problems with input data

Table 24.3 Examples of mail item attribute names and definitions

Mail item attribute name	Definition
.ID	The unique identifier of the mail item
.Machinable	Indicates mail item processability by automated equipment
.Addressed	Indicates if the mail item carries specific addresses or is unaddressed
.NonDeliveryDisposition	The value of this attribute is taken from a code list to indicate what actions are to be taken when the mail item cannot be delivered
.Product.ProductCode	The identifier of a postal product taken from a code list
.ReceptacleType	The type of receptacle holding the mail item (e.g. tray, sack)
.SortMethod	The method used to group smaller mail items into a larger mail unit – the value of this attribute is taken from a code list
.StackableFlag	A flag which, when set to be 'true', indicates that the mail units (containers) can be stacked (one on the top of another)

quality. Specifically, it appears that effective cost accounting depends on knowledge of volumes of different mail products apportioned by activities that are required for the processing and delivery of these products. The sensitivity of cost estimates to errors in volume measurement could have a significant impact on the pricing of postal products. Postal operators have traditionally relied on methods such as engineering studies, sampling surveys and econometric techniques for cost accounting purposes.

We recommend giving serious consideration to the readily available and almost completely unused mailer-generated data. We have provided a detailed analysis of the information that could be obtained from mailers and briefly described the already existing and standardized process of structuring and communicating this information (SMS). Our suggestions concerning the use of data collected from mailers could be combined with internal improvements to MODS data and could also apply to Royal Mail operational data. If accepted, this could create an information-rich environment where data elements obtained from different uncorrelated sources could be compared with each other to establish their accuracy and validity.

NOTES

* This chapter expresses personal views that do not necessarily represent the views of the authors or Pitney Bowes, Inc. We are grateful to Paul Kleindorfer, Michael Crew and Tom Bozzo for many valuable comments and suggestions. Jeff Colvin helped us in finding reference materials.

1. Another way to look at mail item and postal product attributes as composite goods with hedonic properties was recently proposed by Fenster et al. (2006). The purpose of that paper was to understand the behavior of the structure for US domestic mail tariffs over a period of 30 years beginning from 1976, using econometric research techniques. The results obtained revealed that the structure of domestic tariffs as a composite of several hedonic parameters (properties) has been stable (i.e. relative contributions from different properties did not change dramatically with time). The practical implications of this result for postal cost accounting and ratemaking are unclear.

REFERENCES

Awerbuch, S. and A. Preston (2000), 'Postal ABC', in M. Crew and P. Kleindorfer (eds), *Current Directions in Postal Reform*, Boston, MA: Kluwer Academic, pp. 195–215.

Bozzo, T., PRC Docket 2006-1, USPS-T-12.

Bradley, M. and J. Colvin (2000), 'Measuring the cost of universal service for posts', in M. Crew and P. Kleindorfer (eds), *Current Directions in Postal Reform*, Boston, MA: Kluwer Academic Publishers, pp. 29–46.

Bradley, M., J. Colvin and M. Smith (1993), 'Measuring product costs for ratemaking: the United States Postal Service', in M. Crew and P. Kleindorfer (eds), *Regulation and the Nature of Postal and Delivery Services*, Boston, MA: Kluwer Academic Publishers, pp. 133–57.

Bradley, M., J. Colvin and J. Panzar (1997), 'Issues in measuring incremental cost in a multi-functional enterprise', in M. Crew and P. Kleindorfer (eds), *Managing Change in Postal and Delivery Industries*, Boston, MA: Kluwer Academic Publishers, pp. 3–21.

CEN/TS 15523 Postal service – Statement of mailing submission (2006).

Cohen, R., C. Pace, M. Robinson, G. Scarfiglieri, R. Scocchera, V. Comandini, J. Waller and S. Xenakis (2002), 'A comparison of the burden of universal service in Italy and the United States', in M. Crew and P. Kleindorfer (eds), *Postal and Delivery Services*, Boston, MA: Kluwer Academic Publishers, pp. 87–106.

CRA (2005), Postal Rate Commission PRC Docket 2006-1, USPS-LR-L-2 – Cost and Revenue Analysis, Fiscal Year 2005; http://www.prc.gov/show_document.asp?docid=48481

Crew, M. and P. Kleindorfer (2000), 'Cost estimation and economically efficient prices', in M. Crew and P. Kleindorfer (eds), *Current Directions in Postal Reform*, Boston, MA: Kluwer Academic Publishers, pp. 149–70.

Crew, M. and P. Kleindorfer (2005), 'Competition, universal service and the graveyard spiral', in M. Crew and P. Kleindorfer (eds), *Regulatory and Economic Challenges in the Postal and Delivery Sector*, Boston, MA: Kluwer Academic Publishers, pp. 1–30.

Fenster, L., D. Monaco, E.S. Pearsall, C. Robinson and S. Xenakis (2006), 'US postal services as composites goods with hedonic properties', in M. Crew and P. Kleindorfer (eds), *Liberalization of the Postal and Delivery Sector*, Cheltenham, UK and Northampton, MA, USA: Edward Elgar, pp. 369–88.

Gori, S., E. Piccinin, S. Romito and G. Scarfiglieri (2006), 'On the use of cost functions in the assessment of the impact of liberalization on postal universal service burden (restricted versus flexible specifications)', in M. Crew and P. Kleindorfer (eds), *Progress toward Liberalization of the Postal and Delivery Sector*, New York: Springer, pp. 59–74.

LECG (2006), 'Future efficient costs of Royal Mail's regulated mail activities', report; http://www.psc.gov.uk/postcomm/live/policy-and-consultations/consultations/price-control/LECG_Efficiency_Report_Top_Down_Final_Conclusions.pdf

Moriarty, R., S.Yorke, G. Harman, J. Cubbin, M. Meschi and P. Smith (2006), 'Economic analysis of the efficiency of Royal Mail and the implications for regulatory policy', in M. Crew and P. Kleindorfer (eds), *Liberalization of the Postal and Delivery Sector*, Cheltenham, UK and Northampton, MA, USA: Edward Elgar, pp. 165–82.

NERA Economics Consulting (2004), 'Economics of postal services: final report'; http://ec.europa.eu/internal_market/post/doc/studies/2004-nera-final-postal-report_en.pdf

Panzar, J. (2001), 'Funding universal service obligations: the costs of liberalization', in M. Crew and P. Kleindorfer (eds), *Future Directions in Postal Reform*, Boston, MA: Kluwer Academic Publishers, pp. 101–15.

PRC Docket 2005-1, Postal Rate Commission, PRC-LR-14 – Cost Attribution; http://www.prc.gov/docs/47/47301/PRC_LR-14.zip

PRC Docket 2006-1, Postal Rate Commission, USPS-LR-L-93 – PRC Version/Base Year 2005 CRA Model, Data Files, and Report, http://www.prc.gov/docs/48/48574/USPS-LR-L-93.exe

Roberts, M. (2002), 'An empirical model of labor demand for mail sorting operations'; http://econ.la.psu.edu/~mroberts/

Roberts, M. (2006), 'An economic framework for modeling mail processing costs'; http://econ.la.psu.edu/~mroberts/

Index